Phillis Browne

A Year's Cookery

Giving Dishes for Breakfast, Luncheon, and Dinner

Phillis Browne

A Year's Cookery
Giving Dishes for Breakfast, Luncheon, and Dinner

ISBN/EAN: 9783744789493

Printed in Europe, USA, Canada, Australia, Japan

Cover: Foto ©Lupo / pixelio.de

More available books at **www.hansebooks.com**

A YEAR'S COOKERY.

GIVING DISHES FOR

BREAKFAST, LUNCHEON, AND DINNER,

FOR

Every Day in the Year,

WITH

PRACTICAL INSTRUCTIONS FOR THEIR PREPARATION; AND A SPECIAL SECTION ON FOOD FOR INVALIDS.

PHYLLIS BROWNE.

TWENTY-SECOND THOUSAND.

CASSELL & COMPANY, Limited:
LONDON, PARIS & MELBOURNE.
1892.

PREFACE.

THIS book is intended to supply ménus for every day in the year, with recipes for the dishes recommended, and practical instructions for their preparation. So far as I know, no work of the kind on this plan exists. I have specially addressed myself to people of moderate income, with moderate domestic help and ordinary kitchen utensils. I have endeavoured to show how waste may be avoided, and also how, by thinking beforehand, by making one day work in with another, and by choosing materials that are in season, and therefore likely to be reasonable in price, a family might, throughout the year, be provided daily with food excellent in quality, varied in its nature, well cooked and well served, at a reasonable cost.

The ideal family that I have had before me has consisted of about half a dozen persons. I have tried, however, to calculate the quantities and to give the recipes in such a way that the marketing lists can be easily altered to suit varying circumstances.

No particular year has been taken. The book begins where it does, simply because it would not be easy, on account of Sunday, to commence providing for a family either at the beginning or the end of the week. The movable feasts are put down at a likely time of the year, because of the special dishes that are connected with them. In any year, therefore, in order to follow the course, it will be necessary only to note the first Sunday in the year, and work from that.

Three meals have been provided for daily: Breakfast, Luncheon, and Dinner. Those, however, who dine in the middle of the day, and who require Supper, will find that very nearly all the luncheon dishes may be served at Supper.

It will be seen that I have largely recommended soups in this volume. I have done so because I believe their more frequent use amongst us would tend to promote both health and economy.

In drawing up the marketing lists I have only named perishable articles usually bought from day to day. Such things as groceries of all kinds, flour, butter, cheese, eggs, and flavourings, may be bought in quantities, and are, therefore, not mentioned.

I have said that ordinary kitchen utensils would be sufficient to work out these recipes. I shall be glad if it may be understood that these include a wire or a hair sieve and a frying-basket. The former is indispensable; purées must be rubbed through a sieve if they are to be worth anything; the latter is desirable. Both can be bought for a trifling sum.

Those who do not care to follow the ménus in their entirety may find recipes for particular dishes by consulting the Index at the end of the work.

In a book of this nature it is exceedingly difficult to be quite exact in every detail. I have had tested afresh every recipe here given, but I shall esteem it a favour if any of my readers will favour me, through my publishers, with any improvements their experience in working out these ménus may suggest.

I have added to this edition, in the form of an appendix, a new chapter on Food for Invalids.

PHYLLIS BROWNE.

A Year's Cookery.

January 1st.

Breakfast.	Luncheon.	Dinner.
Savoury Eggs.	Baked Rabbit.	Fried Cod.
Potted Beef.	Italian Macaroni.	Stewed Steak.
Hot Rolls or Toast.	Bread and Butter.	Potatoes and Brussels Sprouts.
Honey.		Boiled Apple Dumpling with Sweet Sauce.
Bread and Butter.		Cheese and Celery.
Porridge.		

Marketing.

For the Day.—Five slices, half an inch thick, from the middle of a large Cod; three pounds tender Steak; two moderate-sized Rabbits; one pound rashers of Bacon; Potatoes, Brussels Sprouts, Celery; half a pound of Macaroni. Macaroni should be bought in small quantities. Six ounces of firm Beef Suet.

The flesh of the fish should be firm to the touch, and should rise immediately when pressed with the finger. (*See* Marketing, January 3rd.)

Rump steak is the best steak that can be chosen for this purpose, but it is expensive, and on this account buttock steak may be used in its place. Meat is likely to be tender when it yields to pressure, and when a little taken between the finger and thumb can be crumbled. The steak should be cut evenly, and should be about an inch and a half in thickness. If there is any fear that it will not be tender, it may be brushed lightly over with vinegar before being used. See also recipe for Sea Pie (March 14th).

For hints upon the choice of rabbits, *see* January 24th.

The larger portion of the bacon is for the Rabbits, the remainder for the Kidneys. (Before choosing bacon, *see* January 3rd.)

For To-morrow.—Four Sheep's Kidneys—fine, plump, and perfectly fresh; a large Neck of Mutton, as free from fat as possible (the neck should be hung in an airy place); Sardines. (*See* January 12th.)

BREAKFAST.—*Savoury Eggs.*—Take as many small tins as there are eggs to be cooked—one for each person and one over is a usual allowance. Dariole moulds will be suitable for the purpose; but, wanting these, queen-cake tins or deep patty-pans may be used. Butter the tins well inside, and sprinkle in them a savoury mixture, made by mincing a slice of cold boiled ham (fat and lean together), parsley, pepper, and salt. Two ounces of ham and a tea-spoonful of chopped parsley will be sufficient for three eggs. Break an egg carefully into each tin, put them side by side into a saucepan of fast-boiling water, and poach them gently till the white is thoroughly set. Have ready, in a hot dish, small circles of toasted bread, one for each egg. Turn the eggs carefully upon these, and serve. If liked, a small piece of broiled ham can be substituted for the buttered toast. Potted Beef (January 23rd); Porridge (January 25th).

LUNCHEON.—Baked Rabbit (July 8th); Italian Macaroni (July 7th).

DINNER.—*Fried Cod.*—Sprinkle the slices of cod with pepper and salt, and let them lie for an hour. Dip them in milk on a plate, and flour them thoroughly. Fry them in plenty of hot fat (January 17th). They will take about twenty minutes. When done enough, drain them on kitchen paper and place them on a hot dish, with *maître d'hôtel* butter under them and *maître d'hôtel* sauce round them (April 15th, May 6th). If preferred, Caper Sauce can be used (March 19th). Stewed Steak (January 31st); Boiled Apple Dumpling (July 19th); Sweet Sauce (July 19th); Potatoes (April 7th); Brussels Sprouts (June 4th); Cheese (June 8th).

Things that must not be Forgotten.

1. Pour the fat used for frying into a basin as soon as it is done with. If left on the fire it will spoil.

2. The outer sticks of celery ought always to be preserved, as also should be the rind of the bacon and the remains of the fish and sauce.

3. Let the cook after every meal look carefully over the fragments left from the meal. The pieces of fat should be put on one dish, and afterwards melted down for frying purposes (Note 5, February 19th). The meat, bones, skin, and gristle should be put on another dish, to be afterwards stewed for stock. This business should be done every day; it will prevent waste, and will, during the year, save the purchase of many a pound of gravy-beef and lard for frying. There is nothing disagreeable about it, because, of course, the remnants will not have been touched with anything more objectionable than a knife and fork.*

4. Stew the bones and inferior parts of the rabbit with the bacon-rind, scalded and scraped, in three pints and a half of water. Stew till the liquid is reduced to a little more than a quart (Stock, February 13th). Pour it out and leave it in a cool place.

5. (*See* Remarks on Broken Bread, January 2nd.)

---

* Every one will understand that it is not for one moment supposed that stock made from bones and remnants is equal to stock made from fresh meat. Nevertheless, this stock is both palatable and nourishing, and excellent soup may be made of it (*see* Preface). To make stock from fresh meat (July 30th); from bones (February 13th).

January 2nd.

Breakfast.	Luncheon.	Dinner.
Sardines. Kidneys and Bacon. Toast. Marmalade. Bread and Butter. Milk Porridge.	Cod Pie. Pancakes.	Celery Soup. Irish Stew. Potatoes and Savoy. Lemon Pudding. Cheese and Watercress.

Marketing.

For the Day.—Three Lemons; one dozen large Oysters for the Cod Pie. If native oysters may not be afforded, Portuguese or American oysters may be used; or, if these cannot be procured, tinned oysters will answer for the purpose. If a little sauce were left as well as fish, the oysters can be dispensed with altogether. If scallop-shells are not in the house, half-a-dozen of the deep shells of the oysters should be scoured and taken care of; they will do for scalloped fish. Vegetables—Potatoes, Savoy, and Watercress.

For To-morrow.—Bloaters (one will probably be enough for each person); one tin Collared Tongue; four pounds of the Fillet of the Rump of Beef. (*See* Marketing, January 10th.) Tongues are now to be procured in tins already cooked; they need only to be turned out, to have a napkin or frill pinned round them, and to be garnished with parsley. They are very good, and it is cheaper in the first instance to buy them in this way than to prepare them at home, although the bought tongues are so mellow that they do not "go" very far. (*See also* February 4th.)

The fillet of the rump of beef is a very tender piece of meat. It generally is sold at a price very little below that asked for rump steak, but there is no bone or skin belonging to it, so that it cannot be called an expensive joint. If there is any difficulty about getting this weight of the fillet (and there very likely will be), the butcher may be told to cut through and give a portion of the rump also. There will then be a small piece of skirting, a little fat, and a very little bone, and the meat ought to be charged 2d. or 3d. less per pound. As soon as it is sent home, it should be brushed all over with a table-spoonful of vinegar, have a little pepper and salt sprinkled lightly over it, and be hung in a cool, airy place. Of course the hook must not be stuck into the fleshy part of the meat, but into a portion of the skin.

BREAKFAST.—*Kidneys and Bacon.*—Trim away the fat; skin and cut each kidney into slices the round way. Mix on a plate a table-spoonful of flour, a salt-spoonful of salt, and half a salt-spoonful of pepper. Dip each slice into the mixture. Melt a little bacon fat or butter in the frying-pan. When it is melted, put in the rashers of bacon procured for the purpose yesterday. They must be cut very thinly into small pieces convenient for serving. Fry them very gently over a slow fire, and turn them repeatedly. When done enough, put them on the dish on which they are to be served, and fry the slices of kidney in the same fat. In one minute turn them; in about four minutes they will be done enough, and may be put on the dish with the bacon. They ought to be slightly under-done. Pour away the superabundant fat, sprinkle a tea-spoonful of flour into the remainder, and mix it thoroughly, beating it smooth with the back of a wooden spoon. Add gradually as much water as will make a tolerably thick sauce. Stir this over the fire till it boils, then strain it over the kidneys. A dessert-spoonful of mushroom ketchup may be added to the gravy, and, if liked, a table-spoonful of claret may be thrown in. Kidneys cooked in this way will go half as far again as broiled kidneys. Milk Porridge (June 13th); Sardines (*see* Marketing, January 12th).

Every day, after breakfast, the mistress of a house should go on a tour of inspection through the kitchens and pantries. She can then see what was left from yesterday, and can easily arrange what is to be done for the day. One great means of avoiding waste is to use what is on hand before purchasing fresh materials. It is most probable that to-day there will be found in the pantry the remains of the cold cod; the stock produced by stewing the rabbit-bones and bacon-rind; the outer sticks of celery; and the neck of mutton. This being the case, she will do well to order Cod Pie to be made of the remnants of cod, Celery Soup of the stock and celery, and Irish Stew of the best end of the neck of mutton. The scrag end should be boiled separately, and used as hereafter directed. The batter for the pancakes should be made early in the day, because it is so much better for standing a few hours. Broken pieces of bread should be collected every day, for they constitute a fruitful source of waste in many households, although in others they are scarcely to be seen. They may be used to make bread-crumbs for frying fish, and for this purpose they should be put into a cool oven, dried thoroughly, and lightly crisped, then crushed with a rolling-pin and passed through a fine wire-sieve. They should then be put into a perfectly dry bottle, and stored for use. It is often very inconvenient to be obliged to prepare bread-crumbs each time they are wanted; and if the cook will make them beforehand, when she has time, she will find it a great help. Stale bread may be used in many other ways (*see* Index).

LUNCHEON.—*Cod Pie.*—Take the flesh from the bones of cod, and be careful that no bones or little bits of skin are left in it. Beard the oysters, and stew the skin and the bones of the fish and the beards in a little water. When the goodness is drawn from them, boil the liquid quickly till it is very much reduced. Strain it, add to it the oyster liquor and an equal quantity of milk, and thicken it by adding to it a little flour mixed with a small quantity of water. Stir into this sauce a few drops of essence of anchovy, put the oysters into a strainer, and hold them in the sauce for three seconds. Butter a pie-dish, lay the pieces of fish in it, pour the sauce over, and add the oysters. Spread over the top a covering of mashed potatoes which have either been left from yesterday or have been boiled for the purpose. Make the top of the potato rough with a fork, bake it in a moderate oven, and send it to table lightly browned. If any fish sauce were left, it can be poured over the fish instead of the oysters. When tinned oysters are used, the liquor can be mixed with the sauce, but the oysters need not be boiled in it. This pie must not be *moist* when sent to table. For Pancakes, *see* February 24th.

DINNER.—Celery Soup (December 3rd); Irish Stew (March 10th);

Potatoes (May 12th); Savoy (June 4th); Lemon Pudding (August 12th); Cheese (June 8th).

Things that must not be Forgotten.

1. The bacon and kidney must be fried *slowly*. If cooked quickly they will be hard and indigestible.

2. The bloaters must be put far away from all other food, as anything that they come in contact with will taste of them.

3. Sugar browning is wanted in the house. It may be made to-day. Put a quarter of a pound of brown sugar into an old but clean saucepan, and stir it over the fire till it melts and becomes slightly coloured. Draw it back and let it bake slowly, stirring it every now and then till it is nearly black, without being at all burnt. Pour upon it a pint of water, let it boil for five or six minutes, strain it through muslin into a glass bottle, cork it up, and keep it for use. This browning is so useful that a store should always be kept on hand. An easier way of making browning is to pour a quart of boiling water upon a quarter of a pound of chicory. Let it stand. In half an hour the liquid will be ready to be poured off and bottled for use. This browning, however, does not keep well.

4. It is a good plan for the cook to make a point every Friday of making pastry (April 17th), fruit pies, plain cakes, rolls, buns, Vienna bread, scones, &c., that will be required for three or four days. It is a great help to have little things of this kind in the house; and if the work is so arranged that the business is done regularly there will be no difficulty about it. To-day a cranberry tart (August 7th), Vienna bread (August 26th), Mutton Pies (January 3rd), and a Plain Cake (June 26th) can be made.

January 3rd.

Breakfast.	Luncheon.	Dinner.
Bloaters.	Mutton Pies.	Milk Soup.
Collared Tongue.	Rice Pudding.	Fillet of Beef.
Vienna Bread.		Vegetables—Baked Potatoes and Mashed Parsnips.
Marmalade.		
Bread and Butter.		Boiled Batter Pudding.
Bread and Milk.		Cheese and Celery.

Marketing.

For the Day.—Potatoes, Parsnips, Celery.

For To-morrow.—Half a pound of Streaky Bacon cut into thin rashers; one bottle of Gorgona Anchovies; one large dried Haddock; one pair of moderate-sized but thick Soles; the best end of a Loin of Mutton, as free from fat as may be; a quarter of a pound of Kidney Suet; a quarter of a pound of German Sausage (March 28th); Celery; Apples; one stick of Horse-radish; Jerusalem Artichokes; Potatoes; two Batavian Endive; one

Beet-root; one-pennyworth of Parsley. Parsley is wanted so continually in cookery and for garnishing dishes, that when it cannot be grown (and this can be done easily with ever such a small piece of ground) a point should be made of buying a pennyworth twice a week, say on Wednesdays and Saturdays. If the stalks are put in water, the parsley will keep fresh for two or three days. Some people dry parsley, and this is wise, but for garnishing dishes it is better to be fresh, and it can be obtained in most places without much difficulty all the year round. When bacon is to be used, the quantity required is given in the marketing column for the day. It is not, however, recommended that bacon should be bought a few ounces at a time. It is a good plan to keep it in the house, so that when a little is wanted it can be cut off as required. Bacon should have fine skin, and should possess an agreeable odour. The lean should be of a bright red colour, and intermixed with fibres of fat; whilst raw, it should adhere strongly to the bone. The fat should be firm and white, with a slightly reddish tinge.

In deciding upon the kind of fish to be procured, the state of the market should always be considered. The supply of fish is so uncertain and its price so variable, that the housekeeper will find it to be the wisest plan to pay a visit to the fishmonger and see what lies upon his slab before deciding upon the kind of fish to be bought. In drawing up these *menus*, fish has been fixed upon that is in full season, and therefore likely to be in good condition and reasonable in price at the date given. If, however, it is found that, owing to unforeseen circumstances, the particular variety named is scarce on a certain day, it will be better and more economical to choose a kind that is plentiful, and leave the other for another time. The whereabouts of the recipes for cooking different varieties of fish may be discovered by looking in the Index. It should be remembered that whiting, mackerel, and fresh herrings *must* be cooked when fresh, as they very quickly decompose. Nearly all fish is best when fresh; but there are some kinds, and soles are amongst them, which in cold weather can be kept until the second day without much harm being done; and, therefore, when soles can be obtained quite fresh on the Saturday (as in towns they usually can be), they may be kept for Sunday. Soles should be firm as well as thick. It is one sign of freshness when the skin is difficult to draw off. Fish is fresh when it feels firm and stiff, when the gills are bright red and the eyes bright. If the eyes are dull and the flesh flabby the fish is good for nothing.

A loin of mutton, like a saddle of mutton, is generally considered an expensive dish, and so it is if very fat. The butcher should be asked to supply well-hung mutton, to bone the joint, to trim away as much fat as he can, and to detach the fillet from the under-side. If when it is brought home there is still more fat on it than is likely to be eaten, let it be cut away and rendered for frying purposes. Suet should be firm, hard, and close. Beef kidney suet is the best.

BREAKFAST.—*Bloaters.*—Cut off the heads of the fish, split them open, and grill them upon a gridiron. It is usual to broil bloaters whole; and if perfect cleanliness could be secured that would be the best way. It is not every cook, however, who possesses the knack of cleansing the fish whole, and therefore it is safest to have them opened. Rub the gridiron with a piece of mutton fat, place the bloaters on it, and broil them over a gentle fire for four or, at most, five minutes. Place them on a hot dish, skin downwards, rub them over with a lump of butter, or, better still, a little *maître d'hôtel* butter (April 15th), and they are ready to serve. If more convenient, they can be baked instead of being broiled. Collared Tongue (Marketing, January 2nd); Vienna Bread (August 26th); Bread and Milk (January 25th).

LUNCHEON.—*Mutton Pies.*—Pick the meat carefully from the scrag end of the neck of mutton that was boiled separately when the Irish stew was made. Free it from skin and fat, mince it not too finely, and put it in a basin. Supposing there is half a pound of meat, add two table-spoonfuls of strong gravy (made by boiling the bones and rapidly reducing the liquor), a little pepper and salt, a few drops of essence of anchovy, and a dessert-spoonful of chopped parsley. Mix thoroughly together. Line some tartlet or patty-pans with good short crust (June 19th), fill them with the prepared mince, cover them with paste, ornament them in the usual way, egg them over, and bake in a quick oven. They will take from twenty minutes to half an hour. Serve very hot, neatly arranged on a dish covered with a napkin. If liked, the mutton can be flavoured with a little piece of shallot and two or three mushrooms chopped small, and this will make an agreeable variety. If pastry is made on Friday, these pies could be made at the same time. Rice Pudding (February 24th).

DINNER.—*Milk Soup.*—Put a quart of water on the fire. Peel and throw into cold water two large potatoes, or three small ones, and one leek ; the white part only of the leek should be taken. If a leek cannot be procured, a small onion may be used instead, but the flavour will not be so delicate. When the water boils, throw in the vegetables, add an ounce of butter and a little pepper and salt. Boil for an hour. Pass the soup through a colander, and press the vegetables through with the back of a wooden spoon. Return pulp and soup to the saucepan, add three-quarters of a pint of milk, and stir till it boils. Sprinkle in gradually a heaped table-spoonful of crushed tapioca, and boil for about a quarter of an hour ; keep stirring all the time, or the tapioca may get into lumps. This crushed tapioca may be bought in packets specially prepared for purposes of this kind, or, if preferred, tapioca siftings can be bought by the pound of the corn-chandler. Serve the soup as hot as possible. Fillet of Beef (February 11th); Boiled Batter Pudding (May 18th); Baked Potatoes (May 4th); Mashed Parsnips. [Proceed as for Mashed Turnips (September 30th), but scrape the Parsnips instead of paring them]. Cheese (June 8th).

Things that must not be Forgotten.

1. Make a hole in the centre of each little mutton pie, to keep it from bursting whilst it is being baked.

2. When carving the collared tongue, cut a tolerably thick slice straight from the top ; lay this aside, and put it in its place again before putting the tongue away. This will help to keep the meat from getting dry The slice of tongue can be used afterwards in another way.

Sunday, January 4th.

On Sunday it is very usual for families who dine late on other days to have an early dinner, tea, and supper. This arrangement is therefore followed here.

Breakfast.	Dinner.	Tea.	Supper.
Dried Haddock.	Filleted Soles.	Hot Buttered Toast.	Cold Mutton.
Toasted Bacon.	Rolled Loin of Mutton.	Dry Toast.	Pickles.
Honey.	Mashed Potatoes.	Bread and Butter.	Endive Salad.
Vienna Bread.	Jerusalem Artichokes.	Jam.	Baked Apples.
Dried Toast.	Chocolate Pudding.	Plain Cake.	Cheese.
Bread and Butter.	Cheese.		
Corn Flour Milk.			

BREAKFAST.—The beverage served at breakfast must be determined by the taste of the members of the family. Tea and coffee are the most popular, although cocoa and chocolate are now very extensively taken also. Almost every housekeeper believes that she understands thoroughly how to make these simple beverages, and, doubtless, the majority are right in this belief; nevertheless, a few simple rules on the best way of making each may be useful.

Tea.—A very important item in the preparation of tea is the teapot. It is very commonly said that an earthenware tea-pot is to be preferred to a metal one; but let any housekeeper try the two and compare the infusions, and she will not long retain this opinion. The only reason why an earthenware tea-pot is to be recommended is that it is easily kept clean; and if a little pains is taken to keep the metal tea-pot clean, very much better tea can be made out of the latter than out of the former, with an equal quantity of the dried leaf. A tea-pot should be rinsed out with clean boiling water, and afterwards dried thoroughly each time it is used, and the inside should be as bright as the outside. Two or three minutes before the tea is made a little boiling water should be poured into the pot to heat the metal, then drained off before the tea is put in. By this means less heat will be abstracted from the infusion. As to the quantity of tea to be used, perhaps no better rule can be given than the old-fashioned one of allowing "a spoonful of tea for each person and one for the pot." Another good old rule, known to every one, is that the water must be boiling—"Unless the kettle boiling be, filling the tea-pot spoils the tea." It is not so generally known, however, that this water should be *freshly* boiled. If the kettle has been steaming away for ever so long, the water in it is not fit for making tea; and in order to extract the full aroma from the leaf the water should not have boiled more than one minute. Good tea cannot be made with hard water. When soft water cannot be obtained, a very tiny pinch of soda may be dropped into the tea-pot after the water is poured on the leaves. Soda should, however, be most sparingly used; if too much is put into the tea-pot the tea will be entirely spoilt. Boiling water should be poured very gently upon the dried leaves, and in quantity sufficient to half fill the tea-pot. The lid should at once be shut down, and a "cosy" put over the vessel, and after this the tea is left to "draw." The length of time given to this process must vary with the quality of the tea. Tea of superior quality may stand for ten minutes before the tea-pot is filled up; for the coarser kinds of tea five minutes will be enough; and if a longer time is given it is likely that the infusion will be bitter rather than fragrant. Fine tea can very rarely be purchased at a cheap rate; and it is so frequently adulterated that it is only safe to buy the article of a respectable dealer. Black tea is generally supposed to be purer than green tea, although a mixture of the two is frequently preferred. When the quantity of tea provided is not sufficient, and it is necessary to make fresh tea, the old leaves should be turned quite out, the tea-pot rinsed with boiling water, and the whole process commenced anew. Unless this is done, the bitterness of the old leaves will overpower the flavour of the new ones. So long as additional water is to be added, the tea-pot should never be quite drained before being re-filled. Dried Haddock (January 27th); Toasted Bacon (January 19th); *also* Fried Bacon (January 2nd); Vienna Bread (August 26th); Corn Flour Milk (June 19th).

DINNER.—*Filleted Soles—Sautés.*—It is most economical to fillet the soles at home, as nourishing fish stock for sauce can be made of the skin and bones. Prepare the fish an hour or two before it is to be dressed. Wash the sole and lay it on a board. Cut off with a sharp knife the head, tail, and outer fins, and draw off the skin from the tail to the head, first cutting through a little piece of the skin near the tail, so as to get hold of it. Make a deep incision all down the spinal bone, then dexterously slip the knife between the flesh and the bone, and remove the flesh entire, and as free from jags as possible. Do this to both sides of the fish alike, thus obtaining four long fillets from each sole. Trim the fillets neatly, and divide each one across the centre. Sprinkle pepper and salt lightly on them, flour them well, and wrap them in a cloth, and leave them in the kitchen for an hour or more. This is to dry them thoroughly before cooking them. Unless it is done the egg and bread-crumbs will not adhere to the fish. Beat the yolk and a little of the white of an egg in a plate, and put a large breakfast-cupful of properly prepared bread-crumbs (January 2nd and February 1st) in some paper. Pass the fish through the egg on both sides, and throw the crumbs well over it. Melt a slice of butter in the frying-pan, put in the fillets, and cook them gently till they are brown on one side, then turn them, and brown them upon the other. Put them between sheets of kitchen paper to free them from grease, and dish them like cutlets, with one fillet overlapping another. Pour over them a little *maître d'hôtel* (May 6th) or shrimp sauce (January 30th), or, if it may be afforded, some Dutch sauce (May 14th). All kinds of flat fish can be cooked in this way. If preferred, the egg and bread-crumbs can be omitted, and the fillets floured and dried by being wrapped in a cloth for au hour or two before being cooked. Rolled Mutton (April 22nd); Mashed Potatoes (May 12th); Jerusalem Artichokes (November 30th); Chocolate Pudding (July 24th); Cheese (June 8th).

TEA.—Plain Cake (June 26th).

SUPPER.—Endive Salad (March 13th); Baked Apples (February 9th).

Things that must not be Forgotten.

1. Take care of the bacon fat.
2. Stew the skin and bones of the fish, and make the fish sauce with the stock.
3. Before sending the cold mutton up to supper put it on a clean dish and garnish it with parsley. Carefully preserve any gravy that may have run from it.

January 5th.

Breakfast.	Luncheon.	Dinner.
Collared Tongue. Boiled Eggs. (If any filleted Sole were left, it could be prepared according to the recipe (Jan. 2nd), and served instead of the boiled eggs.) Brown and White Bread and Butter. Marmalade. Milk Toast.	Hambro' Salad. Royal Sandwiches. Cranberry Tart.	Crécy Soup. Beef, with Sharp Sauce; or, if the Beef is used, Steak, with Onions. Potatoes and Winter Greens. Brown Bread Pudding. Cheese and Rusks.

Marketing.

Monday is not a good day for marketing. Customers who make large purchases on this day (unless they buy what is wanted of large first-class dealers) stand in danger of having the surplus stock left from Saturday presented to their notice. Where there is a family to provide for, it will, of course, be necessary to make some purchases, but the housekeeper will do well to defer buying anything that is very important until Tuesday. A Melton Mowbray Pork Pie should be bought for breakfast to-morrow, and a small salad for to-day.

BREAKFAST.—The collared tongue left on Saturday may be served again to-day, and *Boiled Eggs* can be added as an accompaniment. As in the case of savoury eggs, one egg should be allowed for each person, and one over. One would think that it was the easiest thing in the world to boil eggs properly, yet there are not many cooks who are certain to send them up *always* right. Perhaps the reason of this is that the quality of the egg is not considered in calculating the time required for boiling, but the orthodox three minutes is allotted to all eggs, new-laid and stale alike. New-laid eggs need four minutes to "set;" eggs that have been kept for some days will need only three minutes. Eggs should be put into *boiling* water, and should be quite covered; unless this is done they will not be equally cooked. They should be gently boiled. Eggs with very thin shells are less likely to burst if they are put into cold water and brought gently to the boiling point. They will be lightly set when the water boils. If wanted well done, they should be left in the hot water off the fire for a minute. An egg that has been laid twelve hours will generally be preferred to one that is perfectly fresh —warm from the nest. Milk Toast (June 17th).

LUNCHEON.—*Royal Sandwiches.*—Put three eggs into boiling water, and boil them gently for ten minutes. Take them up, and put them into a basin of cold water for five minutes. Take six anchovies, wash them, wipe them in a cloth, cut off the heads and fins, and scrape away the skin. With the fingers and thumb split them open down the back, and take the fillets or sides from the back-bone. Clean and dry perfectly the small salad. Cut six thin slices of stale brown bread, free from crust. Butter these well, and lay between each two one of the eggs, shelled and cut into thin slices, a layer of small salad cut up small, and the fillets of two anchovies. Press the slices together, with a sharp knife divide them into small squares, and arrange them neatly on a dish covered with a napkin. Hambro' Salad (August 8th); Cranberry Tart (August 7th).

DINNER.—*Crécy Soup.*—Scrape and cut up in slices eight good-sized carrots. Put these in a stew-pan with a slice of butter or dripping, the pieces of bacon-rind left from Sunday, two onions, six or eight peppercorns, and four or five outer sticks of celery left from Saturday. Shake the vegetables over the fire for three or four minutes, then put a good-sized crust of stale bread with them, and pour upon them a pint of the stock made from the mutton bones, and let them simmer gently until quite soft. Drain them, bruise them in a mortar, and rub them through a hair-sieve with the back of a wooden spoon, moistening them frequently with the liquor in which they were stewed. Put pulp, liquor and all, into a stew-pan, add an additional quart of stock, and stir the soup over the fire till it boils. Draw it to the side of the fire, and let it simmer gently to throw up the grease, and skim this away carefully as it rises. Add a pinch of sugar, pepper and salt to taste, and a dessert-spoonful of the rich gravy which lies under the cake of fat poured from the roast beef. Serve very hot, and send bread, toasted and cut into dice, to table on a separate dish. This soup ought to be as thick as cream, and of a deep red colour. Beef with Acid Sauce can be made of the remains of the cold beef, cut into neat slices the third of an inch thick, free from fat and gristle. If there is not sufficient cold beef left for this, three pounds of steak must be bought for dinner, and may be stewed with onions according to the recipe given. Those who do not like the flavour of onions should avoid this dish, and then the fresh beef can be stewed in the usual way (January 31st). Whether there are plenty of slices of cold beef or not, there is sure to be plenty of meat upon the bone, and every bit of this should be cut off. The fat portions should be put aside to be rendered, and the skin and gristle stewed with the bone. The lean portions of broken beef can be made into rissoles for luncheon to-morrow. They should be kept covered until they are to be made, to prevent their getting dry. The remains of collared tongue can be put with them. Beef with Sharp Sauce (December 4th); Beef stewed with Onions (November 3rd); Potatoes (May 12th); Winter Greens (June 4th); Brown Bread Pudding (July 20th); Cheese (June 8th).

Things that must not be Forgotten.

1. Purées like the one mentioned above *must* be rubbed through a sieve. The process calls both for time and patience, but the result amply repays both.

2. Before putting the bacon-rind into the stew-pan, scald it in boiling water, and scrape the rough part with a sharp knife.

3. Break the beef bone into small pieces, and stew these for stock according to the recipe given (February 13th). This stock can be used to make parsnip soup for January 8th.

4. Keep the anchovies closely corked down and covered with liquor.

January 6th.

Breakfast.	Luncheon.	Dinner.
Eggs in Brown Butter. Melton Mowbray Pork Pie. Hot and Dry Toast. Brown and White Bread and Butter. Porridge.	Rissoles. Fried Potatoes. Compôte of Apples. (Any remains of the Brown Bread Pudding can be used instead of the Apples. *See* Remains of Pudding Toasted, March 6th.)	Cod's Head and Shoulders. Roast Loin of Pork, with Savoury Pudding. Mashed Potatoes, Savoy. Semolina Pudding. Cheese

Marketing.

For the Day.—About six pounds of Cod. Choose a fish that is thick about the neck, plump and round near the tail, with the hollow behind the head deep, the eyes bright and full, and the flesh firm and white. Be careful that a portion of the liver and of the roe is sent with the fish. Apples, Potatoes, Savoy.

A Loin of Pork. There is no meat that requires to be chosen so carefully as pork; for if the animal from which it is taken were diseased or badly fed, the flesh will be most unwholesome, and is almost certain to produce illness. The safest plan is to buy the meat of the feeder, or, when this cannot be, it should be purchased of a thoroughly respectable dealer. Good pork is firm and finely grained, with the lean of a clear pinkish white, delicately veined with fat and cool to the touch, and the fat fine and white. The skin should be thin and elastic to the touch. Pork should be quite fresh; it will not keep unless salted. It is economical to buy a whole fore loin; roast the best end, and use the chump end for sausages.

For To-morrow.—Order to be sent in the morning two plump young Ostend Rabbits, trussed; half a pound of strips of Bacon (*see* Marketing, January 3rd); six or eight small Soles—"slips" (*see* January 3rd); Muffins (January 29th); Hominy (Marketing, February 10th).

BREAKFAST.—*Eggs in Brown Butter.*—Allow one egg for each person, and one over. Take either an earthenware dish that will stand the fire or a tin dish. The earthenware dish is to be preferred, because the eggs may be sent to table upon it. Put in this a little bacon fat (preserved from Sunday): an ounce will be enough for four eggs. If the bacon fat has been used, butter must be taken instead. Let this not only melt in the oven, but become a rich brown without being at all burnt. Break the eggs into it carefully, so as not to break the yolks, and let them cook slowly till they are set. Sprinkle a little pepper over them, pour upon them a table-spoonful of hot vinegar, and serve. If butter is used instead of bacon fat, salt and pepper must be sprinkled over the eggs. The pork pie should be served on a dish, covered with a napkin. Porridge (January 25th).

LUNCHEON.—*Rissoles.*—Take the pieces of beef and the remains of the collared tongue, and mince all well together, leaving out the skin and gristle. Add a pinch of finely-minced shallot, or, wanting this, of onion boiled till tender, a little pepper and salt, and a few drops of the essence of anchovy. Melt an ounce of butter in a small saucepan, stir in a heaped table-spoonful of flour, and beat the mixture with the back of a wooden spoon. Add one gill of stock, milk, or water, and mix thoroughly. Stir in the minced meat, turn the preparation upon a dish, and leave it till cold. Make a small quantity of good pastry, roll it out to the thickness of the eighth of an inch, and divide it into two parts. Put little balls of the minced meat upon one-half, leaving about two inches distance between each. Moisten the paste round each ball with water, and cover the whole with the unused piece of pastry. Press the edges of pastry closely together round each ball of meat. Stamp them out in rounds with a cutter, place them on a floured dish; place them side by side in a frying-basket, and fry them in plenty of hot fat, as fish is fried (January 17th). If a frying-basket is not at hand, it may be dispensed with. The appearance of the rissoles will be improved if they are brushed over with beaten egg and dipped into crushed vermicelli before being fried. If preferred, the pastry can be omitted altogether, and the minced meat can be made into balls about the size of large walnuts, and dipped in egg and bread-crumbs before being fried, thus making croquettes instead of rissoles. Serve either croquettes or rissoles hot on a dish covered with a napkin, and garnish with fried parsley (January 13th). If liked, a little good brown gravy can be sent to table in a tureen. Fried Potatoes (February 2nd); Compôte of Apples (August 5th and Note 3, September 12th).

DINNER.—Cod's Head and Shoulders (December 6th); Roast Pork (March 4th); Savoury Pudding (September 29th); Mashed Potatoes (May 12th); Savoy (June 4th); Semolina Pudding (March 12th); Cheese (June 8th).

Things that must not be Forgotten.

1. Drain the rissoles and the fried potatoes on kitchen paper as soon as they are taken out of the fat, in order to free them from grease.

2. Preserve the stock in which the cod is boiled.

3. Cut the meat off the chump end of the loin of pork, and make it into sausages (March 18th). Stew the bones of the pork for stock, and keep this stock in a separate vessel.

4. *Thickening*, or *Roux*, is wanted in the house, and may be made to-day. Take equal quantities of flour and good butter; it is no economy to use common butter, because common butter is generally adulterated, and a good deal of it will be lost in clarification. Spread the flour on a paper, and put it before the fire to dry; then pass it through a fine wire-sieve, so as to have it free from lumps. Clarify the butter; that is, melt it, and when it has stood to settle for a while, skim the surface, and pour away the pure oily portion, leaving untouched the thick curd-like substance that will have settled at the bottom. This pure oil is the only part that should be used for the roux. Put the oiled butter into an enamelled saucepan, and mix the flour with it gradually, stirring it briskly to make it quite smooth. Keep stirring it over the fire till it is well cooked, but not at all coloured, then pour half of it into a clean earthenware jar. This will be white thickening, and may be used for white sauces. Keep stirring the remainder over the fire till it is brightly coloured; then draw it back, and let it stand till it ceases to bubble, when it may be at once poured into another jar. This thickening will take a long time to make—perhaps a couple of hours; but when once made it will keep for months. Sauce that is thickened with it should always be allowed

to simmer gently for twenty minutes or half an hour to "throw up the grease," as it is called, which grease must be carefully removed as it rises. The roux may be mixed with either hot or cold liquor. If cold, it should be stirred till it boils; if hot, the roux should be moistened with a little of the liquor off the fire, then poured into the remainder, and stirred till it boils. The sauce or soup thickened with it will only acquire its proper consistency after it has been stirred and boiled. No good cook should be without this roux in the house; and therefore it is understood that when the quantity made is finished, it shall be renewed without further reminder. If unfortunately it should happen that it is all used, and a little is wanted for immediate use, melt half an ounce of butter over the fire, and mix smoothly with it (with a wooden spoon) a table-spoonful of flour. Stir it quickly over a gentle fire for three minutes, moisten it gradually with the liquid to be thickened, and boil it, stirring it all the time. This quantity will be sufficient for a pint of stock. Gravy thickened with raw flour is liable to have a puddingy taste.

5. Soak some hominy in cold water (February 10th).

January 7th.

Breakfast.	Luncheon.	Dinner.
Baked Soles.	Remains of Cod, Scalloped.	Oyster Soup, made of the Fish Stock.
Sausages with Fried Bread.	Toad in the Hole.	Boiled Rabbits with Onion Sauce.
Hot Buttered Toast.		Fried Bacon.
Dry Toast.		Potatoes and Brussels Sprouts.
Muffins.		Vermicelli Pudding.
Marmalade.		Cheese.
Boiled Hominy.		

Marketing.

For the Day.—One dozen large Oysters, or if this will not be afforded, one tin of Oysters; one-pennyworth of Parsley. (*See* January 3rd.) Potatoes, Brussels Sprouts.

For To-morrow.—One tin Bovill's Potted Grouse. This potted grouse is most delicious in flavour; it will, however, have a better appearance if it is taken out of the small tin in which it is sold, and is pressed into two or more of the small jars usually used for preparations of this kind, then covered with clarified butter. If this is done it will serve for two or three breakfasts, and will look and taste well to the last. If it is pressed into one jar it should be turned into a fresh one after it has once been used, and should be sent to table with the jar covered with a paper frill, and the meat garnished with parsley. Half a Pig's Head, and two Pig's Feet for brawn. (*See* Marketing, January 6th.) The pork-butcher should be asked to cut away the cheek, that it may be pickled separately, leaving the rest of the head for brawn. Rolls (September 4th).

BREAKFAST.—*Baked Soles.*—Scrape the soles, but do not skin them, roll them in a soft cloth for awhile to dry them thoroughly, and brush them over on the white side with dissolved butter.

Cover them with prepared bread-crumbs, lay them white side uppermost in a baking-tin in which a little butter has been dissolved, and bake them in a brisk oven. They will be done enough in about twenty minutes. They should be brown on the top, and if they are not the tin containing them must be held before the fire for a minute or two. Prepared in this way the soles will not require any sauce.

Sausages on Toast.—Take about one-half of the sausages made yesterday from the chump end of the loin of pork. Put a little dripping in the frying-pan, and before it is melted put in the sausages. Let them get hot very gradually, shake the pan frequently, and keep turning the sausages till they are equally browned all over. Cook them gently; they will take from fifteen to twenty minutes. Put the sausages on a hot dish. Fry some pieces of bread in the fat that has drained from them, and put these round them as a garnish. Muffins (January 30th); Boiled Hominy (February 11th).

LUNCHEON.—*Scalloped Cod.*—Remove the flesh from the remains of the cold cod, and free it from skin and bone; season it with salt, white pepper, and a very little grated nutmeg. Weigh the flesh, take half the weight in fine bread-crumbs, and season these with salt and cayenne. Butter a pie-dish, and put a layer of crumbs in the bottom; lay the fish upon these, put little pieces of butter here and there upon it; cover well with bread-crumbs, and add a little more butter. Bake in a gentle oven till the preparation is hot throughout. Serve immediately in the dish in which it was baked. For another way, *see* January 26th. Toad in the Hole (January 15th) made of the remainder of the sausages.

DINNER.—Oyster Soup (October 1st); Boiled Rabbit (March 6th); Onion Sauce (October 14th); Fried Bacon (January 2nd); Potatoes (May 12th); Brussels Sprouts (June 4th); Vermicelli Pudding (August 1st); Cheese (June 8th).

Things that must not be Forgotten.

1. Wash the pig's cheek, put a handful of salt on it, and leave it to drain until to-morrow.

2. Take the brains out of the head and throw them away; remove the eyes and snout also. Take out the tongue, rub it with salt, and put it on a separate dish; sprinkle a handful of salt over the head, and let it drain until to-morrow. The pig's feet should be rubbed over with salt, any hairs that may have been left on them being first scraped away.

3. Make a mould of corn-flour blancmange for dinner to-morrow (June 15th), with orange garnish and sauce (December 6th).

4. Put the rabbit stock into a perfectly clean earthenware pan, and keep it in a cool place; it will have to be kept for a day or two.

5. *See* Note 1, February 17th.

6. Fillet the anchovies and prepare the stock for breakfast to-morrow.

January 8th.

Breakfast.	Luncheon.	Dinner.
Anchovy Toast, with Poached Eggs. Potted Grouse. Hot Buttered Toast. Dry Toast. Muffins. Honey. Bread and Butter, Brown and White. Fried Hominy.	Minced Pork. Apples, with Tapioca.	Parsnip Soup. Sea Pie. Potatoes and Boiled Carrots. Corn-flour Blancmange, with Orange Garnish and Sauce. Cheese and Celery.

Marketing.

For the Day.—Two and a half pounds of Buttock Steak (see Marketing, January 1st); a quarter of a pound of Suet; Parsnips, Potatoes, Carrots, and Celery.

For To-morrow.—A piece of Kippered Salmon, weighing three or four pounds; a freshly killed young Hare; a Leg of Mutton. The hare is intended for Sunday week, therefore its purchase should be deferred for a few days, unless the weather is cold and dry. A hare will not keep well in damp "muggy" weather. If the body of the hare is stiff it is fresh, if limp it is stale. The cleft in the lip should not be widely spread, the claws should be tolerably sharp, and the ears tender and soft. If the reverse is the case the animal is old. Hang the hare by its hind legs, and do not skin it until a short time before it is cooked. If it is already paunched (and it is better not to be so, at any rate for a few days) it should be emptied, and the inside wiped dry every day. It will be well before buying a piece of salmon to ascertain whether or not it is liked in the house. Some people like it exceedingly, others not at all; indeed, it has been compared to "salted door-mat."

Ask the butcher to supply mutton that, though perfectly sweet, has hung for several days. The Wether leg with the lump of fat on is the best, and small mutton is to be preferred to large mutton.

BREAKFAST.—*Anchovy Toast.*—Allow one egg for each person, and one over, and as many small squares of dry toast as there are eggs. The toast should be free from crust, about half an inch thick, and should be cut from bread one day old. Make a little anchovy butter as follows:—Cleanse six anchovies, cut off their heads, bone them, and pound them in a mortar with two ounces of fresh butter, a tea-spoonful of essence of anchovy, a pinch of cayenne, and a little grated nutmeg. If a mortar is not at hand the ingredients can be mixed on a plate with a broad bladed knife. Fillet as many anchovies as will be required; three will be enough for a round of toast. (See Royal Sandwiches, January 5th.) Spread a little anchovy butter on the pieces of toast, and lay the three filleted anchovies upon them. Poach the eggs in boiling water, into which a table-spoonful of vinegar and a little salt have been thrown. When they are set, take them up, drain them on the slice, and lay each one upon the piece of toast waiting to receive it. Arrange the eggs in a circle, pour a little gravy under them made of the cupful of stock prepared for the purpose. This stock should have been boiled with a piece of carrot, a strip of the bacon-rind, two peppercorns, and the anchovy bones. When reduced to about two table-spoonfuls it should be strained, and a few drops of browning may be added to colour it. Eggs served in this way form a very appetising little dish, and they are not really so troublesome to prepare as might be supposed. Potted Grouse (January 7th); Muffins (January 30th); Fried Hominy (February 12th).

LUNCHEON.—Minced Pork (April 20th); Apples, with Tapioca (February 18th).

DINNER.—Parsnip Soup (December 3rd); Sea Pie (March 14th); Potatoes (April 7th); Corn Flour (June 15th); Orange Garnish (December 6th); Carrots (July 6th); Cheese (June 8th).

Things that must not be Forgotten.

1. Mix thoroughly half an ounce of saltpetre, two ounces of common salt, two ounces of moist sugar, and a tea-spoonful of black pepper. Dry the ingredients before the fire, wipe the salt off the cheek, and rub it well in every part with the mixture.

2. Cleanse the pig's head and the feet. Do this by rubbing it in every part with plenty of salt, taking away all the thin skin and veins, and pieces of bone from the inside. The business is not a very agreeable one, but it must be done thoroughly. When it is quite clean wash the salt away in tepid water, and dry the head. Cleanse the feet also, split them in halves, and if necessary singe the coverings of the toes till they are loose and can be taken off. Mix thoroughly one ounce of saltpetre, six ounces of common salt, six ounces of brown sugar, and three-quarters of an ounce of black pepper. Rub the mixture into every part of the head, ears, and tongue, and leave all in a deep earthenware pan.

3. Cut the shank bone off the leg of mutton, and stew it for stock while it is fresh. Before using the stock pour it away from the sediment which will have settled at the bottom.

4. Put the slices of salmon to soak first thing in the morning (*see* January 9th).

January 9th.

Breakfast.	Luncheon.	Dinner.
Kippered Salmon.	Scotch Collops.	Boiled Brill.
Remains of Potted Grouse.	Macaroni Cheese.	Roast Leg of Mutton.
Hot Buttered Toast.		Yorkshire Pudding.
Dry Toast.		Boiled Potatoes and Jerusalem Artichokes.
Brown and White Bread and Butter.		Cottage Plum Pudding.
Milk Porridge.		Cheese and Pulled Bread.

Marketing.

For the Day.—One pound and a half of Buttock Steak (*see* January 1st); one good-sized Brill. Brill and turbot are, as a rule, dear in winter. At the same time they may occasionally be obtained cheap. Brill does not possess the gelatinous fins and skin of the turbot, so highly prized by epicures. Its fins. instead of being regarded as choice morsels, are cut off before being cooked. Like the turbot, it should be of a yellowish tint, and should be chosen on account of its freshness. (*See* January 3rd.) Potatoes, Artichokes; Macaroni; six ounces of firm Beef Suet.

For To-morrow.—Half a pound of Bacon in rashers. (*See* January 3rd.) Buy a Saddle of Mutton with not very much fat on it, and ask the butcher to hang it till wanted. A saddle of mutton is generally spoken of as an expensive joint. It is not a cheap one, but neither is it a very expensive one, if care is taken to procure it as lean as possible, that is, with as small an allowance of fat as can be. There is no question that it is an exceedingly delicious joint, and excellent soup may be made from the bones. Sea Biscuits.

BREAKFAST.—*Kippered Salmon.*—Cut thin slices from the salmon, as many as are likely to be wanted, and let them soak in cold water all night. Wipe them dry, rub them over with oil or dissolved butter, lay them on the fish gridiron, and broil them over a bright fire for eight or ten minutes. Rub them over with fresh butter, squeeze the juice of a lemon over, and serve very hot. Be careful to hang the unused salmon in a cool, airy place. Slices may be taken from it when wanted. When the piece is finished, more should be procured, as kippered salmon, when it is liked, is so useful to keep in the house for breakfast. (*See* Ham-cured Herrings, January 15th.) Milk Porridge (June 13th).

LUNCHEON.—*Scotch Collops.*—Cut away the fat and any skinny portions there may be about the steak, and mince it finely, seasoning it well with pepper and salt. An onion can be added, if liked, but this is a matter of taste. Melt a little butter in a stew-pan. Put in the mince, and stir it frequently to keep it from getting into lumps. In about eight minutes dredge a little flour over it, and pour upon it a little stock, boiling hot. Let it simmer gently a minute or two longer, and serve very hot. Three-cornered pieces of toasted bread may be put round the dish as a garnish. For Macaroni Cheese, *see* March 20th.

DINNER.—*Boiled Brill.*—Put the fish-kettle on the fire with cold water to cover the fish, and throw into it a good handful of salt, in the proportion of a quarter of a pound of salt to a gallon of water. Bring it to the boil. Clean and wash the brill inside and out, cut off the fins, and rub it over with lemon juice to preserve its whiteness. In order to prevent the white side breaking in boiling, cut a slit just through the dark skin from the head down the back. Lay the fish on the drainer of the fish-kettle, and put it in the boiling water. Let it boil quickly for less than one minute; then draw it back, and let it simmer gently till it is done enough. Watch it carefully, and as soon as the flesh will leave the bone take it up. If it is not wanted for a few minutes, lay a hot cloth on it, and set the drainer with the fish upon it across the kettle, but on no account leave it in the water. The time required can scarcely be given, because it depends upon the thickness of the fish and upon the rate at which the fish is cooked. It is better to let it simmer *gently.* A moderate-sized brill would take about twenty minutes; a large one, half an hour. Put a fish drainer covered with a hot napkin on a hot dish. Slip the brill on it, white side up. Garnish it with cut lemon and tufts of parsley placed lightly round it. Melted butter flavoured with anchovy (July 17th), or, if it may be afforded, Dutch sauce (May 14th) may be served with it. Roast Leg of Mutton (March 4th); Yorkshire Pudding (December 3rd); Potatoes (April 7th); Jerusalem Artichokes (November 30th); Cottage Plum Pudding (June 6th); Cheese (June 8th).

Things that must not be Forgotten.

1. Rub the pig's cheeks with the brine, and turn them over in the pan.
2. Do the same to the feet.
3. Pastry is to be made to-day (April 17th) : two apple pies (August 7th); scones (August 26th); soda cake (August 14th).
4. Preserve the stock in which the brill is boiled, and take care of any remnants. Boil two table-spoonfuls of rice as for curry; it will be required for the kedgeree at breakfast.
5. Soak Normandy pippins.

January 10th.

Breakfast.	Luncheon.	Dinner.
Kedgeree.	Mutton Tart.	Palestine Soup.
Toasted Bacon.	Baked Potatoes.	Hashed Mutton.
Hot Buttered Toast.	Normandy Pippins.	Savoy and Potatoes.
Dry Toast.		Elegant Economist's Pudding.
Scones.		
Brown and White Bread and Butter.		Newmarket Pudding.
Marmalade.		Cheese.
Biscuits and Milk.		

Marketing.

For the Day.—Potatoes, Savoy, Jerusalem Artichokes for soup.

For To-morrow.—Cod's Head and Shoulders; one dozen large Oysters, or half a pint of picked Shrimps for sauce; two pounds of crimped Skate; Turnip Tops; Potatoes; Celery for the cheese; a pennyworth of Parsley (*see* January 3rd); and a tin of Potted Hare (Bovril's). Before choosing cod, *see* January 1st, 3rd, and 6th. If fresh oysters may not be afforded, tinned oysters may be used instead for sauce. Skate is generally sold cut into strips, and curled round, when it is called crimped skate. It should be chosen for its thickness, breadth, and firmness. A little piece of liver should be sold with it, as this is considered a delicacy. Skate is delicious fish at this time of year, but it is positively injurious when out of season. Two ribs of Beef, boned and rolled by the butcher, to weigh about seven pounds. If preferred, a square piece of the brisket may be bought instead of the ribs. The butcher should be asked to provide beef that has been hung a few days. If freshly killed, the meat will not be tender. Good beef is firm and elastic to the touch. The lean is of a bright red colour, neither pink nor purple It should be well marked with little veins of fat. The fat should be white rather than yellow.

BREAKFAST.—*Kedgeree.*—Pick the flesh of the fish from the bones, and break it into flakes free from skin and bone. Remove the skin from the rice also, and break it up with a fork. The fish and rice should be in about equal quantities. Melt a slice of butter in the frying-pan, throw in the rice and fish, and stir all briskly together till the mixture is quite hot, seasoning it rather highly with salt, pepper, and cayenne. Have ready two well-beaten eggs, stir them at the last moment into the kedgeree, and serve it very hot on a silver dish, if one is at hand. For Toasted Bacon, *see* January 19th. Biscuits and Milk (June 14th); Scones (May 23rd).

LUNCHEON.—*Mutton Tart.*—The cook should prepare the mutton early in the day, so that she may have time to make good gravy of the bones. First cut off the meat for the hash in neat slices, about a quarter of an inch thick, and put these on one side and between two dishes, to keep them from becoming hard. Take off the rest of the meat, that which has to be cut into small broken pieces, and mince it finely with a little of the fat, but without any skin and gristle. Break the bones into small pieces, put them into a saucepan, cover them with two quarts of cold water, and let them simmer as long as can be allowed. If an early dinner is served, it will be best to simmer them for an hour or two with a quart of water, and strain this off for the hash; then boil them again with fresh water for stock. Flavour the mince with salt and pepper, a little grated nutmeg, and a very small piece of chopped onion, if liked. Make some good short crust (June 19th). Cover a large tart-dish with this, rolled to the thickness of the eighth of an inch. Lay the mince upon it, moisten it with cold gravy, and cover it with pastry. Ornament the tart prettily, cut a slit in the centre to allow the steam to escape, and bake in a well-heated oven. Serve hot, with a little of the gravy in a tureen. Baked Potatoes (May 4th); Normandy Pippins (August 16th).

DINNER.—Palestine Soup (December 8th); Hashed Mutton (May 18th); Savoy (June 4th); Potatoes (April 7th); Elegant Economist's Pudding to be made of the remains of cottage plum pudding, if there are any (May 12th); if not, Newmarket Pudding (June 2nd); Cheese (June 8th).

Things that must not be Forgotten.

1. The meat in the hash must on no account be allowed to boil. If it does, it will be hard. It must simmer only till it is hot through.

2. Rub the cheek and the pig's head and feet, and turn all over in the brine.

3. Be careful that the kedgeree is served hot—hot with pepper, hot with the fire, on a hot dish, and upon hot plates. Thus only will it be worth anything at all.

Sunday, January 11th.

Breakfast.	Dinner.	Tea.	Supper.
Skate, with Brown Butter.	Cod's Head and Shoulders.	Thin Bread and Butter.	Cold Beef. Apple Pie. Cheese.
Potted Hare.	Shrimp or Oyster Sauce.	Apricot Jam.	
Hot Buttered Toast.		Marmalade.	
Dry Toast.	Rolled Beef, Roasted.	Soda Cake, made on Friday.	
Scones.	Potatoes.		
Brown and White Bread and Butter.	Turnip Tops.		
Honey.	Vermicelli Pudding.		
Milk Toast.	Cheese and Celery.		

BREAKFAST.—*Coffee.*—The great secret of making coffee good is to make it of a sufficiency of freshly roasted and freshly ground coffee. When, therefore, it cannot be roasted at home and used quickly (and a very good and simple machine is sold for doing this), the berries should be bought in small quantities at a time, should never be ground till just before they are wanted, and should be heated in a gentle oven before they are ground, to revive the flavour. The best utensil that can be used for making the coffee in is a tin cafetière, which can be procured either large or small, to suit the requirements of the family. To use it, first fill it with boiling water and let it stand until quite hot, then pour the liquid at once away. Place the coffee upon the perforated bottom of the upper compartment, and press it down with the piston. Put the strainer on the top and pour through it gently and gradually as much boiling water as is required. Cover the cafetière, and leave it in a hot place for a few minutes. When the liquid has drained into the lower pot the coffee is ready for use. If it is to be served in another pot, the vessel which is to receive it must be made hot with boiling water before the coffee is poured in. To make coffee strong, two ounces of ground berries will be needed for a pint of water. If it should happen that the coffee gets cold, the cafetière may be put upon a hot stove and left there until steam appears in the spout, when it should be at once removed. The coffee should not properly, however, be left to get cold in a metal pot. The milk used in making coffee should be added boiling hot. This is the best way of making coffee. In very many households, however, the old-fashioned coffee-pot is used instead of the cafetière, and then a different method must be adopted. Take the quantity of coffee required, put it into the coffee-pot, and set it on the stove or over a slow fire for five minutes to get hot. Pour the boiling water gently over it, and put it back on the fire for a minute or two till it boils up. Take it off, pour out a cupful, and pour it back into the coffee from a good height. Repeat this process three times. Throw a tea-spoonful of cold water into the coffee and leave it by the side of the fire for a few minutes to clear, then put it through the muslin strainer into the coffee-pot, already made hot for it, in which it is to be sent to table. Skate, with Brown Butter (February 12th); Potted Hare (January 7th); Scones (May 23rd); Milk Toast (June 17th).

DINNER.—*Cod's Head and Shoulders.*—Boil the cod in the stock in which the brill was cooked (December 6th). Shrimp Sauce (January 30th); Oyster Sauce (October 16th); Rolled Beef (March 4th); Potatoes (May 12th); Turnip Tops (June 4th); Vermicelli Pudding (August 1st); Cheese (June 8th).

Things that must not be Forgotten.

1. Turn over the pig's cheek and the head and feet in the brine.
2. Preserve the pieces of fish and any sauce there may be.
3. Stew the bones of the rolled beef for stock.

January 12th.

Breakfast.	Luncheon.	Dinner.
Boiled Eggs. Potted Hare. Toast or Hot Rolls. Brown and White Bread and Butter. Honey. Bread and Milk.	Shepherd's Pie of Beef. Apple Pie.	Oyster Soup. Broiled Steak. Baked Potatoes and Brussels Sprouts. Town Pudding. Cheese and Watercress.

Marketing.

For the Day.—Two dozen large Oysters, or a tin of preserved Oysters. A large slice of Rump Steak, not less than one inch thick, and weighing from three to three and a half pounds; six ounces of Beef Suet; Apples, Potatoes, Brussels Sprouts, Watercress.

For To-morrow.—A brace of well-hung Pheasants. The condition of the birds may be easily ascertained by examination, particularly about the vent. If the flesh is white and fresh-looking, and if the birds smell perfectly sweet, the pheasants will, when cooked, taste no better than an ordinary fowl, which may be procured at much less cost. The degree of "highness" which they have attained must be regulated by the taste of the eaters. Two-pennyworth of fresh Mutton Bones; and order three-pennyworth of Cream for the purée to-morrow. One-pennyworth of Parsley. Sardines: in buying Sardines, it will be well to procure a tin that will contain sufficient, and no more, for the requirements of the family. Although sardines will keep for two or three days, they are best when taken from a newly opened tin, and as the fish are preserved in tins of varying size, there need be no difficulty in providing the quantity likely to be used. For the sake of making a change, they may be turned out of the tin to a separate dish, have a little fresh oil poured upon them, and minced capers drained from the vinegar strewed over them. Champagne or forced Rhubarb will probably be obtainable now. Half a bundle will be sufficient for dinner to-morrow.

BREAKFAST.—Boiled Eggs (January 5th); Potted Hare (*see* Potted Grouse (January 7th); Bread and Milk (January 25th).

LUNCHEON—*Shepherd's Pie.*—It may be that the rolled beef will be preferred cold. It is probable, however, that if it has been used for supper as well as dinner what is left of it will not be very presentable. Therefore it will be most economical to make a pie of it. Boil as many potatoes as will be required for the quantity of meat; half-a-dozen large ones would be sufficient for one pound of beef. Mash them smoothly, and beat them up with a little salt, a slice of melted butter, and the yolk of an egg. If any cold potatoes were left yesterday they may be used instead of boiling fresh ones. Cut the meat into thin slices, free from fat, skin, and gristle, or, if preferred, mince it finely. Season it with salt and pepper. Butter a shallow pie-dish, put the meat into it, and moisten it with any gravy that may be left and a table-spoonful of Worcester sauce; cover with another layer of potato, rough the top with a fork, and bake the pie in a moderate oven for about three-quarters of an hour. It ought to be hot through and brown on the top. If there be no gravy to moisten the meat, use stock instead. Apple Pie made on Jan. 9th.

DINNER.—Make the stock for the oyster soup by stewing the bones and skin of the skate and of the cod in the liquor in which the brill was boiled. Oyster Soup (October 1st); Broiled Steak (January 22nd); Potatoes (May 12th); Brussels Sprouts (Cabbage, June 4th); Town Pudding (December 3rd); Cheese (June 8th).

Things that must not be Forgotten.

1. Rub the pig's cheek and head in the brine, and turn these over.
2. Prepare the fish cakes for breakfast to-morrow of the remains of the cod and skate. (See January 13th.)
3. Wash a few sprigs of parsley, and lay them on a cloth to dry, so that they may be ready for frying with the fish cakes in the morning.

January 13th.

Breakfast.	Luncheon.	Dinner.
Fish Cakes or Sardines.	Beef Hash (Economical).	Potato Purée.
Remains of Potted Hare.	Brown Betty.	Roast Pheasants.
Hot Rolls.	(If there be any remains of the Town Pudding they can be used instead of this.)	Bread Sauce and Brown Gravy.
Dry Toast.		Potato Mould.
Brown and White Bread and Butter.		Chestnuts and Brussels Sprouts.
Marmalade.		Stewed forced Rhubarb and Custard.
Porridge.		Cheese.

Marketing.

For the Day.—Six or eight pounds of the silverside of Beef, fresh—the middle cut is the best; Potatoes, Apples, Brussels Sprouts, and Chestnuts—one pint of Chestnuts to two pounds of Sprouts.

For To-morrow.—A fine Neck of Mutton with as little fat as may be.

BREAKFAST.—*Fish Cakes.*—If any cold potatoes were left from dinner the day before, they can be used instead of boiling fresh ones. If there are none, fresh potatoes must be boiled for the purpose, the number to be regulated by the quantity of fish. There should be equal weights of fish and potato. Break the fish, perfectly free from skin and bone, into flakes, and rub the potatoes through a fine sieve. Mix the two together, and season them rather highly with salt and cayenne, and add a few drops of essence of anchovy; put the mixture into a bowl and make it into a stiff paste with a little milk, melted butter, and lightly beaten egg. Half an ounce of butter, a table-spoonful of milk, and half an egg would be sufficient for one pound of fish, and one pound of cold potatoes. The other half of the egg could be used for brushing over the cakes before they were bread-crumbed. Flour the hands lightly. Make the paste into cakes about an inch and a half in diameter and three-quarters of an inch thick. Use as little flour as possible in doing this. Up to this point the cakes may be prepared the day before they are wanted. Brush the cakes over with egg, and toss them in bread-crumbs, and repeat the process a second time; if the cakes are not entirely covered they will burst in frying, as they will also be in danger of doing if much flour is used with them. Half fill a saucepan with frying fat, and let it boil (see Fat for Frying (February 19th and January 17th); arrange the fish cakes in the frying-basket, being careful not to let them touch each other. As soon as a thin blue smoke can be seen rising from the fat, plunge the basket into it, and let it remain until the cakes are a light golden brown; take them out, lay them on kitchen paper to free them from grease. *Parsley to Fry.*—Let the fat get hot again, put the dried sprigs of parsley into the basket, and plunge them into the hot fat for about two seconds. If when taken out the parsley feels crisp, lay it also on the paper for a minute. Pile the cakes neatly on a hot dish, garnish them with the fried parsley, and serve very hot. If a frying-basket is not at hand, the cakes and the parsley may be dropped into the boiling fat, and taken out with a fish-slice. They must have plenty of room in the saucepan, and must not touch each other. The cakes will be nicer if accompanied by egg sauce, but they will be very good without it. Rissoles, croquettes, and similar preparations should all be fried in this way. If there is no fish for fish cakes, sardines may be substituted. Potted Hare (see Potted Grouse, January 7th); Rolls (September 4th). Porridge (January 25th).

LUNCHEON.—Beef Hash, economical, made of any remnants of broiled steak there may be (November 11th); Brown Betty (November 26th).

DINNER. — Potato Purée (January 26th); Roast Pheasants (October 23rd); Bread Sauce (October 18th); Brown Gravy (October 18th); Potato Mould (October 23rd); Chestnuts and Brussels Sprouts (November 8th); Stewed Rhubarb (May 19th); Custard (August 10th); Cheese (June 8th).

Things that must not be Forgotten.

1. The mistress might privately request the carver to abstain if possible from using the legs of the bird, as they will be much nicer

devilled for breakfast to-morrow than eaten to-day. They must be prepared for devilling over-night. (*See* Breakfast, January 14th.)

2. Make some pickle for the beef, enough to cover it entirely when it is put into an earthenware pan about its own size. The proportions are, one pound of salt, three-quarters of an ounce of saltpetre, four ounces of sugar, three quarts of water. The pickle must be boiled for twenty minutes, skimmed well and strained, and allowed to go cold before the meat is put into it. This pickle, if boiled occasionally, will keep for three months this time of the year, though in summer time it will not keep more than three weeks. It should be reboiled with an additional handful of salt each time it is used, and should, as in the first instance, be skimmed, strained, and allowed to go cold before it is used. It will do to salt different kinds of meat. The liquor in which the meat is boiled, however, will be too salt to use for soup, and will have to be thrown away—a painful business to the economical housekeeper. A rather more expensive but better pickle may be made with one pound of bay salt, ten ounces of brown sugar, two ounces of saltpetre, two ounces of salt prunel, a quarter of a pound of common salt to one gallon of water. With this pickle soup can be made of the liquor used for boiling meat. Bay salt makes meat mellow; saltpetre (though it gives it the beautiful red colour so much admired in pickled beef) tends to harden the meat, therefore it should be used sparingly. Meat is much better pickled in brine like this than bought ready salted of the butcher. A piece of thick muslin should be kept over the pickling jar in order to keep out the dust and flies. The look and smell of the brine will testify to its condition; and it is, therefore, supposed that without further notice here it will be thrown away when done with, and fresh will be made if required. Brine that has once been used for pickling a pig's head should be thrown at once away.

3. Turn and rub the pig's cheek, head, &c.
4. Hang the neck of mutton in a cool place.

January 14th.

Breakfast.	Luncheon.	Dinner.
Devilled Pheasant's Legs, with or without Devil Sauce.	Mutton stewed with Vegetables.	Soles, Filleted and Rolled. Salmi of Pheasant.
Eggs on the Dish.	Baked Omelette.	Fried Potatoes; Greens.
Hot Toast. Dry Toast.		Lèche Crème.
Brown and White Bread and Butter.		Cheese, Pulled Bread, and Celery.
Marmalade.		
Corn Flour Milk.		

Marketing.

For the Day.—A pair of Soles, thick and of moderate size (January 3rd); a tin of preserved Mushrooms; half a pound of Ratafias; one Seville Orange.

If there is not enough pheasant left for a salmi, Steak may be bought to make a Sea Pie (March 14th). One-pennyworth of Parsley (January 3rd); Potatoes, Greens.

For To-morrow.—A tin of ham-cured Herrings; Fillet of Beef (January 2nd); Muffins (January 20th); half a pound of Macaroni (January 1st).

BREAKFAST.—If well cooked, the devil will be regarded by the epicure as the best part of the pheasants. The legs must be prepared over-night. With a sharp knife take the skin off the legs, and score the flesh twice crosswise on each side of the bone. Melt two ounces of butter, and mix with it a dessert-spoonful of salt, a tea-spoonful of pepper, a pinch of cayenne, a spoonful of mustard, and half a tea-spoonful of anchovy. Spread this mixture on the legs, and get it in between the scores as much as possible. Put a cover over the legs, and leave them in a cool place till morning. About a quarter of an hour before they are wanted for breakfast lay them on a gridiron (which has first been rubbed all over with a piece of the fat taken off the neck of mutton, and made hot), and put them over a gentle fire. Broil them slowly, turning them every minute. When done enough, serve them on a very hot dish (a hot-water dish will be the best), and send very hot plates to table with them. If properly dressed, the pheasant, though crisp, will not be at all burnt. A little dissolved butter should be poured over them before being sent to table. If it is wished that they should be very hot, they may be peppered once again before being served. The devilled legs may either be eaten dry, or a little grill sauce in a tureen may accompany them. This may be made as follows :—Chop four shallots or young onions finely, and boil them in half a gill of vinegar for five minutes. Put with them an equal quantity of the gravy preserved from the pheasant, and add a pinch of cayenne, half a tea-spoonful of essence of anchovy, and a table-spoonful of sherry, if permitted. If this sauce is used, the dissolved butter need not be poured over the devil. Eggs on the Dish (December 7th); Corn Flour Milk (June 19th).

LUNCHEON.—*Mutton stewed with Vegetables.*—Divide the neck of mutton into three parts; that is, chop off about two inches from the long rib bones, and cut the piece quite off. Toad in the hole may be made of it to-morrow. Halve the remaining portion, leaving the best end with as many cutlets as will be required for haricot mutton on Friday; the other part, or scrag end, may be stewed for to-day. Cut the meat into neat pieces, pepper and salt them, and pack them closely in a stew-pan. Put on the top of them a Spanish onion finely minced, three carrots cut into slices, and two turnips cut into quarters. Cover the saucepan closely, and put it where it will stew as gently as possible in its own gravy. If cooked very slowly indeed, it will not become dry. At the end of an hour and a half turn the meat over. Try the vegetables occasionally, and as soon as they are done enough take them up, and put them in a covered basin in the oven to keep them hot till the meat is ready—that is, till it is tender without being at all ragged. It will require from three to four hours' gentle stewing. Take it up, and throw a little cold water into the stock in order to make the fat rise to the surface. Skim it carefully, and thicken it with a little flour. Mince the vegetables, and toss them in a saucepan over the fire with a little butter. Put the meat into the gravy for a few minutes to make it hot, lay it on a dish, and put the vegetables in heaps round it. Serve very hot Baked Omelette (August 6th).

DINNER.—Soles, filleted and rolled, with brown sauce (March 1st and February 12th); Salmi of Pheasant (October 24th); Fried Potatoes (February 2nd); Greens (June 4th); Lèche Crème (May 7th); Cheese (June 8th).

Things that must not be Forgotten.

1. If there is not enough pheasant left to make a salmi, the bones, including those of the devilled legs, must be stewed for soup. To make this, put the bones into a saucepan with a large carrot scraped to pulp, a small onion stuck with two cloves, a bunch of parsley, three or four outer sticks of celery, one or two strips of bacon-rind scalded and scraped, half a dozen peppercorns, a pinch of salt, a crust of bread toasted, and as much water or stock as will cover. Let the liquid boil, skim it carefully, draw it back, and simmer it gently for three hours. Strain it, rub the vegetables through a sieve, and return the pulp to the soup, boil up again, and serve with fried sippets. Half a glass of sherry thrown in at the last moment will be an improvement.

2. Make the brawn (March 2nd).
3. Rub and turn over the cheeks and the silverside of beef.
4. Do not wash the tin in which the omelette was baked, but wipe it out till it is quite clean with a soft cloth, and keep it in a dry place.

January 15th.

Breakfast.	Luncheon.	Dinner.
Ham-cured Herrings.	Toad in the Hole.	Haddock, stuffed and baked, or Pheasant Soup.
Brawn.	Macaroni Cheese.	Fillet of Beef.
Muffins.		Horse-radish Sauce.
Brown and White Bread and Butter.		Potatoes.
Honey.		Mashed Parsnips.
Porridge.		Rice Pudding.
		Cheese and Watercress.

Marketing.

FOR THE DAY.—If Pheasant Soup is not provided (Note 1, January 14th), a good-sized Haddock. The large haddocks are the best; Horse-radish, Potatoes, Parsnips, Watercress.

BREAKFAST.—*Ham-cured Herrings*, like slices of kippered salmon, are delicious appetisers for breakfast; but as no one could eat very much of them, they should be accompanied by something substantial, as brawn. It is probable that half a herring will be plenty for each person. The tins ordinarily sold, price 1s., contain twelve fish. To prepare them, put as many as will be required in a dish, and cover them with boiling water. Let them stand twenty minutes, then drain off the liquid, and pour on fresh boiling water. At the end of another twenty minutes take them out, remove the skin and backbone, and serve. The herrings left in the tin will keep in a cool dry place for weeks.

Brawn (March 2nd) is more relishing when accompanied by *Brawn Sauce*. To make this, mix two mustard-spoonfuls of mixed mustard with a dessert-spoonful of brown sugar, a table-spoonful of vinegar, and two table-spoonfuls of oil. If there are any oranges in the house, the grated rind and juice of half a sweet orange will be an improvement. Muffins (January 30th); Porridge (January 25th).

LUNCHEON.—*Toad in the Hole.*—Cut the short end of the neck of mutton into pieces, one with a bone and one without. Put into a bowl four large table-spoonfuls of flour and a little salt, and make a smooth paste with milk, being careful to put in a little at a time, and to beat the batter briskly. When it is quite smooth, add the rest of the milk (about three-quarters of a pint) and two well beaten eggs. Make the batter an hour or two before it is wanted, but beat it up again with a small spoonful of baking-powder the last thing before it is used. It ought to have bubbles in it, which show that it is well beaten. Grease a shallow dish, and make it hot in the oven. Put the pieces of mutton into it, and pour the batter over them. Bake in a well-heated oven for about an hour and a half, till the batter is set and lightly browned. Serve very hot. It is impossible to say exactly how much milk will be wanted, because some flours take more milk than others; the batter should, however, be of the consistency of very thick cream. A cheaper but heavier batter may be made with six ounces of flour, one egg, and a pint of milk. If there is too much flour the pudding is solid, with too little it would not be firm. For ordinary purposes, two table-spoonfuls of flour to an egg, with the requisite quantity of milk, is an excellent proportion; and all baked batter puddings may be made from it. Macaroni Cheese (March 20th).

DINNER.—Haddock stuffed and baked (September 4th); Fillet of Beef (March 4th); Horse-radish Sauce (December 3rd); Potatoes (May 6th); Mashed Parsnips (September 30th); Rice Pudding (February 24th); Cheese (June 8th).

Things that must not be Forgotten.

1. Turn the silverside of beef in the brine.
2. Boil up the stock in the pantry that was made from bones, first clearing it carefully from fat. Stew in it very gently the skin and bones of the fish.
3. Put a cupful of white haricot beans to soak all night in cold water

January 16th.

Breakfast.	Luncheon.	Dinner.
Buttered Eggs.	Cold Beef, with Pickles and Endive Salad.	Mulligatawney Soup.
Brawn and Brawn Sauce.		Haricot Mutton, made of the best end of the Neck of Mutton.
Hot Buttered and Dry Toast.	Cranberry Tart.	
Brown and White Bread and Butter.		Potatoes, Haricot Beans.
		Roly-poly Pudding.
Milk Toast.		Cheese.

Marketing.

For the Day.—Six ounces or more of good Kidney Suet for roly-poly pudding (June 25th); one head of Endive; one small Beetroot, and a pennyworth of small Salad; Potatoes; Vegetables for soup.

For To-morrow.—If the brawn is finished, one small tin of Corned Beef; Shoulder of Mutton, not fat; a pennyworth of fresh German Yeast.

BREAKFAST.—*Buttered Eggs.*—Allow one fresh egg for each person, with an egg over, and one ounce of butter to two eggs. Break the eggs into a bowl and beat them till they are light and frothy; put the quantity of butter to be used into a separate basin, place this over boiling water, and stir it till it is melted; put both butter and eggs into an enamelled saucepan, and *keep stirring* them one way over a gentle fire till they are hot through without being allowed to boil. Once or twice during the process turn them into the basin and back again, in order to mix them thoroughly and to ensure their being slowly cooked. Have ready two or three slices of hot buttered toast, a slice for each person. As soon as the eggs are hot turn them upon the toast, sprinkle a little chopped parsley over the top, and serve. If the eggs are not taken from the fire the moment they are lightly set they will be hard and leathery, even if they do not curdle. Brawn (March 2nd); Brawn Sauce (January 15th); Milk Toast (June 17th).

LUNCHEON.—Salad (March 13th); Cranberry Tart (August 7th).

DINNER.—*Mulligatawney Soup.*—Scrape, cut into pieces, and fry in a little fat, one turnip, two good-sized onions, and four sharp apples. Stir them with a wooden spoon for a minute, then add the white part only of two leeks cut up small, a moderate-sized carrot, a bunch of parsley, a bay leaf, a sprig of thyme, and another of sweet marjoram. Let the vegetables fry together for three or four minutes, then pour over them a pint of the stock boiled up yesterday, and simmer till they are tender. Mix with them thoroughly two table-spoonfuls of flour and about a dessert-spoonful of curry powder; more if the soup is liked very hot. Pour in another quart of stock, remove the scum as it rises, and simmer the soup for about half an hour; strain it, and rub the vegetables patiently through a sieve; return the pulp to the liquid, add a little sugar browning and salt, if required, boil for ten minutes, and serve. If any cold lean meat is left, cut it into neat pieces, add these to the soup, and simmer till they are hot through, but they must not boil. A little rice boiled as for curry should be sent to table with this soup on a separate dish (*see* July 21st); Haricot Mutton (April 13th); Potatoes (May 12th); Haricot Beans (June 20th); Roly-poly Pudding (August 18th); Cheese (June 8th).

Things that must not be Forgotten.

1. Pastry and buns are to be made to-day (April 17th). A cranberry tart for to-day, an apple tart, baked custard tart (to make this, *see* January 19th), Vienna bread (August 26th); and rice cake (August 2nd).

2. Turn the silverside of beef in the brine, and turn and rub the pig's cheeks.

January 17th.

Breakfast.	Luncheon.	Dinner.
Kippered Salmon. Corned Beef. Vienna Bread. Hot Buttered Toast. Dry Toast. Brown and White Bread and Butter. Bread and Milk.	Liver and Bacon. Rice Snowball.	Fried Whiting. Shrimp or Anchovy Sauce. Roast Shoulder of Mutton. Boiled Onions. Potatoes. Savoy. Hayrick Puddings. Cheese.

Marketing.

For the Day.—Whiting (*see* January 3rd); Shrimps; one pound and a half of Sheep's Liver (calf's liver is scarce and dear at this time of the year); a pound of streaky Bacon already cut into rashers (*see* Marketing, January 3rd); half of this is for to-day, and half for breakfast on Monday. One-pennyworth of Parsley. Whiting are best in point of flavour when they are about nine inches long. They should be chosen for the firmness of the flesh and the brightness of the eyes and skin. The fishmonger should be asked to prepare them for frying: that is, to clean and skin them, and to fasten the tail in the mouth of the fish. One whiting may be allowed for each person. If asked to do so, the fishmonger will send the shrimps home ready picked for sauce. Spanish Onions, Potatoes, Savoy.

For To-morrow.—Endive or Lettuce for salad for supper on Sunday evening; one pound and a half of tender Buttock Steak for the jugged hare (*see* Marketing, January 1st); one tin of Potted Grouse (Bovill's); a pair of moderate-sized Soles for dinner to-morrow (*see* January 3rd); one well hung Neck of Mutton for Monday: the butcher must be asked to supply it with as little fat as may be. The neck will be better if it is not jointed until the day that it is to be cooked. Therefore, if the cook cannot joint it herself the meat should be ordered to be sent home first thing on Monday morning. Potatoes, Greens; six ounces of Suet; Small Salad.

BREAKFAST.—Kippered Salmon (*see* January 9th and 15th). Corned Beef bought yesterday; Vienna Bread (August 26th); Bread and Milk (January 25th).

LUNCHEON.—*Liver and Bacon.*—Cut the liver into slices a quarter of an inch thick, and dip each slice in flour, seasoned with pepper and a little salt. Trim away the rind from the slices of bacon, and divide into pieces convenient for serving. Melt a piece of dripping in a frying-pan, put in the bacon, and fry it *gently* until it is done enough, but not overdone. When cooked upon one side turn it to the other. Put it on a hot dish, and place it near the fire to keep warm. Lay the slices of liver in the hot pan and fry them in the bacon fat, turning them over when done upon one side. They must be in a single layer, not one upon the top of another, so that if necessary half must be done at once. The slices will take about a quarter of an hour to fry. In order to ascertain whether they are done enough, cut a little piece; if the liver is brown throughout it is done. Put the liver in the centre of the dish on which the bacon was placed; mix a dessert-spoonful of flour smoothly with about a quarter of a pint of water, pour this into the frying-pan, season it to taste, and stir it till it boils and thickens. Pour it through a strainer upon the liver, but let the bacon be round the dish, out of the way of the gravy. Serve very hot. Savoury Hash (February 5th); Boiled Rice Snowball (February 3rd).

DINNER.—*Fried Whiting.*—Flour the whiting, and wrap it in a soft cloth, and let it lie in the kitchen for an hour or more. It is an advantage for fish thus to lie for an hour or two after it is floured. When wanted, half fill an iron saucepan, of a size that will hold the frying-basket, with frying fat (*see* February 19th). Put it on the fire to boil. When water boils it bubbles up quickly, when fat boils it is still. The best way of telling when the fat is ready for the fish is to watch it until, when still, a pale blue smoke rises, and this is a sign that it is ready for the fish. Break an egg, and put the white only into a plate and beat it lightly. Pass both sides of the fish through the egg, hold it up to drain, and roll it in fine dry bread-crumbs which have been mixed with flour, pepper, and salt, in the proportion of a table-spoonful of flour, a small pinch of pepper, and half a salt-spoonful of salt to two ounces of crumbs. As the fish are crumbed lay them on a dish until all are prepared, then put them into the frying-basket, and do not let them touch each other. When the smoke rises, plunge the basket into the boiling fat to quite cover the fish, move it gently about, and let it remain until the whiting are done through and lightly browned. They will take from six to ten minutes, according to their size. Lift the basket out, let the fat drain away, then put the fish on a plate covered with kitchen paper, cover it with another sheet, and let it drain before the fire for three or four minutes; put it on a hot dish covered with a napkin or a fish paper, and garnish it with fried parsley. Whenever in this book it is said that fish is to be fried in plenty of hot fat these directions are to be closely followed. (*See* also Fried Soles, March 24th). If preferred, the fish instead of being egged and breaded can be simply floured well over before being fried; many epicures consider it more palatable when thus prepared.

When, as often happens, there is not a frying-basket in the house, neither sufficient fat to cover the fish entirely, another method may be adopted. Put into an ordinary frying-pan as much good dripping as will cover the bottom all over to the depth of half an inch; let this get quite hot, and when it is still and the blue smoke rises from it, put in the floured fish, and when it is cooked upon one side turn it to the other. Drain it from grease on kitchen paper, and proceed as before. Shrimp (January 30th), or anchovy (July 17th), or Dutch (May 14th) sauce should be sent to table with the fish. (If more convenient, whiting can be baked instead of being fried, *see* August 19th.) Roast Shoulder of Mutton (March 4th); Boiled Onions (October 28th); Potatoes (May 6th); Savoy (June 4th); Hayrick Puddings (March 19th); Cheese (June 8th).

Things that must not be Forgotten.

1. Partially prepare the hare for to-morrow. If the weather is very dry and cold, and if the hare does not appear to have hung long enough, leave it a week longer, and substitute next Sunday's dinner for to-day.

2. Turn the silverside of beef in the brine, and turn and rub the pig's cheeks.

3. Take the fat off the fire as soon as it is done with, and pour it carefully into a basin. Before using it again remove the sediment, which will have settled at the bottom of the cake.

4. Cleanse a little of the small salad bought for supper to-morrow night, and lay it on a cloth to drain. It is to be served with the anchovies. Also fillet the anchovies, to be ready for breakfast, and put the fillets between two dishes (January 18th).

5. Prepare the compôte of apples for to-morrow (August 5th and September 12th).

6. Put a cupful of hominy to soak all night in cold water (February 10th).

Sunday, January 18th.

Breakfast.	Dinner.	Tea.	Supper.
Anchovies, with Hard-boiled Eggs. Potted Grouse. Hot Buttered Toast. Dry Toast. Brown and White Bread and Butter. Boiled Hominy.	Sole au Gratin. Jugged Hare, with Red Currant Jelly. Potatoes. Greens. Golden Pudding. Cheese.	Thin Bread and Butter. Toast. Compôte of Apples. Rice Cake.	Cold Mutton. Salad. Baked Custard Tart. Cheese.

BREAKFAST.—The different varieties of prepared cocoa usually have directions for making them printed on the packets in which they are sold. The method commonly adopted is to mix the quantity of cocoa required to a smooth paste with a little cold milk, and to stir in with this equal quantities of boiling milk and water. These preparations of cocoa are almost always adulterated with arrowroot, sugar, and similar substances. The most wholesome and digestible beverage is made from the cocoa nibs. These should first be broken up into small pieces with a rolling-pin, soaked overnight in cold water, then simmered gently with the same water for six or seven hours. The liquid should then be strained and allowed to go cold, the fat should be skimmed from the top, and the cocoa is ready. The quantities are a tea-cupful of nibs to a quart of water; and during the process of boiling, water should be added at intervals to keep up the original quantity. The beverage thus produced should be clear and bright like coffee, and may be drunk with boiling milk. It has rather a peculiar taste, to which, however, the palate soon becomes accustomed, and it is a far more valuable article of diet than either tea or coffee. It is recommended by the faculty both for strengthening the frame in debility and sustaining it under exertion. It is a good plan to keep an enamelled saucepan specially for making cocoa, and many people keep it always simmering on the side of the stove. It is economical to boil the old nibs with the fresh ones; but this plan, though it makes the cocoa richer and more nourishing, and extracts the goodness more thoroughly from the nibs, also prevents the cocoa having the bright appearance which it would display if made from fresh nibs only. From motives of economy, also, cocoa shells are frequently substituted for cocoa nibs, the mode of preparation being precisely similar. Potted Grouse (January 7th); Boiled Hominy (February 11th).

Anchovies.—Allow three anchovies for each egg, and one egg for each guest. Boil the eggs hard for eight minutes, and let them go cold. Wash the anchovies, and fillet them by splitting them open with the fingers and thumbs of both hands, and removing the backbone. Arrange the fillets crosswise on a dish, put the small salad that was washed overnight round them, and lay on this the hard-boiled eggs chopped into dice. Pour a little salad oil over all, and serve.

DINNER.—Sole au Gratin (May 3rd); Jugged Hare (October 25th); Potatoes (May 6th); Greens (June 4th); Golden Pudding (May 4th); Cheese (June 8th).

TEA.—Compôte of Apples (August 5th and Note 3, September 12th); Rice Cake (August 2nd).

SUPPER.—Mutton left yesterday; Salad (March 13th); Baked Custard Tart (January 19th).

Things that must not be Forgotten.

1. Be especially careful to preserve everything that remains of the hare-bones, inferior joints, gravy, and forcemeat. Excellent soup may be made of these to-morrow.

2. Turn the beef in the brine, and rub the pig's cheek.

January 19th.

Breakfast.	Luncheon.	Dinner.
Toasted Bacon.	Cold Meat Piquante.	Hare Soup.
Potted Grouse.	Fried Potatoes.	Neck of Mutton, boiled, with Parsley Sauce.
Vienna Bread.	Baked Custard Tart.	Potatoes.
Dry Toast.		Mashed Parsnips.
Brown and White Bread and Butter.		Brown Bread Pudding.
Marmalade.		Cheese.
Fried Hominy.		

Marketing.

For the Day.—A Neck of Mutton. The butcher should be asked to joint the meat. Potatoes, Parsnips.

For To-morrow.—If Kippered Salmon is not already in the house, a quarter of a pound of Kippered Salmon, cut into thin slices; Muffins (January 29th).

BREAKFAST.—Potted Grouse (January 7th). *Toasted Bacon.*—Bacon is never so delicate as when it is toasted before the fire, either on a fork or on the pins of an ordinary toaster. Bacon should be evenly cut. When fat it should be rather thick for toasting; lean bacon may be cut thinner. Eggs poached separately in water and drained well may, if liked, be served with the bacon. They will be by many preferred to eggs fried in fat. When bacon is fried, the process of cooking should be carried on gently over a slow fire until the fat looks transparent, without being browned. Bacon fat should always be carefully preserved, as it may be made useful in the preparation of various dishes. Vienna Bread (August 26th); Fried Hominy (February 12th).

LUNCHEON.—Cold Meat Piquante (March 30th); Fried Potatoes (February 2nd). *Baked Custard Tart.*—Put half a pint of milk into a saucepan, with two or three inches of thin lemon-rind, or, if preferred, an inch of stick cinnamon. Let it simmer gently till it is pleasantly flavoured. Sweeten it, let it cool, take out the flavouring ingredients, and add a small pinch of salt. Whisk three eggs lightly, and put them with the milk. Line a shallow tart-dish with good short crust, pour in the custard, grate a little nutmeg over the top, and bake in a gentle oven. If baked quickly the custard will be watery. If preferred, for economy's sake, two eggs may be used, and a small tea-spoonful of corn-flour may be made into a smooth paste with a little cold milk, and boiled in the custard.

DINNER.—*Hare Soup.*—Look over the remains of the hare, pick the best of the meat from the bones, and cut it into neat pieces convenient for serving. Cover these over, and leave them in a cool place till wanted. Put all the rest—inferior joints, bones, trimmings, and any forcemeat and gravy that may be left—into a saucepan, and cover them with stock made from bones, or, if it has all been used, with water, and add an onion and eight or nine sticks of celery. Simmer gently till the bones are quite clean, then take them out, and rub all that remains patiently through a sieve, forcing as much through as possible. Put pulp and liquid back into the stew-pan, and let the soup boil up again. If it is too thin put a small lump of brown thickening with it, then let it simmer for awhile, removing

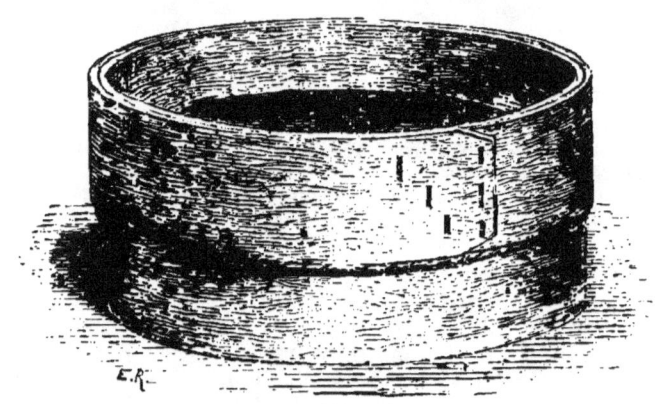

HAIR SIEVE.

the fat as it rises, till it is free from grease. Season it with salt and cayenne to taste, throw in the pieces of meat, and let them remain till they are hot, but they must not boil. Put the soup into the tureen, stir into it a glass of port, a few drops of lemon-juice, and a spoonful of red currant jelly, and serve very hot.

Neck of Mutton, boiled (February 23rd); Parsley or Maître d'Hôtel Sauce (May 6th); Mashed Parsnips (September 30th); Potatoes (May 12th); Brown Bread Pudding (July 20th); Cheese (June 8th).

Things that must not be Forgotten.

1. Turn the beef in the brine, and rub the pig's cheek.
2. Preserve the liquor in which the neck of mutton was boiled.
3. First thing in the morning put the kippered salmon into lukewarm water to soak till the next day.

January 20th.

Breakfast.	Luncheon.	Dinner.
Devilled Salmon.	Minced Mutton, with Poached Eggs.	Milk Soup.
Boiled Eggs.	Stewed Rhubarb and Milk.	Boiled Beef and Carrots.
Muffins.		Mashed Turnips.
Buttered Toast.		Potatoes.
Dry Toast.		Queen's Pudding.
Honey.		Cheese.
Porridge.		

Marketing.

For the Day.—Half a bundle of Champagne Rhubarb; Turnips, Carrots, Potatoes.

For To-morrow.—Three-quarters of a pound of Hard Cod's Roe; eight pounds of the thin end of the Flank of Beef, to be chosen with as little fat as possible, and cut as square as can be. (To choose Beef, *see* January 10th.)

BREAKFAST.—*Devilled Salmon*—(*See* January 8th and 9th.) Prepare the slices of salmon, and grill them as directed in January 9th, remembering only to brush them over with the devil mixture used for the pheasant's drum-sticks (January 14th), instead of simply oiling them. Boiled Eggs (January 5th); Muffins (January 30th); Porridge (January 25th).

LUNCHEON.—*Minced Mutton.*—Pick the meat entirely from the neck of mutton, and free it from all fat, gristle, and sinew. Put the bones and trimmings into a saucepan, with as much cold water as will cover them, and add an onion, half a blade of mace, one clove, six peppercorns, a bouquet garni (that is, a bunch of parsley, a sprig of thyme, and a bay leaf, tied neatly together), and a teaspoonful of flour mixed to a smooth paste with a little cold water. Simmer till the gravy is good. Strain it, season it with salt, and colour it with a few drops of sugar browning. If there be time let it stand, so that the fat can be taken from it. Mince the meat finely, or, better still, pass it through a sausage machine. Put it into a stew-pan, with as much gravy as will barely moisten it. Season it with pepper and salt, put it on the side of the range, and let it heat very slowly for about half an hour, till it is hot through, but of course it must never reach the boiling point, or it will be tough. If liked, a very little Harvey, Worcester, or Chutney sauce can be added to it. Whilst the mince is heating, take a slice of bread an inch thick, remove the crust, and with a sharp knife cut it into four pieces the shape of a heart. If any queen cake tins are in the house the bread can be stamped instead of being cut. Fry these pieces in hot fat till they are brightly browned without being black, and crisp without being hard. When they are done, lay them on a dish covered with kitchen paper to free them from grease. When the mince is almost ready, poach some eggs, allowing one for each person. Place the mince in the centre of a dish, lay the eggs upon it, put the pieces of fried bread, with a little sprig of parsley on each one, round it, and sprinkle a little finely-shred parsley over each egg. Serve very hot. Any kind of cold game, poultry, or meat can be minced in this way, and will form a palatable and pretty-looking dish. For Stewed Rhubarb, *see* May 19th.

DINNER.—Milk Soup (*see* January 3rd). Boiled Beef which has been salted. The meat should be quickly rinsed in cold water before being used, in order to free it from salt (February 23rd). Carrots (July 6th); Mashed Turnips (September 30th); Potatoes (April 7th); Queen's Pudding (August 9th); Cheese (June 8th).

Things that must not be Forgotten.

1. Take the remains of the marrow from the bone in as large pieces as possible. This is for marrow toast for breakfast to-morrow.
2. Be particularly careful not to let the mince boil in the gravy. It must simmer only till it is hot through.
3. Chop small and stew the mutton bones for stock.
4. Boil the brine with an additional handful of salt, and when it is cold lay the thin flank of beef in it.
5. Turn and rub the pig's cheek.
6. Boil the fresh roe in salted water until it is firm. Let it get cold; then cut it into slices the third of an inch thick, and lay these in a pickle made of a table-spoonful of vinegar, a tea-spoonful of salt, a little pepper, and a pinch of mixed spice. Let the roe lie in this till to-morrow, and turn it once or twice during the day.

January 21st.

Breakfast.	Luncheon.	Dinner.
Marrow Toast.	Cold Boiled Beef.	Onion Soup (made of the liquor in which the beef was boiled).
Cod's Roe.	Endive Salad.	Beef Steak and Oyster Pie.
Buttered Toast.	Sweet Macaroni.	Potatoes and Large Savoy.
Dry Toast.		Rice Pudding.
Marmalade.		Cheese.
Brown and White Bread and Butter.		
Bread and Milk.		

Marketing.

For the Day.—Two pounds and a half of tender Steak (*see* January 1st); half an Ox Kidney; one tin preserved Oysters, or, if preferred, two dozen fresh Oysters; one pennyworth of Parsley; Endive, Beetroot, Potatoes, Savoy; half a pound of Macaroni.

For To-morrow.—One tin of Collared Tongue; Bloaters (*see* Note 2, January 2nd).

BREAKFAST.—*Marrow Toast.*—Put the pieces of marrow into a stew-pan with a little water, highly salted. Let it boil for a minute, then drain away the liquor. Have ready one or two slices of toast, spread the marrow on these, and put them into a Dutch oven before a clear fire for about five minutes. Take the toast up, sprinkle over it a little pepper, salt, and finely-chopped parsley, and serve as hot as possible.

Cod's Roe.—Drain the slices of roe from the pickle, dry them and flour them. Break an egg, and separate the yolk from the white. The yolk may be used for Dutch sauce. Beat the white lightly, pass the slices of roe through it, and cover them with seasoned bread-crumbs. Fry them in hot fat till they are brightly browned (*see* Fried Whiting, January 17th); drain them on kitchen paper, and pour over them a little Dutch sauce (May 14th), or, if preferred, anchovy (July 17th) or parsley sauce (May 6th). Bread and Milk (January 25th).

LUNCHEON.—Salad (March 13th); Sweet Macaroni (August 13th).

DINNER.—*Onion Soup.*—Peel half a dozen good-sized onions and two potatoes. Mince them finely, and put them into a stew-pan with a lump of dripping, and let them "sweat" for about ten minutes. They must not brown. Pepper them, pour over them about three pints of the liquor in which the beef was boiled, and add a lump of sugar, a strip of bacon-rind, and one or two outer sticks of celery. Let them simmer gently for about twenty minutes, or till they are tender. Rub the soup through a hair-sieve with the back of a wooden spoon, then return it to the stew-pan. Grate the crumb of a stale loaf into half a pint of boiling milk; stir this into the soup. Serve very hot. Beef Steak and Oyster Pie (March 26th); Potatoes (May 12th); Savoy (June 4th); Rice Pudding (February 24th); Cheese (June 8th).

Things that must not be Forgotten.

1. Be careful to dry the endive thoroughly after washing it.
2. Turn and rub the pig's cheek and the beef.
3. Put two table-spoonfuls of tapioca to soak in one pint of water for luncheon to-morrow.

January 22nd.

Breakfast.	Luncheon.	Dinner.
Bloaters.	Bubble and Squeak.	Vermicelli Soup.
Collared Tongue.	Apples and Tapioca.	Steak à la Béarnaise.
Buttered Toast.		Fried Potatoes.
Dry Toast.		Brussels Sprouts.
Honey.		Newmarket Pudding.
Brown and White Bread and Butter.		Cheese.
Corn Flour Milk.		

Marketing.

For the Day.—A slice of Rump Steak not less than one inch thick, and weighing from three to three pounds and a half. The steak should not be cut from the rump very long before it is used, and, if the weather be favourable, before it is taken the meat should have been hung for some days. To choose steak, see Remarks on Marketing, January 1st. Apples, Potatoes, Brussels Sprouts, Savoy.

For To-morrow.—Order, to come first thing in the morning, about four pounds of the thick Flank of Beef (see January 10th); Pearl Barley; Muffins.

BREAKFAST.—Bloaters (see January 3rd); Collared Tongue (Marketing, January 2nd, and Note 2, January 3rd); Corn Flour Milk (June 19th).

LUNCHEON.—*Bubble and Squeak.*—Cut the remains of the boiled beef into thin slices, fat and lean together. If sufficient cabbage were left, mince it finely; if there be not sufficient, boil a small savoy till done enough, drain, press it well, and cut it small. Fry the slices of meat in a frying-pan over a brisk fire with butter or dripping till they are hot through without being dry or hard. Put them on a hot dish and keep them hot till the cabbage is ready. Turn it over in the frying-pan till it is heated throughout. Pile it on a hot dish, put the pieces of meat round it, and serve immediately. If any other vegetables are left, such as turnips, carrots, or parsnips, they also may be made hot and served with the Bubble and Squeak. No sauce will be required for this dish. Tapioca and Apples (February 18th).

DINNER.—*Vermicelli Soup.*—To be made of the bone stock already in the house, or with essence of beef (see March 22nd).

Broiled Steak with Béarnaise Sauce.—It will be necessary to have a clear bright fire for broiling the steak. Therefore, about three-quarters of an hour before it is to be cooked, clear the dust away from the bottom of the bars, and make up the fire with small coal mixed with coke or cinders that have been broken up. If the fire is blazing instead of being clear, throw a handful of salt upon it. If, however, the steak does not brown properly, make a flare by throwing a little piece of dripping upon the fire. Keep the steak in the warm kitchen for a couple of hours before it is broiled; especially is this necessary if the weather is frosty. A gridiron ought to be kept specially for chops and steaks, another for fish, and, by rights, a third for bloaters. If the same utensil be used for every purpose, it is more than probable that the flavour of the steak will be spoiled. Make the gridiron hot over the fire, clean it well with a piece of paper or rag, rub it over with mutton fat, and again make it hot. Season the steak with pepper and salt, lay it upon the gridiron, move it about for a few seconds for fear it sticks, and then turn it every two minutes till it is done enough. Be, of course, particularly careful not to stick a fork or anything else into the meat, as that would allow the gravy to escape. If a pair of steak-tongs is not at hand, put the fork into the fat. When the steak is black on the outside, and when pressed with the side of a fork it feels firm, not hard to the touch, it is done enough. It is scarcely possible to say how long it will take, because the time required will vary with the state of the fire, the condition and thickness of the meat, and the weather. Under favourable conditions it will be done enough, but with the gravy in it, in ten minutes, well done in twelve minutes, and in the condition known as "under-done" in eight minutes. When taking it from the gridiron stick a fork into the fat, and hold the steak up for a minute to let the fat drain from it, and lay it on a hot dish. Have the plates hot and the Béarnaise sauce (March 23rd) ready; spread the sauce over the steak and serve *immediately*. If liked, a pat of fresh butter may be put under it and another upon it, while the juice of half a lemon and a table-spoonful of Harvey or Worcester sauce may be put with it; the last, however, must be heated separately in a cup in the oven. Or *maître d'hôtel* butter (April 15th) may be rubbed over it, or, if preferred, onion (October 14th), oyster (October 16th), or tomato (July 15th) sauce may be served separately in a tureen. Fried potatoes or fried onions form a suitable garnish for the dish. Fried Potatoes (February 2nd); Brussels Sprouts (June 4th); Newmarket Pudding (June 2nd); Cheese (June 8th).

Things that must not be Forgotten.

1. Boil one of the pig's cheeks (*see* February 1st).
2. Turn the beef, and turn and rub the pig's cheek.
3. Remember to boil the vermicelli separately before adding to the soup, or it will spoil its clearness; also to break it up slightly, so that it will not hang in strings when conveyed from the plate to the mouth.
4. Soak the split peas in cold water all night.
5. Make potted beef for breakfast of the remains of steak. (January 23rd.)

January 23rd.

Breakfast.	Luncheon.	Dinner.
Potted Beef, made of any little pieces left from Broiled Steak. Boiled Pig's Cheek. Muffins. Dry Toast. Marmalade. Bread and Milk.	Tripe. Stewed Rhubarb, with Milk or Cream.	Scotch Broth. Boiled Beef. Turnips and Carrots. Apple Gâteau. Cheese.

Marketing.

For the Day.—One pound and a half of dressed Tripe, perfectly fresh, thick fat, and as white as possible. The honeycomb is usually preferred. In London fresh tripe is generally to be obtained on a Friday. Half a bundle of Forced or Champagne Rhubarb. Beef ordered yesterday to come first thing in the morning. Vegetables required for Scotch broth (March 3rd).

For To-morrow.—A Tin of Pilchards. These fish are preserved and sold in tins, something like sardines. They constitute a pleasant variety for the breakfast table.

BREAKFAST.—*Potted Beef.*—There are almost sure to be some little pieces of steak left in the dish, and these will probably be sufficient to make a small jar of potted beef for breakfast. To make it, trim away all the fat and gristle and burnt outside portions. These can be cut away very sparingly. (The fat can afterwards be rendered for frying purposes.) Cut the lean into thin strips, and afterwards mince it very finely. If it can be passed through a sausage machine so much the better. Pound it in a mortar to a perfectly smooth paste, and as the pounding goes on keep adding the seasoning a little at a time. Half a pound of beef will need half a tea-spoonful of salt, a quarter of a tea-spoonful of pepper, three or four grates of nutmeg, half a tea-spoonful of anchovy essence, and the gravy carefully scraped out of the dish, together with a piece of fresh butter, about the size of an egg, broken up small. If preferred, two ounces of cold boiled bacon fat (taken in this instance from the pig's cheek) can be pounded in the mortar, and used instead of butter. If too much gravy is used the meat will not keep so well. When the seasoning ingredients are thoroughly incorporated put the pulp into a covered jar, set this in a saucepan of boiling water, and let it remain until it is hot all through; take it off the fire, stir it occasionally till nearly cold, then press it firmly into small flat jars, and smooth the top over with a knife; the next day pour on as much dissolved butter or mutton suet as will cover it. Be sure to keep it in a cool place. If this is done, and if paper is tied over it after it is made, it will keep good for some days. Small portions of beef, veal, ham, game, poultry, and fish can always be utilised in this way, and will afford an agreeable addition to the breakfast table. When potted beef is wanted, and there is no cold meat that can be used, it will have to be prepared specially for the purpose. For this take tender meat, the steak or part of the round. Cut it into small pieces, and spread a little beef dripping upon it; lay it in an earthenware jar which has a closely-fitting lid, put a piece of bacon upon it, and pour in a very little cold water. A quarter of a pint of water will be sufficient for two pounds of beef. Put the lid on the pot, set it in a saucepan of boiling water, or in a moderate oven, and let it stew gently till tender, basting it occasionally. Pour away the gravy, and let the beef get cold before potting it, then proceed as directed above. A cake of fat will settle on the top of that which is poured off, and this can be used for cooking purposes; under it will be gravy, which will prove a useful addition to sauces and other preparations. The beef from which beef tea has been made is frequently potted. The more completely the gravy has been drawn from it the less valuable it is. Meat that is quite white and ragged is not worth potting; if, however, there is any goodness at all left in it, seasoning can be added to make it palatable, and so it may serve as a relish, and that is what potted meat is intended for as much as anything. Pig's Cheek (February 1st); Muffins (January 30th); Bread and Milk (January 25th).

LUNCHEON.—Tripe (December 4th); Onion Sauce (October 14th); Stewed Rhubarb (May 19th).

DINNER.—Scotch Broth (March 3rd), with the beef of which it is made for meat; Apple Gâteau (December 9th); Cheese (June 8th).

Things that must not be Forgotten.

1. Pastry had better be made on Saturday this week. As a pigeon pie is to be made for supper on Sunday night, it will be better fresh.
2. Pour the remains of the broth into an earthenware jar, and put it in a cold place. It will be as good the second day as it is the first.
3. Turn the flank of beef, and turn and rub the pig's cheek.

January 24th.

Breakfast.	Luncheon.	Dinner.
Pilchards.	Scotch Broth.	Stewed Eels.
Collared Tongue.	Beef.	Civet of Rabbit.
Buttered Toast.		Potatoes, Boiled Onions, or, if preferred, Greens.
Dry Toast.		
Lemon Marmalade.		Newcastle Pudding.
Milk Toast.		Cheese.

Marketing.

For the Day.—Two pounds of Silver Eels; two moderate-sized Ostend Rabbits. The eels should, when bought, be actually living and moving briskly about. Sharp-nosed eels are the best, and they are finest when rather more than a half-crown piece in circumference, with white bellies, and backs of a bright coppery hue. Yellow eels have a muddy taste. If the fishmonger is to skin the eels, ask him before doing so to pierce the spinal marrow just behind the head with a skewer. This will at once kill the creatures, and prevent the needless barbarity of skinning them alive. Rabbits should be freshly killed and young. If fresh, they will be stiff, with the flesh white and dry; if stale, the flesh will be slimy, and of a bluish tinge. Young rabbits have the claws smooth and sharp, the wool smooth, and the ears tender and easily torn. If the wool is rough, the claws blunt and rugged, and the ears tough, the creature is old. Apples, Potatoes, Onions, or Greens; a pennyworth of German Yeast.

For To-morrow.—A small Codfish, or the tail end of a large fish (see January 1st and 6th); four plump young Pigeons; three pounds of tender Rump Steak (January 1st); a bunch of Rhubarb. The butcher should be asked to cut off steaks until only three pounds are left, and then to take the meat off the bone in one piece, and send this for the purpose required. An additional pound and a half of rump or buttock steak will be needed for the pigeon pie. A quarter of a pound of beef Kidney Suet; one-pennyworth of Parsley. Herbs, &c., for forcemeat, should be in the house, as well as sponge biscuits and ratafias for cabinet pudding. The pigeons, if they are tame, should be freshly killed, and the dark coloured birds are believed to have the highest flavour. Wood pigeons are in season, however, in December and January. If they are chosen, they will be better for having been hung a few days. Potatoes, Greens ingredients for a salad.

BREAKFAST.—Pilchards (Marketing, January 23rd); Collared Tongue; Milk Toast (June 17th).

LUNCHEON.—Scotch Broth; Beef, left yesterday.

DINNER.—*Stewed Eels.*—If the cook has to kill and skin the eels, she should first drive the skewer into the spinal marrow just behind the head, in order to kill it. She should remember not to cut off the creature's head in order to kill it, or it will continue to wriggle as though alive. The fish should be skinned immediately. To do this, cut through the skin round the neck, and turn it down about an inch; then passing a skewer through the head, by which it can be firmly held, take hold of the skin with a rough cloth, and draw it gently off. It will come away with ease and without injuring the flesh. After this, gut the eel without breaking the gall, cut off the bristles which run up the back, divide into pieces about two inches in length, and lay these in strong salt and water for one hour. This will entirely stop the quivering of the flesh, supposing this still continues, in fact or in imagination. Dry the pieces well, roll them in flour seasoned with pepper and salt, and fry them in a little good dripping till they are lightly browned. Let them drain till cold; this will deprive them of the oily taste which often proves so objectionable. Put them into a clean stew-pan, with a bay leaf, an onion stuck with two cloves, a bunch of parsley, an inch of lemon-rind, and about half a pint of stock made from trimmings. Let them simmer gently from twenty to thirty minutes according to their thickness. Take them up, and keep them hot till the sauce is ready. Strain the gravy, thicken it with a little flour, add to it salt and cayenne, a few drops of essence of anchovy, and the juice of half a lemon; let it simmer for ten minutes. If permitted, a glass of red wine may now be added to it. Arrange the pieces of eel on a dish, strain the sauce over them, and garnish with three-cornered sippets. Civet of Rabbit (December 8th); Potatoes (May 12th); Boiled Onions (October 28th); Greens (June 4th); Newcastle Pudding (June 12th); Cheese (June 8th).

Things that must not be Forgotten.

1. Pastry is to be made to-day (April 17th): the pigeon pie (May 15th), one apple pie (August 7th), eight teacakes (August 26th), rice cake (August 2nd).
2. Be particularly careful to preserve the rabbit-bones that are left. They will make excellent stock.
3. Pot the remains of the collared tongue (Note 5, September 26th).
4. Turn the beef, and turn and rub the pig's cheek.

Sunday, January 25th.

Breakfast.	Dinner.	Tea.	Supper.
Pilchards.	Baked Cod.	Brown and White Bread and Butter.	Pigeon Pie.
Potted Tongue.	Roast Rump Steak.	Jam.	Salad.
Boiled Eggs.	Potatoes.	Rice Cake.	Stewed Rhubarb, with Milk.
Hot Teacakes.	Greens.		
Dry Toast.	Cabinet Pudding.		
Brown and White Bread and Butter.	Cheese.		
Porridge.			

BREAKFAST.—Pilchards (Marketing, January 23rd); Potted Tongue (September 26th); Boiled Eggs (January 5th); Hot Teacakes (February 14th).

Porridge.—When there are children in the family it is a good plan, whatever they may have for breakfast, to let them begin the meal either with oatmeal porridge or bread and milk. Porridge is wholesome and nourishing, and will help to make them strong and hearty. Even grown-up people frequently enjoy a small portion of porridge served with treacle and milk. Oatmeal is either "coarse," "medium," or "fine." Individual taste must determine which of these three varieties shall be chosen. Scotch people generally prefer the coarsest kind. The ordinary way of making porridge is the following: Put as much water as is likely to be required into a saucepan with a sprinkling of salt, and let the water boil. Half a pint of water will make a single plateful of porridge. Take a knife (a "spurtle" is the proper utensil) in the right hand, and some Scotch or coarse oatmeal in the left hand, and sprinkle the meal in gradually, stirring it briskly all the time; if any lumps form, draw them to the side of the pan and crush them out. When the porridge is sufficiently thick (the degree of thickness must be regulated by individual taste), draw the pan back a little, *put on the lid,* and let the contents simmer gently till wanted; if it can have one hour's simmering, all the better, but in hundreds of families in Scotland and the North of England it is served when it has boiled for ten minutes or a quarter of an hour; less oatmeal is required when it can boil for a long time, because the simmering swells the oatmeal, and so makes it go twice as far. During the boiling the porridge must be stirred frequently to keep it from burning to the saucepan, but each time this is done the lid must be put on again. When it is done enough it should be poured into a basin or upon a plate, and served hot, with sugar or treacle, and milk or cream. The very best method that can be adopted for making porridge is to soak the coarse Scotch oatmeal in water for *twelve hours* or more (if the porridge is wanted for breakfast it may be put into a pie-dish over night and left till morning). As soon as the fire is lighted in the morning it should be placed on it, stirred occasionally, kept covered, and boiled as long as possible, although it may be served when it has boiled for twenty minutes. When thus prepared it will be almost like a delicate jelly, and acceptable to the most fastidious palate. The proportions for porridge made in this way are a heaped table-spoonful of coarse oatmeal to a pint of water. It is scarcely necessary to give directions for making bread and milk, for every one knows how this is done. It may be said that the preparation has a better appearance if the bread is cut very small before the boiling milk is poured on it, and also that the addition of a small pinch of salt takes away the insipidity. Rigid economists sometimes swell the bread with boiling water, then drain this off, and pour milk in its place. This, however, is almost a pity, for milk is so very good for children; and though recklessness is seldom to be recommended, a mother might well be advised to be reckless about the amount of her milk bill, provided always that the quantity of milk be not wasted, and that the children have it. If it should happen that the little ones got tired of oatmeal porridge, or of bread and milk, a variety might be permitted them in the form of rice and barley porridge (June 15th), rice milk (June 18th), milk porridge (June 13th), and in summer-time plum porridge (August 31st) may be given them.

DINNER.—Baked Cod (February 3rd); Roast Rump Steak: skewer the meat round firmly, and baste it frequently whilst it is being cooked (March 4th); Potatoes (May 12th); Greens (Cabbage, June 4th); Cabinet Pudding (July 12th); Cheese (June 8th).

TEA.—Rice Cake (August 2nd).

SUPPER.—Pigeon Pie made on Saturday; Stewed Rhubarb (May 19th).

Things that must not be Forgotten.

1. Carefully preserve any remains of cod there may be. They can be scalloped for breakfast.
2. Preserve the pigeon-bones and scrapings of the pie to make gravy for the savoury mince at luncheon to-morrow.
3. Turn the beef, and turn and rub the pig's cheek.

January 26th.

Breakfast.	Luncheon.	Dinner.
Scalloped Cod.	Savoury Meat Cake.	Potato Purée.
Pig's Cheek.	Eggs stewed with Cheese.	Boiled Leg of Mutton.
Toasted Teacakes.		Caper Sauce and Mashed Turnips, Carrots, and Potatoes.
Brown and White Bread and Butter.		Roly-poly Pudding.
Dry Toast.		Cheese.
Bread and Milk.		

Marketing.

For the Day.—A well hung Leg of Mutton, weighing about seven pounds; Suet or Dripping for pudding (June 25th); Turnips, Carrots, Potatoes. For

Mutton, *see* January 8th. The best suet for pudding is the kidney fat of beef.

For To-morrow.—Dried Haddock for breakfast.

BREAKFAST.—*Scalloped Cod.*—Take any remains there may be of the baked cod served on Sunday and of the stewed eels of Saturday. Break the flesh into little pieces, entirely free from skin and bone. Season with pepper and salt, and mix lightly in a spoonful of chopped parsley and a few drops of essence of anchovy; moisten with a little melted butter or strong stock made of the bones of the cod. Butter half a dozen scallop shells or deep oyster shells (*see* Marketing, January 2nd), and cover them with finely grated bread-crumbs. Divide the prepared fish into equal portions, one for each shell. Lay the fish upon the bread-crumbs, cover it again with bread-crumbs, and put little bits of butter here and there over the whole. Bake in a quick oven for a quarter of an hour or more, till the fish is hot and the crumbs brightly browned. Lay the shells on a hot dish covered with a napkin, and garnish with parsley. For another way, *see* January 7th. Pig's Cheek, boiled (January 22nd); Bread and Milk (January 25th); Teacakes (February 14th).

LUNCHEON.—*Savoury Meat Cake.*—Take all the scraps of meat left from the pigeon pie and from the steak, mince them finely with a large onion that has been boiled till tender. Take the same quantity by measure of finely grated bread-crumbs that there is of meat. Moisten this with as much boiling stock as it will absorb, and mix all briskly together with a handful of meal, and pepper and salt to taste. Spread the mixture in a shallow dish well greased, lay little bits of dripping here and there on the top, and bake in a good oven. Serve with gravy made from pigeon-bones. Any kind of meat or fish, or a small portion of bullock's liver boiled and chopped small with the onions, may be used in this way, and will afford an inexpensive and nourishing dish. Eggs stewed with Cheese (February 10th).

DINNER.—*Potato Purée.*—Take the stock made of the rabbit-bones, with two pounds of potatoes, weighed after they have been peeled, a stick of celery, and the white part of two leeks; if preferred, two small onions may be used, but the leeks will impart the more delicate flavour. Shred all finely together. Melt a piece of butter about the size of a small egg in a stew-pan. Throw in the vegetables, cover them over, and let them sweat over the fire for a few minutes, being very careful that they do not get at all brown. Pour upon them a quart of the cold stock, and boil all gently together for about half an hour, till the vegetables are quite tender, then rub all through a fine hair-sieve. Put the purée into a clean stew-pan, and season it with salt. When it boils pour it into a hot soup tureen, and add half a pint of boiling cream, or milk if cream may not be afforded. Pick the leaves from two or three sprigs of parsley. Wash the herb in plenty of water, chop it finely, then put it in the corner of a cloth, dip it into cold water, and wring it dry. This second washing lessens the acrid taste which parsley possesses. Sprinkle it into the hot soup and serve. When fresh chervil can be obtained, chervil is to be preferred to parsley. Boiled Leg of Mutton (February 23rd); Caper Sauce (March 19th); Mashed Turnips (September 30th); Carrots, (July 6th); Potatoes (April 7th); Rolypoly Pudding (August 18th); Cheese (June 8th).

Things that must not be Forgotten.

1. Carefully preserve the stock in which the mutton was boiled.
2. Turn and rub the pig's cheek.
3. Boil the salted flank of beef according to the directions given in Note 2, February 23rd, and put it under a weight.
4. Put a cupful of hominy to soak all night in cold water.

January 27th.

Breakfast.	Luncheon.	Dinner.
Dried Haddock.	Macaroni and Bacon.	Six or eight Oysters for each person.
Buttered Eggs.	Cornish Pasties.	Brown Bread, and Butter, with cut Lemon.
Hot Toast.		Curried Mutton.
Dry Toast.		Boiled Rice.
Brown and White Bread and Butter.		Potatoes.
Boiled Hominy.		Brussels Sprouts.
		Lemon Pudding.
		Cheese.

Marketing.

For the Day.—Fresh Oysters. If natives may not be afforded, American or Portuguese oysters may be procured. The thin end of the Flank of Beef, not too fat, and weighing about ten pounds; Potatoes, Brussels Sprouts; six ounces of beef Suet.

For To-morrow.—Three pounds of the muscle of the leg of Beef. As the muscle which lies nearest the hoof is the portion required, it should be cut out whole, and will probably weigh from two to three pounds. Half a pound of bacon in rashers.

BREAKFAST.—*Dried Haddock.*—Either wash the haddock quickly and dry it, or rub it well with a clean soft cloth. It is necessary to do this because a haddock is touched by a good many fingers—some of them perhaps not very clean ones—before it is sent home to the customer. Gradually heat it through by laying it upon a gridiron over a slow clear fire. If preferred, toast it before the fire instead of broiling it. When done enough, put it skin downwards upon a dish, and rub a little fresh butter over it just before sending it to table. Another way of preparing dried haddock is to lay it in a pie-dish that has been made hot by being rinsed with boiling water, pour more boiling water upon it to cover it, lay a plate on the dish to keep in the steam, and let it remain for five or ten minutes, according to the size. When hot through it should be drained, laid on a dish, peppered, rubbed over with fresh butter, and served. If liked, a bay leaf, a little parsley, and a small sprig of thyme may be put into the water with it. When a haddock is prepared in this way care must be taken not to let it lie in the water too long, or it will acquire a sodden taste. Buttered Eggs (January 16th); Boiled Hominy (February 11th).

LUNCHEON.—*Macaroni and Bacon.*—Take the remains of the pig's cheek. It is probable that there will be a portion which is scarcely fit to send to table. About two ounces of this may be taken for the macaroni, and the remainder can be used for breakfast. If none is left, one rasher of bacon, weighing about two ounces, may be used instead in each instance. Cut the bacon into small pieces. Wash half a pound of Naples macaroni, break it up, and throw it into boiling water which has a lump of butter in it. Let it boil for twenty minutes, then throw the water away, and pour in its place a pint of nicely seasoned stock (February 13th); let it boil till tender; when it is soft, without being broken, toss it lightly with a little pepper and salt and the chopped bacon, turn it upon a hot dish, and serve. The commoner the macaroni the more quickly it will be done enough. Good macaroni, if covered with stock, will take about half an hour; it should, however, be looked at frequently, and on no account be allowed to get pulpy. Cornish pasties to be made of the broken remnants of mutton that cannot be taken off in slices for the curry (August 22nd).

DINNER.—Curried Mutton (May 26th); Boiled Rice (July 21st); Potatoes (May 12th); Brussels Sprouts (June 4th); Lemon Pudding (August 12th); Cheese (June 8th).

Things that must not be Forgotten.

1. Boil the brine with an additional handful of salt, and lay the thin flank of beef in it. While the brine is being boiled, scald out the pan and dry it perfectly.
2. Rub and turn the pig's cheek.
3. Trim and glaze the beef (March 21st). This dish will keep for two or three weeks in cold weather, and will be delicious to the last. It should be carved in thin slices.
4. Prepare some bread-crumbs for breakfast to morrow. (January 2nd).
5. Put a breakfast-cupful of white haricot beans to soak in as much water as will cover them.

January 28th.

Breakfast.	Luncheon.	Dinner.
Toasted Bacon.	Pressed Beef.	Haricot Purée.
Scalloped Eggs.	Endive Salad.	Beef Stewed with Vegetables.
Buttered Toast.	Rice, with Stewed Apples and Beetroot.	Potatoes, Mashed.
Dry Toast.		Custard Blancmange.
Brown and White Bread and Butter.		Cheese.
Fried Hominy.		

Marketing.

For the Day.—Endive; Beetroot; one pennyworth of small Salad; Apples, Potatoes.

For To-morrow.—Sheep's Kidneys, one for each person; Bacon, or not, as liked; a small Leg of Pork, one that will weigh seven or eight pounds (see January 6th); one tin of Sardines (see January 12th); one tin of preserved Peaches; one pennyworth of Parsley.

BREAKFAST.—*Scalloped Eggs.*—Take about four table-spoonfuls of finely grated bread-crumbs, season them with pepper and salt, and moisten them with gravy and a little milk or cream. Mince finely also the portion of pig's cheek which was put aside for the purpose (see Macaroni and Bacon, January 27th), and about a table-spoonful of parsley leaves. A small piece of onion may be added, if liked; but it should be boiled before it is minced. Grease a small pie-dish, and line the bottom with the moistened crumbs, then sprinkle upon them the parsley and chopped bacon. Cover the dish, and put it in the oven, and let it remain until it is quite hot. Meanwhile, beat four eggs to a froth, and put with them a spoonful of melted butter, a spoonful of cream, and a little pepper and salt. Pour them gently upon the bacon, put the dish again into the oven without cover, and bake the eggs till they are set. They will take about five minutes. Serve very hot. If scallop-shells are at hand, they may be used instead of the pie-dish; then the ingredients will have to be divided into equal portions, one for each shell; and the shells may be sent to table arranged on a dish, covered with a hot napkin, and garnished with parsley. Toasted Bacon (see January 19th); Fried Hominy (February 12th).

LUNCHEON.—Salad (March 13th). *Rice with Stewed Apples and Beetroot.*—Wash half a pound of rice, and put it into a saucepan with as much water or milk as will cover it. Let it boil gently till it is quite tender and has absorbed the liquor. If necessary, add a little more water or milk during the process of boiling. Whilst the rice is being cooked, put in another saucepan six large baking apples, peeled, cored, and sliced, six slices of beetroot a quarter of an inch thick, and as much water as will prevent burning. Simmer till the fruit is tender; then sweeten to taste. Sweeten the rice, and flavour it with two or three drops of essence of almonds. Put it on a dish, and make a hole in the centre. Beat the apples till smooth, and put them in the hole in the rice. This is a pretty, inexpensive, and wholesome dish. Pressed Beef boiled (January 26th).

DINNER.—Haricot Purée (March 9th); Stewed Beef with Vegetables (March 17th); Mashed Potatoes (May 12th); Custard Blancmange (August 4th); Cheese (June 8th).

Things that must not be Forgotten.
1. Turn the beef in the brine.
2. Turn and rub the pig's cheek.
3. Be particularly careful that the salad is dry before it is mixed.

January 29th.

Breakfast.	Luncheon.	Dinner.
Sardines.	Savoury Rice.	Sole au Gratin.
Broiled Kidneys.	Baked Omelet.	Roast Pork, with Apple Sauce and Sage and Onion Stuffing.
Hot and Dry Toast.		
Marmalade.		Browned Potatoes and Cabbage.
Brown and White Bread and Butter.		Compôte of Peaches from Tinned Fruit.
Porridge.		Cheese.

Marketing.

For the Day.—One large thick Sole (see January 3rd); Potatoes, Cabbage, Apples, Onions, Sage.

For To-morrow.—One pint of split Peas, if these are not already in the house; Kippered Salmon; one Cow-heel from the tripe dealer; two or three Muffins. Muffins are rather troublesome to make, and may be bought at a very cheap rate; so they are not often made at home, excepting in country places. They are generally and rightly considered very indigestible; yet some people are exceedingly fond of them, and will have them.

BREAKFAST.—*Broiled Sheep's Kidneys* are quite an epicure's dish, and also rather an expensive dish. They may be more economically prepared according to the recipes given (January 2nd and July 18th). When they are to be broiled, one will be required for each person. Pass a knife through each kidney from the rounded part, but do not quite separate the halves. Remove the skin and fat, and run a small metal or wooden skewer through the points and across the back, to keep them from curling up whilst they are broiling. Season them with pepper and salt, and oil them in every part. Lay them, the cut side downwards, upon a gridiron that has been made hot and rubbed over with mutton fat, over a bright, clear fire. At the end of four minutes turn them; in as many more dish them. They will take from eight to ten minutes, according to the taste of the eaters. It is a very common fault to over-dress mutton kidneys, and this makes them hard and indigestible. Even when wanted well done, they should always be cooked so that red gravy will run from them when they are cut. Have ready a little *maître d'hôtel* butter (April 15th), about half a tea-spoonful for each kidney. Put the kidneys, the hollow side uppermost, on a very hot dish. Place the allotted portion of *maître d'hôtel* butter in each one, and serve quickly. A little toasted bacon will be found a great improvement to this dish. Sardines (January 12th); Porridge (January 25th).

LUNCHEON.—Savoury Rice (June 17th); Baked Omelet (August 6th).

DINNER.—Sole au Gratin (May 3rd); Roast Pork (March 4th); Apple Sauce (September 29th); Sage and Onion Stuffing (September 29th); Goose Pudding, if liked (September 29th); Potatoes (May 12th); Cabbage (June 4th); Compôte of Peaches (April 11th); Cheese (June 8th).

Things that must not be Forgotten.

1. As soon as the pork comes from the table, lift it upon a clean dish, and carefully preserve any gravy that may have run from it.

2. Turn the beef, and rub the pig's cheek.

3. If any sole is left, it may be made into fish cakes for breakfast; and these will serve instead of the kippered salmon. (*See* January 13th.) If the bones of the sole are not otherwise required, they may be stewed for an hour in as much water as will cover them; and the stock thus made can be put with the bones of the whiting to make fish stock for the lobster soup.

January 30th.

Breakfast.	Luncheon.	Dinner.
Kippered Salmon or Fish Cakes. Pressed Beef. Muffins. Dry Toast. Honey. Brown and White Bread and Butter. Bread and Milk.	Cow Heel, with Parsley Sauce. Stirabout Cheese.	Fried Whiting. Shrimp Sauce. Pork Cutlets, with Apple Sauce. Colcannon. Baked Potatoes. Macaroni Pudding. Cheese.

Marketing.

For the Day.—Whiting, one for each person (*see* January 17th); one pint of Shrimps: the shrimps must be very fresh; one quart of Indian Meal. This meal is not kept by every corn factor, although it may generally be obtained by ordering. It does not keep well, but is exceedingly wholesome and nourishing: Apples, Potatoes, Cabbage.

For To-morrow.—Bloaters for each person (*see* Note, January 2nd); ask the butcher to send, first thing in the morning, a Sheep's Head, chopped half way through. Most butchers kill on Friday, so that the head can be obtained perfectly fresh, which is most important.

BREAKFAST.—Kippered Salmon (January 9th); Fish Cakes (January 13th); Beef boiled (January 26th); Bread and Milk (January 25th). *Muffins.*—Before toasting the muffins, slit them open with the fingers all round the edge to the depth of an inch; hold them before a clear fire, and turn them every minute till they are hot through. Tear them open, butter them liberally, put them on a hot plate, quarter them, and serve quickly.

LUNCHEON.—Cow Heel, with Parsley Sauce (February 20th); Stirabout Cheese (August 1st).

DINNER.—*Fried Whiting* (January 17th)—*Shrimp Sauce.*—Shell the shrimps quickly. Melt an ounce of butter in a small stew-pan, and mix smoothly with it half an ounce of flour. Beat it over the fire till smooth with the back of a wooden spoon, add a gill, or a quarter of a pint of cold water, and stir the sauce till it boils; then add a pinch of cayenne, a few drops of anchovy, and half a gill of cream. Throw in the picked shrimps, and let them get hot through, but the sauce must not boil after they are added. If more convenient a gill and a half of water may be used instead of cream.

Pork Cutlets, with Apple Sauce.—Some people like pork better when it is cold than when it is hot. In this case it will be necessary only to put the meat on a clean dish, garnish it with parsley, and send it to table as it is. A little Brawn Sauce (January 15th) will doubtless be relished with it. If it is preferred that it should be re-dressed, cut the meat from the bone in neat slices, about a quarter of an inch thick. Prepare a tea-cupful of bread-crumbs, and season these with pepper, salt, a pinch of cayenne, and a very little grated nutmeg. Partially dissolve, but do not oil, a slice of fresh butter, draw the slices of pork through the butter, cover them with the bread-crumbs, and place them in a tin dish; mince a small onion finely, strew it over them, put a little butter on the top, and bake in a gentle oven till the onions are tender. Make a little good Apple Sauce (September 29th). Put it into the middle of a hot dish, arrange the cutlets neatly round it, and serve immediately. Colcannon (August 11th); Baked Potatoes (May 4th); Macaroni Pudding (March 27th); Cheese (June 8th).

Things that must not be Forgotten.

1. Turn and rub the pig's cheek; turn the beef in the brine.
2. Break up the bones of the leg of pork and stew them in stock (February 13th). This is for the pea soup for Feb. 2nd.
3. If five or six whiting were used, the heads and bones may be used for fish stock. Cut up a carrot, an onion, and some celery. Fry in butter till lightly coloured, add the heads and bones of whiting, two anchovies, a pinch of herbs, two cloves, and two quarts of water. Stew gently and skim carefully till the liquor is reduced to three pints, then strain into a basin for use.
4. Put six or eight Normandy pippins to soak in cold water.

January 31st.

Breakfast.	Luncheon.	Dinner.
Bloaters.	Stew of Sheep's Head.	Lobster Soup.
Eggs on the Dish.	Normandy Pippins.	Stewed Steak with Minced Vegetables.
Hot Buttered Toast.		Potatoes.
Dry Toast.		Parson's Pudding.
Honey.		Cheese.
Brown and White Bread and Butter.		
Corn Flour Milk.		

Marketing.

For the Day.—Three pounds of tender Steak. (*See* Marketing, January 1st.) It should be cut evenly, and about one inch and a half thick. One tin of Preserved Lobster. For vegetables, *see* recipe January 31st. Potatoes.

For To-morrow.—One large Capon (see that the giblets are sent home with the bird, and if possible procure an additional set); two pounds of best Pork Sausages (to be bought of a thoroughly respectable dealer); one tin of Potted Pheasant (Bovill's), (*see* January 7th); one pennyworth of Parsley; three heads of Celery for chicken salad. Potatoes; Broccoli.

BREAKFAST.—Bloaters (January 3rd); Eggs on the Dish (December 7th); Corn Flour Milk (June 19th).

LUNCHEON.—*Sheep's Head, Stewed.*—Take out the brains of the sheep's head and throw them into cold water. Cleanse the head thoroughly. This is a most important and not particularly agreeable part of the business. The head should be washed in lukewarm water and with plenty of salt; all the soft bones inside the head should be removed, and the blood and matter washed away from the nostrils, the throat, and the ears. The tongue also must be cut away, and the gums rubbed with salt. When finished the head must be laid in salted tepid water, and allowed to soak two hours. Take it out, drain it; and in order that there may be no doubt about its cleanliness, put it into a saucepan with cold water slightly salted, bring it to a boil, then throw the water away. Tie the two halves of the head together in their original position, and put the head again to boil with two quarts of lukewarm water, a dessert-spoonful of salt, and a quarter of a tea-spoonful of pepper. At the same time put the tongue to boil in a separate saucepan, with strongly salted water, one clove, one peppercorn, and a few drops of vinegar. Skim the fat away as it rises, and let the head boil for an hour. At the end of this time put in two turnips, two carrots, three onions, three outer sticks of celery (*see* Note 2, January 1st), a bunch of parsley, and a sprig of thyme. Let the liquor boil up, put the lid again on the saucepan, draw it back, and let it simmer for one hour and a half. Wash the brains well in cold water, and remove the skin and fibres. Half an hour before the head is done enough put them with it into the saucepan, and let them boil for ten minutes. Whilst they are boiling mix smoothly together in a small saucepan over the fire a piece of good dripping or butter the size of a small egg, and a dessertspoonful of flour. When thoroughly blended add gradually a quarter of a pint of the stock in which the head is being boiled. Take up the brains, chop them finely, and put them with the sauce. Skin the tongue and trim it neatly. Put the head on a dish, with the tongue cut into halves. Mash the turnips, and put them in small heaps round the dish, with the carrot between the heaps. Serve very hot. If liked, the tongue and the brain sauce can be served on a separate dish, and either onion, caper, or parsley sauce may be poured over the head. Normandy Pippins (August 16th).

DINNER.—Lobster Soup (May 20th). *Stewed Steak.*—Trim the steak, and cut away the skin and fat. Melt a slice of dripping or butter in a stew-pan, put in the steak, and when it is brown on one side turn it upon the other. Whilst it is browning put a large table-spoonful of flour into a basin, with a salt-spoonful of salt, a salt-spoonful of pepper, half a grain of cayenne, and a tea-spoonful of freshly made mustard. Mix this very smoothly with a little cold water, and add very gradually a pint and a quarter of either water or stock. When the meat is brown pour the sauce over it. Procure a large carrot, a small turnip, an onion, and a stick of celery. Cut up the onion and celery (*see* Note 2, January 1st), and put them with the meat. Scrape the carrot and peel the turnip, then cut the outer part of the two roots into thin ribbons, and to do this peel them round and round with a sharp knife, very much as any one would do who was peeling an apple. Throw the inner portion left after peeling into the saucepan with the steak. Stir the sauce occasionally, to keep it from getting into lumps. When it boils draw it back a little, and let it simmer very gently for an hour and a half. Put the vegetable ribbons on a board, and with a sharp knife shred them very finely, or, if preferred, cut them with a scoop into small balls. Boil them (each kind separately) until tender without being mashed, and drain them thoroughly. Cut the fat of the steak into small pieces, and bake it in a tin in the oven till it is brown and crisp. It is better not to stew the fat with the steak, because it makes the gravy greasy. Place the steak on a hot dish, and put the fat in a heap in the centre of it. Strain the gravy over it, and throw away the vegetables that were stewed with the meat, because by this time they will be no good—all their flavour will have gone into the gravy. After draining the cut vegetables, place them in little heaps upon the steak, arranging them as prettily as possible. If any other vegetables are at hand they may be interspersed with the rest. Serve very hot. Potatoes (April 7th); Parson's Pudding (August 3rd); Cheese (June 8th).

Things that must not be Forgotten.

1. Boil the pig's cheek for breakfast. For directions how to boil it. *see* February 1st.

2. Turn the beef in the brine.

3. Carefully preserve the sheep's head broth.

4. Pastry is to be made to-day (April 17th): one gooseberry pie, one plum pie (August 7th), both made of bottled fruit, tea-cakes (August 26th), sultana cake (August 2nd), baked custard tart (January 19th).

5. Clean the giblets, scald them, and wash them in several waters, then put them in a cool place till the soup can be made. For directions, see Giblet Soup, February 1st.

FRUITS IN SEASON SUITABLE FOR DESSERT IN JANUARY.

Apples (Golden Knobs and Rennets); Oranges (St. Michael, Tangerine, and Malta); Bananas; Grapes; Melons; Pomeloes; Pears (for stewing); Shaddocks; Nuts (Cobs, Filberts, Walnuts, Brazils, Almonds, Barcelonas); Raisins; French Plums; Figs; Dates; Crystallised Fruits; Foreign Preserved Fruits.

FEBRUARY.

In February Seville oranges come into the market, therefore, about the latter end of February or some time in March, marmalade should be made. The business should not be deferred too long, as the oranges are best before they begin to shrivel. As marmalade, even of the best makers, is by no means equal to good home-made marmalade, it is worth while to make as much as will be wanted. The objection generally urged is that the process is so very troublesome. The two recipes here given do not, however, involve an extraordinary amount of labour, and the result of each is excellent, having been proved and approved repeatedly. No. 2 has more consistency than No. 1, the latter being something like a golden jelly with a strong orange flavour. In No. 1, also, Seville oranges only are used. No. 2 can be made of sweet oranges only, or of a mixture of bitter and sweet fruit. In either case it is an improvement to put one lemon with each dozen oranges.

No. 1.—Take any number of Seville oranges of a medium size with dark smooth skins, and one lemon to each dozen oranges. Weigh them, then with a very sharp knife cut them into as thin slices as possible, removing the pips, but nothing else. Put both juice and fruit into a large jar, and pour on two pints and a half of water to each pound of fruit. Let it stand all night. Next day turn it into a preserving pan and boil it till the rind is quite tender. In home-made marmalade the rind is frequently hard. To prevent this it should be boiled till tender before the sugar is put with it.

It will take about two hours from the time it simmers equally all over. Remove it from the fire, and let it go cold, then weigh it again, and to each pound of stock put one pound and a half of loaf sugar. Boil again till the syrup will jelly, which will be in about twenty minutes. The addition of one or two lemons will greatly improve the flavour of this marmalade.

No. 2.—Boil the oranges whole in plenty of water till they can be pierced quite easily with a pin. They will take about three hours, but can scarcely be done too much. Peel the fruit, taking the skin in large pieces, and preserving as much of the white as possible, and throw the skins into cold water. When all are peeled drain and put the skins to boil in plenty of cold water. As soon as they are on the point of boiling pour off the liquid and take fresh water, then boil for another hour, drain again thoroughly, and preserve the water. Bruise and squeeze the fruit to extract the juice, and throw the refuse into cold water. A pint will be sufficient for a dozen oranges. Just before it is wanted pour it through a jelly-bag, and preserve the liquid for making syrup. Lay the skin in folds, and cut it into thin shreds about an inch long. Measure the juice and weigh the shred peel, and to each pint of the former, as well as to each pound of the latter, allow a pound and a half of loaf sugar, and a pint and a half of the liquid obtained from the squeezed fruit, the quantity being made up, if necessary, with the liquid in which the skins were last boiled. Boil sugar and liquid together for twenty minutes, add the juice, and boil again till the liquid forms a thick syrup, being careful to remove the scum as it rises. Last of all, throw in the shred peel, and boil till the marmalade will jelly when a little is put on a plate.

Sunday, February 1st.

Breakfast.	Dinner.	Tea.	Supper.
Pig's Cheek. Potted Pheasant. Toast, Buttered and Dried. Marmalade. Brown and White Bread and Butter. Milk Toast.	Giblet Soup. A Large Capon, or two Fowls Stuffed Sausages. Potatoes and Boiled Broccoli. Gooseberry Pie made of Bottled Gooseberries. Cream if it may be allowed. Cheese.	Brown and White Bread and Butter. Greengage Jam. Sultana Cake.	Chicken Salad (made of small pieces left from dinner). Baked Custard Tart.

BREAKFAST.—A pig's cheek that had been dried after being pickled would need to lie in soak for awhile; but if it were taken straight from pickle, as this would be, it would be necessary only to wash before cooking it. After washing put it into a saucepan, cover it with cold water, and let it boil gently till tender. In this instance the stock in which the pork bones were boiled may be used instead of water. A moderate-sized cheek taken straight out of the pickle would need to boil gently for about two hours and a half; a dried cheek half an hour longer. When done enough draw off the skin, shake bread-raspings over it through a strainer, and lightly cover it, and put it before the fire for five minutes or longer, till the crumbs are set. A pig's cheek boiled in this way is a very agreeable addition to the breakfast table. Bread-raspings may be bought of the baker, a small bagful for twopence. These will need only to be crushed with a rolling-pin and passed through a fine wire sieve. Or they may be prepared at home, and bits of bread that would otherwise be wasted may be used for the purpose. (*See* January 2nd.) When wanted immediately pass stale crumb of bread through a wire sieve, and brown lightly in the oven. Potted Pheasant (January 7th); Milk Toast (June 17th).

DINNER.—*Giblet Soup.*—Wash the giblets well in two or three waters, and scald them in boiling water, then scrape them till clean. Cut off the heads and throw them away; skin the necks, which are sometimes very bloody, and divide each one into three pieces. Put the claws and the legs into boiling water, to loosen the outer skin, and draw this off entirely. The top skin of the gizzard must be cut through. There is a sort of pipe leading from one side to the other, and this must be cut from end to end. In cleaning the liver care must be taken not to break the gall-bag, or the soup will be made bitter. Divide the heart and liver into halves. Put the giblets into cold water, bring this to a boil, and throw the water away. Dry the giblets, and fry them in good butter or dripping till lightly browned, with two or three strips of bacon rind scalded and scraped, then throw them into cold water to free them from fat. Put them into a stew-pan with a large carrot, a leek, a small onion, a turnip, three or four outer sticks of celery, a bunch of parsley, a sprig of thyme, a bay leaf, a blade of mace, and two cloves. A sprig of basil and sweet marjoram may be added if liked, or half a tea-spoonful of savoury herbs may be used instead of the herbs named. These herbs may be brought ready mixed in bottles. Pour over all about two quarts of stock made from bones. Bring this to a boil, skim it carefully, and boil it gently for two hours. Take out the giblets, and pick out such as will do to put into the soup; trim them neatly, and put them aside. Throw the rest again into the stock, and boil for another hour. If thick giblet soup is wanted put a piece of brown thickening the size of a large walnut into a basin. Mix this with a little hot stock to dissolve it, stir it into the soup, and keep stirring till it boils. Draw the saucepan back, and let it simmer gently for twenty minutes to throw up the grease, and skim this carefully away. If brown thickening is not at hand a little may be made (*see* Roux, January 6th). Strain the soup into a hot tureen, add salt and cayenne to taste, and the pieces of giblets, and stir in half a tea-spoonful of lemon-juice and a glass of sherry. The latter may be omitted. Serve very hot. If *clear* giblet soup is wished it will have to be made earlier, to give time for clarifying it. To clarify Soup, *see* Julienne (April 9th); Capon stuffed with Veal Forcemeat (June 30th); Sausages (January 7th); Potatoes (April 7th); Boiled Broccoli (April 25th); Fruit Pie (August 7th); Cheese (June 8th).

TEA.—Sultana Cake (August 2nd).

SUPPER.—Chicken Salad (August 30th); Baked Custard Tart (January 19th).

Things that must not be Forgotten.

1. As soon as dinner is over pick away every morsel of meat from the chicken bones in as neat pieces as possible, and put them between two dishes, to keep them from getting dry. The chicken bones must be preserved; they will make excellent soup.
2. Put one pint of split peas to soak in as much water as will cover them, and throw away those that float—they are not good
3. Peel and slice the potatoes for breakfast to-morrow (*see* February 2nd).
4. Turn and rub the thin flank of beef.

February 2nd.

Breakfast.	Luncheon.	Dinner.
Pressed Beef. Fried Potatoes. Buttered and Dry Toast. Brown and White Bread and Butter Porridge.	Shepherd's Pie, made of the remains of Pressed Beef. Plum Pie, made on Saturday, with a little milk.	Pease Soup. Ribs of Beef, Italian. Potatoes, Haricot Beans. Tinned Pine Apple, with Custard. Cheese.

Marketing.

For the Day.—One Rib of Beef, taken from the middle ribs, boned, rolled, and weighing about four pounds; or if preferred, a slice of tender Steak can be chosen, two inches thick, and weighing about three pounds. (*See* recipe below for the ingredients required.) One Tin Preserved Pine Apple; Potatoes.

BREAKFAST.—*Fried Potatoes.*—Take one good-sized potato for each person. Kidney potatoes are the best for the purpose. Peel and wash them, and cut them the round way into slices, as thin as a shilling. As they are done, throw them into cold water, to free them from the potato flour. They may, if liked, be prepared thus far over night. Put some fat into a saucepan and let it boil (Fried Fish, January 17th). Drain the potatoes, and dry them on a clean napkin; put them, a few at a time, into a frying-basket, and plunge them into the boiling fat. Let them remain till they are of a light brown colour. Turn them upon a dish covered with kitchen paper, let the fat again boil and put in another basketful of potatoes, and repeat until all are fried. Sprinkle salt and pepper over them, and serve. If a frying-basket is not at hand, the potatoes may be fried in the frying-pan, with enough fat to cover them completely. They must be done in single layers, and must be taken out carefully with a slice. If the fat is not boiling the potatoes will be greasy. Porridge (January 25th); Pressed Beef, left from January 30th.

LUNCHEON.—Shepherd's Pie (January 12th); Plum Pie (August 7th).

DINNER.—Pease Soup (follow the directions given for making lentil soup, April 1st, substituting peas for lentils). *Ribs of Beef, Italian Fashion.*—Put the rolled beef into a saucepan with a lump of dripping melted, and let it brown. When done upon one side, turn it to the other. Lift it up (of course being careful not to stick a fork into the fleshy part), and put it into a brown earthenware pan, not too large. Have ready a handful of parsley leaves, and the white part of two leeks cut into dice. Fry these in the fat in which the meat was browned, and when they are cooked without being at all burnt, drain them, and put them upon the beef. Add also two pickled gherkins chopped small, four cloves, and one or two outer sticks of celery cut into one-inch lengths. Pour over all a pint of the stock in which the chicken bones were stewed, and sprinkle a little pepper and salt over the meat. Cover the pan closely, and bake in a gentle oven for an hour and a half, then add a moderate-sized turnip and a carrot, cover again and bake for another hour. Take up the turnip and carrot; cut them separately into dice, and toss them in a saucepan over the fire with a small piece of butter. Put the meat on a hot dish, strain the gravy over it, and by way of garnish place the minced vegetables in little heaps here and there upon it. Serve immediately upon hot plates. Potatoes (May 12th); Haricot Beans (June 20th); Pine Apple, tinned (April 8th); Custard (August 10th); Cheese (June 8th).

Things that must not be Forgotten.

1. Make a Semolina Mould for dinner to-morrow (Note 2, July 23rd).

2. Turn and rub the thin flank of beef.

February 3rd.

Breakfast.	Luncheon.	Dinner.
Remains of Potted Pheasant. Pig's Cheek. Hot Buttered and Dry Toast. Brown and White Bread and Butter. Bread and Milk.	Rissoles (made of remains of beef). Baked Potatoes. Rice Boiled with Raisins.	Cod-fish Stuffed and Baked. Rabbit Pie. Potatoes. Stewed Celery. Semolina Mould. Cheese.

Marketing.

For the Day.—One moderate-sized and perfectly fresh Cod-fish, or if preferred, the tail end of a large fish (see January 1st and 6th). Ingredients for veal forcemeat, if not in the house (June 27th). One freshly killed young Ostend Rabbit (January 24th); a slice of Ham, weighing about three-quarters of a pound (January 3rd); Potatoes, Celery.

For To-morrow.—Order to be sent first thing in the morning, from seven to eight pounds of the Top side of the Round of Beef. This is one of the most economical joints for family use, as it has not much fat, and very little bone. (See January 10th.) A fresh Leg of Pork may also be ordered, and pickled for boiling. (See January 6th.) It is best and most delicate when weighing about four pounds, but if this is too small for the requirements of the family, it certainly should not weigh more than six pounds. To pickle it all that is necessary is to rub it every day with plenty of common salt, the hands being previously washed in cold water. Muffins for breakfast (see January 29th).

BREAKFAST. — Potted Pheasant (January 7th); Pig's Cheek boiled (January 31st); Bread and Milk (January 25th).

LUNCHEON.—Rissoles (January 6th); Baked Potatoes (May 4th). *Rice Boiled with Raisins.*—Take four ounces of good rice; wash it in two or three waters, and pick out the discoloured grains. Mix it with a quarter of a pound of raisins, and tie in a well-floured cloth, leaving plenty of room for the rice to swell. If too much room is given the pudding will be watery, if too little it will be hard. Experience will soon teach the cook the degree of looseness required. Put the pudding into a saucepan with plenty of cold water, bring it slowly to a boil, let it boil gently from an hour and a quarter to an hour and a half. Turn it out carefully, and send it to table with plain sweet sauce poured over it. If liked, one pound of baking apples cored and sliced can be used instead of the raisins. This is a palatable wholesome dish for nursery use.

DINNER.—*Cod-fish baked with Forcemeat.*—Mince finely one ounce of the fat from the pig's cheek. Even if the cheek is nearly finished it is probable that this quantity can be picked from the bones. If cooked bacon-fat were not in the house, an ounce of finely shred beef suet could be used instead. Mix with the fat an equal quantity of finely grated bread-crumbs, and add half a tea-spoonful of chopped parsley, a very small pinch of dried thyme, a few drops of the essence of anchovies, a little pepper and salt. Bind the forcemeat together with a well-beaten egg. Make an incision down each side of the backbone of the fish, press the forcemeat in, and lay the fish in a tin baking-dish. Pour round it three-quarters of a pint of thin melted butter, which has been flavoured with anchovy and lemon-juice. Bake in a moderate oven till the flesh leaves the bone easily, and baste the fish frequently with the sauce. It will be done enough in about an hour; remove it carefully to a hot dish, strain the sauce over it, sprinkle a few bread-raspings upon the top, and serve very hot. If preferred, the fish can be cooked according to the recipe given for Haddock Stuffed and Baked (September 4th). Rabbit Pie (September 11th); Potatoes (May 12th); Stewed Celery (December 2nd); Semolina Mould (Note 2, January 23rd); Cheese (June 8th).

Things that must not be Forgotten.

1. Carefully preserve any remains of cod-fish there may be, and make into fish cakes for breakfast (*see* January 13th); or prepare according to the recipe given January 7th.
2. Make the hydropathic pudding for dinner to-morrow, and leave it in a cold place, with a weight on the top of it (June 16th).
3. Strain the fat in which the rissoles are fried into a basin as soon as done with (February 19th).
4. Boil the sheep's head broth. Soup can be made of it for Feb. 5th.
5. Turn and rub the beef in the brine.
6. Soak a cupful of green lentils in cold water.

February 4th.

Breakfast.	Luncheon.	Dinner.
Fish Cakes. Savoury Eggs. Muffins. Dry Toast. Brown and White Bread and Butter. Porridge.	Australian Mutton, cold, with Pickles and Baked Potatoes. Cake Pudding, made of broken bread.	Smelts. Top side of the Round of Beef. Yorkshire Pudding. Baked Potatoes. Lentils. Hydropathic Pudding. Cheese.

Marketing.

For the Day.—One four-pound tin of Australian Mutton; Smelts, one for each person and one over; one pennyworth of Parsley. Smelts are delicious little fish, and are very generally used as a garnish for large fish, but they are very good served alone. They should be quite fresh, and when in this condition smell like cucumber. The bodies should be stiff and firm, the eyes bright, and the skin transparent. Potatoes.

For To-morrow.—A lunch Tongue. Small tins are now sold about 1s. 3d. each. They contain calves' tongues, and are excellent. A pennyworth of small Salad, and a bottle of Anchovies, if none are in the house.

BREAKFAST.—Fish Cakes (January 13th); Savoury Eggs (January 1st); Muffins (January 30th); Porridge (January 25th).

LUNCHEON.—*Australian Meat* is at its best when served *cold* with pickles. It should be turned out of the tin very carefully, and the dripping that lies on it should be taken away, and will prove a valuable addition to the household stock of dripping to be used in cookery. When the ring dish that is made expressly for Australian meat is not at hand, the meat should be put upon an ordinary dish and garnished with parsley. The jelly should be preserved—it will make excellent gravy; and in order that there may be no waste the tin should be rinsed with warm water for gravy. Baked Potatoes (May 4th). *Cake Pudding.*—This pudding is both economical and wholesome, and is generally a favourite with the children. To make it, gather together a number of pieces of broken bread and put them into a bowl. Pour upon them as much boiling water as will cover them, put a plate upon the bowl, and let them soak until soft, then drain away the water. Beat them up with a fork until smooth, and take out any pieces that still remain doughy. Stir into the mass a good lump of dripping, a pinch of salt, a little grated nutmeg, moist sugar to taste, and a few picked and dried currants, or, if these are objected to, sultana raisins may be used. Grease a pie-dish, turn the mixture into it, and bake in a well-heated oven till the pudding is brightly browned on the top. A little jam is a great improvement to this pudding, and wine sauce makes it seem very much better than it really is. It must not be drained *too* dry.

DINNER.—*Smelts.*—Be particularly careful in cleaning these fish. Do not open them, but pull out the inside through the gills, and leave in the milt or roe, then wipe them lightly with a soft cloth, and dredge them with flour. Let them lie for an hour or two, then egg and bread them, or, if liked, simply dredge them once more with flour. Fry them till brightly browned, according to the directions already given for frying fish. (*See* January 17th.) The smelts may be neatly arranged, with the tails meeting in the centre of the dish, and with a wreath of fried parsley round them. It is very usual to serve them without sauce, but shrimp or anchovy sauce, and more than either, Tartar sauce, will be found to constitute a palatable accompaniment to them. If preferred, they may be baked instead of being fried. Top side of the round (March 4th); Yorkshire Pudding (December 3rd); Baked Potatoes (May 4th); Lentils (March 2nd); Hydropathic Pudding (June 16th); Cheese (June 8th).

Things that must not be Forgotten.

1. It is not likely that the whole of the Australian meat will be used. The remains must be carefully put away, and can be used for luncheon to-morrow.

2. Turn and rub the leg of pork.

3. Boil the stock made from the chicken bones. Very good soup may be made of it for Feb. 6th.

4. Cleanse the small salad, and lay it on a cloth to dry; **also** fillet the anchovies to be ready for breakfast, and put the fillets between two dishes.

5. Turn and rub the beef in the brine.

February 5th.

Breakfast.	Luncheon.	Dinner.
Anchovies with Hard-boiled Eggs. Tongue. Buttered and Dry Toast. Honey. Brown and White Bread and Butter. Milk Toast.	Savoury Hash of Australian Meat. Baked Batter Pudding.	Parsnip Soup made of Sheep's Head Broth. Cold Beef. Salad. Cutlets with Piquante Sauce. Fried Potatoes. Brussels Sprouts. Apple Gâteau. Cheese.

Marketing.

For the Day.—A Neck of Mutton; Parsnips and Gherkins, if these are not in the house; Salad. The butcher should be asked to pare away as much of the fat from the mutton as he can. It is economical to buy the whole of the neck of mutton rather than the best end. The scrag end can always be served separately. If asked to do so, the butcher will divide the cutlets. The best end of the neck will afford seven, three without bones and four with them. If not wanted immediately, the neck should hang in a cool place. Potatoes, Brussels Sprouts, Apples, Split Peas.

BREAKFAST.—Anchovies with hard-boiled eggs (January 18th); Lunch Tongue (January 2nd and 3rd); Milk Toast (June 17th).

LUNCHEON.—*Savoury Hash of Australian Meat.*—We will suppose there is a pound and a half of meat. Take a dessert-spoonful of chopped herbs, consisting of two-thirds parsley and one-third marjoram and thyme. Cut the meat into pieces convenient for serving, and sprinkle over each one a little pepper and salt, and a portion of the mixed herbs. Take half a pint of melted butter made of the jelly of the meat dissolved in stock or hot water, and thickened with a small nut of brown thickening; and if this is not at hand, with an ounce of butter and half an ounce of flour stirred over the fire together till brown. Let the gravy boil, then stir in two pickled gherkins finely minced. Put the meat into the gravy, and let it remain for five or six minutes till it is warmed through. Add a dessert-spoonful of Harvey or Worcester Sauce, and serve immediately. If the sauce is not sufficiently browned, a few drops of brown thickening may be added to it.

Baked Batter Pudding.—Make some batter according to the recipe given for batter in Toad in the Hole (January 15th). Grease a pie-dish and pour in the batter, and bake in a brisk oven. It will be done enough when the batter is set in the middle, and is coloured brightly, and will take about an hour and a half. It is usual to choose a dish that the batter will not quite fill, but the pudding will be more acceptable to many people if the batter is not more than three-quarters of an inch thick. Cold butter and sugar, or jam, may be served as accompaniments. A pleasing variety will be afforded by filling the dish half full of good baking apples cored and sliced before pouring the batter in. Or a thin layer of batter at the bottom of the dish may be first baked, and when it is set jam may be spread upon it, and the remainder of the batter poured upon this.

DINNER.—Parsnip Soup (December 3rd); Beef—top side of the round left yesterday; Salad (March 13th); Cutlets, to be taken from the best end of the neck, with Piquant Sauce (April 30th); Potatoes (February 2nd); Brussels Sprouts (June 4th); Apple Gâteau (September 24th); Cheese (June 8th).

Things that must not be Forgotten.
1. Turn and rub the leg of pork.
2. On no account let the Australian meat *boil* in the gravy. It is already rather over-cooked, and needs only to be warmed through.
3. Make rissoles for breakfast in the morning with the remains of the cold beef. (*See* January 6th.)
4. Put two table-spoonfuls of tapioca in a basin with a pint of water to soak all night.
5. Turn and rub the beef in the brine.
6. Put a cupful of peas to soak all night in cold water.

February 6th.

Breakfast.	Luncheon.	Dinner.
Rissoles.	Stewed Giblets.	Gravy Soup made of Stock from Chicken Bones.
Poached Eggs.	Jam and Bread Pudding	Boiled Pork.
Hot Buttered and Dry Toast.		Pease Pudding.
Lemon Marmalade.		Cabbage and Potatoes.
Porridge.		Tapioca and Apples.
		Cheese.

Marketing.
For the Day.—Two sets of Chickens' or Ducks' Giblets (fresh). These may probably be procured for a few pence. The giblets consist of the head, neck, feet, gizzard, and liver of the birds. The whole or part of a large fresh Ox-cheek; Cabbage, Potatoes, Apples.

For To-morrow.—A tin of preserved Prawns. These prawns offer a pleasant variety for breakfast. They are economical because not very much can be used at once; and besides being used as a relish, they are useful for garnishing dishes; or two or three chopped small and added to melted butter will make a good sauce for fish. The price at the present time is one shilling per tin.

BREAKFAST.—Rissoles (January 6th). *Poached Eggs.*—Have ready a wide saucepan or frying-pan with gently boiling water, into

F

which a pinch of salt and a table-spoonful of vinegar have been thrown. Break the eggs separately into a cup, and slip them one at a time carefully into the water. They must be kept apart, and there must be enough water to cover them. Keep the pan at the side of the stove, and on no account let the water boil fast, or the eggs will break. When the white is set, and the yoke is seen through a thin white covering, the eggs are done enough. Take them up carefully with an egg-slice, and be sure to drain them well. The vinegar in the water will make the eggs white, but if they are not drained thoroughly it will give them an acid taste. Trim away the loose untidy pieces of white that may hang about the eggs, and dish them either on a separate dish or, if preferred, with the rissoles. For Porridge, *see* January 25th.

LUNCHEON.—*Stewed Giblets.*—Clean the giblets according to the directions already given (February 1st). When thoroughly washed, dry them well and roll them in flour. Put the gizzards and feet into a saucepan with half a pint of water or stock, and six peppercorns. Let them stew gently for three-quarters of an hour, then add the rest of the giblets, another pint of water, a small onion stuck with one clove, the red part of a large carrot scraped to pulp, a bunch of parsley, a sprig of thyme, a bay-leaf, and a stick of celery; stew for an hour and a half longer. Take out the herbs; put the giblets upon a dish: if necessary, add a little liquid browning to it, and serve very hot. This is an inexpensive, nourishing and appetising dish. For Browning, *see* January 2nd; Jam and Bread with Milk (February 23rd).

DINNER.—Gravy Soup (August 31st); Boiled Pork (February 23rd); Pease Pudding (December 4th); Cabbages (June 4th); Potatoes (April 7th); Tapioca and Apples (February 18th); Cheese (June 8th).

Things that must not be Forgotten.

1. Wash one pound of prunes and throw away the water. Put them into a basin with as much water as will cover them, and leave them to soak all night.

2. Pastry is to be made to-day (April 17th)—cheese-cakes (August 18th), a few jam tartlets and a rhubarb pie (August 7th), Vienna bread (August 26th), rice cake (August 2nd).

3. Roll tightly and boil the beef (February 23rd). Put it under a weight.

4. Boil the brine with an additional handful of salt. *See* Brine (January 13th).

5. Sprinkle a little salt on the cheek and leave it for two or three hours. Wash it thoroughly with plenty of salt, and take away the soft bone where the slime lodges. Wash it again and wipe it dry, and put it into the brine when this is cold.

February 7th.

Breakfast.	Luncheon.	Dinner.
Tinned Prawns. Cold Pork, with Brawn Sauce. Hot Buttered Toast. Vienna Bread. Brown and White Bread and Butter. Damson Jam. Bread and Milk.	Poor Man's Goose. Semolina Mould.	Cabbage Soup. Curried Rabbit. Boiled Rice. Potatoes. Stewed Endive. Stewed Prunes. Custard. Cheese.

Marketing.

For the Day.—The Fry of a small Pig, about one and a half pounds. This must be perfectly fresh, or it will not be good. One good-sized Ostend Rabbit, to weigh about three and a half pounds; a fine young Cabbage, with a good heart, for soup; Potatoes, Endive.

For To-morrow.—One good-sized Brill (see January 9th); two fine Fowls, trussed for boiling; three heads of Celery. Fowls will be very dear soon, therefore it will be well to have a couple while they are still to be had at a reasonable price. Fowls for boiling should have small but not black legs, and the flesh should be as white as possible. One pound of Bacon, cut into thin rashers (see Bacon, January 3rd); two Batavian Endives; a small Beet-root; one-pennyworth of Parsley; quarter of a pint of picked Shrimps; three-pennyworth of fresh Cream; a couple of fresh unsalted Pig's Feet, ready cleaned by the butcher. The feet of large pigs will be better than those of small ones.

BREAKFAST.—*Tinned Prawns.*—The prawns are contained in a bag inside the tin. Take them out carefully, and arrange the prawns on a dish covered with a fish paper, and garnish with parsley. They look very pretty piled in a pyramid shape, and, if liked, a lemon or a piece of bread may be put in the midst of them to support them in their position. Pork, left yesterday; Brawn Sauce (January 15th); Vienna Bread, made yesterday; Bread and Milk (January 25th).

LUNCHEON.—*Pig's Fry, or Poor Man's Goose.*—Scrub and wash well three pounds of potatoes. Put them into a saucepan with as much cold water as will cover them, and bring the water to a boil. Take the potatoes up, peel them, and cut them into slices a quarter of an inch thick. Boil also a Spanish onion, and mince it finely. Mix together a tea-spoonful of salt, two salt-spoonfuls of pepper, and a tea-spoonful of dried sage. Wash and dry the fry, cut each part into moderately thin slices, and sprinkle a little of the seasoning over each slice. Grease a pie-dish, and fill it with alternate layers of potato and fry, being careful that potatoes shall constitute the first and the last layers. Fill the dish with stock or water, and lay a greased paper over the top, then bake in a moderate oven for about an hour and a half. If liked, a little Apple Sauce can accompany this dish. Semolina Mould (July 23rd).

DINNER.—*Cabbage Soup.*—Wash and trim the cabbage, shred it finely, and cut the shreds across, to shorten the filaments. Throw these into a quart of boiling water, and let them boil till tender. Put with them a quart of the liquor in which the pork was boiled, add pepper and salt, and a good-sized lump of sugar; boil together and serve very hot. The soup ought to be thick with the shred cabbage. Curried Rabbit (July 16th); Boiled Rice (July 21st); Potatoes (May 12th); Stewed Endive (December 5th); Stewed Prunes (February 27th); Custard (August 10th); Cheese (June 8th).

Things that must not be Forgotten.

1. Sprinkle a little salt on he brill before putting it in the larder.

2. Take up the weights from the beef; trim and glaze it. The liquor in which it was boiled can be made into glaze (March 21st).

3. Prepare the pig's feet for breakfast to-morrow. To do this wash them well in boiling water, and scrape off any hairs that may be left on. Put them into a saucepan with as much cold water as will cover them, and add an onion stuck with two cloves, a carrot, a little salt, six peppercorns, and a bay-leaf. Let the saucepan stand by the side of the fire, and keep the feet simmering gently till the bones can be drawn out easily. They will need to simmer nearly all day. When done enough, split each one in halves, bone them, and let them get cold. Melt a little butter in a plate, pass each half through it, and cover with fine and perfectly dry breadcrumbs. In the evening when the fire is low, put the feet on a gridiron, place them over the fire, turn them occasionally, and let them remain until they are hot through and brightly browned. When cold they are ready for use, and will constitute a pleasant variety as a breakfast dish. Brawn Sauce may be served with them (January 15th). They should be neatly arranged on a dish covered with a napkin, and garnished with parsley. If quickly boiled the meat will be hard and indigestible. The preparation of this dish requires time rather than trouble.

4. If rice milk is to be used for breakfast instead of oatmeal porridge, partially prepare it over-night. (Note 3, June 17th.)

5. Turn and rub the ox-check.

Sunday, February 8th.

Breakfast.	Dinner.	Tea.	Supper.
Ham-cured Herrings.	Brill, with Neapolitan Sauce.	Brown and White Bread and Butter.	Rolled Beef. Salad.
Pig's feet, with Brawn Sauce.	Boiled Fowls, with Egg Sauce.	Greengage Jam. Rice Cake.	Rhubarb Pie. Cheese.
Vienna Bread.	Toasted Bacon.		
Marmalade.	Potatoes.		
Brown and White Bread and Butter.	Stewed Celery. Jam Tartlets.		
Rice Milk.	Stone Cream. Cheese.		

BREAKFAST.—Ham-cured Herrings (January 15th); Pig's Feet (Note 3, February 7th); Brawn Sauce (January 15th); Vienna Bread (August 26th); Rice Milk (June 18th).

DINNER.—*Brill.*—Boil the brill according to the directions already given in January 9th. If liked, *Neapolitan Sauce* can be served with it, instead of any of the sauces mentioned there. To make this sauce, put into a small enamelled saucepan four shalots finely minced, a dessert-spoonful of bruised capers, five or six peppercorns, and the juice of a lemon. Stir these ingredients over the fire for three or four minutes, then add a cupful of stock made from bones, a pinch of cayenne, a small clove, half a bay-leaf, a small piece of mace, not quite half a blade. Simmer gently for twenty minutes, and pour out till cool. When it is wanted dissolve a piece of butter about the size of an egg in a separate stewpan. Mix with it over the fire a dessert-spoonful of flour, and work the paste with the back of a wooden spoon till quite smooth; add the cooled liquor, and stir the sauce till it boils. Strain it, put it again into the saucepan, and let it boil, lift it from the fire, put in the shrimps, and stir in the cream. Add a few drops of anchovy essence, and, if liked, a few drops of lemon-juice, and serve immediately. Boiled Fowl, with Egg Sauce (September 6th); Toasted Bacon (January 19th); Potatoes (May 6th); Stewed Celery (December 2nd); Jam Tartlets (August 7th); Stone Cream (July 1st); Cheese (June 8th).

TEA.—Rice Cake (August 2nd).

SUPPER.—Rolled Beef, boiled on Feb. 6th; Salad (March 13th); Fruit Pie (August 7th).

Things that must not be Forgotten.

1. Be sure to take care of the bacon-rind (January 1st and Note 2, January 5th).
2. Take care of the liquor the fowls were boiled in, and stew their bones in it for two or three hours.
3. Preserve the stock in which the fish was boiled.
4. Turn and rub the ox-cheek.

February 9th.

Breakfast.	Luncheon.	Dinner.
Remains of Tinned Prawns (see Note 3 below). Remains of Pig's Feet. Brown Sauce. Hot Buttered Toast. Dry Toast. Watercress. Brown and White Bread and Butter. Porridge.	Rolled Beef. Pickled Walnuts. Baked Potatoes and a little cold Butter. Baked Apples with Sugar.	Victoria Soup (made of chicken stock). Beef Olives. Potatoes. Cabbage. Golden Pudding. Cheese.

Marketing.

For the Day.—Three pounds of tender Steak (*see* January 1st); half a pound of Beef Suet for the golden pudding; or good dripping may be used instead.

For To-morrow.—A whole Scrag of Mutton. According to the usual method of cutting up sheep, the neck is divided into two halves. Get the butcher to leave the part near the head whole. It will furnish an excellent and economical joint, weighing about three pounds. The meat must be perfectly fresh. One tin of preserved Tomatoes; a bundle of dried Sprats; half a dozen Muffins.

BREAKFAST.—Tinned Prawns (*see* February 7th); Pig's Feet (February 7th); Brawn Sauce (January 15th); Porridge (January 25th).

LUNCHEON.—Beef, Boiled (February 6th). *Baked Apples.*—Take some good baking apples, one for each person and one or two over. Wipe them thoroughly, and without paring them put them side by side in a shallow earthenware dish, not to touch each other. Put them into a cool oven and let them bake as gently and slowly as possible until cooked throughout. Take up, put them on a dish, and let them get cold. Before serving sift white sugar thickly over them. Baked Potatoes (May 4th).

DINNER.—*Victoria Soup*, made of the liquor the chickens and the bones were boiled in, with bacon-rind. Take about three pints of the liquor in which the fowls were boiled. Put this in a stewpan with the crushed bones and remnants of the birds, two or three strips of bacon-rind, scalded and scraped (the remainder will be needed for the Tomato Purée to-morrow), an onion, two outer sticks of celery, or, wanting these, as much celery seed as would lie on a three-penny piece (the seed must be tied in muslin), a small carrot, a bay-leaf, six peppercorns, a bunch of parsley, a sprig of thyme, and three ounces of good rice that has been washed in two or three waters. Place the stewpan by the side of the fire and let its contents simmer very gently for about an hour and a half till the rice is tender. Take it up, remove the bones and vegetables from the liquor, and rub the rice patiently through a fine hair sieve. Half an hour before it is to be served boil it once more, season it with a sufficiency of salt, pour it into the hot soup tureen, and stir into it a pint of boiling milk. If cream may be afforded the soup will, of course, be so much the better, but it will be very good and delicate made with milk. Fried bread may be sent to table on a separate dish. Beef Olives (September 5th); Potatoes (May 4th); Cabbage (June 4th); Golden Pudding (May 4th); Cheese (June 8th).

Things that must not be Forgotten.

1. Turn and rub the ox-cheek.
2. When making the soup, preserve about half of the liquor for the stewed mutton to-morrow—it will be better than water.
3. If any of the brill were left it may be served for breakfast instead of the prawns, which could then be used another day (*see* Fish Cakes, January 13th).

February 10th.

Breakfast.	Luncheon.	Dinner
Dried Sprats.	Rissoles (made of remains of rolled beef).	Tomato Purée.
Rolled Beef.		Stewed Mutton with vegetables.
Honey.	Eggs stewed with Cheese.	
Hot Toast.		Broccoli.
Muffins.		Potatoes.
Brown and White Bread and Butter.		Piquant Sauce.
		The Guest's Pudding.
Bread and Milk.		Cheese.

Marketing.

For the Day.—Capers and a quarter of a pound of Suet, if these are not in the house. Beef kidney suet is the best. It should be perfectly sweet and firm to the touch. Potatoes, Broccoli.

For To-morrow.—Four pounds of the Fillet of the Rump of Beef (see Marketing, January 2nd); a bag of Hominy. Hominy is beginning to be much used in England. Three sizes are sold; the middle size is the best. It furnishes excellent, nourishing, and inexpensive food. Dried Pears.

BREAKFAST. — Dried Sprats (February 28th); Rolled Beef, Boiled (February 6th); Muffins (January 30th); Bread and Milk (January 25th).

LUNCHEON.—Rissoles (January 6th). *Eggs stewed with Cheese.*—Melt an ounce of butter or sweet dripping in a saucepan over the fire. Take some eggs—one for each person; break them separately into a cup, and turn them carefully into the pan, and do not let them touch each other. Sprinkle a little pepper and salt upon them; and when they are just set firm, lift them upon a dish with an egg slice; lay very thin slices of soft cheese upon them, and put the dish before the fire till the cheese is melted. Serve very hot with brown bread and butter, and toasted bread as an accompaniment.

DINNER.—Tomato Purée (March 11th). *Stewed Mutton with Vegetables.*—Wash the joint quickly in cold water, dry it with a soft cloth, pepper and salt it, and dredge flour over it. Melt a large lump of dripping in a good-sized stewpan; put in the meat, and when it is brown upon one side turn it to the other. Take it up; put it into another stewpan, and pour over it as much boiling stock as will barely cover it. Let the stock boil up, then put with it three onions, three carrots, three turnips, and a sprig of parsley; place the lid on the saucepan and draw it back, and let its contents simmer very gently indeed for fully four hours. It should be looked at occasionally, and the vegetables should be taken out as soon as they are done enough. If allowed to simmer after they are done their flavour will go into the gravy, and this is not desirable, as they are to be served with the meat. When the mutton is perfectly tender pour the gravy from it; put the liquor in a cold place to make the fat rise to the surface. Skim this off entirely, and thicken about a pint of the gravy with a little brown thickening (*see* January 6th). Strain it again over the mutton and let it stew very gently till the meat is once more hot through. Meantime, mince the vegetables stewed with the meat and sauté them—that is, shake them for three or four minutes over the fire in a small saucepan with a piece of butter. Put the mutton on a dish, strain part of the sauce over it, and arrange the minced vegetables as a sort of wall round it. Chop three pickled gherkins finely; put them with the remainder of the sauce and send this to table in a tureen. The meat should be cut off the bone in long slices. For a similar method, see January 14th. Potatoes (May 12th); Broccoli (April 25th); Guest's Pudding (April 14th); Cheese (June 8th).

Things that must not be Forgotten.

1. Brush the fillet of beef over with vinegar, sprinkle pepper and salt over it, and hang it in a cool larder.

2. Turn and rub the ox-cheek in the brine.

3. Wash a tea-cupful of the hominy in plenty of water and rub it between the hands. Remove the grains that rise to the surface; they are not good. Wash it again in one or two waters; drain it and let it soak till morning in a quart of water. A cover should be put over the dish which contains it.

4. Put half a pound of dried pears or Normandy pippins to soak all night.

February 11th.

Breakfast.	Luncheon.	Dinner.
Hominy.	Liver and Bacon.	Soles, filleted and rolled, with Maitre-d'Hôtel Sauce.
Ox-eyes.	Stewed Pears (dried like Normandy Pippins).	
Hot Buttered Toast.		Roast Fillet of Beef.
Dry Toast.		Potatoes.
Brown and White Bread and Butter.		Broccoli.
Marmalade.		Lèche Crème.
(The hominy will take the place of the porridge.)		Cheese.

Marketing.

For the Day.—One pound and a half of fresh Liver; one pound of Streaky Bacon, cut into rashers; half of this is for to-day, and half for to-morrow (see Marketing, January 3rd); a pair of moderate-sized but thick Soles (see January 3rd); half a pound of Ratafias; a pennyworth of Parsley.

For To-morrow.—Four Sheep's Kidneys, fine, plump, and perfectly fresh; a well-kept Leg of Mutton (see January 8th).

BREAKFAST.—*Boiled Hominy.*—As soon as the kitchen fire is lighted put a tea-spoonful of salt into the water with the hominy, and put it with the water in which it was soaked into a stewpan, and set it by the side of the fire to simmer gently. If there is any difficulty about cooking it over a gentle heat it will be safer to put it in a jar, and set this in a kettle of boiling water, for if allowed to boil quickly it will burn. It will be done enough in about an hour; when it has absorbed the liquid, it should be well stirred, turned into a dish, and eaten either with fresh butter, or melted butter sauce, or with sugar like rice. It is a good plan to make rather more than is wanted for the day, and what is left can be fried for breakfast to-morrow, or can be made into a cake. Ox-eyes (June 5th).

LUNCHEON.—Liver and Bacon (January 17th); Stewed Pears (same as Normandy Pippins, August 16th).

DINNER.—Soles, filleted and rolled, with Maître-d'Hôtel Sauce (March 1st). *Roast Fillet of Beef.*—Bind a slice of fat bacon over the underside of the joint of beef, and roast it gently (March 4th). It should be underdone rather than otherwise; pour round it good brown gravy thickened with roux to the consistency of cream. It is probable that a little gravy was left from the mutton yesterday, and this mixed with the gravy that runs from the meat will answer the purpose admirably. Potatoes (May 4th); Broccoli (April 25th); Lèche Crème (May 7th); Cheese (June 8th).

Things that must not be Forgotten.

1. Take care of the bacon-rind.
2. Cut the shank bone off the leg of mutton and stew it at once for gravy. (*See* Note 3, January 8th.)
3. Turn and rub the ox-cheek.
4. Wash a cupful of haricot beans and put them to soak in plenty of cold water.
5. Make stock from fresh bones for the ox-tail soup on Feb. 13. (*See* February 13th.)

February 12th.

Breakfast.	Luncheon.	Dinner.
Fried Hominy.	Shepherd's Pie (made of remains of cold Beef).	Skate with Brown Butter.
Kidneys and Bacon.	Plain Rice Pudding without Eggs.	Roast Leg of Mutton.
Hot Buttered Toast.		Yorkshire Pudding.
Dry Toast.		Potatoes.
Brown and White Bread and Butter.		Jerusalem Artichokes.
Marmalade.		Haricot Beans.
(The hominy will take the place of the porridge.)		Vermicelli Pudding.
		Cheese.

Marketing.

For the Day.—Two pounds of crimped Skate (January 10th); Potatoes, Artichokes.

For To-morrow.—An Ox-tail; a tin of Collared Tongue (*see* January 2nd, Note, January 3rd; also Marketing, February 4th); one dried Haddock; Watercress.

BREAKFAST.—*Fried Hominy.*—The cold hominy will be quite firm. Cut it into thick slices, flour these, and lightly brush them over with the yolk of an egg. Fry them in hot fat, drain on paper, and serve hot. The hominy will be an agreeable accompaniment to the kidneys and bacon. Kidneys and Bacon (*see* January 2nd).

LUNCHEON.—Shepherd's Pie (January 12th); Plain Rice Pudding (February 24th).

DINNER.—*Skate with Brown Butter.*—Wash the skate and put it into a saucepan with as much cold water as will barely cover it, and add salt and a little vinegar. Let the water boil, skim it, draw the saucepan to the side of the fire, and simmer gently for about ten minutes. Five minutes before the fish is done enough, put the liver into the pan and boil it also. Take up the fish, drain it, put a little of the liver at each end ; have ready a little brown butter sauce, pour it over the fish, and serve immediately. It will be a great improvement to the appearance of the dish if a few sprigs of fried parsley are piled in the centre. To make the *Brown Butter Sauce*, put a good slice of fresh butter, from two to three ounces, into an omelet pan, and stir it over a quick fire till it is brown without being burnt. Skim off the froth, add salt and pepper, and take the butter from the fire. Boil a wine-glassful of vinegar very quickly till it is reduced to a table-spoonful. Mix the brown butter with this, and the sauce is ready. Common butter will do as well for this sauce as the best butter, as the fresh flavour is destroyed in cooking ; sometimes half tarragon vinegar and half plain vinegar are used. Skate prepared thus tastes better than it looks. It is a great favourite with epicures. Roast Leg of Mutton (March 4th) ; Yorkshire Pudding (November 26th) ; Potatoes (April 7th) ; Jerusalem Artichokes (November 30th); Haricot Beans (June 20th) ; Vermicelli Pudding (August 1st); Cheese (June 8th).

Things that must not be Forgotten.

1. Turn and rub the ox-cheek.

2. Preserve any gravy there may be left from the kidneys, to put with the liquor from the shank for gravy for the leg of mutton.

3. As soon as the leg of mutton comes from the table put it away on a clean dish, and carefully preserve any gravy that may be left. If it is to be eaten cold to-morrow it should be carved neatly, or it will have a very unsightly appearance.

4. If any hominy still remain, keep it to make a hominy cake to-morrow.

February 13th.

Breakfast.	Luncheon.	Dinner.
Dried Haddock. Collared Tongue. Hot Buttered Toast. Dry Toast. Brown and White Bread and Butter. Watercress. Porridge.	Tripe and Onion Sauce. Plain Suet Pudding with Jam, Treacle, or, if preferred, Gravy.	Ox Tail Soup. Stock made from fresh bones. Cold Mutton. (If this is objected to the mutton may be re-dressed. For various ways see Index.) Baked Potatoes. Salad of Haricot Beans and Lettuce. Cottage Plum Pudding. Cheese.

Marketing.

For the Day.—One pound and a half of fresh tripe, as thick and white as can be procured. Salad: Two Lettuces, half an Endive, a halfpennyworth of Mustard and Cress, a halfpennyworth of boiled Beet-root. Suet if not in the house, or good dripping may be used instead. From ten to twelve pounds of the thin end of the Flank of Beef. Ask the butcher to supply a piece with as little fat as possible. Potatoes.

For To-morrow.—Half a pound of Bacon, if this is not in the house. One dressed Cow-heel for Beef à la Mode. One pennyworth of Mustard and Cress.

BREAKFAST.—Collared Tongue (Note, January 3rd); Dried Haddock (January 27th); Porridge (January 25th).

LUNCHEON.—Tripe and Onion Sauce (December 4th); Plain Suet Pudding (May 13th).

DINNER.—Ox-tail Soup (February 22nd). *To Make Stock from Bones either Cooked or Uncooked.*—Break the bones into small pieces; put them into a stewpan with cold water in the proportion of one quart of water to a pound of bones. Bring the water to a boil, and when it is nearly boiling throw in a little salt to raise the scum. Carefully remove this with an iron spoon as it rises, draw the stewpan to the side of the fire, cover it closely, and let its contents simmer very gently for five hours, by which time it will be reduced to half the quantity. Strain the liquid through a sieve into a clean bowl and leave it in a cool place till next day. Before using it skim away every particle of fat, and in pouring it out leave untouched the sediment which will most likely be at the bottom of the bowl. This liquor will constitute what is called "unflavoured stock." If it is to be used quickly the flavouring ingredients may be stewed with the bones, but if not it is best to add them afterwards—first, because the stock will keep longer without them; and secondly, because the flavourers can then be varied to suit the kind of soup which is to be made from the stock. When the flavouring ingredients are added on the day they should be boiled for the last two hours only. One carrot, one small turnip, one leek, or failing this, one onion, one clove, two outer sticks of celery, or a quarter of a tea-spoonful of celery seed tied in muslin, one bay-leaf, a bunch of parsley, a sprig of thyme, half a small blade of mace, and six peppercorns will be needed to flavour a quart of liquid, and a small knob of sugar will help to bring out the flavour. The vegetables will not be of any use afterwards, as all their goodness will have gone into the stock, therefore if vegetables are wanted they must be cooked separately. It is not well to let the stock boil more than five hours, as if it did so it might taste unpleasantly of the pan. If there were not time to boil the stock in one day it should on no account be left in the saucepan all night, but rather it should be put into a bowl and finished the next day, and the stewpan should be well washed, scoured, and dried before the stock was put into it again. Stock thus made will in cool weather keep good for several days if kept in a cool place. In summer it should be boiled up every day, and the bowl which contains it should be washed and dried before it is turned into it again. When white soups are wanted a white saucepan should be used, and the stock should be made of veal bones, or the liquor in which fowls, turkeys, and rabbits have been boiled. Brown soups can be made from beef and mutton bones also. The bones and trimmings that are left on plates and dishes should never be thrown away until they have been stewed in this way, and the cook should keep one stewpan for the purpose of making stock; an ordinary iron stewpan will serve the purpose admirably If bones are thrown away without stewing, good food will have been wasted. The soups given in this book are made of unflavoured stock, a supply of which ought to be constantly on hand. Its consumption will vary with the tastes as well as the numbers of a family, and therefore it is scarcely possible to say when the supply from cooked bones will fall short. But if the cook should find that she is short of stock, she should procure two-pennyworth of bones and make it so that she may never be without. A spoon that has been dipped in boiling water should be used to take the fat from the stock. Mutton, Roasted (February 12th); Baked Potatoes (May 4th); Salad (March 13th); Cottage Plum Pudding (June 6th); Cheese (June 8th).

Things that must not be Forgotten.

1. Boil the ox-cheek and put it into a mould with seasoning (April 6th).

2. Boil the brine with a little more salt, and when it is cold put the thin flank of beef into it.

3. Pastry to be made to-day (April 17th):—One Rhubarb Pie; One Plum Pie (Bottled Fruit) (August 7th); One Baked Custard Tart (January 19th); Tea-cakes (August 26th); Hominy Cake (October 16th).

February 14th.

Breakfast.	Luncheon.	Dinner.
Toasted Bacon. Collared Tongue. Tea-cakes. Dry Toast. Brown and White Bread and Butter. Mustard and Cress. Bread and Milk.	Spicy Pie (made of the broken meat from the leg of mutton). Remains of Cottage Plum Pudding, cut into slices and fried.	Six or eight Oysters for each person, with Brown Bread and Butter and a cut Lemon. Beef à la Mode. Potatoes; Brussels Sprouts. Lemon Pudding. Cheese.

Marketing.

For the Day.—Fresh Oysters. Anglo-Dutch, American, or Portuguese Oysters will be found excellent, and are much lower in price than natives. About two pounds of Beef. Any part that is lean and tender will do, but it should be cut thick; a piece from the buttock, or a portion of the thick flank, the clod, or sticking, or even some ox-cheek will answer the purpose Potatoes, Brussels Sprouts; half a pound of beef Suet.

For To-morrow.—One Guinea Fowl (or a pair of birds may be procured if necessary). Guinea fowls are in season from February to June, and offer a welcome substitute for game, which is scarce at the time. The bird should be well kept, and then is not unlike pheasant in taste and appearance. The flesh is both palatable and digestible. A slice of fat Bacon (cured without saltpetre if it can be procured); half a pound of "Julienne." Julienne consists of dried vegetables ready turned for soups. It is sold by the pound, and will be found both economical and convenient. It may be obtained at the Italian warehouses, at about 1s. 2d. per pound, and half a pound will last for three or four months. A jar of Liebig's Extract of Meat; one tin of preserved Pineapple; one-pennyworth of Parsley; a little dried Tarragon if this is not at hand; one tin of Turkey and Tongue for supper on Sunday evening; a tin of Sardines for breakfast on Monday.

BREAKFAST.—Toasted Bacon (January 19th); Collared Tongue (January 2nd). *Tea-cakes, to serve.*—Tea-cakes may either be made hot in the oven, cut through the centre, buttered liberally, cut into quarters, and restored to their original form; or they may be cut through the centre and toasted before being buttered. In either case they should be served very hot. If liked, they can be sent to table cold, in which case they are simply cut into fingers, buttered liberally, and piled crosswise on a plate. Bread and Milk (January 25th).

LUNCHEON.—Spicy Pie (May 7th); Cold Pudding (March 6th).

DINNER.—*Beef à la Mode.*—Wash the cow-heel and cut it into pieces. Cut the beef also into neat pieces and flour them well. Weigh the beef and the cow-heel, and afterwards allow one pint of liquid to each pound of meat. Melt an ounce of dripping in a frying-pan, and put in the meat and two large onions cut into slices. Fry for about ten minutes, and stir the pieces occasionally, being very careful that the onions do not burn, nor the pieces of meat stick to the bottom of the pan. Transfer both meat and onions to a stewpan, add the cow-heel, and gradually as much stock or water (boiling) as is required. Throw in also three carrots cut into slices, a bunch of parsley, a sprig of thyme, two bay-leaves, two allspice, six peppercorns, two cloves, and a little salt. Mix two small table-spoonfuls of flour to a smooth paste with a little cold water. Stir this into the stew, and keep stirring till it boils, being careful to remove the scum as it rises. Cover the stewpan closely, that there may be no evaporation, draw it back, and let its contents simmer very gently for three hours. Skim it every now and then, and before dishing it add pepper and salt if necessary. Put the meat upon a dish, pour the gravy over it, and garnish with the pieces of cow-heel and the carrots. It is an improvement to send to table separately about a dozen small onions of the same size, cooked apart and glazed. To prepare the onions cut off the ends, blanch them by putting them into boiling water for about twenty minutes, then drain and cool them, and take off the two outer skins. Put into a small saucepan a piece of butter the size of an egg, a table-spoonful of pounded white sugar, pepper and salt, and as much stock as will cover the onions. Let them boil gently till tender. Take them up, and boil the gravy quickly till it is reduced to a glaze. If the lid is left off the stewpan the gravy will reduce more quickly. Put the onions in the glaze, shake them in it till they are coated, and baste them every ten minutes till wanted. Onions glazed in this way form an excellent garnish for various meat dishes. Potatoes (May 12th); Brussels Sprouts (June 4th); Lemon Pudding (August 12th); Cheese (June 8th).

Things that must not be Forgotten.
1. Turn and rub the thin flank of beef.
2. Preserve the bacon-rind for flavouring.
3. Break up and stew the leg of mutton bone for stock (*see* February 13th).
4. If there are any remains of the beef à la mode the meat will be excellent potted for breakfast, and the gravy will be a valuable addition to soup.
5. If cream is to be permitted for the rhubarb pie on Feb. 16th it should be ordered to-day.

Sunday, February 15th.

Breakfast.	Dinner.	Tea.	Supper.
Ox-cheek Brawn.	Julienne Soup (quickly made).	Tea-cakes.	Preserved Turkey and Tongue (Tinned).
Boiled Eggs.	Guinea Fowl.	Brown and White Bread and Butter.	Plum Pie.
Tea-cakes.	Brown Gravy.	Damson Jam.	Cheese.
Brown and White Bread and Butter.	Bread Sauce.	Hominy Cake.	
Porridge.	Mashed Potatoes.		
	Broccoli.		
	Preserved Pineapple.		
	Custard.		
	Cheese.		

BREAKFAST.—Ox-cheek Brawn (April 6th); Boiled Eggs (January 5th); Tea-cakes (February 14th); Porridge (January 25th).

DINNER.—*Julienne Soup quickly made.*—Peel an onion, stick two cloves into it, and put it into a saucepan with about a quart of water, a dessert-spoonful of good gelatine, two outer sticks of celery, three peppercorns, a pinch of mixed herbs tied in muslin, and anything else that is at hand that will help to make it tasty. Simmer gently till the water is flavoured, then strain the liquor, stir into it as much Liebig's Extract as will colour it and make it taste good, and thicken it very slightly by boiling in it a little arrowroot mixed to a smooth paste with water. Soak a dessert-spoonful of the Julienne in cold water for three-quarters of an hour. Pour off the water, put the vegetables into a saucepan with fresh cold salted water, and boil them like fresh vegetables. Put them with the soup, boil all together for a quarter of an hour, turn the whole into a heated soup-tureen, and serve immediately. Guinea Fowl (April 5th); Brown Gravy (October 18th); Bread Sauce (October 18th); Mashed Potatoes (May 12th); Broccoli (April 25th); Tinned Pine-apple (April 8th); Custard (August 10th); Cheese (June 8th).

TEA.—Tea-cakes (February 14th); Hominy Cake (October 16th).

SUPPER.—Preserved Turkey and Tongue (*see* Remarks on Potted Grouse, January 7th); Plum Pie (August 7th).

Things that must not be Forgotten.

1. Preserve the bones and remnants of the Guinea Fowl; soup may be made of them for to-morrow.
2. Turn and rub the beef.

February 16th.

Breakfast.	Luncheon.	Dinner.
Sardines.	Ox-cheek Brawn.	Guinea Fowl Soup.
Turkey and Tongue.	Macaroni Cheese.	Broiled Steak with Oyster Sauce,
Hot Buttered Toast.		Fried Potatoes.
Dry Toast.		Rhubarb Pie (a little Cream if permitted).
Brown and White Bread and Butter.		Cheese.
Milk Toast.		

Marketing.

For the Day.—Half a pound of Pipe Macaroni, if it is not in the house. Steak for Broiling (*see* January 22nd). One Tin of Oysters or, if preferred, one dozen large Oysters for Oyster Sauce; Potatoes.

For To-morrow.—One Tin of Potted Grouse (*see* January 7th). Fresh Whiting for breakfast (*see* January 17th).

BREAKFAST.—Sardines (January 12th); Turkey and Tongue (Potted Grouse, January 7th); Milk Toast (June 17th).

LUNCHEON.—Ox-cheek Brawn (April 6th); Macaroni Cheese (March 20th).

DINNER.—*Guinea Fowl Soup.*—Take the remains of the Guinea

Fowl; pick the meat from the bones, and put it aside. Bruise the bones, and put them into a stewpan with the skin and trimmings, any forcemeat there may be, two or three strips of bacon-rind scalded and scraped, three outer sticks of celery that have been preserved for flavouring, a sprig of thyme, a shalot, a small onion stuck with two cloves, a bay-leaf, and six peppercorns. Pour over all about three pints of the stock made from the leg of mutton, bring the liquor to a boil, skim it carefully, and simmer it gently for two hours. Mince the meat, and pound it in a mortar with a slice of the crumb of bread soaked in the stock; season it pleasantly with salt, pepper, and a little grated nutmeg. It will be smoother if it is pressed through a hair sieve after it is pounded, but the operation is rather tedious, and may be dispensed with. Strain the soup, return it to the saucepan, add the pounded meat mixed to a paste with a spoonful or two of cold water. Boil twenty minutes longer, season with pepper and salt if required, and serve very hot. A few drops of brown colouring can be added if necessary. Broiled Steak (January 22nd); Oyster Sauce (October 16th); Fried Potatoes (February 2nd); Rhubarb Pie made on Friday; Cheese (June 8th).

Things that must not be Forgotten.

1. Prepare the ground rice blanc-mange for dinner to-morrow (August 7th).
2. Turn and rub the thin flank of beef.
3. Be careful to preserve about a pint and a half of the leg of mutton stock for the civet of rabbit to-morrow.
4. Turn the potted grouse into a jar, and ornament it with a neatly-cut paper frill, for breakfast (*see* January 7th).
5. Ask the fishmonger to prepare the whiting for frying—that is, skin them, and fasten their tails in their mouths.
6. If hominy is to be used for breakfast it will need to be soaked (*see* February 10th).

February 17th.

Breakfast.	Luncheon.	Dinner.
Fried Whiting.	Shepherd's Pie, made of remnants of Steak.	Baked Gurnet.
Potted Grouse.	Brawn.	Civet of Rabbit.
Tea-cakes.	Baked Custard.	Stewed Celery.
Brown and White Bread and Butter.		Potatoes.
Honey.		Ground Rice Blanc-mange with Jam.
Boiled Hominy.		Cheese.

Marketing.

For the Day.—Gurnets or Gurnards, although they are at their best in October, will probably be still offered for sale, and will afford a pleasant variety for the dinner-table for a few weeks later than this. The flesh is firm and well-flavoured. The freshness of gurnet is determined like that of other fish (*see* January 3rd). A moderate-sized fish will be enough for two people. **Two**

moderate-sized Rabbits, Ostend or Wild, whichever is preferred (*see* January 24th); three heads of Celery; quarter of a pound of Bacon, if this is not in the house (*see* January 3rd); Potatoes.

For To-morrow.—A well-hung Shoulder of Mutton; three pounds of Jerusalem Artichokes; six-pennyworth of Spanish Onions; if allowed, four-pennyworth of Cream for Palestine Soup to-morrow.

BREAKFAST. — Fried Whiting (January 17th); Potted Grouse (January 7th); Tea-cakes (February 14th); Boiled Hominy (February 11th).

LUNCHEON.—Shepherd's Pie (January 12th); Brawn left yesterday; Baked Custard (January 19th).

DINNER.—*Baked Gurnet.*—Cleanse the gurnets like other fish, being careful to cut away the fins and remove the gills. Fill the insides with good veal forcemeat (June 27th)); sew them up securely, and truss the fish with the tail in the mouth. Lay a good slice of fat bacon upon each, and lay them side by side in a baking dish or tin that has been well greased with dripping, and bake in a moderately hot oven till done enough. They will take about half an hour or more, according to size. Serve on a hot dish without a napkin, and pour the sauce round, but not over the gurnets. Good melted butter (July 17th), or maître d'hôtel sauce (May 6th), made acid with lemon-juice, chili vinegar, or caper pickle, will be a suitable accompaniment, or anchovy sauce (July 17th) may be preferred. Civet of Rabbit (December 8th); Stewed Celery (December 2nd); Potatoes (May 12th); Ground Rice Blanc-mange (August 7th); Cheese (June 8th).

Things that must not be Forgotten.

1. Put two table-spoonfuls of tapioca to soak all night in a pint of water, with three or four inches of very thin lemon-rind, cut without any of the white pith, which is objectionable because it is bitter.
2. Turn and rub the beef in the brine.
3. Be careful to stew the rabbit bones for stock.
4. If liked, the outer stalks only of the celery can be stewed, and the inner ones may be served with the cheese course.

February 18th.

Breakfast.	Luncheon.	Dinner.
Remains of Potted Grouse. Savoury Eggs. Hot Buttered Toast. Dry Toast. Brown and White Bread and Butter. Fried Hominy.	Rice and Cheese. Baked Omelet.	Palestine Soup. Shoulder of Mutton. Onion Sauce. Baked Potatoes. Greens. Tapioca and Apples. Cheese

Marketing.

For the Day.—Two pounds of good baking Apples; Potatoes, Greens; one pennyworth of Parsley.

For To-morrow.—Haricot Beans; small Soles, "Slips" (*see* January 3rd); half a pound of rashers of Bacon, if not in the house (*see* January 3rd).

BREAKFAST.—Potted Grouse (January 7th); Savoury Eggs (January 1st); Fried Hominy (February 12th).

LUNCHEON.—*Rice and Cheese.*—Cheese that has become too hard for the table may be used for this dish. It will need to be grated on a coarse grater before being used. Wash a quarter of a pound of rice in two or three waters, put it in a saucepan with plenty of cold water, and let the water boil. Pour it away, and in its place put three gills of milk, and simmer for about twenty minutes, or till the rice is tender without being in a pulp, then season it with pepper and salt. Whilst the rice is simmering grate the cheese; two ounces will be required for this quantity of rice. Grease a shallow dish, spread half the rice upon it, and sprinkle over this half the grated cheese, add the remainder of the rice and the rest of the cheese, and place little pieces of dripping here and there over the top. Put the preparation in a hot oven till it is brightly browned, and serve very hot. Baked Omelet (August 6th).

DINNER.—Palestine soup made of the stock in which the rabbit bones were stewed (December 8th); Shoulder of Mutton (March 4th); Onion Sauce (October 14th); Baked Potatoes (May 4th); Greens (June 4th). *Tapioca and Apples.*—Take half-a-dozen good-sized baking apples, peel, core, and cut them into quarters. Remove the lemon-rind, and put the tapioca and the water in which it was soaked into a saucepan, and stir it till it boils, and let it keep boiling for a few minutes till it is clear, and stir frequently, lest it should get lumpy, then sweeten it with a little white sugar. Put the quarters of apples into a pie-dish with two or three spoonfuls of cold water, some brown sugar, and two cloves. When slightly softened put them at the bottom of the saucepan, cover them with the tapioca, and let them simmer very gently till they are tender without being broken. Lift them upon a dish, colour the tapioca with a little cochineal, pour it over the fruit, and serve cold. If liked, large-grained sago can be used instead of tapioca for this dish, and cinnamon or ginger can be used instead of lemon-rind for flavouring. Prunes or other fruit can, if preferred, be used instead of apples. Cheese (June 8th).

Things that must not be Forgotten.

1. Turn and rub the beef in the brine.
2. Put the mutton upon a clean dish as soon as it comes from the table.
3. Before putting the pickles away, see that they are quite covered with vinegar.
4. Put half a pint of haricot beans to soak all night in plenty of cold water. A little piece of soda the size of a nut may be put with them to help to soften them.

February 19th.

Breakfast.	Luncheon.	Dinner.
Baked Soles. Toasted Bacon. Hot Buttered Toast. Dry Toast. Marmalade. Brown and White Bread and Butter. Porridge.	Cold Mutton with Pickles. Baked Potatoes. Jam and Bread.	Haricot Purée. Beef Steak à l'Italienne. Broccoli. Potatoes. Ground Rice Pudding. Cheese.

Marketing.

For the Day.—A large slice of Rump Steak, weighing from three to four pounds, and cut evenly not less than two inches thick (*see* January 22nd). Potatoes; Broccoli.

For To-morrow.—One large Neck of Mutton with as little fat as may be (*see* February 5th). One cow-heel for luncheon to-morrow. Six pennyworth of Spanish Onions. A small tin of corned beef for breakfast. One pennyworth of Small Salad; Anchovies.

BREAKFAST.—Baked Soles (January 7th); Toasted Bacon (January 19th); Porridge (January 25th).

LUNCHEON.—Mutton left yesterday; Baked Potatoes (May 4th).

DINNER.—Haricot Purée (March 9th); Beef Steak à l'Italienne (February 2nd); Broccoli (April 25th); Potatoes (April 7th); Ground Rice Pudding (August 21st); Cheese (June 8th).

Things that must not be Forgotten.

1. Turn and rub the beef in the brine.
2. Be careful to preserve the bacon rind for flavouring purposes.
3. If any of the beef is left it may be potted and used for breakfast instead of the corned beef.
4. Fillet the anchovies and prepare the cress for breakfast. (*See* January 18th).
5. Be careful to render the fat left from the shoulders of mutton. Fat cooked and uncooked must be rendered down before it can be used. When rendered it is better than common butter for pastry, puddings, and cakes, because common butter is made of no one but the makers thereof know what; and it is better than lard for frying purposes because it is not so greasy. To render it, cut it (both cooked and uncooked) into small pieces, and throw any skin or lean meat there may be with it into the stock-pot. Put it into an old but perfectly clean iron saucepan, cover it with cold water, and boil it quickly with the lid off the pan till the water has evaporated, that is, till the liquid fat looks like clear oil. Stir it frequently during the time to prevent it burning to the bottom of the pan; draw it back, and let it continue to boil but very gently till the pieces of fat look dry and shrivelled, then let it cool for a few minutes, and pour it through an old sieve into a basin. If it were poured out while boiling it would crack the basin. All kinds of fat can be

thus clarified; beef and mutton fat, the fat skimmings of saucepans, and bacon fat, and they only need to be clarified once. The same fat can be used for frying purposes for a long time if passed through a fine strainer after being used. Fat should never be allowed to remain on the fire when not wanted. When it becomes impure it should be melted over the fire with an equal quantity of cold water, then boiled, poured out and allowed to go cold, when the impurities will sink to the bottom and should be scraped off with a knife. When the joints used in the household do not supply a sufficient quantity of fat for cooking purposes, fresh fat can be bought at a low price and rendered down. The best kind for the purpose is the ox flare or caul, or, better still, the twist, that is, the fat which comes from the top side of the round of beef. Not all butchers, however, can supply their customers with the twist. Both ox flare and twist yield a soft fat which is much better than hard fat for cakes and pastry. After fat is rendered, the "craps" or pieces that are left can be rubbed into flour instead of dripping for plain pudding.

February 20th.

Breakfast.	Luncheon.	Dinner.
Anchovies with Hard-boiled Eggs. Corned Beef. Buttered Toast. Dry Toast. Brown and White Bread and Butter. Corn Flour Milk.	Cow Heel with Parsley Sauce. Baked Batter Pudding.	Skate with Brown Butter Sauce. Irish Stew. Potatoes. Apple Pie. Cheese.

Marketing.

For the Day.—Two pounds of Skate (*see* January 10th); Potatoes, Apples, bottled Red Currants; German Yeast.

For To-morrow.—Bloaters for breakfast, one for each person.

BREAKFAST.—Anchovies with hard-boiled Eggs (January 18th); Corned Beef bought yesterday; Corn Flour Milk (June 19th).

LUNCHEON.—*Cow Heel with Parsley Sauce.*—Wash the heel, split it, and soak it for an hour, put it into a saucepan with as much cold water as will quite cover it. Bring it to a boil, skim it carefully, then boil it gently for about four hours, or till the bones can be drawn out. Put it upon a dish without removing the skin, season it with pepper and salt, and cover it with parsley and butter. This dish when properly cooked is both wholesome and delicious. Baked Batter Pudding (February 5th).

DINNER.—Skate with Brown Butter Sauce (February 12th) Irish Stew (March 10th). The best end only of the neck of mutton will be needed for this dish. the scrag end will be wanted for luncheon to-morrow; Potatoes (May 6th); Apple Pie (August 7th); Cheese (June 8th).

Things that must not be Forgotten.

1. Turn and rub the beef in the brine.
2. Pastry is to be made to-day (April 17th). An apple pie; a red currant tart, made of bottled fruit (August 7th); a seed cake (August 14th), and tea-cakes (August 26th).
3. Be careful to preserve the stock in which the cow-heel was boiled. It will be excellent for soup.
4. Make the batter early in the day; it will be better for standing awhile.
5. Keep the bloaters on a dish apart from other food. (*See* Note 3, January 1st.)

February 21st.

Breakfast.	Luncheon.	Dinner.
Bloaters.	Scrag end of Neck of Mutton, with Rice.	Celery Soup.
Corned Beef.	Cake Pudding.	Sausages and Mashed Potatoes.
Tea-cakes, Hot.		Roly-poly Pudding.
Dry Toast.		Cheese.
Marmalade.		
Brown and White Bread and Butter.		
Porridge.		

Marketing.

For the Day.—Two or three pounds of best Sausages, if these can be bought of a trustworthy dealer: if there is any doubt about the matter, buy two pounds of fresh Pork (March 18th); two or three heads of Celery; one pennyworth of Parsley; half a pound (or less) of good beef Suet; Potatoes.

For To-morrow.—One good-sized Ox-tail; two or three Ptarmigan. These birds, which, when plentiful, are usually sold at a reasonable price, are in season from February to April. Birds that have been well kept should be chosen. Ptarmigan are not large (about the size of red grouse), and therefore it is well to have something tolerably satisfying with them. Ox-tail soup will answer this description. When the family is large, a dish of mutton cutlets can be provided as well; in this case two or three pounds of neck of mutton must be ordered (February 5th). If one bird more than is likely to be used at dinner can be procured, it may be made into a salad for supper. (*See* Game or Chicken Salad.) Three heads of French Lettuce; a basket of small Salad; a pennyworth of boiled Beet-root; four sheep's Kidneys and half a pound of streaky Bacon, if this is not in the house (January 3rd); a tin of potted Hare, and a dried Haddock for breakfast on Monday.

BREAKFAST. — Bloaters (January 3rd); Corned Beef bought February 19th; Tea-cakes (February 14th); Porridge (January 25th).

LUNCHEON.—*Scrag End of Neck of Mutton.*—Joint the scrag, and lay it in a large stewpan, and pour over it three quarts of cold water. Bring the liquor to a boil, skim it carefully, and throw into it six ounces of well-washed rice, and let it simmer for an hour; add three carrots, three onions, two turnips, eight peppercorns, and a little salt, and stew gently for two hours longer; serve very hot. Cake Pudding (*see* February 4th).

DINNER.—Celery Soup (December 3rd); Sausages (January 7th); Mashed Potatoes (May 12th); Roly-poly Pudding (August 18th); Cheese (June 8th).

Things that must not be Forgotten.

1. Turn and rub the beef in the brine.
2. In making the celery soup remember that the hearts can be eaten with cheese. The outer sticks only will need to be used for the celery soup.
3. Preserve any liquid that may be left from stewing the neck of mutton.
4. Ask the butcher to joint the ox-tail.
5. Put a teacupful of white haricot beans to soak in plenty of cold water.
6. Make a little mayonnaise sauce for the salad to-morrow evening (August 30th).

Sunday, February 22nd.

Breakfast.	Dinner.	Tea.	Supper.
Sardines.	Ox-tail Soup.	Tea-cakes.	Ptarmigan Salad.
Kidneys and Bacon.	Roast Ptarmigan.	Brown and White Bread and Butter.	Red Currant Tart.
Tea-cakes.	Brown Gravy.		Cheese.
Dry Toast.	Bread Sauce.	Mustard and Cress.	
Honey.	Potatoes.	Seed Cake.	
Brown and White Bread and Butter.	Haricot Beans.		
Bread and Milk.	Chocolate Pudding.		
	Custard.		

BREAKFAST. — Sardines (January 12th); Kidneys and Bacon (January 2nd); Tea-cakes (February 14th); Bread and Milk (January 25th).

DINNER. — *Ox-tail Soup.* — Cut the tail into inch and a-half lengths. Trim away the fat, and fry the pieces in a stewpan, with a little dripping, for five minutes, or till they are brightly browned. Pour over them two quarts of stock or water. (In this instance, any stock left after stewing the scrag of mutton can be used.) Bring the liquor to a boil, and throw in a tea-spoonful of salt. Skim it carefully, and put with it a small carrot, a turnip, an onion, with two cloves, a blade of mace, half a small tea-spoonful of dried savoury herbs (or, wanting these, a bunch of parsley, a sprig of thyme, and a bay leaf), six peppercorns, and a stick of celery. Stew gently for two hours and a half. Strain the stock, and put the pieces of tail into cold water in order to set the fat, and so facilitate its removal. Melt an ounce and a half of butter in a small stewpan, stir in till smooth a table-spoonful of flour, and add the stock gradually. Let the soup simmer by the side of the fire for twenty minutes, and skim away the fat as it rises. Make the meat hot in the soup. Just before serving, add a spoonful of liquid browning, a few drops of lemon juice, and a glass of port. Clear ox-tail is made just in the same way, but the thickening is omitted, and the soup is clarified, (*see* Clear Soup, July 30th). Roast Ptarmigan (Grouse, August (30th); Brown Gravy and Bread Sauce (October 18th); Mutton Cutlets, with Piquant Sauce

(April 30th); Potatoes (May 4th); Haricot Beans (June 20th); Chocolate Pudding (July 24th); Custard (August 10th); Cheese (June 8th).

TEA.—Tea-cakes (February 14th); Seed Cake (August 14th).

SUPPER.—Ptarmigan Salad (August 30th); Red Currant Tart (August 7th).

Things that must not be Forgotten.

1. Be sure that the lettuce is perfectly dry before mixing the salad.
2. Turn and rub the beef in the brine.
3. If the legs of the birds are left they may be devilled for breakfast.

February 23rd.

Breakfast.	Luncheon.	Dinner.
Dried Haddock.	Australian Meat, Cold.	Game Soup.
Potted Hare.	Pickles.	Stewed Steak.
Marmalade.	Baked Potatoes.	Potato Snow.
Hot Buttered Toast.	Jam and Bread, with Milk.	Cabbage.
Dry Toast.		Guest's Pudding.
Brown and White Bread and Butter.		Cheese.
Milk Toast.		

Marketing.

For the Day.—One two-pound tin of Australian meat; three pounds of tender Buttock Steak (*see* January 1st); Potatoes, Cabbage; a quarter of a pound of Suet.

For To-Morrow.—One dozen Scallops for breakfast.

BREAKFAST. — Dried Haddock (January 27th); Potted Hare (January 7th); Milk Toast (June 17th).

LUNCHEON.—Australian Meat, cold (*see* February 4th); Baked Potatoes (May 4th). *Jam and Bread Pudding* (economical).—Spread a little jam on slices of bread, cut about a quarter of an inch thick; lay them on a dish, and pour over them hot milk as much as will cover them. Let them soak awhile, and serve hot or cold. This simple pudding is generally liked by children.

DINNER.—Game Soup, made of bones and remains of Ptarmigan. This soup will have a peculiar but not disagreeable flavour. (*See* February 16th.) Stewed Steak (January 31st); Potato Snow (April 7th); Cabbage (June 4th); Guest's Pudding (April 14th); Cheese (June 8th).

Things that must not be Forgotten.

1. Prepare the scallops for breakfast to-morrow. Note 3, March 7th.
2. Boil the beef. Scrape it with a knife and wash it quickly in cold water. Salt meat may be washed, because if that is done, and the brine recommended before has been used, soup can be made of

the stock if that is wished. Fresh meat must on no account be washed, as that would draw out the juices. Dry it well, and remove the bones. Cut it in half, and lay one piece on the top of the other. (The butcher could probably do this better than it could be done at home.) Bind tape round it to make it safe. Lay an old plate at the bottom of a stewpan, put in the meat, and pour over it as much lukewarm water as will quite cover it ; let it just boil. Skim the liquor, draw the saucepan back, and let the contents simmer very gently till the meat is done enough. It will take about five hours, or half an hour per pound. If it is to be eaten cold, it may be left in the liquor till it is cool, and then it should not be boiled quite so long. Put it between two dishes, lay a heavy weight on the topmost one, and leave it for twelve hours. Strain the liquid, pour it into an earthenware pan, and leave it till cold. When the fat has been taken from it, it may be boiled to glaze (March 21st). The water in which the meat is boiled is to be lukewarm, because the meat is salt ; it is used in order to extract some of the salt before hardening the outside of the meat. *Fresh* meat should be put into fast boiling water, boiled for four minutes to harden the outside, and so keep in the juices, and afterwards have a cupful of cold water added to lower the temperature, then be simmered gently till done. For meat that is to be eaten hot and not pressed, less time will be required for boiling ; but the length of time depends upon the thickness as well as the size of the joint. As a general rule, a quarter of an hour per pound may be allowed for all meat but pork, which needs five minutes per pound extra. The meat must *simmer*, not *boil*, if it is to be tender. There is nothing so difficult as to persuade inexperienced cooks of this fact.

February 24th.
(Supposed to be Shrove Tuesday.)

Breakfast.	Luncheon.	Dinner.
Scallops. Potted Hare. Buttered Toast. Dry Toast. Brown and White Bread and Butter. Porridge.	Savoury Hash of Australian Meat. Cold Potatoes Fried. Plain Rice Pudding.	Sole au Gratin. Roast Loin of Mutton. Boiled Onions or Onion Sauce. Mashed-Potatoes. Broccoli. Pancakes with sugar, cut Lemons. Cheese.

Marketing.

For the Day.—A pair of thick Soles (*see* January 3rd). A well-hung Loin of Mutton, about six pounds. Lemons, if not at hand ; Onions, Potatoes, Broccoli.

For To-morrow.—About five pounds of good Salt Cod. Parsnips. A piece of the gammon of Bacon, weighing about four pounds. Muffins for breakfast (*see* January 29th). Half-a-dozen fresh Herrings (*see* January 3rd). The fish should be bright and silvery looking. The more scales they have, the fresher they are likely to be.

BREAKFAST.—Scallops (Note 3, March 7th); Potted Hare (January 7th); Porridge (January 25th).

LUNCHEON.—Savoury Hash (February 5th). Cold Potatoes, browned (December 26th). *Plain Rice Pudding.*—Wash half a tea-cupful of rice, and throw away the grains that float. Drain the rice, put it

BREAD FOR PANCAKES.

into a pie-dish, and pour over it a quart of skim milk; add a quarter of an inch of cinnamon or a little piece of lemon rind, and a piece of butter the size of a sixpence. Do not stir the pudding, but bake it in a moderate oven till it is covered with a bright brown skin, when it is ready to serve. It will take about an hour and a half.

PANCAKES LAID OVER THE BREAD.

DINNER.—Sole au Gratin (May 3rd); Roast Loin of Mutton (March 4th); Onion Sauce (October 14th); Potatoes (May 12th); Broccoli (April 25th). *Pancakes.*—Two pancakes may be allowed for each person. An ounce and a half of flour, one egg, and a quarter of a pint of milk will make about four pancakes, supposing a small frying-pan is used five or six inches in diameter. Put the flour into a bowl with a little salt; add the eggs and a spoonful of milk, and beat till quite smooth. Add the rest of the milk gradually, and keep beating till the batter is light. The more the batter is beaten the better it will be, and it is best when made some hours before it is wanted. Wipe out the frying-pan, and melt a little dripping in it; pour in enough batter to barely cover the bottom of the pan, and set it over a clear fire. Loosen the edges of the pancake, jerking the pan occasionally to keep the batter from sticking. Turn one side of the pancake over with the point of a knife to see whether the under-side is browned, and if it is toss the pancake over and let the other side brown. Lay the pancake upon kitchen paper to free it from grease, sprinkle some sugar upon it, and squeeze lemon juice over this; and as the pancakes are finished pile them on a hot dish, and keep them as hot as possible till they are to be served. Add a little fresh fat to the pan for each pancake. Sometimes it is preferred that the pancakes should lie open on the dish, and then the first one is placed upon a round piece of crumb of bread cut rather smaller than the pancake itself. This is to keep the pancake from sinking down in the middle. Cheese (June 8th).

Things that must not be Forgotten.

1. Wash the salt fish and put it to soak all night. If very salt, do this early in the day.

2. Reduce the liquid in which the beef was boiled to glaze, and garnish the beef (March 21st).

3. Make the batter for the pancakes some hours before they are to be fried.

4. Prepare the herrings for breakfast to-morrow (August 20th).

5. Make croquettes for breakfast of the remains of cold mutton. (*See* Rissoles, January 6th).

February 25th.

(*Supposed to be Ash Wednesday.*)

Breakfast.	Luncheon.	Dinner.
Rolled Herrings. Croquettes. Muffins. Dry Toast. Brown and White Bread and Butter. Bread and Milk.	Pressed Beef. Baked Plum Pudding.	Salt Fish. Parsnips. Egg Sauce. Roast Neck of Veal. Gammon of Bacon. Potatoes. Stewed Endive. Wyvern Puddings. Cheese.

Marketing.

For the Day.—The best end of a Neck of Veal weighing about six pounds. Veal should be small, finely grained, with firm fat, of a pinkish-white colour. If the lean be flabby and discoloured, or in the least degree green, it is tainted. It should not be kept more than two or three days after it is killed, but if eaten too fresh it will be hard. A pennyworth of fresh Parsley; a quarter of a pound of Beef Kidney Suet, half a Pig's Head and two Pig's Feet for Brawn (*see* Marketing, January 7th); Muffins (*see* January 29th).

Breakfast.—Herrings (August 20th); Croquettes (January 6th); Muffins (January 30th); Bread and Milk (January 25th).

Luncheon.—*Baked Plum Pudding.*—Chop finely four ounces of good beef suet. Mix thoroughly in a bowl three-quarters of a pound of flour, a heaped tea-spoonful of baking powder, and a pinch of salt. Add the chopped suet, four ounces of stoned raisins, four ounces of picked and dried currants, four ounces of sugar, and two ounces of candied peel chopped small. Break an egg into a cup; if perfectly fresh remove the speck, and beat the egg well with a table-spoonful of milk. Moisten the pudding with the mixture, and, if necessary, add more milk; some flours require more moisture than others. It may be remembered, however, that the pudding when mixed should be very stiff—stiff enough for the knife to stand up in it. Grease a dripping-tin with dripping, put the mixture into it, and bake in a well-heated oven. It will be done enough in about an hour. Cut it into squares, sift white sugar over it, and serve. If preferred, dripping can be rubbed into the flour instead of adding chopped suet, and an additional tea-spoonful of baking-powder can be substituted for the egg. Pressed Beef, prepared February 24th.

Dinner.—Salt Fish (April 10th); Parsnips (September 30th); Egg Sauce (April 10th); Roast Neck of Veal (May 28th); Gammon of Bacon (March 30th); Potatoes (April 7th); Stewed Endive (December 5th); Wyvern Puddings (May 9th); Cheese (June 8th).

Things that must not be Forgotten.

1. Preserve the liquor in which the bacon has been boiled. A portion of it can be put with different kinds of stock to flavour it.
2. For the pig's head, *see* Notes 1 and 2, January 7th.
3. Prepare any remains of salt fish there may be for breakfast to-morrow (April 11th).

February 26th.

Breakfast.	Luncheon.	Dinner.
Salt Fish Réchauffé.	Minced Veal.	Macaroni Soup.
Pressed Beef.	Slices of Bacon, Cold or Broiled.	Curried Rabbit.
Muffins.	Baked Apples.	Boiled Rice.
Buttered Toast.		Potatoes.
Dry Toast.		Newmarket Pudding.
Brown and White Bread and Butter.		Cheese.
Honey.		
Porridge.		

Marketing.

For the Day.—Two fine and fresh Ostend Rabbits (*see* January 24th); a quarter of a pound of pipe Macaroni, if not in the house; Apples, Potatoes; Sea Biscuits.

For To-morrow.—Six or eight small Soles, "Slips" (*see* January 3rd); two-pennyworth of Watercress.

BREAKFAST.—Salt Fish, Réchauffé of (April 11th); Pressed Beef, prepared February 24th); Muffins (January 30th); Porridge (January 25th).

LUNCHEON.—Minced Veal (May 11th). *Bacon made Hot.*—Cut the remains of the boiled bacon into thin slices, sprinkle over these fine bread-crumbs that have been slightly seasoned with cayenne, put them on a wire toaster and make them hot through, then serve. Bacon warmed in this way is very good for breakfast. Baked Apples (February 9th).

DINNER.—*Macaroni Soup.*—This soup is made of gravy soup, to which boiled macaroni has been added. For special occasions clear soup would be needed, and for this it would be necessary to clarify the soup (Clear Soup, April 9th). For every-day use, however, good well-flavoured stock will answer the purpose excellently. In this particular instance it will have been made by stewing the veal and mutton bones with vegetables (Stock, February 13th). Macaroni should always be boiled separately before being put into soup, as the outside part is apt to be dirty, and the impurities can only be removed by being dissolved. If the macaroni were boiled in plain water, it would impart a slightly insipid taste to the soup. It is best, therefore, to prepare a savoury stock for it by boiling one or two bacon bones or strips of bacon rind, a leek, and six peppercorns for half an hour in a quart of water. The macaroni will be done enough in about half an hour; the time required, however, varies with the quality of the macaroni. It should be soft and tender without being pulpy. When sufficiently boiled it should be drained, washed once more in cold water, cut into small pieces about a quarter of an inch long, and put into the soup tureen. When ready to be served the hot soup can be strained over it. A quarter of a pound of macaroni is sufficient for three pints of soup. Curried Rabbit (July 16th); Rice (July 21st); Potatoes (April 7th); Newmarket Pudding (June 2nd); Cheese (June 8th).

Things that must not be Forgotten.

1. Put the beef upon a clean dish, and keep it in a cool place. It is to be used for supper on March 1st.

2. Wash a pound of prunes, and put them to soak in a pint and a half of water.

3. Put a breakfast-cupful of white haricot beans to soak in cold water to cover them.

4. Clean the pig's head (*see* Note 2, January 8th); boil the brine in which the beef was pickled, and when it is cold put the head and feet into it.

5. Boil some eggs hard for breakfast to-morrow. One egg may be allowed for each person. Prepare also (for five or six eggs) half a teacupful of bread-crumbs.

6. If any rice were left, put it on a separate dish, and be careful that the curry does not touch it.

February 27th.

Breakfast.	Luncheon.	Dinner.
Small Soles, Baked. Devilled Eggs. Watercress. Buttered Toast. Dry Toast. Brown and White Bread and Butter. Biscuits and Milk.	Liver and Bacon. Stewed Prunes.	Kidney Soup. Haricot Mutton. Haricot Beans. Potatoes. Boiled Rice Pudding, made of the remains of the rice left from the curry. Cheese.

Marketing.

For the Day.—One pound and a half of Sheep's Liver. (It is not probable that calf's liver can be procured, therefore sheep's liver must be used.) Half a pound of streaky Bacon cut into rashers (*see* January 3rd); half an Ox Kidney, or two Sheep's Kidneys ; Potatoes.

For To-morrow.—Two Ox-tails ; a good-sized, tender Neck of Mutton ; one tin of Devilled Turkey and Tongue. (Retail price, 1s.) Dried Sprats, one bundle for each person ; a pennyworth of fresh German Yeast ; four-pennyworth of Cream for soup.

BREAKFAST.—Baked Soles (*see* January 7th). *Devilled Eggs.*—Cut the hard-boiled eggs into halves. Take out the yolks, put them into a basin, season them with a little salt and cayenne, and add bread-crumbs to make them crumbly. The quantity of cayenne must be regulated by individual taste; the more there is used the more devilish the eggs will be. Cut a little piece off the ends of the eggs to make them stand ; fill the hollow places with the prepared yolk, piling it rather high. Place the eggs on a dish, and arrange the watercress between and around them. If liked, finely shred lettuce can be substituted for the watercress. This dish is both pretty and palatable. Biscuits and Milk (June 14th).

LUNCHEON.—Liver and Bacon (January 17th). *Stewed Prunes.*—Simmer the prunes gently in the water in which they were soaked for a couple of hours until they are quite soft. An inch of lemon rind and two cloves may be stewed with them. Drain them, let them cool a little, and put them into a glass dish. Sweeten the syrup, and thicken it slightly with corn-flour or arrowroot. Strain it over the fruit, and serve cold. Milk or custard is an excellent addition to this dish.

DINNER.—*Kidney Soup.*—Cut the kidney into thin slices, and these again into small pieces about half an inch square. Season them with pepper and salt, and dredge flour over them. Wash and prepare one moderate-sized turnip, one large carrot, one small onion, and two outer sticks of celery, and cut all into small pieces. Melt a slice of dripping in a stewpan, put in the kidney, and stir it over the fire for a minute or two, then add the vegetables. Pour in two quarts of cold water and a bouquet garni—that is, a bunch of parsley, a sprig of thyme, and a bay leaf tied together—and simmer all gently for two hours, being careful to remove the scum as it rises : then take out the herbs. Mix two tablespoonfuls of flour to a smooth paste with cold water, add a little of the boiling liquid, and turn the whole into the soup. Let it boil a minute or two ; then add a table-spoonful of ketchup, some liquid browning to make it a rich, deep colour, and a little pepper. Boil once more, and serve very hot. Haricot Mutton (made of the best end of the neck of mutton, April 13th) ; Haricot Beans (June 20th) ; Potatoes (May 4th) ; Rice Mould Réchauffé (April 27th) ; Cheese (June 8th).

Things that must not be Forgotten.

1. Pastry is to be made to-day (April 17th) : one Rhubarb Pie ; one Gooseberry Pie, made of bottled gooseberries (August 7th) ; Lemon Cheese-cakes (August 18th), Vienna Bread (August 26th) ; Rice Cake (August 2nd).

2. Turn the pig's head in the brine.

February 28th.

Breakfast.	Luncheon.	Dinner.
Dried Sprats.	Scrag of Mutton stewed with Vegetables.	Potatoe Purée.
Devilled Turkey and Tongue (tinned).	Hasty Pudding.	Ox-tails Stowed.
Marmalade.		Mashed Potatoes.
Buttered Toast.		Turnips.
Dry Toast.		Baked Omelet.
Brown and White Bread and Butter.		Cheese.
Porridge.		

Marketing.

For the Day.—A pennyworth of Parsley ; Potatoes, Turnips, Vegetables for Mutton.

For To-morrow.—Two well-hung Prairie Birds ; a pair of thick Soles, filleted (*see* January 3rd) ; one pound of streaky Bacon (half for Sunday and half for Monday morning) ; a quarter of a pound of Beef Suet ; one small tin of Sardines ; four heads of Celery, and a Beetroot. Since the facilities for conveying food from one part of the world to another have been increased, prairie birds which at one time were a great rarity have become more common, and they may frequently at this time of the year be obtained at a very moderate price. Though small they are profitable, for the flesh is so firm that it goes a long way, and a couple of prairie birds would quite take the place of a pair of good-sized fowls. Prairie birds should be well kept before being cooked, and the same rules hold good in dressing them that are to be observed with partridges and pheasants. If it may be permitted, three-pennyworth of Cream for rhubarb tart. Potatoes, Apples.

BREAKFAST.—*Dried Sprats.*—Grease the gridiron, make it hot, put the sprats on it, and broil them over a clear fire for two or three minutes. Pile them on a dish covered with a fish paper, and garnish them with parsley. They must be served *very hot*, or they will be comparatively worthless. Devilled Turkey and Tongue (*see* Remarks on Potted Grouse, Marketing, January 7th) ; Porridge (January 25th).

LUNCHEON.—Scrag of Mutton stewed with Vegetables (*see* January 14th); Hasty Pudding (March 30th).

DINNER.—Potatoe Purée (January 26th) ; Ox-tails Stewed (May 8th); Potatoes (May 12th); Mashed Turnips (September 30th); Baked Omelet (August 6th) ; Cheese (June 8th).

Things that must not be Forgetton.

Pluck and truss the birds for to-morrow. Preserve the feathers and dry them for making pillows. To do this, cut away the hard quills, and put all the feathers into a large paper bag. Turn the top over securely to keep them from flying about, and whenever there is an opportunity put them in a cool oven or by the side of the stove when the fire is low, till all the life is baked out of them. They are ready to be put away when the stalks of the feathers can be scraped to fine white powder with the finger-nail. If when thus scraped the quill is sticky, the feathers need to be baked a little longer. They will take ten days or a fortnight if put into the oven every evening. A large bag should be made to keep the cured feathers in until a sufficient quantity have been collected for use.

FRUITS IN SEASON SUITABLE FOR DESSERT IN FEBRUARY.

Apples ; Oranges (St. Michael, Tangerine, and Malta) ; Bananas; Grapes ; Pomeloes ; Shaddocks ; Nuts (Filberts, Cobs, Walnuts, Brazils, Almonds, Barcelonas) ; Almonds and Raisins ; French Plums; Figs; Dates; Crystallised Fruits; Foreign Preserved Fruits.

DISHES FOR INVALIDS.

BROTHS.

BEEF TEA.—The roll of the blade-bone of beef is the best part for making beef tea; what is wanted is fresh-killed, lean, juicy meat. Take away every little bit of fat and bone, cut the meat into very small pieces, and pour cold water over it in the proportion of a pint of water to a pound of beef. Let it stand for an hour or two till the water is red and the meat is white; turn it into a perfectly clean saucepan, place it on the fire, and just before it begins to simmer skim it once carefully ; put on the lid, and simmer for about a quarter of an hour. Strain it through a coarse colander to keep back the meat only. When cold, remove the fat, and stir the tea up before serving it, as the sediment is the most nutritious portion. It is better not to season the beef unless specially requested to do so, as an invalid generally likes to season for himself. If a larger quantity of water is used, the tea should be simmered five or six hours.

Beef Tea (another way).—Cut up the beef as before, pour cold water over it (a pint to a pound), and turn into a stone jar, which has a closely fitting lid; put it into a saucepan of boiling water, the water to come half way up the jar, and let it simmer on the side of the fire for three hours.

Beef Tea quickly made.—Mince half a pound of beef, and put it into a saucepan with half a pint of water. Bring it to the boil, simmer for a few minutes, and serve.

Veal Broth.—Cut a pound of knuckle of veal into small pieces, put these into a stewpan with three pints of water and half a teacupful of rice. Boil gently for an hour and a half. If liked, to vary the flavour, a few parsley leaves, a sprig of thyme, and a lettuce leaf may be chopped small, and simmered with the veal for five or six minutes, not longer, or the flavour will be spoilt; or a small blade of mace, a sprig or two of parsley, and one of thyme and marjoram, can be used.

Mutton Broth.—Take one pound of neck of mutton, as lean as can be procured, pour over it a quart of cold water, and simmer gently for four hours. When the broth is cold remove the fat, and make the broth hot before serving. If liked, half a teacupful of pearl barley can (after being boiled up once with half a pint of water and drained) be stewed with the broth and the white part of a chopped leek, and a small turnip can be simmered with the meat.

Chicken Broth.—Pluck the fowl, remove the inside, being careful not to break the gall-bag, and skin the bird like a rabbit, and be careful to take away every bit of fat from both the inside and the outside. Remove the head and feet, wash the bird well, and cut it into neat pieces; put these into a stewpan with two quarts of cold water. The liver and gizzard of the fowl may be cut into slices and put with the rest. Stew gently for about two hours. Take out the pieces of fowl, and leave the broth until the next day; take off the fat, warm again, and serve. Pepper and salt to be added by the nurse or invalid. If flavoured broth be desired, three or four slices of celery, a blade of mace, and a sliced onion may be stewed with the meat. The meat may be picked from the bones and potted.

Barley Cream.—Take one pound of lean veal, cut it into dice, and pour over it a pint and a half of cold water. Put a heaped tablespoonful of pearl barley into a small saucepan with a teacupful of cold water. Bring it to a boil, then pour away the water, and throw the barley in with the veal, and simmer all gently together for an hour and a half. Strain the liquor, and pound the barley and the veal together, then force all the pulp through a hair sieve with the back of a wooden spoon. Keep moistening it with hot liquor to make it go through more easily. When wanted for use, add salt and a quarter of a pint of sweet cream.

Sunday, March 1st.

Breakfast.	Dinner.	Tea.	Supper.
Sardines.	Soles, filleted, rolled, and baked.	Brown and White Bread and Butter.	Pressed Beef.
Devilled Turkey.			Celery and Beetroot Salad.
Vienna Bread.	Prairie Birds.	Vienna Bread.	
Dry Toast.	Bacon.	Orange Marmalade.	Rhubarb Pie.
Honey.	Brown Gravy.	Rice Cake.	
Brown and White Bread and Butter.	Bread Sauce.		
	Stewed Celery.		
	Potatoes.		
Porridge.	Apple Gâteau.		

BREAKFAST.—Sardines (January 12th); Devilled Turkey served as Grouse (January 7th); Vienna Bread (August 26th); Porridge (January 25th).

DINNER.—*Soles, Filleted, Rolled, and Baked.*—Fillet the soles (*see* Filleted Soles, January 4th), smooth the fillets with a knife, and roll them up, with the white skin *inside*. Grease a baking-tin with butter, stand the rolled fillets in this, and sprinkle over each one salt, white pepper, and a few drops of lemon-juice. Grease a piece of kitchen paper and lay it over the fish to keep it from browning, and put the tin in the oven for five, or at most ten, minutes. Drain the fillets on paper, put them on a hot dish, and garnish by placing different coloured heaps alternately on the top of each little roll. A piece of chili chopped small, a little chopped parsley, chopped egg-yolk, pink ham finely minced, or, when it is to be had, a little heap of chopped truffle, will answer the purpose. Pour maître d'hôtel sauce (May 6th) round the rolls, or, if preferred, brown butter sauce may be used (February 12th). The stock for maître d'hôtel sauce may be made by stewing the heads, tails, and fins of the fish in a pint of cold water.

Prairie Birds.—Cook these birds just like grouse (August 30th), and send rashers of bacon, brown gravy, and bread sauce to table with them. Bacon (July 19th); Gravy (October 18th); Bread Sauce (October 18th); Stewed Celery (December 2nd); Potatoes (May 12th); Apple Gâteau (September 24th); Cheese (June 8th).

SUPPER.—Celery and Beetroot Salad (March 13th).

Things that must not be Forgotten.

1. Stew the outer sticks of the celery, and reserve the inner portion for the salad to be served at supper.

2. If the requirements of the family are so limited that the legs of the birds can be left untouched at dinner-time, they will be excellent devilled for breakfast. (*See* Devilled Drumsticks, January 14th.)

3. If any boiled beetroot is left it should be covered with vinegar and preserved. It will keep for a long time, and will be excellent for salads.

4. Put a breakfast-cupful of German lentils to soak in plenty of cold water.

March 2nd.

Breakfast.	Luncheon.	Dinner.
Toasted Bacon.	Rissoles (made of remains of Pressed Beef).	Game Soup.
Toasted Eggs.		Stewed Steak.
Vienna Bread.	Tapioca and Rice, baked.	Boiled Lentils.
Honey.		Potatoes.
Dry Toast.		Gooseberry Tart.
Brown and White Bread and Butter.		Cheese.
Bread and Milk.		

Marketing.

For the Day.—Three pounds of tender Steak, cut evenly and about one and a half inches thick. (See Marketing, January 1st.) Potatoes.

For To-morrow.—To be sent first thing in the morning, four pounds thick Flank of Beef; a bundle of Rhubarb. Scotch Barley and Dried Peas will be wanted.

BREAKFAST.—Toasted Bacon and Toasted Eggs (January 19th); Vienna Bread (August 26th); Bread and Milk (January 25th).

LUNCHEON.—Rissoles (January 6th). *Tapioca and Rice, Baked.*—Wash half a tea-cupful of rice and half a tea-cupful of tapioca. Put them into a pie-dish, and pour over them about three pints of skim milk (fresh milk is, of course, to be preferred). Place a small piece of butter the size of a threepenny-piece in the dish, and bake in a moderately-heated oven. When a brown skin covers the surface of the pudding it is done enough. It will take from one and a half to two hours.

DINNER. — Game Soup, from the bones and trimmings of the prairie hen (February 16th). Stewed Steak (January 31st). *Boiled Lentils.*—Drain the lentils, and boil them in about three times their bulk of water. In about half an hour they will be tender without being broken at all. Drain them, and return them to the saucepan, with a slice of fresh butter, a little pepper and salt, and a table-spoonful of vinegar. Shake them over the fire till they are quite hot, and serve immediately. To make them very good, melt an ounce of butter in a clean stewpan, and throw in a small onion finely chopped. Stir in a tea-spoonful of flour, add pepper and salt to taste, and sufficient stock and vinegar mixed to make a thick sauce. Put in the lentils, and simmer for ten or fifteen minutes. Potatoes (April 7th); Gooseberry Tart (August 7th); Cheese (June 8th).

Things that must not be Forgotten.

1. *To make Brawn.*—Wash the pig's head lightly, cut off the ears, and put them, with the pig's feet, in a small saucepan, and boil them for an hour and a half. Take them up, drain them, and put them, with the head, into a larger pan; cover all with cold water, and boil for about two hours—less or more, according to the size of

the head, but they should boil until the flesh can be removed from the bones. Lift the head out, remove the bones, skin the tongue, bone the ears, and cut all into small pieces. Put the bones back into the saucepan with two pints of the liquor in which the head was boiled. Throw in a large onion cut into slices, two blades of mace, six cloves, six allspice, and a small tea-spoonful of peppercorns, two bay leaves, and a sprig of thyme. Bring the liquor to a boil, then take off the lid and boil the stock quickly for half an hour, or until half a pint has boiled away. Strain it, put it back into the saucepan with the cut meat, boil up once more, taste it, and, if necessary, season it further; put it into a wet mould (or into two moulds), and let it stand till firm. Turn it out upon a dish, garnish with parsley, and it is ready to serve. If liked, a pound or two of salted beef or of gammon of bacon can be boiled with the brawn, and the addition will be a great improvement. When a whole pig's head is taken the butcher may be asked to cut out the cheeks, and these can be cured and boiled separately. (*See* January 7th and 8th.)

2. The brine must be thrown away after a pig's head has been pickled in it.

3. Make a rhubarb mould for to-morrow (June 3rd).

4. Put a tea-cupful of split peas to soak all night in cold water.

March 3rd.

Breakfast.	Luncheon.	Dinner.
Ox Eyes.	Poor Man's Goose.	Scotch Broth.
Brawn, with Brawn Sauce.	Lemon Cheesecakes.	Boiled Beef.
Buttered Toast.		Potatoes.
Dry Toast.		Rhubarb Mould.
Brown and White Bread and Butter.		Cheese.
Milk Toast.		

Marketing.

For the Day.—About one pound and a half of the Fry of a small Pig (February 7th); Potatoes and Vegetables for Scotch Broth (*see* recipe).

For To-morrow.—Whiting (*see* Marketing, January 17th); a well-hung Leg of Mutton (January 8th).

BREAKFAST.—Ox Eyes (June 5th); Brawn (March 2nd); Brawn Sauce (January 15th); Milk Toast (June 17th).

LUNCHEON.—Poor Man's Goose (February 7th); Lemon Cheesecakes (August 18th).

DINNER.—*Scotch Broth and Boiled Beef.*—Take a tea-cupful of pearl barley, wash it well, and (supposing there are four pounds of beef) put it into a saucepan with four quarts of cold water. Whilst it is heating prepare the vegetables—that is, a moderate-sized cabbage, three leeks, a large turnip, and a large carrot. Cut the cabbage into fine shreds and the turnip into dice. Trim away the green part and the outside leaves of the leeks, and cut the white part into small pieces. Throw the vegetables (excepting only the carrot) into cold water till they are wanted, and before using drain them. Scrape the carrot to pulp. When the water boils, put in the beef, and throw in all the vegetables. Boil for three minutes, then draw the stewpan back, and simmer all gently till the meat is tender. It will take about four hours altogether. When the meat is done enough—which it will be in about two hours—take it up and put it away, then put it back in time to get hot again before it is wanted. Serve the broth in a tureen, like soup, and serve the meat on a separate dish. If liked, mutton or lamb can be used instead of beef. Scotch broth, made hot, is as good the second day as it is the first. Potatoes (April 7th); Rhubarb Mould (June 3rd); Cheese (June 8th).

Things that must not be Forgotten.

Be particularly careful in making the Scotch broth to skim it frequently. Also remember to cover the Pig's Fry with paper before baking it.

March 4th.

Breakfast.	Luncheon.	Dinner.
Fried Whiting. Brawn, with Brawn Sauce. Buttered Toast. Dry Toast. Honey. Brown and White Bread and Butter. Corn-flour Milk.	Scotch Broth. Beef.	Stewed Eels. Roast Leg of Mutton. Yorkshire Pudding. Baked Potatoes. Turnip Tops. Lèche Crème. Cheese.

Marketing.

For the Day.—Two pounds of Silver Eels (*see* Marketing, January 24th); half a pound of Ratafias; a pennyworth of Parsley; Potatoes, Turnip-tops.

For To-morrow.—If Ham is not already in the house, a slice from the middle of a lately-cured Ham.

BREAKFAST. — Fried Whiting (January 17th); Brawn (March 2nd); Brawn Sauce (January 15th); Corn-flour Milk (June 19th).

LUNCHEON.—*Scotch Broth and Beef.*—The beef may, if liked, be made hot in the soup, or, if preferred, it can be eaten cold with pickles. If broken remnants only are left, they may be made into croquettes.

DINNER.—Stewed Eels (January 24th). Roast Leg of Mutton. *To Roast Meat.*—Meat is best when it is roasted before an open fire, and that is about the only thing for which an open range is to be preferred. The first thing to be looked after is the fire, and this should be made up an hour before it is wanted. The dust must be thoroughly cleared out from the bottom of the grate, the hot coals pushed to the front, and fresh coals put at the back. These should not be *thrown* on, but laid on with the fingers, the pieces being packed rather closely, but still arranged so that air can pass freely between them when the fire is clear, bright, and fierce. Just at the same time the hearth should be cleared up, and the cinders, mixed with a little coal-dust slightly wetted, should be thrown at the back. The meat should now be looked over, and any unsightly jagged pieces there may be trimmed away. In a leg of mutton or lamb, the knuckle-bone should be cut off, and the piece of flank, as well as the thick piece of skin from the part near the loin, removed. In the sirloin and ribs of beef, the soft pipe that runs down the bone should be cut out. If there is any doubt about the cleanliness of the joint, it should be well scraped, and wiped with a damp cloth. If it can be avoided, however, it should not be washed, as that draws out its goodness. If, however, it is at all tainted, it should be washed quickly with vinegar and water, and wiped dry as quickly as possible. The dripping-tin, with a large lump of dripping in it, should be put before the fire a quarter of an hour before the meat is hung on the spit; at the same time the meat-screen, if there be one, should be placed ready, and the meat should be so hung that the thickest part catches the heat from the centre of the fire. For the first five minutes or so the joint should be put *near* the fire, in order that the surface may be quickly hardened, and so the juice may be kept in; afterwards the joint should be drawn back and roasted more slowly. An exception to this rule should be made with frozen meat, which should at first be hung at a distance from the fire and drawn gradually nearer. Basting with the dripping melted for the purpose should commence almost immediately after the joint is hung on the spit, and should be repeated as frequently as possible, for on constant basting the excellence of a roasted joint greatly depends. Of course, it is the lean part that needs basting. Poultry and game need to be very well basted. The time required for roasting depends upon the quality, nature, and thickness of the meat, and its distance from the fire. As a general rule, brown meats should be allowed a quarter of an hour per pound and a quarter of an hour over; white meats, twenty minutes to the pound and twenty minutes over; but even brown meats, when they are boned, or when they are very solid, such as the topside of the round of beef, rolled ribs of beef, or rolled loin of mutton, need twenty minutes to the pound if they are to be well done. In deciding the time required for roasting, the thickness of meat should be considered as well as its weight. If the joint is not a good colour, it may be drawn nearer again at the end, when a little salt (and salt only, not flour) may be sprinkled over it. All white meats are improved by being wrapped in greased paper before they are put down to the fire. This paper should be removed twenty minutes or so before the joint is taken down, in order that it may acquire colour. With regard to the dripping in the tin and the gravy to be served with roasted joints, *see* June 9th. For roasting, or rather baking, joints in a close range, *see* March 9th. Yorkshire Pudding (November 26th); Baked Potatoes (May 4th); Turnip-tops (June 4th); Lèche Crème (May 7th); Cheese (June 8th).

Things that must not be Forgotten.

1. Stew the shank-bone to make gravy.
2. Turn the dripping that was in the tin into a basin. It will be excellent for various purposes, and when cold will have some very good gravy underneath it.

March 5th.

Breakfast.	Luncheon.	Dinner.
Fried Ham.	Stewed Ox Kidney.	Sole au Gratin.
Fried Eggs.	Plain Suet Dumpling.	Cold Mutton.
Buttered Toast.		Salad.
Dry Toast.		Baked Potatoes.
Marmalade.		Treacle Pudding.
Brown and White Bread and Butter.		Cheese.
Porridge.		

Marketing.

For the Day.—One fresh Ox Kidney; a pair of good-sized thick Soles (*see* January 3rd); two Lettuces; half an Endive; a pennyworth of Watercress; a half-pennyworth of small Salad; a pennyworth of boiled Beetroot; half a pound of firm beef Suet; Potatoes.

For To-morrow.—Bloaters (one for each person will probably be sufficient); a Silverside of Beef, weighing about eight pounds (*see* January 13th); ingredients for making Brine (*see* January 13th).

BREAKFAST.—*Fried Ham.*—Melt a little bacon fat or dripping in a frying-pan; put in the ham, and fry it very gently till done enough. Turn it six or eight times during the process, or it will be hard. *Fried Eggs.*—When done enough, lift the ham upon a hot dish, and put a little more fat into the frying-pan. Break the eggs separately into a cup, then slip them dexterously into the hot fat, and fry them gently till set. As many eggs as the pan will contain may be put in at one time, provided always that they do not touch each other. The ham will be done enough in about ten minutes; the eggs in about two minutes. Porridge (January 25th).

LUNCHEON.—Stewed Ox Kidney (April 2nd); Plain Suet Dumpling (May 13th).

DINNER.—Sole au Gratin (May 3rd); Mutton roasted yesterday; Salad (March 13th); Baked Potatoes (May 4th); Treacle Pudding (March 28th); Cheese (June 8th).

Things that must not be Forgotten.

1. Keep the bloaters apart from any other food.
2. Make brine (January 13th), and when it is cold put the silverside of beef into it.

3. If any beetroot is left, put it into a jar and cover it with vinegar. It will keep for some time, and may be used either for salad or as pickle.

March 6th.

Breakfast.	Luncheon.	Dinner.
Bloaters. Brawn and Brawn Sauce. Buttered Toast. Dry Toast. Brown and White Bread and Butter. Marmalade. Bread and Milk.	Mutton Tarts, made of remains of cold mutton. Remains of Suet Dumpling toasted, and served with Jam.	Half-a-dozen Oysters each, with Brown Bread and Butter and cut Lemon. Boiled Rabbits. Bacon. Onion Sauce. Mashed Potatoes. Town Pudding. Cheese.

Marketing.

For the Day.—Fresh Oysters (February 14th); a couple of Ostend Rabbits, trussed for boiling (January 21th); Bacon, about two pounds, to be boiled (*see* Marketing, January 3rd); Spanish Onions, Potatoes, Rhubarb, Apples; German Yeast.

For To-morrow.—A couple of fresh, unsalted Pig's Feet (February 7th); **one** tin of preserved Prawns.

BREAKFAST. — Bloaters (January 3rd); Brawn (March 2nd); Brawn Sauce (January 15th); Bread and Milk (January 25th).

LUNCHEON.—It is probable there will be only unsightly pieces of meat left on the mutton-bone; these may be minced and made into mutton pies (January 3rd), or mutton tart (January 10th). (*See* Note 4 below.) *Remains of Suet Dumpling, Toasted.*—Cut the dumpling into neat slices half an inch thick. Place these on the pins of a Dutch-oven, and toast them before the fire till hot through and lightly browned. Or, if preferred, put them in a dripping-tin and make them hot in the oven. Serve on a hot dish, with treacle or jam.

DINNER.—*Boiled Rabbits.*—If requested to do so, the poulterer will skin and truss the rabbits. Should he omit the business, however, proceed as follows:—Make a slit under the body, and take out all that is inside. Break the first joint, and cut round the skin of each leg. Begin to draw off the skin at the hind legs, and draw it over the fore legs, and, last of all, over the head. Take out the eyes; wash the rabbits inside and out, and let them soak for ten minutes in lukewarm water. Wipe them well, and truss them, with the hind legs forward, the fore legs backward, the head fastened to the side by means of a skewer passed through the eyes and body. Put the rabbits into boiling water, as much as will cover them; let them boil up, skim the liquor, and simmer them gently till done enough. They will take from three-quarters of an hour to an hour. Lift them upon a hot dish, and cover them quite over with onion sauce, and serve more onion sauce in a tureen. The bacon may either be boiled to serve with the rabbit or it may be cut into rashers and toasted (*see* January 19th). Some cooks cut the rabbits into joints before sending them to table. Liver sauce may be substituted for onion sauce if the flavour of onions is disliked. Bacon (March 30th); Onion Sauce (October 14th); Liver Sauce (December 22nd); Mashed Potatoes (May 12th); Town Pudding (December 3rd); Cheese (June 8th).

Things that must not be Forgotten.

1. Turn the beef in the brine.
2. Stew the mutton-bone in water for stock (*see* February 13th).
3. Carefully preserve the liquor in which the rabbit was boiled.
4. Pastry to be made to-day (April 17th). Rhubarb pie, apple pie, open jam tart (August 7th); also tea-cakes (August 26th), sultana cake (August 2nd). The trimmings of the pies can be used to make the mutton pies for luncheon to-day, and the apple balls for to-morrow (March 7th).
5. Prepare the pig's feet for breakfast to-morrow (*see* Note, February 7th).

March 7th.

Breakfast.	Luncheon.	Dinner.
Tinned Prawns. Pigs' Feet, with Brawn Sauce. Tea-cakes. Dry Toast. Honey. Brown and White Bread and Butter. Milk Porridge.	Rabbit Gâteau (made of the remnants of rabbit). Apple Balls (made with trimmings of pastry).	Croûte au Pot. Beef Stewed with Vegetables. Potatoes. Rhubarb Pie. Cheese.

Marketing.

For the Day.—Three pounds of the Muscle of the Leg of Beef, cut in one piece from large meat. (*See* Marketing, January 27th.) Potatoes.

For To-morrow.—One pennyworth of Parsley; one dozen fresh Scallops. The fish are alive if they close their shells when touched. A good Sirloin of Beef (the fillet end is the best), weighing about eight pounds (*see* January 10th); a fresh Cocoa-nut, or a small tin of Desiccated Cocoa-nut; two Endive; a pennyworth of Beetroot; two pennyworth of Watercress; and two pennyworth of small Salad; a tin of Preserved Peaches. For breakfast on Monday—one tin of Potted Pheasant; a bottle of Anchovies, if the others were finished. Potatoes; Celery.

BREAKFAST.—Tinned Prawns (February 7th); Pigs' Feet prepared last night; Brawn Sauce (January 15th); Tea-cakes (February 14th); Milk Porridge (June 13th).

LUNCHEON.—Rabbit Gâteau (July 9th). *Apple Balls.*—Pare some large baking apples, and core without dividing them. Roll out some pastry, and stamp two circles about four inches in diameter for each apple. Press one half on one side, the apple and the other half on the opposite side. Wet the edges, and join the two pieces securely, thus covering the apple entirely with pastry. Lay the balls on a greased tin, and bake in a moderately-heated oven till the pastry is crisp. They will take about three-quarters of an hour.

DINNER.—Croûte au Pot (May 25th); Muscle of Beef stewed with Vegetables (March 17th); Potatoes (May 12th); Rhubarb Pie (August 7th); Cheese (June 8th).

Things that must not be Forgotten.

1. Turn the beef in the brine.
2. Cut off the flap of the sirloin of beef, and put it in the brine.
3. Prepare the scallops for breakfast to-morrow—it will save time to-morrow morning. For this, open the shells and trim away the beards and the black portion, leaving only the yellow part and the white, which looks something like the flesh of a crab's claw. Wash the parts that are to be used, and drain them. Mince the meat, and mix with it a third of its bulk in finely-grated bread-crumbs, a liberal allowance of pepper and salt, and a little chopped parsley. A heaped tablespoonful of chopped parsley will suffice for a dozen scallops. Scour out the deeper scallop shells, wash and dry them, and allow one shell for three scallops. Butter the inside thickly, sprinkle breadcrumbs over; put in the minced fish, cover it again with breadcrumbs, and lay little pieces of butter here and there on the top. Put the shells in a hot oven, or in a Dutch-oven before the fire, and let them remain until the preparation is brown on the surface and heated throughout. Serve (very hot) in the shells. Send vinegar to table with the fish. The scallop shells should be taken care of, as they can be used again and again for scalloped fish.

Sunday, March 8th.

Breakfast.	Dinner.	Tea.	Supper.
Scallops. Pigs' Feet, with Brawn Sauce. Tea-cakes. Watercress. Dry Toast. Brown and White Bread and Butter. Milk Toast.	Potatoe Purée. Roast Sirloin of Beef. Mashed Potatoes. Stewed Celery. Cocoa-nut Pudding. Cheese.	Brown and White Bread and Butter. Preserved Peaches. Sultana Cake.	Cold Beef. Salad. Open Jam Tart. Cheese.

BREAKFAST.—Scallops (see Note 3, March 7th); Pigs' Feet left from breakfast yesterday; Prawn Sauce (January 15th); Tea-cakes (February 14th); Milk Toast (June 17th).

DINNER.—Potatoe Purée (January 26th). *Roast Sirloin of Beef.*—To Roast, or, to speak correctly, to *Bake* meat in the oven of a kitchener.—The majority of joints are never so good as when roasted before an open fire. This plan involves, however, such a waste of fuel that close ranges are now used, and what is very commonly called *roasted* meat is meat baked in an oven provided with a ventilator, which allows the vapours given off by the meat to escape. Besides the ventilator, many ovens have a thermometer fastened to them, by which the heat may be regulated. To bake meat, this should reach 240° Fahr. The method of heating the oven varies with the description of the range, full instructions being given by the makers who supply the article. To bake the meat, trim it neatly, and in the case of a sirloin of beef cut away the soft pipe that runs down the bone, and the superfluous suet, leaving it about an inch deep all along. In order to keep the tin and the meat from burning, a hot-water tin is much to be preferred for baking meat. This tin is provided with an under-tin for holding warm water, on the top of which is a tray on which the meat-stand can be placed. In a corner of the tray there is a hole for the steam to escape. In filling the under-tin care should be taken to supply only as much water as will be sufficient to come just below the hole, but not to cover it. But whether this hot-water tin is used or not, there must be a raised stand upon which the meat can be laid, for if it is baked in its own dripping it will be sodden and quite spoilt. When the oven is hot enough, put the meat on the stand, the fat side uppermost, to begin with, and close the ventilator for about five minutes, till the surface of the meat is hardened, to keep in the juices. At the end of this time open the ventilator that the steam may escape, and baste the meat liberally every quarter of an hour. With the oven properly heated it will take ten minutes for every pound, and ten minutes over. Solid pieces of meat, however, such as rolled ribs of beef or the top side of the round, should be allowed a quarter of an hour to a pound, and a quarter of an hour over. When the meat is half cooked, turn it over. The reason for putting the fat part to the top first is that the upper part cooks more quickly, and, therefore, as the fat melts it drops down upon the lean under portion, and serves to baste it. Joints that are not fat should be covered over with kitchen paper, upon which dripping has been thickly spread. Ten minutes before the joint is taken up sprinkle a little salt over it, baste it well, and then do not baste it any more, or the outer cut will taste greasy. Put the joint on a hot dish, and place it near the fire where it will keep hot. Pour the gravy round but not over it, and serve very hot. Gravy (June 9th); Mashed Potatoes (May 12th); Stewed Celery (December 2nd); Cocoa-nut Pudding (August 8th); Cheese (June 8th).

TEA.—Preserved Peaches (April 11th); Sultana Cake (August 2nd).

SUPPER.—Salad (March 13th); Open Jam Tart (August 7th).

Things that must not be Forgotten.

1. Turn the beef in the brine.
2. When preparing the salad, remember to keep half of the mustard and cress for breakfast on March 9th.
3. Put a breakfast-cupful of white haricot beans to soak all night in cold water.

March 9th.

Breakfast.	Luncheon.	Dinner.
Anchovies, with hard-boiled Eggs.	Flap of Beef, boiled with Turnips and Carrots.	Haricot Purée.
Potted Pheasant.	Plain Sago Pudding.	Croquettes, made of remains of Beef.
Tea-cakes.		Best end of Neck of Mutton, roasted.
Dry Toast.		Baked Potatoes.
Watercress.		Apple Pie.
Brown and White Bread and Butter.		Cheese.
Porridge.		

Marketing.

For the Day.—A whole Neck of Mutton, not too fat (*see* February 5th); Turnips, Carrots, Potatoes.
For To-morrow.—A four-pound tin of Australian Mutton.

BREAKFAST.—Potted Pheasant (January 7th); Anchovies, with hard-boiled Eggs (January 18th); Tea-cakes (February 14th); Porridge (January 25th).

LUNCHEON.—Flap of Beef, cut from the Sirloin, boiled with Turnips and Carrots (*see* February 23rd). *Plain Sago Pudding.*—Wash a tea-cupful of sago, put it into a dish, pour over it a pint of milk and a pint of water, and let it soak for half an hour. Put with it an inch or two of lemon-rind, or any suitable flavouring, and a little piece of butter the size of a threepenny-piece. Bake it in a gentle oven till done enough. It will take about two hours and a half. Send sugar to table with it.

DINNER.—*Haricot Purée.*—Slice an onion, put it with the haricot beans, and boil them in three pints of water for four hours. Pass the liquid through a sieve, and rub the beans through with the back of a wooden spoon. Season the soup with pepper and salt, and make it hot; put a pint and a half of boiling milk with it, and serve. Toasted bread cut into dice should be sent to table with the purée. Croquettes made of remains of Beef (Rissoles and Croquettes, January 6th); Best end of the Neck of Mutton, roasted (Meat, to Roast, March 4th); Baked Potatoes (May 4th); Apple Pie (August 7th); Cheese (June 8th).

Things that must not be Forgotten.

1. Turn the beef in the brine.
2. Stew the beef-bone in the liquor in which the flap of beef was boiled (February 13th).

3. Render down the unused fat of the beef (*see* February 19th).

4. Wash a pound of prunes, and put them to soak in a pint of water.

March 10th.

Breakfast.	Luncheon.	Dinner.
Savoury Eggs. Potted Pheasant. Hot Toast. Dry Toast. Honey. Brown and White Bread and Butter. Milk Toast.	Australian Meat, cold, with Baked Potatoes. Stewed Prunes.	Skate, with Brown Butter Sauce. Irish Stew. Potatoes. Wyvern Puddings. Cheese.

Marketing.

For the Day.—Two pounds of Crimped Skate (*see* January 10th). If it seem as though there would not be enough mutton for dinner, an additional scrag end of the Neck of Mutton may be bought; Potatoes.

For To-morrow.—A Tin of Sardines; four Sheep's Kidneys, fine, plump, and perfectly fresh; half a pound of Bacon (if not in the house); one tin of preserved Tomatoes; Muffins. (*See* Marketing, January 29th.)

BREAKFAST.—Savoury Eggs (January 1st); Potted Pheasant (*see* Remarks on Potted Grouse, Marketing, January 7th); Milk Toast (June 17th).

LUNCHEON. — Australian Meat, cold (February 4th); Baked Potatoes (May 4th); Stewed Prunes (February 27th).

DINNER. — Skate, with Brown Butter Sauce (February 12th). *Irish Stew.*—Take the remains of the neck of mutton: there will probably be about three pounds. Trim away very nearly all the fat, cleanse the scrag end of the neck, and cut the meat into pieces convenient for serving. Weigh the trimmed meat; pare some potatoes, and take twice the weight of the meat in pared potatoes. Take also six or eight onions, the quantity to be increased or diminished according to taste. Skin them, cover them with boiling water for a few minutes, and cut them into slices crossways, so that they will fall into rings. Boil the potatoes for a quarter of an hour, drain them, and cut them in slices. Season the pieces of meat plentifully with pepper and slightly with salt; put them in a stewpan, cover them with cold water, and simmer very gently for half an hour. Pour off the liquor into a basin, and let this stand, surrounded by cold water, till the grease rises and can be cleared from it. Irish stew ought not to be greasy, and by this means the grease can be removed. Cover the bottom of the pan with slices of potatoes and onions, put in the meat, with additional pepper and salt if required, cover with potatoes and onions, and pack all rather closely together. Pour on the liquor (free from grease), with water to cover barely the topmost layer; put the lid tightly on the stewpan, and simmer *very gently* for an hour and a half. The stew should taste decidedly peppery. It must not *boil* in cooking. As, if it is properly cooked, the potatoes and onions will be almost reduced to a mash, it is likely that additional potatoes will be required for dinner. Potatoes (April 7th); Wyvern Puddings (May 9th); Cheese (June 8th).

Things that must not be Forgotten.
1. Turn the beef in the brine.
2. Take care of the fat cut from the neck of mutton; it can be rendered down for frying purposes.
3. Before serving the Australian meat, carefully pick off the fat (to be melted down for frying), and take away the jelly, which will be a valuable addition to stock or gravy.

March 11th.

Breakfast.	Luncheon.	Dinner.
Sardines.	Savoury Hash of Australian Meat.	Tomato Purée (made of preserved Tomatoes).
Kidneys and Bacon.	Stewed Rhubarb.	Stewed Steak.
Muffins.		Potatoes.
Dry Toast.		Turnip Tops.
Marmalade.		Brown Bread Pudding.
Brown and White Bread and Butter.		Cheese.
Milk Porridge.		

Marketing.
For the Day.—Three pounds of tender Steak cut evenly, and an inch and a half thick. (Marketing, January 1st.) Rhubarb, Potatoes, and Turnip-tops.

For To-morrow.—A tin of Collared Tongue (*see* Marketing, January 2nd and February 4th); two-pennyworth of Watercress; and a pennyworth of young Radishes; Parsley, Apples, and Beetroot.

BREAKFAST. — Sardines (January 12th); Kidneys and Bacon (January 2nd); Muffins (January 30th); Milk Porridge (June 13th).

LUNCHEON.—Savoury Hash of Australian Meat (February 5th); Stewed Rhubarb (May 19th).

DINNER.—*Tomato Purée.*—Mince finely a shalot and a small onion, and fry these with either a slice of bacon cut small or with one or two strips of bacon-rind, and the contents of a two-pound tin of preserved tomatoes. When fresh tomatoes are in season, half-a-dozen fresh tomatoes cut into slices should be used, and are, of course, to be preferred. Pass the tomatoes through a hair sieve. Boil about three pints of nicely-flavoured stock. When boiling, stir in two table-spoonfuls of crushed tapioca; keep stirring till the tapioca looks clear; add the tomatoes; make all hot together, season with pepper and a little salt, if required, and serve. Stewed Steak

(January 31st); Potatoes (May 12th); Turnip Tops (June 4th); Brown Bread Pudding (July 20th); Cheese (June 8th).

Things that must not be Forgotten.

1. Turn the beef in the brine.
2. Remember that the brown bread pudding can be made of broken pieces of brown bread, if there are any.
3. Put the stalks of the watercress into water all night.
4. If liked, the rice for luncheon to-morrow can be prepared overnight (January 28th).
5. Leave a rasher of bacon for the macaroni on March 12th.

March 12th.

Breakfast.	Luncheon.	Dinner.
Collared Tongue.	Macaroni and Bacon.	Fried Whiting.
Watercress and Radishes.	Rice with Apples and Beetroot.	Boiled Silverside of Beef.
Hot Buttered Toast.		Mashed Turnips.
Dry Toast.		Carrots.
Brown and White Bread and Butter.		Potatoes.
Porridge.		Semolina Pudding.
		Cheese.

Marketing.

For the Day.—Whiting, one for each person (*see* January 17th); eight pounds of the thin end of the Flank of Beef, cut as square as possible; Turnips, Carrots, Potatoes.

For To-morrow.—A tin of Oysters; a pint of Split Peas.

BREAKFAST.—Collared Tongue (*see* Marketing, January 2nd). *Watercress and young Radishes.*—Cut the stalks off the watercress and lay it in a dish. Wash the radishes and take the tops off, scrape the roots slightly, and slit each one twice across to make it look something like an open flower. Make a bed of watercress in a dish, lay the cut radishes on this, and place a small salt-cellar in the middle of the dish, which is now ready for the table. Watercress and radishes thus arranged have a very pretty effect, and afford a pleasant variety for the breakfast-table.—Porridge (January 25th).

LUNCHEON.—Macaroni and Bacon (January 27th); Rice with Apples and Beetroot (January 28th).

DINNER.—Fried Whiting (January 17th); Boiled Silverside of Beef (February 23rd); Mashed Turnips (September 30th); Carrots (July 6th); Potatoes (April 7th). *Semolina Pudding.*—Put a pint and a half of milk into a saucepan with three table-spoonfuls of semolina. Put the saucepan on the fire, and stir the milk occasionally till it boils and the semolina swells. Let it cool, then stir into it two well-beaten eggs, and add moist sugar to sweeten it. Butter a quart pie-dish, pour the mixture into it, grate a little nutmeg over the top, and bake in a well-heated oven. When the pudding is set, and a coloured skin forms on the top, it is done enough. It will take about three-quarters of an hour. Cheese (June 8th).

Things that must not be Forgotten.

1. Take the marrow out of the beef-bone when it comes from table. It can be made into marrow toast for breakfast to-morrow.
2. Boil the brine with an additional handful of salt, and when it is cold put the thin flank of beef into it.
3. Put a breakfast-cupful of split peas to soak in cold water all night.

March 13th.

Breakfast.	Luncheon.	Dinner.
Marrow Toast. Collared Tongue. Dry Toast. Brown and White Bread and Butter. Marmalade. Bread and Milk.	Scalloped Oysters (made of tinned Oysters). Baked Plum Pudding.	Pea Soup. Cold Beef. Salad. Baked Potatoes. Cocoa-nut Pudding. Cheese.

Marketing.

For the Day.—A bundle of Rhubarb; three heads of Lettuce; one pennyworth of Beetroot; a half-pennyworth of small salad; Watercress; one fine Cocoa-nut, or a tin of Desiccated Cocoa-nut, if there is none in the house; Potatoes, Yeast.

For To-morrow.—A good-sized dried Haddock; a Melton Mowbray Pork Pie; half or the whole of a Canadian Ham. If it be permitted, order three-pennyworth of Cream for the Rhubarb Pie on Sunday evening.

BREAKFAST.—Marrow Toast (January 21st); Collared Tongue (January 2nd); Bread and Milk (January 25th).

LUNCHEON.—Scalloped Oysters (April 27th); Baked Plum Pudding (February 25th).

DINNER.—Pea Soup (Lentil Soup, April 1st). Beef, boiled yesterday. *Salad.*—Pick off any decayed portions there may be, cleanse the vegetables, drain and dry them. The excellence of a salad consists to a considerable extent on its being thoroughly dry. In a French kitchen the lettuces are not supposed to be washed at all; they are picked to pieces, and each leaf is cleaned separately with a soft napkin. In England, however, it is too frequently the custom to let the salad lie in water for two or three hours before it is wanted, "to make it taste fresh," and the result is the utter ruin of the salad. If any moisture is allowed to hang about the leaves, the dressing, instead of coating the salad, will sink to the bottom of the bowl like a sauce, and the preparation will taste hot and damp, instead of cool and refreshing. The easiest way of drying a salad when it must be washed (as is certainly the case very often) is to place it, a small portion at a time, in a clean dry towel, then drawing the four corners of the cloth together shake it well to make the moisture leave the vegetable and sink into the cloth. When thoroughly dried, the leaves may be arranged in the salad bowl, due care being taken to make them look as pretty as possible, by contrasting the colours. The dressing ought not to be mixed with the vegetables until the last moment; indeed, many people prefer that the business should be performed by one of the family at the table. Salad-dressings of various kinds are sold ready prepared. Many of them are very good; but as a rule they are expensive, and it will be found that the true epicure prefers the simple cruet-sauce to the best of them. This for a bowl of salad may be made as follows. Put into the salad-spoon a small spoonful of salt and half a tea-spoonful of pepper. Mix the ingredients to a paste with a little vinegar, then add more vinegar to make a brimming spoonful. Toss the salad lightly, but very thoroughly, in this for a minute or two; then add three table-spoonfuls of fine Lucca oil. Toss the salad first with the oil and then with its appropriate garniture, and serve. The garniture must vary with the time of year, and with the nature of the salad. For endive salad a *chapon*—that is, a crust of bread that has been rubbed with a clove of garlic—is excellent; or, where garlic is objected to, two sliced tomatoes may be used instead. For celery salad, shalot and parsley can be used. For lettuce, a *ravigote*—that is, a sprinkling of chopped tarragon, chervil, burnet, and chives—is better than anything else. Fortunately, the herbs are most easily to be obtained when the lettuce is in perfection. When they are not to be had, a little tarragon vinegar may be mixed with the French vinegar, and a shalot, or young onion, may be taken; if a very mild onion flavour be preferred, chives can be used. Very superior salads may be made of almost all kinds of cold vegetables, such as cold boiled potatoes, cauliflower, Brussels sprouts, green peas, boiled asparagus, celery, French beans, Windsor beans, sea-kale, haricot beans, lentils, and beetroot. All that is necessary is to mix three or four kinds together, slice them, and then toss them up lightly at the last moment with the cruet-sauce described above. The addition of cold meat, cut into thin slices, cold fish torn into flakes, anchovies, sardines, or bloaters filleted, or cold chicken or cold game cut into neat pieces, will be a great improvement to a salad.—Baked Potatoes (May 4th); Cocoa-nut Pudding (August 8th); Cheese (June 8th).

Things that must not be Forgotten.

1. Turn the flank of beef in the brine.
2. Pastry is to be made to day (April 17th): an open jam tart (August 7th), lemon cheese-cakes (August 18th), and rhubarb pie (August 7th); also tea-cakes (August 26th) and sultana cake (August

2nd). Half a bundle of rhubarb will be enough for the pie; the remainder may be kept till to-morrow, to make the rhubarb mould for Sunday.

3. Wash a breakfast-cupful of German lentils, and put them in cold water to soak all night.

4. Boil about half a Canadian ham (Note 4, May 27th).

March 14th.

Breakfast.	Luncheon.	Dinner.
Dried Haddock. Melton Mowbray Pork Pie. Tea-cakes. Dry Toast. Honey. Brown and White Bread and Butter. Corn Flour Milk.	Bubble and Squeak. Remains of Baked Plum Pudding cut into slices and toasted.	Fried Whiting. Sea Pie. Potatoes. Boiled Lentils. Fig Pudding. Cheese.

Marketing.

For the Day.—Fresh Whiting (*see* January 17th); two and a-half pounds of Buttock Steak (*see* Marketing, January 1st); quarter of a pound of Suet; half a pound of Figs; two or three baking Apples; one-pennyworth of Parsley; Potatoes; Cabbage.

For To-morrow.—A tin of Mock Turtle Soup; a Fillet of Veal weighing about eight pounds (*see* February 25th). The fillet of veal is the thick part of the leg. The butcher will be prepared to take out the bone, and should send a piece of loose skin with the meat. Half a pound of Bacon, if this is not in the house (*see* January 3rd); two-pennyworth of Watercress; Dried Sprats for breakfast on Monday; a bundle may be allowed for each person.

BREAKFAST.—Dried Haddock (January 27th), bought March 13th; Tea-cakes (February 14th); Corn Flour Milk (June 19th).

LUNCHEON.—Bubble and Squeak (*see* January 22nd); Plum Pudding, served a second time (*see* Suet Dumpling, March 6th).

DINNER.—Fried Whiting (*see* January 17th). *Sea Pie.*—Cut the buttock steak into neat pieces, convenient for serving. If the meat is cut with the grain it will be more likely to be tender. Skin, wash, and cut into small pieces, a moderate-sized carrot, a moderate-sized turnip, and a small onion; a couple of potatoes can be added if liked. If not wanted immediately, turn the vegetables into cold water. Put a layer of meat into a saucepan, sprinkle pepper and salt over, then put in the cut-up vegetables and the rest of the meat; pour in as much cold water as will barely cover the meat; put it on the fire to boil while the crust is being made. If it should reach the boiling-point before the crust is ready, draw it back and let it simmer. To make the crust, skin the suet, free it from fibres, and chop it very finely. In many kitchens there is a mincing machine, which saves both time and labour in chopping suet. When this is not the case, and the suet has to be chopped with a knife, it is best

I

to shred it first very finely, then turn the pieces round and chop the suet a little at a time, using the knife as a lever—that is, keeping it down at the point, and raising the upper part only. When it gets sticky, a little flour should be sprinkled over it. In freeing the knife from suet, the fingers should not be drawn *down the length* of the blade, as that would cause the suet to come off in a lump that would have to be chopped over again. Rather it should be taken off with the fingers at once, and in small quantities. When the suet is chopped as fine as sifted bread-crumbs, rub it into three-quarters of a pound of flour, add a pinch of salt and a teaspoonful of baking powder, and make it into a stiff paste with cold water. Roll it out, and make it round to fit the saucepan; lay it upon the beef; put on the lid, and simmer the pie gently for an hour and a half. Pass the knife round it occasionally to keep it from burning. When it is done enough, put the meat and vegetables on a dish, cut the suet-crust in quarters and lay these on the top, pour the gravy over all, and serve. A Sea Pie is both wholesome and palatable, but its appearance is not very elegant. Potatoes (April 7th); Boiled Lentils (March 2nd); Fig Pudding (June 3rd); Cheese (June 8th).

Things that must not be Forgotten.

1. Turn and rub the beef in the brine.
2. Prepare the rhubarb mould for dinner, and the stone cream for supper to-morrow evening (June 3rd and July 1st).
3. Make the mayonnaise sauce for the Italian salad to-morrow. When made, it can be put into a clean, dry bottle, and corked closely; it will keep for some time (August 30th).
4. Also, to save time on Sunday evening, fillet the anchovies for the salad. They will not spoil if they are kept between two plates in a cool place.

Sunday, March 15th.

Breakfast.	Dinner.	Tea.	Supper.
Boiled Ham.	Mock Turtle Soup (from tinned soup).	Brown and White Bread and Butter.	Italian Salad.
Poached Eggs on Toast.	Fillet of Veal stuffed and roasted.	Damson Jam.	Stone Cream.
Dry Toast.	Toasted Bacon.	Tea-cakes.	Lemon Cheese-cakes.
Tea-cakes.	Seakale.	Sultana Cake.	Cheese and Water-cress.
Brown and White Bread and Butter.	Potatoes.		
Porridge.	Rhubarb Mould.		
	Cheese.		

BREAKFAST.—Boiled Ham (March 13th); Poached Eggs on Toast (February 6th); Tea-cakes (February 14th); Porridge (January 25th).

DINNER.—*Mock Turtle Soup, from tinned Soup.*—Take about

three-quarters of a pint of stock made from bones; put it into a stewpan with a piece of carrot, a pinch of aromatic seasoning (if at hand), a bunch of parsley, a small onion stuck with one clove, a bay leaf, one or two outer sticks of celery, or, wanting this, a pinch of celery-seed in muslin, a strip of bacon-rind scalded and scraped, and a little salt and cayenne; simmer all together for about an hour, then strain the stock. Half an hour before the soup is to be served turn it out of the tin; put it with the newly-flavoured stock into a fresh stewpan, and make it hot. Put the soup into a tureen; taste it, and, if necessary, add a little more seasoning; throw in a wine-glassful of sherry, and serve. The addition of the fresh liquor will correct the tinny taste, which is so very objectionable in preserved soups. If there should not be any stock in the house, water in which a spoonful of Liebig's extract of meat has been dissolved may be used instead. This recipe may be followed with all tinned soups. Fillet of Veal stuffed and baked (June 28th); Toasted Bacon (January 19th); Seakale (June 14th); Potatoes (May 12th); Rhubarb Mould (June 3rd); with custard if liked (August 10th); Cheese (June 8th).

SUPPER.—Italian Salad (April 26th); Stone Cream, made yesterday; Lemon Cheese-cakes, made on March 13th.

Things that must not be Forgotten.

1. Turn the beef in the brine.
2. When the veal is done with, put it upon a clean dish, and carefully preserve any stuffing, gravy, or bacon that may be left.
3. Put a breakfast-cupful of German lentils to soak all night in cold water.

March 16th.

Breakfast.	Luncheon.	Dinner.
Dried Sprats. Boiled Ham. Tea-cakes. Dry Toast. Marmalade. Brown and White Bread and Butter. Bread and Milk.	Preserved Tomatoes, with Gravy and Potatoes. Plain rolled Pudding, with Jam, Treacle, or Marmalade.	Lentil Soup. Minced Veal. Toasted Bacon. Potatoes. Turnip Tops. Open Jam Tart. Cheese.

Marketing.

For the Day.—One two-pound tin of preserved Tomatoes; Potatoes, Turnip Tops.

For To-morrow.—One tin of potted Grouse (January 7th); half a pound of Macaroni; half a pound of Normandy Pippins, if they are not in the house; and three pounds of muscle of Beef. (*See* Marketing, January 27th.) Six or eight small Soles, "Slips" (January 3rd).

BREAKFAST.—Dried Sprats (February 28th); Boiled Ham (May 27th); Tea-cakes (February 14th); Bread and Milk (*see* January 25th).

LUNCHEON.—*Preserved Tomatoes.*—Turn half the contents of a tin of preserved tomatoes into a frying-pan with plenty of salt and a slice of butter. Fry the tomatoes till they are done enough, and covered with rich gravy. Have ready three or four slices of toast, one for each person. Let these soak in the gravy, turn upon a dish, and serve very hot. Send baked potatoes to table in a tureen. *Plain Rolled Pudding.*—Put a pound of flour into a bowl. Add a pinch of salt and a teaspoonful of baking powder, and rub in half a pound of sweet dripping. Stir in as much cold water as will make a stiff paste, roll it out, and then turn it over and over to make it in shape of a bolster. Cover it with a floured cloth, tie the ends securely, and plunge the pudding into fast-boiling water. Keep it boiling till enough; it will take about an hour and a half. Let it cool a minute, turn it upon a hot dish, and send treacle, jam, or marmalade to table with it.

DINNER.—Lentil Soup (April 1st); Minced Veal (May 11th); Toasted Bacon (January 19th); Potatoes (May 12th); Turnip-tops (June 4th); Open Jam Tart, made on March 13th; Cheese (June 8th).

Things that must not be Forgotten.

1. Turn the beef in the brine.
2. Put the Normandy pippins to soak in cold water.

March 17th.

Breakfast.	Luncheon.	Dinner.
Baked Slips.	Macaroni and Ham.	Salmon Shad.
Potted Grouse.	Normandy Pippins.	Stewed Beef with Vegetables.
Hot Buttered Toast.		Potatoes.
Dry Toast.		Wyvern Puddings.
Marmalade.		Cheese.
Brown and White Bread and Butter.		Watercress.
Biscuits and Milk.		

Marketing.

For the Day.—A Shad weighing about four pounds. This fish is often to be had very cheap at this time of the year; and very likely it is on this account that it is not so highly esteemed as it deserves to be. Its freshness is determined by the rules that hold good with other fish. Potatoes, Watercress, Vegetables for beef.

For To-morrow.—Three-pennyworth of Cream for the potato purée; Oranges for orange cream and compôte; Sardines for breakfast. Remember to buy a tin a size larger than will be needed for breakfast, as sardines will be needed for the Hambro salad on Wednesday.

Breakfast.—Baked Slips (January 7th); Potted Grouse (*see* Marketing, January 7th); Biscuits and Milk (June 14th).
Luncheon.—Macaroni and Ham (April 3rd); Normandy Pippins (August 16th).
Dinner.—*Salmon Shad.*—Boil the shad just like salmon, and send anchovy (July 5th) sauce to table with it; or, if it be preferred, egg and bread-crumb it and fry it (March 24th). Be careful that the roe is fried also. *Stewed Beef with Vegetables.*—Leave the muscle of the leg of beef ordered yesterday in one piece. Season it with pepper and salt, put it in a stewpan, then proceed in all things according to the directions given in Mutton Stewed with Vegetables (January 14th). It must have fully three hours' gentle stewing, and should be tender without being ragged. Potatoes (April 7th); Wyvern Puddings (May 9th); Cheese (June 8th).

Things that must not be Forgotten.

1. Turn the beef in the brine.
2. Wash two tablespoonfuls of tapioca, and put them to soak in cold water all night.
3. Put half a pint of green or German lentils to soak all night. They should lie in soak for twenty-four hours.
4. Make the orange cream for dinner to-morrow (December 6th). If more convenient, the garnish for the cream can be left until two or three hours before it is wanted.
5. If possible, leave a little boiled ham for the Hambro salad to-morrow.

March 18th.

Breakfast.	Luncheon.	Dinner.
Sardines.	Hambro Salad.	Potatoe Purée.
Potted Grouse.	Apples, with Tapioca.	Lentils and Sausages.
Hot Toast.		Potatoes.
Dry Toast.		Orange Cream.
Marmalade.		Compôte of Oranges.
Brown and White Bread and Butter.		Cheese.
Porridge.		

Marketing.

For the Day.—Three pounds of best Pork Sausages, or two and a-half pounds of fresh Pork, fat and lean together, from the chump end of the fore loin (*see* recipe below). To choose pork *see* January 6th. Potatoes, Apples, Parsley.

For To-morrow.—Bloaters; one will probably be enough for each person. Apples, Potatoes, Watercress.

BREAKFAST.—Sardines (*see* Marketing, January 12th); Potted Grouse (*see* Marketing, January 7th); Porridge (January 25th).

LUNCHEON.—Hambro Salad (August 8th); Apples, with Tapioca (February 18th).

DINNER.—Potatoe Purée (January 26th). *Sausages* as generally sold are composed of such very questionable ingredients that where it is at all practicable it is much the best to prepare them at home. If there is a sausage-machine in the house that will both mince the meat and fill the skins, this can easily be done; but if not, the business is a troublesome one. The skins (especially if they are ordered beforehand) can be obtained of the pork-butcher, and they should be carefully washed inside and out before being used. If more convenient, they can be dispensed with altogether, and the sausage-meat can be made into small balls, and floured lightly before being fried. The following is an excellent recipe for the preparation of home-made sausages:—Cut the meat from the bones, and stew the latter with as much water as will barely cover them till a strong gravy is obtained. Weigh the pork, and for each pound of lean take half a pound of fat. If the proportion of fat is too small, it can be increased; but tastes vary very much on this point. Cut the meat into small pieces, and pass it through the machine. With each pound of meat put two tablespoonfuls of bread that has been rubbed through a wire sieve, and add a teaspoonful of salt, half a teaspoonful of pepper, and half a teaspoonful of dried sage, or, if liked, a mixture of sage and marjoram can be used. Mix the herbs and seasoning first with the bread-crumbs, and then add the whole to the meat, being careful to blend the ingredients thoroughly. Moisten the mince with a tablespoonful of gravy for each pound of meat, and it is ready either to be put into skins or made into balls. Sausages are always best when quite fresh. If they are bought ready made, they should be procured of a highly respectable dealer, for if purchased indiscriminately they may be made of no one knows what. For Lentils and Sausages *see* April 4th; Potatoes (May 12th); Orange Cream made yesterday; Compôte of Oranges (December 6th); Cheese (June 8th).

Things that must not be Forgotten.

1. Turn the meat in the brine.
2. Preserve any sausages that may be left. They can be used for luncheon to-morrow.
3. Keep the bloaters apart from everything else.
4. Wash one pound of prunes, and put them to soak in plenty of cold water.

March 19th.

Breakfast.	Luncheon.	Dinner.
Bloaters.	Toad in-the-hole.	Kidney Soup.
Buttered Eggs.	Stewed Prunes.	Boiled Leg of Mutton;
Buttered Toast.		Caper Sauce.
Dry Toast.		Carrots, Mashed Parsnips.
Watercress.		Potatoes.
Brown and White Bread and Butter.		Hayrick Puddings.
Milk Toast.		Cheese.

Marketing.

For the Day.—Half an Ox Kidney; a well-hung Leg of Mutton for dinner, and another one, small, plump, and freshly killed, to prepare for dinner on Sunday week. Potatoes, Carrots, Parsnips. It is probable that Turnips will be too old for mashing, or they might be used.

For To-morrow.—One tin of preserved Salmon; half a pint of Mushrooms. Forced mushrooms are usually to be had at a cheap rate at this time of year. One tin of Bovill's potted Partridge; two-pennyworth of Radishes.

BREAKFAST.—Bloaters (January 3rd); Buttered Eggs (January 16th); Milk Toast (June 17th).

LUNCHEON.—Toad-in-the-hole, made of the remains of sausages (January 15th); Stewed Prunes (February 27th).

DINNER.—Kidney Soup (February 27th); Boiled Leg of Mutton (*see* February 23rd). *Caper Sauce.*—Take a good tablespoonful of capers, and bruise them well with a wooden spoon. Make half a pint of good melted butter (July 17th), and stir the mashed capers into this. Taste the sauce; if not sufficiently acid, add a little vinegar, and serve. Carrots (July 6th); Mashed Parsnips (September 30th); Potatoes (May 12th). *Hayrick Puddings.*—Put two ounces of fresh butter into a small jar, and place this in a large bowl of hot water till the butter is nearly melted. The water must not go into the jar. Beat the melted butter to cream, and throw in gradually, whilst beating, two well-whisked eggs. Add, a little at a time, two ounces of fine flour, the grated rind of a fresh lemon, and two tablespoonfuls of sugar. Just before baking, stir in a small pinch of baking powder. Warm some dariole moulds, grease them inside with butter, three-parts fill them with the mixture, and bake in a well-heated oven till they are well risen and brown. They will take about twenty minutes. *Lemon Syrup.*—Squeeze the juice of a lemon into a small cupful of water, and boil it with five moderate-sized lumps of sugar till it is a clear thin syrup, then colour it with six drops of cochineal. Turn the puddings upon a hot dish, pour the sauce round them, and serve. The appearance of the dish will be improved if white sugar is sifted over, and if a little ring of angelica is placed upon each pudding (July 12th). Cheese (June 8th)

Things that must not be Forgotten.

1. Turn and rub the beef in the brine.
2. Before putting away the bottle of capers, be careful to fill it up with fresh vinegar. This will help to preserve the flavour and prevent mould.
3. Make a pickle with half a pint of vinegar, a quarter of a pint of water, one onion stuck with six cloves, two bay-leaves, and a little salt and whole pepper. Put the fresh leg of mutton into this, and turn and rub it every day till wanted.
4. Make a little mayonnaise for the salmon salad to-morrow (August 30th).

March 20th.

Breakfast.	Luncheon.	Dinner.
Mushrooms. Potted Partridge. Hot Buttered Toast. Dry Toast. Radishes. Brown and White Bread and Butter. Corn Flour Milk.	Salmon with Salad (made of tinned salmon). Macaroni Cheese.	Skate with Brown Butter Sauce. Curried Mutton (made of cold leg of mutton). Boiled Rice. Turnip Tops. Potatoes. Red Currant Dumpling (made of bottled fruit). Cheese.

Marketing.

For the Day.—Two heads of Lettuce; a pennyworth of Watercress; small Salad; two pounds of crimped skate (see January 10th); Turnip Tops, Potatoes, bottled Currants, Rhubarb; German Yeast.

BREAKFAST.—*Stewed Mushrooms on Toast.*—Pull out the stems of the mushrooms, and peel them. Melt a good slice of butter in a stewpan, then add a teaspoonful of salt, half a teaspoonful of white pepper, and a very small pinch of powdered mace. Put in the mushrooms, the upper side downwards, and let them stew gently till they are tender; they will take fifteen or twenty minutes. Take a slice of bread the size of the dish on which they are to be served. Toast it, or, better still, fry it in butter; turn the mushrooms upon it, and serve very hot. If liked, white sauce can be poured over the mushrooms. Radishes (March 12th). The green tops of the radishes can be used instead of watercress in the dish. Potted Partridge (see Potted Grouse, January 7th); Corn Flour Milk (June 19th).

LUNCHEON.—*Salmon Salad.*—Mix salmon with the salad (March 13th), and use half the contents of the tin instead of fresh fish (Note 4, March 19th). *Macaroni Cheese.*—Wash half a pound of Naples macaroni, drain it, throw it into boiling water with a lump of butter in it, and boil it for twenty minutes. Throw the water away; pour upon it a pint of milk, and let it simmer gently till it is tender without being pulpy. (The time macaroni takes to boil depends upon the quality; the commoner the kind, the sooner it will be done enough.) Grate two ounces of dry cheese. Parmesan cheese is the best for the purpose, but this is a convenient method of using the dry portions of other cheeses. Turn half the macaroni, milk and all, on a greased dish; sprinkle pepper and salt and a grain or two of cayenne upon it, together with a little of the grated cheese, and repeat until the ingredients are used. Sprinkle grated cheese and a spoonful of bread-raspings on the top of all, and pour over half an ounce of melted butter. Brown the preparation in front of the fire, and serve very hot.

DINNER.—Skate with Brown Butter Sauce (February 12th); Curried Mutton (May 26th); Rice for Curry (July 21st); Turnip Tops (June 4th); Potatoes (May 12th); Red Currant Dumpling, made of bottled fruit (July 19th); Cheese (June 8th).

Things that must not be Forgotten.

1. Turn and rub the mutton in the pickle.
2. Take up the beef, remove the bones, and roll the meat very tightly; bind it with tape, and boil it till tender (*see* February 23rd). Leave it in the liquor off the fire for an hour, and put it between two dishes with a weight upon the top; let it stand all night. Preserve the liquor to make glaze.
3. Pastry is to be made to-day (April 17th): a baked custard (January 19th), and a rhubarb pie (August 7th); a sultana cake (August 2nd) and a few Sally Lunns (August 26th) will also be wanted.
4. Make fish cakes of what is left of the preserved salmon for breakfast to-morrow (*see* January 13th).
5. Soak some hominy for breakfast to-morrow (*see* February 10th).

March 21st.

Breakfast.	Luncheon.	Dinner.
Fish Cakes.	Beef Stew Economical.	Parsnip Soup (made of the liquor the mutton was boiled in).
Potted Partridge.	Jam and Bread.	Civet of Rabbit.
Sally Lunns.		Potatoes.
Dry Toast.		Savoy.
Brown and White Bread and Butter.		Lemon Pudding.
Marmalade.		Cheese.
Hominy.		

Marketing.

For the Day.—Two pounds of lean Steak (*see* January 1st); two plump Ostend Rabbits (*see* January 21th); one pennyworth of Parsley; one tin of Oysters; a set of Pigs' Feet (*see* February 7th); Potatoes; six ounces of Beef Suet.

For To-morrow.—A tin of Pilchards (*see* January 23rd); a couple of Guinea Fowls (*see* February 14th); half a pound of streaky Bacon, if this is not in the house; fresh Salad for supper; two heads of Lettuce; one-pennyworth of Beetroot; two-pennyworth of Watercress (half for breakfast); and one-pennyworth of small Salad; Potatoes; Seakale.

BREAKFAST.—Fish Cakes made yesterday; Potted Partridge (January 7th); Sally Lunns (June 4th); Hominy, boiled (February 11th).

LUNCHEON.—*Beef Stew Economical.*—Cut the steak evenly, with a sharp knife, into slices an inch thick. Brown them on both sides with a little dripping, dredge flour upon them, and put in the pan a large carrot, a turnip, an onion, and a bay-leaf. Pour in the liquor from the tinned oysters with as much stock or water as will cover the bottom of the pan, but not the meat. Cover the stewpan closely, and simmer the meat very gently for about an hour and a half, or till it is tender; add pepper and salt to taste. Put the oysters into a basin and make them hot in the oven. Lay the meat on a dish, place the oysters upon it, and after freeing the gravy from fat, strain it over all. Serve very hot. If liked, mushrooms can be used instead of oysters. Jam and bread, or cheese and bread.

DINNER.—Parsnip Soup (December 3rd); Civet of Rabbit (December 8th); Potatoes (May 12th); Savoy (June 4th); Lemon Pudding (August 12th); Cheese (June 8th).

Things that must not be Forgotten.

1. Turn and rub the mutton in the pickle.
2. Make glaze of the liquor the beef was boiled in, and glaze the beef. To do this, first clear the liquor thoroughly from fat, and boil it quickly without having a lid on the saucepan, being careful to remove the scum as it rises. When it is reduced to about a quart turn it into a small stewpan and boil it again—but more gently —till it is a thick syrup. Try a little in a spoon, and if, when cold, it sets like a jelly, it is ready. When it reaches this stage it is in great danger of burning, and if it burns it is spoiled. Put it into a jar. Paint the meat with it, using for the purpose an ordinary gum-brush that has been soaked for a while in cold water. The glaze should be laid lightly on the surface of the meat, and when one coat is cold and stiff a second may be given. Any glaze that is left should be put into a small dry jar; it will keep for a long time. When wanted, it should be melted as glue is; that is, the jar which contains it should be put into a saucepan surrounded half-way up with boiling water, and kept boiling till it is dissolved. An easy way of making glaze is to soak a spoonful of gelatine in cold water, and dissolve it in twice its bulk of strong, brown gravy. Or glaze may be bought ready-made in skins. This glaze, however, does not taste so well as home-made glaze.
3. Pluck the Guinea Fowl for to-morrow, and preserve and cure the feathers (*see* February 28th).
4. Preserve any cold hominy that may be left; it can be fried for breakfast to-morrow.
5. Prepare the Pigs' Feet for Breakfast (Note 3, February 7th).

Sunday, March 22nd.

Breakfast.	Dinner.	Tea.	Supper.
Pilchards.	Vermicelli Soup.	Brown and White Bread and Butter.	Rolled Beef.
Pigs' Feet.	Guinea-fowl roasted		Salad.
Sally Lunns.	Toasted Bacon.	Plum Jam.	Baked Custard.
Dry Toast.	Bread Sauce.	Sultana Cake.	Cheese.
Watercress.	Potatoes, Seakale.		
Brown and White Bread and Butter.	Queen's Pudding.		
Fried Hominy.	Cheese.		

BREAKFAST.—Pilchards (*see* Sardines, January 12th); Pigs' Feet (February 7th); Sally Lunns (June 4th); Fried Hominy (February 12th).

DINNER.—*Vermicelli Soup.*—Take three ounces of vermicelli, break it lightly with the hands in order that it may be conveniently carried from the plate to the mouth. Put it into a saucepan of cold water, and set it over the fire for a few minutes to cleanse it thoroughly by dissolving the outside dust. Let it cool, then drain it and pour away the water. Have ready three pints of nicely-flavoured stock. Let it boil, then drop the vermicelli into it, and let it boil again for ten minutes, or till the vermicelli is tender; stir it gently once or twice to keep the vermicelli from getting into lumps. Properly Clear Soup should be used (July 30th), or Clear Soup quickly made (February 15th); but for ordinary consumption, stock made from bone, nicely flavoured, strained, and freed from fat, will answer the purpose very well. Roasted Guinea Fowl (April 5th); Bacon (January 19th); Bread Sauce (October 18th); Potatoes (May 12th); Seakale (June 14th); Queen's Pudding (August 9th); Cheese (June 8th).

TEA.—Sultana Cake (August 2nd).

SUPPER.—Rolled Beef. Put the glazed meat on a dish, and garnish it with parsley; Salad (March 13th); Baked Custard Tart Jaunary 19th).

Things that must not be Forgotten.

1. Turn the mutton in the pickle.
2. If the carver can quite conveniently leave the legs of the Guinea Fowl untouched, they may be devilled for breakfast (*see* January 14th); if not, Eggs on the Dish (December 7th) may be served instead.
3. Take care of the bones and trimmings of the birds. Soup can be made of them for dinner to-morrow.

March 23rd.

Breakfast.	Luncheon.	Dinner.
Devilled Drum-sticks or Eggs on the Dish. Pigs' Feet. Buttered Toast. Dry Toast. Brown and White Bread and Butter. Marmalade. Porridge.	Rolled Beef, with baked Potatoes and cold Butter. Plain Rice Pudding.	Guinea Fowl Soup. Steak à la Béarnaise. Fried Potatoes. Rhubarb Pie. Cheese.

Marketing.

For the Day.—A slice of Rump Steak, not less than one inch thick, and weighing from three to three and a-half pounds (*see* January 22nd); Potatoes.

For To-morrow.—Bloaters for breakfast. One for two persons will probably be enough. One tin Collared Tongue (*see* January 2nd).

BREAKFAST.—Devilled Drum-sticks (January 14th); Eggs on the Dish (December 7th); Pigs' Feet (February 7th); Porridge (January 25th).

LUNCHEON.—Beef, Boiled (March 20th); Baked Potatoes (May 4th); Plain Rice Pudding (February 24th).

DINNER.—Guinea Fowl Soup (February 16th); Steak à la Béarnaise. For broiling the steak (January 22nd). *Béarnaise Sauce.*—Allow one egg for two persons, and one ounce of butter for each egg. The yolks only of the eggs will be required; the whites should be preserved, and can be used for the lemon sponge to-morrow. Beat the yolks lightly, put them into a small stewpan, and stir them without ceasing till they begin to thicken. Take the pan off the fire, and put in one-third of the quantity of butter that is to be used. Stir the sauce again over the fire for two minutes, when another third portion of the butter may be introduced *off* the fire. After simmering once more for two minutes, repeat the process for the third time. Take the sauce off the fire, add salt and pepper to taste, and when it has cooled for a minute or two, stir in a little tarragon vinegar till it is sufficiently acid to suit the palate. Have ready (for three eggs) a tablespoonful of finely-chopped tarragon, or, when this is not to be had, a tablespoonful of fresh green parsley, and mix this with the sauce. Just before serving the broiled steak spread the Béarnaise Sauce over the surface and serve very hot. Fried Potatoes (February 2nd); Rhubarb Pie (August 7th); Cheese (June 8th).

Things that must not be Forgotten.

1. Turn the mutton in the pickle.
2. Boil the brine with an additional handful of salt, wash the pan, and pour it back again.

March 24th.

Breakfast.	Luncheon.	Dinner.
Bloaters on Toast. Collared Tongue. Hot Buttered Toast. Dry Toast. Marmalade. Brown and White Bread and Butter. Bread and Milk.	Devilled Eggs. Baked Plum Pudding.	Fried Soles. Shoulder of Mutton. Browned Potatoes. Lemon Sponge. Cheese. Pulled Bread.

Marketing.

For the Day.—Two heads of Lettuce; a pair of Soles (January 3rd); a well-hung Shoulder of Mutton, not too fat; a piece of Silverside of Beef, weighing about eight pounds; Potatoes; a quarter of a pound of good Beef Suet.

For To-morrow.—A tin of Sardines; two-pennyworth of Mustard and Cress.

BREAKFAST.—*Bloaters on Toast.*—Put the bloaters into boiling water, and let them simmer gently two or three minutes, till the skin can be taken off easily. Skin them, and lift the flesh from the bones in fillets. Brush these over with butter, and season them with pepper; then lay them between slices of buttered toast; cut them into neat squares; put them in the oven for a few minutes, and serve very hot. Collared Tongue (*see* Note 2, January 3rd); Bread and Milk (January 25th).

LUNCHEON.—Devilled Eggs (February 27th); Baked Plum Pudding (February 25th).

DINNER.—*Fried Soles.*—Prepare the fish for frying three or four hours before it is wanted. Of late years, authorities have recommended that the fish should not be skinned, as so much nourishment and flavour lies in the skin. It is most usual, however, to remove the skin. When cleaning soles hold them up to the light; if a dark streak can be seen at the side of the roes, the latter should be removed before frying; if not, they may be left. Wipe the fish with a soft cloth, and rub it all over with flour; then roll in a clean cloth, and leave it for an hour or two. If it is thoroughly dry it need not be covered with anything more than flour before it is fried; but if preferred, it may either be egged and breaded, or dipped in a thin smooth batter of flour and water before frying. Large soles may either be filleted or cut through the bone into neat pieces. If fried whole, the frying-basket would, of course, not be required for large flat fish—the frying-pan would rather be needed; but with this exception, when frying soles, the directions can be followed which are given for fried whiting (*see* January 17th). It should be remembered, however, that the black or skinned side should first be placed downwards in the pan, and that in lifting it out of the pan the fork should be stuck into the fish close to the head. When it is preferred that the sole should be egged and breaded instead of being floured, it is a convenience to use brown bread-raspings instead of plain bread-crumbs, as, if this is done, the fish is sure to have a good appearance. Shoulder of Mutton (*see* March 4th and December 16th); Browned Potatoes (October 18th); Lemon Sponge (August 10th), to be made of the whites of eggs left from the Béarnaise Sauce; Cheese (June 8th); Pulled Bread (August 27th).

Things that must not be Forgotten.
1. Turn the mutton in the pickle.
2. Put the silverside of beef into the brine.

March 25th.

Breakfast.	Luncheon.	Dinner.
Sardines with Capers.	Cold Shoulder of Mutton.	Crécy Soup.
Collared Tongue.	Mint Sauce.	Lancashire Hot Pot.
Buttered Toast.	Salad.	Greens.
Dry Toast.	Baked Apples.	Baked Batter with Jam.
Mustard and Cress.		Cheese.
Brown and White Bread and Butter.		
Porridge.		

Marketing.

For the Day.—Two heads of Lettuce, a pennyworth of Watercress, a halfpennyworth of small Salad, and a halfpennyworth of Beetroot; a small Neck of Mutton; three Sheep's Kidneys; a pennyworth of Parsley; Mint, Apples, Potatoes, Greens; a tin of Oysters; Onions.

For To-morrow.—A bottle of Anchovies, if they are not in the house; half a pound of Streaky Bacon, if not at hand.

BREAKFAST.—Sardines with Capers (January 12th); Collared Tongue (Note 2, January 3rd); Porridge (January 25th).

LUNCHEON.—Mutton, Roasted (March 24th). *Mint Sauce.*—Be sure that the mint is fresh and young. Pick the leaves from the stalks, wash them well, and dry them in a cloth. Chop them as fine as possible; then measure the mint; and for every even tablespoonful, allow half the quantity of pounded sugar. Mix the sugar and mint thoroughly, and let it lie for a couple of hours; then pour over it two table-spoonfuls of good vinegar for each tablespoonful of mint. The flavour of the mint will be more thoroughly extracted if it is allowed to lie with the sugar for a while without the vinegar. If it is considered that there is too large a proportion of sugar, less may be used; but the sauce as thus made is very generally approved. Salad (March 13th); Baked Apples (February 9th).

DINNER.—Crécy Soup (January 5th). *Lancashire Hot Pot.*—Take the best end of the neck of mutton, the sheep's kidneys, a moderate-sized onion, and the tinned oysters; free the mutton almost entirely from fat, and cut it into neat chops. Take a wide brown earthenware stewpot, and fill it with alternate layers of the chops, the kidneys, cut into thin slices, some sliced potatoes, and the onion very finely minced. Before putting in the meat, season each piece with pepper and salt. Place whole potatoes over the topmost layer; put in the liquor from the oysters, and add half a pint of stock or water. Cover the stewpan closely, and bake it in a gentle oven for about three hours. If there is any danger that the dish will be too dry, add a little more stock. When the meat is tender lift it on a not dish, and add the oysters, which have been made hot by being put upon a dish in the oven for a few minutes; pour the gravy over all, and serve very hot. The sliced potatoes should be dissolved in the gravy. Greens (June 4th); Baked Batter Pudding with Jam (February 5th); Cheese (June 8th).

Things that must not be Forgotten.

1. Turn and rub the mutton in the pickle.
2. Turn and rub the beef in the brine.
3. Take care of the fat from the neck of mutton. It can either be melted down for frying purposes, or it may be used for making suet crust for puddings.
4. Fillet half-a-dozen anchovies, and lay them between two plates ready for to-morrow morning.
5. Mince very finely a little of the first cut of the collared tongue, and put it between dishes to keep moist.

March 26th.

Breakfast.	Luncheon.	Dinner.
Mock Woodcock. Toasted Bacon. Dry Toast. Marmalade. Brown and White Bread and Butter. Milk Toast.	Scrag end of Neck of Mutton with Rice. Stewed Rhubarb.	Milk Soup. Beef Steak and Mushroom Pie. Savoy. Potatoes. Chocolate Pudding. Cheese.

Marketing.

For the Day.—A bundle of Rhubarb; two pounds of Rump or Buttock Steak (see January 1st); half an Ox Kidney; a quarter of a pint of Mushrooms; a quarter of a pound of powdered Chocolate; Potatoes; Savoy.

For To-morrow.—A tin of Prawns; a slice, half an inch thick, from the middle of a Canadian Ham, if this is not in the house; a Cow Heel from the tripe shop; two-pennyworth of Mustard and Cress; a pennyworth of Watercress.

BREAKFAST.—*Mock Woodcock.*—Beat two eggs and mix with them a table-spoonful of cream. Warm the anchovies before the fire, put them with the eggs into a small saucepan, and stir them briskly over the fire for a minute or two till the sauce thickens. Add the minced tongue, spread the preparation on toast, and serve immediately. Toasted Bacon (January 19th); Milk Toast (June 17th).

LUNCHEON.—Scrag end of Neck of Mutton with Rice (February 21st); Stewed Rhubarb (May 19th).

DINNER.—Milk Soup (January 3rd). *Beef Steak and Mushroom Pie.*—Mix together on a plate a table-spoonful and a half of flour, a heaped tea-spoonful of salt, and half a tea-spoonful of pepper. Take away the fat and the skin from the meat and kidney, and cut both into thin slices. Put a slice of kidney upon each slice of meat, dip the two into the seasoning mixture, and roll them into little rolls. Put a layer of the rolls at the bottom of a dish, put the mushrooms (chopped) upon them, and add the rest of the meat. Pour in stock or water to three-parts fill the dish. Make some good Rough Puff Pastry (May 29th); roll this out once till it is the third of an inch thick, and rather larger than the dish it is intended to cover. Cut off a strip all round the edge, and leave the oval piece in the middle the same size as the pie. Moisten the edge of the dish with water, lay the strip of paste on it, and stick the ends together with a little water. Brush the surface of the strip with water, cover the pie with paste, and press the edges together all round. Cut the edge of the pie evenly all round with a floured knife; ornament the top with any paste that may be left, brush the top of the pie with egg, make a hole in the centre to allow the steam to escape, and bake in a moderate oven. The pie should first be put in the hot part of the oven till the pastry rises and is firm, it should then be moved to the cooler part till the meat is done enough. It will take from two to three hours. If it is in danger of being too deeply coloured, a greased paper should be laid upon it. This method may be followed for all meat pies. Fresh rump steak, or the inside of a sirloin, or the tender part of the round, are the best portions that can be taken for a beef-steak pie, although a very good pie may be made of buttock steak. If liked, fresh oysters, or tinned oysters with their liquor, can be substituted for the mushrooms, or a few parboiled potatoes cut into slices can be introduced. It is always best to have a little good gravy boiling hot ready to be put into the pie through the hole in the top after it is baked. Savoy (June 4th); Potatoes (May 12th); Chocolate Pudding (July 24th); Cheese (June 8th).

Things that must not be Forgotten.

1. Turn and rub the mutton in the pickle.
2. Turn and rub the beef in the brine.
3. Make the Ground Rice Mould for luncheon to-morrow (August 7th).

March 27th.

Breakfast.	Luncheon.	Dinner.
Prawns.	Cow Heel, with Parsley Sauce.	Half a dozen Oysters each, with Brown Bread and Butter and Cut Lemon.
Fried Ham and Eggs.	Ground Rice Mould, with Jam.	Boiled Rabbits and Bacon.
Hot Buttered Toast.		Onion Sauce.
Dry Toast.		Mashed Potatoes.
Mustard and Cress.		Macaroni Pudding.
Brown and White Bread and Butter.		Cheese and Watercress.
Corn Flour Milk.		

Marketing.

For the Day.—Fresh Oysters (February 14th); two moderate-sized Ostend Rabbits (January 24th); half a pound of streaked Bacon, cut in rashers, if not in the house (*see* January 3rd); Potatoes; Onions; German Yeast; Macaroni.

For To-morrow.—A pennyworth of Radishes and a pennyworth of Watercress; six pennyworth of Cream, half for the Palestine soup, and half for the gooseberry pie.

BREAKFAST.—Prawns (February 6th and 7th); Fried Ham and Eggs (March 5th); Corn Flour Milk (June 19th).

LUNCHEON.—Cow Heel, with Parsley Sauce (February 20th); Rice Mould made yesterday.

DINNER.—Oysters (February 14th); Boiled Rabbits (March 6th); Bacon (January 19th); *Macaroni Pudding.*—Break six ounces of macaroni into one-inch lengths, put these into a saucepan with plenty of hot water, and let them boil, without a lid on the saucepan, for twenty minutes. Drain away the water, and pour on a quart of milk, and add a slice of butter and three spoonfuls of sugar. Boil again till the macaroni is tender, without being at all pulpy. It will need about twenty minutes longer, but the time will vary with the quality of the macaroni. Let the mixture cool. Break two eggs into a bowl, grate a little nutmeg into them, and stir them lightly in with the macaroni and milk; pour into a greased dish, and bake in a moderately-heated oven till the pudding is firm and of a light-brown colour. It will take about an hour. Onion Sauce (October 14th); Mashed Potatoes (May 12th); Cheese (June 8th).

Things that must not be Forgotten.

1. Turn and rub the mutton in the pickle.
2. Turn and rub the beef in the brine.
3. Pastry is to be made to-day (April 17th): one plum pie, one gooseberry pie, both made of bottled fruit (August 7th); also rice cake (August 2nd), and Vienna bread (August 26th).
4. Carefully preserve any little pieces of fried ham that may be left. They may be made into ham toast for breakfast to-morrow.

March 28th.

Breakfast.	Luncheon.	Dinner.
Prawns. Ham Toast. Radishes and Watercress. Dry Toast. Brown and White Bread and Butter. Porridge.	Gâteau of Rabbit. Treacle Pudding.	Palestine Soup, made of the Rabbit Stock. Pork à l'Italienne. Browned Potatoes. Greens. Gooseberry Pie. Cheese.

Marketing.

For the Day.—A leg of small Pork, weighing not more than four pounds; quarter of a pound of best Kidney Suet for the treacle pudding; three pounds of Jerusalem Artichokes for soup—artichokes will very likely be scarce now, as they are going out of season; two pennyworth of Parsley, a larger quantity than usual will be needed because of the maître d'hôtel sauce; Potatoes, Greens.

For To-morrow.—A pair of thick Soles (January 3rd); four Sheep's Kidneys—fine, plump, and perfectly fresh; half a pound of rashers of Bacon, if this is not in the house; one tin preserved Tomatoes; two fresh Lettuces; one pennyworth of Beetroot; two pennyworth of small Salad; half a pound of German Sausage for breakfast on March 30th. Very thick German sausage is not usually so good as that made of a small size. The former will not keep more than a day; the latter, though more expensive, will keep for some time. Potatoes; Sea Biscuits.

BREAKFAST.—Prawns (February 7th); *Ham Toast.*—Take the remains of the dressed ham, weigh it, and supposing there is a quarter of a pound, proceed as follows:—Mince it as finely as possible, and put it into a small stewpan with two table-spoonfuls of the rabbit stock, one table-spoonful of cream (or of milk if cream is not to be had), a grate of nutmeg, and a grain of cayenne. Stir the mixture over a gentle fire till it is hot through. Have ready—toasted and buttered—a slice of bread the size of the dish on which the mince is to be served, pour the mince upon this, and serve very hot. Porridge (January 25th).

LUNCHEON.—Gâteau of Rabbit (July 9th). *Treacle Pudding.* —Clear the suet from skin and fibre, and chop it until it looks like fine oatmeal. Mix with it half a pound of fine flour, a tea-spoonful of moist sugar, an even tea-spoonful of baking powder, and half a pound of treacle. Add milk to make a *thick* batter. Grease a plain mould, pour in the mixture, and lay a greased paper on the top of the pudding. Steam for three hours. *To Steam a Pudding* put it into a saucepan which contains boiling water that will reach half way up the mould; it must on no account be so high that the water can enter the mould or touch the paper; and keep the water boiling round it till done enough. If in any case the water touches the paper, it will absorb the moisture all through. The buttered paper keeps the condensed steam from falling into the pudding. Let the pudding stand a minute or two before turning it out, and send treacle sauce or sweet sauce to table with it (July 19th).

DINNER.—Palestine Soup (December 8th); Pork à l'Italienne

(December 18th); Browned Potatoes (October 18th); Greens (June 4th); Gooseberry Tart made yesterday; Cheese (June 8th).

Things that must not be Forgotten.
1. Turn and rub the mutton in the pickle.
2. Turn and rub the beef in the brine.
3. Put a large breakfast-cupful of white haricot beans to soak all night in cold water.
4. Make custard blancmange for dinner to-morrow (August 4th).

Sunday, March 29th.

Breakfast.	Dinner.	Tea.	Supper.
Savoury Eggs. Kidneys and Bacon. Vienna Bread. Dry Toast. Brown and White Bread and Butter. Biscuits and Milk.	Filleted Soles, à la Maître d'Hôtel. Sour Mutton. Potato Snow. White Haricot Beans. Custard Blancmange with Lemon Syrup. Cheese.	Brown and White Bread and Butter. Vienna Bread. Strawberry Jam. Rice Cake.	Cold Sour Mutton. Haricot Salad. Plum Pie. Cheese.

BREAKFAST.—Savoury Eggs (January 1st); Kidneys and Bacon (January 2nd); Biscuits and Milk (June 14th); Vienna Bread (August 26th).

DINNER. — *Filleted Soles à la Maître d'Hôtel.* — Follow the directions given for soles filleted, rolled, and baked (March 1st), but serve Maître d'Hôtel Sauce (May 6th) with the fish instead of Beurre Noir. *Sour Mutton.*—This is a German dish, but almost every one who tastes it likes it. Drain and wipe the mutton that has been in pickle, and roast it in the usual way. Half an hour before it is done enough, pour a cupful of the pickle into the tin with it, and baste the meat well with the liquor. In Germany this joint is always baked, and a couple of potatoes are put into the baking-tin to thicken the gravy. Potato Snow (April 7th); White Haricot Beans (June 20th); Custard Blancmange with Lemon Syrup (August 4th and March 19th); Cheese (June 8th).

TEA.—Vienna Bread (August 26th); Rice Cake (August 2nd).

SUPPER.—*Haricot Salad.*—Prepare the salad in the usual way (*see* March 13th); arrange it round a dish; toss the haricot beans in the same kind of sauce used for the lettuce; pile them in the centre of the dish, and serve. Plum Pie (August 7th).

Things that must not be Forgotten.
1. Turn and rub the beef in the brine.
2. Fillet the anchovies for breakfast to-morrow morning (January 18th).
3. When preparing the salad, leave a little small salad to be served with the anchovies to-morrow.

March 30th.

Breakfast.	Luncheon.	Dinner.
Anchovies and Hard-boiled Eggs. German Sausage. Vienna Bread. Dry Toast. Brown and White Bread and Butter. Porridge.	Mutton à la Sauce Piquante. Hasty Pudding.	Tomato Purée. Boiled Salt Beef. Potatoes. Carrots. Parsnips. Apple Gâteau. Cheese.

Marketing.

For the Day.—Two pounds of Apples; Potatoes, Carrots, Parsnips.

For To-morrow.—Quarter of a pound of Normandy Pippins, if not in the house; a piece of Gammon of Bacon, weighing about four pounds; the whole or part of a large fresh Ox Cheek.

BREAKFAST.—Anchovies and Hard-boiled Eggs (January 18th); German Sausage (June 6th); Vienna Bread (August 26th); Porridge (January 25th).

LUNCHEON.—*Mutton à la Sauce Piquante.*—Cut what is left on the leg of mutton into neat slices. Mince very finely a piece of garlic about the size of a small pea, and one shalot. Melt in a saucepan a piece of butter about the size of a walnut, throw in the garlic and shalot, and add a table-spoonful of flour. Mix all over the fire for a minute or two; add a tea-spoonful of chopped parsley, a table-spoonful of vinegar, and a wine-glassful of stock, and boil together for a quarter of an hour. Put in the sliced meat; let it get hot in the sauce, but it must not boil. Serve immediately with toasted sippets and pickled gherkins round the dish. *Hasty Pudding.*—Put as much milk as will be required into a saucepan with a pinch of salt. Let it boil up, then sprinkle flour slowly in with the left hand, at the same time stirring the pudding briskly with a spoon held in the right hand. If any lumps collect, draw them to the side of the fire and press them out with the back of the spoon. When the pudding is a thick paste, let it boil a minute or two longer, still stirring it, then put it into a pie-dish with a slice of fresh butter, and serve. Treacle or sugar and cream may be eaten with this pudding. Hasty pudding may be eaten at breakfast instead of porridge.

DINNER.—Tomato Purée (March 11th); Boiled Beef (February 23rd); Carrots (July 6th); Parsnips (September 30th); Apple Gâteau (September 24th); Cheese (June 8th).

Things that must not be Forgotten.

1. If the bacon is very dry soak it for three or four hours. In any case wash it well and scrape the under part. Put it into a stewpan with the cold water and cover it; bring it to the boil, skim, and simmer very gently for two hours, half an hour to the pound. Draw off the skin, sift bread-raspings over the top, and the bacon is ready. It can

be used for breakfast to-morrow morning. For bread-raspings *see* Remarks after Breakfast, January 2nd.

2. Boil the brine; let it go cold, then follow the directions given in Note 5, February 6th.

3. Soak half a pound of Normandy pippins in cold water.

4. When cutting the German sausage take a slice off the end, and put this in its place again before putting the sausage away; it will then be kept from getting dry.

March 31st.

Breakfast.	Luncheon.	Dinner.
Boiled Bacon.	Macaroni Cheese.	Fried Smelts.
Poached Eggs on Toast.	Normandy Pippins.	Cold Beef.
Vienna Bread.	Milk.	Mashed Potatoes.
Brown and White Bread and Butter.		Salad.
Marmalade,		Golden Pudding.
Porridge.		Cheese.

Marketing.

For the Day.—Smelts, one for each person and one over (*see* Marketing February 4th); Parsley, Potatoes, Salad; six ounces of Suet.

For To-morrow.—One tin of Pilchards (January 23rd); a pennyworth of Watercress.

BREAKFAST.—Bacon, boiled yesterday; Poached Eggs (February 6th); Vienna Bread (August 26th); Porridge (January 25th).

LUNCHEON.—Macaroni Cheese (March 20th); Normandy Pippins (August 16th).

DINNER.—Fried Smelts (February 4th). The beef boiled yesterday can be served cold with salad. Many people are particularly fond of cold boiled beef. Mashed Potatoes (May 12th); Carrots (July 6th); Golden Pudding (May 4th); Cheese (June 8th).

Things that must not be Forgotten.

1. Turn and rub the ox-cheek in the brine.
2. Wash a pound of prunes, and put them to soak all night in cold water.
3. Put a cupful of green lentils to soak in cold water.

FRUITS IN SEASON SUITABLE FOR DESSERT IN MARCH.

Apples; Oranges; Bananas; Grapes; Pomeloes; Shaddocks; Nuts (Filberts, Cobs, Walnuts, Brazils, Almonds, Barcelonas); Almonds and Raisins; French Plums; Figs; Dates; Crystallised Fruits; Foreign Preserved Fruits.

APRIL.

Towards the end of April or at the beginning of May rhubarb jam may be made. It is best to preserve rhubarb at the latter end of the season, because then it does not contain so much water. Take as much rhubarb as may be thought right, peel it and cut it into small pieces. Weigh it, and with each pound of fruit take one pound of loaf sugar, the thin rind of half a lemon chopped fine, a quarter of an ounce of sweet almonds blanched and chopped fine, and a quarter of an ounce of butter. Bring the fruit slowly to the boil, add the sugar, stir it constantly and skim carefully; then boil it rather quickly, till a little will set when it is put upon a plate. It will take about one hour and a half from the time it simmers equally all over. Just at the last stir in a wine-glassful of whiskey for each seven pounds of fruit. Put the jam into jars, and tie these down in the usual way.

April 1st.

Breakfast.	Luncheon.	Dinner.
Pilchards. Boiled Bacon. Hot Toast. Dry Toast. Watercress and Radishes. Brown and White Bread and Butter. Porridge.	Bubble and Squeak. Stewed Prunes.	Lentil Soup. Stewed Ox-tails. Potatoes. Broccoli. Wyvern Puddings. Cheese.

Marketing.

For the Day.—Broccoli; two Ox-tails (the butcher should be asked to send these home ready jointed); a pennyworth of Parsley; Potatoes, Broccoli, Carrots, Turnips, Onions.

For To-morrow.—Scallops for breakfast (March 7th); German Sausage; Fresh Rolls (September 3rd).

Breakfast.—Pilchards (January 23rd); Bacon, Boiled (March 30th); Radishes (March 12th); Porridge (January 25th). .

Luncheon.—Bubble and Squeak (January 22nd), made of the unsightly remains of the boiled beef. Stewed Prunes (February 27th).

Dinner.—*Lentil Soup.*—Make the soup of the beef liquor, first tasting it to make sure that it will not be too salt. A little of the bacon liquor will be an improvement. Drain the lentils, and put them into a stewpan with the stock, and throw in two onions, two carrots, a turnip, a bunch of parsley, a pinch of savoury herbs, a bay leaf, and, more important than all, either half-a-dozen outer sticks of celery or half a tea-spoonful of bruised celery seed, and a crust of stale bread. Let the liquor boil, skim it occasionally to take off the dark film that keeps rising to the surface, and boil gently for about four hours till the lentils are thoroughly soft. Strain the soup through a wire sieve, take out the parsley, and rub everything else patiently through the sieve into a basin. Keep a small portion of the liquor hot wherewith to moisten the pulp now and then, and so make it go through more easily. Boil the soup again before sending it to table, and serve it very hot. Add a few drops of sugar browning to improve its appearance. Stir it frequently whilst boiling it, to keep it from burning. Some people add a cupful of boiling milk to this soup. Stewed Ox-tails (May 8th); Potatoes (May 6th); Broccoli (April 25th); Wyvern Puddings (May 9th); Cheese (June 8th).

Things that must not be Forgotten.

1. Turn and rub the cheek in the brine.
2. Put two table-spoonfuls of tapioca with an inch or two of thin lemon-rind to soak all night in a pint of water.
3. Make the hydropathic pudding for dinner to-morrow of bottled raspberries (June 16th).

April 2nd.

Breakfast.	Luncheon.	Dinner.
German Sausage. Scallops. Rolls. Dry Toast. Marmalade. Brown and White Bread and Butter. Porridge.	Stewed Ox Kidney. Tapioca and Apples.	Parsnip Soup. Chicken Sauté aux Champignons (made of tinned chicken). Potatoes. Seakale. Hydropathic Pudding. Cheese.

Marketing.

For the Day.—One fresh Ox Kidney; a tin of Boiled Chicken; a tin of Champignons, or a few forced Mushrooms; half a pound of thin rashers of streaky Bacon; Potatoes, Seakale.

For To-morrow.—About four pounds of the Fillet of the Rump of Beef. (See Marketing, January 2nd.)

BREAKFAST.—German Sausage (June 6th); Scallops (March 7th); Rolls (September 4th); Porridge (January 25th).

LUNCHEON.—*Stewed Ox Kidney.*—Take the core out of the kidney, and cut it into neat pieces. Put these into a saucepan with a quart of cold water; add an onion stuck with two cloves, and a little pepper and salt; simmer all gently together for about an hour and a half. Twenty minutes before the kidney is to be taken up melt an ounce of butter or dripping in a stewpan, stir in a table-spoonful of flour, and beat to a smooth paste with the back of a wooden spoon. Add gradually a little of the liquor from the kidney, pour it back into the pan, and boil together for a few minutes. Put in a few drops of sugar browning, and serve with toasted sippets round the dish. Potatoes or boiled rice are excellent served with this dish. Tapioca and Apples (February 18th).

DINNER.—Parsnip Soup, made of the rest of the bacon and beef liquor (December 3rd). *Chicken Sauté.*—Put a gill of oil into a small stewpan, let it boil, then fry the pieces of cooked chicken in it. They will take about six minutes. When brown they are ready for serving. Have ready the sauce and the rashers of bacon broiled and neatly rolled. Arrange the chicken and bacon in a circle round a dish, pour the sauce over them and in the centre, and serve. The sauce may be made as follows:—Shred as finely as possible a piece of garlic the size of a pea, a shallot, and five button mushrooms. Melt half an ounce of butter in a stewpan, stir in a dessert-spoonful of flour, and add a quarter of a pint of water and the same quantity of stock, and stir in the minced vegetables. Take the sauce off the fire, add a table-spoonful of cream and a squeeze of lemon-juice, and serve. The sauce must not boil after the vegetables are added. Potatoes (May 6th); Seakale (June 14th); Hydropathic Pudding (June 16th); Cheese (June 8th).

Things that must not be Forgotten.

1. Turn and rub the cheek in the brine.
2. Remember to brush the fillet of beef with vinegar. (*See* Marketing, January 2nd.)

April 3rd.

Breakfast.	Luncheon.	Dinner.
Buttered Eggs.	Macaroni and Ham.	Crécy Soup.
German Sausage.	Cake Pudding.	Fillet of Beef, Roasted.
Hot Toast.		Yorkshire Pudding.
Dry Toast.		Baked Potatoes.
Honey.		Turnip-tops.
Brown and White Bread and Butter.		Newmarket Pudding. Cheese.
Porridge.		

Marketing.

For the Day.—Half a pound of Naples Macaroni; Potatoes, Turnip-tops.
For To-morrow.—A dried Haddock; a tin of Potted Grouse (January 7th).

BREAKFAST.—Buttered Eggs (January 16th); German Sausage (June 6th); Porridge (January 25th).

LUNCHEON.—*Macaroni and Ham.*—Either bacon or ham may be used for this dish, which is excellent. Boil half a pound of macaroni in slightly salted water for about an hour. Whilst it is boiling, mince finely a quarter of a pound of meat from the gammon of bacon, and grate a quarter of a pound of Parmesan or other cheese. Drain the macaroni, and fill a plain mould (a cake-tin will answer the purpose) with alternate layers of macaroni, ham, and cheese, and flavour each layer with pepper and salt. Beat two eggs, and mix them with a little milk. Melt an ounce of butter, throw it over the macaroni, and, lastly, throw the eggs and milk over all. Bake for half an hour in a moderate oven. Tie a napkin round the tin, and send the macaroni to table without turning it out. For economy's sake, one egg may be used and bread-crumbs substituted for the Parmesan. Cake Pudding (February 4th).

DINNER.—Crécy Soup (January 5th); Fillet of Beef, Roasted (February 11th or March 4th); Yorkshire Pudding (November 26th); Baked Potatoes (May 4th); Turnip-tops (June 4th); Newmarket Pudding (June 2nd); Cheese (June 8th).

Things that must not be Forgotten.

1. Turn and rub the ox cheek in the brine.
2. Put a breakfast-cupful of lentils to soak in cold water.
3. Pastry is to be made to-day (April 17th): open jam tart (August 7th), lemon cheesecakes (August 18th), apple pie (August 7th); also make teacakes (August 26th) and Annie's cake (September 25th).
4. Put a tea-cupful of hominy to soak all night in cold water.
5. If any beef be left it may be potted for breakfast, and used instead of the potted grouse (January 23rd).

April 4th.

Breakfast.	Luncheon.	Dinner.
Dried Haddock.	Baked Mackerel.	Milk Soup.
Potted Grouse.	Boiled Hominy.	Lentils and Sausages.
Teacakes.		Potatoes, Fried.
Dry Toast.		Vermicelli Pudding.
Brown and White Bread and Butter.		Cheese.
Porridge.		

Marketing.

For the Day.—Three moderate-sized Mackerel. Mackerel can be bought at such a cheap rate that it is not so much thought of as it would be if it were dearer. It should be procured very fresh, as it quickly becomes tainted. When fresh, the skin is of a beautiful sea-green colour, the eyes very bright, and the gills very red. The fish should be plump, but not over large. Three pounds of best Pork to make sausages (March 18th); two pennyworth of fresh Parsley: Potatoes.

For To-morrow.—A slice of Ham, the third of an inch thick, if this is not in the house; a quarter of a pound of Sorrel, a small Lettuce, and an ounce (that is, about a handful) of Chervil; a pair of Guinea Fowls (*see* Marketing, February 11th); a slice of fat Bacon, it not at hand. One pound of cold boiled new Potatoes, a sour Apple, the remains of the German Sausage, four Sardines, and a few Gherkins and Capers, will be required for the Russian Salad to-morrow evening. A small tin of Sardines; two pennyworth of Watercress to garnish the Guinea Fowl; Potatoes, Seakale.

BREAKFAST.—Dried Haddock (January 27th); Potted Grouse (January 7th); Teacakes (February 14th); Porridge (January 25th).

LUNCHEON.—Baked Mackerel (April 15th); Boiled Hominy (February 11th).

DINNER.—Milk Soup (January 3rd); Lentils and Sausages. To make sausages, *see* March 18th. Fry or bake the sausages (January 7th and December 13th). Boil the lentils (March 2nd). Cover the bottom of a dish with the lentils, arrange the sausages on the top, and serve very hot. Potatoes, Fried (February 2nd); Vermicelli Pudding (August 1st); Cheese (June 8th).

Things that must not be Forgotten.

1. Turn and rub the ox-cheek in the brine.
2. If any hominy is left, preserve it. It can be fried for breakfast on April 6th.
3. Pluck the guinea fowls, and prepare them for roasting to-morrow. Cure the feathers (February 28th).
4. Make a little Mayonnaise sauce for the salad to-morrow (August 30th). If this is put into a bottle and corked well down, it will keep for some weeks. It takes a good deal of making, therefore it will be well not to put it off till Sunday.

Sunday, April 5th.

Breakfast.	Dinner.	Tea.	Supper.
Fried Ham.	Milk Soup.	Brown and White Bread and Butter.	Russian Salad.
Fried Eggs.	Guinea Fowl.	Apple Jelly.	Apple Pie.
Teacakes.	Bread Sauce.	Annie's Cake.	Half of Lemon Cheesecakes.
Dry Toast.	Brown Gravy.		Cheese.
Brown and White Bread and Butter.	Potatoes.		
Porridge.	Seakale.		
	Hayrick Puddings.		
	Cheese.		

BREAKFAST.—Fried Ham (March 5th); Fried Eggs (March 5th); Teacakes (February 14th); Porridge (January 25th).

DINNER.—Milk Soup (January 3rd). *Guinea Fowl.*—Properly, a guinea fowl ought to be larded. The operation is not at all difficult, but if the cook is afraid of it she may dispense with it, and tie a slice of fat bacon over the breasts of the birds. It is best to tie a piece of greased paper also round the birds before putting them down to the fire; this paper can be removed ten minutes before the guinea fowls are taken up. For the rest, *see* June 30th. Brown gravy (October 18th) should be poured into the dish (not over the birds), and more may be sent to table in one tureen and bread sauce in another. The appearance of the birds will be improved if a little clear brown gravy be boiled quickly down to glaze (March 21st) and poured over them, and the dish may be garnished with watercress. A fine young guinea fowl would need about thirty-five minutes' roasting before a clear, quick fire. Bread Sauce (October 18th); Potatoes (April 7th); Seakale (June 14th); Hayrick Puddings (March 19th); Cheese (June 8th).

TEA.—Annie's Cake (September 25th).

SUPPER.—*Russian Salad.*—Pick four ounces of meat from the guinea fowl. (Cooked veal or any white meat might be used for this purpose.) Cut into small pieces one pound of cold boiled potatoes and four sardines, and mince finely a sour apple, pared and cored, and a tea-spoonful of capers. Slice thinly an inch of German sausage and six pickled gherkins. Put all these ingredients into a dish, mix them thoroughly; then toss them up, just before serving, with a quarter of a pint of Mayonnaise sauce. Garnish with hard-boiled egg and strips of boiled beetroot. If more convenient, ham can be used instead of German sausage, and anchovies instead of sardines. Apple Pie (August 7th); Lemon Cheesecakes (August 18th).

Things that must not be Forgotten.

1. Turn and rub the ox-cheek in the brine.
2. Preserve the bones and trimmings of the guinea fowl.
3. If it can be managed without inconvenience, leave the legs of the guinea fowl untouched; then devil them for breakfast (January 14th).

April 6th.

Breakfast.	Luncheon.	Dinner.
Devilled Drum-sticks or Ham Toast. Sardines. Fried Hominy. Dry Toast. Brown and White Bread and Butter. Porridge.	Beef Collops. Lemon Cheesecakes.	Guinea Fowl Soup. Filets de Bœuf à la Béarnaise. Mashed Potatoes. Roly-poly Pudding. Cheese.

Marketing.

For the Day.—The fillet end of the Sirloin of Beef. Choose a piece weighing about ten pounds, with a good undercut. If there is any difficulty in obtaining an undercut of a sufficient size (it is for dinner), a pound of Rump Steak can be obtained and used with it; Potatoes; six ounces of Suet (this can most likely be trimmed from the joint after the butcher has cut off as much as he will).

For To-morrow.—Fresh Whiting (January 3rd).

BREAKFAST.—Devilled Drum-sticks (January 14th); Ham Toast, made of remains of cooked ham (March 28th); Sardines. The remainder of the tin opened for the salad may be put upon the breakfast table. Fried Hominy (February 12th); Porridge (January 25th).

LUNCHEON.—Take the undercut of the sirloin, and cut it out whole. Divide it into neat steaks half an inch thick; trim these evenly, pepper them lightly, rub them with oil, and leave them till wanted. Collect all the trimmings, mince them finely, and make Scotch collops of it (January 9th). Lemon Cheesecakes (August 18th).

DINNER.—Guinea Fowl Soup (February 16th). *Filets de Bœuf à la Béarnaise.*—Cook the fillets on a gridiron over a clear fire (see Broiled Steak, January 22nd). Turn them frequently; they will be done enough in about five minutes. Make a little Béarnaise sauce (March 23rd), and spread a portion of it upon each cutlet. Put mashed potatoes in the centre of a dish, arrange the fillets round it, and serve (May 12th). This dish may be varied in several ways. Oyster sauce (October 16th), tomato sauce (July 15th), or piquante sauce (May 5th) can be served with the steaks; or maître d'hôtel butter (April 15th) can be melted upon them; or, after being dished in a circle, carrots, French beans, boiled chestnuts, or a Macédoine—that is, a mixture of vegetables neatly shaped and cooked—can be put into the centre. Of course, care must be taken to have a sauce and a garnish that are suited to each other. Roly-poly Pudding (August 18th); Cheese (June 8th).

Things that must not be Forgotten.

1. *Ox-cheek Brawn.*—Wash the cheek, put it into plenty of cold water, and boil till the bones can be drawn out easily. It will take about four hours, more or less, according to its size. Take away the bones and prickly portions; cut the meat into neat pieces, season with pepper and salt, and put it while hot into a brawn-tin. Place a weight upon it, let it stand all night, and in the morning it may be turned out and served for breakfast.

2. Boil up the brine, scald and dry the pan, and pour the brine back again.

3. Cut off the flap of beef. Let the brine get cold, then put the flap into it.

4. Put a cupful of white haricot beans to soak all night in cold water.

April 7th.

Breakfast.	Luncheon.	Dinner.
Fried Whiting.	Tomatoes on Toast.	Haricot Purée.
Ox-cheek Brawn.	Rice and Cheese.	Roast Beef.
Hot Buttered Toast.		Potato Snow.
Dry Toast.		Mashed Parsnips.
Marmalade.		Open Jam Tart.
Brown and White Bread and Butter.		Cheese.
Milk Toast.		

Marketing.

For the Day.—One two-pound tin of Preserved Tomatoes; one pennyworth of Parsley; Potatoes; Parsnips.

For To-morrow.—Bloaters (January 2nd).

BREAKFAST.—Fried Whiting (January 17th); Brawn made yesterday; Milk Toast (June 17th).
LUNCHEON.—Tomatoes on Toast (March 16th); Rice and Cheese (February 18th).
DINNER.—Haricot Purée (March 9th); Roast Beef (March 4th or March 8th). *Potato Snow.*—Boil or steam the potatoes in the usual way. Drain them, and put them at the side of the fire till they fall to pieces. Have ready a hot dish to receive them and a hot wire sieve. Rub them through the latter, letting them fall into the tureen in which they are to be served. Do not disturb the mass that falls, but send it to table as quickly as possible. If liked, it can be put before the fire for two or three minutes to brown the surface. *To Boil Old Potatoes.*—Choose the potatoes as nearly of one size as possible, so that they may take the same time to cook. It is best to boil old potatoes in their jackets, and peel them after they are done enough. If they are diseased, however, they must be peeled in the first instance, and the eyes and black parts must be taken out with a sharp knife. In either case they should be thoroughly washed in cold water, and scrubbed with a scrubbing-brush. Careless cooks frequently peel potatoes without washing them, letting them drop as they are finished into the bowl that contains the skins, and they consider that they have done all that is necessary if they rinse the potatoes before putting them on to boil. By this means the potatoes become stained, and it is one reason why they so frequently look black when sent to table. If boiled in their jackets, put the potatoes into a saucepan with as much cold water as will cover them. Bring the water to a boil, sprinkle salt in (a tea-spoonful of salt to a quart of water), put the lid on closely, and simmer gently till a fork will pierce through them easily. They will take from twenty minutes to three-quarters of an hour, according to their size and quality. Let them boil quickly for the last three minutes. Drain away the water, put a clean cloth over the potatoes in the pan, and put it at the side of the fire to let the moisture escape in steam. Draw off the skin without cutting the potato, and serve as quickly as possible. To boil potatoes without their jackets, cover them with cold water, and boil them, without salt, very gently—the slower the better. When they can be pierced through with a fork drain away the water, sprinkle salt over them, and leave the pan uncovered by the side of the fire, shaking it occasionally to make the potatoes look floury. Mashed Parsnips (September 30th); Open Jam Tart (August 7th); Cheese (June 8th).

Things that must not be Forgotten.

1. Keep the bloaters on a separate dish and away from all other food.
2. Turn and rub the small piece of beef in the brine.

April 8th.

Breakfast.	Luncheon.	Dinner.
Bloaters.	Shepherd's Pie (made of remains of Roast Beef).	Croûte au Pot.
Ox Cheek like Tongue.	Boiled Rice.	Spanish Stew.
Buttered Toast.		Potatoes.
Dry Toast.		Greens.
Brown and White Bread and Butter.		Tinned Pineapple.
Porridge.		Cheese.

Marketing.

For the Day.—Two moderate-sized Ostend Rabbits (January 21th). The dealer should be asked to cut them up into neat pieces before sending them home. A tin of preserved Pineapple; a pennyworth of Parsley; Greens; Potatoes; half a pound of Bacon (January 3rd).

For To-morrow.—A tin of Prawns (February 6th); a pennyworth of Watercress; one tin of Potted Pheasant (*see* Remarks on Potted Grouse, January 7th).

BREAKFAST.—Bloaters (January 3rd); Brawn (Note 1, April 6th); Porridge (January 25th).

LUNCHEON.—Shepherd's Pie (January 12th); Boiled Rice (February 3rd).

DINNER.—Croûte au Pot (May 25th). *Spanish Stew.*—Take a deep earthenware jar. Fill it with alternate layers of sliced onion and rabbit, and season each layer with a little pepper and salt. Lay slices of bacon on the topmost layer, and cover the stewpan securely by tying two or three folds of greased paper upon it. Put the jar almost up to its neck in a saucepan of boiling water, and keep it boiling for two hours and a half. It will not be necessary to leave any liquor in the jar with the rabbit, as the onions will yield sufficient moisture to stew the rabbit and to serve as gravy. If the onion flavour is objected to, the rabbits may be cooked in another way (*see* Index). Potatoes, Boiled (April 7th); Greens (June 4th). *Tinned Pineapple.*—Open the tin and draw off the syrup. Boil it up with two or three lumps of sugar, and add a tea-spoonful of brandy. Let it cool. Arrange the slices of pineapple in a glass dish, pour the syrup over, and serve cold. The appearance of the fruit will be improved if a preserved cherry and a small ring of angelica be placed here and there on the dish. Cheese (June 8th).

Things that must not be Forgotten.

1. Turn and rub the beef in the brine.
2. Do not attempt to clear soup the day before it is wanted. The stock may be made, but soup must be freshly clarified, or it will be cloudy.
3. When making the stock (either of bones or fresh meat), be careful to remove the scum as it rises. If this is not done it will be difficult to clarify the soup. Also, before attempting to use the stock free it carefully from fat. It is supposed here that the stock is

made from bones, and is to be clarified with raw beef. It might be so made from fresh meat that it would need no clarification. (*See* Clear Soup made from Fresh Meat, July 30th.)

4. Make the corn-flour blancmange for dinner to-morrow (June 15th).

April 9th.

Breakfast.	Luncheon.	Dinner.
Prawns.	Flap of Beef, Boiled, with Carrots.	Julienne.
Potted Pheasant.		Roast Leg of Mutton.
Buttered Toast.	Rice and Cheese.	Yorkshire Pudding.
Dry Toast.		Potato Croquettes.
Watercress.		Turnip-tops.
Brown and White Bread and Butter.		Corn-flour Blancmange.
Biscuits and Milk.		Cheese.

Marketing.

For the Day.—One pound of Shin of Beef to clarify the bone stock; a well-hung Leg of Mutton (January 8th); Potatoes; Turnip-tops; Yeast.

For To-morrow.—Four pounds of salt Cod; three or four Pigeons. Tame Pigeons can probably be obtained now; they are better for being freshly killed (January 24th). A slice of Rump Steak; Hot Cross Buns (*see* Note); half a pound of Bacon in rashers; Potatoes; Parsnips; Horseradish.

BREAKFAST.—Prawns (February 7th); Potted Pheasant, *see* Remarks on Potted Grouse (January 7th); Biscuits and Milk (June 14th).

LUNCHEON.—Flap of Beef, Boiled (February 23rd); Rice and Cheese (February 18th).

DINNER.—*Julienne* (February 15th).—To make *Clear Soup*, take two or three pints of good stock (July 30th), well skimmed and free from fat. Half a pound of lean beef will clarify one quart of stock. Cut the beef into very small pieces, and discard every particle of fat and sinew. Have ready a carrot cleaned and scraped to pulp, a turnip cut into dice, and the white part of a leek cut into small pieces. Put the stock (*cold*) into a stewpan, stir in the meat and vegetables, and keep stirring till the contents of the stewpan are on the point of boiling. As soon as this point is reached draw the saucepan back, skim the stock carefully, and let it simmer by the side of the fire for twenty minutes. Strain it carefully through a napkin, pouring it in with a cup a little at a time. When it has gone through once pass it through a second time, and be careful not to disturb the sediment in the napkin, as this will act as a filter, and help to make the soup clear. In clearing soups and jellies it is not necessary that a jelly-bag should be used. A perfectly clean cloth wrung out of boiling water, and fastened over the legs of a chair or stool turned upside down, will answer excellently for the purpose. (*See figure.*) If it is not thought desirable to use raw beef for clarifying the soup, white of egg may be used instead; but by the latter method the soup will be impoverished, by the former it will be enriched. Clear soup forms the basis of many varieties of soup. Vegetables, neatly turned, fried in butter, and thrown into it, make it Julienne Soup; the same vegetables boiled in it, without frying, make it Soup à la Jardiniére. The addition to it of early spring

SUBSTITUTE FOR A JELLY BAG.

vegetables makes Spring Soup, or Soup Printanier, and also Soup à la Macédoine. The introduction of homely vegetables, such as onions and cabbage, alter it into the Peasants' Soup—Soup à la Paysanne. Brussels sprouts thrown into it make it into Flemish Soup; while two or three poached eggs laid gently in make it into Colbert's Soup. If crusts of bread are put in it becomes Croûte au Pot; if macaroni, it is Macaroni Soup; if vermicelli is added, it is Vermicelli Soup. The process of making this soup, however, involves a good deal of trouble, and this is a consideration in households where the number of servants is limited. Roast Leg of Mutton (March 4th or March

8th); Yorkshire Pudding (November 26th); Potato Croquettes (November 4th); Turnip-tops (*see* Cabbage, June 4th); Corn Flour Blanc-mange (June 15th); Cheese (June 8th).

Things that must not be Forgotten.

1. Put the salt fish to soak in cold water all night.
2. Make the pigeon pie (May 15th) and also the rice mould for dinner to-morrow (October 7th). To-morrow is supposed to be Good Friday, therefore the pastry would be better made to-day: an apple pie (August 7th), and a currant cake (June 6th), besides the pigeon pie.
3. *Hot cross buns* may be ordered of the baker, or they may be made at home. If the latter plan is adopted, an ounce of *fresh* German yeast will be required. Take three pounds of fine flour, mix a pinch of salt with it, and rub in eight ounces of good butter. Turn the yeast into a basin, and beat it up well with a table-spoonful of moist sugar till it is a liquid. Add a pint and a half of lukewarm water or milk and two well-beaten eggs, and mix all with the flour to make a batter. Sprinkle a little flour over the dough, cover the bowl with a cloth, and let the dough rise before the fire for a couple of hours; then knead it up well with ten ounces of sugar, half a pound of washed and dried currants, and a little grated nutmeg. Make the dough into buns. Lay these in rows on baking-tins, with an inch or two between each, cut them twice on the top with a knife to make the sign of a cross, and let them rise before the fire for ten minutes. Bake in a quick oven. This quantity will make about three dozen buns. The buns can be toasted and buttered, or made hot in the oven, like teacakes, before serving.

April 10th.
(Supposed to be Good Friday.)

Breakfast.	Luncheon.	Dinner.
Prawns.	Mutton Croquettes.	Salt Fish.
Toasted Bacon.	Sago Pudding.	Egg Sauce.
Hot Cross Buns, Toasted and Buttered.		Boiled Parsnips.
Cold Buns, Buttered.		Hashed Mutton.
Brown and White Bread and Butter.		Pigeon Pie.
Marmalade.		Potatoes.
Corn Flour Milk.		Rice Mould, with Compôte of Oranges.
		Cheese.

BREAKFAST.—Prawns (February 7th); Toasted Bacon (January 19th); Hot Cross Buns (Note 3, April 9th); Corn Flour Milk (June 19th).

LUNCHEON.—Neat slices can be cut from the cold leg of mutton to make hash for dinner, and the unsightly remnants can be used for the croquettes (January 6th); Sago Pudding (March 9th).

DINNER.—*Salt Fish.*—Take the fish out of the water in which it has been soaked, wash it well, and put it into a fish-kettle with plenty of cold water. Bring it gently to a boil, clear off the scum, and let it simmer till the flesh will leave the bone easily. A piece weighing three or four pounds will take from half to three-quarters of an hour. Drain it, put it on a dish covered with a napkin, garnish with parsley and tufts of scraped horseradish. Send egg sauce to table in a tureen, and boiled parsnips as an accompaniment. *Egg Sauce.*—Boil three eggs for ten minutes till they are hard. When cold, shell them and cut them up, first in slices and afterwards in dice. Have ready half a pint of melted butter, stir the egg into it, make it hot without allowing it to boil, and serve. Boiled Parsnips (September 30th); Hashed Mutton (May 18th); Pigeon Pie (May 15th); Potatoes (May 12th); Rice Mould made yesterday (October 7th); Compôte of Oranges (December 6th); Cheese (June 8th).

Things that must not be Forgotten.
1. Make stock of the leg of mutton bone (February 13th).
2. Boil the brine and scald the pan.

April 11th.

Breakfast.	Luncheon.	Dinner.
Boiled Eggs. Potted Pheasant. Hot Buttered Toast. Dry Toast. Brown and White Bread and Butter. Porridge.	Salt Cod Réchauffé. Brown Betty.	Vermicelli Soup. Stewed Steak. Baked Potatoes. Greens. Preserved Peaches. Custard. Cheese.

Marketing.

For the Day.—Three pounds of tender Steak. It should be cut evenly, and be about an inch and a half thick (*see* Marketing, January 1st). One tin of Preserved Peaches; one pennyworth of Parsley; Potatoes, Greens, Turnips, Carrots, Onions, and a few baking Apples; eight pounds of the middle cut of the Silverside of Beef.

For To-morrow.—One two-pound tin of Preserved Tomatoes; fore-quarter of Lamb; quarter of a pound of Chocolate; new Potatoes, a bunch of Mint, Watercress; ingredients for Salad (March 13th). A fore-quarter of lamb is the prime joint. It should be fresh, as, like all young meat, it taints quickly. The quality of the fore-quarter may be determined by the appearance of the jugular vein or vein of the neck. If this is blue and firm the animal is freshly killed, if yellow or green it is stale. The shoulder, too, should be examined. If this has but little flesh upon it the lamb is not fine. Lamb, like mutton, should have the lean clear and red, the fat firm and white. It should be thoroughly cooked. When it cannot be dressed immediately it should be examined frequently, and wiped to remove any moisture that may form on it. Sardines (January 12th); and Melton Mowbray Pork Pie for April 13th.

BREAKFAST.—Boiled Eggs (January 5th); Potted Pheasant, *see* Remarks on Potted Grouse (January 7th); Porridge (January 25th).

LUNCHEON.—*Salt Cod Réchauffé.*—Take the remains of the salt cod left from yesterday. Put the flesh (freed from bone and skin) into a pie-dish, pour what was left of the egg sauce over it, and pepper it lightly. Mash a few potatoes with milk or butter, place these round the edge of the fish, and bake for about half an hour, or till the potatoes are brightly coloured. If there were no egg sauce left, fresh melted butter may be made to moisten the fish. Brown Betty (November 26th).

DINNER.—Vermicelli Soup (March 22nd); stock made of Leg of Mutton bone (February 13th); Stewed Steak (January 31st); Baked Potatoes (May 4th); Greens (*see* Cabbage, June 4th). *Preserved Peaches.*—Follow in all respects the directions given for serving tinned pineapple (April 8th), but add two or three drops of essence of almonds to the syrup before pouring it over the fruit. Custard (August 10th); Cheese (June 8th).

Things that must not be Forgotten.

1. Make potted beef of any little pieces of stewed beef that may be left (January 23rd).
2. Put the silverside of beef into the brine.
3. Chop the mint for mint sauce, and put sugar on it to draw out the flavour (March 25th).

Sunday, April 12th.

Breakfast.	Dinner.	Tea.	Supper.
Savoury Eggs. Potted Beef. Buttered Toast. Dry Toast. Watercress. Brown and White Bread and Butter. Bread and Milk.	Tomato Purée. Fore-quarter of Lamb. Mint Sauce. New Potatoes. Salad. Chocolate Pudding. Cheese.	Brown and White Bread and Butter. Strawberry Jam. Currant Cake.	Cold Lamb. Mint Sauce. Potato Salad. Apple Pie.

BREAKFAST.—Savoury Eggs (January 1st); Potted Beef made yesterday (January 23rd); Bread and Milk (January 25th).

DINNER.—Tomato Purée (March 11th). *Fore-quarter of Lamb* (March 4th or March 8th).—When the lamb is ready for the table the shoulder should be raised from the ribs with a sharp knife, and a slice of butter, a sprinkling of salt, and a squeeze of lemon-juice thrown over the meat. After this the shoulder can be put back again, and the lamb served with a frilled paper fastened round the shank. Mint Sauce (March 25th). *New Potatoes.*—Wash the new potatoes in cold water, and scrape them with a knife. Put them into boiling water, sprinkle a little salt over them, put the lid on the pan, and boil them till the centre feels tender when pierced with a fork; they will take about a quarter of an hour. Pour off all the water, lay a clean cloth over the potatoes, put the lid on again, and let the pan stand by the side of the fire till the potatoes are dry. Take them up, and serve on a hot dish. *Potatoes à la maître d'hôtel.* Pour a little maître d'hôtel sauce over the potatoes before serving them. Salad (March 13th); Chocolate Pudding (July 24th); Cheese (June 8th).

Tea.—Currant Cake (June 26th).

Supper.—*Potato Salad.*—Cut any new potatoes that may be left from dinner into thin slices. Put these on a dish with a few salad leaves of any kind finely shred. Toss them up in the usual way with pepper, salt, oil, and vinegar. Sprinkle a little finely-minced parsley and shallot on the top, and garnish with beetroot, hard-boiled eggs cut into rings, tufts of watercress, small radishes, shred cucumber or nasturtium leaves and flowers, or whatever else may be convenient. If potatoes alone are made into salad, it will be better for being mixed half an hour before it is wanted. If salad leaves are put with it it, must not be mixed till the moment of serving. Almost all vegetables plainly cooked are excellent served as a salad when cold. Potato salad is very good mixed with a few sardines or a herring. (*See* Russian Salad, April 5th.) Apple Pie (August 7th).

Things that must not be Forgotten.
1. Turn and rub the beef in the brine.
2. Put a tea-cupful of white haricot beans to soak in cold water.

April 13th.

Breakfast.	Luncheon.	Dinner.
Sardines.	Cold Lamb.	Mullagatawny Soup.
Melton Mowbray.	Mint Sauce.	Haricot Mutton.
Hot Buttered Toast.	Baked Omelette.	Haricot Beans.
Dry Toast.		Mashed Potatoes.
Marmalade.		Roly-poly Pudding.
Porridge.		Cheese.

Marketing.
For the Day.—A fine Neck of Mutton; one pound of good Beef Suet.
For To-morrow.—Dried Sprats (February 27th); a small tin of Corned Beef.

Breakfast.—Sardines (January 12th); Pork Pie ordered April 13th; Porridge (January 25th).

Luncheon.—Lamb served yesterday; Mint Sauce (March 25th); Baked Omelette (August 6th).

Dinner.—Mullagatawny Soup (January 16th). *Haricot Mutton.*—Take the best end of the neck of mutton, trim away most of the fat, and divide the meat into neat chops. Prepare also three turnips, three carrots, one onion, and the white part of two leeks. Cut these into any shape that may be preferred, and throw them into cold water till wanted. Melt a little butter in a frying-pan, put in the chops, and fry them for a minute till they are lightly browned on each side. Take them up, and fry the vegetables in the same fat for a few minutes, and turn them about to keep them from changing colour. Dredge flour over the chops, put them in a stewpan, lay the fried vegetables upon them, and pour in gradually as much warm water or stock as will just cover the whole. Bring the liquor to a boil, then draw it to the side of the fire, and simmer it gently till the chops are tender. It will take about an hour and a half. Pour off most of the liquor, and put it in a basin surrounded by cold water to cool. Carefully take off all the fat, season the gravy with pepper and salt, and add a table-spoonful of walnut or mushroom ketchup and a few drops of sugar browning. Put it on the fire once more till very hot; arrange the chops neatly on a dish, pour the gravy over them, and serve. Haricot Beans (June 20th); Mashed Potatoes (May 12th); Roly-poly Pudding (August 18th); Cheese (June 8th).

Things that must not be Forgotten.
1. Turn and rub the beef in the brine.
2. Hang the scrag of mutton in a cool place.

April 14th.

Breakfast.	Luncheon.	Dinner.
Dried Sprats.	Liver and Bacon.	Fried Salmon Shad.
Corned Beef.	Fried Roly-poly.	Mutton, stewed with vegetables.
Hot Buttered Toast.		
Dry Toast.		Caper Sauce.
Brown and White Bread and Butter.		Boiled Potatoes.
		Guest's Pudding.
Milk Toast.		Cheese.

Marketing.
For the Day.—A pound and a half of Calf's Liver; half a pound of streaky Bacon, cut into rashers (January 3rd); a Salmon Shad, weighing about four pounds (March 17th); Potatoes; another Scrag of Mutton, if necessary.

For To-morrow.—A tin of Pilchards (January 23rd); Muffins (*see* Marketing, January 29th); Sea Biscuits.

BREAKFAST.—Dried Sprats (February 28th); Corned Beef bought yesterday; Milk Toast (June 17th).

LUNCHEON.—Liver and Bacon (January 17th); Roly-poly, sliced (March 6th).

DINNER.—Fried Salmon Shad (March 17th). *Scrag of Mutton, Stewed with Vegetables* (February 10th).—If liked, to make variety, the meat can be taken up when done enough, brushed over with yolk of egg, have bread raspings sprinkled over it, and be browned in a Dutch oven before the fire, then served as before. Caper Sauce (March 19th); Boiled Potatoes (April 7th). *Guest's Pudding.*—Take eight ounces of bread-crumbs that have been passed through a wire sieve. Put half of these into a bowl, and pour upon them half a pint of boiling milk. Lay a plate on the top, and let them soak for a while; then add the remainder of the bread-crumbs, three ounces of crushed ratafias, four ounces of moist sugar, four ounces of chopped candied-peel, four ounces of chopped suet, the grated rind of a fresh lemon, a pinch of salt, and a tea-spoonful of baking powder. Mix the dry ingredients thoroughly, then add four eggs, one at a time, and stir the mixture well. Pour the preparation into a buttered mould, lay a buttered paper on the top, and steam for two hours. (*See* Treacle Pudding, March 28th.) Let the pudding stand a minute or two, turn it out carefully, and serve with sweet sauce. If liked, half a pound of stale bread can be used instead of fresh bread-crumbs; but if this were done, the bread would need to be beaten well with a fork after soaking, and any lumps there might be would have to be taken away. Also, for economy's sake, two eggs and a little more milk might be used instead of four eggs. Cheese (June 8th).

Things that must not be Forgotten.

1. Turn and rub the beef in the brine.
2. Take care of any little remnants of bacon there may be. They can be used for luncheon to-morrow.
3. If supper is taken, it will be well to substitute Australian meat for liver and bacon, as the latter would be rather indigestible taken at night.
4. Put a cupful of green lentils to soak in plenty of cold water.

April 15th.

Breakfast.	Luncheon.	Dinner.
Pilchards.	Baked Mackerel.	Lentil Soup.
Corned Beef.	Macaroni and Bacon.	Top side of the Round of Beef.
Muffins.		Yorkshire Pudding.
Dry Toast.		Mashed Potatoes.
Brown and White Bread and Butter.		Seakale.
Biscuits and Milk.		Lèche Crème.
		Cheese.

Marketing.

For the Day.—Three moderate-sized Mackerel (April 4th); half a pound of Macaroni; the top side of the Round of Beef; eight ounces of Ratafias; two pennyworth of Parsley; Potatoes, Seakale.

For To-morrow.—Six or eight small Soles, Slips (January 3rd); two Sheep's Kidneys, to be stewed with the pork kidney; a Loin of Pork, weighing about five pounds. The butcher should be asked to joint it and score it as if it were to be cooked directly; Muffins.

BREAKFAST.—Pilchards (January 23rd); Curried Beef bought April 13th; Muffins (January 30th); Biscuits and Milk (June 14th).

LUNCHEON.—*Baked Mackerel.*—Wash the mackerel in cold water, cut off the tails and heads, and open the fish down the back. Wipe them inside and out with a soft cloth, and lay them open, skin downwards, in a well-greased baking-tin. Sprinkle salt and pepper on them, squeeze a little lemon-juice over, and cover them with a piece of well-greased kitchen paper to keep them from burning. Bake in a moderate oven for about twenty minutes or till done enough. Have ready two ounces of maître d'hôtel butter; spread a portion of this upon each fish, and serve. Mackerel cooked thus is excellent, and is very quickly and easily prepared. *To make Maître d'Hôtel Butter,* pick some parsley from the stems, wash it, and chop it finely. After chopping it, wash it a second time, by putting it in a corner of a cloth, dipping it in cold water, and wringing it dry. This second washing takes away the acrid taste which is so objectionable in uncooked parsley. Put the parsley on a plate with its bulk in fresh butter, a little pepper and salt, and a few drops of lemon-juice. Work the ingredients together with the point of a knife till the mixture is smooth and of the consistency of very thick cream, when it is ready for use. If the butter is made a little time before it is wanted, keep it in a cool place, as, if melted, it would turn oily and be spoilt. Macaroni and Bacon (January 27th), made of remains of bacon.

DINNER.—Lentil Soup (April 1st); Roast Beef (March 4th or March 8th); Yorkshire Pudding (November 26th); Seakale (June 14th); Mashed Potatoes, moulded (October 23rd); Lèche Crème (May 7th); Cheese (June 8th).

Things that must not be Forgotten.

1. Turn and rub the beef in the brine.

2. It was recommended on the 13th of March that a small Canadian ham should be procured. If this were done, and if it has been used since, it is probable that now it will be nearly finished. Instead of keeping it longer and allowing it to deteriorate in quality, it will be best to make *Potted Ham* of what is left. Cut off all the meat and weigh it, and for every pound of lean take a quarter of a pound of fat. Mince it finely, or, if practicable, pass it through a sausage machine, and put half a salt-spoonful of cayenne, a quarter of a nutmeg grated, and a pinch of pounded mace with each pound and a half of meat. Mix the ingredients thoroughly, press the mince into a dish, and lay a greased paper on the top. Bake it for about twenty-five minutes, put it into small potting jars, in which it can be served, press it down very closely, and cover the top with a layer of melted lard. Store in a cool place. The ham will keep good for months. The ham bone will be a very valuable addition to the stock-pot.

3. Make custard blancmange for dinner to-morrow. If this is inconvenient, the blancmange can be made first thing in the morning. It will set at this time of the year if it is poured into very small moulds (August 4th).

4. Make a pickle with a quart of vinegar, a quart of cold water, and thirty peppercorns. Tarragon vinegar is to be preferred, or a portion of tarragon vinegar mixed with plain vinegar may be used. Rub the pickling pan quickly across with garlic, rub the pork with powdered sage, and lay the meat in the pickle. Add three fresh sage leaves, and leave it for three days, turning and rubbing it every day. The kidney may be taken out and stewed for breakfast to-morrow.

April 16th.

Breakfast.	Luncheon.	Dinner.
Baked Slips.	Devilled Eggs.	Skate au Beurre Noir.
Stewed Kidney.	Boiled Rice.	Cold Beef.
Muffins.		Salad.
Dry Toast.		Potato Mould
Brown and White Bread and Butter.		Custard Blancmange, with Lemon Syrup.
Marmalade.		Cheese.
Corn Flour Milk.		

Marketing.

For the Day.—Two pounds of Skate (January 10th); two heads of Lettuce; twopennyworth of small Salad; a half-pennyworth of boiled Beetroot; one pennyworth of Watercress; Potatoes.

For To-morrow.—A Cow-heel for luncheon; Gorgona Anchovies will be wanted for breakfast; Rolls (September 4th).

BREAKFAST.—Baked Slips (January 7th). *Mutton or Pork Kidneys Stewed.* — Skin the kidneys, and without cutting them take out the fat, then cut them, the round way, into slices the thickness of a penny piece. Mix in a plate two tea-spoonfuls of chopped parsley, half a tea-spoonful of powdered thyme, and a little salt, pepper, and cayenne. Sprinkle this mixture over the sliced kidneys. Melt two ounces of butter in a pan, put in the kidneys, and let them brown quickly on both sides. Dredge a table-spoonful of flour over them, and hold them over the fire for a minute or two, shaking them well to keep them from burning. Pour on a quarter of a pint of stock, and add the juice of half a lemon and a table-spoonful of mushroom ketchup. Bring the liquor to the point of boiling, arrange the slices of kidney on a dish, let the gravy boil for one minute, then pour it over them. If liked, toasted sippets may be put round the dish. Muffins (January 30th); Corn Flour Milk (June 19th).

LUNCHEON.—Devilled Eggs (February 27th); Boiled Rice (February 3rd).

DINNER.—Skate au Beurre Noir (February 12th); Beef, served yesterday; Salad (March 13th); Potato Mould (October 23rd); Custard Blancmange (August 4th); Cheese (June 8th).

Things that must not be Forgotten.

1. Turn and rub the beef in the brine.
2. Turn and rub the pork in the pickle.
3. Preserve half of the small salad and half of the watercress bought with the salad for breakfast to-morrow. Cleanse it overnight, and lay it on a cloth to drain.
4. Fillet the anchovies for breakfast to-morrow (January 18th), and put the fillets between two dishes.

April 17th.

Breakfast.	Luncheon.	Dinner.
Anchovies, with Hard-boiled Eggs.	Cow-heel, with Parsley Sauce.	Milk Soup.
Potted Ham.	Apple Balls.	Beef, with Acid Sauce.
Hot Rolls.		Turnip-tops.
Dry Toast.		Potatoes.
Watercress.		Cottage Plum Pudding.
Brown and White Bread and Butter.		Cheese.
Porridge.		

Marketing.

For the Day.—Six or eight baking Apples; Turnip-tops; Potatoes; German Yeast.
For To-morrow.—Dried Haddock; one tin of Collared Tongue.

BREAKFAST.—Anchovies, with hard-boiled Eggs (January 18th); Potted Ham, made April 15th; Rolls (September 4th); Porridge (January 25th).

LUNCHEON.—Cow-heel, with Parsley Sauce (February 20th); Apple Balls (March 7th).

DINNER.—Milk Soup (January 3rd); Beef, with Acid Sauce (December 4th); Turnip-tops (*see* Cabbage, June 4th); Mashed Potatoes (May 12th); Cottage Plum Pudding (June 6th); Cheese (June 8th).

Things that must not be Forgotten.

1. Turn and rub the beef in the brine.
2. Turn and rub the pork in the pickle.
3. Wash a pound of prunes, and put them to soak in plenty of cold water.
4. Pastry is to be made. Apple balls (March 7th); for luncheon to-day, minced meat tart (made of the broken remnants of beef) for luncheon to-morrow (*see* Mutton Tart, January 10th), rhubarb pie (August 7th), jam turnovers (September 25th); also make Annie's cake (September 25th) and Sally Lunns (August 26th). The kinds of pastry most frequently used in domestic cookery are—1, Puff Paste (April 24th); 2, Short Paste (June 19th); and 3, Suet Crust, for boiled puddings and dumplings (June 25th). The first of these is the most

difficult to make. It is suited for superior pastry of all kinds, vol-au-vents, patties, tarts, meat pies, &c. Short Crust is employed principally for fruit pies and tartlets. There is a variety named Rough Puff (May 29th), which is easier to make than real Puff Paste, and another variety named Flaky Crust (August 7th), excellent for pies and tarts. An attempt will be made in this book to describe clearly the method of making all these pastes. Fine wheat flour should always be employed in making pastry, and for Puff Paste and the best Short Crust it will be advisable to use Vienna flour for the purpose. This flour is expensive, and it is also difficult to obtain genuine in country places ; but it is so very superior to even the best English flour, and, moreover, it rises so well and is so fine and white, that it is not to be compared with any other. Butter, too, if it is used at all in making pastry, should be good and sweet, for nothing imparts its own unpleasant taste to everything it comes near more decidedly than common butter. Salt butter is not objectionable if it is well washed before it is used, then squeezed in a cloth to free it from moisture. Slightly rancid butter may be washed first in new milk, and afterwards in cold water, to sweeten it. The way to wash butter is to knead it with the hands in the cold fluid, very much as bread is kneaded. Good beef dripping, clarified (Note 5, February 19th), makes very good Short Crust for common use, especially if a little baking powder is put with it. Soft dripping is, of course, to be preferred, such as is obtained from roasted joints or that made by rendering down soft fat, as the twist from the top side of the round or ox flare. Mutton dripping is not to be recommended for making pastry, although hard mutton fat is almost as good as suet for making puddings and boiled paste. A small portion of good firm lard mixed with either butter or dripping is very much liked by some cooks; this, however, is a matter of taste.

5. Put a cupful of green lentils to soak all night in cold water.

April 18th.

Breakfast.	Luncheon.	Dinner.
Dried Haddock.	Minced Meat Tart.	Potato Purée.
Collared Tongue.	Stewed Prunes.	Pork, German way of cook-
Sally Lunns.		ing, to imitate Wild Boar.
Dry Toast.		Lentils.
Brown and White Bread		Potatoes.
and Butter.		Hydropathic Pudding (made
Marmalade.		of bottled red currants).
Bread and Milk.		Cheese.

Marketing.

For the Day.—Potatoes ; Bottled Fruit ; one pennyworth of Parsley.

For To-morrow.—Half or the whole, according to the size, of a Calf's Head. It may be either with or without the skin ; it is more expensive and better with the skin. The butcher should be asked to prepare it for boiling. Half a dozen small Mackerel (April 4th); three or four pounds of Gammon of Bacon; Sardines (January 12th); a tin of Salmon; a tin of preserved Pineapple; two Lettuces; a pennyworth of small Salad; a pennyworth of Beetroot; two pennyworth of Watercress (half for breakfast); Potatoes, Greens. If it may be permitted, order three pennyworth of Cream, to be served with the rhubarb tart to-morrow evening.

BREAKFAST.—Dried Haddock (January 27th); Collared Tongue (January 2nd); Sally Lunns, served like Teacakes (February 14th); Bread and Milk (January 25th).

LUNCHEON.—Minced Meat Tart, made yesterday; Stewed Prunes (February 27th).

DINNER.—Potato Purée (January 26th). *Pork, German fashion.*—Take the pork out of the pickle, rub it over once more with powdered sage, cover the skin with greased kitchen paper, and roast or bake it in the usual way (March 4th or March 8th). Baste it with the pickle in which it was soaked. For sauce, take a cupful of the pickle, and make it hot in a saucepan; throw a good-sized lump of sugar into it, thicken with flour and butter, and add a few drops of sugar browning and a glassful of red wine. In cooking, allow twenty minutes for each pound of meat. Lentils (March 2nd, the second method); Potatoes, browned in a mould (October 23rd); Hydropathic Pudding (June 16th); Cheese (June 8th).

Things that must not be Forgotten.

1. Turn and rub the beef in the brine.
2. As soon as the calf's head is delivered, take out the brains, and throw them into cold water until wanted.
3. To save trouble on Sunday evening, make a little Mayonnaise sauce, put it into a bottle, and cork it closely (August 30th).
4. Pickle half a dozen small mackerel (August 28th).

Sunday, April 19th.

Breakfast.	Dinner.	Tea.	Supper.
Sardines.	Milk Soup.	Brown and White Bread and Butter.	Salmon Salad (made of tinned salmon).
Cold Pork.	Calf's Head.	Dry Toast.	Rhubarb Tart.
Brawn Sauce.	Boiled Bacon.	Strawberry Jam.	Cream.
Sally Lunns.	Greens.	Annie's Cake.	Cheese.
Dry Toast.	Potato Snow.		
Watercress.	Tinned Pineapple.		
Brown and White Bread and Butter.	Custard.		
Milk Toast.	Cheese.		

BREAKFAST.—Sardines (January 12th); Pork left yesterday. Brawn Sauce (January 15th); Sally Lunns (August 26th); Milk Toast (June 17th).

DINNER.—Milk Soup (January 3rd). *Calf's Head.*—Take out the tongue, and if the head is not already perfectly cleansed wash it thoroughly. Put it into boiling water for ten minutes to blanch it; take it up, put it into a stewpan with cold water to cover it, and bring it to the boil; skim the liquor carefully, draw the pan back, and simmer the head gently till it is done enough. It will take from two hours and a half to three hours, according to its size, and it will require boiling half an hour longer with the skin on than without it. Remove the skin and fibres which hang about the brains, drain away the water, and put them into a stewpan with water to which a table-spoonful of vinegar has been added. Skim the liquor carefully, and boil for a quarter of an hour. Boil the tongue with the head (it should be put into the water three-quarters of an hour before the head is taken up), and when done enough trim and skin it. A short time before the head is to be served, chop the brains rather coarsely, put them into a saucepan, with half a cupful of good melted butter, a table-spoonful of chopped parsley, and three powdered sage leaves, if liked. Add pepper and salt to taste, and a few drops of lemon-juice, and simmer gently for a few minutes. Put the tongue, skinned, in the middle of a hot dish, pour the brain sauce round, and serve. Dish the head on a separate dish, and garnish with cut lemon and parsley, or with sprigs of boiled broccoli round it. Send parsley sauce to table in a tureen, and serve ham, bacon, or pickled pork as an accompaniment. Boiled Bacon (March 30th); Greens (June 4th); Potato Snow (April 7th); tinned Pineapple (April 8th); Custard (August 10th); Cheese (June 8th).

TEA.—Annie's Cake (September 25th).

SUPPER.—*Salmon Salad* (see Mayonnaise of Salmon, May 24th); Rhubarb Tart (August 7th).

Things that must not be Forgotten.

1. Turn and rub the beef in the brine.
2. Preserve the liquor the calf's head was boiled in.
3. Preserve also the liquor in which the bacon was boiled.
4. Put a breakfast-cupful of split peas to soak all night in cold water.
5. Turn the mackerel in the vinegar.

April 20th.

Breakfast.	Luncheon.	Dinner.
Pickled Mackerel.	Minced Pork.	Pease Soup.
Bacon made hot.	Jam Turnovers.	Calf's Head, Hashed.
Sally Lunns.		Boiled Bacon.
Dry Toast.		White Broccoli.
Brown and White Bread and Butter.		Potatoes.
Marmalade.		Semolina Pudding.
Corn Flour Milk.		Cheese.

Marketing.

For the Day.—A pound of Apples; White Broccoli; Potatoes.

BREAKFAST.—Pickled Mackerel (August 28th); Bacon left yesterday, made hot (February 26th); Sally Lunns (June 4th); Corn Flour Milk (June 19th).

LUNCHEON.—*Minced Pork.*—Carefully cut away every particle of meat from the leg of pork, mince it finely, take away all the fat and skin, and weigh it. Rub a stewpan quickly across with garlic, melt a slice of butter in it, and, supposing there is one pound of meat, put in four apples and four onions that have been pared, cored, and chopped small. Stir them over a gentle fire for a minute or two, then add a gill of the gravy left from the pork, or, if there is none of this, substitute two table-spoonfuls of the liquor the calf's head was boiled in and a table-spoonful of vinegar. Season the minced pork with salt and pepper, and, supposing there is one pound of meat, add a spoonful of mustard and a dessert-spoonful of flour. Stir the mince into the sauce, and let it simmer gently till it is heated throughout, but it must not boil. Serve with toasted sippets round the dish. Jam Turnovers (September 25th).

DINNER.—*Pease Soup.*—Follow in all respects the directions given (April 1st) for making Lentil Soup, remembering only that the browning will not be required. The soup may be made of a mixture of the calf's head liquor and the bacon liquor. It will be found that this stock is very greasy, therefore it will be well, after skimming away the fat that has risen to the surface, to simmer the stock for awhile by the side of the fire to make it throw up the grease, and then to skim this away as it rises. *Calf's Head, Hashed.*—Cut the remains of the calf's head into neat pieces convenient for serving. Season these lightly with pepper, salt, and cayenne, flavour them with a pinch of grated lemon-rind, and dredge them well with flour. Supposing there is one pound of meat, take a pint of the liquor in which the head was boiled. Melt a slice of fresh butter in a stewpan, put in the meat, and shake it over the fire for a minute or two till the butter is absorbed. Add the liquor, a shallot finely minced, and a tea-spoonful of lemon-juice, and simmer all gently together for a quarter of an hour. The meat, of course, must not boil. Arrange the pieces of meat on a hot dish, pour the gravy over, and serve immediately. A glassful of sherry can be added, if liked. Boiled Bacon made hot (*see* Luncheon, February 26th); White Broccoli (April 25th); Potatoes (May 12th); Semolina Pudding (March 12th); Cheese (June 8th).

Things that must not be Forgotten.

1. Turn and rub the beef in the brine.
2. If there is still any calf's head left, make it into a mould for breakfast. *Calf's Head Mould.*—Cut the meat into small neat pieces. Make also a little clear savoury jelly. Soak a plain mould in cold water, put a little of the jelly into it, and let it stiffen. Arrange the pieces of meat in it, and to improve the appearance of the dish mix with the meat something that contrasts in colour,

such as sprigs of parsley, hard-boiled eggs cut into rings or slices of pink ham. Leave a space between the ingredients so that the jelly can run between them. Almost fill the mould with meat, pour in the jelly and set the mould in a cold place. When wanted, turn it out, and garnish it with parsley. It will be a very good breakfast dish. When there is no cold calf's head Australian cooked meat can be used as a substitute. To make the clear savoury jelly see November 14th.

3. When making the soup, remember to leave a little of the liquor for the hash and the calf's head mould.

April 21st.

Breakfast.	Luncheon.	Dinner.
Calf's Head Mould.	Collared Tongue.	Fried Plaice.
Ham Toast.	Macaroni Cheese.	Dutch Sauce.
Hot Buttered Toast.		Boiled Beef.
Dry Toast.		Carrots.
Marmalade.		Mashed Parsnips.
Brown Bread and Butter.		Potatoes.
Porridge.		Brown Bread and Butter Pudding.
		Cheese.

Marketing.

For the Day.—Half a pound of Macaroni; a thick Plaice (January 3rd). Although plaice may be had almost all the year, it is at its best from now to the end of September. It is a cheap fish and but lightly esteemed; indeed, a great culinary authority has said that the worst cookery could do plaice no wrong, and the best could not do it good. It must be acknowledged that small plaice does not form a very appetising dish, but the same cannot be said of thick plaice. Cooked according to the recipe given below it is excellent; and if a little Dutch sauce may be allowed also it is almost sure to meet with approval. Carrots; Parsnips; two or three pounds of the belly piece of Pork.

For To-morrow.—Half a bundle of Rhubarb; Mustard and Cress. Order, to be sent to-morrow, from three to four pounds of a loin of Mutton; the best end to be preferred (January 3rd). The butcher should be asked to bone the joint. Sea Biscuits.

BREAKFAST.—Calf's Head Mould, made yesterday; Ham Toast, made of remains of boiled bacon (March 28th); Porridge (January 25th).

LUNCHEON.—Collared Tongue left from Saturday; Macaroni Cheese (March 20th).

DINNER.—*Fried Plaice.*—Fillet the plaice. If asked, the fishmonger will do this, or if there is any difficulty about it, do not try to skin the fish, but in all else proceed according to the directions given for filleting soles (January 4th). Cut the fillets into neat pieces about two inches wide, dry them well by laying them in a cloth for a while, then roll them in flour. Fry them in plenty of hot fat (January 13th and March 24th) till they are brightly browned all over, drain them on kitchen paper, serve them piled on a dish covered with a fish paper, and garnish with fried parsley. Care must be taken that the pieces of fish do not touch each other whilst frying. If preferred, the plaice can be egged and breaded, or dipped in batter before being fried. Dutch Sauce (May 14th). *Boiled Beef.* —Take the beef out of the brine, wash it quickly in cold water or wipe it with a cloth, and boil it (February 23rd). Carrots (July 6th); Mashed Parsnips (September 30th); Potatoes (April 7th); Brown Bread and Butter Pudding (July 20th); Cheese (June 8th).

Things that must not be Forgotten.
1. Boil the brine and scald the pan.
2. Make the rhubarb mould for dinner to-morrow (June 3rd).
3. Put the pork into the pickle. It will be ready for boiling April 25th. If preferred, a piece of pork can be bought on that day ready pickled.

April 22nd.

Breakfast.	Luncheon.	Dinner.
Boiled Eggs.	Cold Beef.	Scallops.
Potted Ham.	Salad.	Rolled Loin of Mutton.
Mustard and Cress.	Plain Rice Pudding.	Browned Potatoes.
Hot Buttered Toast.		Turnip-tops.
Dry Toast.		Rhubarb Mould.
Brown and White Bread and Butter.		Custard.
Biscuits and Milk.		Cheese.

Marketing.

For the Day.—Two heads of Lettuce; a pennyworth of Endive; a pennyworth of Beetroot; two pennyworth of Watercress (half for breakfast to-morrow); Scallops (March 7th and January 3rd); Turnip-tops; Potatoes; a pennyworth of Parsley; a square piece of the thin Flank of Beef, weighing eight or ten pounds.

For To-morrow.—Bloaters (January 2nd); a quarter of a pound of Macaroni, if not in the house.

BREAKFAST.—Boiled Eggs (January 5th); Potted Ham made April 15th; Biscuits and Milk (June 14th).

LUNCHEON.—Beef boiled (April 21st); Salad (March 13th); Plain Rice Pudding (February 24th).

DINNER.—Scallops (Note 3, March 7th). *Rolled Loin of Mutton.* —Mince the fillet of mutton, and mix with it its bulk in finely-grated bread-crumbs, an ounce of mutton suet chopped, a shallot finely minced, a tea-spoonful of chopped parsley, a little pepper and salt, a grate of nutmeg and the same of lemon-rind, and enough egg to bind the mixture together. Spread the forcemeat equally over the inner side of the mutton, roll it neatly lengthwise, bind it tightly with tape, flour it well, and roast or bake it, as most convenient (March 4th or March 8th). Rub the inside of a saucepan lightly with garlic, put in the mutton bones, and add a shallot, a piece of carrot, a stick of celery or a pinch of celery seeds, and a pint of water or stock. Stew gently for a couple of hours. Strain the gravy, thicken it with flour, add a few drops of sugar browning, a tablespoonful of ketchup, and (if permitted) the same of port. Put the meat on a dish, pour the gravy round, and serve. A few glazed onions will be an excellent garnish for this dish (February 14th.) Browned Potatoes (October 18th); Turnip-tops (June 4th); Rhubarb Mould made yesterday; Custard (August 10th); Cheese (June 8th).

Things that must not be Forgotten.

1. Put the thin flank of beef into the brine.
2. Keep the bloaters on a separate dish and apart from everything else in the larder.
3. Turn and rub the pork in the pickle.

April 23rd.

Breakfast.	Luncheon.	Dinner.
Bloaters. Scalloped Eggs. Hot Buttered Toast. Dry Toast. Watercress. Brown and White Bread and Butter. Corn Flour Milk.	Bubble and Squeak. Jam and Bread Pudding, Economical.	Macaroni Soup. Rump Steak à la Béarnaise. Potatoes Soufflées. Wyvern Puddings. Cheese.

Marketing.

For the Day.—From three to three pounds and a half of Rump Steak (*see* Marketing, January 22nd). Potatoes.

For To-morrow.—Half a pint of forced Mushrooms; German Sausage for breakfast; one Ox-tail; the scrag of a whole Neck of Mutton (*see* Marketing, February 9th).

BREAKFAST.—Bloaters (January 3rd); Scalloped Eggs (January 28th); Corn Flour Milk (June 19th).

LUNCHEON.—Bubble and Squeak (January 22nd); Jam and Bread Pudding, Economical (February 23rd).

DINNER.—Macaroni Soup (February 26th); Broiled Steak à la Béarnaise (January 22nd); Sauce (March 23rd). *Potatoes Soufflées; Potato Chips.*—Take fine kidney potatoes, wash them, peel them, and cut them into slices as thick as a penny piece. As they are turned out of hand throw them into a bowl of cold water to free them from the potato-flour, which will be likely to prevent their being successfully fried. Half fill an iron saucepan with clarified dripping; put this on the fire. Drain the potatoes on a cloth, and when dry, put them, a few at once, into a wire basket. When the fat boils—that is, when it is still and a steam rises—put in the potatoes, and shake them to keep them from sticking together. Draw the saucepan back, and let them simmer for about five minutes, or until a little piece pressed between the finger and thumb feels quite tender. The fat will by this time have cooled considerably, therefore take the basket out, and make the fat boil again. Put the potatoes into it, draw it back once more, and in two minutes the slices will be ready, inflated, and of a beautiful golden brown colour. Dry them on paper, put them on a hot dish, sprinkle salt over them, and serve immediately. These are Potatoes Soufflées. For a change, they may be peeled round and round into ribbons before being immersed in the fat; then they will be Potato Chips. The French cut potatoes into plugs about two inches long and half an inch wide, and fry them as described above (*see* also Potatoes, Fried, February 2nd). Wyvern Puddings (May 9th); Cheese (June 8th).

Things that must not be Forgotten.

1. Carefully preserve any little pieces of rump steak that may be left. They can be made to-morrow into Cornish pasties (August 22nd) and beef patties.
2. Turn the beef and the pork in the brine.

April 24th.

Breakfast.	Luncheon.	Dinner.
Stewed Mushrooms on Toast. German Sausage. Dry Toast. Marmalade. Brown and White Bread and Butter. Bread and Milk.	Cornish Pasties. Preserved Tomatoes, with Gravy.	Ox-tail Soup. Scrag of Mutton, Stewed with Vegetables. Mashed Potatoes. Queen's Pudding. Cheese.

Marketing.

For the Day.—One two-pound tin of Preserved Tomatoes; a pennyworth of fresh German Yeast; about two-pennyworth of Ice from the fishmonger, if the weather is at all warm, for making puff paste. Carrots, Turnips, Potatoes.

For To-morrow.—One tin of Pilchards (January 23rd); one dressed Cow-heel from the tripe shop, for Beef à la Mode.

BREAKFAST.—Stewed Mushrooms on Toast (March 20th); German Sausage (June 6th); Bread and Milk (January 25th).

LUNCHEON.—Cornish Pasties, to be made with pastry to-day (August 22nd); Preserved Tomatoes, with Gravy (March 16th).

DINNER. — Ox-tail Soup (February 22nd); Scrag of Mutton, Stewed with Vegetables (February 10th); Mashed Potatoes (May 12th); Queen's Pudding (August 9th); Cheese (June 8th).

Things that must not be Forgotten.

1. Turn and rub the beef in the brine.
2. Pastry is to be made to-day: Cornish pasties (August 22nd)

L

and meat patties (July 17th) made of the remnants of steak (a few scraps will be all the meat required for these); red-currant pie, of bottled fruit (August 7th); lemon cheesecakes (August 18th); also teacakes (August 26th); and plain seed cake (August 14th) may be made. *To make Puff Paste.*—Choose the coolest part of the kitchen for making the pastry, and a few minutes before commencing wash the hands in hot water to cool them. If there is not a refrigerator in the house, have a basin filled with ice put ready in a cool part of the larder. In cold weather the ice may be dispensed with. Take equal weights of sweet butter and Vienna flour (for an ordinary pie, ten or twelve ounces of butter will be enough for one pound of flour).

PASTRY FOLDED OVER THE BUTTER.

Put the flour on a board, mix a little salt with it, and make it into a smooth paste with a few drops of lemon-juice and cold water. It must not be too stiff. Knead it well, and roll it about till it is like putty: this is to make it workable; then leave it for about five minutes. Squeeze the butter in a cloth till every drop of liquid is expelled from it. The butter should be very cold; but if the paste is made in winter, and the butter is hard, it may be worked till smooth. Press it with the knuckles to a square shape. Roll the paste out quite straight and one way till it is of such a size that when the butter is put upon it the four corners of the paste can be folded over to meet evenly and securely in the middle. Roll it once till it is about the third of an inch thick, and be careful to roll it straight, or when it is baked the flakes will be one-sided. It is to be *rolled*, not pushed, and care must be taken not to let the butter break through the paste. Shake a little flour over and under the paste when necessary; but do this very sparingly, or it will be mottled. Fold over one-third of the length, flatten this lightly with the rolling-pin, and fold the other third over the top. This operation is called *giving a turn*. Put the paste on ice, or, if this is not at hand, in a draught of

air, to cool it, for a quarter of an hour. Put it again on the board, with the rough edges towards the cook, and give it two turns : that is, roll it and turn it over twice. Then put it again upon ice, and repeat until it has had seven turns. Leave it on ice once more for a few minutes, roll it till it is a quarter of an inch thick, and it is ready for use. Paste prepared like this should puff up to at least five times its original height. In summer time the yolk of an egg may be mixed with the cold water to make the paste in the first instance, but in winter this may be dispensed with. It is easier to make puff paste on a marble slab than on a wooden board. It will be understood that in making puff paste the great object is to keep the butter and paste in separate layers, and it is for this that it is so necessary to cool the paste between the turns. When puff paste is intended for fruit tarts and cheesecakes, a little sifted white sugar can be added to the flour. (*See* Rough Puff, May 29th).

April 25th.

Breakfast.	Luncheon.	Dinner.
Pilchards.	Cauliflower au Gratin.	Baked Mackerel.
Beef Patties.	Baked Plum Pudding.	Beef à la Mode.
Toasted Teacakes.		Onions.
Dry Toast.		Potatoes.
Brown and White Bread and Butter.		Baked Batter, with Jam.
Porridge.		Cheese.

Marketing.

For the Day.—A good-sized Cauliflower. The true cauliflower is out of season just now, but white Broccoli, which is often called by the same name, will answer the purpose excellently. A quarter of a pound of Beef Suet. Two moderate-sized Mackerel; two pounds of tender lean Beef (February 14th); Onions; Potatoes; a pennyworth of Parsley.

For To-morrow.—A two-pound tin of Preserved Tomatoes; a pair of Prairie Birds (February 28th); half a pound of Rashers of Bacon, if not at hand; Potatoes; Asparagus. Anchovies and Olives will be needed; also materials for a salad—Lettuce, Watercress, Beet-root, &c.; a few Radishes and Watercress may be ordered for breakfast.

BREAKFAST.—Pilchards (January 23rd); Beef Patties made yesterday; Teacakes (February 14th); Porridge (January 25th).

LUNCHEON.—*Cauliflower and Broccoli, To Boil; Cauliflower au Gratin; Sauce Blanche.*—Boil a cauliflower in the usual way. To do this, sprinkle a little salt over it, pour cold water upon it to dislodge the insects, cut the ends of the stalks (the tops would be likely to discolour the vegetable), and remove any withered leaves there may be. Lay the cauliflower, head downwards, in salted water for an hour, wash it in two or three waters, and examine it carefully to be sure there are no insects in it. Have ready a large saucepan full of boiling water, throw a table-spoonful of salt into this, let it boil a minute, and skim it carefully. Unless this is done the cauliflower will be a bad colour. Put in the cauliflower head downwards, and if it should turn over in the water turn it back, and *do not put the lid on the saucepan.* Boil the vegetable gently till the centre of the flower is quite tender. It will take from fifteen to twenty-five minutes, according to the size. It will be necessary to turn it round and try it when it has been boiling a certain length of time, as this is the only way of determining whether or not it is done enough. If it is left till the stalks are tender the flower may be boiled too much. Take it up with a slice, and it is ready to serve. Melted butter in a tureen may be sent to table with it ; or when it is wanted very good, a little *Sauce Blanche* may be laid over it by table-spoonfuls to completely cover the flower. This is made as follows :—Melt an ounce of butter in a small stewpan, stir in three-quarters of an ounce of flour, and beat the mixture over the fire with the back of a wooden spoon till it is quite smooth and well cooked. The sauce will not oil if the flour and butter be well cooked together. Add gradually half a pint of cold water, and keep stirring till the sauce is smooth. Stir in a pinch of salt and the yolk of an egg, and the sauce is ready. For *Cauliflower au Gratin*, boil the cauliflower as above directed. Have ready two ounces of grated Parmesan. Mix in a stewpan half an ounce of butter and one ounce of flour; add gradually a quarter of a pint of cold water, and keep stirring till the sauce boils and thickens. Add a table-spoonful of cream, a little salt, and a small pinch of cayenne; take the sauce off the fire, and stir in one ounce of the grated cheese. Cut away the outside green leaves, and with a cloth squeeze the water from the cauliflower. Put it on a dish, lay the sauce upon it, sprinkle the rest of the cheese over it, and brown it before the fire. Serve very hot. The rind of cheese that has gone dry may be grated and used for this dish instead of Parmesan; indeed, it affords a very agreeable mode of using old pieces of cheese. Baked Plum Pudding (February 25th).

DINNER.—Baked Mackerel (April 15th); Beef à la Mode (February 14th); Onions, Glazed (February 14th); Potatoes (April 7th); Baked Batter Pudding, with Jam (February 5th); Cheese (June 8th).

Things that must not be Forgotten.

1. Turn the beef in the brine.
2. Boil the *Pickled Pork*. To do this, put it into a saucepan, cover it with cold water, and bring it gently to the boil. Draw the pan back, and simmer gently for about twenty minutes to the pound, or more if very thick. The skin should be left on, and the pork served without bread raspings.
3. Pluck the birds and cure the feathers (Note, February 28th).
4. Make the Mayonnaise and bottle it (August 30th), and fillet the anchovies for supper to-morrow night.
5. Make a mould of rice, and put it in a cool place (October 7th).

Sunday, April 26th.

Breakfast.	Dinner.	Tea.	Supper.
Pilchards.	Tomato Purée.	Brown and White Bread and Butter.	Italian Salad.
Pickled Pork.	Roast Prairie Hens.	Teacakes.	Red Currant Tart.
Teacakes.	Fried Bacon.	Apple Jelly.	A Mould of Rice.
Dry Toast.	New Potatoes.	Seed Cake.	Cheese.
Brown and White Bread and Butter.	Asparagus.	Lemon Cheesecakes.	
Radishes and Watercress.	Oiled Butter.		
Milk Toast.	General Favourite Pudding.		
	Cheese.		

BREAKFAST.—Pilchards (January 23rd); Pickled Pork, boiled yesterday; Teacakes (February 14th); Radishes and Watercress (March 12th); Milk Toast (June 17th).

DINNER.—Tomato Purée (March 11th); Roast Prairie Hens (March 1st); Fried Bacon (Kidneys and Bacon, January 2nd). New Potatoes (April 12th); Asparagus (June 14th); Oiled Butter (June 14th); General Favourite Pudding (May 17th); Cheese (June 8th).

TEA.—Teacakes (February 14th); Seed Cake (August 14th); Lemon Cheesecakes (August 18th).

SUPPER.—*Italian Salad.*—An Italian salad may be made at any time of the year of any vegetable that is in season, or a suitable mixture of cooked vegetable may be taken for it. If lettuces and endive are used for it, let them be dried perfectly before being used. Shred the lettuce finely, and toss it lightly with tarragon vinegar and salt. Place it on a dish that has been made as cool as possible, with a dozen filleted anchovies rolled in parsley and a tea-spoonful of capers. Just before serving toss the salad lightly with a quarter of a pint of mayonnaise (August 30th), garnish with boiled beet-root cut into strips and four hard-boiled eggs cut into quarters. Crown the whole with stoned olives, and serve. Red Currant Pie (August 7th); Rice Mould (October 7th).

Things that must not be Forgotten.

1. Turn the beef in the brine.
2. If the legs of the birds are not wanted at dinner-time leave them untouched, and devil them for breakfast to-morrow (January 14th).
3. Asparagus is very good served by itself, when the meat is done with. If this plan is adopted, oiled butter (June 14th), or, better still, Dutch sauce (May 14th), should be served with it.

April 27th.

Breakfast.	Luncheon.	Dinner.
Devilled Drum-sticks. Pickled Pork. Teacakes. Dry Toast. Marmalade. Brown and White Bread and Butter. Bread and Milk.	Scalloped Oysters. Réchauffé of Rice Mould.	Game Soup. Beef Steak à l'Italienne Potatoes. Brown Bread and Butter Pudding. Cheese.

Marketing.

For the Day.—A tin of Preserved Oysters; a slice of tender Steak two inches thick, and weighing about three pounds (January 10th); Potatoes; Normandy Pippins.

For To-morrow.—A small tin of Corned Beef; a penny-worth of small Salad. Order a well-hung Shoulder of Mutton, to be sent to-morrow morning. Choose one that has not an undue proportion of fat. Muffins (January 29th).

BREAKFAST.—Devilled Drum-sticks (January 14th); Pickled Pork (Note 2, April 25th); Teacakes (February 14th); Bread and Milk (January 25th).

LUNCHEON. — *Scalloped Oysters.* — Open the tin, take out the oysters, put them on a dish in the oven, and let them get hot through. Strain the oyster liquor; melt one ounce of butter in a small stewpan, mix with it an ounce of flour, and work it to a smooth paste with the back of a wooden spoon. Add the oyster liquor and an equal measure of milk; stir the sauce till it boils and thickens. Season it with salt and cayenne, strain it over the oysters, and serve immediately. Send pepper and vinegar and a little brown bread and butter to table with this dish. *Réchauffé of Rice Mould.*—Beat up the rice with half a gill of milk, and add one beaten egg (or two eggs if a considerable portion of the rice were left), a spoonful of washed currants, and a little grated nutmeg. Press the rice into a mould, lay a buttered paper on the top, and steam it for an hour and a half (Treacle Pudding, March 28th). Serve with sweet sauce (July 19th).

DINNER.—Game Soup, made of the bones and trimmings of the prairie birds (February 16th); Beef Steak à l'Italienne (February 2nd); Potatoes, Steamed (May 6th); Brown Bread and Butter Pudding (July 20th); Cheese (June 8th).

Things that must not be Forgotten.

1. Turn and rub the beef in the brine.
2. Put half a pound of Normandy pippins to soak in cold water.
3. Carefully preserve any scraps of beef that may be left; shepherd's pie can be made of them for luncheon to-morrow (January 12th).
4. Wash a breakfast-cupful of haricot beans, and put them to soak in cold water. Throw away any that float.

April 28th.

Breakfast.	Luncheon.	Dinner.
Savoury Eggs.	Shepherd's Pie.	Haricot Purée.
Corned Beef.	Normandy Pippins, with Cold Milk.	Roast Shoulder of Mutton.
Muffins.		Browned Potatoes.
Dry Toast.		Seakale.
Small Salad.		Pancakes.
Brown and White Bread and Butter.		Cheese.
Corn Flour Milk.		

Marketing.

For the Day.—Potatoes and Sea-kale.
For To-morrow.—A tin of Mock-Turtle Soup; Watercress; Anchovies; Gooseberries.

BREAKFAST.—Savoury Eggs (January 1st); Corned Beef, bought April 27th; Muffins (January 30th); Corn Flour Milk (June 19th).

LUNCHEON.—*Shepherd's Pie* (January 12th). Normandy Pippins (August 16th).

DINNER.—Haricot Purée (March 9th); Roast Shoulder of Mutton (March 4th and December 16th); Browned Potatoes (October 18th); Seakale (June 14th); Pancakes (February 24th); Cheese (June 8th).

Things that must not be Forgotten.

1. Turn and rub the beef in the brine.
2. As soon as the mutton leaves the table put it upon a clean dish.
3. Fillet half a dozen anchovies, and lay them between two plates ready for to-morrow morning.

April 29th.

Breakfast.	Luncheon.	Dinner.
Mock-Woodcock.	Hashed Mutton.	Mock-Turtle Soup.
Corned Beef.	Hasty Pudding.	Veal and Ham Pie.
Watercress.		New Potatoes.
Hot Toast.		Macaroni Pudding.
Dry Toast.		Cheese.
Brown and White Bread and Butter.		
Gooseberry Fool.		

Marketing.

For the Day.—Two pounds of Veal from the best end of the neck or the breast, and six ounces of mild Ham cut very thin; if permitted, three or four Mushrooms will be an improvement to the pie; new Potatoes; six ounces of Macaroni; a pennyworth of Parsley; three or four fresh Mackerel (April 4th).
For To-morrow.—Three or four plump Sheep's Kidneys; a pennyworth of Radishes.

BREAKFAST.—Mock-Woodcock (March 26th); Corned Beef, bought April 27th. Gooseberry Fool (June 24th) to be taken with Bread and Butter.

LUNCHEON.—Hashed Mutton (May 18th); Hasty Pudding (March 30th).

DINNER.—Mock-Turtle Soup (March 15th). *Veal and Ham Pie.*—Cut the veal into slices the size of an oyster-shell and a quarter of an inch thick, and the ham into very thin rashers. Mix on a plate two tea-spoonfuls of salt, a tea-spoonful of white pepper, half a tea-spoonful of pounded mace, and half a tea-spoonful of grated lemon-rind. Fill the pie-dish with alternate layers of veal and ham, and sprinkle a portion of the seasoning over each layer of veal. Let ham form the uppermost layer. If it be allowed, put the yolks of three or four eggs, boiled hard, and four or five mushrooms between the layers. Pour a very little cold water over the meat, line the edges of the dish with pastry, cover with a good crust, ornament according to fancy, make a hole for the steam to escape, and bake in a good oven. The pie will be done enough in about two hours and a half. As soon as the crust is risen and set, a greased paper must be laid over the pie, and it must be put in the coolest part of the oven. If mushrooms and the yolks of eggs are allowed for this pie, Puff Paste (April 24th) will be the most suitable covering for it, or Rough Puff (May 29th) will answer excellently. For a plain family pie Short Crust (June 19th) will be sufficient. Boil the veal bones in slightly salted water for a couple of hours; pour the liquor out, and free it from fat; make it boiling hot, and just before the pie is to be served pour it in by means of a funnel. New Potatoes (April 12th); Macaroni Pudding (March 27th); Cheese (June 8th).

Things that must not be Forgotten.

1. Turn and rub the beef in the brine.
2. Pickle the mackerel bought to-day (August 28th).
3. Put a cupful of hominy to soak all night in cold water (February 10th).

April 30th.

Breakfast.	Luncheon.	Dinner.
Pickled Mackerel.	Remains of Veal and Ham Pie.	Vermicelli Soup.
Stewed Kidney.	Boiled Hominy.	Mutton Chops, with Piquante Sauce.
Radishes.		Mashed Potatoes.
Hot Buttered Toast.		Broccoli.
Dry Toast.		Treacle Pudding.
Brown and White Bread and Butter.		Cheese.
Milk Toast.		

Marketing.

For the Day.—About four pounds of the best end of a Loin of Mutton; Potatoes; Broccoli; a jar of Liebig's Extract of Meat. Neck of mutton cutlets are frequently objected to because they are so expensive; it will be found more profitable, therefore, to take them from the loin, and prepare

as recommended below. The butcher should be asked to cut off the top of the loin, to be stewed separately. A quarter of a pound of firm sweet Suet.
For To-morrow.—A slice of Ham from the middle of the leg; Watercress.

BREAKFAST.—Pickled Mackerel (August 28th); Stewed Kidney (April 16th); Milk Toast (June 17th).

LUNCHEON.—Veal and Ham Pie served yesterday; Boiled Hominy (February 11th).

DINNER.—*Vermicelli Soup.*—The stock for this soup may be made by stewing the bones of the shoulder of mutton with vegetables, and adding a little extract of meat to the liquor (March 22nd). *Mutton Cutlets, with Piquante Sauce.*—It is often found that when mutton chops are sent to table the piece of meat in the middle is eaten; the rest is wasted. To prevent this, cut the meat out with as much fat as is likely to be used in one piece. Divide it into cutlets half an inch thick. The fillet or undercut of the loin should be taken out first of all, and may be formed into separate cutlets. Beat an egg thoroughly, and mix with it a tea-spoonful of oil, a tea-spoonful of water, and a little pepper and salt. Have ready a tea-cupful of stale bread that has been rubbed through a wire sieve. Brush the cutlets over with the egg mixture, then cover them entirely with the bread-crumbs. Melt about an ounce of butter or clarified dripping in a frying-pan, lay in the cutlets, and pour two ounces of butter or fat over them. Cook them over a quick fire till done enough; they will take about seven minutes. When brown on one side turn them to the other. Lift them out carefully, of course remembering not to stick the fork into the lean part, and free them from fat by pressing them between two folds of kitchen paper. Have ready half a pint of piquante sauce (May 5th). Put some mashed potatoes (May 12th) in a mound in the middle of a hot dish, arrange the cutlets round it, and with a table-spoon lay the sauce upon them. Serve very hot. If preferred, the chops can be cooked as above after being cut from the loin in the usual way, but there is less waste attending this method. Broccoli (Cauliflower, To Boil, April 25th); Treacle Pudding (March 28th); Cheese (June 8th).

Things that must not be Forgotten.

1. Turn and rub the beef in the brine.
2. If any hominy were left, preserve it, to be fried for luncheon to-morrow.
3. Put a tea-cupful of green lentils to soak all night in cold water.
4. Stew the top of the loin of mutton, to be served at luncheon to-morrow (Luncheon, May 1st).

FRUITS IN SEASON SUITABLE FOR DESSERT IN APRIL.

Apples (Golden Knobs and Rennets), Oranges, Bananas, Grapes, Nuts, Almonds and Raisins, French Plums, Figs, Dates, Crystallised Fruits, Foreign Preserved Fruits.

DISHES FOR INVALIDS.

PLAIN DRINKS.

Toast Water.—This simple beverage is rarely well made. Take a slice of stale bread (crust is to be preferred, as the crumb will soon turn sour), toast it very slowly all through without burning it at all. Pour over it a quart of boiling water, and let it stand, covered, till cold. If liked, it may be flavoured with lemon-rind.

Rice Water.—Valuable in diarrhœa. Wash a quarter of a pound of best Carolina rice, put it in a saucepan with a quart of water, and let it boil for ten minutes. Strain it off and add more water, and repeat until there is no more goodness in the rice. The liquor is ready to drink when cold. If liked, an inch of stick cinnamon or a piece of ginger may be boiled with the rice, or if the patient be not feverish a little cream may be added. A pinch of salt is sometimes considered an improvement.

Barley Water.—Useful in colds, chest affections, hectic fever, and diseases of the bladder. There are two varieties—clear barley water and thick barley water. For *Clear Barley Water.*—Wash a table-spoonful of pearl barley in two or three waters, put with it two lumps of sugar, the thin rind of one lemon, and the juice of half a one. Pour on it a quart of boiling water, and let it stand for two hours or more. Strain and serve. If preferred, orange-rind and juice, currant jelly, or sliced liquorice can be used as a flavourer. *Thick Barley Water.*—Wash two ounces of barley, and put it in a stewpan with a quart of cold water. Boil gently for two hours. Strain it into a jug, put the thin rind of half a lemon with it, and let it go cold. Take out the lemon-rind, sweeten to taste, and serve.

Linseed Tea.—Used by patients suffering from diseases of the throat and chest, diarrhœa, dysentery, inflammation of the bowels, and inflammatory complaints. Take one ounce of linseed and half an ounce of sliced liquorice-root. Put these ingredients into a jug, pour over them a quart of boiling water, and place the vessel by the side of the fire for two or three hours. Strain through muslin, and take a couple of spoonfuls occasionally. Sliced lemon and sugar-candy may be added to improve the flavour.

Lemonade.—Pare off the yellow rind of a fresh lemon, and be careful not to take any of the thick white pith, as that would make the lemonade bitter. Put this into a jug with the strained juice of two lemons and about an ounce of loaf sugar. Pour over all a pint and a half of boiling water, and let this stand till cold. Strain the liquor, and it is ready for use.

May 1st.

Breakfast.	Luncheon.	Dinner.
Fried Ham. Fried Eggs. Watercress. Hot Buttered Toast. Dry Toast. Brown and White Bread and Butter. Porridge.	Top of the Loin of Mutton, Stewed, with Potatoes. Salad. Fried Hominy.	Stewed Eels. Rolled Ribs of Beef. Lentils. Steamed Potatoes. Lemon Pudding. Cheese.

Marketing.

For the Day.—Two pounds of Silver Eels (Marketing, January 24th); one or two ribs of Beef, boned and rolled. If asked to do so, the butcher will bone and roll the beef. Potatoes; ingredients for a small Salad; a pennyworth of fresh German Yeast; six ounces of Suet.

For To-morrow.—A tin of Sardines (January 12th); a tin of Potted Pheasant (*see* Remarks on Potted Grouse, January 7th); Preserved Oysters.

BREAKFAST.—Fried Ham (March 5th); Fried Eggs (March 5th); Porridge (January 25th).

LUNCHEON.—*Loin of Mutton, Stewed.*—Put the meat in a stewpan, fat downwards; cover the pan closely, and fry gently till the fat is considerably melted. Take up the meat and pour off the fat, and put a gill of cold water with it. Let it stand till cold, then take the fat from the top, and put the gravy that is under it back into the stewpan with the meat, a small onion finely minced, and a little pepper and salt. Stew gently for half an hour. Let the meat go cold, and serve with salad and pickles. Salad (March 13th); Fried Hominy (February 12th).

DINNER.—Stewed Eeels (January 24th); Rolled Ribs of Beef, Roasted (March 4th or March 8th); Lentils (March 2nd); Steamed Potatoes (May 6th); Lemon Pudding (August 12th); Cheese (June 8th).

Things that must not be Forgotten.

1. Boil the beef that has been in the brine (*see* February 23rd).
2. Boil the brine with an additional handful of salt, and scald the pan (January 13th).
3. Pastry is to be made to-day (April 17th): rhubarb pie (August 7th); jam turnovers (September 25th); baked custard (January 19th); also rice cake (August 2nd); and Vienna bread (August 26th).

May 2nd.

Breakfast.	Luncheon.	Dinner.
Sardines.	Mackerel au Gratin.	Milk Soup.
Potted Pheasant.	Suet Dumpling, with Jam.	Cold Beef.
Vienna Bread.		Salad.
Dry Toast.		Baked Potatoes.
Marmalade.		Pickles.
Brown and White Bread and Butter.		Cocoa-nut Pudding.
Bread and Milk		Cheese.

Marketing.

For the Day.—Two moderate-sized Mackerel (April 4th); half a pound of firm Beef Kidney Suet; two heads of Cabbage Lettuce; a pennyworth of small Salad; a half-pennyworth of boiled Beet-root; two-pennyworth of Watercress (half of the last is for breakfast to-morrow); a good-sized Cocoa-nut or a tin of Desiccated Cocoa-nut; Potatoes; a pennyworth of Parsley.

For To-morrow.—A pair of thick Soles (January 3rd); a Fore-quarter of Lamb; Asparagus; new Potatoes; Mint, for sauce; three-pennyworth of Cream, if permitted; either a small tin of Mushrooms or two good-sized Mushrooms.

For May 4th.—German Sausage.

BREAKFAST.—Sardines (January 12th); Potted Pheasant (*see* Remarks on Potted Grouse, January 7th); Vienna Bread (August 26th); Bread and Milk (January 25th).

LUNCHEON.—*Mackerel au Gratin.*—Wash the fish in cold water and wipe them in a cloth. Cut off the heads and tails and open them down the back. Lay the mackerel on a board and draw out the bones. Be careful also to remove the dark substance which lies close to the backbone near the head, as this often imparts a bitter taste to the fish. Wash and pick a bunch of parsley; chop it finely, fasten it in the corner of a cloth, dip it in cold water, and wring it dry. This second washing is intended to remove its acrid taste. Chop small a piece of onion the size of a large bean, mix it with the parsley, and add a dessert-spoonful of finely-grated bread-crumbs, a teaspoonful of mixed herbs—lemon, thyme, and marjoram—a little pepper and salt, and a few drops of lemon-juice. Sprinkle the mixture upon the inner part of one mackerel, and lay the other mackerel upon it. Put the fish thus placed one on the top of the other in a greased tin; lay small pieces of dripping here and there upon them, cover with a dish or greased paper, and bake in a moderate oven for half an hour. Baste occasionally with the dripping. Lift the fish carefully upon a hot dish and serve. Fresh herrings are very good dressed in this way. Suet Dumpling (May 13th).

DINNER.—Milk Soup (January 3rd); Cold Beef left from yesterday; Salad (March 13th); Baked Potatoes (May 4th); Cocoa-nut Pudding (August 8th); Cheese (June 8th).

Things that must not be Forgotten.

1. Reduce the liquor in which the beef was boiled and glaze the beef (March 21st).
2. Make rissoles for breakfast to-morrow of the cold beef left yesterday (January 6th).
3. Chop the mint and put sugar upon it for mint sauce (March 25th).

Sunday, May 3rd.

Breakfast.	Dinner.	Tea.	Supper.
Rissoles.	Sole au Gratin.	Vienna Bread.	Pressed Beef.
Potted Pheasant.	Fore - quarter of Lamb.	Brown and White Bread and Butter.	Potato Salad.
Vienna Bread.	Mint Sauce.	Rice Cake.	Rhubarb Tart.
Dry Toast.	New Potatoes.	Damson Jam.	Cheese.
Brown and White Bread and Butter.	Asparagus.		
Watercress.	Hayrick Puddings.		
Corn Flour Milk.	Cheese.		

BREAKFAST.—Rissoles (January 6th); Potted Pheasant (*see* Remarks on Potted Grouse, January 7th); Vienna Bread (August 26th); Corn Flour Milk (June 19th).

DINNER.—*Sole au Gratin.*—For a pair of soles mix on a plate a bunch of parsley washed in two waters (Mackerel au Gratin, May 2nd), half a shallot, and either eight small mushrooms or two large ones, all chopped small. Rub a slice of stale bread through a wire sieve, put the crumbs on a tin, and brown them in the oven. Wash the soles and dry them in a cloth. Cut off the outside fins with a sharp knife, nick through the skin across the head and tail, push the little finger up to loosen the skin, and draw it off on both sides. Grease a tin large enough to hold the fish side by side, sprinkle half the chopped mushroom on it, and add a little pepper and salt and a few drops of lemon-juice. Nick the soles in two or three places, and lay them, the nicked side uppermost, on the tin. Sprinkle the rest of the mixture upon them, with a little pepper and salt and a tea-spoonful of lemon-juice, and the browned bread-crumbs. Lay little pieces of butter here and there on the top, and pour over last of all a gill of strong stock that has been boiled till it is so much reduced that it will jelly when cold. Bake in a brisk oven for ten minutes or thereabout. When a steel knife will go easily through the thickest part of the fish they are done enough. Lift them carefully upon a clean hot dish, pour the sauce round, and serve. Fore-quarter of Lamb, Roasted (March 4th and April 12th); Mint Sauce (March 25th); New Potatoes (April 12th); Asparagus (June 14th); Hayrick Puddings (March 19th); Cheese (June 8th).

TEA.—Vienna Bread (August 26th); Rice Cake (August 2nd).

SUPPER.—Beef boiled May 1st; Potato Salad (April 12th); Rhubarb Tart (August 7th); Cheese (June 8th).

Things that must not be Forgotten.

1. If any new potatoes are left, excellent salad can be made by slicing them and tossing them up with the usual dressing.
2. If any asparagus is left, make it into asparagus toast for breakfast to-morrow.
3. As soon as the lamb comes from table lay it upon a clean dish.

May 4th.

Breakfast.	Luncheon.	Dinner.
German Sausage.	Pressed Beef.	Julienne, quickly made.
Asparagus, with Eggs.	Baked Potatoes.	Cold Lamb.
Vienna Bread.	Baked Custard.	Mint Sauce.
Dry Toast.		New Potatoes.
Brown and White Bread and Butter.		Golden Pudding.
Marmalade.		Cheese.
Milk Toast.		

Marketing.

For the Day.—One pound Kidney Suet for Puddings to-day and to-morrow; Old Potatoes and New Potatoes. If there is no Mint Sauce left, a pennyworth of Mint.

For To-morrow.—A quarter of a pound of streaky Bacon, in rashers; Radishes.

BREAKFAST.—German Sausage (June 6th). *Asparagus, with Eggs.*—Take the asparagus that is left, and cut all the green part into pieces the size of peas. Supposing there are a dozen heads of asparagus, melt an ounce of butter in a stewpan, put with it a tablespoonful of cream or milk, a table-spoonful of gravy, a little pepper and salt, and three well-beaten eggs. Throw in the asparagus, stir the eggs quickly over the fire for half a minute till they are set, pour the mixture upon a hot dish, garnish with toasted sippets, and serve very hot. Vienna Bread (August 26th); Milk Toast (June 17th).

LUNCHEON.—Pressed Beef boiled May 1st. *Baked Potatoes.*—Choose large potatoes, and as much of one size as possible. Wash them in lukewarm water, and scrub them till thoroughly clean. Dry them with a cloth, and put them in a moderately heated oven. Turn them about occasionally, and bake them until they are done enough, that is, until a skewer will pierce them easily. Press each one till it bursts slightly, as that will keep the potatoes from becoming heavy, and serve very hot on a dish covered with a napkin. They will take from one and a half to two and a half hours, according to their size and the heat of the oven. Baked Custard Tart (January 19th).

DINNER.—Julienne, quickly made (February 15th); Lamb served yesterday; Mint Sauce (March 25th); New Potatoes (April 12th). *Golden Pudding.*—Mix thoroughly together six ounces of finely-shred beef suet, a pinch of salt, half a pound of fine bread-crumbs, half a pound of marmalade. Add half a tea-spoonful of baking powder, two eggs, and as much milk as is needed to make a stiff paste. Put the mixture into a greased mould, lay a buttered paper on the top, and steam for four hours (March 28th). Let the pudding stand a minute or two, turn it upon a hot dish, and serve with sweet sauce. A little sherry is a very agreeable accompaniment. Cheese (June 8th).

Things that must not be Forgotten.

1. Lamb is so very delicious served cold that it seems a shame to warm it up in any way. Those, however, who object to cold meat may prefer (supposing there is any meat still left upon it) to have the bladebone devilled, grilled, and served with piquante sauce. For this it must be prepared over-night. Trim away the skin and fat, and score the meat deeply at half-inch distances. Supposing there is about a pound and a half of meat on the bone, make a hot mixture by working together with the point of a knife a slice of butter, two tea-spoonfuls of mixed mustard, a tea-spoonful of salt, and a salt-spoonful of cayenne. Rub this mixture into the scores. To-morrow all that will be necessary will be to lay the meat on a gridiron at a good height over a clear fire, and turn it frequently till it is hot through and a light brown colour. It will take about a quarter of an hour.

May 5th.

Breakfast.	Luncheon.	Dinner.
Toasted Bacon.	Stewed Cheese.	Milk Soup.
Pressed Beef.	Jam Turnovers.	Grilled Shoulder of Lamb.
Radishes.		Piquante Sauce.
Hot Buttered Toast.		Veal Rolls.
Dry Toast.		Spinach.
Brown and White Bread and Butter.		New Potatoes.
		Guests' Pudding.
Gooseberry Fool.		Cheese.

Marketing.

For the Day.—One pound and a half of lean Veal, from the fillet or loin. If there is no lamb left, more veal than this will be needed (February 25th). Spinach; New Potatoes; Broccoli; a quarter of a pound of Ratafias.

For To-morrow.—Half a pound of Forced Mushrooms.

BREAKFAST.—Toasted Bacon (January 19th); Beef boiled May 1st; Gooseberry Fool (June 24th).

LUNCHEON.—*Stewed Cheese.*—Cut a quarter of a pound of cheese into thin slices, and put it into a stewpan with as much ale as will barely cover it. Keep stirring it till it melts, then let it cool a minute, and stir in a spoonful of mustard and the yolk of one egg well beaten. Stir over the fire again for half a minute, pour the preparation upon a dish, stick three-cornered sippets of toast in the middle, and all round, and serve very hot. Jam Turnovers (September 25th).

DINNER.—Milk Soup (January 3rd); Grilled Shoulder of Lamb

(Note, May 4th). *Piquante Sauce.*—Make a quarter of a pint of good melted butter. Stir in half a tea-spoonful of anchovy sauce, and add a table-spoonful of vinegar, a dessert-spoonful of very finely chopped pickled gherkins, and the same of chopped capers, with a shallot finely chopped, if liked. Boil together, skim, and serve. *Veal Rolls.*—Cut the veal into thin slices, three or four inches long and two inches broad. Spread a little forcemeat (June 27th) over, roll each one neatly, and fasten it securely with twine. Melt a slice of butter in a stewpan, put in the rolls, and turn them about till they are browned all over. Barely cover them with stock or water, and simmer them very gently for an hour and a half. Thicken the gravy with bread-crumbs, arrange the rolls in a dish, strain the gravy over, and place round small tufts of broccoli, boiled and drained well. If convenient, sausage meat might be spread over the veal instead of forcemeat, and chopped parsley, shallot, allspice, pepper, and salt sprinkled over to flavour it. Spinach (May 10th); New Potatoes (April 12th); Guests' Pudding (April 14th). Cheese (June 8th).

Things that must not be Forgotten.

1. Broken remnants of cheese, if not too dry, can be stewed instead of fresh cheese.
2. Preserve the bacon-rind. It will be valuable for flavouring soups.

May 6th.

Breakfast.	Luncheon.	Dinner.
Mushroom Toast. Devilled Eggs. Watercress. Dry Toast. Brown and White Bread and Butter. Milk Porridge.	Croquettes (made of remnants of beef). Stewed Rhubarb.	Fried Plaice. Neck of Mutton, with Maitre d' Hôtel Sauce. Steamed Potatoes. Turnip-tops. Macaroni Pudding. Cheese.

Marketing.

For the Day.—A thick Plaice (April 21st); a Neck of Mutton, not too fat (February 5th); Potatoes; Turnip-tops; half a bundle of Rhubarb; two pennyworth of Parsley.
For To-morrow.—Bloaters (Note 2, January 2nd). Rolls (September 3rd).

BREAKFAST.—Mushroom Toast (March 20th); Devilled Eggs (February 27th); Milk Porridge (June 13th).
LUNCHEON.—Croquettes (*see* Rissoles, January 6th); Stewed Rhubarb (May 19th).
DINNER.—Fried Plaice (April 21st); Neck of Mutton, with Parsley Sauce (February 23rd). *Parsley Sauce,* called also *Maître d'Hôtel Sauce.*—Wash a sprig or two of parsley, pick the leaves from the stalk, and chop them very finely. Put the parsley in the corner of a cloth, dip it in water, and wring it dry. This second washing

M

takes away the acrid taste. Melt one ounce of butter in a small saucepan, stir in half an ounce of flour, and beat the mixture over the fire with the back of a wooden spoon till it is quite a smooth paste. Stir in gradually half a pint of cold water, and keep stirring till the sauce boils. Add a pinch of salt, and just before serving the sauce stir in the chopped parsley. *Steamed Potatoes.*—Old potatoes only can be steamed. Wash and scrub the potatoes, and, if liked, peel them. It is best, however, to steam them in their jackets, and peel them quickly when done enough. Fill the saucepan belonging to the steamer with water and put it on the fire. When the water boils put the potatoes in the steamer, sprinkle a little salt over them, put the lid down closely, and place the steamer over the hot water. In about half an hour try the potatoes. If a skewer can be easily pierced through them they are done enough. If they have been peeled before being steamed, shake the steamer to make the potatoes floury. If they have not been peeled, skin them quickly and serve. Turnip-tops (*see* Cabbage, June 4th); Macaroni Pudding (March 27th); Cheese (June 8th).

Things that must not be Forgotten.

1. Keep the bloaters apart from all other food.
2. Preserve the liquor in which the mutton was boiled; it can be used for the soup to-morrow.

May 7th.

Breakfast.	Luncheon	Dinner.
Bloaters.	Spicy Pie.	Mullagatawny Soup.
Buttered Eggs.	Semolina Mould.	Stewed Beef.
Rolls.		Mashed Potatoes.
Dry Toast.		Spring Cabbage.
Honey.		Leche Crème.
Brown and White Bread and Butter.		Cheese.
Porridge.		

Marketing.

For the Day.—Three pounds of tender Steak (Marketing, January 1st). It should be cut evenly, and about an inch and a half thick. Half a pound of Ratafias; Potatoes; Cabbage.

For To-morrow.—Dried Haddock; a pennyworth of Mustard and Cress; one four-pound tin of Australian Meat.

BREAKFAST.—Bloaters (January 3rd); Buttered Eggs (January 16th); Rolls (September 3rd); Porridge (January 25th).

LUNCHEON.—*Spicy Pie.*—Make a little plain pastry with three-quarters of a pound of flour, a pinch of salt, a quarter of a pound of clarified dripping, and half a tea-spoonful of baking-powder (Short Crust (June 19th). Cut the meat from the cold mutton, and keep the fat and lean separate. Throw the bones into the mutton liquor and stew them well to improve the stock. Mince the lean meat very finely, measure it; mix thoroughly with it its bulk in fat, chopped finely, stoned and dried currants, chopped raisins, chopped apples, and moist sugar. Season with salt and a very little grated nutmeg. Put the mixture into a pie-dish, cover with pastry in the usual way, and bake in a well-heated oven. Serve either hot or cold. Semolina Mould (July 23rd).

DINNER.—Mullagatawny Soup (January 16th); Stewed Steak (January 31st); Mashed Potatoes (May 12th); Spring Cabbage (June 4th.) *Lèche Crème.*—Put a pint and a quarter of milk into a stewpan with two table-spoonfuls of powdered sugar, a pinch of salt, and four drops of ratafia flavouring. Make it hot over the fire, but do not let it boil. Mix two table-spoonfuls of flour to a smooth paste with a quarter of a pint of milk, and add the well-beaten yolks of three and the white of one egg. Stir a little of the warm milk with the eggs; add the rest; gradually return the whole to the saucepan, and stir till the mixture begins to thicken. Pour it gently upon six ounces of ratafias which have been laid at the bottom of a shallow dish; arrange the remaining two ounces of ratafias on the top, and serve when cold. If liked, the yolks of two, instead of three, eggs can be used. Cheese (June 8th).

Things that must not be Forgotten.

1. There are sure to be a few scraps of meat left from the stew at dinner; make these into potted beef for breakfast (January 23rd).

2. Put a breakfast-cupful of white haricot beans to soak all night in cold water.

3. If convenient, make the custard blancmange for dinner to-morrow (August 4th).

4. The white of egg left from the Lèche Crème can be whisked to a firm froth and put into the sultana cake mixture to-morrow.

May 8th.

Breakfast.	Luncheon.	Dinner.
Dried Haddock.	Australian Meat, cold, with Pickles.	Fried Whiting.
Potted Beef.	Baked Potatoes.	Stewed Ox-tails.
Mustard and Cress.	Plain Rice Pudding.	Haricot Beans.
Hot Toast.		Boiled Potatoes.
Dry Toast.		Custard Blancmange.
Brown and White Bread and Butter.		Lemon Syrup.
Marmalade.		Cheese.
Bread and Milk		

Marketing.

For the Day.—Fresh Whiting, one for each person (January 3rd and 17th); two fine Ox-tails. The butcher should be asked to send these home ready jointed. Ox-tails may usually be bought at a cheaper rate in summer than in winter, because they will not keep so well. Three-quarters of a pound of Rump or Buttock Steak; four plump young Pigeons (January 24th); a Leg of Mutton; Potatoes.

BREAKFAST. — Dried Haddock (January 27th); Potted Beef (January 23rd); Bread and Milk (January 25th).

LUNCHEON.—Australian Meat, cold (February 4th); Baked Potatoes (May 4th); Plain Rice Pudding (February 24th).

DINNER.—Fried Whiting (January 17th). *Stewed Ox-tails.*—Wash the tails, divide them into joints, throw them into boiling water, and boil them for ten minutes. Drain them, and trim them neatly to make them look smooth and round. Put them into a stewpan with a carrot, an onion stuck with six cloves, a bunch of parsley, half a blade of mace, a few celery seeds tied in muslin, a dozen peppercorns, a spoonful of salt, and two quarts of stock or water. Let the liquor boil, skim it carefully, cover it closely, draw it to the side of the fire, and simmer gently for two hours, or till the pieces of tail are tender. Pour off the gravy, and put it into a basin surrounded with cold water, and remove the fat, which will rise to the surface. Take two good-sized carrots and two turnips, and cut them into neat shapes, balls or dice; prepare also eight moderate-sized onions. Strain the stock, put it with the vegetables into a stewpan, season it with pepper and salt, and boil all together till the vegetables are done enough. Put the pieces of tail into a clean stewpan, and place the turned and boiled vegetables with them. Skim the sauce, and if it is not sufficiently rich and thick boil it down quickly to reduce it, or, if preferred, thicken it with brown thickening. When it is quite ready, pour it over the ox-tail, simmer all together for ten minutes, and serve neatly arranged in a hot dish. In summer time, when ox-tails may frequently be had at a low rate, they are very good served with green peas (July 12th). For this they should be cooked as described above, then laid in a circle on a dish, the peas being placed in the centre. The gravy should then be boiled till very thick and poured round the base. For variety's sake, dressed spinach, French beans, or mixed vegetables may be substituted for the peas, or mushrooms may be boiled in the gravy. Haricot Beans (June 20th); Boiled Potatoes (April 12th); Custard Blancmange (August 4th); Lemon Syrup (March 19th); Cheese (June 8th).

Things that must not be Forgotten.

1. Carefully preserve any gravy that may be left from the ox-tail; it will be a valuable addition to the savoury hash to-morrow. If any pieces of ox-tail were left they may be breaded, and served at breakfast to-morrow.

2. Make the pickle for the sour mutton (March 19th), and put the leg of mutton into it.

3. Pastry is to be made to-day (April 17th); minced meat rolls, made of a portion of the Australian meat (*see* Sausage Rolls, (November 6th); pigeon pie, for dinner to-morrow (May 15th); plum pie of bottled fruit (August 7th); also milk rolls (August 26th); and sultana cake (August 2nd).

May 9th.

Breakfast.	Luncheon.	Dinner.
Ox-tail, Grilled, if any were left; if not, Savoury Eggs. Minced Meat Rolls. Dry Toast. Milk Rolls. Marmalade. Brown and White Bread and Butter. Porridge.	Savoury Hash of Australian Meat. Rice and Cheese.	Potato Purée. Pigeon Pie. Mashed Potatoes. Greens. Wyvern Puddings. Cheese.

Marketing.

For the Day.—Potatoes; Greens; a pennyworth of Parsley.
For To-morrow.—Half a pound of Bacon, in rashers; a pair of thick Soles (January 3rd); a fillet of Veal, weighing about eight pounds (February 25th and March 11th). See that the bone is sent with the veal. A good-sized tin of Sardines (January 12th); a pound of Swiss Roll; New Potatoes (two pounds more than are likely to be used at dinner); Spinach; a tin of Collared Tongue; Anchovies, Capers, and Gherkins will be wanted; Watercress.

BREAKFAST.—Savoury Eggs (January 1st); Minced Meat Rolls, Sausage Rolls (November 6th); Milk Rolls (August 26th); Porridge (January 25th).

LUNCHEON.—Savoury Hash of Australian Meat (February 5th); Rice and Cheese (February 18th).

DINNER.—Potato Purée (January 26th); Pigeon Pie (May 15th); Mashed Potatoes (May 12th); Greens (*see* Cabbage, June 4th). *Wyvern Puddings.*—Make some batter two or three hours before dinner-time (*see* Toad in the Hole, January 15th). Grease some patty-pans, pour a little of the batter into each, and bake in a quick oven. Turn the puddings out of the tins, put a little jam upon each one, and serve. When it is decided to have Yorkshire pudding as an accompaniment to roast meat, the batter may be baked in small tins like this instead of being cooked in the dripping-tin under the meat, and the puddings can then be neatly arranged round the joint. Cheese (June 8th).

Things that must not be Forgotten.

1. Put a cupful of hominy to soak all night in cold water.
2. In serving the sardines at breakfast to-morrow, remember to keep back four or six for the Russian salad at night.
3. If the mayonnaise made a fortnight ago were used entirely, make a little more and bottle it (August 30th).
4. If any pigeon pie were left, it will be excellent served at breakfast to-morrow instead of the collared tongue.
5. Make a ground rice mould (August 7th) for supper to-morrow evening.
6. Turn and rub the mutton in the pickle.
7. Stew the veal bone for white stock, to be used on May 11th.

Sunday, May 10th.

Breakfast.	Dinner.	Tea.	Supper.
Sardines.	Soles, Filleted and Rolled, with Brown Butter.	Brown and White Bread and Butter.	Russian Salad.
Collared Tongue.		Strawberry Jam.	Plum Pie.
Milk Rolls.		Sultana Cake.	Ground Rice Mould.
Dry Toast.	Roast Fillet of Veal.		Cheese.
Watercress.	Toasted Bacon.		
Brown and White Bread and Butter.	New Potatoes.		
Hominy.	Spinach.		
	Raspberry Sandwich Pudding.		
	Cheese.		

BREAKFAST.—Sardines (January 12th); Collared Tongue (January 2nd); Milk Rolls (August 26th); Hominy (February 11th).

DINNER.—Soles, Filleted and Rolled, with Brown Butter Sauce (March 1st and February 12th); Fillet of Veal (June 28th); Toasted Bacon (January 19th); New Potatoes (April 12th). *Spinach.*—Spinach sinks so much in boiling that it will require a good bowlful to make a dish. It needs to be washed in several waters, because, as it grows so near the ground, there is usually a good deal of grit in it. When it is being washed it should be lifted out of the water with the hands: by this means the grit sinks to the bottom of the pan. When thoroughly cleansed double each leaf together, and tear away the stalk and its continuation quite down the back of the leaf. Put the spinach with the water that clings to it into a large iron pan. Do not put on the lid, but keep stirring the spinach to prevent its burning. In a very short time it will have yielded sufficient water to do away with any fear of this. Let it boil quickly till tender; it will take from ten to fifteen minutes. Pour it into a colander and press the water from it with a vegetable presser or the back of a plate. Put it on a board and chop it as finely as possible, or, if it is wanted very good, rub it through a wire sieve. Melt an ounce of butter in a stewpan, add a little pepper and salt, a table-spoonful of cream, and the spinach, and keep stirring till thoroughly mixed and quite hot. Press the vegetable into a mould, turn upon a hot dish, and serve. If liked, poached eggs can be laid upon it and fried sippets served round it. Sometimes a tea-spoonful of flour is mixed smoothly with the butter before the cream is stirred in. Raspberry Sandwich Pudding (November 29th); Cheese (June 8th).

TEA.—Sultana Cake (August 2nd).

SUPPER.—Russian Salad (April 5th); Plum Pie (August 7th); Ground Rice Mould (August 7th).

Things that must not be Forgotten.

1. Preserve any hominy that may be left.
2. Turn and rub the mutton in the pickle.

May 11th.

Breakfast.	Luncheon.	Dinner.
Boiled Eggs.	Rice and Cheese.	Victoria Soup.
Collared Tongue.	Hasty Pudding.	Minced Veal.
Hot Buttered Toast.		Fried Bacon.
Dry Toast.		New Potatoes.
Honey.		Cottage Plum Pudding.
Brown and White Bread and Butter.		Cheese.
Fried Hominy.		

Marketing.

For the Day.—Six ounces of Bacon in rashers (January 3rd); Potatoes; six ounces of Suet.

For To-morrow.—A quarter of a pound of German Sausage; one Cow's Heel; Fillet of Beef (January 2nd).

BREAKFAST. — Boiled Eggs (January 5th); Collared Tongue (January 2nd); Fried Hominy (February 12th).

LUNCHEON.—Rice and Cheese (February 18th); Hasty Pudding (March 30th).

DINNER.—Victoria Soup (February 9th). *Minced Veal.*—Take the remains of the fillet of veal, trim away the skin and nearly all the fat; cut the meat into slices, then into strips, and then into very small squares. Do not, however, chop the meat. Mix with it a very small pinch of pounded mace and a grate or two of lemon-rind, and dredge flour thickly over it. Put the trimmings, skin, and bone into a saucepan with—supposing there is a pound and a half of meat—a pint and a half of the stock made from the veal bone, an inch of lemon-rind, two sprigs of parsley, and one of thyme. Cover closely, and stew gently for about an hour, till the gravy is strong and good. Let it go cold and free it from fat. Melt an ounce of butter in a stewpan, beat an ounce of flour smoothly with it, and add a quarter of a pint of the stock and the same of milk. Stir the sauce till it boils. Season it with salt and very slightly with pepper; a spoonful or two of cream may be added, and is a great improvement. Put in the mince and make it hot through, but on no account let it boil. Turn it upon a hot dish and surround it with toasted sippets. Send strips of bacon to table with it. If preferred, minced veal may be coloured brown with a little brown thickening. Fried Bacon (January 2nd, Bacon fried with Kidneys); New Potatoes (April 12th); Cottage Plum Pudding (June 6th); Cheese (June 8th).

Things that must not be Forgotten.

1. Turn the mutton in the pickle.
2. Put a cupful of haricot beans to soak all night in cold water.
3. Brush the beef lightly over with vinegar, sprinkle pepper and salt over it, and hang it in a cool airy place (January 2nd).

May 12th.

Breakfast.	Luncheon.	Dinner.
German Sausage.	Cow's Heel, with Parsley Sauce.	Haricot Purée.
Eggs, with Brown Butter.	Elegant Economist's Pudding.	Fillet of Beef.
Hot Buttered Toast.		Broccoli.
Dry Toast.		Mashed Potatoes.
Marmalade.		Brown Bread Pudding
Brown and White Bread and Butter.		Cheese.
Porridge.		

Marketing.

For the Day.—Broccoli ; Potatoes.
For To-morrow.—A Melton Mowbray Pork Pie ; Forced Mushrooms ; Watercress ; a two-pound tin of Tomatoes ; half a pound of good Kidney Suet.

BREAKFAST.—German Sausage (June 6th) ; Eggs, with Brown Butter (January 6th) ; Porridge (January 25th).

LUNCHEON.—Cow's Heel, with Parsley Sauce (February 20th). *Elegant Economist's Pudding.*—Cut the remains of the cottage plum pudding into neat slices and lay them in a buttered pie-dish, pressing them down to make them adhere. Make as much custard as will fill the dish ; let it go cold. Pour it upon the pudding ; cover the top with thin slices of pudding, and bake in a gentle oven. When the custard is set the pudding is done enough. It will take from half an hour to an hour, according to its size. The custard may be plain or rich, according to taste (August 10th).

DINNER.—Haricot Purée (March 9th) ; Fillet of Beef, Roasted (February 11th) ; Broccoli (Cauliflower, April 25th). *Mashed Potatoes.*—Boil or steam two pounds of potatoes, and when done enough rub them quickly through a wire sieve. Melt an ounce of butter in a stewpan, pour over it a quarter of a pint of milk, and add pepper and salt to taste. When the milk boils stir in the sifted potatoes, beat all briskly together over the fire for a minute or two, turn into a hot tureen, and serve. If liked, the potatoes can be pressed into a buttered mould, turned out in a shape, and browned before the fire or in a brisk oven. Late in the season, when old potatoes are full of eyes, to mash potatoes is to adopt one of the best methods of serving them (*see also* Potato Croquettes, November 4th). Brown Bread Pudding (July 20th) ; Cheese (June 8th).

Things that must not be Forgotten.

1. Turn the mutton in the pickle.
2. Preserve the liquor in which the cow's heel was boiled. It will make very good stock.

May 13th.

Breakfast.	Luncheon.	Dinner.
Pork Pie.	Cold Beef.	Tomato Purée.
Mushrooms on Toast.	Salad.	Leg of Lamb.
Watercress.	Suet Pudding, with Jam,	Mint Sauce.
Hot Buttered Toast.	Treacle, or Gravy.	New Potatoes.
Dry Toast.		Spinach.
Brown and White Bread and Butter.		Wyvern Puddings. Cheese.!
Corn Flour Milk.		

Marketing.

For the Day.—Two heads of Lettuce; a half-pennyworth of boiled Beetroot; a pennyworth of small Salad; a half-pennyworth of Spring Onions; a Leg of Lamb; New Potatoes; Spinach; a pennyworth of Parsley; Mint for Sauce.
For To-morrow.—A small tin of Corned Beef; half a pint of Shrimps; Radishes.

BREAKFAST.—Pork Pie bought yesterday; Mushrooms on Toast (March 20th); Corn Flour Milk (June 19th).

LUNCHEON.—Salad (March 13th). *Suet Pudding.*—Trim away all skin and fibre, and chop the suet as finely as possible. Put it into a basin, and with half a pound of suet mix thoroughly one pound of flour, a tea-spoonful of baking powder, and a pinch of salt. Add cold water to make a *stiff* paste. Wring a pudding-cloth out of boiling water, flour it well, and put the paste into it. Tie it securely with string, remembering to leave room for the pudding to swell, and plunge it into plenty of fast-boiling water. Boil for two hours, or longer if convenient. This pudding will be lighter if made with equal portions of stale bread-crumbs and flour rather than with flour alone. For the sake of variety, a little grated lemon-rind and the juice of a lemon or a little grated ginger may be put with it to flavour it.

DINNER.—Tomato Purée (March 11th); Leg of Lamb (March 4th); Mint Sauce (March 25th); New Potatoes (April 12th); Spinach (May 10th); Wyvern Puddings (May 9th); Cheese (June 8th).

Things that must not be Forgotten.

1. Turn and rub the mutton in the pickle.
2. It is a very great improvement to sauté new potatoes, and indeed almost all vegetables, before serving them. To do this, boil them in the usual way, melt a slice of butter in a saucepan, and toss the potatoes in it.
3. Pot the shrimps for breakfast to-morrow (November 12th).

May 14th.

Breakfast.	Luncheon.	Dinner.
Potted Shrimps.	Minced Lamb.	Fried Plaice.
Corned Beef.	Plain Rice Pudding.	Dutch Sauce.
Radishes.		Broiled Steak, with Maitre
Hot Buttered Toast.		d'Hôtel Butter.
Dry Toast.		Potato Snow.
Brown and White Bread		Semolina Pudding.
and Butter.		Cheese.
Bread and Milk.		

Marketing.

For the Day.—A thick Plaice (April 21st); a slice of Rump Steak, weighing from three to three pounds and a half (*see* Marketing, January 22nd); Potatoes.
For To-morrow.—Four plump young Pigeons; a quart of Gooseberries.

BREAKFAST.—Corned Beef bought yesterday; Shrimps (November 12th); Bread and Milk (January 25th).

LUNCHEON—*Minced Lamb.*—Cut the meat off the bone and weigh it. Break up the bone, and stew it with an onion and a piece of carrot till a strong gravy is obtained. Supposing there is a pound of meat, mix with it a tea-spoonful of salt, half a tea-spoonful of white pepper, a shallot finely minced, a tea-spoonful of chopped parsley, very little grated nutmeg, and a table-spoonful of flour. Pour three-quarters of a pint of gravy over this, and simmer it gently, stirring it frequently till it is hot through, but it must not boil. Garnish with toasted sippets. Minced lamb is very good served with boiled spinach. Most people would, however, prefer to have it cold rather than it should be warmed up in any way. Plain Rice Pudding (February 24th).

DINNER.—Fried Plaice (April 21st). *Dutch Sauce.*—Real Dutch sauce is thickened with yolk of egg and no flour. Four yolks of eggs, two table-spoonfuls of cream or water, and two ounces of butter, a grate of nutmeg, and a little pepper and salt are put into a gallipot. This is put into a saucepan half full of cold water, placed over a gentle fire, and whisked briskly with a wooden spoon until it begins to thicken and look like rich cream, when it is taken off the fire, and either lemon-juice or Tarragon or Chili vinegar to taste is stirred into it. Thus made, however, the sauce would be too expensive for every-day use, and a very excellent imitation of it may be made as follows:—Blend smoothly together half a tea-spoonful of flour and an ounce of butter. Put the mixture into a gallipot, with a table-spoonful of water, another of Tarragon vinegar, and the yolk of an egg. Put the gallipot in a saucepan of cold water, place it on a gentle fire, and whisk till the sauce begins to thicken. If liked, add more vinegar or a little lemon-juice, and serve. However the sauce is made, it should be taken from the fire as soon as it is thick, and heated gently, or it will curdle. Broiled Steak (January 22nd); Maitre d'Hôtel Butter (April 15th); Potato Snow (April 7th); Semolina Pudding (March 12th); Cheese (June 8th).

A YEAR'S COOKERY.

Things that must not be Forgotten.
1. Turn and rub the mutton in the pickle.
2. Preserve the remnants of the steak.

May 15th.

Breakfast.	Luncheon.	Dinner.
Boiled Eggs. Corned Beef. Hot Buttered Toast. Dry Toast. Brown and White Bread and Butter. Gooseberry Fool.	Shepherd's Pie. Jam and Bread Pudding, Economical.	Milk Soup. Pigeon Pie. New Potatoes. Spring Cabbage. Lemon Pudding. Cheese.

Marketing.

For the Day.—A Breast of Veal (February 25th). The butcher should be asked to bone the joint before sending it home. A thin slice of lean uncooked Ham; a pound of Suet, for forcemeat and for the Lemon Pudding; New Potatoes; Spring Cabbage; the whole or part of a fresh Ox Cheek; two or three thin slices of Bacon, cured without saltpetre; one pound and a half of Rump Steak, half an inch thick, or, if preferred, the same weight of lean Veal; Gooseberries and Bottled Fruit.

For To-morrow.—Half an Ox Kidney, or three Sheep's Kidneys. Ask the butcher to send in the morning, well assorted, perfectly fresh, and weighing about one pound and a half, a Lamb's Fry. In many places the fry is so much sought after that it is as well to speak for it beforehand. Half a pound of streaky Bacon in rashers; Mustard and Cress.

BREAKFAST.—Boiled Eggs (January 5th); Corned Beef left yesterday; Gooseberry Fool (June 24th).

LUNCHEON.—Shepherd's Pie, made of the scraps and trimmings of the broiled steak (January 12th); Jam and Bread Pudding, Economical (February 23rd).

DINNER.—Milk Soup (January 3rd). *Pigeon Pie.*—Clean the pigeons, cut them in halves, and put in each one a piece of maître d'hôtel butter that has been mixed with the livers parboiled and minced. Cut the steak, or, if it is preferred, the veal, into neat pieces, season these with salt and pepper, and place them at the bottom of the pie-dish. Over them lay the birds, cut in halves, and place the yolk of a hard-boiled egg between these. Lay a thin slice of bacon over each piece of pigeon, and half fill the dish with strong gravy made from bones. If permitted, a few mushrooms will greatly improve the flavour of the pie. Cover with pastry in the usual way. As this is a good pie, Puff Paste (April 24th), or, if this is too much trouble, Rough Puff (May 29th), will answer excellently for it. When ornamenting the pie, scald and clean three of the feet, and place them in the hole at the top, in order to show what kind of pie it is. Brush over with yolk of egg, and bake in a well-heated oven. This pie should not, even in cold weather, be kept more than two days, as it quickly turns sour after it is baked. New Potatoes (April 12th); Spring Cabbage (June 4th); Lemon Pudding (August 12th); Cheese (June 8th).

Things that must not be Forgotten.

1. Turn and rub the mutton in the pickle.
2. If bacon or ham cured without saltpetre cannot easily be procured, lightly boil the bacon before putting it in the pie. Unless this is done it may turn the contents of the pie red.
3. Pastry is to be made to-day (April 17th): the pigeon pie, a gooseberry and red currant tart (August 7th) from bottled fruit, lemon cheesecakes (August 18th); also sultana cake (August 2nd) and milk rolls (August 26th). If the season is early, fresh gooseberries may not be very expensive, and they may then be used.
4. Clean the ox-cheek (Note 5, February 6th), also boil the brine, and let it go cold before using it again (January 13th).
5. If any lemon pudding is left, it can be cut in slices, toasted, and served at luncheon.
6. *Rolled Veal.*—Spread a thin layer of veal forcemeat over the inside of the breast of veal, sprinkle a table-spoonful of finely-chopped pickled gherkins over this, and lay the slice of ham on the top. Roll the veal very tightly, and bind it securely with tape. Put it into a stewpan, with a plate under it to keep it from sticking, barely cover it with stock, and simmer it very gently for about three hours. Put it between two dishes, lay a heavy weight on the top, and let it go cold.
7. If the bones are not required for making glaze, they should be stewed with the veal, and the stock may be used for soup.

May 16th.

Breakfast.	Luncheon.	Dinner.
Remains of Pigeon Pie. Stewed Kidney. Milk Rolls. Dry Toast. Brown and White Bread and Butter. Mustard and Cress. Milk Porridge.	Lamb's Fry. Bacon. Sliced Lemon Pudding.	Crécy Soup. Chops. Piquante Sauce. Mashed Potatoes. Spinach. Vermicelli Pudding. Cheese.

Marketing.

For the Day.—Three or four pounds of Loin Chops, as free from fat as possible (April 30th); Potatoes; Spinach; a pennyworth of Parsley. Lamb's Fry to be sent in for Luncheon.

For To-morrow.—A pair of thick Soles (January 3rd), filleted; Potatoes; Spring Cabbage; a tin of Sardines; two heads of Lettuce; a half-pennyworth of Beetroot; a pennyworth of Radishes; a half-pennyworth of Spring Onions; four pennyworth of Finger Biscuits; Sea Biscuits.

BREAKFAST.—Pigeon Pie served yesterday; Stewed Kidney (April 2nd or April 16th); Milk Rolls (August 26th); Milk Porridge (June 13th).

LUNCHEON.—*Lamb's Fry.*—Look over the fry first thing in the morning, and if there are any hard gristly portions, such as the heart and the melt, trim them neatly, flour them, and turn them over in a frying-pan over the fire till they are lightly browned; then put them into a pie-dish, barely cover them with stock or water, and bake them in a moderate oven for a couple of hours. Turn them about occasionally, to keep them from sticking to the bottom of the dish. Twenty minutes before the fry is to be served dip the pieces in flour, and fry them gently in butter or dripping till done enough. They will take about a quarter of an hour. Take them up, drain them, and put all the fry together on a dish. Mix a dessert-spoonful of flour smoothly with a gill of the gravy from the dish; pour this into the pan, and stir it till it boils and thickens; add a little mushroom ketchup, pepper and salt, and a few drops of browning. Strain the sauce over the fry, and serve very hot. It is an improvement to roll the pieces of fry in egg and bread-crumb, or to dip them in frying batter (October 22nd), before cooking them. Sliced Pudding (March 6th).

DINNER.—Crécy Soup (January 5th). *Mutton Chops.*—Divide the loin into chops, trim away most of the fat (which may be melted down for frying or used to make a pudding), and dip the chops into egg and bread-crumbs. Cook them as directed (April 30th), and serve round mashed potatoes (May 12th), with piquante sauce (May 5th) poured over them. Spinach (May 10th); Vermicelli Pudding (August 1st); Cheese (June 8th).

Things that must not be Forgotten.
1. Turn and rub the mutton in the pickle.
2. Turn and rub the cheek in the brine.
3. Remove the tape from the breast of veal, trim the ends evenly, and brush it over with glaze (*see* March 21st).

Sunday, May 17th.

Breakfast.	Dinner.	Tea.	Supper.
Sardines.	Fillets of Sole, Sautés.	Brown and White Bread and Butter.	Cold Mutton. Salad.
Rolled Veal.	Roast Sour Mutton.	Plum Jam.	Gooseberry Tart.
Milk Rolls.	Potato Snow.	Sultana Cake.	Lemon Cheese-cakes.
Dry Toast.	Spring Cabbage.		Cheese.
Brown and White Bread and Butter.	General Favourite Pudding.		
Biscuits and Milk.	Cheese.		

BREAKFAST.—*Rolled Veal.*—Put the veal on a clean dish, garnish it with parsley, and cut it into very thin slices. It will be excellent either as a breakfast, luncheon, or supper dish. Sardines (January 12th); Milk Rolls (August 26th); Biscuits and Milk (June 14th).

DINNER.—Sole Fillets of, Sautés (January 4th). Roast Sour Mutton (March 29th); Potato Snow (April 7th); Spring Cabbage (June 4th). *General Favourite Pudding.*—Spread a little strawberry jam very thinly over the finger biscuits, arrange them at the bottom of a dish, grate the rind of a lemon over them, and pour upon them half a pint of custard, made with a cupful of milk, the yolks of two eggs, and a little sugar. Let the biscuits soak for awhile. Whisk the whites of three eggs to a stiff froth, stir in lightly an ounce of sifted sugar, and as much finely-powdered and sifted arrowroot as will keep the eggs from falling. Lay the icing on the top of the pudding in broken masses, brown the top quickly in a hot oven or before the fire, and serve cold. The icing will take no harm if made an hour or two before it is wanted.

TEA.—Sultana Cake (August 2nd).

SUPPER.—Salad (March 13th); Goosberry Tart (August 7th); Lemon Cheesecakes (August 18th).

Things that must not be Forgotten.

1. Turn and rub the ox-cheek in the brine.
2. Put the veal in a cool place as soon as it is done with.

May 18th.

Breakfast.	Luncheon.	Dinner.
Rolled Veal.	Hashed Mutton.	Croûte au Pot.
Poached Eggs on Toast.	Red Currant Tart.	Boiled Aitchbone of Beef.
Milk Rolls.		Carrots.
Dry Toast.		Summer Cabbage.
Honey.		Potatoes.
Brown and White Bread and Butter.		Boiled Batter Pudding, with Sweet Sauce.
Bread and Milk.		Cheese.

Marketing.

For the Day.—Aitchbone of Beef. This joint is generally sold at a cheap rate, but it cannot be called economical, because it contains so much bone. When nicely cooked, however, it is very tender, and it is favoured by many. Carrots; Potatoes; Summer Cabbage.

For To-morrow.—A tin of Potted Grouse (January 7th); Bloaters (Note 2, January 2nd); threepennyworth of Cream.

BREAKFAST.—Rolled Veal left yesterday; Poached Eggs (February 6th); Milk Rolls (August 26th); Bread and Milk (January 25th).

LUNCHEON.—*Hashed Mutton.*—Cut the meat from the bone in thin slices (if hash were made of boiled mutton the slices would have to be as thick again), trim them neatly, and put them aside. Break the mutton bone into three or four pieces. Slice two onions, and fry them in a little fat till they are lightly browned. Put them into a stewpan with a pint and a half of cold water, the mutton bones, and a turnip, and stew all gently together for an hour and a half. Strain the liquor into a basin, and set this in a pan of cold water, to make the fat rise; skim it carefully, and put half a pint of the gravy back into the stewpan, with half a tea-spoonful of flour mixed smoothly with water to thicken it. Stir the sauce till it boils, then add the pieces of meat, a little pepper and salt, and a few drops of browning. Heat all very gently together by the side of the fire for half an hour, but on no account let the gravy boil, or the meat will be hard. Just before serving, stir in a tea-spoonful of sherry or a few drops of walnut vinegar, or any other flavouring that may be preferred. Arrange the slices of meat upon a dish, strain the sauce over them, garnish with toasted sippets, and serve. If a very small quantity of meat is on the mutton bone it will be well to mince instead of hashing it (January 20th); Red Currant Tart (August 7th).

DINNER.—Croûte au Pot (May 25th); Boiled Aitchbone of Beef (February 23rd); Carrots (July 6th); Summer Cabbage (June 4th); Potatoes (May 12th). *Boiled Batter Pudding.*—Make some batter according to the recipe given for Toad-in-the-Hole (January 15th), but use a spoonful or two less of milk, or the pudding may not turn out. Grease a pudding-basin that the batter will quite fill, and make it hot; pour in the batter, sprinkle a little flour on the top, and tie securely over it a pudding-cloth that has been wrung out of boiling water and floured. Place the basin in a saucepan with plenty of boiling water, and keep boiling moderately fast for an hour and a half. Sometimes a spoonful of sugar, a grate or two of nutmeg, and a small piece of butter are added to the batter. Let the pudding stand two or three minutes before turning it out, garnish it with bright-coloured jelly, and send sweet sauce to table in a tureen. Sweet Sauce (July 19th); Cheese (June 8th).

Things that must not be Forgotten.

1. Turn and rub the ox-cheek in the brine.
2. Stew the mutton bone again with the gravy that was not used and an additional quart of water. The goodness will not have been drawn from it with only one hour's simmering.
3. Keep the bloaters apart from everything else in the larder.
4. Wash a cupful of hominy, and put it to soak all night in cold water.

May 19th.

Breakfast.	Luncheon.	Dinner.
Bloaters.	Rolled Veal.	Mackerel, à la Maître d'Hôtel.
Potted Grouse.	Boiled Hominy.	Cold Beef.
Hot Toast.		Salad.
Dry Toast.		Cucumber.
Marmalade.		Mashed Potatoes.
Brown and White Bread and Butter.		Stewed Rhubarb.
Porridge.		Cream.
		Cheese.

Marketing.

For the Day.—A pair of moderate-sized Mackerel (April 4th); two heads of Lettuce; a half-pennyworth of Beetroot; a pennyworth of Small Salad; two

pennyworth of Watercress (half for breakfast to-morrow morning); a fresh Cucumber; half a bundle of Rhubarb; Potatoes.
For To-morrow.—A tin of Preserved Lobster; a tin of Pilchards; Muffins (January 29th).

BREAKFAST.—Bloaters (January 3rd); Potted Grouse (January 7th); Porridge (January 25th).
LUNCHEON.—Rolled Veal (Note 6, May 15th); Boiled Hominy (February 11th).
DINNER. — Mackerel, à la Maître d'Hôtel (April 15th); Beef served yesterday; Salad (March 13th). *Cucumber.*—A cucumber may either be sent to table dressed (that is, peeled, cut into thin slices, seasoned with pepper and salt, then covered with one or two spoonfuls of vinegar and oil) or whole, on a dish covered with a napkin. In old-fashioned country-houses one or two small onions are sometimes sliced and mixed with the sliced cucumber. Mashed Potatoes (May 12th). *Stewed Rhubarb.*—Wash the rhubarb and cut it into three-inch lengths. For one pound of fruit make a syrup by boiling a quarter of a pint of water with six ounces of loaf sugar till clear. Put in the rhubarb and simmer it very gently till it is soft without having fallen. As the pieces become tender lift them one by one carefully into a glass dish, and when all are done pour the syrup out to cool. Add two or three drops of cochineal to the syrup to colour it, and pour it over the fruit. Early in the season the rhubarb need not be peeled, but when it gets old the skin must be removed. Champagne, or forced rhubarb, when it can be obtained, is the best for this dish. Stewed rhubarb is most delicious when a little cream is served with it. Cheese (June 8th).

Things that must not be Forgotten.
1. Turn and rub the ox-cheek in the brine.
2. Watch the rhubarb very carefully when stewing it. It falls very quickly after it has once become tender.

May 20th.

Breakfast.	Luncheon.	Dinner.
Pilchards.	Rissoles of Beef.	Lobster Soup.
Potted Grouse.	Fried Hominy.	Roast Shoulder of Mutton.
Muffins.		Potatoes.
Dry Toast.		Onions, Glazed.
Watercress.		Broccoli.
Brown and White Bread and Butter.		Gingerbread Pudding.
Milk Toast.		Cheese.

Marketing.
For the Day.—A well-kept Shoulder of Mutton, not too fat (January 17th); Onions; Potatoes; Broccoli; a pennyworth of Parsley; a pound of Beef Kidney Suet, part of it for to-day and part for to-morrow.

BREAKFAST.—Pilchards (January 23rd); Potted Grouse (January 7th); Muffins (January 30th); Milk Toast (June 17th).

LUNCHEON.—Rissoles of the remains of Beef (January 6th); Fried Hominy (February 12th).

DINNER.—*Lobster Soup.*—Take the stock made from the mutton bones (Note 2, May 18th), and stew it for an hour with a carrot, a turnip, a small onion, a very small pinch of celery-seed tied in muslin, and half a dozen peppercorns. Rub the soup through a sieve, and to each pint of liquor add a dessert-spoonful of corn-flour mixed smoothly with half a pint of milk. Stir the soup till it boils, then add pepper and salt to taste, and a quarter of a tea-spoonful of essence of anchovy. Break the yolk of an egg into the soup tureen, stir in the soup, and add the preserved lobster, cut into neat pieces. Let these stand for five or six minutes, and serve. The lobster must on no account boil in the soup. Roast Shoulder of Mutton (December 16th); Glazed Onions (February 14th); Boiled Potatoes (April 7th); Broccoli (April 25th). *Gingerbread Pudding.*—Take six ounces of stale bread-crumbs that have been rubbed through a wire sieve; mix with them three ounces of flour, six ounces of finely-chopped beef suet, a tea-spoonful of powdered ginger, and a tea-spoonful of baking-powder. Dissolve two table-spoonfuls of treacle in a gill of milk, add three drops of almond-flavouring, and make a smooth stiff paste by stirring the liquid into the dry ingredients. Turn the mixture into a buttered mould, lay a greased paper on the top, and steam the pudding for three hours. This pudding may be more easily, and rather more economically, made by rubbing a slice of beef dripping into flour instead of mixing bread-crumbs and flour with chopped suet. Cheese (June 8th).

Things that must not be Forgotten.

1. Turn and rub the ox-cheek in the brine.
2. Pot what is left of the veal roll. It can be used for breakfast to-morrow. (*See* Potted Beef, January 23rd.)

May 21st.

Breakfast.	Luncheon.	Dinner.
Potted Veal and Ham.	Cauliflower au Gratin.	Fried Whiting.
Savoury Eggs.	Baked Plum Pudding.	Minced Mutton Cakes, with Tomato Sauce.
Hot Buttered Toast.		Calf's Liver and Bacon.
Dry Toast.		New Potatoes.
Brown and White Bread and Butter.		Spinach.
Porridge.		Guest's Pudding.
		Cheese.

Marketing.

For the Day.—A large white Broccoli; fresh Whiting (January 17th); a two-pound tin of Tomatoes; one pound and a half of Calf's Liver; one pound of

Streaky Bacon, cut into rashers (half for to-day and half for breakfast to-morrow); New Potatoes; Spinach.

For To-morrow.—One Dried Haddock; half a pound of Macaroni.

BREAKFAST.—Potted Veal and Ham, made yesterday. Savoury Eggs (January 1st); Porridge (January 25th).

LUNCHEON.—Cauliflower au Gratin (April 25th); Baked Plum Pudding (February 25th).

DINNER.—Fried Whiting (January 17th). *Minced Mutton Cakes.*—Cut the lean meat from the shoulder of mutton, and mince it according to the directions given (January 20th), being careful to stew the bones and trimmings until the gravy is so strong that it will jelly when cold. If there is any difficulty about this, dissolve a tea-spoonful of gelatine in the gravy. Put only so much gravy with the meat as will bind it together: four table-spoonfuls will be enough for one pound of mince. Spread the mince upon a dish, and when it is cold and stiff form it into cakes about two inches in diameter. Flour these lightly and brush them over with egg and bread-crumb; let them lie for an hour, and then repeat the operation. Put them into a frying-basket, plunge them into boiling fat, and let them remain till brightly browned (*see* Fish Cakes, January 13th). They will be done enough in from six to eight minutes. Drain them on kitchen paper, arrange them round a dish, and pour tomato sauce into the centre (July 15th). Liver and Bacon (January 17th); New Potatoes (April 12th); Spinach (May 10th); Guest's Pudding (April 14th); Cheese (June 8th).

Things that must not be Forgotten.

1. Turn and rub the ox-cheek.
2. Preserve any bacon that may be left. It can be used for luncheon to-morrow.
3. If any pudding were left at luncheon it can be sliced and toasted for to-morrow.
4. Preserve one or two rashers of bacon for braising the loin of lamb.

May 22nd.

Breakfast.	Luncheon.	Dinner.
Dried Haddock.	Macaroni and Bacon.	Potato Purée.
Fried Bacon.	Sliced Pudding.	Loin of Lamb, Braised.
Hot Buttered Toast.		Spinach.
Dry Toast.		New Potatoes.
Brown and White Bread and Butter.		Roly-poly Pudding.
Bread and Milk.		Cheese.

Marketing.

For the Day.—A Loin of Lamb, or, if this is not sufficient for the requirements of the family, a Saddle of Lamb—that is, two loins joined together. Be sure

that the butcher joints the meat. Spinach; New Potatoes; half a pound of Beef Suet for to-day and to-morrow.
For To-morrow.—Half a pound of Forced Mushrooms; a pennyworth of Watercress.

BREAKFAST.—Dried Haddock (January 27th); Fried Bacon (January 2nd); Bread and Milk (January 25th).
LUNCHEON.—Macaroni and Bacon (January 27th); Sliced Pudding (March 6th).
DINNER.—Potato Purée (January 26th). *Loin of Lamb, Braised.*—Take a close-fitting and thick stewpan, just large enough to hold the meat. Put two or three thin slices of bacon at the bottom of the pan, and add a table-spoonful of chopped mint and a table-spoonful of lemon-juice. Put in the lamb, lay a slice or two of bacon on the top, and add half a pint of stock or as much as will about half cover the meat. Simmer very gently indeed for an hour and a half, and when the meat is half cooked turn it over. Take it up, drain it, and keep it hot. Take the fat off the gravy, and boil it quickly to reduce it. When it is very strong season it with pepper and salt, put the lamb in it for a few minutes to make it hot, and serve it with the gravy strained over it. Spinach (May 10th); New Potatoes (April 12th); Roly-poly Pudding (August 18th); Cheese (June 8th).

Things that must not be Forgotten.

1. Boil the ox-cheek (April 6th). Press it between two dishes and place a heavy weight on the upper one.
2. Pastry is to be made to-day (April 17th): rhubarb pie, open jam tart (August 7th), jam turnovers (September 25th), rice cake (August 2nd), scones (August 26th).
3. Make a ground rice mould for dinner to-morrow (August 7th).

May 23rd.

Breakfast.	Luncheon.	Dinner.
Mock Tongue (Ox-cheek).	Scotch Collops.	Fried Plaice.
Stewed Mushrooms.	Baked Batter Pudding.	Dutch Sauce.
Scones.		Stewed Savoury Beef.
Dry Toast.		Mashed Potatoes.
Brown and White Bread and Butter.		Ground Rice Mould, with Red Currant Jam.
Milk Toast.		Cheese.

Marketing.

For the Day.—Fresh Sheep's Hearts: one will probably be sufficient for two persons. A thick Plaice (April 21st); about four pounds of the Leg of Mutton piece, or a small piece of the Round of Beef. Brush the beef quickly over with vinegar before cooking it. Potatoes; a pennyworth of Parsley.
For To-morrow.—A Cabbage Lettuce; an ounce of Chervil; three-pennyworth of Cream; half or the whole of a Calf's Head; four pounds of Gammon of Bacon; New Potatoes; Broccoli; Sea-kale; half a pound of Ratafias, for Mountain Pudding; a tin of Preserved Salmon of a good brand; Ingredients for a Salad, with additional Watercress for breakfast.

BREAKFAST.—Stewed Mushrooms (March 20th). *Scones* (August 26th).—Make the scones hot in the oven, open and butter them. Milk Toast (June 17th).

LUNCHEON. — Sheep's Hearts (July 2nd). Baked Batter Pudding (February 5th) may be eaten either with the meat and gravy or separately with sugar or jam.

DINNER.—Fried Plaice (April 21st); Dutch Sauce (May 14th). *Stewed Savoury Beef.*—Cut two thin slices from the gammon of bacon, and lay one under and one upon the beef. Grease an earthenware jar with a close-fitting lid, put in the beef, and throw in a bunch of parsley, half a blade of mace, two cloves, and six peppercorns. Pour over all three-quarters of a pint of stock or cold water, lay a slice of dripping on the beef, fasten down the jar, and set it in a moderately-heated oven. Let it stew gently for two hours, and baste it occasionally with the liquor. When the meat is done enough pour off the gravy, strain it, and free it from fat. Make it hot in a saucepan, thicken it by stirring into it a tea-spoonful of flour mixed smoothly with a little cold water, season it with pepper and salt, and stir into it a table-spoonful of finely-chopped pickled gherkins. Put the meat on a dish, pour the gravy over, and serve with red currant jelly as an accompaniment. This dish is very good *cold.* Mashed Potatoes (May 12th); Ground Rice Mould (August 7th) made yesterday; Cheese (June 8th).

Things that must not be Forgotten.

1. If any savoury stew is left, put it upon a clean dish and serve for breakfast to-morrow.

2. Throw the calf's brains into water as soon as they come in.

3. Make a little mayonnaise and bottle it closely, to serve with the mayonnaise of salmon to-morrow evening (August 30th).

4. Peel and slice five or six potatoes and throw them into cold water, ready to be fried to-morrow morning. They will not be much trouble, and will be a very agreeable addition to the breakfast-table.

Sunday, May 24th.

Breakfast.	Dinner.	Tea.	Supper.
Cold Beef.	Milk Soup.	Brown and White Bread and Butter.	Mayonnaise of Salmon.
Fried Potatoes.	Calf's Head, with Brain Sauce.	Strawberry Jam.	Rhubarb Tart.
Watercress.	Boiled Bacon.	Rice Cake.	Cream.
Scones.	New Potatoes.		Cheese.
Dry Toast.	Sea-kale.		
Brown and White Bread and Butter.	Mountain Pudding.		
Milk Porridge.	Cheese.		

BREAKFAST.—Beef served yesterday. Fried Potatoes (February 2nd, May 23rd); Milk Porridge (June 13th).

Dinner.—Milk Soup (January 3rd); Calf's Head, Boiled (April 19th); Boiled Bacon (March 30th); New Potatoes (April 12th); Broccoli (April 25th); Sea-kale (June 14th); Mountain Pudding (September 20th); Cheese (June 8th).

Tea.—Rice Cake (August 2nd).

Supper.—*Mayonnaise of Salmon.*—Dry the salad in the usual way (March 13th), and shred it finely. Take the salmon out of the tin and break it into neat pieces. Put a layer of salad upon a dish, and place the inferior pieces of salmon on the top; then repeat in alternate layers until the salmon and salad are used, being careful to put the most presentable pieces of fish where they will be seen. Pour a small portion of the sauce over the different layers, so that it may penetrate through the mass, but leave plenty of sauce for the top. Garnish with hard-boiled eggs, olives, beet-root, or anything else that may be at hand. Just before serving pour the mayonnaise sauce (August 30th) over the top of the salad, sprinkle half a tea-spoonful of chopped parsley over all, and the salad is ready. A very pretty way of garnishing the salad is to cut the beet-root into thin strips, and with these to make a kind of open lattice-work round the lower part of the salad, to place hard-boiled eggs cut into quarters lengthwise over this, and to ornament the summit of the pile with olives. Salad and mayonnaise can be arranged in this way with fresh pickled salmon, lobsters, fresh and preserved, filleted herrings, and cold dressed fish of various kinds. A very excellent mayonnaise of salmon may be prepared by boiling a salmon whole, placing it on a dish with lettuce-hearts round it, and mayonnaise sauce as an accompaniment.

Things that must not be Forgotten.

1. If any mayonnaise sauce is left, bottle it and cork it closely.
2. The liquor in which the calf's head was boiled is so greasy that it will be best made into lentil or pease soup on May 26th.

May 25th.

Breakfast.	Luncheon.	Dinner.
Cold Boiled Bacon.	Macaroni and Ham.	Croûte au Pot.
Mock Tongue (Ox-cheek).	Jam Turnovers.	Boiled Leg of Mutton.
Scones.		Caper Sauce.
Dry Toast.		Young Carrots.
Brown and White Bread and Butter.		Mashed Potatoes.
Corn Flour Milk.		Open Jam Tart.
		Custards.
		Cheese.

Marketing.

For the Day.—A plump Leg of Mutton; young Carrots; Potatoes.

For To-morrow.—Bespeak a Lamb's Fry; one pound of American Dried Apples (chips)—*see* Note 1, on next page; Mustard and Cress.

BREAKFAST.—Bacon served with the Calf's Head yesterday. Mock Tongue served the day before yesterday. Scones (May 23rd); Corn Flour Milk (June 19th).

LUNCHEON.—Macaroni and Ham, made of a portion of the boiled gammon (April 3rd). In making the mould preserve a portion of ham for the ham toast to-morrow. Jam Turnovers (September 25th).

DINNER.—*Croûte au Pot.*—Strictly speaking, Croûte au Pot is clear soup with crusts and homely vegetables thrown into it. The process of making clear soup is, however, too troublesome for daily use (July 30th), and an excellent soup, which is literally Croûte au Pot, may be made as follows:—Take two-pennyworth of bones, cooked or uncooked; break them into small pieces, and put them into a stew-pan with two quarts of cold water. When the liquor approaches the boiling point throw in a little salt to raise the scum, and skim with an iron spoon. Meantime, prepare in the usual way two carrots, a turnip, two leeks or one good-sized onion, a pinch of mixed savoury herbs or, wanting these, a bunch of parsley, a sprig of thyme, and a bay-leaf, a little celery-seed, fifteen peppercorns, and, last of all, three stale crusts of bread toasted brown. Throw these ingredients into the soup, let it boil up again, skim it once more, draw it back, and let it simmer gently for two hours. If convenient, the bones might with advantage be stewed longer, but two hours will be enough for the vegetables. Take out the bones, strain the liquor into a bowl, and rub the vegetables and the bread through a hair sieve. Keep a little of the liquor hot: it will help to moisten the pulp and make it go through the sieve more easily. Mix the pulp with the liquor, return it to the stewpan, and let it boil; then add two or three drops of browning if necessary, and the soup is ready to serve. If a dozen pea-shells, or better still, a cupful of green peas can be added to the soup, its flavour will be improved. Soup made in this way and without the bread may be thickened with flour or corn-flour (a table-spoonful to a pint), mixed to a smooth paste with water and stirred into the soup, and boiled for a few minutes till the flour is cooked. It is then called *Brown Soup.* The majority of people would, however, much prefer a soup thickened with bread rather than flour, and the method is convenient because it enables the cook to use profitably pieces of bread that would otherwise be wasted. Not too much bread must be used, however, or the soup will taste pappy. Boiled Leg of Mutton (February 23rd); Caper Sauce (March 19th); Carrots (July 6th); Mashed Potatoes (May 12th); Custard (August 10th); Cheese (June 8th).

Things that must not be Forgotten.

1. *Dried Apples,* imported from America and sold by grocers, are excellent for cooking purposes when properly prepared, and they are much more economical than fresh fruit. Wash one pound of chips, and put them with a quart of water into the oven when it is cool and not wanted for other purposes. Let them stew for twelve hours (they

can remain in the oven all night), and they are ready to be sweetened, flavoured, and used.
 2. Wash two table-spoonfuls of tapioca and soak it in water all night.
 3. Soak a cupful of green lentils in cold water.
 4. Make a mould for breakfast of the remains of the calf's head (April 20th).

May 26th.

Breakfast.	Luncheon.	Dinner.
Calf's Head Mould.	Lamb's Fry.	Lentil Soup.
Ham Toast.	Tapioca and Apples.	Curried Mutton (made of cold Boiled Mutton).
Dry Toast.		Boiled Rice.
Brown and White Bread and Butter.		Treacle Pudding.
Mustard and Cress.		Cheese.
Bread and Milk.		

Marketing.

For the Day.—A fresh Lamb's Fry; a quarter of a pound of fresh Beef Suet; if hams were not cured at home in the season, a sugar-cured Ham, weighing about twelve pounds (September 17th); a piece of the thin flank of Beef, weighing from eight to ten pounds.

BREAKFAST.—Calf's Head Mould (April 20th); Ham Toast (March 28th); Bread and Milk (January 25th).

LUNCHEON.—Lamb's Fry (May 16th); Tapioca and Apples (February 18th).

DINNER.—Lentil Soup (April 1st). *Curried Mutton.*—Curry may be made either of fresh or cooked meat. Veal, chicken, rabbits, and similar meats, are particularly suited to this mode of cookery. To curry fresh meat, see July 16th. For cooked meat proceed as follows:—Cut the meat from the cold mutton into small neat pieces, and trim away the skin and gristle, but not the fat. Leave on the bone the broken remnants of meat: they can be minced for luncheon to-morrow. Peel six good-sized onions and chop them small; then fry them in a little butter or dripping till they are lightly browned. Take them up with a slice, and fry in the same fat two sour apples that have been pared and chopped small. When these are soft drain away the fat, return the onions to the stewpan, pour on a pint of the liquor in which the mutton was boiled, and simmer gently till the onions and apples are perfectly tender, then rub them through a hair sieve. Mix smoothly with the pulp a dessert-spoonful of Captain White's curry-paste, a tea-spoonful of curry-powder, a dessert-spoonful of ground rice, and a few drops of browning. Stir in the pint of liquor, and boil the same over the fire, stirring it frequently, till it is thick and smooth like very thick gruel. Taste it, and if it is not sufficiently acid add a few drops of lemon-juice. Draw the pan back, put in the slices of meat, cover them with the sauce, and let them heat gently by the side of the fire for half an hour. The liquid must on no account boil, or the meat will be hard. Just before serving hold it over the fire for a minute to make it hot (but still, do not let it boil), put it on a dish, pile the rice round it like a wall, and serve. The sauce for curry should not be liquid, but thick. If apples are not at hand, green gooseberries or lemon-juice will supply the acidity required. The addition of a little freshly-grated cocoa-nut or grated Brazil nuts gives a pleasant variety of flavour. Good curry, if accompanied, as it should be, by rice, boiled so that every grain is separate, does not need potatoes with it. To boil rice for curries, see July 21st. Curry is an excellent dish for hot weather, and is highly esteemed in hot countries. Treacle Pudding (March 28th); Cheese (June 8th).

Things that must not be Forgotten.

1. Boil up the brine, or, if necessary, make fresh brine (January 13th), and lay the flank of beef in it.

2. Cut off one-third of the sugar-cured ham and soak it all night in cold water. If very dry, a ham should be soaked for twenty-four hours.

May 27th.

Breakfast.	Luncheon.	Dinner.
Buttered Eggs.	Minced Mutton.	Sole au Gratin.
Calf's Head Mould.	Plain Rice Pudding.	Stewed Steak.
Hot Buttered Toast.		Mashed Potatoes.
Dry Toast.		Turnip-tops.
Honey.		Hayrick Puddings.
Brown and White Bread and Butter.		Cheese.
Milk Porridge.		

Marketing.

For the Day.—A pair of thick fresh Soles (January 3rd); three pounds of tender Steak, cut evenly and about an inch and a half thick (see Marketing, January 1st); Potatoes; Turnip-tops; one-pennyworth of Parsley.

For To-morrow.—A keg or a bottle of Anchovies, if there are none in the house; Muffins (January 29th).

BREAKFAST.—Buttered Eggs (January 16th); Milk Porridge (June 13th).

LUNCHEON.—*Minced Mutton* (January 20th); Plain Rice Pudding (February 24th).

DINNER.—Sole au Gratin (May 3rd); Stewed Steak (January 31st); Mashed Potatoes (May 12th); Turnip-tops (see Cabbage, June 4th); Hayrick Puddings (March 19th); Cheese (June 8th).

Things that must not be Forgotten.

1. Preserve any little pieces of steak that may be left; they can be used for the Shepherd's Pie to-morrow.

2. Fillet the anchovies and prepare the stock for anchovy toast to-morrow (January 8th).
3. Make the rhubarb mould for dinner to-morrow (June 3rd).
4. Boil the piece of ham. To do this, trim, scrape, and brush it well, and put it in a stewpan with plenty of cold water to cover it. Let it heat slowly, skim it carefully; after boiling for two minutes draw it back, and simmer it very gently but continuously till done enough. A piece of ham will take about half an hour to the pound from the time the water boils; a whole ham of a good size would need six hours, a small ham about four hours. When the meat can be pierced easily with a skewer and the skin will peel off readily it is done enough. If it is to be eaten cold, it is an improvement to leave it in the liquor till half cold. This, however, must not lead to its being left in the saucepan all night. Draw off the skin, trim the ham, and shake bread-raspings (January 2nd and February 1st) over it. Put it in the oven or before the fire to set the crumbs, and the ham is ready to serve. The flavour of the ham will be improved if a carrot or even a little celery-seed and a bunch of herbs are boiled with it. It will be remembered that a ham should be soaked for awhile before it is boiled (Note 2, May 26th).
5. Turn and rub the beef in the brine.

May 28th.

Breakfast.	Luncheon.	Dinner.
Anchovy Toast. Boiled Ham. Muffins. Dry Toast. Brown and White Bread and Butter. Corn Flour Milk.	Shepherd's Pie. Hasty Pudding.	Vermicelli Soup. Neck of Veal, Rolled and Roasted. Spinach. New Potatoes. Rhubarb Mould. Custard. Cheese.

Marketing.

For the Day.—Five pounds of the best end of a Neck of Veal (Feb. 25th). Ask the butcher to cut it for rolling, and bone the joint. Potatoes; Spinach.
For To-morrow.—A four-pound tin of Australian Meat; a bottle of Preserved Raspberries.

BREAKFAST.—Anchovy Toast (January 8th); Ham boiled yesterday; Muffins (January 30th); Corn Flour Milk (June 19th).

LUNCHEON.—Shepherd's Pie, made of remnants of steak and cold mashed potatoes, if there be any (January 12th); Hasty Pudding (March 30th).

DINNER.—Vermicelli Soup (March 22nd). *Neck of Veal, Rolled and Roasted.*—Lay the boned veal flat on the table, and sprinkle upon it a little chopped parsley and powdered thyme, with pepper and salt, or, if preferred, spread forcemeat upon it. Lay thin slices of the fatty part of the ham upon it, roll it very tightly, and bind it with tape. Rub it over with bacon fat and roast it before a clear fire, basting it frequently (March 4th). It will take about half an hour to the pound. Take two or three strips of bacon-rind and fry them with the veal bones. Put them into a stewpan, pour over them a pint and a half of stock or water, and let them simmer gently for an hour. Put in a bunch of parsley and a sprig of thyme, half an inch of lemon-rind, and half a small blade of mace, and simmer again till the gravy is considerably reduced. Strain it and free it from fat. Stir into it a tea-spoonful of corn-flour mixed smoothly with water, and boil it, stirring it all the time, for two or three minutes till thick. Add a little sugar browning and two table-spoonfuls of cream, if it is to be had, with pepper and salt to taste. Put the meat in a tin before the fire, and baste it with its gravy for about ten minutes. Put it on a hot dish, strain the gravy over it, and garnish with sliced lemon. Spinach (May 10th); New Potatoes (April 12th); Custard (August 10th); Cheese (June 8th).

Things that must not be Forgotten.

1. Reserve a little of the gravy made from the bones for *Veal Cake* to be made to-morrow. To make it, cut the veal into neat slices, and take an equal number of slices of lean ham. Arrange the meat in layers in a mould, and put hard-boiled eggs cut in slices, with a sprinkling of chopped parsley, pepper, and salt between each layer. Fill the mould with the gravy, bake in the oven for about half an hour, and turn the shape out when cold. Garnish the cake with parsley, and serve.

2. Wash a pound of prunes, and put them to soak in cold water all night.

3. Make hydropathic pudding of the bottled raspberries, for dinner to-morrow (June 16th).

4. Turn and rub the beef in the brine.

May 29th.

Breakfast.	Luncheon.	Dinner.
Boiled Eggs.	Australian Meat, Cold.	Fried Plaice.
Boiled Ham.	Baked Potatoes.	Calf's Liver and Bacon.
Hot Buttered Toast.	Pickle.	Mutton Chops, Stewed in their own Gravy.
Dry Toast.	Stewed Prunes.	
Brown and White Bread and Butter.		New Potatoes.
Milk Toast.		Spring Cabbages.
		Hydropathic Pudding.
		Cheese.

Marketing.

For the Day.—A thick Plaice (April 21st and January 3rd); a pound and a half of Calf's Liver; half a pound of Streaky Bacon, cut into rashers. As it is possible that the liver will be too much for the digestion of some of the

diners, it will be well to have also a dish of Mutton Chops stewed in their own gravy. The chops, as many as may be required, will be best taken from the loin. New Potatoes; Spring Cabbages; one-pennyworth of fresh German Yeast.
For To-morrow.—Two-pennyworth of Watercress.

BREAKFAST.—Boiled Eggs (January 5th); Boiled Ham (Note 4, May 27th) ; Milk Toast (June 17th).
LUNCHEON.—Australian Meat, Cold (February 4th); Baked Potatoes (May 4th); Stewed Prunes (February 27th).
DINNER.—Fried Plaice (April 21st); Calf's Liver and Bacon (January 17th). *Mutton Chops, Stewed in their own Gravy.*—Trim away the fat entirely, dip each chop quickly in and out of cold water, sprinkle pepper lightly upon it, and dredge it well on both sides with flour. For each chop that is to be cooked put a tablespoonful of water or broth into a thick iron saucepan, lay the chops side by side in a single layer, put on the lid, and simmer as gently as possible, but without ceasing, for an hour and a half. Turn them over when half cooked. Just before serving throw a tea-spoonful of chopped parsley into the gravy. If the gravy should be dried up, another spoonful or two of water may be added, but there will not be much fear of this if the chops are *gently* stewed. Chops prepared in this way are tender and easily digested, and suitable for invalids. New Potatoes (April 12th); Spring Cabbages (June 4th); Hydropathic Pudding (June 16th); Custard (August 10th); Cheese (June 8th).

Things that must not be Forgotten.

1. Make a veal cake of the remains of the dressed veal (Note 1, May 28th).
2. Turn and rub the beef in the brine.
3. Pastry is to be made to-day : gooseberry pie of bottled gooseberries, or of fresh gooseberries if the season is an early one (August 7th); lemon cheesecakes (August 18th); treacle tart (August 7th); also Vienna bread (August 26th); Annie's cake (September 25th). *Rough Puff Paste.*—Many housekeepers would consider puff paste (April 24th) too troublesome to make, as well as too expensive, and, it might be added, too indigestible to be used excepting on very special occasions. When this is the case the directions given in the following recipe may be followed, and the pastry will be found excellent, being suited for superior pies, tarts, and tartlets. Put half a pound of fine flour (Vienna flour if it is allowed) upon a board, with six ounces of butter, and chop the butter in the flour with a knife. A dexterous cook may *break*, not rub, the butter in the flour. Make a well in the centre of the flour, and drop into it half a tea-spoonful of lemon-juice, a pinch of salt, and the yolk of an egg. The latter may be omitted. Mix the pastry lightly with water; the water should be added gradually and mixed in with the fingers. Keep the board and the

hand floured, to prevent the pastry sticking to it. The pastry should not be too stiff, or it will not be light. Flour the rolling-pin and give the pastry three good rolls, and after each roll fold the pastry over in half and turn the rough edges to the front. If the pastry bladders or cracks as it is rolled, it is a sign that it is good. To make a pie, moisten the edge of the dish, and lay on it a strip of paste three-quarters of an inch thick. Moisten the edge again, and roll the paste for the top, but much thinner than for the strip. Brush the top, but not the sides, of the pastry over with yolk of egg, and bake it in a well-heated but not fierce oven. The oven must not be fierce because the pastry is to rise; if too hot it would stiffen the surface at once without giving it a chance of rising. When the pastry is done enough the pie should be put in the top or cooler part of the oven to cook the inside. An easy way of making Puff Paste is to brush white of egg over the paste between the turns.

4. Boil the piece of ham that is in the house (Note 4, May 27th).

May 30th.

Breakfast.	Luncheon.	Dinner.
Eggs on the Dish.	Australian Savoury Hash.	Pickled Salmon.
Boiled Ham.	Treacle Tart.	Chicken Sauté aux Champignons.
Vienna Bread.		New Potatoes.
Dry Toast.		Cabbage.
Brown and White Bread and Butter.		Golden Pudding.
Watercress.		Cheese.
Porridge.		

Marketing.

For the Day.—Half a pound of Mushrooms, or, failing these, a small tin of Champignons; a tin of Preserved Salmon; a two-pound tin of Roast Chicken; six ounces of Beef Suet; a pennyworth of Parsley.

For To-morrow.—A pair of thick Soles (January 3rd); the fishmonger should be asked to fillet the fish. A Fore-quarter of Lamb (April 11th); four moderate-sized fresh Mackerel (April 4th); two-pennyworth of young Mint; New Potatoes; materials for the Salad on Sunday night; Spinach; a bunch of Asparagus; a tin of Preserved Peaches. Order also three pennyworth of Cream for the Gooseberry Pie.

BREAKFAST.—Veal Cake (May 28th); Ham boiled May 29th; Vienna Bread (August 26th); Porridge (January 25th).

LUNCHEON.—Savoury Hash of Australian Meat (February 5th); Treacle Tart (August 7th), made yesterday.

DINNER.—*Pickled Salmon.*—To pickle preserved salmon, take the salmon out of the tin an hour or two before it is wanted, divide it into neat pieces (this will make it look more like fresh salmon), and pour over it a pickle made of equal parts of vinegar and water, boiled with peppercorns, and allowed to go cold. When the salmon is to be served put the pieces on a dish, pour a little of the liquor round, and garnish with curled endive. Fresh salmon that has been cooked may be pickled in the same way, but it should lie at least twelve hours covered with vinegar. Uncooked salmon should be lifted in good-sized pieces from the bone, laid in an earthen pan, sprinkled over with salt, covered with vinegar, tied down securely, and baked in a gentle oven till done enough, then left in the pickle till wanted. A dozen peppercorns or more should be placed in the dish with it. Chicken Sauté aux Champignons (April 2nd); New Potatoes (April 12th); Cabbage (June 4th); Golden Pudding (May 4th); Cheese (June 8th).

Things that must not be Forgotten.
1. Turn and rub the beef in the brine.
2. Pickle the mackerel for breakfast to-morrow (August 28th).

Sunday, May 31st.

Breakfast.	Dinner.	Tea.	Supper.
Pickled Mackerel.	Soles, Filleted and Rolled, with Brown Butter.	Brown and White Bread and Butter.	Cold Lamb.
Boiled Ham.		Damson Jam.	Mint Sauce.
Vienna Bread.		Annie's Cake.	Salad.
Dry Toast.	Roast Quarter of Lamb, with Mint Sauce.		Gooseberry Tart.
Marmalade.			Cream.
Brown and White Bread and Butter.	New Potatoes.		Cheese.
Porridge.	Spinach.		
	Asparagus.		
	Dutch Sauce.		
	Tinned Peaches.		
	Custard.		
	Cheese.		

BREAKFAST.—Veal Cake (May 28th); Pickled Mackerel (August 28th); Ham boiled May 29th; Vienna Bread (August 26th); Porridge (January 25th).

DINNER.—Soles, Filleted, Rolled, and Baked (March 1st), with Brown Butter Sauce (February 12th); Roast Quarter of Lamb (March 4th and April 12th); Mint Sauce (March 25th); New Potatoes (April 12th); Spinach (May 10th); Asparagus (June 14th); Dutch Sauce (May 14th); Preserved Peaches (April 11th); Custard (August 10th); Cheese (June 8th).

TEA.—Annie's Cake (September 25th).

SUPPER.—Salad (March 13th); Gooseberry Pie (August 7th).

Things that must not be Forgotten.
1. Turn and rub the beef in the brine.
2. If any mackerel is left, return it to the pickle and keep it covered.

3. If there is enough meat on the ribs of lamb to supply what is wanted for supper, leave the shoulder of lamb untouched; it can be served at dinner to-morrow.

4. Put aside a few heads of asparagus for breakfast.

FRUITS SUITABLE FOR DESSERT IN MAY.

Apples, Oranges, Grapes, Nuts (Filberts, Brazils, Barcelonas, Almonds), Raisins, French Plums, Figs, Dates, Crystallised Fruits, Foreign Preserved Fruit.

DISHES FOR INVALIDS.

SPOON MEAT.

Water Gruel (No. 1).—Mix a table-spoonful of oatmeal into a smooth paste with a little cold water, and add gradually a pint of boiling water. Boil for a quarter of an hour, stirring all the time; season with salt or sugar, according to taste, strain, and serve. If the gruel is not well boiled it will produce flatulency.

Water Gruel (No. 2).—Mix a table-spoonful of patent groats to a smooth paste with water, add a pint of boiling water, and stir over the fire for ten minutes; season, and serve. Gruel is more nourishing when made with milk instead of water.

Sago.—Soak a table-spoonful of sago for a couple of hours, to take away the earthy taste. If there is not time for this it may be dispensed with. Boil it in a pint of water, stirring it all the time, till it is quite transparent. Pour it into a basin, sweeten it with sugar, and flavour it with brandy or wine, if approved, or with a little orange-flower water. If liked, a little orange or lemon-rind may be boiled with the sago, which may be made with milk instead of water.

Tapioca.—This is prepared like sago.

Arrowroot.—Mix a dessert-spoonful of arrowroot to a smooth paste with a little water, pour upon it half a pint of boiling water or milk, and stir it over the fire for a minute or two till it is on the point of boiling; sweeten and flavour to taste, and serve.

Rice Gruel.—Mix a table-spoonful of ground rice to a smooth paste with water, add a pint of cold water, and boil well for half an hour. Sweeten and flavour to taste. Two or three table-spoonfuls of cranberries may be added to rice gruel, if approved.

Panada.—Take the crumb of half a stale penny loaf, pour a pint of water upon it, and boil it for five minutes. Beat it till smooth, put with it a piece of butter, a little sugar and grated nutmeg, and a little black currant jelly, if liked, with as much more water as is agreeable; stir it over the fire for ten minutes, and serve. Sometimes the white meat from the breast of a roasted chicken is chopped, pounded in a mortar, and mixed with the soaked bread; or the flesh of game, young pheasant, partridge, or rabbit, is substituted for that of the chicken.

Thick Milk.—Mix a good table-spoonful of corn-flour with a pint of cold milk, and boil for twenty minutes; sweeten to taste, add a spoonful of brandy and two or three drops of vanilla, and serve.

Savoury Custard.—Mix a dessert-spoonful of corn-flour to a smooth paste with water, and add half a pint of either beef tea or mutton or chicken broth. Stir over the fire for five minutes, add salt, and serve. For another Savoury Custard, see July 30th.

Cocoa made from Cocoa-nibs.—*See* January 18th.

June 1st.

Breakfast.	Luncheon.	Dinner.
Asparagus on Toast.	Minced Ham.	Sago Soup.
Pickled Mackerel.	Toasted Sippets.	Cold Shoulder of Lamb.
Vienna Bread.	Lemon Cheesecakes.	Cucumber.
Brown and White Bread and Butter.		Fresh Salad.
Honey.		Wyvern Puddings.
Bread and Milk.		Cheese.

Marketing.

For the Day.—A tin of Sardines (January 12th); a collared Tongue (January 2nd); a pound of American dried Apples, "chips"; a Cucumber. As soon as a Cucumber is brought in, it should be put (the stalk end downwards) into a jug of cold water.

BREAKFAST.—Asparagus with Eggs (May 4th); Pickled Mackerel (August 28th); Vienna Bread (August 26th); Bread and Milk (January 25th).

LUNCHEON.—*Minced Ham* (made of the scraps cut from the boiled ham).—Prepare the ham as for ham toast (March 28th). Put the mince on a dish, garnish with toasted sippets, and send baked potatoes to table with it. Lemon Cheesecakes (August 18th).

DINNER.—*Sago Soup.*—Wash two ounces of the best pearl sago in plenty of water, and boil it with a quart of good stock till transparent. Season with salt, a pinch of cayenne, a lump of sugar, and as much powdered mace as would lie on a threepenny-piece; squeeze a few drops of lemon-juice into it, add a glass of sherry, if permitted, and serve. Lamb served yesterday; Cucumber (May 19th); Potato Salad (April 12th); Wyvern Puddings (May 9th); Cheese (June 8th).

Things that must not be Forgotten.

1. Turn and rub the beef in the brine.
2. Prepare the apple chips (Note 1, May 25th); stew them with the sliced beet-root after they have been taken from the jar.

June 2nd.

Breakfast.	Luncheon.	Dinner.
Sardines. Collared Tongue. Hot Toast. Dry Toast. Marmalade. Brown and White Bread and Butter. Milk Porridge.	Eggs, Stewed with Cheese. Rice, with Apples and Beet-root.	Potato Soup. Broiled Steak, à la Béarnaise. Fried Potatoes. Newmarket Pudding. Cheese.

Marketing.

For the Day.—A slice of Rump Steak, not less than one inch thick, and weighing from three to three and a half pounds (Marketing, January 22nd); Kidney Potatoes; Apples; Beetroot.

For To-morrow.—A quart of fresh green Gooseberries; Muffins (January 29th).

BREAKFAST.—Sardines (January 12th); Collared Tongue (January 2nd); Milk Porridge (June 13th).

LUNCHEON.—Eggs, Stewed with Cheese (February 10th); Rice, with Apples and Beet-root (January 28th).

DINNER.—Potato Purée (January 26th); Broiled Steak (January 22nd); Béarnaise Sauce (March 23rd); Fried Potatoes (February 2nd). *Newmarket Pudding.*—Cut some slices of very thin bread and butter, and with them three-parts fill a buttered pie-dish, and sprinkle a few washed currants between the layers. Make as much custard as will fill the dish, sweeten it, and flavour it pleasantly by boiling the milk with a strip of thin lemon-rind, a bay-leaf, or a small piece of stick cinnamon. With a pint of milk put the yolks of two eggs and the white of one and a tea-spoonful of corn-flour. If more eggs are permitted the pudding will be correspondingly improved, and then the corn-flour may be omitted. Bake in a well-heated oven till the custard is set and the pudding is lightly browned upon the surface. A very pleasant variety of this pudding may be made by spreading a little marmalade upon the slices of bread instead of sprinkling currants between the layers. The name of the pudding will then be changed to *Marmalade Bread and Butter Pudding.* Cheese (June 8th).

Things that must not be Forgotten.

1. Turn and rub the beef in the brine.
2. Make rissoles of any scraps of broiled steak that may be left (January 6th). They can be made to-night, and will be easily fried in the morning for breakfast. Also make the Gooseberry Fool (June 24th).

June 3rd.

Breakfast.	Luncheon.	Dinner.
Beef Rissoles. Collared Tongue. Muffins. Dry Toast. Brown and White Bread and Butter. Gooseberry Fool.	Savoury Meat Cake. Baked Plum Pudding	Fried Whiting. Loin of Mutton, Boned, Stuffed, and Rolled. Mashed Potatoes. Broccoli. Fig Pudding. Cheese.

Marketing.

For the Day.—Half a pound of good Beef Suet, half for the baked plum and half for the fig pudding; fresh Whiting (January 17th); a Loin of Mutton, with as little fat as possible (the butcher should be asked to bone the joint); half a pound of Figs; a pennyworth of Parsley; Potatoes; Broccoli.

For To-morrow.—Six or eight small Soles, "slips" (*see* Marketing, January 3rd); one tin of Potted Grouse (January 7th); Sally Lunns; half a bundle of Rhubarb.

BREAKFAST.—Rissoles (January 6th); Collared Tongue (January 2nd); Muffins (January 30th); Gooseberry Fool (June 24th).

LUNCHEON.—Savoury Meat Cake, Economical (January 26th); Baked Plum Pudding (February 25th).

DINNER.—Fried Whiting (January 17th); Loin of Mutton, Boned and Rolled (April 22nd); Mashed Potatoes (May 12th); White Broccoli (April 25th). *Fig Pudding.*—Cut the figs into thin slices and chop them finely. Chop finely a quarter of a pound of suet and two ounces of apples, weighed after being peeled and cored; rub a quarter of a pound of stale bread through a wire sieve; grate as much ginger as would fill a salt-spoon, and as much nutmeg as would thinly cover a threepenny-piece. Put a quarter of a pound of flour into a bowl, mix the ingredients already mentioned thoroughly with it, and add a pinch of salt, a tea-spoonful of baking-powder, and two ounces of raw sugar. Beat up an egg, and mix about half a pint of milk with it; stir it, and bind the mixture together to a stiff batter. Turn the pudding into a greased mould that it will quite fill. Cover it with a cloth wrung out of boiling water and floured, and plunge it into plenty of fast-boiling water. Keep it boiling gently for four hours. If the water boils away, add more boiling. Turn it upon a hot dish, and send sweetened sauce (July 19th) to table with it. Cheese (June 8th).

Things that must not be Forgotten.

1. Turn and rub the beef in the brine.
2. The remains both of the baked plum pudding and of the fig pudding should be preserved, and can be used at luncheon to-morrow.
3. Make a *Rhubarb Mould* for dinner to-morrow. Wash (this time of the year), skin, and cut into short lengths as much rhubarb as will

fill a quart basin. Boil this gently with a gill of water, a pound of loaf sugar, and the strained juice and grated rind of half a lemon. Stir it occasionally, to prevent burning, until it has fallen. Soak half an ounce of gelatine in water while the rhubarb is boiling, then dissolve it with two table-spoonfuls of boiling water. Stir it into the rhubarb, beat it briskly for a minute or two, and add three or four drops of almond flavouring, and three or four drops of cochineal to colour it. Turn it into a mould that has been soaked in cold water, and put it in a cool place to set. Serve it on a glass dish, with cream, Devonshire cream, or custard as an accompaniment.

June 4th.

Breakfast.	Luncheon.	Dinner.
Baked Slips.	Mutton à la Sauce Piquante.	Mackerel à la Maitre d'Hôtel.
Potted Grouse.	Sliced Pudding.	Beef Stewed with Vegetables.
Sally Lunns.		New Potatoes.
Dry Toast.		Cabbage.
Brown and White Bread and Butter.		Rhubarb Mould.
Porridge.		Custard.
		Cheese.

Marketing.

For the Day.—Two or three moderate-sized Fresh Mackerel; about three pounds, in one piece, of the Muscle of the Leg of Beef (January 27th); New Potatoes; Spring Cabbage.

For To-morrow.—A pennyworth of Watercress.

BREAKFAST.—Baked Slips (January 7th). Potted Grouse (January 7th). *Sally Lunns.*—Prepare the Sally Lunns in all things like the tea-cakes (February 14th), remembering only to split them into three instead of into halves. Porridge (January 25th).

LUNCHEON.—Mutton à la Sauce Piquante, made of the remains of mutton served June 3rd (March 30th); Sliced Pudding (March 6th).

DINNER.—Mackerel, Baked, à la Maître d'Hôtel (April 15th); Maître d'Hôtel Sauce (May 6th); Beef à la Jardinière (March 17th); New Potatoes (April 12th). *Cabbage (Savoys, Greens, and Brussels Sprouts).*—Trim away the outer leaves, cut the cabbage into halves through the heart, put these into a bowl, sprinkle a little salt upon them, and pour cold water gently into the crevices to dislodge the insects. Pour cold water all over them, and let them lie in it for an hour; then wash them in two or three waters, and drain them in a colander. Have ready a saucepan with plenty of fast-boiling water in it; throw salt into this, in the proportion of a table-spoonful to half a gallon of water. If the vegetables are old or stale a very little carbonate of soda—as much as would barely cover a threepenny-piece—may be added also; but this is not necessary when the vegetables are young and freshly gathered.

Put in the cabbage, press it down occasionally, and boil till tender. *Do not put the lid on the saucepan during the whole time.* When done enough, turn it into a colander, press the water from it with the back of a plate, and put it into a hot tureen. Score it several times across the top with a knife, sprinkle pepper and salt over it, and serve. A small cabbage will be done enough in about twenty minutes; a large one will take from half to three-quarters of an hour. Savoys, Turnip-tops, and Brussels sprouts may be cooked in the same way: that is, trimmed and cleansed, then thrown into plenty of fast-boiling water, and boiled with the lid off the pan till done enough. Sprouts, however, should be kept whole and drained lightly, and they should not be pressed or cut across. Rhubarb Mould (June 3rd); Custard (August 10th); Cheese (June 8th).

Things that must not be Forgotten.

1. Turn and rub the beef in the brine.
2. Remember that the cabbage water must not be poured down the sink or down any drain belonging to the house. The best way of getting rid of it is to pour it on the ground outside.

June 5th.

Breakfast.	Luncheon.	Dinner.
Ox Eyes. Potted Grouse. Hot Buttered Toast. Dry Toast. Brown and White Bread and Butter. Corn Flour Milk.	Swiss Stew. Baked Omelet.	Croûte au Pot. Veal and Ham Pie. New Potatoes. Gooseberry Fool. Cheese.

Marketing.

For the Day.—Two pounds of Veal for the pie, one pound for the Swiss Stew; six ounces of mild Ham; a quart of fresh green Gooseberries; a pennyworth of German Yeast; Potatoes.

For To-morrow.—A tin of Pilchards; half a pound of German Sausage; two good-sized Ox-tails, ready jointed; six ounces of good Beef Suet.

BREAKFAST.—*Ox Eyes.*—Take some stale bread and cut it into slices three-quarters of an inch thick. Stamp these into rounds with the top of a tea-cup, and out of the middle of each one take a smaller round the size of the top of an egg-cup. Butter a dish that can be put into the oven, lay the rings in, then cover them with milk or cream (if sour cream is at hand it is to be preferred), and let them soak till soft. Drain away the milk and put a raw egg into the middle of each ring, sprinkle a little pepper and salt upon them, and put a tea-spoonful of milk on each egg. Bake in a hot oven until the whites are set, but they must not brown. If the dish on which they are baked cannot be sent to table, take the ox eyes up carefully with a slice, lay them on a hot dish, and garnish with watercress. Potted Grouse (January 7th); Corn Flour Milk (June 19th).

LUNCHEON.—*Swiss Stew.*—Cut a pound of veal into neat pieces, season these with pepper and salt, and brown them in a little dripping in a stewpan. Wash and pare six large potatoes, and one onion; cut them into halves, let them boil for a few minutes, then drain them, and put them with the veal. Mince the onion, and put it also with the meat, and add a tea-spoonful of vinegar, and a pint and a half of stock. Cover the pan closely, and simmer gently for an hour; thicken the gravy with flour, let it boil up, put a table-spoonful of ketchup with it, and serve. Baked Omelet (August 6th).

DINNER.—Croûte au Pot (May 25th); Veal and Ham Pie (April 29th); New Potatoes (April 12th); Gooseberry Fool (June 24th); Cheese (June 8th).

Things that must not be Forgotten.

1. Boil the beef (February 23rd), and lay it between two dishes with a weight upon it.
2. Preserve the liquor to make glaze to-morrow.
3. Pastry (April 17th) is to be made to-day: Veal and ham pie (April 29th); red currant pie of bottled fruit (August 7th); jam turnovers (September 25th); also a plain cake (June 26th); and teacakes (August 26th).

June 6th.

Breakfast.	Luncheon.	Dinner.
Pilchards.	Macaroni Cheese.	Vermicelli Soup.
German Sausage.	Jam and Bread Pudding, Economical.	Stewed Ox-tails.
Teacakes.		New Potatoes.
Dry Toast.		Greens.
Brown and White Bread and Butter.		Cottage Plum Pudding.
Marmalade.		Cheese.
Porridge.		

Marketing.

For the Day.—Half a pound of Naples Macaroni; Potatoes; Greens; a pennyworth of Parsley; three ounces of Vermicelli.

For To-morrow.—A moderate-sized but thick Turbot. Moderate-sized fish are the best. The under-side should be of a yellowish-white colour. Turbot will keep for a day if lightly salted. If Lobster Sauce is wanted, a small hen Lobster or a little Spawn. Fishmongers generally keep the spawn on hand corked down, and, if asked to do so, will send a little with the fish. A young Goose. Michaelmas is generally considered the time for geese, but young or green geese are excellent also at this time of the year, and they are less expensive than at Michaelmas. Potatoes; Lentils; a tin of Preserved Pineapple; two pennyworth of Watercress, half for breakfast; a Dried Haddock; two Lettuces; a half-pennyworth of Beetroot, and the same of small Salad; a small sugar-cured Ham (September 17th).

BREAKFAST.—Pilchards (January 23rd). *German Sausage.*—To serve the German sausage, cut it into thin slices, arrange them neatly on a dish, and garnish with parsley. Teacakes (February 14th); Porridge (January 25th).

LUNCHEON.—Macaroni Cheese (March 20th); Jam and Bread Pudding, Economical (February 23rd).

DINNER.—Vermicelli Soup (March 22nd); Stewed Ox-tails (May 8th); New Potatoes (April 12th). *Greens.*—Follow in all respects the directions given for boiling cabbage (June 4th). *Cottage Plum Pudding.*—Chop very finely six ounces of beef suet, free from skin and sinew. Put it into a bowl, and mix with it a pinch of salt, a quarter of a pound of currants, picked and dried, a quarter of a pound of chopped raisins, two tea-spoonfuls of baking-powder, six ounces of flour, two ounces of stale bread that has been rubbed through a wire sieve, a quarter of a nutmeg grated, and three ounces of moist sugar. Mix the ingredients thoroughly, then make them into a stiff paste with two well-beaten eggs and a little milk. Wring a cloth out of boiling water, flour it well, turn the pudding into it, tie it securely, and leave room for swelling; plunge it into boiling water, and keep boiling for four hours. Half these quantities will be sufficient for a small family. Cheese (June 8th).

Things that must not be Forgotten.

1. Make the mayonnaise sauce for to-morrow, if there is none in the house (August 30th); bottle it, and cork it closely.
2. Glaze the beef (March 21st).
3. Soak a cupful of green lentils in water all night.

Sunday, June 7th.

Breakfast.	Dinner.	Tea.	Supper.
Pilchards.	Boiled Turbot.	Brown and White Bread and Butter.	Pressed Beef.
Fried Ham.	Lobster Sauce or Dutch Sauce.	Apple Jelly.	Salad.
Fried Eggs.	Green Goose.	Plain Cake.	Red Currant Tart.
Teacakes.	Gooseberry Sauce.		Cheese.
Dry Toast.	New Potatoes.		
Watercress.	Green Lentils.		
Brown and White Bread and Butter.	Tinned Pineapple.		
Porridge.	Cheese.		

BREAKFAST.—Pilchards (January 23rd); Fried Ham; for this, take a slice, a third of an inch thick, from the middle of the ham bought yesterday (March 5th); Fried Eggs (March 5th); Teacakes (February 14th); Porridge (January 25th).

DINNER.—*Boiled Turbot.*—Empty and cleanse the fish. To prepare turbot for boiling, scrape it from tail to head, rub a little salt on, wash it in two or three waters, dry it with a cloth, and rub it over either with lemon-juice or vinegar: this is to make it white. If there are any red spots, rub them with salt and lemon-juice. Leave on the fins, as they, with the gelatinous skin, are considered the tit-bits. Make a slit through the middle of the dark side of the fish, to keep the white side from breaking. Place the fish on the drainer, and put it in plenty of boiling water, well salted and skimmed. Let it boil, then draw it back, and simmer very gently till the fish is done enough. A moderate-sized fish will take about twenty minutes. Watch and skim if required. As soon as the flesh seems to shrink from the bone it is done, and should be taken up immediately, as it will soon spoil. If not wanted immediately, it can be left on the drainer over the kettle, with a cloth laid over it. Serve, the white side up, on a hot dish covered with a napkin, and garnish with parsley and cut lemon; or, if lobster sauce is served with it, a little lobster coral may be used for garnishing. All fish, with one exception, may be boiled according to the directions given here: that is, cleaned, put into boiling salted water, boiled one minute, then drawn back, and *simmered gently* till done enough. The exception is mackerel, which should be put into warm, not boiling, water, for fear of breaking the skin. *Sauces for Turbot.*—Lobster, Dutch, anchovy, shrimp, oyster, and maître d'hôtel sauces are all suitable accompaniments to boiled turbot; the kind should be made to suit taste and convenience. Lobster sauce is perhaps generally preferred; and, as already stated, a little spawn can frequently be obtained of the fishmonger, for making it. This is not always the case, however, and a mistress who endeavours to provide for the wants of the household with a due regard to economy would perhaps think it extravagant to buy a lobster for no other purpose than to make sauce. From a moderate-sized hen lobster both lobster butter for sauce, and lobster salad might be made. Lobster butter, though best when fresh, will keep for a time, and as lobsters containing coral and spawn cannot always be had, the cook, when she does get any, should make a supply, so that lobster sauce can be made when wanted. *Lobster Butter* is made with both coral and spawn. The small beads lying under the body of the lobster are spawn, the deep red portions in the neck and down the back are coral. To make lobster butter, put the spawn on a tin and bake it gently for a few minutes, then pound both seeds and coral in a mortar with about twice the quantity of butter, and season with cayenne. *Be careful to break the seeds.* As the butter is precious, care should be taken not to waste even a little bit of it, and therefore the mortar should be carefully scraped out, either with a silver knife or with a piece of raw potato cut into the shape of a wedge. Rub the butter through a hair sieve with the back of a wooden spoon, and it is ready for use. To make *Lobster Sauce*, melt an ounce of butter in a small stewpan over the fire. Stir in half an ounce of flour, and beat the mixture to a smooth paste with the back of a wooden spoon. Pour in the third of a pint of cold water, and stir the sauce over the fire till it thickens. Add pepper and salt, and a table-spoonful of cream. Boil the sauce again, take it off the fire, and stir in enough lobster butter to colour it brightly. Add a few drops of lemon-juice, and serve. If it is to be had, a little of the lobster flesh, chopped small, can be stirred into the sauce, and will be considered an improvement. It is, however, oftener absent than present, as the meat is generally wanted for other purposes. Dutch Sauce (May 14th). Anchovy Sauce (July 17th); Shrimp Sauce (January 30th); Oyster Sauce (October 16th); Maître d'Hôtel Sauce (May 6th). *Green Goose.*—Proceed as for Roast Goose (September 29th), but do not stuff the bird. Season it, however, liberally inside with pepper and salt. *Gooseberry Sauce.*—Boil unripe gooseberries, drain them, and rub them through a sieve. Add a pat of butter to the pulp, season with sugar and salt if liked, and serve. This sauce is often served with mackerel. New Potatoes (April 12th); Lentils (March 2nd); Tinned Pineapple (April 8th); Cheese (June 8th).

TEA.—Plain Cake (June 26th).

SUPPER.—Beef, boiled (June 5th); Salad (March 13th); Red Currant Tart (August 7th).

Things that must not be Forgotten.

1. Preserve any cold turbot that may be left. Excellent fish cakes may be made of it for luncheon to-morrow.
2. Put half a pound of Normandy pippins to soak all night in cold water.
3. Also put a cupful of haricot beans to soak in cold water.

June 8th.

Breakfast.	Luncheon.	Dinner.
Dried Haddock. Pressed Beef. Toasted Teacakes. Dry Toast. Marmalade. Brown and White Bread and Butter. Corn Flour Milk.	Fish Cakes. Normandy Pippins.	Oyster Soup (made of the liquor the turbot was boiled in and tinned oysters). Haricot Mutton. Haricot Beans. Young Carrots. New Potatoes. Pancakes. Cheese.

Marketing.

For the Day.—A tin of Preserved Oysters; three or four pounds of Chops from the Loin for Haricot Mutton; Young Carrots; New Potatoes; the middle cut of the Silverside of Beef, weighing about eight pounds.

For To-morrow.—Anchovies, if not in the house; Radishes; Watercress.

BREAKFAST.—Dried Haddock (January 27th); Beef, boiled (June 5th); Toasted Teacakes (February 14th); Corn Flour Milk (June 19th).

LUNCHEON.—Fish Cakes (January 13th); Normandy Pippins (August 16th).

Dinner.—Oyster Soup (October 1st); Haricot Mutton (April 13th); Young Carrots (July 6th); Haricot Beans (June 20th); New Potatoes (April 12th); Pancakes (February 24th). *Cheese, To serve.*—Cheese may either be brought upon the table whole or cut; or, better still, it may be cut before dinner into small square pieces and handed round by the waiter. Fresh sweet butter, formed into small pats, balls, or rolls, and garnished with parsley; pulled bread (August 27th), rolls, biscuits, or rusks, with watercress, celery, salad, radishes, or cucumber, should always be sent to table with cheese. If this be done, and if care and judgment be exercised in the selection of the cheese, the course may be made most enjoyable. Foreign cheeses have become very popular of late (Roquefort, Camembert, Gorgonzola, Neufchatel, and Gruyère), and afford a most agreeable change even from the time-honoured Stilton. Small portions of two or three different kinds of cheese may be handed on the same salver. When cheese becomes hard and dry it should on no account be wasted, as it may be used in various ways (Index: Cheese, Dry, To Use).

Things that must not be Forgotten.

1. Boil the brine with an additional handful of salt. When cold, put the silverside of beef into it.
2. Make mutton pies for breakfast to-morrow of scraps of mutton that may be left (January 3rd).
3. If any haricot beans remain from dinner, let them be put aside to make haricot salad, to be served with the pressed beef at luncheon to-morrow.
4. Wash a tea-cupful of small tapioca, and let it soak all night in a pint of cold water.
5. Soak also a cupful of green lentils.

June 9th.

Breakfast.	Luncheon.	Dinner.
Mock Woodcock.	Pressed Beef.	Croûte au Pot.
Mutton Pies.	Plain Tapioca Pudding.	Rolled Ribs of Beef.
Radishes and Watercress.		New Potatoes.
Hot Buttered Toast.		Cauliflower.
Dry Toast.		Lemon Pudding.
Brown and White Bread and Butter.		Cheese.
Bread and Milk.		

Marketing.

For the Day.—About eight pounds of the Ribs of Beef (January 10th), boned and rolled; six ounces of Beef Suet; Potatoes; Lemons; Cauliflower.
For To-morrow.—Half a dozen fresh Mackerel of a moderate size (April 4th); half a pound of Bacon in rashers; a two-pound tin of Preserved Tomatoes; a bottle of Preserved Raspberries; Mustard and Cress for breakfast. Order three pennyworth of Cream for to-morrow.

BREAKFAST.—Mock Woodcock (March 26th); Mutton Pies (January 3rd); Radishes (March 12th); Bread and Milk (January 25th).

LUNCHEON.—*Plain Tapioca Pudding.*—Put the tapioca, with the water in which it was soaked and a pint of milk, into a greased pie-dish. Throw into it half an inch of stick cinnamon or five or six inches of thin lemon-rind, and add a piece of butter about the size of a threepenny-piece. Bake in a gentle oven until the tapioca is transparent and the pudding is covered with a brown skin. It will take about three hours. Serve with sugar or jam.

DINNER.—Croûte au Pot (May 25th); Rolled Ribs of Beef, Roasted (March 4th or 8th). *Gravy.*—Roasted joints should be served with a little brown, clear, bright gravy, as free from fat as it can be obtained. If the gravy that belongs to the joint is to be served, the cook should, when the meat is sufficiently roasted, take up the dripping-tin and carefully and slowly pour away the fat. As soon as brown sediment begins to run away as well as fat she should stop, and pour about a quarter of a pint more of boiling water into the tin, stirring and scraping well those parts where the gravy has dried and become hard. When the liquor looks dark and rich, she should strain it through a fine strainer into a small stewpan, and make it hot, without absolutely allowing it to boil, put a pinch of salt with it, and pour it into the dish but not over the joint. Two or three table-spoonfuls of gravy only should be thus served, however, as it is most objectionable for the carver to have very much gravy in the dish, and the juices which run from the meat when it is cut will add to the quantity as well as improve the quality of that which is provided. Many cooks pour half the gravy at their disposal into the dish, and send the rest in hot a few minutes later, and this course is to be recommended. Gravy will be stronger if stock instead of water be stirred into the dripping-tin, and very often what is called "gravy beef" is purchased to make it with. This is as extravagant as it is unnecessary. In a house where meat is used daily the cook can always, if she likes, put on one side scraps and trimmings to make gravy. Stock, made for the purpose beforehand, can be used instead of the sediment in the dripping-tin, which sediment may be allowed to go cold, and be used the next time gravy is wanted; the obvious advantage being that in both instances the gravy can be served perfectly free from fat. Stock for beef gravy may be made as follows:—Slice a small onion, and fry it very lightly in a little butter. Pour upon it half a pint of water, and add a small pinch of celery-seed, a sprig of parsley, a strip of bacon-rind scalded and scraped, and a small piece of turnip, together with scraps of meat or bone (the shank bone of a leg of mutton is excellent for making gravy). Simmer gently and skim carefully, till the liquor is reduced one-half, then strain it into a basin; when cold, free it entirely from fat, and make it hot when wanted. Of course, if liquor from boiled meat can be substituted for water in a case like this, so much the better. This flavoured stock would do very well for beef, but not for mutton; mutton and lamb should have a tasteless gravy. New Potatoes (April 12th); Cauliflower (April 25th); Lemon Pudding (August 12th); Cheese (June 8th).

Things that must not be Forgotten.
1. Turn and rub the beef in the brine.
2. Pickle the mackerel for breakfast to-morrow (August 28th).
3. See that the butcher sends home the fresh bones taken from the rolled beef. They must be stewed for stock (February 13th).
4. Make the Hydropathfc Pudding for dinner to-morrow (June 16th).

June 10th.

Breakfast.	Luncheon.	Dinner.
Pickled Mackerel.	Shepherd's Pie.	Tomato Purée.
Toasted Bacon.	Custard Sippets.	Cold Rolled Beef.
Mustard and Cress.		Salad.
Hot Toast.		New Potatoes.
Dry Toast.		Raspberry Hydropathic Pudding.
Brown and White Bread and Butter.		Cream.
Bread and Milk.		Cheese.

Marketing.

For the Day.—Two heads of Lettuce; a pennyworth of Watercress; a half-pennyworth of boiled Beetroot; a half-pennyworth of small Salad; New Potatoes: a pennyworth of Parsley.

For To-morrow.—A tin of Bovill's Potted Hare (*see* Remarks on Potted Grouse, January 7th); Muffins (January 29th).

BREAKFAST.—Pickled Mackerel (August 28th); Toasted Bacon (January 19th); Bread and Milk (January 25th).

LUNCHEON.—Shepherd's Pie, made of the remains of the pressed beef (January 12th). *Custard Sippets.*—Break an egg into a plate, beat it well, and put with it the third of a pint of milk, sugar and flavouring to taste. Cut stale bread, as much as may be required, into slices half an inch thick, divide them into neatly-shaped pieces, and soak them in the custard. Take them up before they are soft enough to break, lay them in a clean cloth with a cupful of flour, and shake the corners of the cloth to throw the flour over them, and so coat them with it. Put them carefully on a hair sieve, and shake it to free them from superfluous flour, and fry them in a frying-pan half-filled with hot fat till they are lightly browned on both sides. Lay them between two pieces of kitchen paper to free them from grease, sift white sugar thickly over them, and serve hot.

DINNER.—Tomato Purée (March 11th); Salad (March 13th); New Potatoes (April 12th); Raspberry Hydropathic Pudding (June 16th) Cheese (June 8th).

Things that must not be Forgotten.

1. Turn and rub the beef in the brine.
2. Turn the pieces of mackerel in the vinegar. If this is done daily the fish will keep for three or four days.
3. Make the ground rice mould for luncheon to-morrow (August 7th).
4. Wash and soak a large cupful of hominy (Note 3, February 10th).

June 11th.

Breakfast.	Luncheon.	Dinner.
Boiled Eggs.	Pickled Mackerel.	Fried Halibut.
Potted Hare.	Ground Rice Mould, with Apple Jelly.	Roast Leg of Lamb.
Muffins.		Mint Sauce.
Dry Toast.		New Potatoes.
Brown and White Bread and Butter.		Broccoli.
Boiled Hominy.		Lèche Crème.
		Cheese.

Marketing.

For the Day.—As many slices of Halibut, an inch thick, as are likely to be required. Halibut is a most excellent fish, and it is astonishing that it is not more popular than it is. In the north of England, indeed, it is valued according to its deserts; but in the south of England it is but little known, excepting to Jews, with whom it is a great favourite. Very likely it is held in low estimation because it is cheap. It grows to an enormous size, but those fish are the best which weigh from thirty to forty pounds. It may be cooked in various ways, but the one which is least to be recommended is boiling. Fishmongers would be glad to get it if they were asked for it and thought there was a chance of selling it, because in spring and summer it is generally brought abundantly to market. In choosing it, remember that the same rules hold good with it as with other fish. A Leg of Lamb; half a pound of Ratafias; New Potatoes; Broccoli; Mint.

For To-morrow.—A tin of Sardines (January 12th); half a pound of Mushrooms.

BREAKFAST.—Boiled Eggs (January 5th); Potted Hare (*see* Potted Grouse, January 7th); Muffins (January 30th); Boiled Hominy (February 11th).

LUNCHEON.—Pickled Mackerel (August 28th). *Ground Rice Mould* (August 7th).—Turn the mould upon a glass dish, and garnish it with bright-coloured jelly or jam.

DINNER.—Fried Halibut (June 23rd); Roast Leg of Lamb (March 4th); Gravy (June 9th); Mint Sauce (March 25th); New Potatoes (April 12th); White Broccoli (April 25th); Lèche Crème (May 7th); Cheese (June 8th).

Things that must not be Forgotten.

1. Preserve any fish that may be left. It can be made into a fish pie for luncheon to-morrow.
2. Turn and rub the beef in the brine.
3. The remains of boiled hominy can be fried for breakfast to-morrow.

June 12th.

Breakfast.	Luncheon.	Dinner.
Sardines.	Fish Pie.	Lobster Soup, of Fresh Lobster.
Stewed Mushrooms.	Cold Lamb.	Beef Steak Pie.
Dry Toast.	Mint Sauce.	Potatoes.
Marmalade.	Potato Salad.	Greens.
Brown and White Bread and Butter.		Newcastle Pudding.
Fried Hominy.		Cheese.

Marketing.

For the Day.—Two pounds of Rump or Buttock Steak (January 1st); half an Ox Kidney; a quarter of a pint of Mushrooms; a small fresh Lobster (*see* remarks on Lobster Butter, June 7th); a pennyworth of German Yeast for Scones, or Baking-powder (August 2nd) may be used; Potatoes; Greens; Gooseberries.

For To-morrow.—Order a Lamb's Fry; a pennyworth of Watercress.

BREAKFAST.—Sardines (January 12th); Stewed Mushrooms (March 20th); Fried Hominy (February 12th).

LUNCHEON.—Fish Pie (*see* Cod Pie, January 2nd); Lamb and Mint Sauce served yesterday; Potato Salad (April 12th).

DINNER.—*Lobster Soup.*—Follow the recipe given May 20th, but use fresh lobster instead of tinned lobster, and stock made from rolled beef bone instead of fish stock. Beef Steak Pie (March 26th); Potatoes (April 12th); Greens (*see* Cabbage, To Boil, June 4th). *Newcastle Pudding.*—Butter the inside of a pint basin, and fill it with thin slices of stale bread and butter which have had white sugar and grated lemon sprinkled upon each slice. Make a custard by mixing half a pint of new milk with two well-beaten eggs. Flavour this also with lemon. Pour the custard over the bread, lay a buttered paper on the top, and steam it very gently for about an hour (*see* Treacle Pudding, March 28th). Turn out carefully, and serve with fruit or lemon syrup (March 19th). If liked, a more delicate pudding may be made by using sponge biscuits instead of bread, and then one egg only will be required for the custard. Cheese (June 8th).

Things that must not be Forgotten.

1. Turn and rub the beef in the brine.
2. Make potted beef of any little pieces of meat that may be left in the pie (January 23rd).
3. Pastry is to be made to-day (April 17th): beef-steak pie (March 26th), green gooseberry pie, of fresh fruit (August 7th), open jam tart (August 7th); also scones (August 26th) and seed cake (August 14th).

June 13th.

Breakfast.	Luncheon.	Dinner.
Potted Beef.	Cauliflower au Gratin.	Milk Soup.
Buttered Eggs.	Baked Plum Pudding.	Lamb's Fry.
Scones.		Bacon.
Dry Toast.		Potatoes.
Watercress.		Spring Cabbage.
Brown and White Bread and Butter.		Open Jam Tart.
		Plain Rice Pudding.
Milk Porridge.		Cheese.

Marketing.

For the Day.—A large Cauliflower; a quarter of a pound of Beef Suet; a good-sized Lamb's Fry; one pound of Bacon in strips; Potatoes; Spring Cabbage; a pennyworth of Parsley.

For To-morrow.—One or two Leverets are probably needed for a dish, but of course this must depend upon the requirements of the family. Like hares, leverets should be kept for awhile before being dressed. They may generally be bought ready for cooking, but if it is preferred to hang them at home it should be remembered that they will not keep long in warm weather. A leveret may be known by the knob on the first joint of the fore-leg. Two or three sets of Chickens' or Ducks' Giblets; Half a pound of French Chocolate; four plump Sheep's Kidneys; a tin of Collared Tongue (January 2nd); three heads of Lettuce; a pennyworth of boiled Beetroot; a pennyworth of Watercress; a half-pennyworth of Small Salad; Potatoes; Cauliflower; Asparagus; Gherkins; half a pint of Mushrooms, or a small tin of Champignons: Capers and Anchovies or Sardines will be needed for Russian Salad; one pound of Sea Biscuits.

BREAKFAST. — Potted Beef (January 23rd); Buttered Eggs (January 16th). *Milk Porridge.*—Boil a pint of milk. Whilst it is boiling mix a table-spoonful of oatmeal smoothly with a little cold milk, stir the boiling milk into this, and boil it for ten minutes, stirring it all the time. Add a pinch of salt or a little sugar, if preferred, and eat with bread and butter.

LUNCHEON.—Cauliflower au Gratin (April 25th); Baked Plum Pudding (February 25th).

DINNER.—Milk Soup (January 3rd); Lamb's Fry (May 16th); Bacon (Liver and Bacon (January 17th); Potatoes (April 12th); Cabbage (June 4th); Open Jam Tart (August 7th); Plain Rice Pudding (February 24th); Cheese (June 8th).

Things that must not be Forgotten.

1. When the lamb's fry is cooked, and before sending to table, put aside a little of the sweetbread for Russian salad to-morrow evening.
2. If mayonnaise is not in the house, make a little and bottle it closely (August 30th).
3. Turn and rub the beef in the brine.
4. Remember that old dry cheese may be used for the cauliflower au gratin.
5. Clean and blanch the giblets, so as to keep them sweet (Feb. 1st).
6. Put the white ends of the asparagus one inch deep in cold water till wanted.

Sunday, June 14th.

Breakfast.	Dinner.	Tea.	Supper.
Fried Kidneys and Bacon.	Giblet Soup.	Brown and White Bread and Butter.	Russian Salad.
Watercress.	Civet of Leveret.	Apple Jelly.	Gooseberry Pie.
Scones.	Potatoes.	Seed Cake.	Cream.
Dry Toast.	Cauliflowers.		Cheese.
Brown and White Bread and Butter.	Asparagus and Dutch Sauce.		
Biscuits and Milk.	Chocolate Pudding.		
	Custard.		
	Cheese.		

BREAKFAST.—Fried Kidneys and Bacon (January 2nd); Scones (May 23rd). *Biscuits and Milk.*—Break up as many sea biscuits as are likely to be needed. Put them into a bowl, and pour boiling water on them to cover them; put a plate over them, and let them soak for about ten minutes. Drain away the water; put milk in its place and a little sugar, and serve. This dish may be served for the children's breakfast as a change from porridge or bread and milk.

DINNER.—Giblet Soup (February 1st). *Civet of Leveret.*—Supposing there is one leveret, trim a quarter of a pound of bacon, and soak it in water for a few minutes to extract the salt. Divide the leveret into neat joints. Cut the bacon into inch-square pieces and fry them; take them up, and fry the leveret in the bacon fat. Now take up the leveret, put back the bacon, and add an onion, a shallot, a small carrot, a small turnip, a bunch of parsley, a sprig of thyme, and a bay-leaf. Turn all over in the frying-pan a few times; add the pieces of leveret, half a pint of mushrooms neatly trimmed and sliced, and as much stock as will cover the meat. Let the gravy boil, then draw the saucepan back, and stew gently till the pieces of leveret are tender. They will take about an hour and a half. Add a table-spoonful of flour mixed to a smooth paste with water, and season with salt and pepper. Put the meat on a dish; boil the sauce, skim it carefully, stir a glass of dark wine into it, strain it over the leveret, and serve. Potatoes (April 12th); Cauliflower (April 25th). *Asparagus.—To boil Asparagus and Seakale.*—Asparagus is best when freshly cut. Scrape the stems slightly and throw them into cold water as they are done, but do not keep them in more than a minute or two. Cut the white ends evenly, to make the stalks the same length, and tie them in bundles with tape or rag, as twine would be likely to cut the stalks. Choose a stewpan large enough to hold the asparagus without bending the stalks. Half fill it with water, throw a little salt into it, skim it, and when it boils quickly put in the asparagus. Leave the lid off the pan, and boil gently till tender. Asparagus will need to boil from twenty to thirty minutes, according to the thickness, and it should be taken up as soon as it is done enough, or it will lose colour and flavour. Drain it, and lay it on a round of toast half an inch thick, well browned on both sides, and that has been dipped into the asparagus water. Send rich Melted Butter (July 17th), *Oiled Butter* (that is, butter melted but not allowed to brown, then poured away from the curd that settles at the bottom, and slightly salted), Dutch sauce (May 14th), Mayonnaise Sauce (August 30th), or Brown Butter Sauce (February 12th), to table with it. Asparagus is frequently served by itself after the joint. Sauce should never be *poured over* asparagus, but served in a tureen. *Seakale* is boiled just like asparagus, though it needs only to be washed and trimmed before it is boiled. When very young it will be done enough in about twenty minutes; large seakale will require boiling from half an hour to three-quarters. Melted butter may, if liked, be poured over the seakale in the tureen. Chocolate Pudding (July 24th); Custard (August 10th); Cheese (June 8th).

TEA.—Seed Cake (August 14th).

SUPPER.—Russian Salad (April 5th); Gooseberry Pie (August 7th).

Things that must not be Forgotten.

1. Turn and rub the beef in the brine.
2. Preserve all the bones and trimmings of the leveret. Excellent soup may be made of them for to-morrow.
3. If any asparagus is left it can be cooked with eggs for breakfast to-morrow, instead of savoury eggs (May 4th).

June 15th.

Breakfast.	Luncheon.	Dinner.
Savoury Eggs.	Macaroni and Tongue.	Leveret Soup.
Collared Tongue.	Cake Pudding.	Boiled Beef.
Scones.		Young Carrots.
Dry Toast.		Potatoes.
Brown and White Bread and Butter.		Corn-flour Blancmange.
		Lemon Syrup.
Milk Porridge.		Cheese.

Marketing.

For the Day.—Half a pound of Macaroni; Carrots; Potatoes; an Ox-cheek.

For To-morrow.—Six or eight small Soles, "Slips," for breakfast (January 3rd); Watercress. Order three pennyworth of Cream.

BREAKFAST.—Savoury Eggs (January 1st); Collared Tongue (January 2nd); Scones (May 23rd); Milk Porridge (June 13th).

LUNCHEON.—*Macaroni and Tongue.*—Follow the recipe given for macaroni and ham (April 3rd), using a slice of collared tongue instead of ham. Cake Pudding (February 4th).

DINNER.—*Leveret Soup.*—Follow in all respects the directions given for making hare soup (January 19th). Boiled Beef (February 23rd); Young Carrots (July 6th); Potatoes (April 12th). *Corn-flour Blancmange.*—Measure one pint of milk; put two ounces of corn-flour into a basin, and mix it smoothly with a little of the cold milk. Put what is left of the milk, with an ounce of sugar, into a saucepan, and make it hot without letting it boil. Mix the corn-flour with it, and stir it well till it thickens, and five minutes afterwards put two or three drops of almond or vanilla flavouring with the corn-flour; turn it into a damp mould, and put it into a cool place till wanted. Serve it upon a glass dish, and garnish it with jam or with a compôte of fresh fruit (August 5th). If the mould is flavoured with lemon, lemon syrup coloured with cochineal may be poured round it. Lemon Syrup (March 19th); Cheese (June 8th).

Things that must not be Forgotten.

1. Cleanse the ox-cheek (*see* Note 5, February 6th).
2. Boil the brine, and when it is cold put the cheek into it.
3. Make a rhubarb mould (June 3rd) for dinner to-morrow.
4. When the beef comes from table, take the marrow from the bone.
5. Put a cupful of green lentils to soak in cold water all night.
6. Make *Rice and Barley Porridge* for breakfast. To do this, wash a quarter of a pound of rice and a quarter of a pound of Scotch barley, and stew them very gently in two quarts of water till they are quite soft. They will take two or three hours. Turn into a dish, and before serving them to-morrow boil up again with a little milk, and sugar or treacle to taste. If a little cream can be served with this porridge it will be very agreeable.
7. *See* Note 2, January 3rd.

June 16th.

Breakfast.	Luncheon.	Dinner.
Marrow Toast.	Cold Boiled Beef.	Lentil Soup.
Baked Slips.	Salad.	Mutton Chops, with Piquante Sauce.
Dry Toast.	Plain Sago Pudding.	Potatoes.
Watercress.		Rhubarb Mould.
Brown and White Bread and Butter.		Cream.
Rice and Barley Porridge.		Cheese.

Marketing.

For the Day.—Two heads of Lettuce; a half-pennyworth of Beetroot; ditto of Small Salad; a pennyworth of Endive; three or four pounds of the best end of a Loin of Mutton (Marketing, April 30th); Potatoes.

For To-morrow.—Bottled Red Currants.

BREAKFAST.—Marrow Toast (January 21st); Baked Slips (January 7th); Porridge made yesterday.

LUNCHEON.—Beef served yesterday; Salad (March 13th); Plain Sago Pudding (March 9th).

DINNER.—Lentil Soup (April 1st), to be made of the beef liquor if it is not too salt; Mutton Chops, with Piquante Sauce (April 30th); Rhubarb Mould (June 3rd); Potatoes (April 12th); Cheese (June 8th).

Things that must not be Forgotten.

1. Turn and rub the cheek in the brine.

2. Make hydropathic red currant pudding for dinner to-morrow. *Hydropathic Pudding* may be made with fruit of all kinds, fresh or bottled. If fresh fruit is used, it must be stewed with water and sugar until it is about as much cooked as it would be in a fruit pie. If bottled fruit is used, the syrup only should be boiled with sugar, and the fruit simmered in it for a minute or two. Take some stale bread. Cut a round piece the size of half-a-crown and lay it at the bottom of a basin, and arrange around it strips or fingers of bread about half an inch wide, remembering to leave a space the width of the finger between the strips. When the fruit is ready, and while it is still hot, put it in a spoonful at a time, so as not to displace the bread, and, as a further means to this end, put the heavier part of the fruit—the pulp and skin and stones, if there are any—at the bottom of the mould, and the juice last of all. Cover the top entirely with stale bread cut into very small dice; lay a plate on the pudding, put a weight on the plate, preserving the juice that rises above the plate, and set the pudding in a cool place till wanted. If it is well pressed down it will turn out in a shape, and will be found an excellent pudding. This dish is thus named because it is served at the hydropathic establishments as a substitute for fruit pies and tarts, as pastry is not considered wholesome. In cold weather it will turn out if it is made three or four hours before it is wanted, but in warm weather it needs to be made overnight.

3. Preserve the bones from the mutton chops. Stewed with the bones from the breast of veal served to-morrow, they will make excellent stock (February 13th).

June 17th.

Breakfast.	Luncheon.	Dinner.
Fried Ham. Fried Eggs. Dry Toast. Marmalade. Brown and White Bread and Butter. Milk Toast.	Bubble and Squeak. Savoury Rice.	Fried Plaice. Dutch Sauce. Rolled Breast of Veal. Potatoes. Spinach. Hydropathic Red Currant Pudding. Cream or Custard. Cheese.

Marketing.

For the Day.—A thick Plaice (April 21st); the fishmonger should be asked to fillet the fish. A Breast of Veal; the butcher should be asked to bone the

P

meat. One pound of Bacon, cut into rashers (half for to-day and half for to-morrow); Suet, for forcemeat; Potatoes; Spinach; a pennyworth of Parsley. Ham bought June 6th is supposed to be in the house.

For To-morrow.—A tin of Prawns.

BREAKFAST.—Fried Ham (March 5th); Fried Eggs (March 5th). *Milk Toast.*—Toast lightly and butter as much stale bread as is likely to be needed. Have ready boiling milk to fill the dish. Season it with salt; stir a small piece of butter in till melted; lay the toast on a flat dish, pour the milk over, and serve. The children might, for a change, like to have marmalade spread on the toast instead of butter.

LUNCHEON.—Bubble and Squeak (January 22nd). *Savoury Rice.*—Wash a small tea-cupful of rice, drain it, and put it into a stewpan, with an onion, a carrot, a pint of nicely-flavoured stock, and a small piece of butter. Let it stew gently till it has absorbed the liquor. Make a custard with three-quarters of a pint of milk and one egg. Put this with the rice, add a table-spoonful of chopped parsley, a shallot finely minced, and season with pepper and salt. Put the rice into a buttered dish, and bake in a gentle oven till it is covered with a brown skin. The rice will be very good if it is simply boiled in the stock till tender, and then served.

DINNER.—Fried Plaice (April 21st); Dutch Sauce (May 14th). *Rolled Breast of Veal.*—Lay the boned breast on a table, and spread veal forcemeat evenly upon it (June 27th). Roll it up very tightly, and bind it round and round with tape. Wrap it in a greased paper, and bake it in a moderate oven. Baste it frequently over the paper. Half an hour before it is taken up remove the paper, that it may brown. Serve it on a hot dish, and garnish it with thin slices of fried bacon and cut lemon. Pour a little brown gravy (June 28th) over it, and send more to table in a tureen. Half an hour per pound should be allowed for baking. Potatoes (April 12th); Spinach (May 10th); Pudding made yesterday; Custard (August 10th); Cheese (June 8th).

Things that must not be Forgotten.

1. Turn and rub the ox-cheek in the brine.
2. Stew the mutton and veal bones for stock.
3. Partially prepare the rice milk for breakfast. Wash half a pound of rice, and put it into a saucepan, with a little salt and a quart of water. Let it boil very gently for an hour and a quarter. Turn it into a bowl, and leave it till morning.

June 18th.

Breakfast.	Luncheon.	Dinner.
Prawns. Collared Tongue. Hot Buttered Toast. Dry Toast. Honey. Brown and White Bread and Butter. Rice Milk.	Baked Mackerel, à la Maître d'Hôtel. Gingerbread Pudding.	Victoria Soup. Minced Veal. Fried Bacon. Potatoes. Cauliflower. Wyvern Puddings. Cheese.

Marketing.

For the Day.—Two moderate-sized Mackerel (April 4th); Potatoes; Cauliflower.

For To-morrow.—A dried Haddock; a quarter of a pound of German Sausage. Order a Lamb's Fry and four plump young Pigeons. Mustard and Cress.

BREAKFAST.—Prawns (February 7th); Collared Tongue served June 15th. *Rice Milk.*—Take the rice that has been already boiled in water. Let it boil up in a pint and a half of milk, sweeten it to taste with honey or sugar, and serve.

LUNCHEON.—Baked Mackerel (April 15th); Gingerbread Pudding (May 20th).

DINNER.—Victoria Soup (February 9th); Minced Veal (May 11th); Fried Bacon (January 2nd); Potatoes (April 12th); Cauliflower (April 25th); Wyvern Puddings (May 9th); Cheese (June 8th).

Things that must not be Forgotten.
1. Turn and rub the ox-cheek in the brine.
On no account allow the mince to boil in the gravy.

June 19th.

Breakfast.	Luncheon.	Dinner.
Dried Haddock. German Sausage. Hot Buttered Toast. Dry Toast. Mustard and Cress. Brown and White Bread and Butter. Corn-flour Milk.	Lamb's Fry. Plain Rolled Pudding, with Treacle.	Crécy Soup. Pigeon Pie. Potatoes. Spring Cabbage. Queen's Pudding. Cheese.

Marketing.

For the Day.—A Lamb's Fry; a pound and a half of Rump Steak, an inch thick, for the pigeon pie; Potatoes; Spring Cabbage; a pennyworth of fresh German Yeast.

For To-morrow.—A tin of Bovill's Potted Pheasant; a tin of Pilchards; a Cow's Heel, from the tripe shop.

BREAKFAST.—Dried Haddock (January 27th); German Sausage (June 6th). *Corn-flour Milk.*—Put a little lemon-rind or a laurel-leaf into a pint of milk, and set it by the side of the fire till it is nicely flavoured, then bring it to the boil. Beat two table-spoonfuls of flour to a smooth paste with half a tea-cupful of milk, and add two well-beaten eggs. Stir the boiling milk into the corn-flour, return the whole to the saucepan, let the preparation boil once more, and stir it over the fire five minutes afterwards. Sweeten with honey, sugar, or treacle, and serve.

LUNCHEON. — Lamb's Fry (May 16th); Plain Rolled Pudding (March 16th).

DINNER.—Crécy Soup (January 5th); Pigeon Pie (May 15th); to be made with pastry to-day; Potatoes (April 12th); Spring Cabbage (June 4th); Queen's Pudding (August 9th); Cheese (June 8th).

Things that must not be Forgotten.

1. Turn and rub the ox-cheek in the brine.

2. Pastry is to be made to-day (April 17th); Pigeon pie (May 15th); jam tarts (August 7th); lemon cheesecakes (August 18th); open jam tart (August 7th); also Vienna bread (August 26th); and rice cake (August 2nd). Rough Puff Paste (May 29th) will be very good for the pigeon pie. What is called Short Crust is very good for pies and tarts. The difference between Puff Paste and Short Crust is this: in Puff Paste the butter and flour are not mixed together, but are kept separate in thin layers. In Short Crust the butter and flour are intermixed by kneading. Short Crust is of two qualities: one for superior pastry, and the other for household pastry. *To Make Superior Short Crust.*—Put six ounces of flour on a board, and rub four ounces of butter into it till it looks like fine oatmeal. Mix in a very small pinch of salt and an ounce of fine white sugar. Make a well in the centre of the flour, and put into it the yolk of an egg, two drops of lemon-juice, and a large table-spoonful of cold water. Yolk of egg and lemon-juice help to make the paste workable. Mix the whole to a smooth stiff paste with two fingers; knead the paste lightly, and keep the board and the fingers floured, to prevent their being sticky. Fold the paste over, and roll it *once only* to the size and thickness that is needed. *Economical Short Crust.*—Put a pound of flour into a bowl, with a pinch of salt and a heaped tea-spoonful of baking-powder; mix thoroughly, then rub in six ounces of clarified dripping; add water to make a stiff paste, roll out once, and use.

3. Put a cupful of white haricot beans to soak all night in cold water.

June 20th.

Breakfast.	Luncheon.	Dinner.
Pilchards. Potted Pheasant. Vienna Bread. Dry Toast. Brown and White Bread and Butter. Oatmeal Porridge.	Cow's Heel, with Parsley Sauce. Custard Sippets.	Croûte au Pot. Haricot Mutton. Haricot Beans. Potatoes. Roly-poly Pudding. Cheese.

Marketing.

For the Day.—The best end of a neck of Mutton; six ounces of Beef Suet, for roly-poly; a pennyworth of Parsley.
For To-morrow.—A rather small Turbot; ask the fishmonger to fillet the fish before sending it home (January 3rd and June 6th). Half a pint of Shrimps, for sauce; a couple of Ducklings; Green Peas, if not too expensive. Choose ducklings with plump, firm breasts. A tin of Salmon, or a pound or two of Fresh Salmon, for supper; Ingredients for Salad.

BREAKFAST. — Pilchards (January 23rd); Potted Pheasant (see Potted Grouse, January 7th); Vienna Bread (August 26th); Oatmeal Porridge (January 25th).

LUNCHEON.—Cow's Heel, with Parsley Sauce (February 20th); Custard Sippets (June 10th).

DINNER.—Croûte au Pot (May 25th); Haricot Mutton (April 13th). *Haricot Beans, Boiled.*—Drain the beans, and put them in a saucepan with plenty of cold water, slightly salted. Let them boil gently till tender, but not pulpy. They will take about two hours. Pour away the water, and let the beans stand by the fire a minute or two, shaking them once or twice, to dry them. Put a little piece of butter with them and a little pepper and salt, and serve them as hot as possible. For a change, the beans when drained may be put into a stewpan, with a slice of butter, pepper, salt, a table-spoonful of lemon-juice, and a table-spoonful of chopped parsley; or an ounce of butter may be melted, mixed smoothly with half an ounce of flour, a quarter of a pint of stock or water, and a table-spoonful of parsley, and the beans may be shaken over the fire in this sauce. Still another change may be made by chopping one or two onions very finely, then frying them in a little butter, mixing them with the boiled beans, and moistening the whole with a spoonful or two of gravy. It must not be forgotten that any haricot beans that are left will be excellent served as a salad. If it should happen that they have not been soaked overnight, they may still be prepared for dinner, care being taken to throw half a cupful of cold water in with them every half hour whilst they are boiling. In this case they will not need to boil much longer than they would if soaked. Potatoes (April 12th); Roly-poly Pudding (August 18th); Cheese (June 8th).

Things that must not be Forgotten.

1. Turn and rub the ox-cheek in the brine.
2. Boil what remains of the Canadian ham (*see* Note 4, May 27th).
3. Cleanse the goose giblets (February 1st); and fry them in a little butter; this will keep them good till June 22nd.
4. Soak a breakfast-cupful of hominy in water all night (February 10th).
5. Preserve the liquor in which the cow-heel is boiled for soup on June 22nd.

Sunday, June 21st.

Breakfast.	Dinner.	Tea.	Supper.
Boiled Eggs.	Filleted Turbot.	Brown and White Bread Pudding.	Pickled Salmon.
Boiled Ham.	Shrimp or Lobster Sauce.	Damson Jam.	Salad.
Vienna Bread.	Roast Ducklings.	Cheesecakes.	Open Jam Tart.
Dry Toast.	New Potatoes.		Cheese.
Brown and White Bread and Butter.	Green Peas or Spinach.		
Marmalade.	Hayrick Puddings.		
Boiled Hominy.	Cheese.		

BREAKFAST.—Boiled Eggs (January 5th); Ham boiled yesterday; Vienna Bread (August 26th); Boiled Hominy (February 11th).

DINNER.—*Filleted Turbot.*—Divide the fillets into neat pieces about the size of two fingers, dry them, season them, pepper and salt them, and put them, side by side, in a frying-pan, with a slice of butter melted and a tea-spoonful of lemon-juice. Put them over the fire for a few minutes, and turn them over when they are half cooked. They will take about ten minutes. Drain them on kitchen paper; arrange them in a circle on a dish, pour the shrimp sauce over them, and place a little fried parsley (January 13th) in the centre. If more convenient, the fillets can be baked in the oven. Shrimp Sauce (January 30th); Lobster Sauce (June 7th); Roast Ducklings (July 26th); New Potatoes (April 12th); Green Peas (July 12th); Spinach (May 10th); Hayrick Puddings (March 19th); Cheese (June 8th).

TEA.—Lemon Cheesecakes (August 18th).

SUPPER.—Pickled Salmon (May 30th); Salad (March 13th); Open Tart Jam (August 7th).

Things that must not be Forgotten.

1. When the pickled salmon is brought from the table, put it in the vinegar till wanted again.
2. Preserve any hominy that may be left; it can be fried for breakfast to-morrow.

June 22nd.

Breakfast.	Luncheon.	Dinner.
Pickled Salmon.	Cauliflower au Gratin.	Gravy Soup.
Boiled Ham.	Lemon Cheesecakes.	Braised Loin of Lamb.
Vienna Bread.	Rice Pudding.	New Potatoes.
Dry Toast.		Spinach.
Honey.		Queen's Pudding.
Brown and White Bread and Butter.		Cheese.
Fried Hominy.		

Marketing.

For the Day.—A large Cauliflower or White Broccoli; a Loin of Lamb (May 22nd); New Potatoes; Spinach; six or eight pounds of the thin Flank of Beef, cut square, and with as little fat as possible.

BREAKFAST.—Pickled Salmon (May 30th); Ham, boiled (June 20th); Vienna Bread (August 26th); Fried Hominy (February 12th).

LUNCHEON.—Cauliflower au Gratin (April 25th); Lemon Cheesecakes (August 18th); Rice Pudding (February 24th).

DINNER.—Gravy Soup (August 31st); Braised Loin of Lamb (May 22nd); New Potatoes (April 12th); Spinach (May 10th); Queen's Pudding (August 9th); Cheese (June 8th).

Things that must not be Forgotten.

1. Take up the ox-cheek and boil it (April 6th).
2. Boil the brine (January 13th); let it go cold, then put the thin flank of beef into it.
3. If the boiled ham is nearly finished, cut the meat from the bone, mince it as finely as possible, and put it between two plates to keep it moist, ready for to-morrow morning.

June 23rd.

Breakfast.	Luncheon.	Dinner.
Ox-cheek.	Eggs, Stewed with Cheese.	Halibut Cutlets.
Ham Toast.	Baked Batter Pudding, with Jam.	Rolled Steak, with Forcemeat.
Dry Toast.		Potatoes.
Brown and White Bread and Butter.		Cabbage.
Marmalade.		Macaroni Pudding.
Milk Porridge.		Cheese.

Marketing.

For the Day.—About four pounds of Halibut from a large fish; ask the fishmonger to divide the fish into slices three-quarters of an inch thick (June 11th). A slice of Beef, weighing about three pounds, and from an inch to an inch and a half thick, cut from the middle of the rump; a quarter of a pound of Suet, for forcemeat; Potatoes; Cabbage; six ounces of Naples Macaroni.

For To-morrow.—A pennyworth of Watercress. (Sea Biscuits if required).

Breakfast.—Ox-cheek (April 6th); Ham Toast (March 28th); Milk Porridge (June 13th).

Luncheon.—Eggs, Stewed with Cheese (February 10th); Baked Batter Pudding (February 5th).

Dinner.—*Halibut Cutlets.*—Dry the fish and flour it well. Put it into a frying-pan half full of boiling fat, and when it is done enough upon one side turn it to the other with a slice. It will take from ten to twelve minutes. Drain it upon paper, and serve, with brown butter sauce (February 12th) poured over it. If liked, the slices can be dipped in a thin batter of flour and water, or they can be sprinkled over with lemon-juice before being fried. *Rolled Steak.*—Lay the steak flat on the table, season it with pepper and salt, and lay at one end a roll of nicely-flavoured forcemeat (*see* June 27th). Roll the steak tightly round and round, and bind it securely across and at the ends with twine, to prevent the forcemeat escaping. Melt a little butter in a stewpan, put in the steak, and turn it about till it is browned equally all over. Pour upon it as much stock as will half cover it, and stew it gently for two hours. Turn it over when it is half cooked. Thicken the gravy by adding a table-spoonful of corn-flour mixed to a smooth paste with water; boil the sauce, and add a few drops of sugar browning, and pepper and salt to taste. Put the rolled beef on a hot dish, strain part of the gravy over it and the rest into a tureen, and serve very hot. If liked, the meat can be covered with a greased paper and baked in the oven, instead of being stewed. It will then need to be basted well, and twenty minutes before it is served the greased paper will have to be removed, and the beef floured and basted, in order to brown it. Twenty minutes per pound must be allowed for roasting. Potatoes (April 12th); Cabbage (June 4th); Macaroni Pudding (March 27th); Cheese (June 8th).

Things that must not be Forgotten.
1. Turn and rub the thin flank of beef in the brine.
2. Save any halibut that may be left for fish cakes to-morrow.
3. Remember when boiling the cabbage to pour the cabbage water not down the sink, but upon the ground outside the house.

June 24th.

Breakfast.	Luncheon.	Dinner.
Buttered Eggs.	Fish Pie.	Potato Soup.
Ox-cheek.	Gooseberry Fool.	Loin of Mutton, Boned, Rolled, and Stuffed.
Hot Toast.		
Dry Toast.		Potatoes.
Watercress.		Cauliflower.
Brown and White Bread and Butter.		Golden Pudding.
Biscuits and Milk.		Cheese.

Marketing.

For the Day.—One pound of Green Gooseberries; Old Potatoes, to mash for the fish pie and potato soup; the best end of a not very fat Loin of Mutton; the butcher should be asked to bone the joint. Cauliflower; New Potatoes; six ounces of Beef Suet, for pudding; a pennyworth of Parsley.

For To-morrow.—A tin of Sardines (January 12th); Potted Hare (*see* Potted Grouse, January 7th); Muffins (January 29th).

BREAKFAST.—Buttered Eggs (January 16th); Ox-cheek (April 6th); Biscuits and Milk (June 14th).

LUNCHEON.—Fish Pie (*see* Cod Pie, January 2nd). *Gooseberry Fool.*—Take the tops and tails from the gooseberries, and put them into a stewpan, with a cupful of cold water and half a pound of sugar. Let them stew gently until quite soft. Rub them through a colander or coarse sieve with the back of a wooden spoon, so as to get the pulp and keep back the skins, which must be thrown away. Let the pulp go quite cold, then mix with it gradually cold milk, to make the pulp the thickness of cream. Taste, and add more sugar if not sufficiently sweet for the taste, but the fool will be more refreshing if slightly acid. This dish, though old-fashioned, is very wholesome and a general favourite. It is very palatable and generally acceptable served with bread and butter as a breakfast dish for children. If a richer dish is required, cream, or half cream and half milk, may be used instead of milk only; but the preparation is excellent made with milk only.

DINNER.—Potato Soup (January 26th); Loin of Mutton, Boned and Rolled (April 22nd); Potatoes (April 12th); Cauliflower (April 25th); Golden Pudding (May 4th); Cheese (June 8th).

Things that must not be Forgotten.

1. Turn and rub the beef in the brine.
2. Prepare the rice and barley porridge for breakfast (Note 6, June 15th).

June 25th.

Breakfast.	Luncheon.	Dinner.
Sardines.	Cold Mutton.	Boiled Brill.
Potted Hare.	Salad.	Neapolitan Sauce.
Muffins.	Stewed Rhubarb.	Beef-steak Pudding, with Mushrooms.
Dry Toast.		Potatoes.
Brown and White Bread and Butter.		Custard Blancmange.
Marmalade.		Almond Syrup.
Rice and Barley Porridge.		Cheese.

Marketing.

For the Day.—Two heads of Lettuce; a half-pennyworth of Beetroot, a half-pennyworth of Small Salad; a pennyworth of Watercress; half a bundle of Rhubarb; a Brill (January 9th); two pounds of tender Steak and half an Ox Kidney (*see* January 1st). The undercut of a sirloin of beef would make an excellent pudding, or instead of buttock steak a tender slice from a round might be taken, though it would be well to beat it lightly with the rolling-pin before cutting it up. Besides kidneys, a dozen mushrooms, fresh oysters, when they are in season (or, for economy's sake, tinned oysters), or chopped shallot and parsley, may be added to beef-steak pudding or pie; or, when

game is plentiful, the addition of a partridge or a grouse, well cleaned and cut in pieces, will be found a great improvement. Beef Suet for the pudding, six, eight, or ten ounces, according to the degree of richness required.
For To-morrow.—Four fresh Mackerel. Order to be sent in the morning a Shoulder of Mutton, not too fat (January 17th).

BREAKFAST.—Sardines (January 12th); Potted Hare (*see* Potted Grouse, January 7th); Muffins (January 30th); Rice and Barley Porridge (Note 6, June 15th).

LUNCHEON.—Mutton served yesterday; Salad (March 13th); Stewed Rhubarb (May 19th).

DINNER.—Boiled Brill (January 9th); Neapolitan Sauce (February 8th). *Beef-steak Pudding.*—Put the meat, with only a small allowance of fat, on a board, trim away the skin, and cut it into neat slices convenient for serving. Flour the pieces well, and season each one with pepper and salt. If mushrooms are used, they should have the stems cut away and be skinned, and, if large, be cut into neat pieces, then rinsed quickly in cold water, drained, and laid between the folds of a soft cloth to dry. If oysters are used, they should be put into a stewpan, with their liquor, and barely brought to the boil. The liquor should then be strained from them to be mixed with the gravy from the pudding, and the beards and hard parts of the oysters should be cut away. Parsley or shallot should be finely chopped. *To make Suet Crust for Meat Puddings, Roly-poly Puddings, Fruit Dumplings, &c.*—Weigh one pound of flour, and also six, eight, or ten ounces of suet, whichever is approved. Very good suet crust may be made with six ounces of suet if a tea-spoonful of baking-powder is also introduced. Of course the larger the quantity of suet used the richer will be the pastry. Trim away all the skin and chop the suet (March 14th). Mix it with the flour, add a pinch of salt and baking-powder, if it is to be used; then mix in thoroughly enough cold water to make a stiff paste. Sprinkle flour on the board and on the rolling-pin, to keep the paste from sticking. Take one-third of the pastry and set it aside for the cover. Choose a pudding-basin that will hold about three pints (one with a rim is to be preferred). Roll the pastry till it is twice the size of the top of the pudding and about a third of an inch thick. Line the basin with the paste, and with a floured knife trim it evenly with the edge of the basin. Put in the meat, with the kidney, mushrooms, oysters, or whatever is to be used, and pour in with it a small cupful of gravy or water, and wet the edge of the basin with cold water. Lay on the cover and press the edges well together. Wring a pudding-cloth out of boiling water, flour it well, lay it over the top of the basin, and tie it on firmly round the rim. Turn the corners back and pin them over the top, plunge the pudding into boiling water, and keep it boiling until done enough. This pudding, which will be a good-sized one, will take four hours to boil; a smaller pudding will need three hours and a half. When taken up, and before attempting to turn the pudding out, hold the bottom of the basin in cold water for half a minute, put a dish on the top, and turn the basin gently over. These instructions may be followed in making all kinds of boiled fruit dumplings, substituting, of course, fruit and sugar for the meat and gravy. Potatoes (April 12th); Custard Blancmange (August 4th). *Almond Syrup.*—Make a syrup by boiling together loaf sugar and water, and flavour it by adding two or three drops of essence of almonds. Cheese (June 8th).

Things that must not be Forgotten.
1. If any beef-steak pudding is left, carefully preserve it; it will be excellent warmed up for luncheon to-morrow.
2. Pickle the mackerel bought this morning (August 28th).
3. Turn and rub the beef in the brine.

June 26th.

Breakfast.	Luncheon.	Dinner.
Pickled Mackerel. Potted Hare. Hot Buttered Toast. Dry Toast. Brown and White Bread and Butter. Marmalade. Bread and Milk.	Beef-steak Pudding, warmed. Savoury Rice.	Bisque Soup. Roast Shoulder of Mutton. Onion Sauce. New Potatoes. Cauliflower. Newmarket Pudding. Cheese.

Marketing.
For the Day.—A small Crab; Potatoes; Cauliflower; Onions; Gooseberries; bottled Cherries.
For To-morrow.—Half a pint of Mushrooms.

BREAKFAST.—Pickled Mackerel (August 28th); Potted Hare (*see* Potted Grouse, January 7th); Bread and Milk (January 25th).

LUNCHEON.—*Beef-steak Pudding, warmed.*—Butter the inside of a small clean basin, and lay the cold pudding in it. Tie a cloth over the top, and place a plate on that. Put the basin in a stewpan one-third filled with boiling water; cover the pan, and steam the pudding till it is quite hot. It will take about an hour. Serve on a hot dish, with a little fresh gravy, if it is to be had. Savoury Rice (June 17th).

DINNER.—Bisque Soup (October 17th); Roast Shoulder of Mutton (March 4th); Gravy (June 9th); Onion Sauce (October 14th); New Potatoes (April 12th); Cauliflower (April 25th); Newmarket Pudding (June 2nd); Cheese (June 8th).

Things that must not be Forgotten.
1. Turn and rub the beef in the brine.
2. When the mackerel is taken from the breakfast-table, turn it over in the vinegar before putting it away. If this is done, and if it is kept in a cool place, it will keep for several days.
3. Pastry is to be made to-day (April 17th): Gooseberry pie,

cherry pie of bottled fruit (August 7th), treacle tart; also scones (August 26th) and plain cake. A very *Good Cheap Cake* may be made as follows:—Put a pound of flour into a bowl, with a pinch of salt and a dessert-spoonful of baking-powder. Rub in four ounces of butter, dripping, or lard, the latter being the least desirable. A mixture of butter and dripping is to be preferred. When the flour looks like fine oatmeal, and is quite free from lumps, add four ounces of moist sugar, half a pound of currants picked and dried, an ounce of candied peel chopped small, and a quarter of a nutmeg grated. Mix thoroughly and beat to a stiff paste with milk or water. One great secret of making plain cakes light is to mix them *stiffly*, as both sugar and shortening when melted help to moisten the cake. Very much, too, depends upon the baking. Small cakes should be put into a brisk oven to begin with, to make them rise, but the heat should not be increased after they have begun to bake, or the outer portions will be burnt while the inside is pasty. Large cakes need a moderate oven, in order that they may be baked through. A cake is done enough when a skewer plunged into the centre of it comes out clean. When done enough, the cake should be turned out of the tin and put on its side, leaning against something till cold. This will keep it from becoming heavy. (To clean Currants, *see* Note 4, December 7th).

4. Bone the beef, roll it very tightly, and boil it (February 23rd). Put it under a weight.

June 27th.

Breakfast.	Luncheon.	Dinner.
Savoury Eggs.	Cold Shoulder of Mutton.	Milk Soup.
Mushrooms on Toast.	Salad.	Liver and Bacon.
Scones.	Treacle Tart.	Potatoes.
Dry Toast.		Cabbages.
Brown and White Bread and Butter.		Boiled Rhubarb Pudding.
Milk Toast.		Cheese.

Marketing.

For the Day.—Materials for Salad both for luncheon to-day and supper to-morrow night: Lettuce Salad for the one, and Potato Salad for the other. One pound and a half of Calf's Liver; one pound of Streaky Bacon (half for to-day and half for to-morrow); Potatoes; Cabbages; half a pound of Suet for rhubarb pudding and for forcemeat; Parsley.

For To-morrow.—Plump Sheep's Kidneys (one for each person); a thick pair of Soles, filleted (January 3rd); a Fillet of Veal, weighing about eight pounds (March 14th); Anchovies, if not in the house; Sponge Biscuits and Lemon required; Watercress; Dried Haddock for June 29th; Potatoes; Spinach.

BREAKFAST.—Savoury Eggs (January 1st); Mushrooms on Toast (March 20th); Scones (May 23rd); Milk Toast (June 17th).

LUNCHEON. — Mutton served yesterday; Salad (March 13th); Treacle Tart (August 7th).

DINNER.—Milk Soup (January 3rd); Liver and Bacon (January

17th); Potatoes (April 12th); Cabbages (June 4th). *Boiled Rhubarb Pudding.*—Follow the directions given for making beef-steak pudding (June 25th), substituting rhubarb (skinned and cut into one inch lengths) for the meat, and sugar for the flavourings. Cheese (June 8th).

Things that must not be Forgotten.

1. Boil the liquor in which the meat was boiled. Glaze and brush the beef over with this (March 21st).

2. To save time to-morrow, prepare the *Forcemeat for the Veal* to-day. For this take half a pound of bread-crumbs that have been rubbed through a colander. Put with them three table-spoonfuls of finely-chopped suet, a table-spoonful of chopped parsley, a tea-spoonful of powdered thyme, a little piece of lemon-rind about the size of a thumb-nail, finely chopped, and a little pepper and salt. Put the mixture in a cool place, and leave it till wanted. Before using it bind it together with a beaten egg, but this should not be put in until to-morrow.

3. Fillet the anchovies, and prepare the stock for anchovy toast to-morrow (January 8th).

4. Partially prepare the rice milk for breakfast to-morrow (Note 3, June 17th).

5. Stew the veal bone, to make gravy for the joint. A little of this stock may be used for the anchovy toast (*see* Gravy for Veal, June 28th).

Sunday, June 28th.

Breakfast.	Dinner.	Tea.	Supper.
Anchovy Toast.	Soles, Filleted, Rolled, and Baked, with Brown Butter Sauce.	Brown and White Bread and Butter.	Rolled Beef.
Broiled Kidneys.		Damson Jam.	Salad.
Scones.		Plain Cake.	Cherry Pie.
Dry Toast.			Cheese.
Watercress.	Roast Fillet of Veal.		
Brown and White Bread and Butter.	Fried Bacon.		
Rice Milk.	Potatoes.		
	Spinach.		
	General Favourite Pudding.		
	Cheese.		

BREAKFAST.—Anchovy Toast (January 8th); Broiled Kidneys (January 29th); Scones (May 23rd); Rice Milk (June 18th).

DINNER.—Soles, Filleted, Rolled, and Baked (March 1st); Brown Butter Sauce (February 12th). *Fillet of Veal, Baked or Roasted.*—Put the forcemeat into the space from which the bone was taken; cut the flap slightly with a sharp knife, and lay forcemeat under it. Skewer the joint into a good round shape, bind it firmly with tape, lay the loose skin (usually sent for the purpose by the butcher) over the forcemeat and over the fat. Flour the fillet, put it into a baking-tin with deep sides, and lay a greased paper over it. Baste it frequently over the paper. Let it bake twenty minutes to the pound and twenty minutes over. When done enough, take off the paper and let it brown, if required. Remove the tape, skewers, and loose skin, and put in a silver skewer to keep the meat in shape. Pour thick brown gravy over the veal, and garnish with strips of bacon, toasted, and sliced lemon. A fillet of veal is better to be baked than roasted, because it is so difficult to keep in the stuffing when the joint is hung on the spit. *Gravy for Veal.*—Break the veal bone into several pieces, and put these into a stewpan with a quart of cold water, a bunch of parsley, a small sprig of thyme, a square inch of thin lemon-rind, a blade of mace, and six peppercorns. Cover closely, and stew gently for an hour and a half, or till the liquor is reduced to a pint. Strain it into a bowl, and let it go cold. So far the gravy can be made the day before it is wanted. Melt an ounce of butter in a small stewpan, beat into it an ounce of flour and half a pint of stock previously freed from fat. Stir it till it boils. Pour off the fat from the pan in which the veal was baked, keeping back the brown sediment. Pour in the sauce, and scrape the brown gravy from the bottom of the pan. Return the sauce to the stewpan, add salt to taste, and a few drops of sugar browning, if required; strain the gravy over the meat, and serve. Fried Bacon (January 2nd); Potatoes (April 12th); Spinach (May 10th); General Favourite Pudding (May 17th); Cheese (June 8th).

TEA.—Plain Cake (June 26th).

SUPPER.—Beef, boiled (June 26th); Salad (March 13th); Cherry Pie (August 7th).

Things that must not be Forgotten.

1. Be careful not to put too much lemon into the forcemeat. The quantity named in the recipe, though small, will be quite sufficient; and many people strongly object to it.

2. If a little of the stock made from the veal bone can be preserved, it will serve to make gravy for the chickens on June 30th, then the chicken giblets can be made into soup.

June 29th.

Breakfast.	Luncheon.	Dinner.
Dried Haddock.	Rolled Beef.	Vermicelli Soup.
Boiled Eggs.	Potato Salad.	Minced Veal.
Scones.	Gooseberry Pie.	Fried Bacon.
Hot Buttered Toast.		Potatoes.
Dry Toast.		Hydropathic Pudding of Raspberries and Red Currants.
Honey.		
Brown and White Bread and Butter.		Cheese.
Oatmeal Porridge.		

Marketing.

For the Day.—Bacon, if required; Potatoes; Bottled Raspberries and Red Currants.

For To-morrow.—Sardines (January 12th); a large fine Fowl or a couple of Chickens. Poultry should now begin to be reasonable in price, and will be cheaper as the summer advances. They are cheapest in October and November. Young poultry are known by their smooth legs, pliable feet, and fine, white, clean-looking skin. They should be plump and heavy. White-legged fowls are generally considered the best for boiling, while those with black legs are preferred for roasting. In cool weather a fowl should hang for a day or two before being cooked, but care must be taken that it does not become tainted. The flesh will be firmer if it is plucked the night before it is cooked. If the poulterer is to truss the birds, ask him to prepare them for roasting. Order a Lamb's Fry for to-morrow. Three-quarters of a pound of Beef Suet.

BREAKFAST.—Dried Haddock (January 27th); Boiled Eggs (January 5th); Scones (May 23rd); Oatmeal Porridge (January 25th).
LUNCHEON.—Beef, boiled (June 26th); Potato Salad (April 12th).
DINNER.—Vermicelli Soup (March 22nd); Minced Veal (May 11th); Fried Bacon (January 2nd); Potatoes (April 12th); Hydropathic Pudding (June 16th); Cheese (June 8th).

Things that must not be Forgotten.

1. If any cold potatoes were left at dinner yesterday, let them be used for the potato salad.
2. Peel and slice the potatoes, and throw them into cold water, ready for to-morrow (February 2nd).
3. Pluck the fowl for to-morrow, and remember to draw the feathers out without turning them backward, and so tearing the skin (February 28th).

June 30th.

Breakfast.	Luncheon.	Dinner.
Sardines.	Lamb's Fry.	Potato Purée.
Rolled Beef.	Plain Suet Pudding, with Gravy.	Roast Chickens.
Fried Potatoes.		Bacon.
Hot Toast.		Bread Sauce.
Dry Toast.		Potatoes.
Marmalade.		Cabbage.
Brown and White Bread and Butter.		Lemon Pudding.
Bread and Milk.		Cheese.

Marketing.

For the Day.—Lamb's Fry, and Fowl, or a couple of Chickens, ordered yesterday, to be trussed for roasting; half a pound of Bacon; Potatoes; Cabbage.
For To-morrow.—A Bath Chap; a quarter of a pound of German Sausage; Muffins (January 29th); two fine Ox-tails (April 1st).

BREAKFAST.—Sardines (January 12th); Fried Potatoes (February 2nd); Bread and Milk (January 25th).
LUNCHEON.—Lamb's Fry (May 16th); Plain Suet Pudding (May 13th): this can be served with the fry, if liked.
DINNER. — Potato Purée (January 26th). *Chicken or Fowl, Roasted.*—Skewer the fowl firmly, flour it well, and cover it with

well-greased kitchen-paper. Put it, neck downwards, to a clear fire, and baste it frequently with butter or dripping. A chicken would take about half an hour; a large fowl one hour. If two fowls are roasted together they should be placed back to back on the spit, and the backs should be turned to the fire for a minute or two before serving. Large fowls are frequently stuffed with veal forcemeat (June 27th) or sausage meat (March 18th), as they "go further" when thus prepared. Brown gravy, made of stock or of the giblets, and bread (October 18th), or oyster (October 16th) sauce should be served with the fowls. Bacon rolls (July 19th) may be used to garnish the dish. Potatoes (April 12th); Cabbage (June 4th); Lemon Pudding (August 12th); Cheese (June 8th).

Things that must not be Forgotten.

1. Soak and boil the Bath chap (Note 1, August 25th).
2. Preserve the remains of the rolled beef.
3. Scald the giblets. If necessary, make them into gravy (October 18th), or use them for soup to-morrow (February 1st).

FRUITS IN SEASON SUITABLE FOR DESSERT IN JUNE.

Oranges and Apples (going out); Apricots (from France). Towards the end of the month, Cherries, Strawberries, Black, Red, and White Currants, Black, Red, and White Grapes, and West Indian Pineapples.

PRESERVING FRUIT.

At the latter end of June or the early part of July, Gooseberries, Strawberries, Currants (Red, White, and Black), and Raspberries may be preserved. The precise time must depend upon the state of the weather. When the season is early and the weather dry, it is wise to take advantage of the opportunity and boil the fruit, because the weather may break, and jam made from wet fruit will not keep.

Fruit for preserving should be fine in quality, sound, fresh, dry, and free from dust. It should be prepared with as little handling as possible, and care should be taken not to bruise it. The sugar used for it should be of superfine quality, and should be in lumps, not powder. There is no economy in using common sugar for jams. The difference in price between it and refined sugar is quite made up for by the larger amount of scum thrown up by the inferior sugar. The different kinds of fruit may be boiled alone or in suitable combinations. The following mixtures are to be recommended:—Strawberries and Raspberries, Strawberries and Red or White Currants, Raspberries and Red Currants, Raspberries and Rhubarb, Raspberries and Gooseberries, Raspberries and Cherries, and Blackberries and Apples are also very good boiled together. In each instance double the quantity of raspberries is taken to that of the accompanying fruit.

The method of making ordinary jam with these fruits is very much the same for each. The fruit should first be weighed, then boiled alone till it bubbles equally all over. It should be well skimmed, though not too early, as that would cause waste. The sugar should then be added, and the jam boiled till a little put upon a plate will set. Both the colour and the flavour of the fruit will be better preserved if the fruit is boiled first. When an open range is used, the preserving-pan should on no account be placed flat upon the fire, as that would be sure to make the jam burn. The fruit also should be well stirred from the sides and bottom of the pan ; especially should this be done after the sugar is added. When two kinds of fruit are used together, such as rhubarb and raspberries, the harder kind (in the instance named, the rhubarb) should be boiled longer than the kind which falls easily.

As to the proportionate weight of sugar to be used, that must vary with the nature of the fruit. Acid fruit, such as rhubarb and green gooseberries, requires one pound of sugar to one pound of fruit. Strawberries, raspberries, currants, and cherries, and most plums, need three-quarters of a pound of sugar to one pound of fruit; indeed, cherries, raspberries, and black currants, when no water is used, are often boiled with half their weight in sugar. Damsons, too, are an acid fruit, and they are boiled with equal weights of fruit and sugar ; but with them it is best to allow a tablespoonful of water to each pound of fruit. If too large a proportion of sugar is used the jam will *set* more quickly, and will not need to boil away so much, but the delicate flavour of the fruit will be lost, and the jam will be likely to candy on the surface with keeping.

When jam is sufficiently boiled it should be turned into perfectly sound jars or glasses (the latter are the best, because in them any deterioration in the quality of the jam can be at once perceived). A little tissue-paper dipped in spirit of wine should then be laid on the fruit, and the glass should either be tied down securely or be covered with gummed paper, or else with paper dipped in white of egg ; and the jam should be stored in a cool, dry, airy place.

Red, Black, or White Currant Jelly.—Take dry, clean fruit. Put it into a jar, cover it closely, set it in a saucepan three-parts filled with cold water, and let it simmer till the juice flows freely. Pour the fruit into a jelly-bag to drain away the juice, but do not squeeze the fruit. Measure it, and put it into a preserving-pan, with a pound of sugar (in lumps) to a pint of juice, and boil till a little put upon a plate will set. Carefully skim it during the boiling. Put it into small jars for keeping. If this jelly is thought too sweet, a smaller proportion of sugar can be used. The jam will then need to boil a little longer. Blackberry or Raspberry Jelly can be made in this way. If the fruit is not squeezed, it can be boiled for every-day use with half the weight of sugar. It must, however, be used right away ; it will not keep.

July 1st.

Breakfast.	Luncheon.	Dinner.
Bath Chap.	Baked Mackerel.	Giblet Soup.
German Sausage.	Spiced Pie, made of remnants of Beef.	Stewed Ox-tails.
Muffins.		Potatoes.
Dry Toast.		Greens.
Mustard and Cress.		Stone Cream.
Brown and White Bread and Butter.		Cheese.
Corn-flour Milk.		

Marketing.

For the Day.—Two fresh Mackerel (April 4th); Potatoes; Greens; a square piece of Brisket of Beef, weighing about eight pounds: a sugar-cured Ham, weighing about twelve pounds.
For To-morrow.—Watercress.

BREAKFAST.—Bath Chap (August 25th); German Sausage (June 6th); Muffins (January 30th); Corn-flour Milk (June 19th).
LUNCHEON.—Baked Mackerel (April 15th); Spiced Pie (May 7th).
DINNER.—Giblet Soup (February 1st); Stewed Ox-tails (May 8th); Potatoes (April 12th); Cabbage Greens (June 4th). *Stone Cream.*—Make a pint of blancmange with gelatine (December 11th), or corn-flour (June 15th). Put two stale sponge biscuits sliced at the bottom of a glass dish, and lay a little good jam upon them. Grate the rind of a lemon upon them, and squeeze on them the strained juice. Cover the dish with the blancmange while it is still in a liquid condition, and let it stand in a cool place till stiff. Ornament it with knobs of the same jam that is spread on the cakes, or, if preferred, garnish it with blanched almonds. The substitution of cream for milk in the blancmange will make this into a very superior dish. Cheese (June 8th).

Things that must not be Forgotten.

1. Soak a cupful of hominy in water (Note 3, February 10th).
2. Be careful not to pour the cabbage water down any of the drains belonging to the house, but get rid of it by pouring it on the ground outside.

July 2nd.

Breakfast.	Luncheon.	Dinner.
Bath Chap.	Scotch Collops.	Tomato Purée.
Scalloped Eggs.	Yorkshire Pudding, Baked in tins.	Breast of Lamb, Stewed with Mushrooms.
Hot Buttered Toast.		Green Peas.
Dry Toast.		New Potatoes.
Brown and White Bread and Butter.		Brown Bread Pudding.
Marmalade.		Cheese.
Boiled Hominy.		

Marketing.

For the Day.—A pound and a half of Buttock Steak (January 1st); five or six Tomatoes; fresh tomatoes may probably now be procured, and they will, of

course, be much better than the tinned fruit. A Breast of Lamb; half a pint, or a tin of Mushrooms; Green Peas; New Potatoes; two or three rashers of Fat Bacon, if not in the house.
For To-morrow.—A tin of Collared Tongue; Watercress.

BREAKFAST.—Scalloped Eggs (January 28th); Boiled Hominy (February 11th).
LUNCHEON.—Scotch Collops (January 9th). *Batter Pudding, baked in Tins.*—Follow the recipe given for Wyvern puddings (May 9th), and instead of putting jam on the pudding serve them with the gravy.
DINNER.—Tomato Purée (March 11th); *Breast of Lamb, Stewed with Mushrooms.*—Draw out the bones from the lamb. Melt a little butter in a saucepan, put in the meat, and turn it about till it is equally browned all over. Sprinkle a little salt and pepper over it, and put with it a teaspoonful of chopped parsley, a shallot, or a small onion finely minced, and the mushrooms. Pour in stock to barely cover the meat, and simmer very gently for an hour. Ten minutes before the meat is taken up add a few drops of lemon-juice to the gravy. Put the lamb on a hot dish, place the mushrooms round it, and strain the gravy over all; serve immediately. Green Peas (July 12th); New Potatoes (April 12th); Brown Bread Pudding (July 20th); Cheese (June 8th).

Things that must not be Forgotten.

1. Boil the brine, with an additional handful of salt, and lay the brisket of beef in it.
2. Make a ground rice shape for dinner to-morrow (August 7th).

July 3rd.

Breakfast.	Luncheon.	Dinner.
Collared Tongue. Watercress. Hot Buttered Toast. Brown and White Bread and Butter. Fried Hominy.	Macaroni and Bacon. Gooseberry Fool.	Boiled Brill. Shrimp Sauce. Veal, simply Braised. Spinach. Potatoes. Ground Rice Shape, with Red Currant Jelly. Cheese.

Marketing.

For the Day.—A quart of Gooseberries; a thick Brill (January 9th); half a pint of picked, or one pint of unpicked, Shrimps; a slice from the Fillet of Veal, about four inches thick, and weighing about four pounds; ask the butcher to remove the bone. Spinach; Potatoes; a pennyworth of fresh Yeast; Macaroni.
For To-morrow.—Bespeak half an Ox-kidney for to-morrow.

BREAKFAST.—Collared Tongue (January 2nd); Fried Hominy (February 12th).

LUNCHEON.—Macaroni and Bacon (January 27th); Gooseberry Fool (June 24th).

DINNER.—Boiled Brill (January 9th); Shrimp Sauce (January 30th). *Veal, simply Braised.*—Cut away the skin, bind the veal into a compact piece with tape, and flour it well. Melt a small slice of butter in a stewpan, put in the veal, and fry it till it is brown on one side, then turn it upon the other. Take it up, and put into the stewpan a large carrot cut into slices, an onion, a bunch of parsley, a sprig of thyme, a bay-leaf, half a blade of mace, and half a dozen peppercorns. Cover the vegetables with one or two thin slices of fat bacon, lay the meat on the top, and pour in as much stock or water as will just cover the vegetables without touching the veal. Lay a round of buttered paper on the meat. Cover the stewpan closely, put it at the side of the stove, and let the veal cook as slowly as possible for quite four hours. Baste it frequently with the liquor, in order that it may absorb the flavour of the vegetables. When done enough take it up and keep it hot. Strain the gravy, and boil it quickly for a few minutes till it is thick and smooth. If necessary, add salt to it, but possibly the bacon will have supplied all that is required. Add a few drops of browning if necessary, pour the sauce over the meat, and serve. The meat should be tender and mellow, but not at all ragged. This dish will look very pretty garnished with a Macedoine or mixture of turned cooked vegetables. This is rather troublesome to prepare at home, but may be bought in a tin ready prepared and needing only to be made hot. Ground Rice Shape made yesterday; Cheese (June 8th).

Things that must not be Forgotten.

1. Turn and rub the beef in the brine.
2. If any brill is left, lift it from the bone; it can be used to make fish cakes (January 13th) for luncheon to-morrow.
3. Pastry may be made to-day (April 17th): Cherry pie, gooseberry pie (August 7th), jam turnovers (September 25th), soda cake (August 14th), scones (August 26th). If any sour milk is in the house it may be used to make scones.

July 4th.

Breakfast.	Luncheon.	Dinner.
Fried Ham.	Fish Cakes.	Kidney Soup.
Fried Eggs.	Veal Rissoles.	Mutton Chops, with Piquante Sauce.
Scones.		
Dry Toast.		Broccoli. Potatoes.
Honey.		Rothe Grütze.
Brown and White Bread and Butter.		Cheese.
Milk Porridge.		

Marketing.

For the Day.—Half an Ox Kidney ordered yesterday; Mutton Chops (Marketing, April 30th); a pound of Red Currants, and half a pound of Raspberries;

Broccoli, Potatoes. Old potatoes will be required for the fish cakes; a pennyworth of Parsley. Ham bought July 1st.

For To-morrow.—About four pounds of the middle cut of a Salmon. Salmon when good has the gills and flesh red, the body stiff, the scales bright, the eyes prominent, and the belly firm and thick. The redness of the gills is not alone to be relied upon as a sign of the goodness of the fish, as this appearance is frequently given artificially. A couple of Ducks. Young ducks have the breast plump and firm and the skin clear and fresh-looking. If the breast is lean and flabby it may be suspected that the bird is old. Green Peas, new Potatoes. Materials for a salad: two lettuces, a half-pennyworth of beetroot, a half-pennyworth of small Salad, two pennyworth of Watercress, half for breakfast; one pound of fresh Strawberries; a quarter of a pound of Bacon in rashers; Sea Biscuits if not in the house; and a tin of Potted Grouse (January 7th); Dried Haddock for July 6th.

BREAKFAST.—Fried Ham (March 5th); Fried Eggs (March 5th); Scones (May 23rd); Milk Porridge (June 13th).

LUNCHEON.—Fish Cakes (January 13th). *Veal Rissoles.*—Mince very finely all that remains of the cold veal, and mix with the mince one-fourth of its bulk in cooked bacon or ham, and also in bread-crumbs that have been rubbed through a colander. Add three or four drops of essence of anchovy, a little pepper and salt, and a table-spoonful of finely-chopped parsley. Moisten the mixture, and bind it together with beaten egg and a little of the gravy that the veal was stewed in. Make up the preparation into balls the size of walnuts, flour these lightly, and fry them to a light brown colour. Serve them with a little of the veal gravy if there be any left.

DINNER.—Kidney Soup (February 27th); Mutton Chops, with Piquante Sauce (April 30th); Cauliflower (April 25th); Potatoes (April 12th); Rothe Grütze (December 10th); Cheese (June 8th).

Things that must not be Forgotten.

1. Turn and rub the beef in the brine.
2. Make a strawberry gâteau for supper to-morrow night (*see* Cherry Gâteau, July 11th).
3. Salt the short bones of the chops and put them aside; they can be stewed with the scrag of mutton served July 6th.

Sunday, July 5th.

Breakfast.	Dinner.	Tea.	Supper.
Devilled Eggs.	Boiled Salmon.	Plum Jam.	Pickled Salmon.
Toasted Bacon.	Anchovy Sauce.	Soda Cake.	Salad.
Scones.	Roast Ducks.		Strawberry Gâteau.
Dry Toast.	Green Peas.		Cheese.
Watercress.	New Potatoes.		
Brown and White Bread and Butter.	Cherry Pie. Cheese.		
Biscuits and Milk.			

BREAKFAST.—Devilled Eggs (February 27th); Toasted Bacon (January 19th); Scones (May 23rd); Biscuits and Milk (June 14th).

DINNER.—*Boiled Salmon.*—Scrape the scales from the fish, clean it, and be careful that no blood is left in it. Put it into boiling salted water, that has had a little vinegar or lemon-juice put into it, let it boil two minutes, then draw it back, and simmer it gently till done enough. It will take from six to ten minutes per pound, according to the thickness of the fish. When the flesh leaves the bones easily it is done enough. Take it up immediately; if too much boiled it will be tasteless and colourless. If it is not wanted on the instant it may be kept on the fish drainer across the fish kettle with a thick cloth laid upon it. Put it on a napkin or fish paper, garnish with parsley and cut lemon, and send anchovy sauce to table with it. If preferred, shrimp (January 30th) or Dutch sauce (May 14th) may be used instead of anchovy sauce. Anchovy Sauce (*see* Melted Butter, July 17th). Lemon-juice or vinegar is put into the water to set the colour of the salmon. Roast Duck (July 26th); Green Peas (July 12th); New Potatoes (April 12th); Cherry Pie (August 7th); Cheese (June 8th).

TEA.—Soda Cake (August 14th).

SUPPER.—Pickled Salmon (May 30th); Salad (March 13th); Strawberry Gâteau (*see* Cherry Gâteau, July 11th).

Things that must not be Forgotten.

1. As soon as the salmon leaves the table, lift the flesh from the bone in neat pieces; put these in a dish, and cover them with vinegar They can be served at supper.
2. Turn and rub the beef in the brine.

July 6th.

Breakfast.	Luncheon.	Dinner.
Dried Haddock. Potted Grouse. Scones. Dry Toast. Brown and White Bread and Butter. Milk Toast.	Scrag of Mutton with Rice. Gooseberry Fool.	Croûte au Pot. Boiled Neck of Mutton with Maître d'Hôtel Sauce. Potatoes. Young Carrots. Viennoise Pudding. Cheese.

Marketing.

For The Day.—A fine Neck of Mutton not too fat. (Be sure that the butcher joints the meat.) The Scrag is to be served at luncheon, the best end is for dinner. A quart of Green Gooseberries. Old Potatoes, Young Carrots.

For To-morrow.—Half a Pound of Macaroni. (Marketing, January 1st.) A pennyworth of small Salad. Anchovies if not in the house. A pound of Red Currants; half a pound of Raspberries; Cream.

BREAKFAST.—Dried Haddock (January 27th); Potted Grouse (January 7th); Scones (May 23rd); Milk Toast (June 17th).

LUNCHEON.—Scrag of Mutton with Rice (February 21st). The short bones of the chops served July 4th may be stewed with this. Gooseberry Fool (June 24th).

DINNER.—Croûte au Pot (May 25th); Boiled Neck of Mutton (February 23rd). A neck of mutton should, after boiling five minutes, simmer for fifteen minutes per pound, and fifteen minutes over. Maître d'Hôtel Sauce (May 6th). Potatoes (April 12th). *Carrots, To Boil.*—Young carrots should be simply washed before boiling, then rubbed with a clean cloth when they are tender. Old carrots should be washed, scraped with a knife, and cut either to the shape of young carrots or to a fancy shape. After preparing the carrots throw them into plenty of boiling water lightly salted, and let them boil till tender. Quite young carrots will be done enough in about twenty minutes, old carrots will take from three-quarters of an hour to an hour and a half. When tender drain them and put them into a stewpan with enough stock to barely cover them, a lump of sugar, and a slice of fresh butter. Boil the sauce quickly, with the lid off the pan, till it is thick and coats the carrots. Shake them in the glaze, and serve. *Viennoise Pudding.*—Take five ounces of stale bread, and cut it into very small pieces. Pour a glass of sherry on this if permitted, and with the wine milk that has been coloured darkly with sugar browning (January 2nd) to make a pint. If a superior pudding is required, a mixture of milk and cream may be used, but there must be a pint of liquid altogether. Let the bread soak for awhile, then beat it well with a fork, and add three ounces of sultana raisins, three ounces of moist sugar, two ounces of candied peel chopped small, the grated rind of a lemon. Mix thoroughly. Beat the yolks of one, two, three, or four eggs in a bowl, and add them to the pudding. If one or two eggs only are used a tea-spoonful of flour should be stirred into the pudding to bind it together, or it will not turn out. Put the mixture into a well-buttered mould, lay a round of buttered paper on the top, and steam it (Treacle Pudding, March 28th) for an hour and a half. When it is firm in the centre it is done enough. Let it stand a minute before turning it out. Sweet sauce or brandy sauce may be served with this. Cheese (June 8th).

Things that must not be Forgotten.

1. Turn and rub the beef in the brine.
2. Boil the neck of mutton in the liquor used for the scrag of mutton, and preserve any that may be left.
3. Make the rothe grütze for to-morrow (December 10th).
4. See Note 4 (January 17th).
5. Partially prepare the rice and barley porridge for breakfast to-morrow. (Note 6, June 15th.)
6. Save the whites of the eggs used for the pudding; cover them and keep them in a cool place till Wednesday. The Plaice at Luncheon can be egged with them, then covered with bread-crumbs

instead of being floured only before frying. Or, if preferred, they can be whisked and stirred into the Wyvern puddings just before they are baked.

July 7th.

Breakfast.	Luncheon.	Dinner.
Anchovies and Hard-boiled Eggs.	Baked Mackerel.	Sliced Halibut.
Potted Grouse.	Italian Macaroni.	Loin of Lamb, braised, with Tomatoes.
Hot Buttered Toast.		New Potatoes, Spinach.
Dry Toast.		Rothe Grütze.
Marmalade.		Cheese.
Brown and White Bread and Butter.		
Rice and Barley Porridge.		

Marketing.

For The Day.—Two moderate-sized fresh Mackerel (April 4th); as many slices of Halibut an inch thick as are likely to be required (June 11th). A Loin of Lamb (Marketing, May 22nd). Half a dozen Tomatoes. Foreign tomatoes are not usually expected until August, and English tomatoes until September, but for the last year or two very fine Lisbon tomatoes have been brought into the London market by the end of June. New Potatoes; Spinach.

For To-morrow.—A dozen fresh Herrings (January 3rd), soft roed fish are to be preferred; a pound of Bacon in rashers, half for breakfast, and half for the Rabbit; a pennyworth of Mustard and Cress.

BREAKFAST.—Anchovies and Hard-boiled Eggs (January 18th); Potted Grouse (January 7th); Rice and Barley Porridge (June 15th).

LUNCHEON.—Baked Mackerel (April 15th). *Italian Macaroni.*—Put the half pound of macaroni into two quarts of boiling water with a tea-spoonful of salt and half the quantity of pepper, and let it simmer for twenty minutes or longer if required. It should be tender when pressed between the finger and thumb. Drain it well, and put it back into the stewpan with half a pint of stock or milk (in Italy stock is used), and simmer it for two or three minutes. Have ready grated a quarter of a pound of cheese, mixed Parmesan and Gruyère, if they are to be had, if not, any mild dry English or American cheese can be used. Put half the cheese into the macaroni, shake it about, add a slice of butter and shake again, then put in the rest of the cheese, and when this also is thoroughly mixed serve immediately.

DINNER.—Fried Halibut (June 23rd); Loin of Lamb, braised (May 22nd). The Tomatoes may be baked by themselves, and may be either placed round the lamb as a garnish, or served on a separate dish. *Baked Tomatoes.*—Cut off the stalks and put the tomatoes into a greased pie-dish, sprinkle a little pepper and salt over them, and cover the top with finely-grated bread-crumbs. Bake in a moderate oven for about half an hour till the tomatoes are quite soft. If preferred, the tomatoes can be cut into thick slices before being baked. New Potatoes (April 12th); Spinach (May 10th); Rothe Grütze made yesterday. Cheese (June 8th).

Things that must not be Forgotten.
1. Turn and rub the beef in the brine.
2. Pickle the herrings for breakfast to-morrow (August 20th).
3. Partially prepare the rice milk for breakfast (Note 3, June 17th).

July 8th.

Breakfast.	Luncheon.	Dinner.
Pickled Herrings.	Fried Plaice.	Vermicelli Soup.
Mustard Sauce.	Dutch Sauce.	Baked Rabbit.
Toasted Bacon.	China Chilo.	Potatoes.
Hot Buttered Toast.	Rice Boiled for Curry.	Cauliflower.
Dry Toast.		Wyvern Puddings.
Brown and White Bread and Butter.		Cheese.
Mustard and Cress.		
Rice Milk.		

Marketing.
For the Day.—A thick Plaice (April 21st); a pair of tame Rabbits. Ostend Rabbits have by this time gone out of season, but Tame Rabbits are to be had in summer time, and furnish excellent food. To choose Rabbits, *see* January 24th. A pound and a half of Mutton, taken from the Loin or Neck; Potatoes; Cauliflowers; a pennyworth of Parsley; two Lettuces and Green Peas for China Chilo.

For To-morrow.—Fine plump Sheep's Kidneys, one for each person; a pennyworth of Watercress; six ounces of firm Beef Suet, for Roly-poly Pudding.

BREAKFAST.—Pickled Herrings, prepared last evening. When serving the herrings put them on a glass dish, pour a little of the vinegar round, and garnish with parsley. *Mustard Sauce.*—Make a little maître d'hôtel sauce (May 6th); stir a tea-spoonful of mixed mustard into it, and serve. The pickled herrings will be very good without sauce. Toasted Bacon (January 19th); Rice Milk (June 18th).

LUNCHEON.—Fried Plaice (April 21st); Dutch Sauce (May 14th). *China Chilo.*—Cut the meat from the bones in the loin of mutton, and retain a small portion only of the fat. Mince the meat finely, and wash and shred the lettuces. Put the meat into a stewpan with the shred lettuces, a pint of freshly-shelled green peas, a slice of sweet butter, a little pepper and salt, and a quarter of a pint of stock or water. Stir the ingredients over a gentle fire till hot, then cover the stewpan closely, draw it back, and let its contents simmer very gently for two hours. Boil a cupful of rice as for curry. Put the preparation on a dish, place the rice round it, and serve very hot. If liked, a large onion finely minced, or a small cucumber cut into dice, or a few mushrooms may be stewed with the vegetables; and when green peas are not in season, carrots, turnips, French beans, or cauliflower sprigs may be used in their place.

DINNER.—Vermicelli Soup (March 22nd). *Baked Rabbit.*—Skin, and empty the rabbits, and cut them into neat joints, convenient for serving. Pepper these lightly, and put them side by side (not one on the top of another) into a baking-tin, and lay a rasher of bacon upon each one. Bake in a moderate oven till the rabbit is sufficiently cooked. It will take about an hour and a half. Put the pieces of rabbit on a dish, garnish with the bacon, pour the gravy over all, and serve. The heads of the rabbits need not be put on the dish, but the flesh can be picked off to put with the remains of the rabbit in the gâteau to-morrow, and the bones stewed will make excellent stock. Potatoes (April 12th); Cauliflower (April 25th); Wyvern Puddings (May 9th); Cheese (June 8th).

Things that must not be Forgotten.

1. Turn and rub the beef in the brine.
2. Prepare and slice the potatoes, and throw them into cold water, to be ready for frying to-morrow morning (February 2nd).

July 9th.

Breakfast.	Luncheon.	Dinner.
Broiled Kidneys.	Rabbit Gâteau.	Sole au Gratin.
Fried Potatoes.	Compôte of Cherries.	Veal Stew Piquante
Hot Buttered Toast.		New Potatoes.
Dry Toast.		Green Peas.
Brown and White Bread and Butter.		Roly-poly Pudding.
Watercress.		Cheese.
Oatmeal Porridge.		

Marketing.

For the Day.—One pound of Kentish Cherries; a slice of Veal from the Fillet, weighing two and a half or three pounds; a small Cucumber; a Lettuce; New Potatoes; Green Peas.

For To-morrow.—A pint of freshly-boiled Shrimps; a small tin of Corned Beef. Bespeak a Lamb's Fry for to-morrow.

BREAKFAST.—Broiled Kidneys (January 29th); Fried Potatoes (February 2nd); Oatmeal Porridge (January 25th).

LUNCHEON.—*Rabbit Gâteau.*—Take the remains of baked rabbit, pick all the meat from the bones, and leave out the hard outer skin and the sinews, which will be a valuable addition to the stock-pot. Weigh the meat, put a slice of bacon with it, if there is any, and mince all finely together. Take half the weight in stale crumb of bread; soak this in milk, squeeze it dry, and pound it with the minced rabbit; season with pepper and salt. Bind the mixture together with yolk of egg, and at the last moment mix in the white of egg beaten to a stiff froth. Turn the preparation into a plain tin mould well buttered, put a greased paper on the top, and steam the gâteau for an hour and a half as puddings are steamed (March 28th). Take half a pint of nicely flavoured stock (this can be made with a portion of the rabbit bones if necessary); thicken it by boiling in it a dessert-spoonful of corn-flour mixed smoothly with a little cold water; add a few drops of sugar browning, and a glass of sherry, if permitted. Turn the gâteau on a dish, pour the gravy round, and serve. Cold meat of different kinds can be served a second time in this way. Compôte of Cherries (August 5th).

DINNER.—Sole au Gratin (May 3rd); Veal Stew Piquante (October 2nd); New Potatoes (April 12th); Green Peas (July 12th); Rolypoly Pudding (August 18th); Cheese (June 8th).

Things that must not be Forgotten.

1. Turn and rub the beef in the brine.
2. Shell the shrimps overnight, and put them between two dishes.

July 10th.

Breakfast.	Luncheon.	Dinner.
Buttered Shrimps.	Lamb's Fry.	Boiled Brill.
Corned Beef.	Boiled Rice.	Neapolitan Sauce.
Hot Buttered Toast.		Scotch Hotch Potch.
Dry Toast.		Hayrick Puddings.
Honey.		Cheese.
Brown and White Bread and Butter.		
Corn Flour Milk.		

Marketing.

For the Day.—A Lamb's Fry (May 16th); a moderate-sized Brill (January 9th); three to four pounds of a Loin of Mutton divided into neat chops. Procure a loin with as little fat as possible. If preferred, a neck of mutton or the ribs of lamb may be chosen. Plenty of vegetables for the hotch potch: young Turnips, young Carrots, a lettuce, a good-sized Cauliflower, a whitehearted Cabbage, and some young Onions, together with about two pecks of Green Peas. There should be as many mixed vegetables as will fill a quart measure or more, and three pints of freshly-shelled green peas. The excellence of hotch potch consists in the presence of a superabundance of peas. New Potatoes; a pennyworth of German Yeast.

For To-morrow.—A tin of Sardines (January 12th). Order four pennyworth of Cream, if permitted.

BREAKFAST.—Buttered Shrimps (July 23rd); Corned Beef, bought yesterday; Corn Flour Milk (June 19th).

LUNCHEON.—Lamb's Fry (May 16th); Boiled Rice (February 3rd).

DINNER.—Boiled Brill (January 9th); Neapolitan Sauce (February 8th). *Scotch Hotch Potch.*—Prepare the mixed vegetables, all but the carrots, cut them up and shred them finely, and put with them a handful of parsley chopped small. Put them into a stewpan with four quarts of boiling stock or water, and add the yellow part only of three young carrots finely grated, a pint and a half of green peas, or half the quantity provided, and the loin or neck of mutton cut into neat chops. If lamb is preferred it should be kept whole. Boil gently for an hour and a half, season with pepper and salt, add the rest of the peas, boil half an hour longer, and serve. The cutlets should be put into the tureen with the hotch potch. This dish is called a soup, but it is much more like a stew. Of course, if thought well, it can be served as a soup, and meat can be sent to table after it is removed. Hayrick Puddings (March 19th); Cheese (June 8th).

Things that must not be Forgotten.

1. Cut the brisket of beef that has been in salt in two pieces, tie one half securely on the top of the other, and boil it till tender, then press it under a weight (February 23rd).

2. Pastry is to be made to-day (April 17th): red currant pie of bottled fruit (August 7th); jam turnovers (September 25th); also teacakes (August 26th), and good currant cake (June 26th).

July 11th.

Breakfast.	Luncheon.	Dinner.
Sardines.	Fish Pie (made of remains of Brill).	Potato Purée.
Corned Beef.		Calf's Liver and Bacon.
Teacakes.	Hotch Potch made hot.	Potatoes. Cabbage-Greens.
Dry Toast.	Jam Turnovers.	Red Currant Pie.
Brown and White Bread and Butter.		Cream.
Marmalade.		Cheese.
Bread and Milk.		

Marketing.

For the Day.—A pound and a half of Calf's Liver: half a pound of streaky Bacon cut into rashers; a pennyworth of Parsley: Potatoes, Greens.

For To-morrow.—Fresh Strawberries, and half a pint of milk for each child for breakfast; Watercress; four or five Tomatoes; a moderate-sized but thick Turbot, with a little Lobster Spawn, if Lobster Sauce is required; two Leverets (June 13th); three-quarters of a pound of Bacon in rashers—half a pound of this is for breakfast; half a pint of Mushrooms, or, if these are not to be had, a small tin of Champignons; Green Peas, New Potatoes; eight stale sponge fingers and three or four Ratafias. Materials for a salad: Lettuce, Beetroot, and Endive; a pound of Cherries for the gâteau; if permitted, order half a pint of double cream for the gâteau. A Ham bought July 1st is supposed to be in cut.

BREAKFAST. — Sardines (January 12th); Corned Beef, bought July 9th; Teacakes (February 14th); Bread and Milk (January 25th).

LUNCHEON.—Fish Pie (*see* Cod Pie, January 2nd); Hotch Potch served yesterday; Jam Turnovers (September 25th).

DINNER.—Potato Purée (January 26th); Calf's Liver and Bacon (January 17th); Potatoes (April 12th); Cabbage Greens (June 4th); Red Currant Pie (August 7th); Cheese (June 8th).

Things that must not be Forgotten.

1. Glaze the beef (March 21st).
2. Do not pour the cabbage water down any of the drains of the house.
3. Make the *Cherry Gâteau* for supper to-morrow. Soak one ounce of gelatine in a cupful of water for an hour. Remove the stalks and stones from one pound of cherries. Boil a quarter of a pound of loaf sugar in half a pint of water for ten minutes; throw in the cherries, and let them boil for ten minutes. Dissolve the gelatine in a little of the syrup, add it to the cherries, throw in a few cherry kernels, and colour the gâteau with cochineal. Put the preparation into a damp mould which has a gallipot fixed in the centre. When wanted turn it into a glass dish, and put a little cream or custard (August 10th) in the place which was occupied by the gallipot. Various fruits may be used instead of cherries.
4. Carefully preserve any cold turbot that may be left, and make fish cakes of it for breakfast to-morrow (January 13th).

Sunday, July 12th.

Breakfast.	Dinner.	Tea.	Supper.
Fish Cakes.	Boiled Turbot.	Brown and White Bread and Butter.	Pressed Beef.
Tomatoes and Bacon.	Lobster Sauce.	Strawberry Jam.	Salad.
Toasted Teacakes.	Civet of Leveret.	Cake.	Cherry Gâteau.
Dry Toast.	Green Peas.		Cheese.
Watercress.	New Potatoes.		
Brown and White Bread and Butter.	Cabinet Pudding.		
Strawberries with Cold Milk, and Bread and Butter.	Cheese.		

BREAKFAST.—Fish Cakes (January 13th). *Tomatoes and Bacon.*—Cut the stalks from the tomatoes, and if liked, cut them into thick slices; or they may be left whole. Fry the bacon very gently over a slow fire till it is done enough. Lift it upon a hot dish and gently fry the tomatoes till tender in the fat that has run from the bacon. They will be done enough in a few minutes. Put them on the dish with the bacon, and serve immediately. Teacakes (February 14th); Strawberries bought yesterday.

LUNCHEON.—Boiled Turbot (June 7th); Lobster Sauce (June 7th); Civet of Leveret (June 14th). *Green Peas.*—Peas are best when young and freshly shelled. Put plenty of water with a pinch of salt into a saucepan. When it is quite boiling put in the shelled peas and let them boil till almost tender. If liked, two or three sprigs of mint can be boiled with them. The lid must not on any account be placed on the saucepan. The peas will be done enough in from fifteen to twenty minutes, according to their age and size. It is best to try them now and then, as if boiled till they break they will be spoilt. Drain them well, and put them into a shallow pan with a slice of butter the size of a walnut for a tureen full of peas. Sprinkle a tea-spoonful of white sugar and a pinch of salt over them, and shake them over the fire to coat them with the butter. Turn into a tureen and serve. If the peas are old, or have been long gathered, a very small pinch of carbonate of soda may be put into the water in which they are boiled; but this is not necessary, and is better to be omitted when the peas are young and freshly shelled. Potatoes (April 12th.) *Cabinet Pudding.*—Choose a pint mould, or if a larger pudding is required, increase the quantities of the ingredients proportionately to the size. Butter the mould and ornament it inside according to taste. Angelica cut into strips, preserved cherries and pistachio kernels make a very pretty garnish for sweet dishes of all kinds, the dark green of the angelica and the lighter green of the pistachios contrasting very effectively with the bright colour of the cherries. These ingredients are generally avoided because they are regarded as expensive. If carefully used, however, it would be found that half a pound of each would suffice for the moderate requirements of a family for five or six months. The cherries and pistachios must be kept separate in covered jars, and the angelica must be kept in a cool place excluded from the air. The pistachios before being used must be blanched as almonds are, that is, they must be put into a saucepan with the cold water and heated gently till on the point of boiling, when the skins can be easily slipped off, leaving the beautiful green kernel exposed to view. Half a dozen kernels, half an inch of angelica, and a dozen cherries, would make a plain pudding or blancmange look quite a superior dish. Break the biscuits and ratafias into moderate-sized pieces. After ornamenting the buttered mould put in the biscuit, carefully, not to disturb the ornamentation, and pour gently in a custard made of two-thirds of a pint of milk, the yolks of two, and the white of one, egg. Sweeten to taste and flavour with vanilla or almond. Lay a round of buttered kitchen paper on the top of the pudding, and steam it till it is firm in the centre. (Treacle Pudding, March 28th.) It will take about three-quarters of an hour, and the water should be *boiled gently.* Let it stand a minute, turn it carefully upon a hot dish, and pour a little good sauce round it. If the pudding is preferred cold, boil the custard and mix an ounce of dissolved gelatine with it. Cheese (June 8th).

TEA.—Currant Cake (June 26th).

SUPPER.—Salad (March 13th). Whipped Cream (December 12th).

Things that must not be Forgotten.

1. The white of egg that is not used will be a valuable addition to the batter pudding to-morrow.
2. Preserve the liquor in which the turbot is boiled. Fish soup can be made of it for to-morrow.
3. Put a cupful of green lentils to soak all night in cold water.

July 13th.

Breakfast.	Luncheon.	Dinner.
Fried Ham.	Fish Cakes.	Fish Soup, Simple.
Fried Eggs.	Baked Batter Pudding.	Roast Ribs of Beef, Rolled
Teacakes.		Boiled Lentils.
Dry Toast.		Potatoes.
Honey.		Newmarket Pudding.
Brown and White Bread and Butter.		Cheese.
Corn Flour Milk.		

Marketing.

For the Day.—One or two ribs of Beef, according to the requirements of the family. The butcher should be asked to bone the meat, roll it, and skewer it firmly. Potatoes; two pounds of old potatoes will be wanted for the fish cakes; a fresh Ox Tongue. If this is not to be procured immediately it can be ordered of the butcher and pickled as soon as convenient. A tongue is never so good as when boiled straight out of the pickle.

For To-morrow.—A pennyworth of Watercress.

BREAKFAST.—Fried Ham (March 5th); Fried Eggs (March 5th); Teacakes (February 14th); Corn Flour Milk (June 19th).

LUNCHEON.—Fish Cakes (January 13th); Baked Batter Pudding (February 5th).

DINNER.—*Fish Soup, Simple.*—Take the bones, head, and all that is left of the turbot, after using the flesh for fish cakes, and stew them for two hours in about three pints of the liquor the fish was boiled in. Strain the soup, and return it to the stewpan with two table-spoonfuls of well-washed rice, an onion stuck with one clove, and half a blade of mace, and simmer again for half an hour. Season the soup with pepper and salt, and mix a large breakfast-cupful of boiling milk with the liquor, and pour it into the tureen. Have ready a table-spoonful of well-washed and finely-chopped parsley, throw it into the tureen at the last moment, and serve very hot. Roast Ribs of Beef. (To Roast Meat, March 4th); Gravy (June 9th); Potatoes (April 12th); Lentils (March 2nd); Newmarket Pudding (June 2nd); Cheese (June 8th).

Things that must not be Forgotten.

1. Trim the tongue, rub it well all over with salt, put it on an earthenware dish, and let it lie for twenty-four hours. This is to clear it of slime.

2. *Potted Leveret.*—Pick every particle of meat from the bones of the leveret. Mince it finely, and pound it till smooth, and take out all sinew and outside skin. Season the meat agreeably with pepper and salt, and sparingly with pounded mace and pounded cloves. Moisten the meat with butter whilst pounding it, press it into a potting pot, and cover it with clarified butter. It will be excellent for breakfast or luncheon. The bones, skin, and gravy that remain can be made into soup (*see* Hare Soup, January 19th).

3. Put a cupful of hominy to soak all night in cold water (February 10th).

July 14th.

Breakfast.	Luncheon.	Dinner.
Eggs in Brown Butter.	Baked Mackerel.	Leveret Soup.
Potted Leveret.	Savoury Rice.	Cold Beef.
Teacakes.		Salad.
Dry Toast.		Potatoes.
Brown and White Bread and Butter.		Pancakes.
Watercress.		Cheese.
Boiled Hominy.		

Marketing.

For the Day.—Two moderate-sized Mackerel (April 4th); a fine Lettuce, half an Endive, a half-pennyworth of Beetroot, Watercress, small Onions; a small plump Leg of Mutton.

For To-morrow.—A dozen fresh Herrings with soft roes; one pound of Tomatoes, or, if more convenient, a small bottle of Preserved Tomatoes, can be procured instead of the fresh fruit. The Ham to be boiled to-morrow is understood to be already in the house.

BREAKFAST.—Eggs in Brown Butter (January 6th); Potted Leveret made yesterday; Teacakes (February 14th); Boiled Hominy (February 11th).

LUNCHEON.—Baked Mackerel (April 15th); Savoury Rice (June 17th).

DINNER.—Leveret Soup (*see* Hare Soup, January 19th); Beef roasted July 13th; Salad (March 13th); Potatoes (April 12th); Pancakes (February 24th); Cheese (June 8th).

Things that must not be Forgotten.

1. Boil the brine with an additional handful of salt, and let it go cold.

2. Drain away the slime from the ox tongue, wash it lightly, and put it in the brine. Be careful to cover it well. It must be turned and rubbed every day for a fortnight or more.

3. Make a pickle for sour mutton (March 19th), and put the leg of mutton into it.

4. Make the batter for the pancakes an hour or two before it is wanted.

5. Pickle the herrings, and leave them in a dish covered with vinegar (August 20th).

6. Prepare the tomato sauce for breakfast to-morrow. It can be made hot in the morning (July 15th).

July 15th.

Breakfast.	Luncheon.	Dinner.
Pickled Herrings.	Boiled Ham.	Fried Plaice.
Eggs in Sunshine.	Broad Beans.	Dutch Sauce.
Hot Buttered Toast.	Maître d'Hôtel Sauce.	Chicken Fricasseed.
Dry Toast.	Suet Pudding.	Potatoes.
Marmalade.		Cauliflower.
Brown and White Bread and Butter.		Brown Bread and Butter Pudding.
Fried Hominy.		Cheese.

Marketing.

For the Day.—About half a peck of Broad or Windsor Beans; two pennyworth of Parsley; a thick Plaice (April 21st); a couple of plump young Chickens (June 29th); a quarter of a pound of firm Kidney Suet; Potatoes; Cauliflower.

For To-morrow.—Muffins (January 29th); half a pound of Naples Macaroni. Order for to-morrow one or a couple of tame Rabbits. A quarter of a pint of Cream, for the curry.

BREAKFAST.—*Eggs in Sunshine.*—Take an earthenware dish that will stand the fire and also that can be sent to table. Butter it well, sprinkle a little salt upon it, break into it as many eggs as are required, and put it on the top of the range, or in the oven for a couple of minutes till the eggs are set. Have ready some good tomato sauce, pour it over the eggs, and serve. If preferred, the tomatoes can be simply baked (July 7th) and laid on the eggs. *To make Tomato Sauce.*—Take half a dozen ripe tomatoes. Trim away the stalks, scoop out the seeds, cut the fruit in slices, and put them in a stewpan, with a quarter of a pint of water, an ounce of butter, and a little pepper and salt. If liked, a sliced onion, a bay-leaf, and a pinch of thyme can be added. Simmer gently with the stewpan well covered for about three-quarters of an hour, or till the tomatoes are quite tender. Stir them frequently, or they will burn. Rub them through a sieve. Melt an ounce of butter in a stewpan, and mix smoothly with it half an ounce of flour. Beat it over the fire with the back of a wooden spoon till it is well cooked. Take the pan off the fire, add gradually the tomato purée, and a gill of stock. Return the sauce to the stewpan, boil again till thick, and serve. *Tomato Sauce from Preserved Tomatoes.*—If preserved tomatoes are to be used instead of fresh tomatoes, proceed exactly as directed above, using the pulp from the bottle instead of the purée that has been rubbed through a sieve. If the shallot flavour is liked, one or two sliced shallots, a bay-leaf, and a sprig of thyme, can be stewed with the sauce, and removed before serving. Half these quantities will be enough for breakfast. Fried Hominy (February 12th).

LUNCHEON.—Boiled Ham (Note 4, May 27th); *Broad Beans.*—Follow the recipe given for boiling green peas (July 12th). Young beans will be done enough in twenty minutes, old ones will need to boil half an hour or more. Maître d'Hôtel Sauce (May 6th); Plain Suet Dumpling (May 13th).

DINNER.—Fried Plaice (April 21st); Dutch Sauce (May 14th); Chicken Fricasseed (July 28th); Potatoes (April 12th); Cauliflower (April 25th); Brown Bread and Butter Pudding (July 20th); Cheese (June 8th).

Things that must not be Forgotten.

1. Turn and rub the tongue in the brine.
2. Turn and rub the mutton in the pickle.
3. Turn over the herrings in the vinegar.
4. Make hydropathic red currant pudding for to-morrow (June 16th).

July 16th.

Breakfast.	Luncheon.	Dinner.
Pickled Herrings	Scotch Collops.	Gravy Soup.
Boiled Ham.	Italian Macaroni.	Tame Rabbits, Curried.
Muffins.		Boiled Rice.
Dry Toast.		Potatoes.
Brown and White Bread and Butter.		Hydropathic Red Currant Pudding.
Milk Porridge.		Cheese.

Marketing.

For the Day.—A pound and a half of Buttock Steak (January 1st); one pound of Red Currants.

For To-morrow.—A tin of Sardines (January 12th); Sea Biscuits. When the weather is very hot, cold meat is often preferred to hot meat. If this is the case, the Leg of Lamb which is intended for dinner to-morrow may be bought and cooked to-day, then put into a meat safe, and salad can be served instead of green peas.

BREAKFAST.—Pickled Herrings (August 20th); Boiled Ham (Note 4, May 27th); Muffins (January 30th); Milk Porridge (June 13th).

LUNCHEON.—Scotch Collops (January 9th); Italian Macaroni (July 7th).

DINNER.—Gravy Soup (September 22nd), stock made of chicken bones. *Tame Rabbits Curried.*—The quantities given are for one rabbit. Skin the rabbit, wash it quickly, and cut it into neat joints convenient for serving. Dry them in a cloth. Pare and chop small two onions. Fry them in a good slice of butter or sweet dripping, and when they are brown, without being at all burnt, take them up, and fry the pieces of rabbit in the same fat. Turn them about for about ten minutes and let them be equally fried all over. Take them up, and let them drain. Put the fried onions in a stewpan with a sour apple chopped small (or half a dozen green gooseberries, if more convenient), and a pint of stock. Mix in a basin a dessert-spoonful of Captain White's curry paste, a tea-spoonful of curry powder, half a tea-spoonful of salt, and a dessert-spoonful of ground rice. Beat this to a smooth paste with a little stock, stir it into the sauce, and simmer till the onions are soft, then rub the whole carefully through a hair sieve. Return the sauce to the stewpan, add the pieces of rabbit, and simmer as gently as possible for two hours. At the end of that time stir in a quarter of a pint of cream. Lift the curry off the fire, taste it, if not sufficiently acid add a little lemon-juice, and serve with boiled rice round the dish. A pound and a half of lean veal or a chicken can be substituted for the rabbit in this recipe. Boiled Rice (July 21st); Potatoes (May 12th); Hydropathic Red Currant Pudding (June 16th); Cheese (June 8th).

Things that must not be Forgotten.
1. Turn and rub the tongue in the brine.
2. Turn and rub the mutton in the pickle.
3. Pick the meat from the ham-bone and pot the ham for breakfast to-morrow (April 15th); cooked ham will not need to be baked.
4. Wash a tea-cupful of large sago, and let it soak all night in a pint and a half of cold water.

July 17th.

Breakfast.	Luncheon.	Dinner.
Sardines.	Meat Patties.	Soles Fried.
Potted Ham.	Sago Mould.	Anchovy Sauce
Hot Toast.		Roast Leg of Lamb.
Brown and White Bread and Butter.		Mint Sauce.
		Potatoes.
Marmalade.		Green Peas.
Biscuits and Milk.	.	Devonshire Junket.
		Fresh Strawberries.
		Cheese.

Marketing.
For the Day.—A pair of thick Soles; a plump Leg of Lamb; fresh Mint; New Potatoes; Green Peas; a bottle of prepared Rennet from the chemist's; half a pint of Red Currants for the sago; fresh Strawberries; a pennyworth of fresh German Yeast; Cherries, for the pie.

For To-morrow.—Anchovies, if not in the house; three or four plump Sheep's Kidneys; one pound of Vienna Flour; a pennyworth of Small Salad.

BREAKFAST.—Sardines (January 12th); Potted Ham (April 15th); Biscuits and Milk (June 14th).

LUNCHEON.—*Meat Patties.*—Collect the remnants of meat from

the fricasseed chickens, the potted ham, and the Scotch collops. Trim away the skin, and mince the meat as finely as possible. For three-quarters of a pound of meat melt an ounce of butter in a stewpan, and stir in smoothly an ounce of flour, and afterwards a quarter of a pint of strong stock made from the chicken bones. When the sauce is thick add half the quantity of cream, if it is to be had; if not, milk must be used, and season with pepper and salt to taste, and a very little grated nutmeg. Take the pan off the fire and mix the mince with the sauce. If three or four mushrooms or champignons can be added the mince will be all the nicer. Turn the preparation on a dish, cover it with greased paper, and let it remain till cold. When the pastry (April 17th) is being made to-day take as much as is likely to be required, roll it out to the thickness of an eighth of an inch, and stamp it with a cutter into rounds two inches in diameter. Gather the trimmings, roll them again, and stamp them with the same cutter until there are as many rounds as are required. Place a spoonful of the mince on the centre of one half of the rounds, moisten the pastry round the edge with water, and lay the other rounds evenly on the top. Press the rounds together with the top of a cutter, brush them over with egg, place them on a greased baking-tin, and bake in a well-heated oven till the pastry is done enough. Scrape a little of the pastry off the bottom of each patty, and serve hot on a dish covered with a napkin. If liked, fruit can be substituted for the mincemeat in this recipe. Sago Mould (October 8th).

DINNER.—Soles, Fried (March 24th). *Anchovy Sauce.*—Stir a table-spoonful of anchovy sauce into half a pint of melted butter. To make *Melted Butter.*—Melt an ounce of butter in a small saucepan. Draw the pan back, and mix in gradually half an ounce of flour. Cook the paste for a minute, beating it all the time with the back of a wooden spoon. If this is done the sauce will not be likely to oil; then add half a pint of cold water, a little at a time, and stir the sauce till it boils. Boil for three minutes, and serve. This sauce forms the basis of many sauces. Roast Leg of Lamb (March 4th); Mint Sauce (March 25th); Potatoes (April 12th); Green Peas (July 12th); Devonshire Junket (September 17th); Cheese (June 8th).

Things that must not be Forgotten.

1. Turn and rub the tongue in the brine.
2. Turn and rub the mutton in the pickle.
3. Pastry is to be made to-day (April 17th): Meat patties, cherry pie (August 7th), also Sally Lunns (August 26th), and Annie's cake (September 25th).
4. Make a semolina mould for luncheon to-morrow (July 23rd).
5. Prepare the anchovies and the small salad for breakfast to-morrow (*see* Note 4, January 17th).
6. Partially prepare the rice and barley porridge for to-morrow (Note 6, June 15th).

July 18th.

Breakfast.	Luncheon.	Dinner.
Anchovies and Hard-boiled Eggs. Stewed Kidneys. Sally Lunns. Dry Toast. Brown and White Bread and Butter. Honey. Rice and Barley Porridge.	Cold Lamb. Mint Sauce. Semolina Mould.	Milk Soup. Norman Haricot. Green Peas. Custard Blancmange, with Compôte of Cherries. Cheese.

Marketing.

For the Day.—Half a peck of Peas; one pound of Cherries; a slice of lean Veal from the fillet, weighing from two to three pounds, or, if preferred, Veal Cutlets can be taken from the neck or loin; one pound of Bacon in rashers (half of this is for breakfast to-morrow).

For To-morrow.—Small Soles, "Slips" (see January 3rd); two pounds or more of the tail end of a large Salmon. The tail end is the cheapest part of the fish. A little more should be procured than is likely to be wanted for dinner, as Salmon Mayonnaise is to be served for supper. A couple of Chickens; Potatoes; Cauliflower; one pound of Red Currants; a dozen Apricots, if cheap; ingredients for Salad, two Lettuces, Small Salad, &c.; six ounces or more of firm Kidney Suet for the Fruit Dumpling; Bloaters, for July 20th.

BREAKFAST.—Anchovies and Hard-boiled Eggs (January 18th). Stewed Kidneys (April 16th); Sally Lunns (June 4th); Rice and Barley Porridge (June 15th).

LUNCHEON.—Lamb served yesterday; Mint Sauce (March 25th); Semolina Mould (July 23rd).

DINNER.—Milk Soup (January 3rd); Norman Haricot (August 24th); Green Peas (July 12th); Custard Blancmange (August 4th); Compôte of Cherries (August 5th); Cheese (June 8th).

Things that must not be Forgotten.

1. Turn the tongue in the brine and the mutton in the pickle.
2. Make mayonnaise for supper to-morrow night (August 30th).

Sunday, July 19th.

Breakfast.	Dinner.	Tea.	Supper.
Baked Slips. Toasted Bacon. Sally Lunns. Dry Toast. Brown and White Bread and Butter. Milk Toast.	Salmon Cutlets. Boiled Chickens, with Golden Rain. Rolled Bacon. Potatoes. French Beans. Red Currant Dumpling. Sweet Sauce. Cheese.	Brown and White Bread and Butter. Compôte of Apricots. Annie's Cake.	Mayonnaise of Salmon. Cherry Pie. Cheese.

BREAKFAST. — Baked Slips (January 7th); Toasted Bacon (January 19th); Sally Lunns (June 4th); Milk Toast (June 17th).

DINNER.—*Salmon Cutlets.*—Divide the salmon into neat rounds a quarter of an inch thick, and about three inches across. Dip each one in a mixture of flour and curry powder, and fry the cutlets in hot fat till they are lightly browned (January 17th). They will be best done in a frying-basket, but they can also be cooked by being put into a frying-pan with a slice of butter melted, being turned over when half done. Mince half a shallot finely, fry it in a little butter, and sprinkle over it a tablespoonful of flour and another of curry powder. Add half a pint of stock, and stir the sauce till it thickens, and throw in a large table-spoonful of mixed pickles finely chopped. Arrange the cutlets in a dish, pour the sauce upon them, and serve. If preferred, the salmon cutlets can be egged and breaded, or even floured simply, then fried in fat, and accompanied by Anchovy (July 17th), Shrimp (January 30th), Caper (March 19th), Dutch (May 14th), or Béarnaise Sauce (March 23rd). Boiled Fowls, with Golden Rain (September 6th). *Rolled Bacon.*—Cut some bacon into very thin slices about three inches long and an inch and a half wide, roll them up, and fasten them with a small skewer to keep them in shape. Lay them on a tin, and put them in the oven till sufficiently cooked; they will take five or six minutes. Remove the skewer, and serve them round the chickens. Potatoes (April 12th); French Beans (August 16th). *Red Currant Dumpling.*—Make this pudding, and all boiled fruit puddings, according to the recipe given for beef-steak pudding (June 25th), substituting red currants, or any other fruit, with a little sugar and water, for the meat and gravy. If much sugar is put into the pudding it will be heavy. Boil from two hours and a quarter to two hours and three-quarters, according to the size of the pudding and the hardness of the fruit. Serve with powdered white sugar or sweet sauce. *Sweet Sauces for Puddings.*—A very plain sauce may be made by adding sugar to melted butter (July 17th), while the addition of wine or brandy would turn this into Wine Sauce or Brandy Sauce. A slightly superior sauce may be made by following the recipe for melted butter, but using milk instead of water, and flavouring the sauce with nutmeg, vanilla, or lemon; and the addition of the beaten yolk of an egg, stirred in after the sauce has cooled for a minute, would still further enrich this sauce. A very good sauce for simple *dry* puddings is made by pouring half a pint of boiling water upon a dessert-spoonful of arrowroot mixed to a smooth paste with cold water, then adding sugar, lemon-juice, and nutmeg to taste. Cheese (June 8th).

TEA.—Compôte of Apricots (August 5th); Annie's Cake (September 25th).

SUPPER.—Mayonnaise of Salmon (May 24th); Cherry Pie (August 7th).

Things that must not be Forgotten.

1. Turn and rub the tongue in the brine and the mutton in the pickle.

July 20th.

Breakfast.	Luncheon.	Dinner.
Eggs on the Dish.	Chicken Kromeskies.	Fried Plaice.
Bloaters.	Raspberry Fool.	Dutch Sauce.
Sally Lunns.		Hotch-potch.
Dry Toast.		Brown Bread Pudding.
Brown and White Bread and Butter.		Cheese.
Honey.		
Corn-flour Milk.		

Marketing.

For the Day.—One pound of Raspberries. If these are not procurable, green gooseberries, strawberries, or rhubarb may be used instead. A thick Plaice (April 21st); materials for Hotch-potch (Marketing, July 10th); four fresh Mackerel.

For To-morrow.—A quarter of a pound of Bacon in rashers; three or four fresh Tomatoes.

BREAKFAST.—Eggs on the Dish (December 7th); Bloaters (January 3rd); Sally Lunns (June 4th); Corn-flour Milk (June 19th).

LUNCHEON.—Chicken Kromeskies (July 29th). *Raspberry Fool.*—Proceed as directed for Gooseberry Fool (June 24th).

DINNER.—Fried Plaice (April 21st); Dutch Sauce (May 14th); Hotch-potch (July 10th). *Brown Bread Pudding.*—Collect the pieces of stale brown bread there may be in the house, break them up into very small pieces, and put as many as will weigh 6 ozs. in a basin. Pour upon them the third of a pint of boiling milk, place a plate on the basin, and let the bread soak till soft. Squeeze the pudding dry, beat it well with a fork, and take out any hard pieces there may be in it; then add two ounces of good brown sugar, the grated rind of a *large* fresh lemon, and twenty drops of Vanilla essence. Mix thoroughly, and add two well-beaten eggs. Put the mixture into a pint mould that has been well buttered, place a piece of greased paper on the top, and steam it for an hour and a quarter. Turn it on a hot dish, and serve. For a superior pudding, the yolks of four eggs and the whites of two may be used, and a little cream may be put with the milk. When two eggs only are used, the pudding must be squeezed dry before the eggs are added, or it will not turn out. This pudding will be much improved if a little whip sauce is poured round it. *Whip Sauce.*—Put the yolks of two eggs into a gallipot, with a dessert-spoonful of sifted sugar, a glass of common white wine (orange wine will do for the purpose), the grated rind of a lemon, and a very small piece of cinnamon. Set the gallipot in a small stewpan which has in it hot water to the depth of two inches, put it on the fire, and whisk the sauce till it comes to a thick froth, then pour it round the pudding. If preferred, fruit syrup and a little milk may be used instead of wine. This sauce must not be allowed to boil. Cheese (June 8th).

Things that must not be Forgotten.

1. Turn and rub the tongue in the brine and the mutton in the pickle.
2. Pickle the mackerel for breakfast to-morrow (August 28th).

July 21st.

Breakfast.	Luncheon.	Dinner.
Pickled Mackerel.	Remains of Hotch-potch.	Soles, Rolled and Baked, with Brown Butter Sauce.
Tomatoes and Bacon.	Devilled Eggs.	Curried Veal.
Hot Buttered Toast.		Boiled Rice.
Dry Toast.		Red Rice.
Brown and White Bread and Butter.		Cheese.
Milk Toast.		

Marketing.

For the Day.—A pair of thick Soles, filleted (January 3rd); a slice of lean Veal from the Fillet, weighing from two and a half to three pounds; a pound and a half of Red Currants and a pottle of Raspberries for the pudding.

For To-morrow.—A small tin of Corned Beef; Muffins (January 29th); half a pound of Naples Macaroni (January 1st).

BREAKFAST.—Pickled Mackerel (August 28th); Tomatoes and Bacon (July 12th); Milk Toast (June 17th).

LUNCHEON.—Hotch Potch served yesterday; Devilled Eggs (February 27th).

DINNER.—Soles, Rolled and Baked (March 1st); Brown Butter Sauce (February 12th). *Curried Veal.*—Follow in all respects the recipe given for Curried Rabbit (July 16th). *Rice Boiled for Curry.*—Patna rice is the best for this purpose. Wash the rice well two or three times in cold water to take away the raw taste from it. Pick away the discoloured grains, and throw it into plenty of fast-boiling water slightly salted, and let it boil quickly until a grain feels tender when taken between the thumb and finger. It will take fifteen or twenty minutes, and should on no account be allowed to boil until it forms a pulpy mass, as it is an object to keep the grains separate. Drain it in a colander, and let cold water run on it a minute or two to separate the grains. Dry the stewpan near the fire, put the rice into it, let it stand on the range with the lid half on, and shake it occasionally till it is dry and quite hot. Pile it round the curry like a wall, and serve. Red Rice (December 10th); Cheese (June 8th).

Things that must not be Forgotten.

1. Turn the tongue in the brine and the mutton in the pickle.
2. Turn the pieces of mackerel in the pickle, and keep in a cool place. If this is done, the fish will keep for three or four days.
3. Take care of any rice that may be left. Very good pudding can be made of it for to-morrow.

July 22nd.

Breakfast.	Luncheon.	Dinner.
Pickled Mackerel. Corned Beef. Muffins. Dry Toast. Brown and White Bread and Butter. Oatmeal Porridge.	Macaroni à la Milanaise. Baked Plum Pudding.	Croûte au Pot. Sour Mutton. Potatoes. French Beans. Rice Mould. Cheese.

Marketing.

For the Day.—A quarter of a pound of Beef Suet; French Beans; a pennyworth of Parsley; a pennyworth of Mint; a pound of ripe Tomatoes.

For To-morrow.—Half a pint of freshly boiled picked Shrimps. If the shrimps are not quite fresh they will not be good to-morrow. Watercress; fresh Fruit for breakfast.

BREAKFAST.—Pickled Mackerel (August 28th); Corned Beef bought yesterday; Muffins (January 30th); Oatmeal Porridge (January 25th).

LUNCHEON.—*Macaroni à la Milanaise.*—Follow the recipe given for Italian macaroni (July 7th). Have ready a little tomato sauce (July 15th), and just before serving the macaroni pour the tomato sauce over it. One or two mutton cutlets will be very good served with this dish. If preferred, to save trouble, the tomatoes can be baked (July 7th). Baked Plum Pudding (February 25th).

DINNER.—Croûte au Pot (May 25th); Sour Mutton (March 29th); Potatoes (April 12th); French Beans (August 16th); Rice Mould (April 27th); Cheese (June 8th).

Things that must not be Forgotten.

1. Turn and rub the tongue in the brine.
2. Put the shrimps in a cool place and cover them with muslin.

July 23rd.

Breakfast.	Luncheon.	Dinner.
Buttered Shrimps. Corned Beef. Hot Buttered Toast. Dry Toast. Brown and White Bread and Butter. Watercress. Fresh Fruit with Milk.	Stuffed Tomatoes. Toad-in-the-Hole.	Halibut Cutlets. Cold Mutton. Salad. Cucumber. New Potatoes. Newmarket Pudding. Cheese.

Marketing.

For the Day.—Five or six large ripe Tomatoes; a pound and a half of Buttock Steak; three or four pounds of Halibut (Marketing, June 23rd); a fresh cucumber; a Lettuce; a half-pennyworth of Beet-root; a half-pennyworth of young Onions; Potatoes.

For To-morrow.—Four plump young Kidneys; half a pound of Bacon in rashers; Mustard and Cress.

BREAKFAST.—*Buttered Shrimps.*—Melt an ounce of butter in a saucepan, and mix an ounce of flour smoothly with it. Add gradually half a pint of stock, and stir the sauce till it thickens. Put in the shrimps, and let them simmer for a minute or two, but not boil. Toast a round of bread, and butter it well, pour the preparation upon it, and serve very hot. If liked, milk or cream can be used instead of stock.

LUNCHEON.—*Stuffed Tomatoes.*—Make a savoury forcemeat by mixing together a slice of the corned beef, finely minced, and an ounce of lean ham, half a shallot chopped small, a table-spoonful of chopped parsley, two table-spoonfuls of bread-crumbs, two or three mushrooms, if they are to be had, and a little butter. Bind the forcemeat together with the yolk of an egg. Take a slice from the stalk end of the tomatoes; scoop out the seeds without breaking the fruit, and fill the vacant place with the mince. Shake brown bread-raspings (January 2nd) on the top, put the tomatoes, side by side, in a greased baking-tin, invert a dish over them to cover them, and bake in a brisk oven for about a quarter of an hour till they are cooked. If liked, a little brown gravy may be served round the tomatoes, but they are very good without. Toad-in-the-Hole (January 15th). Use the buttock steak for this dish.

DINNER.—Halibut Cutlets (June 23rd); Mutton served yesterday. If hot meat is preferred, *see* Index. In hot weather cold meat and salad often proves very acceptable. Salad (March 13th); Cucumber (May 19th); New Potatoes (April 12th); Newmarket Pudding (June 2nd); Cheese (June 8th).

Things that must not be Forgotten.

1. Turn the tongue in the brine.
2. Make a *Semolina Mould* for luncheon to-morrow. Mix two table-spoonfuls of semolina with cold milk, and add more milk to make the quantity up to one pint. Put the mixture into a saucepan, stir it without ceasing for ten minutes, and then draw it back and let it simmer for an hour, stirring it occasionally. Sweeten it to taste, and turn it into a damp mould. To-morrow it can be turned out, and will be very good eaten with jam or sugar and cream.
3. When preparing the watercress for breakfast, put aside a sprig or two for the salad.

July 24th.

Breakfast.	Luncheon.	Dinner.
Fried Kidneys and Bacon.	Mutton, Minced.	Boiled Brill.
Mustard and Cress.	Semolina Mould, with	Neapolitan Sauce.
Hot Buttered Toast.	Rhubarb Jam.	Fricassee of Chicken.
Dry Toast.		Bacon Rolls.
Brown and White Bread and Butter.		Cauliflower.
Corn-flour Milk.		Potatoes.
		Chocolate Pudding.
		Cheese.

Marketing.

For the Day.—A moderate-sized Brill (January 9th); quarter of a pint of picked Shrimps, for sauce; one or two plump Chickens; quarter of a pound of Streaky Bacon; Cauliflower; Potatoes; half a pound of best French Chocolate.

For To-morrow.—Muffins (January 29th); half a pound of Red Currants for juice. The Ham is supposed to be in the house.

BREAKFAST.—Kidneys and Bacon (January 2nd); Corn-flour Milk (June 19th).

LUNCHEON.—Cut all the meat from the leg of mutton, mince it, and serve with sippets (January 20th); Semolina Mould make yesterday.

DINNER.—Boiled Brill (January 9th); Neapolitan Sauce (February 8th); Fricassee of Chicken (July 28th); Bacon Rolls (July 19th); Cauliflower (April 25th); Potatoes (April 12th). *Chocolate Pudding.*—Boil half a pound of grated chocolate in one-third of a pint of milk for ten minutes. Stir in when hot an ounce of butter and an ounce and a half of sugar, and when cool add the yolks of two eggs. Beat the whites of the eggs to a froth, and break them in lightly just before steaming the pudding. Butter the inside of a mould with the fingers, and sprinkle two ounces of powdered rusks upon the butter. Put in the chocolate, lay a buttered paper on the top of the pudding, and steam it for an hour and a quarter. (Treacle Pudding, March 28th). Turn out carefully, and serve with a pint of good custard (August 10th) round the pudding. Cheese (June 8th).

Things that must not be Forgotten.

1. Turn and rub the tongue in the pickle.
2. Pastry is usually made on Friday, but as a pigeon pie is to be made for Sunday, and as it will not keep well for more than a day or so, it will be better to defer the business until to-morrow.
3. Make the sago mould for luncheon to-morrow, and let it stand in a cool place till wanted (October 8th).

July 25th.

Breakfast.	Luncheon.	Dinner.
Fried Ham.	Rice and Cheese.	Soles au Gratin.
Fried Eggs.	Sago Mould.	Veal, Stewed.
Muffins.		Green Peas.
Dry Toast.		Young Carrots.
Brown and White Bread and Butter.		Potatoes. Viennoise Pudding.
Bread and Milk.		Cheese.

Marketing.

For the Day.—A pair of thick Soles (January 3rd); three or four pounds of the Loin, Neck, or Breast of Veal; Green Peas; Young Carrots; New Potatoes; three plump Young Pigeons; a slice of Beef or Veal (May 15th).

For To-morrow.—A moderate-sized Turbot, filleted (June 6th); a couple of Ducks (July 4th); Green Peas; Endive; ingredients for a Salad; six ounces of firm Beef Suet; one or two pairs of Lambs' Sweetbreads; Bacon.

BREAKFAST.—Fried Ham (March 5th); Fried Eggs (March 5th); Muffins (January 30th); Bread and Milk (January 25th).

LUNCHEON.—Rice and Cheese (February 18th); Sago Mould made yesterday.

DINNER.—Soles au Gratin (May 3rd). *Veal Stewed.*—Divide the veal into chops or neat pieces convenient for serving. Melt a slice of butter in a stewpan, put in the veal, which has been peppered, salted, and dredged with flour, and let it fry until it is lightly coloured upon both sides. Pour in gradually boiling stock or water to cover it, and let the meat simmer very gently for an hour. Put with it a dozen young carrots, half a dozen young onions, if the flavour is liked, a bunch of parsley, a sprig of thyme, and a little pepper and salt. Then simmer till the vegetables are done enough. Place the meat and vegetables upon a dish, put with the sauce two ripe tomatoes broken small, and a little mushroom ketchup. Boil the sauce two or three minutes (if not sufficiently acid add a little lemon-juice), pour it round the meat, and serve. Send new potatoes (April 12th) and green peas (July 12th) to table as accompaniments to this dish. Viennoise Pudding (July 6th); Cheese (June 8th).

Things that must not be Forgotten.

1. Turn and rub the tongue in the brine.
2. Put a cupful of hominy to soak (February 10th).
3. Wash and trim the sweetbreads, and boil them gently till they are firm in as much stock as will cover them (Note 3, July 4th).
4. Pastry is to be made to-day (April 17th): a pigeon pie (May 15th) and a cherry pie (August 7th); also teacakes (August 26th), and rice cake (August 2nd).
5. The custard blancmange may be made for supper to-morrow night (August 4th).

Sunday, July 26th.

Breakfast.	Dinner.	Tea.	Supper.
Lambs' Sweetbreads.	Filleted Turbot.	Brown and White Bread and Butter.	Pigeon Pie.
Rolled Bacon.	Roast Ducklings.		Salad.
Teacakes.	Green Peas.	Strawberry Jam.	Custard Blancmange.
Dry Toast.	Cherry Pie.	Rice Cake.	
Marmalade.	Cheese.		Lemon Syrup.
Brown and White Bread and Butter.			Cheese.
Boiled Hominy.			

BREAKFAST.—Lambs' Sweetbreads (July 4th); Bacon Rolls (July 19th); Teacakes (February 14th); Boiled Hominy (February 11th).

DINNER.—Filleted Turbot (June 21st). *Roast Ducklings.*—Stuff the ducks with sage and onion stuffing such as is used for roast goose (September 29th). If this is objected to, it can be omitted. Put the birds down to a brisk clear fire, and baste them well till done enough. Send them to table with good brown gravy (made by stewing the necks, gizzards, and livers with onions) poured round but not over them (September 29th). Besides green peas, stewed endive, young turnips tossed in butter, and any kind of salad may be served as an accompaniment. Both ducks and ducklings should be *well* cooked. Ducklings require fully half an hour's roasting; ducks about one hour. Green Peas (July 12th); Stewed Endive (December 5th); Cherry Pie (August 7th); Cheese (June 8th).

TEA.—Rice Cake (August 2nd).

SUPPER.—Pigeon Pie (May 15th); Salad (March 13th); Custard Blancmange made yesterday; Lemon Syrup (March 19th).

Things that must not be Forgotten.

1. Turn and rub the tongue in the brine.
2. Carefully preserve any fish and sauce that may be left.

July 27th.

Breakfast.	Luncheon.	Dinner.
Remains of Pigeon Pie.	Fish Pie.	Potato Purée.
Boiled Eggs.	Baked Batter Pudding.	Rolled Loin of Mutton.
Teacakes.		Potatoes.
Dry Toast.		French Beans.
Brown and White Bread and Butter.		Treacle Pudding.
Fried Hominy.		Cheese.

Marketing.

For the Day.—About three pounds of the best end of a Loin of Mutton; Potatoes; French Beans; four ounces of Beef Suet for the treacle pudding.

When the weather is hot, it is very desirable that the purchase of large joints should be avoided, and that no more meat should be procured than is likely to be immediately used. In cold weather beef and mutton are made more tender by being kept for awhile, but in hot weather meat taints quickly, and therefore it is not safe to keep it. Young meat, such as veal and lamb, is better for being freshly killed. In hot weather it is important that all pipes and veins should be cut away from meat as soon as it comes into the house, and the joint should either be put into the meat-safe or covered with muslin and hung till wanted in a cool airy place. Many cooks pepper the joint to keep away the flies. It is better not to lay it on a dish, as the pressure might cause taint on the under part. If meat *must* be kept for a day or two, it should be examined frequently, say twice a day, and if there is any sign that it is likely to become decomposed, it should be washed in vinegar and water and cooked as soon as possible; or if this is inconvenient, it may, after washing, be plunged into boiling water which has a little piece of charcoal in it, boiled quickly for four minutes, dried thoroughly, and hung up again. Meat that is slightly tainted should be washed in water in which a little permanganate of potash, enough to redden the liquid, has been dissolved. This can be procured for threepence or fourpence of any chemist. If the meat is very decidedly tainted it should not be used, as it is sure to be unwholesome. In hot weather cold meat is very generally preferred to hot meat, therefore Beef, Mutton, or Lamb may with advantage be cooked and served cold, rather than be kept when it is not likely to keep.

For To-morrow.—A tin of Sardines (January 12th).

BREAKFAST.—Pigeon Pie served yesterday; Boiled Eggs (January 5th); Teacakes (February 14th); Fried Hominy (February 12th).

LUNCHEON.—Fish Pie (January 2nd); Baked Batter Pudding (February 5th).

DINNER.—Potato Purée (January 26th); Rolled Loin of Mutton (April 22nd); Potatoes (April 12th); French Beans (August 16th); Treacle Pudding (March 28th); Cheese (June 8th).

Things that must not be Forgotten.

1. Boil the tongue. A tongue is never so good as when cooked straight from the pickle. Wash it in one or two waters, put it in a pan with cold water, bring it slowly to a boil, and simmer it gently till done. It will take from three and a half to four hours, but it should be tried occasionally, and if the skin will peel off easily it is a sign that it is sufficiently boiled. It should be skinned whilst hot. The most economical way of serving it is to roll it tightly with the tip of the tongue turned inside, and press it into a round cake-tin or jar, and put a plate with a heavy weight on the top of it. When prepared in this way the root and all can be used. If liked, the liquor in which it is boiled can be made into glaze and brushed over the sides of the tongue (March 21st). If it is not convenient to cook the tongue at once, it should be hung to dry in a cool place, and wrapped in cotton when dry.

2. If the brine can be used again, it will be well to pickle another tongue, as the liquor can scarcely be used for beef after the tongue has been in it

July 28th.

Breakfast.	Luncheon.	Dinner.
Sardines. Rolled Tongue. Teacakes. Dry Toast. Brown and White Bread and Butter. Marmalade. Milk Porridge.	Cold Mutton. Salad. Macaroni Cheese.	Milk Soup. Fowl Fricasseed. Potatoes. French Beans. Lèche Crème. Cheese.

Marketing.

For the Day.—A Cos Lettuce; small Salad; Watercress; Beetroot; half a pound of Naples Macaroni (January 1st); French Beans; Mint; Parsley; a plump young Fowl; half a pint of fresh Mushrooms or a tin of Champignons; half a pound of Tomatoes; New Potatoes; Ratafias.

For To-morrow.—Order a Tame Rabbit to be sent in the morning.

BREAKFAST.—Sardines (January 12th); Rolled Tongue, boiled yesterday; Teacakes (February 14th); Milk Porridge (June 13th).

LUNCHEON.—Mutton roasted yesterday; Salad (March 13th); Macaroni Cheese (March 20th).

DINNER.—Milk Soup (January 3rd). *Fowl Fricasseed.*—Draw the fowl, and cut it into small, neat joints convenient for serving. Put these into a stewpan, with shallot, two or three strips of bacon-rind scalded and scraped, or an ounce of lean ham, two cloves, two small carrots, a bouquet garni (that is, a bunch of parsley, a sprig of thyme, and a bay-leaf tied together), and half a blade of mace. Pour over all enough stock to barely cover the fowl, add pepper and salt, and simmer gently for half an hour. At the end of that time put the pan on one side, drain the stock into a basin, and when it is cold free it from grease. Meantime wash and peel the mushrooms, and put them into a separate stewpan, with a small slice of butter, a squeeze of lemon-juice, and half a gill of cold water. Let them boil once and turn them upon a plate. If champignons are used this may be omitted. Melt two ounces of butter in a stewpan, and mix smoothly with it one ounce and a half of flour, add the chicken stock and the trimmings from the mushrooms, and simmer all gently together, skimming the sauce when necessary till it is reduced to a pint. Put the chicken and the mushrooms into a clean saucepan, strain the stock over them, add a quarter of a pint of milk, or cream, if it is permitted, with pepper and salt to taste, and simmer all gently together till very hot without boiling. Put the meat on a dish, pour the sauce over, and garnish with sippets. Cold chicken may be fricasseed in the same way, but it will not need the preliminary boiling. Potatoes (April 12th); French Beans (August 16th); Lèche Crème (May 7th); Cheese (June 8th).

Things that must not be Forgotten.

1. Preserve any cold chicken that may be left.
2. Take only one or two sprigs of the watercress for the salad. Preserve the rest for breakfast to-morrow.
3. Make a corn-flour blancmange for luncheon to-morrow (June 15th).

July 29th.

Breakfast.	Luncheon.	Dinner.
Buttered Eggs.	Chicken Kromeskies.	Filleted Sole Sauté.
Rolled Tongue.	Corn-flour Blancmange.	Anchovy Sauce.
Hot Toast.		Tame Rabbit, Curried.
Dry Toast.		Boiled Rice.
Brown and White Bread and Butter.		Potatoes.
		Cabbage.
Watercress.		Queen's Pudding.
Biscuits and Milk.		Cheese.

Marketing.

For the Day.—A small piece of fat Bacon; a pair of thick Soles, filleted (January 3rd); one or a pair of tame Rabbits, cut into neat joints; Potatoes; Cabbage; a dozen fresh Herrings.

For To-morrow.—A pennyworth of Small Salad.

BREAKFAST.—Buttered Eggs (January 16th); Tongue boiled day before yesterday; Biscuits and Milk (June 14th).

LUNCHEON.—*Chicken Kromeskies.*—Kromeskies can be made with any kind of cooked poultry, game, fish, veal, or mutton. When mutton is used, the addition of a few oysters, fresh or tinned, is an improvement. They afford an excellent means of presenting cooked meat in an agreeable form. They are not really troublesome to make when once the process is understood. Boil the bacon and let it go cold. Cut all the meat from the chicken bones, mince it finely, and season it with pepper and salt if required. Supposing there is a quarter of a pound of meat, melt an ounce of butter in a stewpan, mix it with an ounce of flour, and add one gill of liquor. It is probable that in this case there will be a little cold sauce that can be used, or if there is none milk can be taken. Stir the mixture over the fire till it is smooth and very stiff, then add the mincemeat; turn the preparation upon a plate, and put it on one side to get cold. Cut some slices, about three inches long and two wide, and as thin as it is possible, from the fat bacon. Make some *Frying Batter* as follows:—Put a quarter of a pound of flour into a bowl, with a pinch of salt, and mix it very smoothly with a gill of lukewarm water, then add two table-spoonfuls of salad oil; this will make the batter smooth instead of leathery. Just before it is to be used beat the whites of two eggs to a firm froth, and *dash* this, not stir it, lightly in. The yolks of the eggs can be used for the pudding. Spread a spoonful of the forcemeat upon each piece of bacon, and roll it securely to the shape of a cork. Half fill a stewpan with clarified dripping, and put it on the fire till it boils, that is, till it is still and a light blue smoke rises from it. When the fat is ready, take the kromeskies, one at a time, in a spoon; dip them into the batter, and put them at once, with the batter that is in the spoon with them, into the boiling fat. When the batter is lightly browned, that is, in less than a minute, the kromeskies will be done enough. Lay them as they are done on kitchen-paper to free them from grease, and when all are fried put them on a dish covered with a fish-paper, garnish with fried parsley, and serve. The kromeskies will not be good if the bacon is not cut thin. The batter, directions for making which are given, can be used for any kind of fruit fritters. Corn Flour Blancmange (June 15th).

DINNER.—Filleted Sole Sauté (January 4th); Anchovy Sauce (July 17th); Rabbit, Curried (July 16th); Rice, Boiled (July 21st); Potatoes (April 12th); Cabbage (June 4th); Queen's Pudding (August 9th); Cheese (June 8th).

Things that must not be Forgotten.

1. Pot the remains of the boiled tongue (Note 5, September 26th).
2. Cleanse the salad, and partially prepare the anchovies (Note 4, January 17th).
3. Pickle the fresh herrings (August 20th).
4. Prepare the rice and barley for breakfast (Note 6, June 15th).
5. Soak a cupful of white haricot beans in cold water all night.

July 30th.

Breakfast.	Luncheon.	Dinner.
Anchovies and Hard-boiled Eggs. Potted Tongue. Hot Buttered Toast. Dry Toast. Brown and White Bread and Butter. Rice and Barley.	Baked Mackerel. Gingerbread Pudding.	Clear Soup, with Savoury Custard. Norman Haricot, with Potatoes. Haricot Beans. Viennoise Pudding. Whip Sauce. Cheese.

Marketing.

For the Day.—Two moderate-sized Mackerel (April 4th); two pounds of Shin of Beef, to make stock from fresh meat. If preferred, half beef and half veal can be used. Carrots; Turnip; Onion; Leek; Celery-seed. Bouquet garni. A slice of lean Veal from the fillet, weighing about three pounds (February 25th); Potatoes.

For To-morrow.—Three or four ripe Tomatoes; half a pound of Bacon. Order two Ox-tails. These are usually cheap at this time of the year, because they will not keep. Four pennyworth of Cream, or a tin of Devonshire Cream, if permitted.

BREAKFAST.—Anchovies and Hard-boiled Eggs (January 18th); Potted Tongue (Note 5, September 26th); Rice and Barley (June 15th).

s

LUNCHEON.—Baked Mackerel (April 15th); Gingerbread Pudding (May 20th).

DINNER.—*Clear Soup* may be made from fresh meat stock, or by using Liebig's Extract of Meat without any stock (Feb. 15th), or it may, with care and skill, be made from fresh meat without needing clarification. *Clear Soup made at once from Fresh Meat.*—Allow a pint of water for each pound of beef and one pint over. For brown soup shin of beef is usually taken, though finer soup would be made from buttock steak; for white soup knuckle of veal is required, and a slice of lean ham is an improvement to both. Cut the meat, free from fat, into small pieces, and lay these at the bottom of a stewpan, with a slice of fresh butter. Cover the pan, and let the meat brown on both sides, but be careful to move it about, that it may not stick to the pan. Add enough hot water to cover the meat, and boil this quickly, still keeping the pan covered, till it is reduced to a kind of brown gum, then add cold water, a little at a time, bringing the liquor gently to the point of boiling; skim it most carefully until the right quantity of water is used. The gradual addition of the cold water will help the scum to rise. Add the vegetables (scalded) and flavouring ingredients; draw the pan back, and simmer gently for about three hours. Strain the liquor through a jelly-bag without squeezing the meat at all, put the stock into a bowl, and when it is cool free it from fat, and pour it away from any sediment that may have settled at the bottom. The meat will be very good served with vegetables. *To make Stock from Fresh Meat.*—Take beef or veal, or a mixture of both, and allow the usual proportions—a pint to a pound and a pint over. Take away every particle of fat, and cut the meat into small dice. Put these into a stewpan, pour on the requisite quantity of cold water, and add a little salt. Put on the lid, bring the liquor quickly to a boil, skim it carefully, throw in the vegetables, and simmer gently for five hours, still skimming the liquor occasionally. A carrot, a turnip, a leek, a bunch of parsley, a sprig of thyme, a bay-leaf, two or three sticks of celery, and a pinch of herbs will be required for three pints of water. Strain the liquor through a sieve into a bowl, and when cold remove the fat from the top. The meat can be boiled again with fresh vegetables. If clear soup is to be made from stock thus prepared it must be clarified either with raw beef, as directed for Clear Soup or Julienne (April 9th), or, if this is considered too expensive, with white of eggs only. For this the whites of the eggs must be whisked with a little cold water and stirred into the soup while it is lukewarm, and whisked till on the point of boiling. It should then be drawn back, boiled gently for twenty minutes, allowed to stand for twenty minutes, and strained through a jelly-bag. The white of one egg will probably be sufficient for a pint and a half of soup. White of egg, however, impoverishes soup, raw beef enriches it, so the latter is much superior to the former. Soup should be clarified the same day that it is to be used, as it goes cloudy with keeping. *Savoury Custard* is very good served in Clear Soup. To make this, take the yolks of two eggs and the white of one; whisk them, and put with them a gill of the clear soup. Turn the custard into a buttered gallipot, cover the top with buttered paper, and place it in a saucepan with hot water two or three inches deep. The water must not touch the paper. Steam the custard very *gently* till it is set; it will take about a quarter of an hour. If it is allowed to boil quickly the custard will be full of little holes instead of being smooth. Let it go cold, then cut it into thin slices with a sharp knife. Shape these into small circles or diamonds, place them in the soup, and serve. Norman Haricot (August 24th); Potatoes (April 12th); Haricot Beans (June 20th); Viennoise Pudding (July 6th); Whip Sauce (July 20th); Cheese (June 8th).

Things that must not be Forgotten.

1. Turn the herrings in the vinegar.
2. Partially prepare the rice milk for breakfast (Note 3, June 17th).

July 31st.

Breakfast.	Luncheon.	Dinner.
Pickled Herrings.	Minced Veal.	Salmon Cutlets.
Tomatoes and Bacon.	Custard Sippets.	Stewed Ox-tails.
Hot Buttered Toast.		Potatoes.
Dry Toast.		French Beans.
Brown and White Bread and Butter.		Devonshire Junket.
		Cream.
Rice Milk.		Cheese.

Marketing.

For the Day.—About a pound and a half of the tail-end of a moderate-sized Salmon. This is the cheapest part of the fish. Potatoes; French Beans; Ox-tails and Cream, ordered yesterday.

For To-morrow.—A tin of Potted Grouse.

BREAKFAST.—Tomatoes and Bacon (July 12th); Rice Milk (June 18th).

LUNCHEON.—Minced Veal (May 11th); Custard Sippets (June 10th).

DINNER.—Salmon Cutlets (July 19th); Stewed Ox-tails (May 8th); Potatoes (April 12th); French Beans (August 16th); Devonshire Junket (September 17th); Cheese (June 8th).

Things that must not be Forgotten.

1. Turn the herrings in the pickle.
2. Pastry is to be made to-day (April 17th): Red Currant Tart (August 7th); and Beef-steak and Mushroom Pie (March 26th); also Scones (August 26th); and Rice Cake (August 2nd).

FRUITS IN SEASON SUITABLE FOR DESSERT IN JULY.

Pine-apples, Apricots, Cherries, Currants (Black, Red, and White), Greengages, Jersey Grapes, Plums, Raspberries, Strawberries.

HERBS.

Herbs should be gathered and dried in the following months:—Chervil, Elder Flowers, Fennel, and Parsley: May, June, and July; Mint, Orange Thyme, and Burnet: June and July; Knotted Marjoram and Winter Savory: about the end of July; Thyme and Lemon Thyme, and Summer Savory and Tarragon: July and August; Basil: August; Sage: August and September.

Herbs are in best condition for drying just before they begin to flower. They should be gathered on a dry day, but not in the heat of the sun. The more quickly they are dried the more effectually will their flavour be preserved. It is a good plan to put them before the fire, being careful that they do not burn. When quite dry the leaves should be picked off the stalks, rubbed to powder, and passed through a wire sieve, then put into small dry bottles, and corked closely till wanted. When all the herbs are dried, a most excellent aromatic seasoning may be made as follows :—

Aromatic Herbaceous Seasoning.—Take three ounces of basil, three ounces of marjoram, two ounces of winter savory, three ounces of thyme, one ounce of dried bay-leaves, two ounces of ground cloves, two ounces of white pepper, one ounce of powdered mace, one ounce of grated nutmeg, half an ounce of cayenne pepper, half an ounce of grated lemon-peel, and two cloves of garlic. Pound all the ingredients together in a mortar, sift them through a wire sieve, put into small dry bottles, and cork for use. This mixture will be found most excellent for flavouring soups and sauces, a small pinch being sufficient for a quart of liquor. It is scarcely possible to improve upon this mixture. It is most important that genuine spices should be provided, and to secure this it is best to grind the ingredients at home. When this is not practicable they should be purchased of a first-class dealer.

Tarragon Vinegar should be made in July. Pick the fresh leaves off the stalks, put them into a bottle, and cover them with vinegar. Let them remain four or six weeks, then strain the vinegar, put it into small bottles, and cork it securely. Two or three drops of this vinegar will prove a valuable addition to salad dressings and to mayonnaise sauce.

Walnuts should be pickled and Walnut Ketchup should be made from the beginning to the middle of July. The earliest walnuts are the best; as the season advances the fruit gets woody. Prick each walnut quite through with a large darning-needle. The hands should be covered with a cloth while this is done, or they will be deeply stained. Make enough brine (made of salt dissolved in boiling water) to cover them. The brine should be so strong that it will float an egg, and should go cold before the walnuts are put into it. Place a board on the fruit to keep it under; let the walnuts lie in the brine for nine days, and make fresh brine every third day. Drain the walnuts, and turn them about in the sun till they go black. Put them into a jar and pour over them hot vinegar to cover them Spices should be boiled in the vinegar: two ounces of whole pepper, one ounce of whole ginger, three or four cloves, and a blade of mace to each quart of vinegar. Tie the jars down securely, and store in a dry place. The walnuts may be used at the end of a month, though it would be best to leave them untouched for six months. At the end of that time the vinegar may be drained off and used as ketchup, and the jars filled up with fresh vinegar. They should in all cases be looked at now and then, and fresh vinegar to cover the walnuts entirely added when necessary.

August 1st.

Breakfast.	Luncheon.	Dinner.
Pickled Herrings. Potted Grouse. Scones. Dry Toast. Brown and White Bread and Butter. Marmalade. Milk Toast.	Scrag of Mutton, with Rice. Stirabout Cheese.	Milk Soup. Beef-steak Pie. Potatoes. Cabbages. Vermicelli Pudding. Cheese.

Marketing.

For the Day.—The scrag end of a Neck of Mutton; two pounds of Rump or Buttock Steak (January 1st); half an Ox Kidney; a quarter of a pint of Mushrooms or a small tin of Champignons; Saltpetre for the butter; a pint of Indian Meal (Marketing, January 30th); Potatoes; Cabbages; a pennyworth of Parsley.

For To-morrow.—A moderate-sized Turbot (June 6th); half a pint of Picked Shrimps or Lobster Spawn; a Fore-quarter of Lamb (April 11th); Beans; Potatoes; ingredients for a Salad; Mint; a pound and a half of Red Currants, and half a pound of Raspberries. Half a small Ham is supposed to be in the house. A little best Kidney Suet for the pudding on August 3rd, and Watercress for the devilled eggs; two or three pounds of Apples. Sometimes apples that have been blown from the trees, windfalls, are to be bought at a cheap rate at this time of the year. If this is the case, a few can be procured to make Parson's Pudding for August 3rd. If not, Treacle Pudding (March 28th) may be substituted for the Parson's Pudding.

BREAKFAST.—Pickled Herrings (August 20th); Potted Grouse (January 7th); Scones (May 23rd); Milk Toast (June 17th).

LUNCHEON.—Scrag of Mutton, Stewed with Rice (February 21st). *Stirabout Cheese.*—Put into a saucepan a pint of milk, a pint of water, and a little salt. Boil, then with one hand sprinkle two ounces of

Indian meal into the liquid, and stir briskly with a knife held in the other hand till the mixture is smooth and thick. Simmer gently for an hour and stir frequently. Add an ounce of butter or dripping, a spoonful of mustard, and two ounces of grated cheese. Turn upon a hot dish and serve. This preparation, when cold, may be cut into slices and fried. Cheese that has become too dry to be used in the ordinary way may be taken for this dish.

DINNER.—Milk Soup (January 3rd); Beef-steak Pie (March 26th); Potatoes (April 12th); Cabbage (June 4th). *Vermicelli Pudding.*—Flavour a pint and a quarter of milk with lemon, cinnamon, or vanilla, and drop into it when boiling four ounces of vermicelli; crush it slightly with one hand whilst sprinkling it in, and stir it to keep it from gathering in lumps or burning. Let it boil gently, stirring it frequently, till it is tender and very thick. Pour it into a bowl, sweeten it to taste, stir a lump of butter into it, and when it is cool add two eggs, lightly beaten. Turn it into a buttered pie-dish, and bake it in a moderately-heated oven till it is brown on the top. A tea-spoonful of brandy and a little cream will improve the pudding, or, for economy's sake, one egg may be used instead of two, and the butter may be omitted. Cheese (June 8th).

Things that must not be Forgotten.

1. Boil the ham for breakfast to morrow (Note 4, May 27th).
2. Put the suet into the flour-bin and cover it with flour till wanted. It will keep there better than anywhere else. It should be remembered that if treacle pudding is to be made a quarter of a pound of suet will be sufficient; for parson's pudding six ounces of suet will be needed.
3. Make Rothe Grütze for dinner to-morrow (December 10th).

Sunday, August 2nd.

Breakfast.	Dinner.	Tea.	Supper.
Savoury Eggs.	Boiled Turbot.	Brown and White Bread and Butter.	Cold Lamb.
Boiled Ham.	Shrimp or Lobster Sauce.	Apple Jelly.	Salad.
Scones.	Quarter of Lamb.	Rice Cake.	Red Currant Tart.
Dry Toast.	Mint Sauce.		Cheese.
Brown and White Bread and Butter.	Potatoes.		
Marmalade.	Cauliflowers		
Corn-flour Milk.	Rothe Grütze.		
	Cheese.		

BREAKFAST.—Savoury Eggs (January 1st); Ham boiled yesterday; Scones (May 23rd); Corn-flour Milk (June 19th).

DINNER.—Boiled Turbot (June 7th); Shrimp Sauce (January 30th); Lobster Sauce (June 7th); Roast Lamb (March 4th and April 12th); Mint Sauce (March 25th); Potatoes (April 12th); Cauliflower (April 25th); Rothe Grütze (December 10th); Cheese (June 8th).

Tea.—For the *Rice Cake*, which was supposed to be made last Friday, proceed as follows:—Rub eight ounces of fresh butter into one pound of flour, add a pinch of salt, three heaped tea-spoonfuls of baking-powder (the recipe for making this is given below), a pound of ground rice, six ounces of sugar, a pound of picked and dried currants, and two ounces of candied peel chopped small. Mix the dry ingredients thoroughly. Add two well-beaten eggs and milk to make a stiff paste. Put the mixture into two small tins lined with buttered paper, and bake in a well-heated oven. When a notched skewer pushed to the bottom of the cake comes out quite clean the cakes are done enough. They will take a little more than an hour to bake. When turned out of the tin, cakes should be at once turned on their sides or on a sieve till cool. If left in the tin they will be likely to be made heavy. To make a plain *Sultana Cake*, weigh ten ounces of flour, and rub into it four ounces of butter or clarified dripping, add two ounces of moist sugar, four ounces of picked sultanas, a tea-spoonful of grated lemon-rind, one ounce of candied peel finely chopped, and two tea-spoonfuls of baking-powder; mix the dry ingredients thoroughly, stir in one egg beaten up with a little milk, just sufficient to moisten the cake, and bake as before. If cakes are made too *moist* in mixing they are sure to be heavy when baked. For a *Sultana Cake* that is a little richer, but still plain and wholesome, take eight ounces of flour, a pinch of salt, one ounce of candied peel, a tea-spoonful of grated lemon-rind, a tea-spoonful of baking-powder, four ounces of butter or dripping, four ounces of sugar, and four ounces of sultanas. Mix the dry ingredients, then moisten with two eggs and about two table-spoonfuls of milk. When eggs are put into cakes of this description it is best to stir in the yolks with the milk or water that is used to moisten the liquid, to whisk the whites to a firm froth, and to stir this lightly into the cake just before it is put into the tin in which it is to be baked.

To make *Baking-powder*.—Take an equal *bulk* of tartaric acid, carbonate of soda, and either ground rice or corn-flour. Mix the ingredients thoroughly, and rub the powder through a wire sieve. As a general rule a tea-spoonful of this powder is required for each pound of dry ingredients used. When baking-powder is used the pastry or cake that it is intended to lighten should be baked as soon as possible after it is moistened.

Supper.—Salad (March 13th); Red Currant Tart (August 7th).

Things that must not be Forgotten.

1 Carefully preserve any cold fish that may be left; it can be used for luncheon to-morrow. Cold potatoes also should be preserved; they can be used both for the fish cakes and for the potato salad.

August 3rd.

Breakfast.	Luncheon.	Dinner.
Devilled Eggs.	Fish Cakes.	Potato Purée.
Boiled Ham.	Plain Rice Pudding.	Cold Lamb.
Scones.		Mint Sauce.
Dry Toast.		Salad.
Brown and White Bread and Butter.		Parson's Pudding.
Bread and Milk.		Cheese.

BREAKFAST.—Devilled Eggs (February 27th); Ham boiled day before yesterday; Scones (May 23rd); Bread and Milk (January 25th).

LUNCHEON.—Fish Cakes (January 13th); Plain Rice Pudding (February 24th).

DINNER.—Potato Purée (January 26th); Lamb served yesterday; Mint Sauce (March 25th); Potato Salad (April 12th). *Parson's Pudding.*—Make some good suet crust (June 25th); roll this out as for Roly-poly Pudding (August 18th), and spread over the surface a mixture made of apples, pared, cored, and chopped small, picked and washed currants, and a little moist sugar. Sprinkle finely-chopped suet on the top, roll the pudding up, fasten the ends securely, put it in a floured cloth, and boil it like roly-poly pudding, serving with sweet sauce (July 19th). This pudding is generally liked by children. Cheese (June 8th).

Things that must not be Forgotten.

1. Make a semolina mould for luncheon to-morrow (July 23rd).
2. Put a cupful of hominy to soak all night in cold water (February 10th).

August 4th.

Breakfast.	Luncheon.	Dinner.
Ham on Toast.	Stewed Pigeons.	Fillets of Sole Sautés.
Boiled Eggs.	Semolina Mould.	Ribs of Beef, Rolled.
Buttered Toast.		Browned Potatoes.
Dry Toast.		Cabbage.
Brown and White Bread and Butter.		Macaroni Pudding.
Marmalade.		Cheese.
Boiled Hominy.		

Marketing.

For the Day.—Three plump young Pigeons (January 24th); three-quarters of a pound of Bacon in rashers, half for to-day and half for to-morrow; a pair of thick Soles, filleted (January 3rd); one rib of Beef to weigh about six pounds; the butcher should be asked to bone and roll the meat. Six ounces of pipe Macaroni (January 1st); Potatoes; Cabbage; a peck of Peas.

For To-morrow.—About four plump fresh Sheep's Kidneys; Watercress; a pint of fresh Fruit of any kind to make juice for the cold sago.

BREAKFAST.—Ham on Toast (March 28th); Boiled Eggs (January 5th); Boiled Hominy (February 11th).

LUNCHEON.—*Stewed Pigeons.*—When peas are plentiful and pigeons are cheap, a very excellent dish may be made by stewing them together as follows :—Pluck three plump young pigeons, and truss 'them with their legs inside. Cut half the bacon bought this morning into very small pieces, throw these into a stewpan with a piece of butter the size of a walnut, and shake them over the fire for a minute. Put the pigeons upon them breast downwards, and turn these about till they are equally and lightly browned all over. Take them up, and mix a table-spoonful of flour smoothly with the bacon and butter, and beat the paste over the fire with the back of a wooden spoon till it is well cooked. Add gradually a pint of stock or water, and throw in a bunch of parsley. Let the sauce boil, add the pigeons, a quart of freshly-shelled green peas, a small lump of sugar, and a little pepper; simmer all gently together for three-quarters of an hour. Place the pigeons on a dish, put the sauce and peas round them, and serve.

DINNER.—Fillets of Sole Sautés (January 4th); Ribs of Beef, Rolled and Roasted (March 4th or March 8th); Browned Potatoes (October 18th); Cabbage (June 4th); Macaroni Pudding (March 27th); Cheese (June 8th).

Things that must not be Forgotten.

1. Do not forget to stew the beef bones. Excellent stock may be made from them.

2. Preserve any boiled hominy that may be left; it can be fried for breakfast to-morrow.

3. Prepare the *Custard Blancmange* for dinner to-morrow. Soak an ounce of gelatine in a cupful of cold water for an hour. Make a pint of custard, either plain or rich (August 10th). Stir the soaked gelatine in this whilst it is hot till it is dissolved. Oil some small moulds of various sizes, fill them with the custard, and put them in a cool place till wanted. When they are to be served, turn the shapes upon a glass dish, pour around them a little brightly-coloured fruit syrup or lemon syrup (March 19th), place a ring of angelica or a preserved cherry upon each mould, and serve. If preferred, a compôte of fresh fruit, such as white currants, red currants, cherries, or strawberries, can be used instead of the syrup (August 5th). When very small moulds are used the blancmange can, for the sake of convenience, be made the day that they are to be served; but of course it is safer, especially in hot weather, to let them stand some hours to stiffen.

4. Make for luncheon to-morrow a mould of cold sago with fruit juice (October 8th).

August 5th.

Breakfast.	Luncheon.	Dinner.
Fried Kidneys and Bacon. Buttered Toast. Dry Toast. Brown and White Bread and Butter. Watercress. Fried Hominy.	Scotch Collops. Sago Mould.	Fried Plaice. Dutch Sauce. Beef, with Acid Sauce. Potatoes. Cauliflowers. Custard Blancmange. Compôte of Fresh Fruit. Cheese.

Marketing.

For the Day.—One pound and a half of Buttock Steak (January 1st); a thick Plaice (April 21st); Potatoes; Cauliflowers; a pint of fresh Fruit for the compôte; a pennyworth of Parsley; Saltpetre for the butter, if wanted (August 27th).

For To-morrow.—Half a pint of freshly-boiled picked Shrimps; a tin of Collared Tongue (January 2nd).

Breakfast.—Fried Kidneys and Bacon (January 2nd); Fried Hominy (February 12th).

Luncheon.—Scotch Collops (January 9th); Sago Mould (October 8th).

Dinner.—Fried Plaice (April 21st); Dutch Sauce (May 14th); Beef, with Acid Sauce (December 4th); Potatoes (May 12th); Cauliflowers (April 25th). *Compôte of Fresh Fruit.*—A compôte consists simply of fresh fruit boiled in syrup until it is cooked sufficiently, but has not lost either its original shape or colour. Compôtes are wholesome and elegant preparations, and are much superior to stewed fruit as it is usually served. To prepare a compôte it is necessary to have a clear syrup, made by boiling together loaf sugar and water. The fruit, sound, ripe, and fresh, should be thrown into this syrup when it is boiling, and simmered gently for a while, the time varying with the nature of the fruit. The preparation should always be removed from the fire as soon as the fruit is done enough, and before it has time to fall. The fruit itself should then be lifted into a glass dish, and the syrup boiled a minute or two longer; but it should always be allowed to cool before it is poured into the dish. The quantity of sugar used must of course depend upon the acidity of the fruit, and a sufficiency must be used, or the syrup will not look bright and clear. Apples, hard pears, strawberries, raspberries, plums of all kinds, cherries, red, white, and black currants, apricots, nectarines, peaches, and blackberries are all excellent made into compôtes. Properly made compôtes will keep for two or three days, and if there is any sign that they are becoming spoilt they may be restored by being boiled for a minute or two. Superior compôtes are excellent as dessert dishes, and fruit preserved in this way may be used to garnish sweet dishes of various kinds. Cheese (June 8th).

Things that must not be Forgotten.

1. Put the shrimps in a cool place, and cover them with muslin.
2. Preserve any broken remnants of beef there may be. Rissoles can be made of them to-morrow.

August 6th.

Breakfast.	Luncheon.	Dinner.
Buttered Shrimps.	Baked Mackerel.	Tomato Purée.
Collared Tongue.	Rissoles.	Curried Chicken.
Hot Buttered Toast.		Rice.
Dry Toast.		New Potatoes.
Brown and White Bread and Butter.		Baked Omelette.
Milk Porridge.		Cheese.

Marketing.

For the Day.—A couple of fresh moderate-sized Mackerel; two pounds of ripe Tomatoes; one Capon or a pair of Chickens (June 29th). Those who keep fowls, and who find it necessary to kill an old bird from time to time, may render it as tender when cooked as a young chicken by adopting the following method. Pluck the bird whilst still warm, wrap it in plenty of vine-leaves, then in an old napkin, and bury it for about twenty-four hours, not in damp ground but in good earth. Take it up, and stew it gently in a small quantity of water. New Potatoes.

For To-morrow.—A quarter of a pound of German Sausage; Sea Biscuits, if not in the house; one Cow-heel, dressed, from the tripe shop; Muffins (January 29th).

BREAKFAST.—Buttered Shrimps (July 23rd); Collared Tongue bought yesterday; Milk Porridge (June 12th).

LUNCHEON.—Baked Mackerel (April 15th); Rissoles made of remnants of Beef (January 6th).

DINNER.—Tomato Purée (March 11th); *Curried Chicken.*—Follow the directions given for currying rabbit (July 16th). Rice, Boiled, for Curry (July 21st); New Potatoes (April 12th). *Baked Omelette.*—Break two eggs or more in a bowl, and whisk them lightly; add sugar and flavouring to taste. Take a small omelette-pan, or wanting this, if two eggs are used, a round cake tin that is kept exclusively for this purpose, and that measures about four inches across, may be used. Put a slice of butter in this and let it get boiling hot. Whisk the eggs till the last moment, pour them into the pan, and bake in a very brisk oven. The omelette will be done enough in five or six minutes. An omelette-pan should never be washed, but wiped out with a dry cloth. If it is washed, the next omelette that is baked or fried in it will almost certainly be a failure. Cheese (June 8th).

Things that must not be Forgotten.

1. If the legs of the chicken can be preserved, they may be devilled for breakfast to-morrow

August 7th.

Breakfast.
Devilled Drumsticks.
German Sausage.
Muffins.
Dry Toast.
Brown and White Bread and Butter.
Biscuits and Milk.

Luncheon.
Beef à la Mode.
Treacle Tart.

Dinner.
Fried Hake.
Mutton Chops, with Piquante Sauce.
Potatoes.
French Beans.
Brown Bread and Butter Pudding.
Cheese.

Marketing.

For the Day.—Two pounds of lean Beef; buttock steak, the clod or sticking or an ox-cheek may be used. About three pounds of Hake, cut into slices about half an inch thick. Hake is a most excellent fish, that is not valued as it ought to be, because it is cheap. It is a large west country fish, very often sold under the name of Devonshire or White Salmon, and it may be cooked in any of the ways recommended for salmon or for cod. The most economical way of buying it for a family is to purchase a whole fish, weighing about twelve pounds, then salt the tail end, which can be boiled the next day, and cut the thick part into steaks. Sometimes it can be obtained fresh and crimped like cod, and then it is really very superior. In choosing it, the same rules hold good with this fish as with others (January 3rd). About three pounds of the best end of a Neck of Mutton; Potatoes; French Beans; a pennyworth of German Yeast.

For To-morrow.—A tin of Sardines; Watercress.

BREAKFAST.— Devilled Drumsticks (January 14th); German Sausage (June 6th); Muffins (January 30th); Biscuits and Milk (June 14th).

LUNCHEON.—Beef à la Mode (February 14th); Treacle Tart (*see below*).

DINNER.—*Fried Hake.*—Follow the directions given for Fried Cod (January 1st). Mutton Chops, with Piquante Sauce (April 30th); Potatoes (May 12th); French Beans (August 16th); Brown Bread Pudding (July 20th); Cheese (June 8th).

Things that must not be Forgotten.

1. Take care of one or two slices of German sausage for the Hambro' salad on Sunday evening.

2. Make a *Ground Rice Mould* for luncheon to-morrow. Take four ounces of ground rice, one quart of milk, three ounces of white sugar, and any flavouring that may be preferred, lemon-rind, almond, or vanilla essence. Put a pint and a half of the milk into a saucepan with the sugar and flavourings, and with the half-pint that remains mix the rice to a smooth paste. Stir the rice into the milk when the latter boils, and let it boil quickly, stirring it all the time till it leaves the saucepan with the spoon. Pour it into a quart mould of china or tin that has been soaking in cold water for a few minutes, and put it in a cool place till wanted. Serve on a glass dish, with treacle, jam, or a compôte of fresh fruit round it (August 5th). If preferred, the

shape can be made of whole rice instead of ground rice; then the rice would be put into the milk when cold, and would be simmered gently till soft. It would need to be well beaten before being turned into the mould.

3. Pastry (April 17th) and rolls are to be made to-day: Greengage Pies, Vienna Bread (August 26th), and Sultana Cake (August 2nd). *Fruit Pies* are made in the same way, whatever kind of fruit is used. The fruit, properly prepared, is put into a pie-dish and heaped up in the middle, and moist sugar, more or less according to the acidity of the fruit, is sprinkled over it. Apples or other fruits that are not fully ripe, and so are not likely to fall well, are often partially baked at this stage. The pastry is then rolled out to the shape of the pie-dish, but larger, and about a quarter of an inch thick. A strip of paste rather larger than the edge of the dish should be cut from the rolled pastry, the edge of the dish should be moistened with water, the strip of paste laid on it being pressed down lightly with the fingers. The strip of pastry can now be moistened again, the cover laid on the pie, and the pastry pressed down with the fingers at the inner part of the edge. The edges are then to be cut evenly all round, and ornamented according to taste, and a slit can be made in the pastry at the side of the pie, with the blade of a small knife, to allow the steam to escape. The pie is now ready for the oven, which should be well heated, and it will be done enough when the pastry is set and of a light brown colour. Superior pies look better when glazed, and for this all that is necessary is to brush the surface of the pie quickly over with cold water, and to sprinkle powdered white sugar over it before putting it in the oven. When fruit is likely to be very juicy, a small cup or jar should be placed bottom uppermost in the middle of the pie to keep the juice from boiling over. *Pies* are made with the pastry over the fruit, *Tarts* with the pastry under the fruit. Tarts are of all sizes and shapes, and are usually baked in tins. In most cases it is best to bake the pastry before filling it, and to prick a few holes in the bottom of the tart, or lay a crust of bread on it, to keep the pastry down and in shape. When, however, a cover is to be placed over it, as, for instance, in cranberry tart, the fruit must be put in its place at first, though even then it is sometimes well to stew it a little, and let it cool before laying it on the pastry. *Treacle Tart* is made by lining a tin with pastry, spreading treacle over it, and covering it with two or three layers of pastry rolled out exceedingly thin, each layer having treacle spread over it. A covering of pastry is placed on the top, and the tart is ready for the oven.

For both pies and tarts a *light* crust is always to be preferred. Puff paste (April 24th) is the best for superior pies and tarts, though good short crust (June 19th) is also excellent for the purpose. When puff-paste is regarded as being either too troublesome to make or too rich for digestion, what may be called *Flaky Crust* will be a very good substitute for it. To make this, put half a pound of flour into a bowl, with a pinch of salt, half a tea-spoonful of sifted sugar, and half a tea-spoonful of baking-powder (August 2nd); mix all thoroughly, and make into a *stiff* paste by stirring in the white of one egg whisked to a stiff froth and a little water. Weigh a quarter of a pound of butter or clarified dripping, and divide this into two portions. Roll out the pastry to the thickness of a quarter of an inch, spread one portion of the butter evenly over it, and dredge flour upon this. Fold the paste in three, turn it round with the edges to the front, and roll it again. Spread the remainder of the butter over it, dredge flour on it again, and roll it to the shape that is required. Bake in a brisk oven. Sometimes this pastry is made by rubbing the butter into the flour, as for short crust, rolling the paste out three or four times, and brushing it over with white of egg each time it is rolled.

4. Partially prepare the rice milk (Note 3, June 17th).

August 8th.

Breakfast.	Luncheon.	Dinner.
Collared Tongue.	Beef à la Mode.	Soles, Filleted and Rolled, with Brown Butter Sauce.
Buttered Eggs.	Ground Rice Mould.	Loin of Lamb, Braised.
Vienna Bread.		New Potatoes.
Dry Toast.		Peas.
Brown and White Bread and Butter.		Cocoa-nut Pudding.
Rice Milk.		Cheese.

Marketing.

For the Day.—A pair of thick Soles (January 3rd); a Loin of Lamb; Potatoes; Green Peas, if they are to be had; Parsley; a fresh Cocoa-nut, or a small tin of Desiccated Cocoa-nut; half a pint of Mushrooms.

For To-morrow.—Half a dozen small fresh Mackerel (April 4th); a tin of Bovill's Potted Pheasant; the tail end, or, if preferred, a cut from the middle, of a moderate-sized Salmon; Shrimps for sauce; a small Cucumber for garnish; a fillet of Veal (March 14th); half a pound of Bacon in rashers; Ingredients for forcemeat (June 27th); Potatoes; Broccoli; Apples, Lettuce, Endive, &c., for Hambro' Salad (see below).

BREAKFAST.—Collared Tongue (Note, January 3rd); Buttered Eggs (January 16th); Vienna Bread (August 26th); Rice Milk (June 18th).

LUNCHEON.—Beef à la Mode and Rice Mould prepared yesterday.

DINNER.—Soles, Filleted, Rolled, and Baked (March 1st); Brown Butter Sauce (February 12th); Loin of Lamb, Braised (May 22nd); New Potatoes (April 12th); Green Peas (July 12th). *Cocoa-nut Pudding.*—Take one cupful of grated cocoa-nut or of desiccated cocoa-nut, pour upon it a pint of boiling milk, let it soak for awhile; put it in a saucepan, bring it again to the boil, and add rather less than a pint of cold milk and a table-spoonful of corn-flour mixed to a smooth paste with a quarter of a gill of milk. Stir the mixture and let it boil again. Pour it out, and when cool add three well-beaten eggs and sugar to taste. Pour into a buttered dish, and bake in a moderate oven for about three-quarters of an hour. If fresh coconut is used the milk of the nut may be added to the pudding when it is cool. Cheese (June 8th).

Things that must not be Forgotten.

1. Pickle the mackerel for breakfast to-morrow (August 28th).
2. *Hambro' Salad* will be required for supper to-morrow evening. It may be partially prepared to-day, that is, the ingredients may be collected, and the anchovies may be filleted and laid between two dishes. To prepare the salad, cleanse the lettuce and endive, dry it thoroughly, and shred it finely. Put it in a salad bowl, and mix with it half a dozen filleted anchovies, a small slice of the boiled salmon torn into flakes, two or three slices of German sausage finely minced, a few slices of cold boiled potatoes, and a sour apple chopped small. Toss the whole lightly and thoroughly together at the moment of serving with the ordinary salad dressing, oil, vinegar, pepper, and salt (March 13th), sprinkle a spoonful of minced German sausage on the top, garnish with hard-boiled eggs, and serve. Strictly speaking, kippered salmon and grated Hambro' beef ought to enter into the composition of this salad, but when they are not at hand ingredients of a like character may take their place.

Sunday, August 9th.

Breakfast.	Dinner.	Tea.	Supper.
Potted Pheasant.	Boiled Salmon.	Brown and White Bread and Butter.	Hambro' Salad.
Pickled Mackerel.	Fillet of Veal, Stuffed and Baked.	Vienna Bread.	Greengage Pie.
Vienna Bread.	Bacon Rolls.	Strawberry Jam.	Cheese.
Dry Toast.	Potatoes.	Sultana Cake.	Pulled Bread.
Brown and White Bread and Butter.	Cauliflower.		
Milk Toast.	Queen's Pudding, with Sugar Icing.		
	Cheese.		

BREAKFAST.—Potted Pheasant (*see* Potted Grouse, January 7th); Pickled Mackerel (August 28th); Vienna Bread (August 26th); Milk Toast (June 17th).

DINNER.—Boiled Salmon (July 5th); Shrimp Sauce (January 30th), Caper Sauce (March 19th), or better still, Dutch Sauce (May 14th) or Béarnaise (March 23rd), are greatly to be preferred. Fillet of Veal, Stuffed and Baked (June 28th); Bacon Rolls (July 19th); Potatoes (May 12th); Cauliflower (April 25th). *Queen's Pudding, with Sugar Icing.*—Rub some stale bread through a wire sieve until half a pint of bread-crumbs have been obtained. Put these into a bowl, pour upon them a pint of boiling milk, add the grated rind of a lemon, three table-spoonfuls of white sugar, an ounce of butter, and the beaten yolks of two eggs (the whites of the eggs should be put aside; they will be wanted presently) Butter a small pudding-dish, or, if preferred, line it with pastry, pour in the mixture, and bake in a well-heated oven till it is set and nicely browned. Put the two whites of eggs upon a plate, and whisk them until the froth can be cut in two with a knife. After they are whisked mix about a spoonful of sifted arrowroot with them to keep the froth firm, add as much white sugar as will sweeten the icing, and place it in broken lumps on the top of the pudding. Put it in the oven till lightly browned on the top, and it is ready to serve. Cheese (June 8th).

Tea.—Vienna Bread (August 26th); Sultana Cake (August 2nd).

Supper.—Hambro' Salad (August 8th); Pie (August 7th); Pulled Bread (August 27th).

Things that must not be Forgotten.

1. If any salmon is left, pickle it as soon as possible after it leaves the table (May 30th).
2. Turn over the mackerel in the vinegar.
3. Put a cupful of white haricot beans to soak all night in cold water.

August 10th.

Breakfast.	Luncheon.	Dinner.
Pickled Salmon.	Chops, Stewed in their own Gravy	Haricot Purée.
Potted Pheasant.		Minced Veal.
Hot Buttered Toast.	Lemon Sponge.	Bacon Rolls.
Dry Toast.		Potatoes.
Brown and White Bread and Butter.		Cabbage.
		Chocolate Pudding.
Marmalade.		Custard.
Oatmeal Porridge.		Cheese.

Marketing.

For the Day.—Two pounds and a half, or more, of Mutton Chops from the loin; three-quarters of a pound of Bacon (half of this is for dinner and half for breakfast to-morrow); Potatoes; Cabbage; half a pound of French Chocolate.
For To-morrow.—Three or four French or Globe Artichokes (these may have to be ordered); a Lamb's Fry (Marketing, May 15th); Tomatoes.

Breakfast.—Pickled Salmon (May 30th); Potted Grouse (January 7th); Oatmeal Porridge (January 25th).

Luncheon.—Chops, Stewed in their own Gravy (May 29th). *Lemon Sponge.*—Custard is to be made later in the day. For this the yolks of the eggs only will be needed, and therefore the whites may be utilised by making them into Lemon Sponge. This dish is a pretty and inexpensive one for a supper or cold collation. Soak an ounce of isinglass or gelatine, and the rind of two lemons thinly pared, in a pint of cold water for an hour. Take out the rind, dissolve the gelatine over the fire, and add three-quarters of a pound of loaf sugar, and the juice of three lemons. Let all boil together for three or four minutes, pour out the mixture, and let it remain till it is cold and beginning to set. Whisk the whites of the two eggs, the yolks of which are to be used for the custard pudding, add them to the mixture, and whisk again for about half an hour till the preparation becomes of the consistence of sponge. Pile it lightly in a glass dish, leaving it rocky in appearance, sprinkle hundreds and thousands on the top, and serve.

DINNER.—Haricot Purée (March 9th); Minced Veal (May 11th); Bacon Rolls (July 19th); Potatoes (April 12th); Cabbage (June 4th); Chocolate Pudding (July 24th).

Custard that is to be served in glasses as an accompaniment to fruit or sweet dishes may be made with cream or milk and with eggs, varying in number from one to eight or nine. The richer the custard the more likely it is to curdle in making. A moderately good custard may be made as follows:—Boil a pint of milk, sweeten it to taste, but if any essence is to be used for flavouring do not put this in until the custard is made. Almond, lemon, vanilla, orange, or brandy are the flavourings usually chosen. A few drops of vanilla essence and a spoonful of brandy are very good together. If lemon or orange flavour be chosen, the very thin rind of the fruit should be boiled in the milk till it tastes pleasantly. While the milk is boiling beat three eggs lightly, pour the boiling milk upon them, put them into an enamelled saucepan, and stir the custard over a slow fire till it begins to thicken. Draw it quite back so that it cannot even simmer, and let it remain, stirring it occasionally, for about a quarter of an hour. By letting it remain at a gentle heat in this way and stirring it well the custard will be considerably enriched. Pour it out, stir it now and then to keep it from skinning on the surface, and when cold it is ready. If almond flavour has been used, a few almonds, blanched and finely shred, may be sprinkled over it in the glasses, or nutmeg may be grated on the surface. A plain custard may be made with a pint of milk, one egg, and a tea-spoonful of flour or corn-flour. The thickening ingredients should be mixed to a smooth paste with cold milk, then added to the boiling milk, and after being boiled up and cooling a minute, the two should be mixed with a beaten egg and the mixture boiled. (Cheese June 8th).

Things that must not be Forgotten.

1. Turn the mackerel in the vinegar.
2. If any cabbage is left it should be preserved, as Colcannon can be made of it for dinner to-morrow.

August 11th.

Breakfast.	Luncheon.	Dinner.
Potted Pheasant.	Lamb's Fry.	Croûte au Pot.
Fried Bacon and Tomatoes.	Boiled Artichokes.	Roast Shoulder of Mutton
Buttered Toast.	Dutch Sauce.	Mint Sauce,
Dry Toast.		Colcannon.
Brown and White Bread and Butter.		Compôte of Plums.
		Custard.
Corn-flour Milk.		Cheese.

Marketing.

For the Day.—A Shoulder of Mutton, not too fat; a pint of Greengages; Cabbage, if none were left yesterday; Mint; Potatoes.

For To-morrow.—A small tin of Corned Beef; Anchovies, if none are in the house; a pennyworth of Small Salad.

BREAKFAST.—Potted Pheasant (see Potted Grouse, January 7th); Fried Bacon and Tomatoes (July 12th); Corn-flour Milk (June 19th).

LUNCHEON.—Lamb's Fry (May 16th). *Boiled Artichokes.*—Soak the artichokes for awhile in strong salt and water, cut the stalks even, trim away the lower leaves, and cut a little piece off the ends of the others. Put the artichokes, stalk uppermost, into quickly-boiling salted water. Leave the lid off the saucepan, and boil the artichokes until the leaves can be drawn out easily. They will take from half an hour to an hour, according to their size and age. Send them to table on a hot dish, with Dutch sauce (May 14th) as an accompaniment. The thick, juicy part of the leaves and the bottom or part that lies under the choke are the only portions of this vegetable that are eaten, and they are delicious. No more agreeable dish for supper or luncheon need be desired than boiled artichokes and Dutch sauce.

DINNER.—Croûte au Pot (May 25th); Roast Shoulder of Mutton (March 4th and December 16th); Mint Sauce (March 25th). *Colcannon.*—Take equal quantities of cold boiled cabbage or savoy and cold boiled potatoes. Crush the potatoes and chop the cabbage finely, then put both into a stewpan, with a slice of butter or dripping and a little pepper and salt. Stir all briskly together over the fire till the vegetables are well mixed. Grease a basin with dripping, press the mixture into it, and put it in the oven till the vegetables are very hot throughout; turn upon a dish, and serve. Compôte of Plums (August 5th); Custard (August 10th); Cheese (June 8th).

Things that must not be Forgotten.

1. Prepare the anchovies as far as possible for breakfast to-morrow (Note 4, January 17th).

2. Shalots come into the market some time in August. Purchase a few, say a pound, put them in an onion bag, and hang them in a cool dry place. They will keep till spring, and are constantly wanted in cookery.

August 12th.

Breakfast.	Luncheon.	Dinner.
Anchovies and Hard-boiled Eggs. Corned Beef. Buttered Toast. Dry Toast. Brown and White Bread and Butter. Bread and Milk.	Toad in the Hole. Cauliflower au Gratin.	Hake Cutlets, Fried. Cold Shoulder of Mutton. Potatoes. Salad. Lemon Pudding. Cheese.

Marketing.

For the Day.—A pound and a half of Mutton for the Toad in the Hole ; a large Cauliflower ; three pounds taken from the middle of a good-sized Hake : ask the fishmonger to cut this into slices half an inch thick (August 7th); Potatoes; a Cos Lettuce ; a half-pennyworth of Small Salad; a half-pennyworth of Beetroot and young Onions ; six ounces of good Beef Suet; Parsley.

For To-morrow.—Bloaters, one for each person ; a quarter of a pound of Pipe Macaroni ; order for to-morrow an Ox Kidney ; Muffins (January 29th).

BREAKFAST.—Anchovies and Hard-boiled Eggs (January 18th); Corned Beef bought yesterday ; Bread and Milk (January 25th).

LUNCHEON.—Toad in the Hole (January 15th); Cauliflower au Gratin (April 25th).

DINNER.—Fried Hake (*see* Fried Cod, January 1st); Mutton served yesterday (*see* Cold Mutton, July 23rd); Salad (March 13th); Potatoes (April 12th). *Lemon Pudding.*—Shred a quarter of a pound of beef suet very finely. Mix with it half a pound of bread-crumbs, quarter of a pound of sugar, the thin rind of two large lemons chopped small, and a pinch of salt. Mix thoroughly; moisten with two well-beaten eggs and the strained juice of two lemons. Turn the mixture into a buttered mould that it will fill, tie a floured cloth over the top, plunge it into boiling water, and keep it boiling for two hours. Let it stand a minute, turn it out, and serve with sweet sauce (July 19th), or with a little sherry, if permitted. If preferred, one egg and a tea-spoonful of baking-powder may be used instead of two eggs ; then a little water will be required to moisten the pudding. Cheese (June 8th).

Things that must not be Forgotten.

1. Remember to keep the bloaters in the larder apart from all other food.

2. Preserve any remains of hake that there may be; fish cakes can be made of them for dinner to-morrow.

3. Put a large cupful of hominy to soak all night in cold water (February 10th).

August 13th.

Breakfast.	Luncheon.	Dinner.
Bloaters on Toast.	Stewed Ox Kidney.	Fish Cakes.
Corned Beef.	Sweet Macaroni.	Fowl, Stewed with Tomatoes.
Muffins.		Potatoes.
Dry Toast.		French Beans.
Brown and White Bread and Butter.		Newcastle Pudding.
Boiled Hominy.		Cheese.

Marketing.

For the Day.—One pound of Bacon in rashers (January 3rd), half for dinner to-day and half for breakfast to-morrow. One large Fowl or a couple of Chickens, according to the requirements of the family. For one fowl half a pound of Tomatoes and three or four Mushrooms, or a tin of Champignons. Potatoes; French Beans; Saltpetre for the butter, if there is none in the house (August 27th).

For To-morrow.—Order to be sent in the morning a couple of Leverets and three plump young Pigeons (January 24th).

BREAKFAST.—Bloaters on Toast (March 24th); Corned Beef served yesterday; Muffins (January 30th); Boiled Hominy (February 11th).

LUNCHEON.—Stewed Ox Kidney (April 2nd). *Sweet Macaroni.*—Boil a quarter of a pound of macaroni in water till tender, but not at all broken. Drain it, put with it half a pint of cream or milk, three ounces of sugar, and any flavouring that may be chosen. Let it simmer again until it is quite thick, and stir it occasionally to keep it from burning, but be careful not to break the macaroni. Turn it upon a dish and serve. A compôte of fresh fruit or a little preserved fruit is a very pleasant accompaniment to sweet macaroni.

DINNER.—Fish Cakes (January 13th); Fowl, Stewed with Tomatoes (September 12th); Potatoes (April 12th); French Beans (August 16th); Newcastle Pudding (June 12th); Cheese (June 8th).

Things that must not be Forgotten.

1. Preserve any hominy that may be left; it can be fried for breakfast to-morrow.

2. If the legs of the fowls were not used, devil them for breakfast to-morrow (January 14th).

August 14th.

Breakfast.	Luncheon.	Dinner.
Devilled Drumsticks.	Stewed Pigeons.	Fried Whiting.
Toasted Bacon.	Stuffed Tomatoes.	Civet of Leverets.
Hot Buttered Toast.		Potatoes.
Dry Toast.		Cabbage.
Brown and White Bread and Butter.		Semolina Pudding.
		Cheese.
Fried Hominy.		

Marketing.

For the Day.—A pair of Leverets (June 13th) and three Pigeons ordered yesterday; half a dozen ripe Tomatoes; fresh Whiting (January 17th); Potatoes; Cabbage; one ounce of fresh German Yeast; half a pound of Bacon; Fruit for Pies.

For To-morrow.—A tin of Sardines; a quarter of a pound of German Sausage; Watercress.

BREAKFAST.—Devilled Drumsticks (January 14th); Toasted Bacon (January 19th); Fried Hominy (February 12th).

LUNCHEON.—Stewed Pigeons (August 4th); Stuffed Tomatoes (July 23rd).

DINNER.—Fried Whiting (January 17th); Civet of Leverets (June 14th); Potatoes (May 6th); Cabbage (June 4th); Semolina Pudding (March 12th); Cheese (June 8th).

Things that must not be Forgotten.

1. Preserve all that is left of the leverets; very good soup may be made of it for to-morrow.

2. Pastry is to be made to-day (April 17th); Plum Pies (August 7th) and open Jam Tart (August 7th); also Scones (August 26th), and plain *Soda Cake.*—Rub six ounces of butter or clarified dripping into one pound of flour; add a pinch of salt, a tea-spoonful of mixed spice, a table-spoonful of caraway seeds or a table-spoonful of picked and dried currants, and six ounces of moist sugar. Mix thoroughly; add a tea-spoonful of vinegar, and half a pint of milk in which a tea-spoonful of carbonate of soda has been dissolved. Turn the mixture into a tin lined with greased paper, and bake in a moderate oven. A richer cake may be made by substituting eggs for a little of the milk. *Seed Cake.*—Follow the directions given for Sultana Cake (August 2nd), but substitute a table-spoonful of caraway seeds for the raisins. *Good Soda Buns* may be made as follows:—Rub six ounces of butter or clarified dripping into a pound of flour; add six ounces of sugar and two ounces of candied peel chopped small. Dissolve a quarter of a tea-spoonful of carbonate of soda in about a table-spoonful of warm milk; stir this into the flour, and drop in, one at a time, the yolks of four and the whisked whites of two eggs. Grease a

baking-tin, put the batter on it in lumps, and bake in a quick oven.
Light Buns, quickly made.—Mix half a tea-spoonful of tartaric acid, half a tea-spoonful of carbonate of soda, and a pinch of salt with a pound of flour; rub in two ounces of butter, and add four ounces of currants, two ounces of sugar, and half a tea-spoonful of caraway seeds. Mix one egg with half a pint of milk, make a hole in the flour, pour in the milk, and beat together with a knife; drop in lumps on a greased tin, and bake in a quick oven. N.B.—The oven for cakes should be brisk at the commencement, but it should not be increased afterwards.

August 15th.

Breakfast.	Luncheon.	Dinner.
Sardines.	Scotch Collops.	Leveret Soup.
German Sausage.	Plain Suet Pudding.	Loin of Lamb, Braised.
Scones.		Potatoes.
Dry Toast.		Cauliflower.
Watercress.		Hayrick Puddings.
Brown and White Bread and Butter.		Cheese.
Milk Porridge.		

Marketing.

For the Day.—Beef for Scotch Collops (January 9th); half a pound of Suet; a Loin of Lamb; Potatoes; Cauliflower; Parsley; Sea Biscuits.

For To-morrow.—Plump Sheep's Kidneys, one for each person; one moderate sized Turbot (June 6th); Shrimps or Lobster Spawn; one good-sized Capon or a pair of Fowls, as required; ingredients for Veal Forcemeat (June 27th); one Lettuce; a half-pennyworth of Small Salad; a half-pennyworth of Beetroot; order four pennyworth of Cream for Normandy Pippins, if permitted; or, better still, a little Devonshire Cream; Potatoes; French Beans; a tin of potted Grouse for breakfast (January 7th).

BREAKFAST.—Sardines (January 12th); German Sausage (June 6th); Scones (May 23rd); Milk Porridge (June 13th).

LUNCHEON.—Scotch Collops (January 9th); Plain Suet Pudding (May 13th).

DINNER.—Leveret Soup (*see* Hare Soup, January 19th); Loin of Lamb, Braised (May 22nd); Potatoes (April 12th); Cauliflower (April 25th); Hayrick Puddings (March 19th); Cheese (June 8th).

Things that must not be Forgotten.

1. Pluck the fowl to-day and prepare the forcemeat, but do not stuff it (February 28th and June 27th).

2. Soak half a pound of Normandy pippins all night in a pint and a half of water.

3. Make a little mayonnaise for the chicken salad to-morrow evening (August 30th).

Sunday, August 16th.

Breakfast.	Dinner.	Tea.	Supper.
Devilled Eggs.	Boiled Turbot.	Brown and White Bread and Butter.	Chicken Salad.
Broiled Sheep's Kidneys.	Shrimp or Lobster Sauce.	Scones.	Plum Pie.
Scones.	Fowl, Stuffed and Roasted.	Strawberry Jam.	Cheese.
Dry Toast.	Bread Sauce.	Seed Cake.	
Brown and White Bread and Butter.	Brown Gravy.		
Marmalade.	Potatoes.		
Biscuits and Milk.	French Beans.		
	Normandy Pippins.		
	Cheese.		

BREAKFAST.—Devilled Eggs (February 27th); Broiled Sheep's Kidneys (January 29th); Scones (May 23rd); Biscuits and Milk (June 14th).

DINNER.—Boiled Turbot (June 7th); Shrimp Sauce (January 30th); Lobster Sauce (June 7th); Fowl, Stuffed and Roasted (June 30th); Brown Gravy (October 18th); Bread Sauce (October 18th); Potatoes (April 12th). *French or Kidney Beans.*—Cut off the stalks and draw away the fibre that runs down both sides; cut the beans into thin strips lengthwise, and throw them into cold water till they are to be cooked. Have ready plenty of fast-boiling water slightly salted. Drain the beans, throw them into the boiling water, and boil them rather quickly, *with the lid off the pan*, till they are tender. If young they will be done enough in a quarter of an hour; if large and old they will want half an hour or more. Drain them in a colander, and serve in a hot tureen. It is a very great improvement to sauté the beans before serving them, that is, to melt a slice of butter in a saucepan and shake the beans in it over the fire till they are coated with the butter. A pinch of salt and a tea-spoonful of white sugar should be sprinkled over them whilst they are in the pan. Beans thus prepared are served in France as a separate course. When fresh beans are not to be had, tinned beans may be used, and will be found excellent. *Normandy Pippins.*—Put the pippins, with the water in which they were soaked, into a pie-dish, and with them the thin rind of a large lemon and two ounces of loaf sugar. Place them in a gentle oven, and bake for about an hour and a half; then add another two ounces of sugar, and bake again, still very gently, till the apples are tender. Strain the syrup, put with it the juice of the lemon, a few drops of cochineal, and a glass of port. Place the apples on a glass dish, pour the syrup (when cool) over them, and serve cold. Devonshire cream is a great improvement to this dish, and if a spoonful be put on each apple its appearance will be improved. If Devonshire cream is not to be had, two or three blanched almonds may be stuck into the apples, and thick cream may be served as an accompaniment. If the pippins are quickly baked they will burst in cooking, and they ought to be kept whole. Dried pears may be prepared in the same way, and one or two cloves may be stewed in the syrup with them. Cheese (June 8th).

TEA.—Scones (May 23rd); Seed Cake (August 14th).
SUPPER.—Chicken Salad (August 30th); Plum Pie (August 7th).

Things that must not be Forgotten.

1. If any mayonnaise is left, put it into a bottle, cork it closely, and it will keep for some time.
2. If any beetroot is left, cut it into slices, cover it with vinegar, and it can be used the next time salad is wanted.
3. Pick the flesh from the turbot as soon as it leaves the table, and boil a little rice to make kedgeree for breakfast to-morrow (January 10th).

August 17th.

Breakfast.	Luncheon.	Dinner.
Kedgeree.	Eggs, Stewed with Cheese.	Croûte au Pot.
Potted Grouse.	Cake Pudding.	Leg of Lamb.
Hot Buttered Toast.		Mint Sauce.
Dry Toast.		Potatoes.
Brown and White Bread and Butter.		Green Peas, if they are to be had.
Marmalade.		Macaroni Pudding.
Milk Porridge.		Cheese.

Marketing.

For the Day.—A plump Leg of Lamb; Mint; Potatoes; Green Peas.
For To-morrow.—Half a pound of Mushrooms; Small Salad, for breakfast; three pennyworth of Cream; a spoonful of Lobster Spawn.

BREAKFAST.—Kedgeree (January 10th); Potted Grouse (January 7th); Milk Porridge (June 13th).

LUNCHEON.—Eggs, Stewed with Cheese (February 10th); Cake Pudding (February 4th).

DINNER.—Croûte au Pot (May 25th); Roast Leg of Lamb (March 4th); Mint Sauce (March 25th); Potatoes (April 12th); Green Peas (July 12th); Macaroni Pudding (March 27th); Cheese (June 8th).

Things that must not be Forgotten.

1. Partially prepare the rice and barley porridge (Note β, June 15th).
2. Put the lamb on a clean dish as soon as it leaves the table.

August 18th.

Breakfast.	Luncheon.	Dinner.
Mushrooms on Toast.	Cold Lamb.	Bisque Soup.
Eggs on the Dish.	Mint Sauce.	Curried Veal.
Hot Buttered Toast.	Salad.	Boiled Rice.
Dry Toast.	Compôte of Plums.	French Beans.
Mustard and Cress.		Roly-poly Pudding.
Brown and White Bread and Butter.		Cheese.
Rice and Barley Porridge.		

Marketing.

For the Day.—A large Lettuce, Beetroot, Watercress, &c.; Plums for compôte; a moderate-sized Crab. Moderate-sized fish are the best. If the crab feels light it is not good. Crabs are at their best from April to October. A pound and a half or more of Veal Cutlet for curry; French Beans; six ounces of Beef Suet for roly-poly pudding; a small, plump Leg of Mutton for pickling; Fresh Fruit for the Rothe Grützе.

For To-morrow.—Small Soles for breakfast (January 3rd); order a Lamb's Fry for to-morrow.

BREAKFAST.—Mushrooms on Toast (March 20th); Eggs on the Dish (December 7th); Rice and Barley Porridge (June 15th).

LUNCHEON.—Lamb served yesterday; Mint Sauce (March 25th); Salad (March 13th); Compôte of Plums (August 5th).

DINNER.—Bisque Soup (October 17th). *Curried Veal.*—Follow the recipe for Curried Rabbit (July 16th), and substitute the veal for the rabbit. Boiled Rice (July 21st); French Beans (August 16th). *Roly-poly Pudding.*—Make some suet crust with one pound of flour (June 25th), roll it out till it is moderately thin, and let it be longer than broad; spread jam over it to within half an inch of the edge all round, wet the edges, roll the pudding up to make it like a bolster, press the edges together, and roll it in a cloth that has been wrung out of boiling water and floured. Tie the ends of the cloth securely close to the pudding, plunge it into boiling water, and keep it boiling without ceasing for an hour and a half. Let it cool a minute, turn it upon a dish, and send sweet sauce (July 19th) to table with it. If preferred, treacle can be substituted for the jam in this recipe. It is a good plan to put an old plate under the pudding in the saucepan, to keep it from sticking to the pan. Cheese (June 8th).

Things that must not be Forgotten.

1. Make some pickle (March 19th) and put the leg of mutton into it.
2. Put a cupful of green lentils to soak all night in cold water.
3. *Lemon Cheesecakes.*—It is a good thing to have on hand some lemon paste for making lemon cheesecakes. This should be made when there is a convenient opportunity. If kept in a cool place it will remain good for years. The following is the recipe:—Grate the rinds of two large lemons upon a coarse grater, and clean the grater with as many bread-crumbs, and no more, as will take off all the rind.

Add half a pound of white sugar and the juice of one of the lemons. Beat six eggs, turn them into a jar with the grated lemon mixture and a quarter of a pound of butter; put the jar into a saucepan with two or three inches of boiling water, place it on the fire, and stir the lemon mixture till it is as thick as honey. It may either be used at once or kept till wanted. When it is to be used, line some patty-pans with pastry, half fill them with the mixture, and bake in a quick oven.

4. Make Rothe Grütze for dinner to-morrow (December 10th).

August 19th.

Breakfast.	Luncheon.	Dinner.
Potted Grouse.	Lamb's Fry.	Baked Whiting.
Baked Slips.	Baked Batter Pudding.	Roast Beef.
Hot Buttered Toast.		Lentils.
Dry Toast.		Browned Potatoes
Brown and White Bread and Butter.		Rothe Grütze.
Marmalade.		Cheese.
Milk Toast.		

Marketing.

For the Day.—Lamb's Fry, ordered yesterday; three or four Whiting (January 17th). Whiting can be obtained at this time of the year, and may be chosen for the sake of variety, but it is at its best from October to March. A Sirloin of Beef weighing about eight pounds; Potatoes; three or four small Mushrooms or a small tin of Champignons; Parsley.

For To-morrow.—A Collared Tongue (January 2nd); a pint of Plums for breakfast. Ask the poulterer to preserve two or three sets of Giblets for to-morrow; they can be stewed for luncheon. Duck's, Goose, or Fowl's Giblets may all be used. Watercress. Grouse (see August 29th).

BREAKFAST.—Potted Grouse served day before yesterday; Baked Slips (January 7th); Milk Toast (June 17th).

LUNCHEON.—Lamb's Fry (May 16th); Baked Batter Pudding (February 5th).

DINNER.—*Baked Whiting.*—Scale, empty, and wash the whiting, then lay them in a cloth to dry them thoroughly. Mince the mushrooms, and have ready a table-spoonful of chopped parsley and a little salt and cayenne. Butter a baking-tin rather thickly, sprinkle half the parsley and mushrooms in it, and lay the whiting on the top. Season them with salt and cayenne, squeeze the juice of a lemon over them, add what remains of the parsley and mushroom, and cover the fish with sifted bread-crumbs that have been browned in the oven. Put a slice of butter, broken into small pieces, here and there upon the fish, pour over it about half a gill of strong stock, to which a spoonful of sherry can be added if liked, and bake in a brisk oven till the fish is done enough. It will take from ten to fifteen minutes. Put the whiting on a hot dish, strain the gravy over, and serve. Roast Beef (March 4th); Lentils (March 2nd); Potatoes (April 12th); Custard Blancmange (August 4th); Cheese (June 8th).

Things that must not be Forgotten.
1. Turn and rub the mutton in the pickle.
2. Prepare the plum porridge for breakfast to-morrow (August 31st).
3. Make a corn-flour blancmange for dinner to-morrow (June 15th).

August 20th.

Breakfast.	Luncheon.	Dinner.
Savoury Eggs.	Stewed Giblets.	Macaroni Soup.
Collared Tongue.	Savoury Rice.	Cold Beef.
Hot Buttered Toast.		Salad.
Dry Toast.		Potatoes.
Brown and White Bread and Butter.		Corn-flour Blancmange.
Watercress.		Lemon Syrup.
Plum Porridge.		Cheese.

Marketing.
For the Day.—Giblets ordered yesterday; a fine Cos Lettuce; Watercress; young Onions; Radishes; Beetroot; Potatoes; Macaroni for soup; Saltpetre (August 27th); a dozen fresh Herrings, half soft and half hard roes.

For To-morrow.—Half a pound of Bacon in rashers; Rhubarb.

BREAKFAST.—Savoury Eggs (January 1st); Collared Tongue (January 2nd); Plum Porridge (August 31st).

LUNCHEON.—Stewed Giblets (February 6th); Savoury Rice (June 17th).

DINNER.—Macaroni Soup (February 26th); Beef served yesterday; Salad (March 13th); Potatoes (May 12th); Corn-flour Blancmange (June 15th); Lemon Syrup (March 19th); Cheese (June 8th).

Things that must not be Forgotten.
1. Turn and rub the mutton in the pickle.
2. Make the rhubarb mould (June 3rd) for luncheon.
3. *Pickle the Fresh Herrings.*—Cut off the heads and tails of the fish, scrape and wash them well, and split each one in halves, taking out the bones. Rub each half with pepper, salt, and mustard, and grate a very small quantity of nutmeg on each. Roll the halves separately, and pack them in a stone jar (one that would hold three pounds of jam or marmalade would be about the right size). Pound the soft roes of the fish, and mix them with half a pint of vinegar and as much water as would cover the herrings. Put a couple of bay-leaves on the top of all, cover the jar tightly, and bake in a gentle oven for about an hour. When the fish is cold it is ready to serve, and will be most excellent for either breakfast, luncheon, or supper. The fish should be turned in the vinegar every day, and will keep good for three or four days even in summer. To serve these herrings, place them on a dish, with two or three parsley-leaves on each small roll. Pour a little of the gravy into the dish.

August 21st.

Breakfast.	Luncheon.	Dinner.
Pickled Herrings.	Croquettes.	Mulligatawney Soup.
Toasted Bacon.	Rhubarb Mould.	Chops, with Piquante Sauce.
Hot Buttered Toast.	Milk.	French Beans.
Dry Toast.		Fried Potatoes.
Brown and White Bread and Butter.		Ground Rice Pudding.
Oatmeal Porridge.		Cheese.

Marketing.

For the Day.—Three to four pounds of the best end of a Loin of Mutton (April 30th); Plums; French Beans; Potatoes; a pennyworth of German Yeast.

For To-morrow.—Lambs' Sweetbreads; Fillet of Beef (January 2nd).

BREAKFAST.—Pickled Herrings (August 20th); Toasted Bacon (January 19th); Porridge (January 25th).

LUNCHEON.—Croquettes, made of the remains of the cold beef (Rissoles, January 6th); Rhubarb Mould (June 3rd).

DINNER.—Mulligatawney Soup (stock made of beef bones, February 13th), (January 16th); Chops, with Piquante Sauce (April 30th); French Beans (August 16th); Fried Potatoes (February 2nd). *Ground Rice Pudding.*—Flavour a quart of milk by heating it gently with some thinly-cut lemon-rind, a little bit of cinnamon, or a couple of laurel-leaves. When pleasantly flavoured, take out the flavouring ingredient and boil the milk. Mix four ounces of ground rice smoothly with a little cold milk, add this to the boiling milk, and stir till thick. Put the rice into a bowl, let it cool, then mix with it a little sugar, a piece of butter the size of a nut, and two well-beaten eggs. Turn into a buttered dish, and bake in a gentle oven. If the oven is hot, the pudding will be watery. A spoonful of brandy will improve the pudding, and an additional egg will enrich it. Cheese (June 8th).

Things that must not be Forgotten.

1. Turn and rub the mutton in the pickle.
2. Partially prepare the lambs' sweetbreads for breakfast to-morrow (Oct. 22nd).
3. Turn the herrings in the vinegar.
4. Pastry is to be made to-day (April 17th); Plum Pies (August 7th); also Teacakes (August 26th) and Annie's Cake (September 25th).
5. Stew the top of the loin of mutton for luncheon to-morrow (May 1st).

August 22nd.

Breakfast.	Luncheon.	Dinner.
Lambs' Sweetbreads. Collared Tongue. Teacakes. Dry Toast. Brown and White Bread and Butter. Marmalade. Corn-flour Milk.	Pickled Herrings. Top of the Loin of Mutton, Stewed. Salad.	Milk Soup. Fillet of Beef. Potatoes. Cauliflower. Plum Pie. Cheese.

Marketing.

For the Day.—Potatoes; Cauliflower; Lettuce; small Salad; Beetroot; young Onions.

For To-morrow.—Three or four Red Mullet. This fish may be had all the year, but it is at its best at the time when it is cheapest, that is, from July to October. It is very variable in price. Generally fish is chosen for its freshness, but red mullet is better for being kept a short time. It is called the woodcock of the sea, and its liver is esteemed a delicacy, while next to the liver stands the head. When taken out of the water it is of a beautiful rose-colour. It is rarely more than twelve inches long. A jar of Anchovy Paste; a Fore-quarter of Lamb (April 11th); Mint; French Beans; Potatoes; ingredients for a Salad; French Chocolate; three pennyworth of Cream, if permitted; a pound of Plums for the gâteau.

BREAKFAST.—Lambs' Sweetbreads (Oct. 22nd); Collared Tongue (January 2nd); Teacakes (February 14th); Corn-flour Milk (June 19th).

LUNCHEON.—Pickled Herrings (August 20th); Stewed Mutton (May 1st); Salad (March 13th).

DINNER.—Milk Soup (January 3rd); Roast Fillet of Beef (February 11th); Potatoes (May 12th); Cauliflower (April 25th); Plum Pie (August 7th); Cheese (June 8th).

Things that must not be Forgotten.

1. Turn and rub the mutton in the pickle.
2. Make a plum gâteau for supper to-morrow evening (July 11th).
3. Cut all the meat from the cold beef, and make *Cornish Pasties* for breakfast to-morrow. They may be made and baked, then warmed in the oven for breakfast, or, if preferred, they can be eaten cold. Cut up the beef into small pieces, and season it with pepper and salt. Wash and peel a few potatoes, half boil them, then cut them up also. Make some short crust (June 19th) with flour, dripping, and baking-powder. Roll this out till it is about a quarter of an inch thick, and divide it into small squares about five inches across. Put a little meat and potato upon each square, moisten the edges, and fold the pastry over the meat, then press the edges securely together. Bake till the pastry is done enough. Sometimes turnips are substituted for potatoes in Cornish Pasties.

Sunday, August 23rd.

Breakfast.	Dinner.	Tea.	Supper.
Anchovy Paste.	Red Mullet, Baked.	Brown and White Bread and Butter.	Cold Lamb.
Cornish Pasties.	Roast Quarter of Lamb.	Teacakes.	Mint Sauce.
Toasted Teacakes.	Mint Sauce.	Raspberry and Red Currant Jam.	Salad.
Dry Toast.	Potatoes.	Annie's Cake.	Plum Gâteau.
Brown and White Bread and Butter.	French Beans.		Cheese.
Bread and Milk.	Chocolate Pudding.		
	Custard.		
	Cheese.		

BREAKFAST.—Anchovy Paste bought yesterday; Cornish Pasties (August 22nd); Teacakes (February 14th); Bread and Milk (January 25th).

DINNER.—*Red Mullet, Baked.*—Red mullet may be broiled or baked, but it should never be boiled, or the liver, which is the titbit with epicures, will be lost. Wash and dry the fish, but do not either scale or open it. Cut off the fins, and carefully take out the gills, with the small thread-like intestine that will adhere to them. Oil some sheets of unglazed paper, one for each fish, and bake them for two or three minutes to harden them. Put a piece of fresh butter in each paper case, and sprinkle pepper and salt upon it. Lay the fish on the butter, put a little butter upon it, fold the paper over, and fasten the ends securely. Put the fish thus fastened in paper into a baking-tin, and bake them in a moderate oven. They will be done enough in about half an hour. They may be served in the paper or not, as approved, but they look better without the paper. A little lemon-juice should be squeezed over them. For sauce, take a quarter of a pint of melted butter (July 17th). Stir into this the gravy in the pan, add salt and cayenne, a glass of sherry, and a tea-spoonful of essence of anchovies. Boil up once, and serve in a tureen. Roast Quarter of Lamb (March 4th and April 12th); Mint Sauce (March 25th); Potatoes (April 12th); French Beans (August 16th); Chocolate Pudding (July 24th); Custard (August 10th); Cheese (June 8th).

TEA.—Teacakes (February 14th); Annie's Cake (September 25th).

SUPPER.—Salad (March 13th); Plum Gâteau (July 11th).

Things that must not be Forgotten.

1. Turn and rub the mutton in the pickle.
2. Put a cupful of hominy to soak all night in cold water (February 10th).

August 24th.

Breakfast.	Luncheon.	Dinner.
Anchovy Paste.	Cold Lamb.	Fried Plaice.
Poached Eggs.	Salad.	Dutch Sauce.
Teacakes.	Boiled Rice, with Raisins.	Norman Haricot.
Dry Toast.		Cauliflower.
Brown and White Bread and Butter.		Young Carrots.
Marmalade.		Cottage Plum Pudding.
Boiled Hominy.		Cheese.

Marketing.

For the Day.—Materials for a Salad; a thick Plaice (April 21st); about three pounds of lean Veal from the fillet; new Potatoes; Cauliflowers; a slice of lean Ham; young Carrots; six ounces of Suet.

For To-morrow.—A dried Haddock; four ripe Tomatoes; half a pound of Bacon (January 3rd); a quarter of a pound of Macaroni; Mustard and Cress.

BREAKFAST.—Anchovy Paste served yesterday; Poached Eggs (February 6th); Teacakes (February 14th); Boiled Hominy (February 11th).

LUNCHEON.—Lamb served yesterday; Salad (March 13th); Boiled Rice, with Raisins (February 3rd).

DINNER.—Fried Plaice (April 21st); Dutch Sauce (May 14th). *Norman Haricot.*—Cut the veal into neat pieces convenient for serving, and about half an inch thick. Brown them on both sides in a frying-pan with a little dripping, and with them the ham, also cut into neat pieces. Take them up, and pour a pint of stock or water into the pan in which they were fried, scrape the pan with a spoon to get all the gravy, and let the water boil up. Put the meat into a stewpan, in a single layer, if possible; pour the gravy over it, and add a bunch of parsley, a sprig of thyme, and a bay-leaf. Let the veal simmer very gently by the side of the fire for about three-quarters of an hour. Take two pounds of small new potatoes, wash and scrape them, throw them into boiling water, and let the water boil up once. Take them up, put them upon the veal, and simmer again until the potatoes are tender. Skim the fat from the gravy, taste it, and add pepper and salt if required. Thicken it with a little corn-flour mixed smoothly with water, and add a little lemon-juice if liked, and browning if necessary. Put the veal on a hot dish, garnish with the potatoes, and serve. Young carrots (July 6th), or, when they can be had, green peas (July 12th), are excellent as an accompaniment to this dish. Cauliflower (April 25th); Cottage Plum Pudding (June 6th); Cheese (June 8th).

Things that must not be Forgotten.

1. Turn and rub the mutton in the pickle.
2. Put a cupful of white haricot beans to soak all night in cold water.

3. Preserve any boiled hominy that may be left; it can be fried for breakfast to-morrow.

August 25th.

Breakfast.	Luncheon.	Dinner.
Dried Haddock. Tomatoes and Bacon. Hot Buttered Toast. Dry Toast. Brown and White Bread and Butter. Mustard and Cress. Fried Hominy.	Baked Mackerel. Macaroni and Mushrooms.	Fresh Herrings. Mustard Sauce. Sour Mutton. Potatoes. Haricot Beans. Cocoa-nut Pudding. Cheese.

Marketing.

For the Day.—Half a pound of Mushrooms; two moderate-sized fresh Mackerel (April 4th); fresh Herrings. One may be allowed for each person. The herrings should be bright and silvery, and should have their scales uninjured; choose plump fish. In this instance the soft-roed fish are to be preferred. Potatoes; a tin of desiccated Cocoa-nut.

For To-morrow.—A tin of Sardines (January 12th); a Bath Chap, that is, a pig's cheek cured like bacon; speak for two sets of fresh Giblets for to-morrow; Watercress; a pound of Fresh Fruit.

BREAKFAST.—Dried Haddock (January 27th); Tomatoes and Bacon (July 12th); Fried Hominy (February 12th).

LUNCHEON.—Baked Mackerel (April 15th). *Macaroni and Mushrooms.*—Boil a quarter of a pound of macaroni in a pint and a half of water, with a little pepper and salt, for twenty minutes, or till a little piece can be crushed between the thumb and finger. Drain the macaroni, put it into a clean stewpan, pour a quarter of a pint of stock over it, with an ounce of butter and an ounce of grated cheese. Stir it over a gentle fire for five minutes; turn on a hot dish. Have ready the mushrooms, put them on the macaroni, and serve. To prepare the mushrooms, wash and skin them, cut them into slices, and put them into a stewpan, with an ounce of butter and a little pepper and salt. Toss them over the fire for ten minutes; take them up, and they are ready.

DINNER.—Fresh Herrings, with Mustard Sauce (September 15th); Sour Mutton (March 29th); Potatoes (April 12th); Haricot Beans (June 20th); Cocoa-nut Pudding (August 8th); Cheese (June 8th).

Things that must not be Forgotten.

1. Soak the bath chap in cold water for three or four hours, then boil it according to the directions already given for pig's cheek (February 1st).
2. Prepare the sago mould for luncheon to-morrow (October 8th).

August 26th.

Breakfast.	Luncheon.	Dinner.
Sardines.	Cold Mutton.	Giblet Soup.
Bath Chap.	Salad.	Pigeon Pie.
Hot Buttered Toast.	Sago, with Fruit Juice.	French Beans.
Dry Toast.		Potatoes.
Brown and White Bread and Butter.		Wyvern Puddings.
Watercress.		Cheese.
Biscuits and Milk.		

Marketing.

For the Day.—Materials for Salad; four plump young Pigeons; a pound and a half of lean Veal from the leg or the loin; French Beans; Potatoes; fresh German Yeast; Carbonate of Soda and Cream of Tartar, for scones.

BREAKFAST.—Sardines (January 12th); Bath Chaps (February 1st); Biscuits and Milk (June 14th).

LUNCHEON.—Mutton, served yesterday; Salad (March 13th); Sago Mould (October 8th).

DINNER.—Giblet Soup (February 1st); Pigeon Pie (May 15th). Rough Puff Paste (May 29th) will be excellent for this pie. Kidney Beans (August 16th); Potatoes (April 12th); Wyvern Puddings (May 9th); Cheese (June 8th).

Things that must not be Forgotten.

1. The remnants of the cold mutton can be minced, and, with the trimmings of the pastry, made into a mutton tart (January 10th) for luncheon to-morrow.

2. If a little additional pastry were made, a plum pie (August 7th) could be made for dinner to-morrow.

3. Preserve any pigeon pie that may be left; it can be used for breakfast to-morrow.

4. As pastry is on hand, and the oven will be hot, it may perhaps be wished to make a few scones or teacakes for breakfast. In hot weather, milk that has gone sour (as it is very likely to do) may be either put into pastry or made into scones. If there is no sour milk, a pint extra could be taken, and kept all night for the purpose. If kept in a warm place it would be almost sure to have turned by morning. *Scones with Sour Milk* (real Scotch recipe).—Mix thoroughly a pound and a half of flour, a pinch of salt, a heaped tea-spoonful of carbonate of soda, and the same of cream of tartar. Mix to a light paste with a pint of sour milk, knead the dough a little, roll it out till about a third of an inch thick, and cut it into three-cornered pieces, each side being about four inches long. Put the scones on a floured tin, and bake in a quick oven. *Scones made with Baking-powder.*—Rub four ounces of butter or clarified dripping into a pound of flour, and add a pinch of salt and a dessert-spoonful of baking-powder.

Make into a rather stiff paste with milk, roll out, and make up as above. If liked, this paste can be rolled and made into horns, like Vienna bread. *Milk Rolls made with Baking-powder.*—Rub two ounces of butter into a pound of flour, and add a small pinch of salt and a heaped tea-spoonful of baking-powder (August 2nd). Stir in milk to make a smooth, stiff, elastic dough, but do not handle it more than is necessary. Divide it into balls, and bake immediately in a brisk oven. When half baked, brush the rolls with milk. This dough may be made into twists or half moons, like Vienna bread. *Vienna Bread.* —Take one pound of Vienna flour, one pound of best biscuit flour, and a pinch of salt. Choose a bowl not over large; one that will hold three times the quantity of flour will be right. Rub in two ounces of butter, dissolve an ounce of German yeast by mixing it with a spoonful of sugar, add gradually a pint of lukewarm milk and two well-beaten eggs. Mix the liquid with the flour, and knead well till the dough is smooth and lithe. Score it with a knife, cover it with a clean towel, leave it in a warm place, where it is free from a current of air, and cover it with a cloth. In summer-time it will very likely be all right on the kitchen table; in winter it would be better to stand on the fender, but it must not be in a draught. It will probably rise sufficiently in two hours or a little more. Make it into plaits, rolls, or crescents, brush the top with beaten egg, and bake in a quick oven. To make a crescent or horn, as it is sometimes called, roll the dough into a kind of equilateral triangle. Of course, it is not necessary to be very exact. Roll the pastry up, beginning at one of the sides, by doing which the middle part will be thicker than the sides, then draw the two ends of the roll towards one another, to make a kind of crescent. *Teacakes.*—Rub six ounces of butter, or three ounces of butter and three ounces of lard, into two pounds of flour, and add a pinch of salt. Dissolve rather less than an ounce of fresh German yeast with half a pint of lukewarm water. Put the flour into a bowl that will hold about three times the quantity, scoop a hole in the middle of it without leaving the bottom of the bowl uncovered, and pour in the dissolved yeast. Draw a little of the flour in from the sides, and stir it into the liquor to make a thin batter; sprinkle flour over this, cover the bowl, and leave it in a warm place, as in Vienna Bread. When bubbles begin to break through the flour it is ready. Beat two eggs, mix them with about two table-spoonfuls of milk, and knead all well together, adding as much lukewarm milk as will make a lithe smooth dough. Score this with a knife, cover the bowl with a cloth, and leave it till well risen. Divide it into ten pieces, roll these into cakes the size of a saucer, put them on a baking-tin before the fire for a few minutes, and bake in a quick oven. They must on no account be turned over in baking. In Yorkshire, where teacakes are very popular, currants are often added to the dough, but they should not be worked in till the dough has risen. A quarter of a pound of currants would be enough for this quantity of flour. *Sally Lunns.*—

Take an ounce of fresh German yeast, a pound and a half of flour, a quarter of a pound of butter, two eggs, and a pinch of salt. Put the flour into a bowl and mix the salt with it. Put the butter and milk into a saucepan over the fire, and stir till the butter is melted. The milk should be rather more than lukewarm. Mix the yeast with sugar till it is liquid, add the milk gradually, and stir this into the flour. Throw in the eggs lightly beaten, and knead to a smooth dough. Divide the dough into four portions, put them into greased round tins, cover them over, and put them in a warm place to rise. When they have risen to almost three times their original size, bake in a quick oven. N.B.—If in the recipes given above Vienna flour, or a portion of Vienna flour, be permitted the rolls will be lighter and whiter. Vienna flour is about double the price of the best biscuit flour. It is used for superior cakes and pastry.

August 27th.

Breakfast.	Luncheon.	Dinner.
Remains of Pigeon Pie. Bath Chap. Teacakes. Dry Toast. Brown and White Bread and Butter. Milk Toast.	Mutton Tart. Plain Rice Pudding.	Boiled Brill. Dutch Sauce. Leg of Lamb, Roasted. Mint Sauce. Potatoes. Cauliflower. Plum Pie. Cheese.

Marketing.

For the Day.—A Brill (January 9th); a plump Leg of Lamb (April 11th); Mint; Potatoes; Cauliflower.

For To-morrow.—Three or four fresh Sheep's Kidneys; a quarter of a pound of Bacon in rashers; a plump Chicken, or two, as required (June 29th and August 6th).

BREAKFAST.—Pigeon Pie and Bath Chap, served yesterday; Teacakes (February 14th); Milk Toast (June 17th).

LUNCHEON.—Mutton Tart (January 10th); Plain Rice Pudding (February 24th).

DINNER.—Boiled Brill (January 9th); Dutch Sauce (May 14th); Roast Lamb (March 4th); Mint Sauce (March 25th); Potatoes (April 12th); Cauliflower (April 25th); Cheese (June 8th). *Pulled Bread* is very much liked with cheese. To make this take a newly-baked loaf of bread, remove the crust, and *pull* the crumb lightly and quickly into rough pieces about three inches long. Bake these in a gentle oven till they are crisp and of a light brown colour.

Things that must not be Forgotten.

1. Make a stone cream for dinner to-morrow (July 1st).
2. As soon as the lamb is taken from table put it on a clean dish.
3. Partially prepare the rice milk (Note 3, June 17th).

4. Pluck the fowls, and hang them in a cool larder (February 28th).

5. *To Keep Butter in Hot Weather.*—In very hot weather it is often found difficult to keep butter firm. Ice keeps it right, but ice is not always to be had, and when this is the case the following method may be adopted. Dissolve half a tea-spoonful of saltpetre in a pint of water, and put this in a pie-dish. Place the butter in a jar, and put the jar in the dish containing the saltpetre water. Lay a clean cloth over the butter, and let the corners rest in the saltpetre water. Keep the butter in as cool and dark a place as can be found, and change the water every day. If butter tastes rancid, wash it well first with new milk and afterwards with cold water. Fresh butter keeps well when kept in water that has tartaric acid dissolved in it. A dessert-spoonful of acid may be allowed for a gallon of water.

August 28th.

Breakfast.	Luncheon.	Dinner.
Fried Kidneys and Bacon.	Cold Lamb.	Salmon Cutlets.
Bath Chap.	Salad.	Chicken Pudding.
Teacakes.	Custard Sippets.	Potatoes.
Dry Toast.		Baked Tomatoes.
Brown Bread and Butter.		Stone Cream.
Marmalade.		Cheese.
Rice Milk.		

Marketing.

For the Day.—Materials for Salad. About a pound and a half of the tail end of a Salmon. This part is chosen because it is the cheapest. Half a dozen ripe Tomatoes; a slice of lean Ham; Potatoes; six or eight fresh Mackerel with soft roes (April 4th); a pennyworth of German Yeast.

For To-morrow.—Half a pound of Mushrooms; Plums and Apples.

BREAKFAST.—Fried Kidneys and Bacon (January 2nd); Bath Chap, served yesterday; Teacakes (February 14th); Rice Milk (June 18th).

LUNCHEON.—Lamb, served yesterday; Salad (March 13th); Custard Sippets (June 10th).

DINNER.—Salmon Cutlets (July 19th). *Chicken Pudding.*—Empty the crop, take out the inside, and divide the chickens into neat pieces. Line a pudding-basin with good suet crust (June 25th); arrange the pieces of chicken neatly inside, interspersed with the ham, which has been also neatly divided. Season with pepper and salt, and pour over all a little strong gravy, made of the chicken giblets. Cover in the usual way (June 25th). The addition of one or two sheep's kidneys will greatly improve this dish, as will also a few mushrooms, or, when they are in season, a few oysters. The pudding should be long and gently boiled. Potatoes (April 12th); Baked Tomatoes (July 7th); Stone Cream (July 1st); Cheese (June 8th).

Things that must not be Forgotten.

1. Preserve the chicken bones; they will be a valuable addition to the stock-pot.
2. Pastry is to be made to-day (April 17th): Plum and apple pie (August 7th); lemon cheesecakes (August 18th); custard tart (January 19th); also seed cake (August 14th) and Vienna bread (August 26th).
3. *Pickled Mackerel.*—The mackerel should be pickled at once. Cut the heads and tails off the fish, clean them, and be careful to remove the brown substance which sticks to the backbone near the head, as this may make the fish taste bitter. Loosen the backbone by pressing it with the thumb and finger of the right hand whilst holding the mackerel in the left hand, and take the bone out whole. Divide the flesh and the roe into neat pieces convenient for serving. Take a stone jar, put in a few pieces of fish, then season with pepper and salt, pour vinegar over, and add a shalot and a bay-leaf. Put in the rest of the fish, pepper and salt it again, and pour vinegar over all. Put the lid on the jar, cover it with paper, tie it on tightly, and bake in a gentle oven for two hours. Turn the fish on a dish, remove the herbs, garnish with fennel and parsley, and serve. For economy's sake one-fourth of water can be put with the vinegar. Mackerel thus prepared should be turned in the liquor every day, and if kept in a cool place will keep a week.
4. Partially prepare the plum porridge for breakfast to-morrow (August 31st).

August 29th.

Breakfast.	Luncheon.	Dinner.
Pickled Mackerel.	Scrag of Mutton, Stewed with Rice.	Boiled Hake.
Mushrooms on Toast.	Hasty Pudding.	Stewed Steak.
Vienna Bread.		Fried Potatoes.
Dry Toast.		Young Carrots.
Brown and White Bread and Butter.		Vermicelli Pudding.
Plum Porridge.		Cheese.

Marketing.

For the Day.—Two or three pounds of the Scrag of Mutton; about three pounds of fresh Hake (August 7th); Steak for stewing (January 31st); Potatoes; Carrots.

For To-morrow.—Two or three pounds of Salmon (July 4th); a couple of Ducks (July 4th); Sage and Onions, for stuffing; Beans; Potatoes; a plump young Chicken, for chicken salad (June 29th), or the Grouse bought August 19th may be used; materials for a Salad; a pound of Plums. Grouse shooting commences on the 12th of August, but the birds should be allowed to hang as long as possible before they are cooked. Grouse is usually regarded by epicures as the finest of all winged game. It is so uncertain in price that if it has to be purchased it can scarcely be placed in the list of provisions which are at the disposal of the economical housekeeper Sometimes, however, owing to exceptional circumstances, it is to be had for a reasonable price, and then it proves a welcome addition to the daily fare. Watercress; Fruit for Cream (*see* Note 2, below). Bloaters (January 29th); and a tin of Collared Sheep's Tongue for breakfast on August 31st.

BREAKFAST.—Pickled Mackerel (August 28th); Mushrooms on Toast (March 20th); Vienna Bread (August 26th); Plum Porridge (August 31st).

LUNCHEON.—Scrag of Mutton, Stewed with Rice (February 21st); Hasty Pudding (March 30th).

DINNER.—Boiled Hake (*see* Salmon, Boiled, July 5th); Stewed Steak (January 31st); Fried Potatoes (February 2nd); Carrots (July 6th); Vermicelli Pudding (August 1st); Cheese (June 8th).

Things that must not be Forgotten.

1. Pluck the ducks and the chicken or grouse, and cure the feathers (February 28th).

2. Make the *Strawberry Cream* for supper to-morrow night. This can be made either with fresh fruit (one pint for half a pint of cream) or with jelly (two good table-spoonfuls to half a pint of cream). The same recipe may be followed in making creams of other fruit, such as raspberries, red currants, apricots, &c. Fresh fruit should have sugar sprinkled over it for an hour or two to make the juice flow freely, and if it is at all hard it should be gently stewed. When jelly is used instead of fresh fruit a little lemon-juice should be added. Soak an ounce of gelatine in a cupful of milk for an hour. Dissolve the jelly, boil it with an ounce of sugar, and put the gelatine with it. Put the half pint of cream in a bowl. Whisk it in a cool place till it begins to thicken, then stop whisking it immediately, or it will curdle. Put the whipped cream with the fruit, and stir the mixture lightly together. Scald a mould with hot water, then rinse it out with cold water. Pour the mixture into it, and put it in a cool place or upon ice till stiff. When fresh fruit is used it should be rubbed through a hair sieve, and the pulp only should be taken. If liked, custard can be substituted for the fruit juice, and so *Italian Cream* can be made. For the custard half a pint of milk, the yolks of three and the white of one egg, and a little sugar will be required (August 10th).

3. Make the mayonnaise (August 30th) for supper to-morrow night.

4. Make the plums into a compôte for to-morrow (August 5th).

5. Roast the grouse or the chicken, and leave it till to-morrow to be made into a salad (June 30th and Note 1, August 30th). If preferred, the grouse could be roasted and served hot for dinner, and the remains, if there were any, could be made into a salad. In this case it would be necessary to provide something else for dinner, as a brace of grouse alone would not go very far.

Sunday, August 30th.

Breakfast.	Dinner.	Tea.	Supper.
Pickled Mackerel.	Boiled Salmon.	Brown and White	Chicken or Grouse
Eggs in Brown Butter.	Caper Sauce.	Bread and Butter.	Salad.
Vienna Bread.	Roast Ducks.	Compôte of Plums.	Strawberry Cream.
Dry Toast.	French Beans.	Seed Cake.	Lemon Cheesecakes.
Brown and White Bread and Butter.	Potatoes.		Cheese.
Watercress.	Plum Pie.		
Porridge.	Cheese.		

BREAKFAST.—Pickled Mackerel (August 28th); Eggs in Brown Butter (January 6th); Vienna Bread (August 26th); Porridge (January 25th).

DINNER.—Boiled Salmon (July 5th); Caper Sauce (March 19th); Roast Ducks (July 26th); French Beans (August 16th); Potatoes (April 12th); Plum Pie (August 7th); Cheese (June 8th).

TEA.—Compôte (August 5th); Seed Cake (August 14th).

SUPPER.—*Chicken or Grouse Salad.*—Cut the grouse into neat joints. Boil three or four eggs hard, and provide materials for a salad (whatever may be in season), mayonnaise sauce, and one or two pickled gherkins. Prepare the salad, and dry it thoroughly (March 13th), but do not dish it till a few minutes before it is to be served. Put a little of the shred salad on a dish, and toss it in a spoonful or two of the mayonnaise. Pile the inferior joints of the game on this, add more salad, and repeat until the ingredients are used. Pour mayonnaise over all, and garnish the salad with hard-boiled eggs cut into quarters, and gherkins cut into thin slices, or anchovies filleted. If chervil or tarragon is to be had, a little may be chopped and thrown over the thick sauce at the last moment, or, if preferred, a spoonful of tarragon vinegar can be used in making the mayonnaise. *Chicken Salad* is made exactly in the same way. Chicken salad is exceedingly good made with celery instead of lettuce, or with a mixture of the two. Strawberry Cream (August 29th).

Things that must not be Forgotten.

1. If it is preferred that the grouse should be roasted and served hot, proceed as follows. *Roast Grouse.*—Let the birds hang as long as possible. Pluck them, and handle them very lightly in doing so, draw them, and wipe them inside and out with a damp cloth, but do not wash them. Truss them firmly, put them down to a sharp clear fire, and baste them liberally all the time. Soak a slice of toast in the dripping-tin and serve them on this. Send brown gravy (October 18th) and bread sauce (October 18th) to table with them They will take about half an hour to roast.

2. Pickle any remains of salmon there may be (May 30th).

3. Preserve the bones and remains of chicken or grouse for making soup.

4. *Mayonnaise Sauce.*—Take a round-bottomed bowl, not over large, put into it the yolk of an egg and beat it for two or three minutes, then drop pure salad oil into it, one drop at a time, and beat the sauce well between every addition till the sauce is thick and dark, and looks something like beeswax. Now put in a few drops of vinegar, then oil again, until as much sauce is made as is required. Stir in more vinegar, a little at a time, to make the sauce taste pleasantly, and add salt, pepper, and a very small pinch of sugar. The sauce when finished, should be a firm creamy substance. A very good sauce may be made with the yolk of one egg, a quarter of a pint of oil, and two table-spoonfuls of vinegar, but if this quantity would not be sufficient, a pint of oil with vinegar in proportion might be put with one egg. A few drops of lemon-juice would help to make it look creamy, and a little tarragon vinegar would improve the taste. It may be noted that mayonnaise sauce will keep for a long time if it is put into a bottle, closely corked, and kept in a cool place. The secret of making mayonnaise sauce is to put in the oil in *drops only* at the beginning, beating well between every addition till the mixture becomes thick, and also to beat the sauce one way. If it were stirred first one way and then another, it would curdle. It should be mixed in a cool place, and the oil should be cold, otherwise the sauce would not thicken. If, notwithstanding all precautions, the sauce should curdle, the addition of a raw egg-yolk or of a small lump of ice, or something that is *cold*, will remedy the mischief. Mayonnaise sauce is so delicious and so universally popular that it is worth making, even though it is a little troublesome. The reason why so many cooks fail in making it is that they cannot believe that it is necessary to attend to the small details mentioned above. This sauce is especially suited for chicken, game, and fish salads of all kinds, and for serving with cold fish. Another very superior sauce, *Tartar Sauce*, is made just in the same way, only it is indispensable that tarragon vinegar should be used for it, and one or two spoonfuls of chopped pickle of some kind (gherkins to be preferred) must be stirred in after it is made; a spoonful of chopped chervil and tarragon should also be added after the sauce is made, but if they are not to be had, chopped parsley may be used instead.

5. Make custard blancmange for dinner to-morrow (August 4th).

August 31st.

Breakfast.	Luncheon.	Dinner.
Bloaters on Toast.	Pickled Salmon.	Gravy Soup.
Collared Sheep's Tongues.	Baked Custard Tart.	Roast Shoulder of Mutton
Vienna Bread.		Mint Sauce.
Dry Toast.		Potatoes.
Brown and White Bread and Butter.		Vegetable Marrow.
Marmalade.		Custard Blancmange.
Bread and Milk.		Cheese.

Marketing.

For the Day.—A Shoulder of Mutton (not very fat); Potatoes; Vegetable Marrow; Mint.

For To-morrow.—A tin of potted Grouse; a quart of any kind of red Plums for Porridge, and Fruit for the Rothe Grütze.

BREAKFAST.—Bloaters on Toast (March 24th); Collared Sheep's Tongues, bought day before yesterday; Vienna Bread (August 26th); Bread and Milk (January 25th).

LUNCHEON.—Pickled Salmon (May 30th); Custard Tart (January 19th).

DINNER.—*Gravy Soup.*—Follow the recipe given for guinea fowl soup (February 16th), using the chicken bones or meat bones instead of the bones and trimmings of game. Roast Shoulder of Mutton (December 16th); Mint Sauce (March 25th); Potatoes (April 12th); Vegetable Marrow (September 3rd); Custard Blancmange (August 4th); Cheese (June 8th).

Things that must not be Forgotten.

1. Make a Rothe Grütze mould for to-morrow (December 10th).
2. Partially prepare the *Plum Porridge* for breakfast to-morrow. For this, put the plums into a stewpan, with half a pint of water, two ounces of sugar, and a small piece of cinnamon. Boil gently to a pulp, then rub the whole through a colander into a basin. So far the porridge can be prepared over night. In the morning mix about a pint of cold milk with the pulp, add a little more sugar if the porridge is not sweet enough, and serve with bread as an accompaniment. All kinds of fresh summer fruit can be served in this way for breakfast, and will be generally approved by the young folks.

FRUITS SUITABLE FOR DESSERT IN AUGUST.

Gooseberries, Currants (Red, White, and Black), Cherries, Strawberries, Raspberries, French Melons, Apricots (from France), Greengages, Jersey and Lisbon Grapes, English Hot-house Grapes, Nectarines, Mulberries, Peaches, Plums, West India Pine-apples, Pears, last year's Nuts.

PICKLES.

Indian Pickle: a very convenient Pickle for Family Use.—Take a quantity of any vegetables that can be procured. Cauliflowers, not too much grown, white cabbage, young carrots, cucumbers, beetroot, French beans, &c., are suitable for this purpose. Prepare the vegetables, by cutting away the outer leaves of the cauliflower and dividing it into small branches, cutting the cabbage into very thin shreds, stringing the beans, skinning the onions, slicing the beetroot, trimming and scraping the carrots. Make a brine strong enough to float an egg, throw the vegetables into it, and let them boil one minute; drain them, and dry them perfectly by shaking a few at a time lightly in a soft cloth. Take as much vinegar as will entirely cover them, and boil it for five minutes with spices in the following proportion; to two quarts of vinegar, one ounce of whole ginger, one ounce of long pepper, one ounce of black peppercorns, and two cloves of garlic. Mix separately with a little cold vinegar in a basin an ounce of turmeric, and an ounce of flour of mustard, and stir this into the vinegar whilst it is boiling. Mix the vegetables thoroughly, and put them into an unglazed jar, and pour the vinegar, boiling, over them: it must entirely cover them. Cover closely, and keep in a cool place. Keep adding any vegetables that are in season, remembering always to boil them in brine for a minute and to dry them before putting them with the rest. Nasturtium seeds, radish pods, chilies, gherkins, and celery cut in lengths will be suitable additions. As the vinegar becomes absorbed more must be poured in, but it must be boiled and allowed to go cold before it is put with the pickle. The preparation can be used in about a fortnight, but it will improve with being kept.

Pickled Onions.—Take the smallest onions that can be obtained. Those called Reading onions are the best for this purpose. They must be quite ripe and dry, and are in the best condition for the purpose just after they have been harvested. Be careful not to use a steel knife in peeling them, as that would spoil their colour. With a silver knife take off the two outer skins, when the onion will look clear and white. Put them, as fast as they are ready, into perfectly dry pickling glasses, and cover them with cold vinegar. Tie them down closely and store; they can be used in three weeks, and will be found excellent. It is a good plan to stand near the fire when peeling onions, or if the eyes water very much the onions can be thrown into hot water. It is best not to do this if it can be helped.

Pickled Red Cabbage.—This pickle may be made in August or September. Choose a cabbage with a firm heart and of a deep red colour. Strip away the outer leaves and cut the cabbage into very thin shreds. Spread these on a dish, sprinkle salt well over them, and leave them for twenty-four hours. Squeeze the salt entirely from them. The more thoroughly this is done the better will be the colour of the cabbage. Put them in a jar, cover with cold boiled vinegar, leave the pickle for twenty-four hours, then tie closely, and store in a cool place. This pickle should be quickly used. It deteriorates with keeping.

September 1st.

Breakfast.	Luncheon.	Dinner.
Boiled Eggs.	Cold Shoulder of Mutton.	Baked Hake.
Potted Grouse.	Salad.	Neck of Veal, Boned and Rolled.
Buttered Toast.	Sago and Rice Pudding.	
Dry Toast.		Potatoes.
Brown and White Bread and Butter.		Cauliflower.
		Rothe Grütze.
Plum Porridge.		Cheese.

Marketing.

For the Day.—Materials for a Salad; about three pounds of Hake, cut from the middle of the fish; four or five pounds of the Neck or Loin of Veal (February 25th); Potatoes; Cauliflower.

For To-morrow.—Two Lambs' Sweetbreads; half a pound of Bacon (January 3rd); four ripe Tomatoes; Mustard and Cress; Muffins (January 29th).

BREAKFAST.—Boiled Eggs (January 5th); Potted Grouse (January 7th); Plum Porridge (August 31st).

LUNCHEON.—Mutton, served yesterday; Salad (March 13th). *Sago and Rice Pudding.*—Take half sago and half rice, and proceed as for plain rice pudding (February 24th).

DINNER.—*Baked Hake.*—Wash the fish in salt and water, rub it over with vinegar, and let it lie for an hour, then roll it in a cloth, and leave it to dry. Take a thick slice of stale bread, and rub it through a wire sieve. Put two ounces of the sifted crumbs upon a plate, and mix with them a little pepper, salt, and grated nutmeg, a pinch of mixed herbs, and a pinch of grated lemon-rind. Brush the fish with beaten egg, and sprinkle half the crumbs over it. Put it on a drainer in a deep baking-dish to raise it, pour round, but not over it a cupful of water and a wine-glassful of vinegar, and add a shalot finely minced, and a small carrot—or, if preferred, a few onions and potatoes—cut into slices. Place the dish in a moderate oven, and bake the fish for about an hour, basting it frequently with clarified dripping. When half cooked, turn it and strew the remainder of the crumbs over it. When done enough, put it on a hot dish, garnish with lemon and parsley, and send anchovy sauce (July 17th) or caper sauce (March 19th) to table with it. A piece from the middle of a cod may be cooked in this way. Neck of Veal, Boned and Rolled (May 28th); Potatoes (April 12th); Cauliflower (April 25th); Rothe Grütze (December 10th); Cheese (June 8th).

Things that must not be Forgotten.

1. Partially prepare the sweetbreads for to-morrow (October 22nd).
2. If any fish is left let it be made into fish cakes (January 13th) or scalloped (January 7th) for breakfast to-morrow, and used instead of the bacon and tomatoes (July 12th).

September 2nd.

Breakfast.	Luncheon.	Dinner.
Lambs' Sweetbreads. Bacon and Tomatoes. Muffins. Dry Toast. Brown and White Bread and Butter. Mustard and Cress. Corn-flour Milk.	Minced Veal. Custard Sippets.	Boiled Brill. Shrimp Sauce. Boiled Leg of Mutton. Caper Sauce. Young Carrots. Mashed Turnips. Potatoes. General Favourite Pudding. Cheese.

Marketing.

For the Day.—A Brill (January 9th), Shrimps for Sauce; a plump Leg of Mutton; Turnips; Carrots: Parsley; Potatoes.
For To-morrow.—Gorgona Anchovies, if not in the house; a pennyworth of Small Salad.

BREAKFAST.—Lambs' Sweetbreads (October 22nd); Bacon and Tomatoes (July 12th); Muffins (January 30th); Corn-flour Milk (June 19th).

LUNCHEON.—Minced Veal (May 11th); Custard Sippets (June 10th).

DINNER.—Boiled Brill (January 9th); Shrimp Sauce (January 30th); Boiled Leg of Mutton (February 23rd); Caper Sauce (March 19th); Young Carrots (July 6th); Mashed Turnips (September 30th); Potatoes (May 12th); General Favourite Pudding (May 17th); Cheese (June 8th).

Things that must not be Forgotten.

1. Preserve the liquor in which the leg of mutton is boiled.
2. Fillet the anchovies, and prepare the small salad for breakfast to-morrow (January 18th).
3. Put a cupful of hominy to soak in cold water all night (February 10th).

September 3rd.

Breakfast.	Luncheon.	Dinner.
Potted Grouse. Anchovies and Hard-boiled Eggs. Hot Buttered Toast. Dry Toast. Brown and White Bread and Butter. Boiled Hominy.	Stewed Ox Kidney. Plain Suet Pudding.	Herrings, with Mustard Sauce. Curried Mutton. Boiled Rice. Vegetable Marrow. Brown Bread Pudding. Cheese.

Marketing.

For the Day.—A fresh Ox Kidney; half a pound of Suet; six or eight fresh Herrings (August 25th); a Vegetable Marrow. These vegetables may be kept far into the winter by simply hanging them in a dry place.

For To-morrow.—A two-pound tin of Spiced Beef; order Rolls to be sent in the morning from the baker's. If requested to do so, the baker will send hot rolls early in the morning for breakfast.

BREAKFAST.—Potted Grouse (January 7th); Anchovies and Hard-boiled Eggs (January 18th); Boiled Hominy (February 11th).
LUNCHEON.—Stewed Ox Kidney (April 2nd); Plain Suet Pudding (May 13th).
DINNER.—Herrings, with Mustard Sauce (September 15th); Curried Mutton (May 26th); Boiled Rice (July 21st). *Vegetable Marrow, Boiled.*—Pare the rind off thinly. If the marrow is large, cut it in halves or quarters, and scoop out the seeds before boiling; if it is small, this may be done after boiling. Put the vegetable into plenty of boiling water slightly salted; bring it to the boiling point, skim the water, then put on the lid and boil till the marrow is tender. A small marrow will take from fifteen to twenty minutes, a large marrow from half to three-quarters of an hour. Have ready a slice of toast, dip it into the boiling water, and put it on a dish. Take up the marrow with a slice, drain it, put it on the toast, and serve. Send melted butter (July 17th) to table as an accompaniment. Brown Bread Pudding (July 20th); Cheese (June 8th).

Things that must not be Forgotten.

1. Preserve any hominy that may be left; it can be fried for breakfast to-morrow.
2. Be sure to boil the mutton liquor.

September 4th.

Breakfast.	Luncheon.	Dinner.
Savoury Omelette.	Lamb's Fry.	Haddock, Stuffed and Baked.
Spiced Beef.	Jam and Bread, with Milk.	Roast Lamb.
Hot Rolls.		Tomato Sauce.
Dry Toast.		Potatoes.
Brown and White Bread and Butter.		Viennoise Pudding.
Fried Hominy.		Cheese.

Marketing.

For the Day.—A Lamb's Fry; a good-sized Haddock. Haddock is an excellent fish, its flesh being firm, delicate, and rich. It is at its best from August to December. The larger fish are to be preferred. The haddock has on it two black spots, one on each side, which are said to be the marks left by St. Peter's finger and thumb when he took the tribute-money out of its mouth. Its freshness is determined by the rules which hold good with other fish (January 3rd). A quarter of a pound of Suet; a Leg of Lamb (April 11th); half a dozen ripe Tomatoes; a pennyworth of Yeast.
For To-morrow.—Small Soles ("slips") for breakfast (January 3rd).

BREAKFAST.—*Savoury Omelette.*—This is a very good breakfast dish, and easily made whenever the process is understood. It i.

important to keep a pan for omelettes only, which pan should never be washed, but should be well wiped with a clean cloth each time it is used. Take chopped parsley to fill a tea-spoon, and three eggs. Beat the eggs for two seconds, and mix with them the parsley and a little pepper and salt. Rub the omelette-pan with a shalot, then melt an ounce of butter in it over a bright clear fire. Pour the eggs upon the hot butter, stir them quickly with a wooden spoon, and shake the pan to keep the eggs from sticking. As soon as the mixture begins to thicken, raise the handle of the pan, and let the omelette remain at the opposite side till it is brown. Turn it over quickly, and put it on a hot dish. The outside should be of a golden colour, and the inside quite soft. Serve immediately. Spiced Beef, bought yesterday. *Hot Rolls* are sent in hot from the baker's. They need only to be split open, buttered, put together again, then placed on a hot dish and covered with a hot napkin. Fried Hominy (February 12th).

LUNCHEON.—Lamb's Fry (May 16th); Jam and Bread, with Milk (February 23rd).

DINNER.—*Haddock, Stuffed and Baked.*—Make a little good forcemeat with a quarter of a pound of bread-crumbs, a quarter of a pound of chopped suet, a little pepper and salt, a table-spoonful of chopped parsley, and a dessert-spoonful of mixed herbs chopped small. Bind together with a beaten egg or with milk. Empty and clean the haddock, wash it, and dry it thoroughly. Fill it with the forcemeat, and sew it up. Put it into a greased dripping-tin nearly its own size, dredge flour upon it, and place little pieces of butter or clarified dripping here and there upon it; put it into a moderate oven and bake it, basting it frequently till done enough. It will take from half to three-quarters of an hour, according to size. Serve it on a hot dish without sauce, if liked, or with anchovy sauce (July 17th) or brown butter sauce (February 12th). Roast Lamb (March 4th); Tomato Sauce (July 15th); Potatoes (April 12th); Viennoise Pudding (July 6th); Cheese (June 8th).

Things that must not be Forgotten.

1. If any haddock is left, free it from skin and bones, tear it into flakes, put it into a pie-dish, and moisten it with sauce or melted butter. Cover it thickly with bread-crumbs, place little pieces of butter here and there upon it. To-morrow morning bake it in a moderate oven till the surface is browned. Serve for breakfast on the dish in which it was baked; send melted butter to table with it, and serve walnut pickle as an accompaniment.

2. Pastry is to be made to-day (April 17th): Plum Pie (August 7th), Treacle Tart (August 7th); also Sally Lunns (August 26th) and Plain Currant Cake (June 26th).

3. Put a cupful of haricot beans to soak all night in cold water.

September 5th.

Breakfast.	Luncheon.	Dinner.
Baked Slips.	Cold Lamb.	Soup for the Shah.
Haddock Pie.	Salad.	Beef Olives.
Sally Lunns.	Treacle Tart.	Potatoes.
Dry Toast.		Haricot Beans.
Brown and White Bread and Butter.		Boiled Plum Pudding (made of fresh fruit).
Milk Porridge.		Cheese.

Marketing.

For the Day.—Materials for a Salad (March 13th); a good-sized Vegetable Marrow; about two pounds of tender Steak (January 1st); two or three slices of Bacon; six ounces or more of Beef Suet for the boiled pudding; a pound and a half of Plums; Parsley; Potatoes.

For To-morrow.—A pair of plump young Fowls (June 29th); two additional sets of Giblets, if they can be procured; it is not likely that these can be bought on Monday when they are to be used; half a pound of Bacon; a moderate-sized fresh Turbot (June 6th); picked Shrimps for sauce; a dozen fresh Herrings (August 25th); Potatoes for dinner and for a Salad; Vegetable Marrow; Cocoa-nut or desiccated Cocoa-nut; a pound of Plums for porridge; Sardines; a sour Apple and Gherkins wanted for the Russian Salad; a Shoulder of Mutton for Monday. If the weather is hot this purchase should be deferred.

BREAKFAST.—Baked Slips (January 7th); Haddock Pie (Note 1, September 4th); Sally Lunns (June 4th); Milk Porridge (June 13th).

LUNCHEON.—Lamb, served yesterday; Salad (March 13th); Treacle Tart (August 7th).

DINNER.—Soup for the Shah, made of the liquor the leg of mutton was boiled in (September 17th). *Beef Olives.*—Divide the steak into thin slices, about four inches long and three wide; put a tea-spoonful of forcemeat in the middle of each piece, roll it, and tie it securely with twine. Put a little butter in a stewpan, and fry the olives, turning them about, till they are equally browned all over. Pour upon them enough stock or water to make gravy, cover the pan, and stew very gently for two hours. Pour off the gravy, thicken it with brown thickening (January 6th), and add a wine-glassful of claret or a little ketchup, if liked, and let it boil up again. Remove the twine, put the rolls in the centre of a hot dish, pour the gravy over them, place the boiled haricot beans round (June 20th), and serve very hot. If preferred, a large cauliflower can be boiled separately, and sprigs of the same can be placed round the meat instead of the beans. The forcemeat can be made with two ounces of bread-crumbs, two ounces of chopped suet, a dessert-spoonful of chopped parsley, a small tea-spoonful of mixed marjoram and thyme, and a little pepper and salt. Boiled Plum Pudding (made of fresh fruit, July 19th); Cheese (June 8th).

Things that must not be Forgotten.

1. Pickle the herrings bought this morning (August 20th).
2. Make the plum porridge for breakfast (August 31st).

3. Make a Stone Cream for supper on Sunday night (July 1st). Pluck and draw the fowls, to be ready for dinner; trim and boil all the giblets (February 1st); unless this is done they will not keep until Monday, when they are to be made into soup. When a fowl is drawn, one should be able to put the fingers right through the body of the bird. Preserve and dry the feathers (February 28th).

4. Make a quarter of a pint of mayonnaise for the Russian salad (August 30th).

Sunday, September 6th.

Breakfast.	Dinner.	Tea.	Supper.
Pickled Herrings.	Boiled Turbot.	Brown and White Bread and Butter.	Russian Salad.
Buttered Eggs.	Shrimp Sauce.	Gooseberry Jam.	Stone Cream.
Sally Lunns.	Fowl, with Golden Rain.	Plain Currant Cake.	Cheese.
Dry Toast.	Bacon Rolls.		
Brown and White Bread and Butter.	Potatoes.		
Plum Porridge.	Vegetable Marrow.		
	Cocoa-nut Pudding.		
	Cheese.		

BREAKFAST.— Buttered Eggs (January 16th); Pickled Herrings (August 20th); Sally Lunns (June 4th); Plum Porridge (August 31st).

DINNER.—Boiled Turbot (June 7th); Shrimp Sauce (January 30th). *Boiled Fowls, with Golden Rain.*—Truss the fowls firmly for boiling. Put them breast downwards into fast-boiling water, which has in it a carrot, an onion, and a bunch of herbs. Boil for one minute, then draw the saucepan back and *simmer very gently* for about three-quarters of an hour, or for an hour if the birds are large. In this particular instance the birds are to be covered entirely with sauce, therefore it does not signify very much whether or not they are very white when boiled; otherwise they would look a better colour if they were wrapped in kitchen paper, thickly buttered, whilst boiling. It is evident, however, that the liquor could be more satisfactorily used if the paper were omitted. *To make the Sauce.*—Boil two eggs for ten minutes, let them go cold, then throw the white part into cold water to preserve the colour, and leave the yolks untouched. Melt an ounce of butter in a stewpan, stir in, off the fire, an ounce of flour, and beat the mixture till smooth with the back of a wooden spoon. Add half a pint of milk, and stir the sauce over the fire till it thickens; then add a gill of cream, and the white of egg cut into dice. Let the sauce boil again, and be careful not to stir it, so that the egg white may not be crushed or broken. Take up the fowls, drain them well, and put the sauce upon them. Do this carefully with a spoon, so as to cover them in every part; rub the yolks of the eggs through a wire sieve upon the breasts of the birds to make the golden rain, and serve. Bacon Rolls

(July 19th); Potatoes (May 6th); Vegetable Marrow (September 3rd); Cocoa-nut Pudding (August 8th); Cheese (June 8th).
TEA.—Plain Currant Cake (June 26th).
SUPPER.—Russian Salad (April 5th); Stone Cream (July 1st).

Things that must not be Forgotten.

1. The Russian salad can be made with a little of the flesh of the boiled chicken, sardines, and a slice of bacon instead of ham.

2. If the legs of the chicken are not used, devil them for breakfast to-morrow; they will have to be prepared over night (January 14th).

3. Carefully preserve the chicken bones; they will greatly improve the stock.

September 7th.

Breakfast.	Luncheon.		Dinner.
Sardines.	Chicken Kromeskies;	or	Giblet Soup.
Devilled Drumsticks.	Croquettes, made	of	Roast Shoulder of Mutton.
Sally Lunns.	Spiced Beef.		Mint Sauce.
Dry Toast.	Baked Batter Pudding.		Potatoes.
Brown and White Bread and Butter.			Beans.
			Brown Bread Pudding.
Milk Toast.			Cheese.

Marketing.

For the Day.—Mint; Potatoes; Beans.

For To-morrow.—Rolls for breakfast (September 3rd); half a pint of full-grown Mushrooms; a Saddle of Mutton. If the weather be favourable, this joint may be hung for nearly a fortnight, and cooked on Sunday week. It should, however, be looked at every day, and cooked earlier if it will not keep.

BREAKFAST.—Sardines (*see* Marketing, January 12th); Devilled Drumsticks (January 14th); Sally Lunns (June 4th); Milk Toast (June 17th).

LUNCHEON.—Chicken Kromeskies (July 29th) or Croquettes (*see* Rissoles, January 6th); Baked Batter Pudding (February 5th).

DINNER.—Giblet Soup (February 1st); Roast Shoulder of Mutton (December 16th); Mint Sauce (March 25th); Potatoes (May 4th); Beans (August 16th); Brown Bread Pudding (July 20th); Cheese (June 8th).

Things that must not be Forgotten.

1. Put a cupful of green lentils to soak all night in cold water.

2. Partially prepare the rice milk for breakfast (see Note 3, June 17th).

3. As soon as the roast mutton leaves the table put it on a clean dish, and preserve any gravy there may be.

v

September 8th.

Breakfast.	Luncheon.	Dinner.
Mushrooms and Bacon. Devilled Eggs. Hot Rolls. Dry Toast. Brown and White Bread and Butter. Rice Milk.	Cold Mutton. Salad. Hasty Pudding.	Boiled Hake. Dutch Sauce. Rolled Ribs of Beef. Lentils. Potatoes. Town Pudding. Cheese.

Marketing.

For the Day.—Materials for a Salad (March 13th); about three pounds of Hake (August 7th); one or two Ribs of Beef. The butcher should be asked to bone and roll the joint, and fasten it firmly. The bones should of course be sent with the meat, and they may be stewed for stock. Two pounds of Apples for Town pudding.

For To-morrow.—A dozen fresh Herrings (August 25th); half soft and half hard roes. Watercress; Muffins (January 29th); a small bottle of preserved Tomatoes; a pint of Blackberries, and two or three Apples.

BREAKFAST.—*Mushrooms and Bacon.*—Cleanse the mushrooms thoroughly. Fry the bacon very gently. When it is almost done enough put in the mushrooms, and fry them also. Lift the bacon on a hot dish as soon as it is sufficiently cooked. Sprinkle pepper and salt on the mushrooms, and place them in the centre of the dish. Serve very hot. Devilled Eggs (February 27th); Rice Milk (June 18th).

LUNCHEON.—Salad (March 13th); Hasty Pudding (March 30th).

DINNER.—Boiled Hake (*see* Boiled Salmon, July 5th); Dutch Sauce (May 14th). Boiled hake is slightly insipid, therefore it requires a piquant sauce to be served with it. Rolled Ribs of Beef (March 4th); Lentils (March 2nd); Potatoes (May 6th); Town Pudding (December 3rd); Cheese (June 8th).

Things that must not be Forgotten.

1. Make a corn-flour blancmange for luncheon to-morrow (June 15th).
2. Boil the blackberries and apples together, with a little sugar, and make a hydropathic pudding for dinner to-morrow (June 16th).
3. Pickle the herrings for breakfast to-morrow (August 20th).

September 9th.

Breakfast.	Luncheon.	Dinner.
Pickled Herrings. Watercress. Muffins. Dry Toast. Brown and White Bread and Butter. Honey. Porridge.	Minced Mutton, with Poached Eggs. Corn-flour Blancmange. Lemon Syrup.	Potato Purée. Cold Beef. Salad. Potatoes. Hydropathic Blackberry Pudding. Cheese.

Marketing.

For the Day.—Materials for a Salad; Potatoes.
For To-morrow.—A moderate-sized fresh Haddock; a pound of Plums; speak for a Lamb's Fry to-morrow.

BREAKFAST.—Pickled Herrings (August 20th); Muffins (January 30th); Porridge (January 25th).
LUNCHEON.—Minced Mutton (January 20th); Corn-flour Blancmange (June 15th); Lemon Syrup (March 19th).
DINNER.—Potato Purée (January 26th); Beef served yesterday; Salad (March 13th); Potatoes (May 12th); Hydropathic Pudding (June 16th); Cheese (June 8th).

Things that must not be Forgotten.

1. Prepare the haddock for breakfast to-morrow: that is, clean it, cut off the head, and *remove the skin*, rub it all over with salt, and hang it in an airy place. The cook must not imagine that the skin can be left on the fish.
2. Make the plums into a compote for luncheon to-morrow (August 5th).
3. Pot any remains of cold beef there may be (January 23rd).

September 10th.

Breakfast.	Luncheon.	Dinner.
Rizzared Haddock.	Lamb's Fry.	Boiled Brill.
Potted Beef.	Compote of Plums.	Anchovy Sauce.
Hot Buttered Toast.		Loin of Lamb, Braised.
Dry Toast.		Baked Tomatoes.
Brown and White Bread and Butter.		Potatoes.
Bread and Milk.		Beans.
		Cottage Plum Pudding.
		Cheese.

Marketing.

For the Day.—A Lamb's Fry ordered yesterday; a moderate-sized Brill (January 9th and January 3rd); a Loin of Lamb (May 22nd); Tomatoes; Potatoes; French Beans; six ounces of Beef Suet.
For To-morrow.—Half a pound of Bacon in rashers (January 3rd); Mustard and Cress.

BREAKFAST.—*Rizzared Haddock.*—Rub the haddock all over with oil or dissolved butter, dredge flour upon it, and broil it over a clear fire. Put a little butter upon it, and serve very hot. Potted Beef (January 23rd); Bread and Milk (January 25th).
LUNCHEON.—Lamb's Fry (May 16th); Compote of Plums (August 5th).
DINNER.—Boiled Brill (January 9th); Anchovy Sauce (July 17th); Loin of Lamb Braised (May 22nd); Baked Tomatoes (July 7th); Potatoes (April 7th); Beans (August 16th); Cottage Plum Pudding (June 6th); Cheese (June 8th).

Things that must not be Forgotten.

1. If any fish is left, make it into fish cakes for breakfast to-morrow (January 13th).
2. If any of the compote remain, put it at once away. It will keep for two or three days.

September 11th.

Breakfast.	Luncheon.	Dinner.
Fish Cakes.	Beef Collops.	Stewed Eels.
Toasted Bacon.	Slices of Plum Pudding, Warmed.	Rabbit Pie.
Hot Buttered Toast.		Potatoes.
Dry Toast.		Cabbage.
Mustard and Cress.		Macaroni Pudding.
Brown and White Bread and Butter.		Cheese.
Corn-flour Milk.		

Marketing.

For the Day.—A pound and a half of Buttock Steak (January 1st); a pound and a half of Eels (January 24th); a plump young Rabbit (January 24th); three-quarters of a pound of lean Veal; a quarter of a pound of mild Bacon cut into thin slices; Potatoes; Cabbage.

For To-morrow.—A Bath Chap: that is, a pig's cheek cured like bacon; a pound of Plums; a plump Chicken, or two Chickens if one will not be sufficient; Apples for pies.

BREAKFAST.—Fish Cakes (January 13th); Toasted Bacon (January 19th); Corn-flour Milk (June 19th).

LUNCHEON.—Scotch Collops (January 9th); Cold Pudding warmed up (March 6th).

DINNER.—Stewed Eels (January 24th). *Rabbit Pie.*—Cut the rabbit into small neat pieces, keep out the breast bone and bone the legs. Cut the veal also into thin pieces two inches square, and divide the bacon into strips. Scald and scrape the bacon-rind, and put it into a saucepan with the bones and breast of the rabbit. Cover with cold water, and add salt, pepper, an onion, and half a blade of mace. Simmer gently for gravy. Put the veal, rabbit, and slices of bacon in layers into a pie-dish, and season each layer with pepper, salt, grated nutmeg, and grated lemon-rind. The dish must not be over full, or the rabbit will be dry. Half a small lemon grated and an eighth part of a nutmeg grated will be sufficient for this quantity. Pour in half a pint of the stock, then line the edges with pastry, and cover with pastry according to the directions given for making beef-steak pie (March 26th). Bake in a well-heated oven for an hour and a half or two hours. As soon as the pastry has risen and is set, lay a sheet of paper over it, to prevent its acquiring too much colour. Rough puff paste (May 29th) would be excellent for this pie, or, if preferred, short crust (June 19th) might be made instead. In winter, when veal is expensive, two young rabbits might be used instead of one rabbit and the veal cutlet. Strain the gravy, and before serving the pie pour this in by means of a funnel placed in the hole of the crust. Rabbit pie is very good eaten cold. Potatoes (May 6th); Cabbage (June 4th); Macaroni Pudding (March 27th); Cheese (June 8th).

Things that must not be Forgotten.

1. Soak the Bath chap and boil it for breakfast to-morrow (Note 1, August 25th).

2. Pastry is to be made to-day (April 17th) : Two apple pies (August 7th) and rabbit pie ; also light buns, quickly made (August 14th); scones, if there is any sour milk (August 26th), or teacakes (August 26th), and soda cake (August 14th).

3. Make plum porridge for breakfast to-morrow (August 31st).

4. Pluck the chicken and hang it in a cool place. Dry the feathers (Note 1, February 28th).

September 12th.

Breakfast.	Luncheon.	Dinner.
Eggs on the Dish.	Rabbit Gâteau.	Croûte au Pot.
Bath Chap.	Suet Dumpling, with Jam.	Stewed Chicken, with Tomatoes and Mushrooms.
Teacakes.		
Dry Toast.		
Brown and White Bread and Butter.		Potato Snow.
Plum Porridge.		Cabbage.
		Apple Pie.
		Cheese.

Marketing.

For the Day.—Half a pound of Suet; three or four Tomatoes ; half a pound of Mushrooms ; Potatoes ; Cabbage ; Parsley.

For To-morrow.—A tin of Potted Pheasant ; a pair of thick Soles (January 3rd); Fore-Quarter of Lamb (April 11th) ; Mint ; Vegetable Marrow ; Potatoes ; Apples, for a compote ; materials for a Salad (March 13th); Tomatoes for breakfast on Monday.

BREAKFAST.—Eggs on the Dish (December 7th); Bath Chap (August 25th); Teacakes (February 14th); Plum Porridge (August 31st).

LUNCHEON.—Rabbit Gâteau, made of the remnants of the rabbit pie (July 9th). If there is enough of it, the pie will be excellent served cold. Suet Dumpling, with Jam (May 13th).

DINNER.—Croûte au Pot (May 25th). *Stewed Chicken, with Tomatoes and Mushrooms.*—Draw the chicken, and cut it into neat pieces. Take a good-sized saucepan and melt a good slice of sweet butter in it. Throw in an onion finely minced and the red part of a carrot scraped, and stir over the fire for three minutes. Put in the pieces of chicken, season them with salt and pepper, and fry them in the butter, moving them occasionally to keep them from sticking to the pan. When lightly browned pour upon them a pint and a half of stock (made from the rabbit bones), add four moderate-sized tomatoes cut into halves, and a table-spoonful of corn-flour mixed to a smooth paste with a little cold water. Stir the sauce till it boils, draw it back, and let it simmer gently for half an hour. Clean the mushrooms and cut them into thin slices ; add a table-spoonful of coarsely chopped parsley, and simmer again for a quarter of an hour. Put the pieces of chicken on a hot dish, pour the sauce over, garnish with fried bread, and serve. Potato Snow (April 7th); Cabbage (June 4th) ; Cheese (June 8th).

Things that must not be Forgotten.

1. Preserve one mushroom from those that are stewed with the chicken for the sole au gratin to-morrow.
2. Soak a large cupful of hominy in cold water all night.
3. Make a compote of apples for supper to-morrow night (August 5th). Apples should be pared, cut into halves, and cored, before being stewed in the syrup. A little lemon-juice may be put with them.

Sunday, September 13th.

Breakfast.	Dinner.	Tea.	Supper.
Potted Pheasant.	Sole au Gratin.	Brown and White Bread and Butter.	Cold Lamb.
Bath Chap.	Quarter of Lamb.		Salad.
Teacakes.	Mint Sauce.	Cold Teacakes.	Compote of Apples.
Dry Toast.	Vegetable Marrow.	Strawberry Jam.	Cheese.
Brown and White Bread and Butter.	Potatoes.	Soda Cake.	
Boiled Hominy.	Hayrick Pudding.		
	Cheese.		

BREAKFAST.—Potted Pheasant (Marketing, *see* Remarks on Potted Grouse, January 7th); Bath Chap (August 25th); Teacakes (February 14th); Boiled Hominy (February 11th).

DINNER.—Sole au Gratin (May 3rd); Roast Quarter of Lamb (April 12th); Mint Sauce (March 25th). Vegetable Marrow (September 3rd); Potatoes (May 12th); Hayrick Puddings (March 19th); Cheese (June 8th).

TEA.—Soda Cake (August 14th).

SUPPER.—Salad (March 13th).

Things that must not be Forgotten.

1. Preserve any hominy that may be left; it can be fried for breakfast to-morrow.
2. Cold Potatoes left to-day may be used for the salad to-morrow.

September 14th.

Breakfast.	Luncheon.	Dinner.
Boiled Eggs.	Cold Lamb.	Tomato Purée.
Potted Pheasant.	Mint Sauce.	Broiled Steak à la Béarnaise.
Teacakes.	Potato Salad.	
Dry Toast.	Macaroni and Bacon.	Fried Potatoes
Brown and White Bread and Butter.		Leche Crème.
Marmalade.		Cheese.
Fried Hominy.		

Marketing.

For the Day.—Half a pound of Macaroni (January 1st); half a dozen ripe Tomatoes; a slice of Rump Steak, not less than an inch thick (January 22nd); Potatoes; half a pound of ratafias.

For To-morrow.—Four plump Sheep's Kidneys; half a pound of Bacon in rashers (January 3rd); Mustard and Cress.

BREAKFAST.—Boiled Eggs (January 5th); Potted Pheasant (*see* Potted Grouse, January 7th); Teacakes (February 14th); Fried Hominy (February 12th).

LUNCHEON.—Lamb and Mint Sauce served yesterday; Potato Salad (April 12th); Macaroni and Bacon; the remains of the Bath Chap may be used for this (January 27th).

DINNER.—Tomato Purée (March 11th); Broiled Steak à la Béarnaise (January 22nd); Fried Potatoes (February 2nd); Lèche Crème (May 7th); Cheese (June 8th).

Things that must not be Forgotten.

1. Carefully preserve any little pieces of steak that may be left.
2. If preferred, Swiss Role can be substituted for ratafins in the pudding.

September 15th.

Breakfast.	Luncheon.	Dinner.
Fried Kidneys and Bacon.	Shepherd's Pie.	Herrings, with Mustard Sauce.
Hot Buttered Toast.	Gingerbread Pudding.	Boiled Leg of Mutton.
Dry Toast.		Caper Sauce.
Brown and White Bread and Butter.		Carrots.
Mustard and Cress.		Mashed Turnips.
Milk Porridge.		Potatoes.
		Newmarket Pudding.
		Cheese.

Marketing.

For the Day.—Fresh Herrings (August 25th): choose fish with soft roes; allow one fish for each person, and one over. A plump, well-kept Leg of Mutton (January 8th); Potatoes; Carrots; Turnips.

For To-morrow.—Bloaters: one for two persons will probably be enough; a tin of Collared Tongue (January 2nd); Rolls for breakfast (September 3rd); Sea Biscuits, if not in the house; order half an Ox Kidney to be sent in the morning.

BREAKFAST.—Fried Kidneys and Bacon (January 2nd); Milk Porridge (June 13th).

LUNCHEON.—Shepherd's Pie, made of the remnants of broiled steak (January 12th); Gingerbread Pudding (May 20th).

DINNER.—*Herrings, with Mustard Sauce.*—Scale and empty the herrings, cut off their heads and tails and open them, take out the backbone carefully, and lay them flat; pepper and salt the inside of the fish, and draw them through a little salad oil that has been poured into a dish. Let them lie for an hour, then put on a greased gridiron, and broil them over a gentle but clear fire till they are done enough, turning them frequently. They will take about a quarter of an hour. Fry the roes separately in a little fat. Put the herrings on a dish with the fried roes, squeeze a little lemon-juice over them, and serve them very hot, with a little mustard sauce (July 8th) in a tureen. Boiled

Leg of Mutton (February 23rd); Caper Sauce (March 19th); Carrots (July 6th); Mashed Turnips (September 30th); Newmarket Pudding (June 2nd); Cheese (June 8th).

Things that must not be Forgotten.

1. Keep the bloaters apart from all other food.
2. Make the *Apple Mould* for dinner to-morrow. Put an ounce of gelatine to soak in a cupful of water. Pare, core, and slice two pounds of good baking-apples, put them into a stewpan with water to cover them, and let them simmer gently till soft. Stir in the soaked gelatine till dissolved, and add sugar to taste, with a little lemon-juice, if liked. Beat the mixture till smooth, put it into a damp mould, and set it in a cool place. Serve with cream or custard.
3. Preserve the liquor that the leg of mutton was boiled in.

September 16th.

Breakfast.	Luncheon.	Dinner.
Bloaters on Toast.	Minced Mutton.	Kidney Soup.
Collared Tongue.	Slices of Gingerbread Pudding, Toasted.	Curried Mutton.
Hot Rolls.		Boiled Rice.
Dry Toast.		Kidney Beans.
Brown and White Bread and Butter.		Apple Mould.
Mustard and Cress.		Custard.
Biscuits and Milk.		Cheese.

Marketing.

For the Day.—Half an Ox Kidney, ordered yesterday; Beans; a dozen fresh Herrings with soft roes (August 25th); Parsley.
For To-morrow.—Muffins; Watercress.

BREAKFAST.—Bloaters on Toast (March 24th); Collared Tongue (*see* Marketing, January 2nd); Hot Rolls (September 4th); Biscuits and Milk (June 14th).

LUNCHEON.—Minced Mutton (January 20th). Neat slices can be cut from the cold boiled leg of mutton and curried for dinner. The unsightly broken pieces that remain can be minced for luncheon. The bone should of course be broken up and stewed for stock (February 13th). Slices of Gingerbread Pudding, Toasted (*see* Remains of Pudding, Toasted, March 6th).

DINNER.—Kidney Soup (February 27th); Curried Mutton (May 26th); Boiled Rice (July 21st); Kidney Beans (August 16th); Apple Mould (September 15th); Custard (August 10th); Cheese (June 8th).

Things that must not be Forgotten.

1. Pickle the fresh herrings as soon as possible after they come in (August 20th).

2. Partially prepare the rice and barley porridge for breakfast (Note 6, June 15th).

3. Put a cupful of haricot beans to soak all night in cold water.

4. Stew the bones of the leg of mutton in the liquor in which it was boiled; the stock can be used for the soup to-morrow.

September 17th.

Breakfast.
Pickled Herrings.
Collared Tongue.
Muffins.
Dry Toast.
Brown and White Bread and Butter.
Watercress.
Rice and Barley Porridge.

Luncheon.
Beef Stew, Economical.
Boiled Rice.

Dinner.
Soup for the Shah.
Roast Sirloin of Beef.
Haricot Beans.
Potatoes.
Devonshire Junket.
Cheese.

Marketing.

For the Day.—Two pounds of lean Steak (see Marketing, January 1st); three or four Mushrooms; a large Vegetable Marrow; a Sirloin of Beef, weighing about eight pounds: choose meat with a good undercut (January 10th); Potatoes; a small bottle of prepared Rennet: this can be bought of any chemist.

For To-morrow.—A Canadian Ham, sugar cured. These hams, which can be bought at a very cheap rate (6d. per pound), are excellent for every day use, though of course they are not so delicious as those cured at home. A plump young Fowl, or two Fowls if required; order Rolls for breakfast (September 4th).

BREAKFAST.—Pickled Herrings (August 20th); Collared Tongue (January 2nd); Muffins (January 30th); Rice and Barley Porridge (June 15th).

LUNCHEON.—Beef Stew, Economical (March 21st); Boiled Rice (February 3rd).

DINNER.—*Soup for the Shah.*—Pare, core, and quarter the vegetable marrow, put it into a stewpan with as much stock as will cover it, and add an onion sliced, a small piece of butter, and a little pepper and salt. Let it simmer gently till quite soft, then rub it through a sieve, and mix with the purée a pint of stock, or a little more if it is very thick: this will depend on the size of the marrow; throw a lump of sugar into it, and make it very hot. Have ready a pint of boiling milk, and add this to the soup at the last moment. If it is liked, in order to enrich the soup, the yolk of an egg may be put into the tureen and slightly beaten, a spoonful of soup may then be stirred in quickly, and the rest added gradually. Soup for the Shah derives its name from the fact that the vegetable marrow is believed to have been brought originally from Persia. When they are in season, a table-spoonful of green peas may be boiled separately, and thrown into the soup at the last moment. These will represent the jewels Orientals delight in. Roast Sirloin of Beef (March 4th); Haricot Beans

(June 20th); Potatoes (May 6th). *Devonshire Junket.*—Heat a quart of milk till it is lukewarm. Meanwhile, put half a tea-spoonful of powdered cinnamon and a table-spoonful of sugar into a cup, pour on a wine-glassful of brandy, and stir till the sugar is dissolved. Add this to the milk, put it into the dish in which it is to be served, and stir in a table-spoonful of the prepared rennet. In three or four hours it will be firm and ready to be served. If it can be procured, a little clotted cream should be spread on the top of the junket, and white sugar sifted over that. Sometimes fresh fruit is eaten with this dish. Cheese (June 8th).

Things that must not be Forgotten.

1. Cut the flap off the sirloin of beef, and sprinkle salt over it if the weather be warm.
2. Turn the herrings in the vinegar, and put them in a cool place.
3. Cut a good-sized piece from the Canadian ham, and boil it for breakfast to-morrow (Note 4, May 27th).
4. Pluck the chicken and hang it in a cool larder; dry the feathers (February 28th).

September 18th.

Breakfast.	Luncheon.	Dinner.
Pickled Herrings.	Flap of Beef, Boiled with Carrots and Turnips.	Filleted Hake.
Boiled Ham.		Fricassée of Chicken.
Rolls.	Rice Réchauffé.	Potatoes.
Dry Toast.		Baked Tomatoes.
Brown and White Bread and Butter.		Chocolate Pudding.
Marmalade.		Custard.
Milk Toast.		Cheese.

Marketing.

For the Day.—A piece of Hake, weighing about two pounds, from the middle of the fish (August 7th); Potatoes; Tomatoes; Turnips; Carrots; an ounce of German Yeast; Plums.

For To-morrow.—Watercress; six or eight small Soles: "Slips" (January 3rd).

BREAKFAST.—Pickled Herrings (August 20th); Boiled Ham (May 27th); Rolls (September 4th); Milk Toast (June 17th).

LUNCHEON.—Flap of Beef, Boiled (February 23rd); Turnips (September 30th); Carrots (July 6th); Rice Réchauffé (April 27th).

DINNER.—Filleted Hake (July 19th). Follow this recipe, substituting only hake for the salmon. Chicken, Fricasséed (July 28th); Potatoes (April 7th); Baked Tomatoes (July 7th); Chocolate Pudding (July 24th); Custard (August 10th); Cheese (June 8th).

Things that must not be Forgotten.

1. Preserve the chicken bones and the liquor the beef was boiled in.
2. Pastry is to be made to-day (April 17th): Plum Pies (August

7th) and Treacle Tart (August 7th); also Milk Rolls (August 26th) and Rice Cake (August 2nd).

3. Partially prepare the rice milk for breakfast (*see* Note 3, June 17th).

4. Soak a cupful of white haricot beans in cold water all night.

September 19th.

Breakfast.	Luncheon.	Dinner.
Baked Slips.	Liver and Bacon.	Boiled Brill and Anchovy
Boiled Ham.	Treacle Tart.	Sauce
Milk Rolls.		Sea Pie.
Dry Toast.		Potatoes.
Brown and White Bread and		Mashed Turnips.
Butter.		Guest's Pudding.
Watercress.		Cheese.
Rice Milk.		

Marketing.

For the Day.—A pound and a half of Calf's Liver; half a pound of Streaky Bacon (January 3rd); a thick Brill (January 9th); two pounds and a half of Buttock Steak (*see* Marketing, January 1st); Turnips; Potatoes; Parsley; ten ounces of firm Suet.

For To-morrow.—A pair of moderate-sized thick Soles (January 3rd). The Saddle of Mutton that has been hanging since last Tuesday week will probably now be ready for the spit. A pound of Plums; Potatoes; Scarlet Runners; three or four Tomatoes; a fresh Haddock; Sardines for Monday; half an Endive, and a pennyworth of Beet-root to garnish the haricot salad; half a pound of Bacon for Monday.

BREAKFAST.—Baked Slips (January 7th); Boiled Ham (May 27th); Milk Rolls (August 26th); Rice Milk (June 18th).

LUNCHEON.—Liver and Bacon (January 17th); Treacle Tart (August 7th).

DINNER.—Boiled Brill and Anchovy Sauce (January 9th and July 17th); Sea Pie (March 14th); Potatoes (April 7th); Mashed Turnips (September 30th); Guest's Pudding (April 14th); Cheese (June 8th).

Things that must not be Forgotten.

1. If the boiled ham is almost finished, cut all that is left from the bone, then mince it, and put it between two plates to keep it moist till morning.

2. Follow the directions given Note 1, September 9th.

3. Boil the haricot beans (June 20th), drain them, and put them away. They are intended for haricot salad to-morrow night.

Sunday, September 20th.

Breakfast.	Dinner.	Tea.	Supper.
Ham Toast. Rizzared Haddock. Milk Rolls. Dry Toast. Brown and White Bread and Butter. Plum Porridge.	Soles, Filleted, Rolled, and Baked, with Brown Butter Sauce. Roast Saddle of Mutton. Venison Sauce. Scarlet Runners. Potatoes. Mountain Pudding Cheese.	Brown and White Bread and Butter. Milk Rolls. Apple Jelly. Rice Cake.	Cold Mutton. Haricot Salad. Sliced Tomatoes. Damson Pie. Cheese.

BREAKFAST.—Ham Toast (March 28th); Rizzared Haddock (September 10th); Milk Rolls (August 26th); Plum Porridge (August 31st).

DINNER.—Soles, Filleted, Rolled, and Baked (March 1st); Brown Butter Sauce (February 12th); Roast Saddle of Mutton (March 4th). *Venison Sauce.*—Melt two table-spoonfuls of red currant jelly, and mix with it a table-spoonful of port or claret. Heat in a small saucepan, and serve very hot. Potatoes (May 6th); Scarlet Runners (*see* Kidney Beans, August 16th). *Mountain Pudding.*—Butter a pie-dish and line it with ratafias, and grate the rind of a lemon over them. Mix two ounces of flour with a little cold milk to a smooth paste, and add cold milk gradually to make a pint. Boil this for ten minutes, stirring all the time. Pour the mixture gently over the ratafias, and soak for ten minutes. Beat the whites of the eggs to a stiff froth. Stir two ounces of sifted sugar to this, and add a little corn-flour or arrowroot to make the icing stiff. Arrange it on the pudding in five or six little mounds to imitate mountains, and put the pudding in the oven till these are lightly browned. Serve cold. This icing will take no harm if it is made two or three hours before it is wanted. Cheese (June 8th).

TEA.—Milk Rolls (August 26th) and Rice Cake (August 2nd).

SUPPER.—Haricot Salad (March 29th). *Sliced Tomatoes.*—Prepare these an hour or so before they are wanted. Rub a small dish with cut garlic or shalot; cut the tomatoes into thin slices, lay these on the dish, and sprinkle plenty of salt and a very little pepper over them. Pour a little oil and vinegar over all. Plum Pie (August 7th)

Things that must not be Forgotten.

1. As soon as the mutton leaves the table put it on a clean dish.
2. If any beans were left at dinner they can be added to the Haricot Salad.

September 21st.

Breakfast.	Luncheon.	Dinner.
Toasted Bacon	Shepherd's Pie.	Mulligatawney Soup.
Sardines.	Sweet Macaroni.	Cold Mutton and Salad, or, if preferred, Hash à la Sauce Piquante.
Milk Rolls.		
Dry Toast.		
Brown and White Bread and Butter.		Potatoes.
Oatmeal Porridge.		Vegetable Marrow.
		Boiled Batter Pudding.
		Cheese.

Marketing.

For the Day.—Half a pound of Macaroni; materials for Salad, if required; Potatoes; Vegetable Marrow.

For To-morrow.—A tin of Corned Beef; one pound of ripe Tomatoes.

BREAKFAST.—Toasted Bacon (January 19th); Sardines (January 12th); Milk Rolls (August 26th); Porridge (January 25th).

LUNCHEON.—*Shepherd's Pie* (January 12th).—This can be made of remnants of meat left from the sea pie. Sweet Macaroni (August 13th).

DINNER.—Mulligatawney Soup (January 16th); Salad (March 13th); Cold Meat à la Sauce Piquante (March 30th); Potatoes (April 7th); Vegetable Marrow (September 3rd); Boiled Batter Pudding (May 18th); Cheese (June 8th).

Things that must not be Forgotten.

1. Partially prepare a little tomato sauce, to be ready for breakfast to-morrow (July 15th). If preferred, the tomatoes can be baked (July 7th).

2. Stew the mutton bones in the stock made from the chicken bones; gravy soup can be made of it to-morrow.

September 22nd.

Breakfast.	Luncheon.	Dinner.
Eggs in Sunshine.	Veal Rolls.	Gravy Soup.
Corned Beef.	Compote of Plums.	Beef-steak and Mushroom Pie.
Hot Buttered Toast.		
Dry Toast.		Mashed Potatoes.
Brown and White Bread and Butter.		Newcastle Pudding.
		Cheese.
Bread and Milk.		

Marketing.

For the Day.—Two and a half or three pounds of lean Veal from the fillet or loin; a quarter of a pound of Suet for forcemeat; two pounds of Rump or Buttock Steak (January 1st); half an Ox Kidney; a quarter of a pint of Mushrooms; one pound of Plums; Potatoes.

For To-morrow.—A Cow Heel; hot Rolls for breakfast; four-pennyworth of Cream.

BREAKFAST.—Eggs in Sunshine (July 15th); Corned Beef procured yesterday; Bread and Milk (January 25th).

LUNCHEON.—Veal Rolls (May 5th); Compote of Plums (August 5th).

DINNER.—*Gravy Soup.*—Take any bones that there may be or stock made from bones, also two or three strips of bacon-rind scalded and scraped. Weigh them, and over three pounds of bones put two quarts of cold water. Bring the liquor to a boil and skim it well, then put into it two carrots scraped and cut into slices, two turnips, an onion stuck with two cloves, a bunch of parsley, a sprig of thyme, a bay-leaf, a blade of mace, and fifteen peppercorns. Simmer gently and skim carefully for two hours. Strain the stock, add salt to taste, and dissolve half a spoonful of Liebig's extract of meat in it. If it is not sufficiently browned, add a few drops of sugar browning; boil up again, and serve. If liked, two or three vegetables can be boiled separately and put into the soup. Beef-steak and Mushroom Pie (March 26th); Mashed Potatoes (May 12th); Newcastle Pudding (June 12th); Cheese (June 8th).

Things that must not be Forgotten.

1. Rough puff paste will be excellent for the beef-steak pie (May 29th).

2. Put a cupful of hominy to soak all night in cold water (February 10th).

September 23rd.

Breakfast.	Luncheon.	Dinner.
Eggs on the Dish.	Cow Heel, with Parsley Sauce.	Baked Halibut.
Corned Beef.	Custard Sippets.	Norman Haricot.
Hot Rolls.		Young Carrots.
Dry Toast.		Wyvern Puddings.
Brown and White Bread and Butter.		Cheese.
Boiled Hominy.		

Marketing.

For the Day.—Two or three pounds of lean Veal for the Norman haricot; three or four slices of Halibut (June 11th); Carrots; Potatoes.

For To-morrow.—Muffins (January 29th); Apples; a slice to be taken from the middle of the Canadian Ham bought September 17th; a pound of Plums for hydropathic pudding.

BREAKFAST.—Eggs on the Dish (December 7th); Corned Beef left from yesterday; Rolls (September 4th); Boiled Hominy (February 11th).

LUNCHEON.—Cow Heel, with Parsley Sauce (February 20th); Custard Sippets (June 10th).

DINNER.—Halibut Cutlets (June 23rd); Norman Haricot (August 24th); Young Carrots (July 6th); Wyvern Puddings (May 9th); Cheese (June 8th).

Things that must not be Forgotten.

1. Be careful to preserve any hominy that may be left; it can be fried for breakfast to-morrow. Also preserve any cold fish that may be left for fish cakes to-morrow.

2. Garlic comes into the market in September. It should be kept like shalots (August 11th).

September 24th.

Breakfast.	Luncheon.	Dinner.
Fried Ham.	Fish Cakes.	Boiled Hake.
Fried Eggs.	Treacle Pudding.	Caper Sauce.
Muffins.		Loin of Lamb, Braised.
Dry Toast.		Baked Tomatoes.
Brown and White Bread and Butter.		Apple Gâteau.
Fried Hominy.		Cheese.

Marketing.

For the Day.—Half a pound of good Beef Suet for the two puddings; about three pounds of Hake (August 7th); a Loin of Lamb (Marketing, May 22nd); a pound of Ripe Tomatoes; one pound of Apples; Parsley.

For To-morrow.—A tin of Collared Tongue (January 2nd); a Cow Heel for beef à la mode; a pint of Blackberries for the hydropathic pudding.

BREAKFAST.—Fried Ham (March 5th); Fried Eggs (March 5th); Muffins (January 30th); Fried Hominy (February 12th).

LUNCHEON.—Fish Cakes, made of cold potatoes and the remnants of halibut (January 13th); Treacle Pudding (March 28th).

DINNER.—*Boiled Hake.*—Proceed as for boiled salmon (July 5th); Caper Sauce (March 19th); Loin of Lamb, Braised (May 22nd); Baked Tomatoes (July 7th). *Apple Gâteau.*—Take some stale bread and rub it through a wire sieve. Weigh six ounces of the crumbs, and put with them six ounces of sugar, four ounces of suet chopped small, the grated rind of one lemon, half a pound of apples, weighed after being pared, cored, and chopped, two table-spoonfuls of flour, half a spoonful of baking-powder, the strained juice of two lemons, and three, or if preferred, two eggs. Put the mixture into a greased tin mould, and steam it for three hours (Treacle Pudding, March 28th). Let the pudding stand two or three minutes before turning it out, and serve it with sweet sauce (July 19th). Cheese (June 8th).

Things that must not be Forgotten.

1. Boil a table-spoonful of rice, as for curry (July 21st).

2. Take care of any hake that may be left; kedgeree can be made for breakfast to-morrow.

3. Make a hydropathic pudding (June 16th) for dinner to-morrow with the blackberries bought in the morning.

September 25th.

Breakfast.	Luncheon.	Dinner.
Kedgeree.	Beef à la Mode.	Haddock, Stuffed and Baked.
Rolled Tongue.	Jam Turnovers.	Curried Rabbit.
Hot Buttered Toast.		Boiled Rice.
Dry Toast.		Cauliflowers.
Brown and White Bread and Butter.		Hydropathic Pudding
Milk Porridge.		Custard.
		Cheese.

Marketing.

For the Day.—Two pounds of lean Beef, cut in a thick slice (February 14th); a good-sized fresh Haddock (September 4th); four ounces of Beef Suet; two moderate-sized Ostend Rabbits (January 24th); Cauliflowers; a pennyworth of German Yeast; Apples and Damsons for pies.

For To-morrow.—A tin of Sardines (January 12th); Sea Biscuits, if not in the house.

BREAKFAST.—Kedgeree (January 10th); Rolled Tongue (January 2nd); Milk Porridge (June 13th).

LUNCHEON.—Beef à la Mode (February 14th). *Jam Turnovers.*—These can be made with the pastry to-day. Take the trimmings of the pastry, and roll it out to the thickness of a quarter of an inch. Stamp it into rounds with a small saucer; spread a little jam upon one half, moisten the edges with water, and turn the other half over. Press the edges of pastry together, brush them over with water, sprinkle a little white sugar on the top, and bake on tins in a brisk oven. If liked, fresh fruit can be used instead of jam, but if it is of a kind that will not fall easily it should be partially stewed before being put into the pastry.

DINNER.—Haddock, Stuffed and Baked (September 4th); Curried Rabbit (July 16th); Boiled Rice (July 21st); Cauliflowers (April 25th); Hydropathic Pudding (June 16th); Custard (August 10th); Cheese (June 8th).

Things that must not be Forgotten.

1. Pastry is to be made to-day (April 17th): Apple and Damson or Blackberry Pies (August 7th), Jam Turnovers, above; also Teacakes (August 26th) and *Annie's Cake.*—Put two pounds of flour into a bowl, and mix with it a salt-spoonful of salt and six heaped tea-spoonfuls of baking-powder (August 2nd). Rub in one pound of butter or clarified dripping, and add a pound of sugar, half a pound of raisins, a pound and a half of currants, four ounces of mixed peel chopped small, and half a tea-spoonful of grated nutmeg. Moisten with four eggs well beaten and a little milk. Turn into tins lined with paper, and bake in a well-heated oven. This quantity will make two good-sized cakes.

2. Soak a cupful of green lentils all night in cold water.

September 26th.

Breakfast.	Luncheon.	Dinner.
Sardines.	Rabbit Gâteau.	Croûte au Pot.
Rolled Tongue.	Apple Pie.	Ribs of Beef, Boned and Rolled.
Teacakes.		Lentils.
Dry Toast.		Browned Potatoes.
Brown and White Bread and Butter.		Newmarket Pudding.
Marmalade.		Cheese.
Biscuits and Milk.		

Marketing.

For the Day.—Two Ribs of Beef, boned and rolled (September 8th); Potatoes. Buy also a piece of the Silverside of fresh Beef, weighing eight or ten pounds.

For To-morrow.—A pair of thick Soles (January 3rd); a dried Haddock; a couple of Ducks (July 1th); Ingredients for a Salad; Apples for apple mould; Parsley. If permitted, order a little Cream for supper to-morrow. A jar of Anchovy Paste.

BREAKFAST.—Sardines (January 12th); Rolled Tongue (January 2nd); Biscuits and Milk (June 14th).

LUNCHEON.—Rabbit Gâteau, made of the flesh of the cold rabbit picked from the bones (July 9th); Apple Pie (August 7th).

DINNER.—Croûte au Pot (May 25th); Ribs of Beef, Boned and Rolled (March 4th or 8th); Lentils (March 2nd); Browned Potatoes (October 18th); Newmarket Pudding (June 2nd); Cheese (June 8th).

Things that must not be Forgotten.

1. Make a little brine (January 13th), and lay the silverside of beef in it.

2. Stew the bones of the beef for stock (February 13th).

3. Pluck the ducks, and scald the giblets for gravy.

4. Partially prepare the rice and barley porridge for breakfast to-morrow (Note 6, June 15th).

5. With the remnants of the collared tongue make *Potted Tongue* for breakfast to-morrow. Take all that remains of the tongue, trim away and scrape off any dark unsightly portions. Cut the rest into thin slices and chop it small, then pound it in a mortar till quite smooth. Whilst pounding keep adding the flavouring ingredients, pepper and cayenne, salt, if required, mustard, and very little grated nutmeg, with dissolved fresh butter to make the preparation mellow. Press the meat into a small potting jar, cover it with dissolved butter, and it is ready.

6. Make the apple mould (September 15th).

Sunday, September 27th.

Breakfast.	Dinner.	Tea.	Supper.
Dried Haddock.	Sole, Fillets of, Sautés.	Brown and White Bread and Butter.	Cold Roast Ribs of Beef.
Potted Tongue.	Maître d'Hôtel Sauce.	Teacakes.	Salad.
Teacakes.	Roast Ducks.	Strawberry Jam.	Apple Mould.
Dry Toast.	Vegetable Marrow.	Annie's Cake	Cream Cheese.
Brown and White Bread and Butter.	Damson or Blackberry Pie.		
Marmalade.	Cream Cheese.		
Rice and Barley Porridge.			

BREAKFAST.—Dried Haddock (January 27th); Potted Tongue (Note 5, September 26th); Teacakes (February 14th); Rice and Barley Porridge (June 15th).

DINNER.—Fillets of Sole Sautés (January 4th); Maître d'Hôtel Sauce (May 6th); Roast Ducks (July 26th); Vegetable Marrow (September 3rd); Damson Pie (August 7th); Cheese (June 8th).

TEA.—Annie's Cake (September 25th).

SUPPER.—Salad (March 13th); Apple Mould (September 15th).

Things that must not be Forgotten.

1. Turn and rub the beef in the brine.
2. Put a cupful of white haricot beans to soak all night in cold water.

September 28th.

Breakfast.	Luncheon.	Dinner.
Anchovy Paste.	Beef Rissoles.	Haricot Purée.
Eggs in Brown Butter.	Macaroni Cheese.	Chicken, Fricasséed.
Teacakes.		Potatoes.
Dry Toast.		Beans.
Brown and White Bread and Butter.		Viennoise Pudding.
Honey.		Cheese.
Milk Toast.		

Marketing.

For the Day.—Half a pound of Macaroni (January 1st); one, or if the requirements of the family call for it, two plump Fowls; Potatoes; Beans.

For To-morrow.—Half a pound of Mushrooms; a pound of Blackberries or other fruit; half a pound of Bacon; Muffins (January 29th); bespeak an Ox Kidney; also order a freshly-killed young Goose. The breast should be plump, the skin white, the feet yellow and pliable. If a set of Chicken Giblets can be procured to-morrow, in addition to the goose giblets, the soup on Wednesday will be so much the better.

BREAKFAST.—Anchovy Paste, bought the day before yesterday; Eggs in Brown Butter (January 6th); Teacakes (February 14th); Milk Toast (June 17th).

LUNCHEON.—Beef Rissoles, made of the remnants of the cold ribs of beef (January 6th); Macaroni Cheese (March 20th).

DINNER.—Haricot Purée (March 9th); Chicken, Fricasséed (July 28th); Potatoes (May 12th); Beans (August 16th); Viennoise Pudding (July 6th); Cheese (June 8th).

Things that must not be Forgotten.
1. Stew the chicken bones for stock (February 13th).
2. It should be remembered that Viennoise pudding can be made with stale bread instead of fresh bread-crumbs.
3. Turn and rub the beef in the brine.

September 29th.

Breakfast.	Luncheon.	Dinner.
Anchovy Paste.	Stewed Ox Kidney.	Cod's Head and Shoulders.
Mushrooms and Bacon.	Stirabout Cheese.	Oyster Sauce.
Muffins.		Roast Goose, with Sage and Onion Stuffing.
Dry Toast.		Apple Sauce.
Brown and White Bread and Butter.		Savoury Pudding.
Honey.		Potatoes.
Compote of Blackberries, with Milk.		Cabbages.
		Baked Batter Pudding, with Jam.
		Cheese.

Marketing.
For the Day.—Cod's Head and Shoulders (January 6th); a dozen fresh Oysters, or, if preferred, a tin of Oysters; Ox Kidney, ordered yesterday; a little Indian Meal, if this is not in the house; Sage; Onions; Apples; a large fresh Lemon; Potatoes; Cabbages; a set of Giblets in addition to the goose giblets; if they can be procured; a pound of Blackberries or other fruit for juice.

For To-morrow.—A tin of Potted Grouse; Bloaters for breakfast; Rolls (September 3rd); Watercress.

BREAKFAST.—Anchovy Paste, served yesterday; Mushrooms and Bacon (September 8th); Muffins (January 30th); Compote of Fresh Fruit (August 5th), to be taken with bread and butter and milk.

LUNCHEON.—Stewed Ox Kidney (April 2nd), Stirabout Cheese (August 1st).

DINNER.—Cod's Head and Shoulders (December 6th); Oyster Sauce (October 16th). *Roast Goose, with Sage and Onion Stuffing:—* Pluck the goose carefully, remove the quill sockets, and singe off the little hairs that may remain by holding a lighted paper close to the skin. Draw the bird, and wash and wipe it inside and out; truss it firmly, with the legs and pinions fastened close to the body. Fill it with sage and onion stuffing, and put a fresh lemon in the centre of the stuffing. The lemon should have had the thin yellow rind taken off, leaving untouched the thick white skin that lies under it. This white pith will absorb the objectionable flavour from the onion, and should be taken out and thrown away before the goose is sent to table. Tie the openings of the bird securely, fasten a greased paper on the breast of the bird, put it neck downwards to a clear brisk fire, and baste it liberally with good dripping till done enough. It is a sign that it is done when the steam draws to the fire (March 4th). It must be *well* roasted. Lift it on a hot dish, take out the skewers, and remove the lemon; pour a little brown gravy round it, and send more gravy and apple sauce to table with it. A small goose will require to be roasted about an hour and three-quarters, a large one two hours or two hours and a half. *Brown Gravy for the Roast Goose.*—Slice an onion, chop it small, and fry it in a little butter till lightly browned. Pour over it a little more than a pint of stock made from bones (February 13th), and add a bunch of parsley, a blade of mace, six peppercorns, a spoonful of sugar browning (January 2nd), and a little salt. Mix a dessert-spoonful of flour to a smooth paste with a little cold water, and stew the gravy gently for an hour or more till it is good and of the thickness of cream. If there is no stock in the house, the giblets can be stewed for gravy (see Brown Gravy from Giblets, October 18th). *Sage and Onion Stuffing.*—Peel four large onions, put them into a saucepan with plenty of cold water, and let them boil till tender. Drain them well, chop them till small, and mix with them four table-spoonfuls of bread-crumbs, four fresh sage-leaves chopped, or six dry ones powdered, and a little pepper and salt. *Apple Sauce for Goose.*—Pare, core, and cut into small pieces two or three pounds of baking apples. The quantity must be regulated by the requirements of the family. Put them into a saucepan with two or three spoonfuls of water, cover them closely, and simmer very gently till the apples are quite soft. Shake the pan occasionally to keep the fruit from burning. When done enough, beat them to pulp, add a small piece of butter and a little sugar, but not enough to remove the acidity of the apples; serve in a tureen. *Savoury Pudding* is in some places considered a suitable accompaniment both to roast goose and roast pork. It is an excellent dish, besides being an economical one, seeing that it makes the goose "go" further. To make it, break into small pieces as much bread as will fill a pint basin, and pour over it as much boiling milk as it will absorb: that will be a little more than a pint. Cover the dish, and let the bread soak till soft. Beat it well with a fork, and remove any hard lumps there may be. Put with it four good-sized onions boiled and chopped, a quarter of a pound of chopped suet, a tea-spoonful of powdered sage, a table-spoonful of oatmeal, and plenty of pepper and salt. Mix thoroughly, and add two well-beaten eggs; add a little more milk if necessary; the pudding should be a *thick* batter. Pour it into a greased dripping-tin that it will cover to the thickness of about three-quarters of an inch, bake it in the oven for about half an hour, then put it under the goose, and turn it about till it is brightly browned all over; let it stand a minute, cut into squares, and serve it as Yorkshire pudding is served *with* the goose. It will take about an hour and a half in all to cook it properly. Potatoes (May 12th); Cabbages (June 4th); Baked Batter, with Jam (February 5th); Cheese (June 8th).

Things that must not be Forgotten.

1. If the giblets do not need to be stewed for gravy, clean them as soon as possible (February 1st), and put them into boiling water for five minutes. This will preserve them for awhile.
2. Make a sago mould for dinner to-morrow (October 8th).
3. Remember to keep the bloaters apart from all other food.
4. Preserve the liquor in which the cod was boiled.
5. Partially prepare the rice milk for breakfast to-morrow (Note 3, June 17th).
6. Turn and rub the beef in the brine.

September 30th.

Breakfast.	Luncheon.	Dinner.
Bloaters on Toast.	Hashed Goose.	Giblet Soup.
Potted Grouse.	Savoury Pudding made hot; wanting this, Custard Sippets.	Boiled Leg of Mutton.
Hot Rolls.		Caper Sauce.
Dry Toast.		Mashed Turnips.
Brown and White Bread and Butter.		Potatoes.
Watercress.		Cold Sago, with Fruit Juice.
Rice Milk.		Cheese.

Marketing.

For the Day.—A plump Leg of Mutton; Turnips; Potatoes; Parsley.
For To-morrow.—Three or four ripe Tomatoes for breakfast; order four-pennyworth of Cream for the soup to-morrow.

BREAKFAST.—Bloaters on Toast (March 24th); Potted Grouse (January 7th); Hot Rolls (September 4th); Rice Milk (June 18th).

LUNCHEON.—*Hashed Goose.*—Prepare the gravy for this dish as early as possible, as it should have time to get cold before being used. Divide what is left of the roast goose into neat pieces. Put the stuffing on a separate dish, and just before it is wanted make it hot in the oven. Draw off the skin of the goose, put it, with the bones and trimmings, into a saucepan, and pour over it the brown gravy left yesterday, with additional stock or water to make about a pint and a quarter. Add a sliced onion, half a blade of mace, and a bunch of parsley, and stew gently for about an hour. Mix a dessert-spoonful of flour to a smooth paste with a little cold water, stir this into the gravy, and boil the sauce a quarter of an hour longer till it is thick and smooth. Strain it, put it aside, and when cold remove the fat that rises to the surface. If there is not time for it to go cold, put it in a basin and set it in cold water, as that will make the fat rise to the surface quickly. Arrange the pieces of goose in a saucepan, sprinkle pepper and salt over them, pour as much gravy over them as will almost, but not quite, cover them, and heat the hash very gently by the side of the fire, without once allowing it to boil. When it is hot through, put the meat on a dish, pour the sauce over it, arrange the stuffing (made hot) in heaps round it, garnish with sippets, and serve. Savoury Pudding (September 29th); Custard Sippets (June 10th).

DINNER.—Giblet Soup (February 1st); Boiled Leg of Mutton (February 23rd); Caper Sauce (March 19th); Potatoes (April 7th); Mashed Turnips. *To Boil Turnips.*—Wash and brush the turnips in cold water. Pare away the thick skin, cutting down till a line can be seen a little way in. This outer part is stringy and bitter to the taste, and should be rejected. Throw the turnips into cold water till they are to be cooked. If very large, cut them in halves, throw them into plenty of boiling water, put the lid on the pan, and boil till tender. Take them up, put them into a stewpan, cover them with stock, add a tea-spoonful of sugar, and boil quickly till the sauce is reduced to a glaze. Shake the pan that the turnips may be coated with the glaze, and serve. The time they will take will depend upon their age; young turnips will be done enough in half an hour or less; fully-grown turnips will need about an hour's boiling; very old turnips no amount of boiling will make tender. *To Mash Turnips.*—Drain the boiled turnips, and squeeze the water from them, mash them well; put them into a saucepan with a small lump of butter, pepper and salt to taste, and a spoonful or two of cream or milk. Turn all over the fire till quite hot, and serve. *Parsnips* may be both boiled and mashed in the same way, but in preparing them, it will be necessary to scrape them only, not to pare them. Cold Sago, with Fruit Juice (October 8th); Cheese (June 8th).

Things that must not be Forgotten.

1. Preserve the liquor in which the leg of mutton was boiled.
2. Be careful that the pieces of goose do not boil in the gravy; they must simmer only.
3. Prepare a cupful of bread-crumbs for breakfast to-morrow.
4. Turn and rub the beef in the brine.

FRUITS SUITABLE FOR DESSERT IN SEPTEMBER.

Grapes, Plums, Melons, Mulberries, Blackberries, Nectarines, Apples, Apricots, Peaches, Pomegranates, Pears, Cob Nuts, Filberts, Walnuts, Hazel Nuts, Figs.

KETCHUP.

Mushroom Ketchup.—Choose mushrooms that are large, fully ripe, perfectly fresh, and gathered in dry weather. If they are taken in wet weather or soon after rain the ketchup will not keep. Cut off the ends of the stalks, look the mushrooms over, and throw aside any that are worm-eaten or decayed. Break the mushrooms into small pieces, put them into an earthen pan, and mix them well with salt, in the proportion of three-quarters of a pound of salt to a peck of mushrooms. Let them stand for three days, and turn them over every now and then with a wooden spoon. Drain the liquor from them without pressure, put the juice into a very clean stewpan, and let it simmer for half an hour. Pour it out and leave it till next day; strain it again, and with every pint of the liquor add a quarter of a tea-spoonful of mace, the same quantity of powdered ginger, and half the quantity of cayenne. Simmer half an hour longer. Let the ketchup stand till quite cold, pour it off free from sediment, put the clear liquor into perfectly dry, but cold, quart bottles, and put a dessert-spoonful of brandy into each bottle. Cork securely with new and sound corks, cut these level with the top of the bottle, and seal them over to thoroughly exclude the air. Sometimes a spoonful of Lucca oil is poured into the ketchup to preserve it. The mushrooms that were left after the clear liquor was poured off may have a little more salt sprinkled over them, then be put into a cool oven for a night, after which the juice can be well pressed from them, and this, with the sediment left after the juice was strained, can be boiled and flavoured highly with a quarter of an ounce each of black pepper, Jamaica pepper, cloves, and bruised ginger, with three anchovies chopped small and a spoonful of port to every quart of ketchup. This will afford a liquor which, though thick and inferior to the other in flavour, will yet be very useful for flavouring stews and hashes.

October 1st.

Breakfast.	Luncheon.	Dinner.
Fried Tomatoes.	Toad-in-the-Hole.	Oyster Soup.
Mutton Collops.	Cauliflower au Gratin.	Curried Mutton.
Buttered Toast.		Boiled Rice.
Dry Toast.		Vegetable Marrow.
Brown and White Bread and Butter.		Golden Pudding.
Marmalade.		Cheese.
Oatmeal Porridge.		

Marketing.

For the Day.—One pound of Buttock Steak for Toad-in-the-hole; a large Cauliflower; Vegetable Marrow; six ounces of Beef Suet; a tin of Oysters or a dozen fresh Oysters.

For To-morrow.—A dried Haddock; order a fine Ox-tail.

BREAKFAST.—*Mutton Collops, with Tomatoes.*—Cut half a dozen thin slices from the cold mutton. Break an egg into a plate and beat it lightly. Draw the slices of mutton through it and toss them in the bread-crumbs, which have been mixed with a tea-spoonful of flour and a little pepper and salt. Melt a slice of butter in a frying-pan, put in the collops, and cook them very gently. When they are brown upon one side turn them to the other. Cut the tomatoes into slices about half an inch thick. Take up the collops, put them on a hot dish, and fry the tomatoes in the same fat. In three or four minutes they will be done. Put them round the collops, sprinkle a few bread-crumbs over them, and serve. Porridge (January 25th).

LUNCHEON.—Toad-in-the-Hole (January 15th); Cauliflower au Gratin (April 25th).

DINNER.—*Oyster Soup.*—Take the liquor in which the cod was boiled, or, if this is not available, the liquor in which the leg of mutton was boiled can be used. Throw a small onion, a little salt, and about a dozen peppercorns into it, and boil it till it is considerably reduced. Skim it well and strain it. Put about a quart of it back into the stewpan, with a bay-leaf and the strained liquor from a tin of oysters. The oysters themselves may be put on a dish in the oven to be made hot. Stir in two table-spoonfuls of flour mixed to a smooth paste with water. Let the liquor boil, put with it the cream ordered yesterday, which has been boiled separately, and add a tea-spoonful of anchovy essence. Place the oysters in a hot soup tureen, pour the soup over them, and serve. If fresh oysters are allowed for this soup, put the liquor from the shells with the quart of stock, beard the oysters, and stew the beards to extract the flavour. Strain, thicken, flavour, and boil the soup as before directed. Just before serving the soup hold a metal strainer in the boiling stock to make it hot, put the oysters in this, let the liquor boil around them for about three seconds, then turn them into the soup tureen, and pour the soup over them. *Curried Mutton.*—Use the remains of the cold boiled leg of mutton for this dish (May 26th). Boiled Rice (July 21st); Vegetable Marrow (September 3rd); Golden Pudding (May 4th); Cheese (June 8th).

Things that must not be Forgotten.

1. Turn and rub the beef in the brine.
2. Boil up the liquor in which the leg of mutton was boiled.

October 2nd.

Breakfast.	Luncheon.	Dinner.
Dried Haddock.	Stewed Ox-tail.	Fillets of Sole Sautés.
Potted Grouse.	Brown Betty.	Maître d'Hôtel Sauce.
Hot Buttered Toast.		Veal Stew Piquante.
Dry Toast.		Bacon Rolls.
Brown and White Bread and Butter.		Potato Snow.
Honey.		Cabbage.
Bread and Milk.		Wyvern Puddings.
		Cheese.

Marketing.

For the Day. Ox-tail, ordered yesterday; a pair of thick Soles; from two to three pounds of lean Veal from the loin or fillet; Apples; small Cucumber; a Lettuce; Potatoes; Cabbage; Parsley; a pennyworth of German Yeast; Plums.

For To-morrow.—Small Soles, "Slips," for breakfast; order a pound and a half of Calf's Liver.

Breakfast.—Dried Haddock (January 27th); Potted Grouse (January 7th); Bread and Milk (January 25th).
Luncheon.—Stewed Ox-tail (May 8th); Brown Betty (November 26th).
Dinner.—Fillets of Sole Sautés (January 4th); Maître d'Hôtel Sauce (May 6th). *Veal Stew Piquante.*—Cut the veal into neat pieces about an inch square. Peel, slice, and flour the cucumber, and shred the lettuce finely. Season the veal with pepper and salt, flour it well, and fry it in a little butter or clarified dripping until it is lightly browned. Fry with it the cucumber and the lettuce, and turn the ingredients over in the pan to keep them from burning. Put them into a saucepan, pour boiling stock or water over to barely cover them, and simmer very gently indeed for an hour, or till the veal is tender. Add a few drops of lemon-juice, and serve very hot. When they are in season, a pint of freshly-shelled green peas stewed with the meat is an improvement. Bacon Rolls (July 19th); Potato Snow (April 7th); Cabbage (June 4th); Wyvern Puddings (May 9th); Cheese (June 8th).

Things that must not be Forgotten.

1. Turn and rub the beef in the brine.
2. Make a Plum Gâteau for luncheon to-morrow (*see* Cherry Gâteau, July 11th).
3. Pastry is to be made to-day (April 17th): Apple Pie, Damson Pie (August 7th); also Milk Rolls (August 26th) and Lemon Cheesecakes (August 18th).
4. Put a cupful of hominy to soak all night in cold water (February 10th).

October 3rd.

Breakfast.	Luncheon.	Dinner.
Baked Slips.	Liver and Bacon.	Mock Turtle Soup.
Buttered Eggs.	Baked Potatoes.	Civet of Rabbit.
Milk Rolls.	Plum Gâteau.	Potatoes.
Dry Toast.		French Beans.
Brown and White Bread and Butter.		Rice Gâteau, with Compote of Blackberries.
Boiled Hominy.		Cheese.

Marketing.

For the Day.—Liver, ordered yesterday; half a pound of Bacon; a tin of Mock Turtle Soup; one good-sized, or if necessary, a couple of Rabbits (January 24th); Potatoes; French Beans; Blackberries to serve with the rice; a dozen fresh Herrings, half soft and half hard roes.

For To-morrow.—Three or four pounds from the middle of a good-sized Cod (January 1st); a pair of plump Fowls; materials for Stuffing; half a pound of Ratafias; a tin of Sardines; a quarter of a pound of German Sausage; Potatoes; Vegetable Marrow; Capers, Gherkins, and Potatoes will be wanted for the Russian salad.

BREAKFAST.—Baked Slips (January 7th); Buttered Eggs (January 16th); Milk Rolls (August 26th); Boiled Hominy (February 11th).

LUNCHEON.—Liver and Bacon (January 17th); Baked Potatoes (May 4th); Plum Gâteau (July 11th).

DINNER.—Mock Turtle Soup, from tinned soup (March 15th); Civet of Rabbit (December 8th); Potatoes (May 12th); French Beans (August 16th). *Rice Gâteau.*—Take four ounces of best Carolina rice and wash it well; if this is done it will not be so likely to burn. Put it in a saucepan with as much water as will cover it, bring it to the boil, and simmer it gently till the water is absorbed, then pour upon it a pint of milk, throw in the thinly-cut rind of half a lemon, add a lump of butter, and simmer gently till the rice is quite soft. Put it in a basin, and take out the lemon-rind. Beat the rice well with the back of a wooden spoon, sweeten it, and let it go cold. Break two eggs, and put the whites on a separate dish. Stir the yolks unbeaten into the rice. Butter a plain mould, throw a handful of finely-grated bread-crumbs into it; whisk the whites of the eggs to a firm froth, at the last moment stir them lightly into the rice, pour the mixture into the mould, and bake in a hot oven. It will be ready in a little less than an hour. Let it stand a minute or two, turn it out, and serve. The Compote of Blackberries (August 5th) may either be served in a glass dish separately, or may be poured round the gâteau. Cheese (June 8th).

Things that must not be Forgotten.

1. Turn and rub the beef in the brine.
2. Preserve any hominy that may be left; it can be fried for breakfast to-morrow.
3. Pickle the fresh herrings bought this morning (August 20th).
4. Pluck the fowls carefully, ready for to-morrow, and leave them in a cool larder. Preserve and dry the feathers (Note 1, February 28th).
5. If there is no mayonnaise in the house, make a little for the Russian salad to-morrow night (August 30th).

Sunday, October 4th.

Breakfast.	Dinner.	Tea.	Supper.
Pickled Herrings.	Baked Cod.	Brown and White Bread and Butter.	Russian Salad.
Boiled Eggs.	Roast Fowls.	Black Currant Jam.	Fruit Pie.
Milk Rolls.	Brown Gravy.	Milk Rolls.	Cheese.
Dry Toast.	Bread Sauce.	Lemon Cheesecakes.	
Marmalade.	Potato Snow.		
Brown and White Bread and Butter.	Vegetable Marrow.		
Fried Hominy.	Lêche Crème.		
	Cheese.		

BREAKFAST.—Pickled Herrings (August 20th); Boiled Eggs

(January 5th); Milk Rolls (August 26th); Fried Hominy (February 12th).

DINNER. — Baked Cod (*see* Baked Hake, September 1st); Roast Fowls (June 30th); Brown Gravy, made from the fowl giblets (October 18th); Bread Sauce (October 18th); Potato Snow (April 7th); Vegetable Marrow (September 3rd); Lèche Crème (May 7th); Cheese (June 8th).

TEA.—Lemon Cheesecakes (August 18th).

SUPPER.—Russian Salad (April 5th); Fruit Pie (August 7th).

Things that must not be Forgotten.

1. If the legs of the fowls can be preserved, devil them for breakfast to-morrow (January 14th).
2. Turn and rub the beef in the brine.
3. Put a cupful of white haricot beans to soak all night in cold water.
4. Preserve the chicken bones; they will be a valuable addition to any stock there may be in the house.
5. Turn the herrings in the vinegar.

October 5th.

Breakfast.	Luncheon.	Dinner.
Devilled Drumsticks.	Australian Meat, Cold.	Victoria Soup.
Pickled Herrings.	Baked Potatoes.	Boiled Beef.
Sardines.	Plain Rice Pudding.	Carrots.
Milk Rolls.		Turnips.
Dry Toast.		Haricot Beans.
Brown and White Bread and Butter.		Potatoes.
		Cocoa-nut Pudding.
Honey.		Cheese.
Corn-flour Milk.		

Marketing.

For the Day.—A four-pound tin of Australian Meat; Carrots; Turnips; Potatoes; a small tin of Desiccated Cocoa-nut; Damsons or Blackberries for a pudding.

For To-morrow.—*Partridges* are now in full season, but they are so uncertain in price that they can scarcely be said to be at the disposal of the strictly economical housekeeper. They should be well kept before being cooked; if dressed when freshly killed they would be flavourless and hard. The length of time that they are to be kept, and their condition when cooked, must depend, however, upon the weather and the taste of those who have to eat them. Young birds are to be preferred, with dark coloured bills and yellow legs. Muffins (January 29th).

BREAKFAST.—Devilled Drumsticks (January 14th); Pickled Herrings (August 20th); Sardines—the remains of the tin opened on Sunday night; Milk Rolls (August 26th); Corn-flour Milk (June 19th).

LUNCHEON. — Australian Meat, Cold (February 4th); Baked Potatoes (May 4th); Plain Rice Pudding (February 24th).

DINNER.—Victoria Soup, the chicken bones to be stewed in the stock (February 9th).—*Boiled Beef* (February 23rd).—Wash and boil the beef that has been in pickle. Carrots (July 6th); Turnips (September 30th); Haricot Beans (June 20th); Potatoes (May 12th); Cocoa-nut Pudding (August 8th); Cheese (June 8th).

Things that must not be Forgotten.

1. Take the pieces of marrow from the beef bone in as large pieces as possible; marrow toast can be made of them for breakfast to-morrow (January 21st).
2. Put a cupful of green lentils to soak all night in cold water.
3. Make a mock calf's head mould with the remains of the Australian meat (April 20th).
4. Make a hydropathic pudding for dinner to-morrow with the fresh fruit bought this morning (June 16th).
5. Boil the brine and let it go cold (January 13th).

October 6th.

Breakfast.	Luncheon.	Dinner.
Marrow Toast.	Scotch Collops.	Lentil Soup.
Calf's Head Mould.	Baked Apples.	Cold Beef.
Muffins.		Salad.
Dry Toast.		Roast Partridges.
Brown and White Bread and Butter.		Brown Gravy.
		Brown Crumbs.
Honey.		Bread Sauce.
Milk Porridge.		Potato Snow.
		Hydropathic Pudding.
		Cheese.

Marketing.

For the Day.—A pound and a half of Buttock Steak (January 1st); materials for a Salad; Potatoes; Apples; a square piece of the thin Flank of Beef, weighing about eight pounds.

For To-morrow.—A tin of Prawns; Watercress.

BREAKFAST.—Marrow Toast (January 21st); Calf's Head Mould April 20th) made yesterday; Muffins (January 30th); Milk Porridge (June 13th).

LUNCHEON.—Scotch Collops (January 9th); Baked Apples (February 9th).

DINNER.—Lentil Soup (April 1st); Cold Beef cooked yesterday; Salad (March 13th). *Roast Partridge.*—In England partridges are almost always roasted. Pluck and draw the birds, and wipe them inside and out. Cut off the head and truss the bird, with the thighs drawn close to the breast, and the legs erect. If liked, tie a slice of fat bacon over the breast to keep it moist, but be careful to remove this before sending the bird to table. Spit the partridge, put it down to a clear bright fire, and begin to baste it at once with good dripping, and baste it every two or three minutes. Small birds will be done enough in about twenty-five minutes, large birds will require thirty-five minutes. Five minutes before the bird is taken up substitute butter for the dripping in basting, take off the bacon, and dredge a little flour on the breast. Serve it *immediately;* if it is kept hot in the oven or anything of that kind it will most likely be spoilt; send good brown gravy and bread sauce (October 18th), and bread-crumbs on a separate dish, to table with it. *Gravy for Game* should be *good*, and will of course need to be made a long time before the birds are put down to the fire. It is therefore worth while to allow a little gravy beef for this purpose, and if any trimmings of chicken bones are at hand so much the better. Take half a pound of lean beef (or half veal and half beef may be used), cut them eat into small pieces, put it in a saucepan with a slice of butter and a minced onion, and move it about till brown; put with it a bay-leaf, two cloves, six peppercorns, a bunch of parsley, a piece of carrot, and a pinch of bruised celery-seed tied in muslin; add also a dessert-spoonful of corn-flour mixed to a smooth paste with water. Stir the sauce till it boils, cover it closely, draw it to the side, and simmer it gently for an hour or more till it is strong. Strain, let it cool, free it from fat, add a little sugar browning if necessary, and salt to taste. When wanted, boil it, put a spoonful or two of sherry into it, pour a little of it round the birds, and serve the rest in a hot tureen. *Bread-crumbs for Game.*—These can, for convenience, be made some time before they are required, then made hot in the oven. Take some stale crumb of bread, rub it through a wire sieve, and crumble it. There must be plenty of crumbs to cover a small dish. Then take a piece of butter about the size of an egg, throw it into an enamelled stewpan, put in the crumbs, and stir them till they begin to colour. Draw them back, and keep stirring till they are brown. Put them on blotting-paper before the fire to free them from grease, and toss them about with a fork. When heating them for use, they must not be allowed to remain in the oven till they are hard, or they will be spoilt. Bread Sauce (October 18th); Potato Snow (April 7th); Hydropathic Pudding made yesterday (June 16th); Cheese (June 8th).

Things that must not be Forgotten.

1. Carefully preserve the bones and trimmings of the game, with any gravy that may be left; excellent soup can be made of it for to-morrow.

2. The remains of the cold beef can be made into Bubble and Squeak for luncheon to-morrow.

3. Put the flank of beef into the brine.

October 7th.

Breakfast.
Ox Eyes.
Calf's Head Mould.
Hot Buttered Toast.
Dry Toast.
Brown and White Bread and Butter.
Watercress.
Biscuits and Milk.

Luncheon.
Bubble and Squeak.
Sweet Macaroni.

Dinner.
Game Soup.
Loin of Mutton, Boned and Rolled.
Potatoes.
Kidney Beans.
Lemon Dumplings.
Cheese.

Marketing.

For the Day.—A large Cabbage; half a pound of Macaroni; about four pounds of the best end of a Loin of Mutton; the butcher should be asked to bone the joint. Potatoes; Kidney Beans; six ounces of Beef Suet.

For To-morrow.—A tin of Prawns; a small sugar-cured Ham; Mustard and Cress; the Fillet of the rump of Beef (Marketing, January 2nd); Fresh Rolls for breakfast (September 3rd); order four-pennyworth of Cream for horse-radish sauce; Sea Biscuits.

BREAKFAST.—Ox Eyes (June 5th); Calf's Head Mould left from yesterday (April 20th); Biscuits and Milk (June 14th).

LUNCHEON.—Bubble and Squeak (January 22nd); Sweet Macaroni (August 13th).

DINNER.—Game Soup (February 16th); Loin of Mutton, Boned and Rolled (April 22nd); Potatoes (May 12th); Kidney Beans (August 16th). *Lemon Dumplings.*—Follow the recipe given for lemon pudding (August 12th). Instead of putting the mixture into one large mould, butter a number of cups or small moulds. Lay a greased paper on the top of each one, and put them into a shallow stewpan, and pour boiling water round them to reach half-way up the sides. Put on the cover, and steam the puddings for three-quarters of an hour or more, according to the size of the moulds. The dumplings should be set in the middle. Let them stand a minute, turn them upon a dish, sift white sugar upon them, and send wine sauce (July 19th) to table with them. Cheese (June 8th).

Things that must not be Forgotten.

1. Turn and rub the beef in the brine.
2. Boil three or four pounds of the ham for breakfast to-morrow (May 27th).
3. Partially prepare the rice and barley porridge for breakfast. (Note 6, June 15th).
4. Make a *Rice Mould* for dinner to-morrow. Wash six ounces of Carolina rice, and put it into a brown earthenware dish, with a pint and a half of milk, and a piece of butter the size of a small nut. Place a cover on the top, and put the dish in a dripping-tin with boiling water in it. Set it in the oven, and keep the water boiling round it till the rice is quite tender and has absorbed the milk. If

necessary, add a little more milk—this will depend on the quality of the rice. It will take two or three hours. Add sugar to taste, and any seasoning that may be preferred—almond, lemon, or vanilla. The rice should be stiff, but not hard. Beat it well with a wooden spoon till it is quite smooth, then pack it lightly in a damp mould, and put it in a cool place all night. When it is to be served, turn it upon a glass dish, and pour round it a little lemon or other fruit syrup (March 19th), or a compote of any fresh fruit (August 5th). If preferred, garnish it with jam, or with orange garnish and syrup (December 6th). If more convenient, the rice can be simmered in a stewpan, but it is much better done in this way.

5. Brush the fillet of beef over with a table-spoonful of vinegar, sprinkle pepper and salt on it, and hang it in a cool, airy place.

October 8th.

Breakfast.	Luncheon.	Dinner.
Tinned Prawns.	Mutton Croquettes.	Gurnet Stuffed and Baked.
Boiled Ham.	Stuffed Tomatoes.	Fillet of Beef.
Breakfast Rolls.	Rice and Cheese.	Horse-radish Sauce.
Dry Toast.		Yorkshire Pudding.
Brown and White Bread and Butter.		Potatoes.
Mustard and Cress.		Vegetable Marrow.
Biscuits and Milk.		Rice Mould.
		Cheese.

Marketing.

For the Day.—Two or more Gurnets (February 17th). Gurnets are at their best in October; half a dozen ripe Tomatoes; Potatoes; Vegetable Marrow; a young root of Horse-radish.

For To-morrow.—A tin of Sardines (January 12th); a pound of Blackberries or Damsons for fruit juice.

BREAKFAST.—Tinned Prawns (February 7th); Ham boiled yesterday (Note 4, May 27th); Rolls (September 4th); Biscuits and Milk (June 14th).

LUNCHEON.—Mutton Croquettes (Rissoles, January 6th); Stuffed Tomatoes (July 23rd); Rice and Cheese (February 18th).

DINNER.—Baked Gurnet (February 17th); Fillet of Beef (February 11th); Horse-radish Sauce (December 3rd); Potatoes (May 6th); Vegetable Marrow (September 3rd); Rice Mould made yesterday (October 7th); Cheese (June 8th).

Things that must not be Forgotten.

1. Turn and rub the beef in the brine.
2. Make a *Sago Mould, with Fruit Juice*, for luncheon to-morrow. —Put the fruit into a brown jar, sprinkle a little moist sugar on it,

and put it in a large stewpan half full of boiling water or into a cool oven till the juice flows freely. Wash a tea-cupful of sago (large sago is to be preferred), soak it for an hour in a pint and a half of cold water, then put it into a saucepan, and stir it till it boils. Draw it back and simmer it gently, stirring it frequently till it looks clear and is thick. Put half a pint of the fruit juice with it, boil together for a few minutes, and add sugar to taste. Pour the preparation into a damp mould, and leave it in a cool place till to-morrow. When wanted, turn it upon a glass dish, sift white sugar over it, and pour milk or, if it will be allowed, cream round it.

October 9th.

Breakfast.	Luncheon.	Dinner.
Sardines.	Shepherd's Pie.	Boiled Brill.
Boiled Ham.	Sago, with Fruit Juice.	Dutch Sauce.
Hot Toast.	Milk or Cream.	Veal and Ham Pie.
Dry Toast.		Potatoes.
Brown and White Bread and Butter.		Cabbage.
		Pancakes.
Marmalade.		Cheese.
Milk Toast		

Marketing.

For the Day.—A good-sized Brill (January 3rd and January 9th); two pounds of lean Veal from the best end of the Neck or the Breast; six ounces of mild Ham; three or four Mushrooms; Potatoes; Cabbage; German Yeast.

For To-morrow.—Half a dozen small Soles, "Slips," for breakfast.

BREAKFAST.—Sardines (January 12th); Ham (boiled the day before yesterday); Milk Toast (June 17th).

LUNCHEON.—Shepherd's Pie, made of the remains of the roast beef (January 12th); Sago, with Fruit Juice (October 8th).

DINNER.—Boiled Brill (January 9th); Dutch Sauce (May 14th); Veal and Ham Pie (April 29th); Potatoes (April 7th); Cabbage (June 4th); Pancakes (February 24th); Cheese (June 8th).

Things that must not be Forgotten.

1. Turn and rub the beef in the brine.
2. Pastry is to be made to-day: Veal and ham pie (April 29th), open jam tart (August 7th), lemon cheesecake (August 18th), light tea-buns (August 14th), teacakes (August 26th).
3. Partially prepare the rice milk for breakfast (Note 3, June 17th).

October 10th.

Breakfast.	Luncheon.	Dinner.
Baked Slips.	Tripe à la Coutance.	Crécy Soup.
Ham Toast.	Lemon Cheesecakes.	Roast Leg of Pork.
Teacakes.		Tomato Sauce.
Dry Toast.		Potatoes.
Honey.		Greens.
Brown and White Bread and Butter.		Apple Gâteau.
Rice Milk.		Cheese.

Marketing.

For the Day.—A pound and a half of the thin part of dressed Tripe; a fresh Leg of Pork. Pork is best for roasting when it weighs six or seven pounds. Half a dozen fresh Tomatoes; Potatoes; Greens; Apples.

For To-morrow.—A moderate-sized Turbot; a pint of Shrimps; a Shoulder of Mutton, not too fat (January 17th); Mint; Potatoes; Beans; materials for a Salad.

BREAKFAST.—Baked Slips (January 7th); Ham Toast (March 28th); Teacakes (February 14th); Rice Milk (June 18th).

LUNCHEON.—Tripe à la Coutance (October 23rd); Lemon Cheesecakes (August 18th).

DINNER.—Crécy Soup (January 5th). *Roast Leg of Pork.*—Cut through the skin, but no deeper, in strips half an inch apart. Rub dripping or salad oil all over it before putting it to the fire, and baste it well whilst it is being roasted (March 4th). When it is about two parts cooked brush it over again with oil. Pour a little brown gravy over it, and send more to table in a tureen. Apple sauce (September 29th) or tomato sauce (July 15th) are suitable accompaniments. Pork should be well cooked, and therefore from twenty to twenty-five minutes should be allowed for each pound of meat. In some parts of the country savoury pudding (September 29th) is served with roast pork. Sage and onion are sent to table in a separate dish. Mashed Potato Mould (October 23rd); Greens (June 4th); Apple Gâteau (September 24th); Cheese (June 8th).

Things that must not be Forgotten.

1. Turn and rub the beef in the brine.
2. Put the roast pork on a clean dish as soon as it leaves the table.
3. Make a corn-flour blancmange for supper to-morrow night (June 15th).

Sunday, October 11th.

Breakfast.	Dinner.	Tea.	Supper.
Savoury Eggs.	Turbot and Shrimp Sauce.	Brown and White Bread and Butter.	Cold Mutton.
Cold Pork.	Roast Shoulder of Mutton.	Greengage Jam.	Salad.
Brawn Sauce.	Mint Sauce.	Light Tea-Buns.	Pickle.
Teacakes.	Potatoes.		Open Jam Tart.
Dry Toast.	Beans.		Corn-flour Blancmange.
Brown and White Bread and Butter.	Cabinet Pudding.		
Honey.	Cheese.		
Biscuits and Milk.			

BREAKFAST.—Savoury Eggs (January 1st); Cold Pork cooked yesterday; Brawn Sauce (January 15th); Teacakes (February 14th); Biscuits and Milk (June 14th).

DINNER.—Boiled Turbot (June 7th); Shrimp Sauce (January 30th); Roast Shoulder of Mutton (March 4th); Mint Sauce (March 25th); Potatoes (April 7th); Beans (August 16th); Cabinet Pudding (July 12th); Cheese (June 8th).

TEA.—Light Tea-Buns (August 14th).

SUPPER.—Salad (March 13th); Open Jam Tart (August 7th); Corn-flour Blancmange (June 15th).

Things that must not be Forgotten.

1. Turn and rub the beef in the brine.
2. Put a cupful of green lentils to soak all night in cold water.
3. Partially prepare the rice and barley porridge (Note 6, June 15th).

October 12th.

Breakfast.	Luncheon.	Dinner.
Fried Ham.	Scalloped Fish.	Lentil Soup.
Fried Eggs.	Wyvern Puddings.	Tomato Beef.
Teacakes.		Potatoes.
Dry Toast.		Town Pudding.
Brown and White Bread and Butter.		Cheese.
Rice and Barley Porridge.		

Marketing.

For the Day.—Three pounds of lean Beef cut in steaks; Half a dozen ripe Tomatoes; Potatoes; Apples; six ounces of firm Suet.

For To-morrow.—A tin of Collared Tongue (January 2nd); Anchovies; small Salad; a plump young Fowl, or two Fowls if required.

BREAKFAST.—Fried Ham, a slice taken from the ham bought on the 7th of October (March 5th); Fried Eggs (March 5th); Teacakes (February 14th); Rice and Barley Porridge (June 15th).

LUNCHEON.—Scalloped Fish: take the remains of the Turbot,

and follow the recipe given for Cod (January 7th); Wyvern Puddings (May 9th).

DINNER.—Lentil Soup (April 1st). *Tomato Beef.*—Cut the tomatoes into slices; butter the inside of a stewpan, cover the bottom with sliced tomatoes, lay on a portion of the beef, and put tomatoes and beef in alternate layers until both are used. Cover the pan closely, place it at the side of the fire, and let its contents simmer gently for an hour and a half. Add pepper and salt, and serve on a hot dish. Potatoes (May 6th); Town Pudding (December 3rd); Cheese (June 8th).

Things that must not be Forgotten.
1. Turn and rub the beef in the brine.
2. Cleanse the small salad, and lay it on a cloth to drain, to be ready for breakfast; also fillet the anchovies, and put the fillets between two dishes.
3. Pluck the fowl and hang it in a cold larder; dry the feathers (February 28th); clean the giblets, and afterwards throw them into boiling water for five minutes. This will help to keep them.

October 13th.

Breakfast.	Luncheon.	Dinner.
Anchovies and Hard-boiled Eggs. Collared Tongue. Hot Buttered Toast. Dry Toast. Brown and White Bread and Butter. Milk Toast.	Ham and Macaroni. Custard Sippets.	Herrings and Mustard Sauce. Fricassee of Fowl. Potatoes. General Favourite Pudding. Cheese.

Marketing.
For the Day.—Half a pound of Macaroni; Fresh Herrings. One for each person and one over (August 25th); Potatoes; half a pint of Mushrooms, or a small tin of Champignons for the Fowl; four-pennyworth of Finger Biscuits; Quinces (*see* Note 4).

For To-morrow.—Watercress; Muffins (January 29th).

BREAKFAST.—Anchovies and Hard-boiled Eggs (January 18th); Collared Tongue (January 2nd); Milk Toast (June 17th).

LUNCHEON.—Ham and Macaroni (April 3rd); Custard Sippets (June 10th).

DINNER.—Herrings and Mustard Sauce (September 15th); Fricassee of Fowl (July 28th); Potato Snow (April 7th); General Favourite Pudding (May 17th); Cheese (June 8th).

Things that must not be Forgotten.
1. Turn and rub the beef in the brine.
2. Preserve any chicken that may be left.

3. Prepare the rice milk (Note 3, June 17th).

4.—Quinces come into the market in October. This fruit mixed with apples makes a most delicious pie or pudding. It can be preserved as follows:—Peel the fruit and divide into quarters. Weigh it and allow three pounds of sugar and a gill of water to five pounds of fruit. Put sugar, water, and fruit into pint jars, tie brown paper on the top, place the jars in boiling water and simmer gently for three hours. Let the fruit go cold, tie it down tightly, and mix a portion with apples when pies are being made. Quinces thus prepared will not keep very long.

October 14th.

Breakfast.	Luncheon.	Dinner.
Collared Tongue.	Chicken Kromeskies.	Potato Purée.
Eggs in Brown Butter.	Baked Plum Pudding.	Boiled Rabbits.
Muffins.		Onion Sauce.
Dry Toast.		Rashers of Bacon.
Watercress.		Potatoes.
Rice Milk.		Cabbage.
		Chocolate Pudding.
		Cheese.

Marketing.

For the Day.—A couple of plump young Ostend Rabbits (January 21th); half a pound of Bacon in rashers; Potatoes; Cabbage; a cake of French Chocolate; a small plump Leg of Mutton, to be put in pickle for sour mutton; a quarter of a pound of suet.

For To-morrow.—Three or four Bloaters; order the muscle of the Leg of Beef (January 27th); a freshly-killed young Hare may be bought to-day (January 8th), and hung in a cool airy place till Sunday week, or any more convenient time.

BREAKFAST.—Collared Tongue left from yesterday; Eggs in Brown Butter (January 6th); Muffins (January 30th); Rice Milk (June 18th).

LUNCHEON.—Chicken Kromeskies, made of the remains of the Fricasseed Chicken (July 29th); Baked Plum Pudding (February 25th).

DINNER.—Potato Purée (January 26th); Boiled Rabbits (March 6th). *Onion Sauce.*—Take four good-sized onions, peel them, cut them into quarters, put them into a saucepan with plenty of cold water to cover them, and let them boil gently till quite tender. Take them up, drain them well, and chop them small. Boil three-quarters of a pint of milk with a thin slice of lemon-rind. Mix a dessertspoonful of flour to a smooth paste with water, add this to the milk, and stir the sauce till it boils. Put in the onions, take out the lemon-rind, add pepper and salt to taste, and move the saucepan to the side of the fire to keep the sauce hot till it is wanted. If the lemon flavour is objected to, the rind can be omitted, but many people regard it as an improvement. Rolled Bacon (July 19th); Potatoes Mashed (May 12th); Cabbage (June 4th); Chocolate Pudding (July 24th); Cheese (June 8th).

Things that must not be Forgotten.
1. Turn and rub the beef in the brine.
2. Make a pickle (Note 3, March 19th), and put the leg of mutton into it.
3. Preserve any cold rabbit that may be left. Also take care of the liquor the rabbits were boiled in. There should be excellent stock from the chicken bones and the rabbit liquor.
4. Put a cupful of hominy to soak all night in cold water.
5. Keep the bloaters apart from all other food.
6. Pot the remains of the collared tongue for breakfast to-morrow (Note 5, September 26th).

October 15th.

Breakfast.	Luncheon.	Dinner.
Bloaters on Toast.	Rabbit Gâteau.	Victoria Soup.
Potted Tongue.	Suet Pudding, with Jam.	Muscle of Beef Stewed with Vegetables.
Hot Buttered Toast.		Potatoes.
Dry Toast.		Stone Cream.
Brown and White Bread and Butter.		Cheese.
Honey.		
Boiled Hominy.		

Marketing.
For the Day.—Half a pound of firm Kidney Suet; Potatoes.
For To-morrow.—Three or four plump Sheep's Kidneys; half a pound of Bacon in rashers; Rolls for Breakfast (September 3rd); order to be sent in three or four plump young Pigeons, trussed for boiling.

BREAKFAST.—Bloaters on Toast (March 24th); Potted Tongue made yesterday (September 26th); Boiled Hominy (February 11th).

LUNCHEON.—Rabbit Gâteau (July 9th); Suet Pudding, with Jam (May 13th).

DINNER.—Victoria Soup (February 9th); Beef à la Jardinière (March 17th); Potatoes (May 6th); Stone Cream (July 1st); Cheese (June 8th).

Things that must not be Forgotten.
1. Turn and rub the beef in the brine.
2. Turn and rub the mutton in the pickle.
3. Put a large cupful of haricot beans to soak all night in cold water.
4. If any hominy is left, preserve it; if not, soak a tea-cupful in cold water. Hominy cake is to be made to-morrow.

October 16th.

Breakfast.	Luncheon.	Dinner.
Broiled Kidneys and Bacon. Hot Rolls. Dry Toast. Brown and White Bread and Butter. Oatmeal Porridge.	Stewed Pigeons. Rice and Cheese.	Cod's Head and Shoulders. Oyster Sauce. Roast Leg of Mutton. Haricot Beans. Browned Potatoes. Hayrick Puddings. Cheese.

Marketing.

For the Day.—About six pounds of Cod's Head and Shoulders (see Note 4 below); a tin of Oysters, or a dozen large fresh Oysters; a well-hung Leg of Mutton (January 8th); Potatoes; French Beans; a pennyworth of German Yeast; Pork, (for fresh sausage (March 18th), or a pound of good Pork Sausages; Quinces; this fruit mixed with apples makes one of the most delicious of pies.
For To-morrow.—Watercress; three-pennyworth of Cream for the Bisque Soup.

BREAKFAST.—Broiled Kidneys (January 29th); Toasted Bacon (January 19th); Hot Rolls (September 4th); Porridge (January 25th).

LUNCHEON.—Stewed Pigeons (August 4th); Boil French Beans separately, and substitute them for the peas in this recipe. Rice and Cheese (February 18th).

DINNER.—Cod's Head and Shoulders (December 6th). *Oyster Sauce* (with fresh oysters).—In opening the oysters, be careful to preserve all the liquor. Put this liquor into a saucepan with a third of a pint of milk, take off the beards of the oysters, and throw them into the liquor. Simmer gently for a little while to draw the flavour from the beards, then strain the milk into a basin. Melt an ounce of butter in a small stew-pan, mix half an ounce of flour smoothly with it, stir in the flavoured milk. Keep stirring till the sauce boils, then add a tea-spoonful of anchovy sauce. Have ready a stewpan with plenty of boiling water in it. Make a metal strainer hot by holding it in the water for a minute. Put in the oysters, and let them remain in the water for about three seconds. Turn them into a very hot sauce tureen, pour the sauce over them, and serve immediately. If a table-spoonful of cream may be permitted, the sauce will be much richer. *Oyster Sauce* (with tinned oysters).—Open the tin, strain off the liquor, and put the oysters on a dish in the oven to get hot. Mix the liquor with a quarter of a pint of milk, melt two ounces of butter in a saucepan, stir in an ounce of flour, and add the milk. When the sauce boils put in a tea-spoonful of anchovy sauce and the oysters. Serve in a hot tureen. It is probable that the contents of a whole tin will not be required for the sauce. When this is the case, half a tin may be used with half the liquor, and scalloped oysters (April 27th) for breakfast or luncheon may be made of the remainder. If covered entirely with the liquor the oysters will keep for a day or two, even though the tin is opened. Roast Leg of Mutton (March 4th); Haricot Beans (June 20th); Browned Potatoes (October 18th); Hayrick Puddings (March 19th); Cheese (June 8th).

Things that must not be Forgotten.

1. Turn and rub the mutton in the pickle.
2. Boil the beef that has been in pickle (February 23rd).
3. Pastry is to be made to-day (April 17th). Apple and Quince pies (October 13th); also sausage rolls with the trimmings of the pastry (November 6th); Vienna bread (August 26th), and *Hominy Cake*.—Take a breakfast-cupful of boiled hominy, a breakfast-cupful of flour, a pinch of salt, a slice of butter melted, half a tea-spoonful of baking powder, and two eggs. Work the mixture with the fingers till smooth, put it in a greased mould, and bake in a quick oven.
4. When the family is moderately large, it is economical to buy a large whole cod instead of part of one, then cut off the tail end, salt it, and the second day fry it in slices. A whole fish can generally be bought for twopence a pound less than the head and shoulders, or the middle of the fish.
5. Boil the remainder of the ham (Note 4, May 27th).

October 17th.

Breakfast.	Luncheon.	Dinner.
Devilled Eggs.	Minced Mutton.	Bisque Soup.
Sausage Rolls.	Small Suet Dumplings.	Mutton à la Sauce Piquante.
Vienna Bread.		Potatoes.
Dry Toast.		Vegetable Marrow.
Brown and White Bread and Butter.		Newcastle Pudding.
Watercress.		Cheese.
Corn Flour Milk.		

Marketing.

For the Day.—A quarter of a pound of Suet for dumplings; a moderate-sized Crab (August 18th); a spoonful of Lobster spawn from the fishmonger; Potatoes; Vegetable Marrow.

For To-morrow.—A pair of Soles (January 3rd); a pair of fine Fowls (June 29th); materials for Forcemeat; ingredients for Salad (March 13th); Potatoes; Celery; a quarter of a pound of Bacon for Bacon rolls; Mustard and Cress for breakfast; Tomatoes for Tomato Sauce if liked.

BREAKFAST.—Devilled Eggs (February 27th); Sausage Rolls made yesterday (November 6th); Vienna Bread (August 26th); Corn Flour Milk (June 19th).

LUNCHEON.—Minced Mutton (January 20th). Neat slices can be cut from the cold leg of mutton for dinner, and the broken remnants can be minced for luncheon. *Small Suet Dumplings.*—Mix the pudding according to the recipe given (May 13th). Let it be very stiff; divide it into balls about the size of an egg. Drop these from the point of a fork into fast-boiling water, and boil them about half an hour. Serve them with the mutton, or with sugar or jam if preferred.

DINNER.—*Bisque Soup.*—Crack the claws of the crab, and take out all the meat, tear it into shreds with two forks, and put it aside, between two dishes, in a cool place. Pick all the rest of the meat from the crab, and put with it half its bulk of rice which has been boiled separately for the purpose. Pound it well, put stock or boiling water with it to make it of the consistency of very thick cream, and rub it through a hair sieve. When wanted, make it very hot, but do not let it reach the boiling point; boil the cream ordered yesterday, and stir it into the soup, add a spoonful of lobster butter (June 7th), to colour the soup, and serve. If lobster butter cannot be had, the soup will taste as good as if it were there, but it will not look so well. Mutton à la Sauce Piquante (March 30th); Potatoes, Mashed (May 12th); Vegetable Marrow (September 3rd); Newcastle Pudding (June 12th); Cheese (June 8th).

Things that must not be Forgotten.

1. Turn and rub the mutton in the pickle.
2. Glaze the beef that was boiled yesterday (March 21st).
3. Pluck the fowls, and hang them in a cool larder; clean the giblets (February 1st), and throw them into boiling water for five minutes. Sauce for the birds can be made of them for to-morrow.
4. Dry the feathers of the poultry (Note, February 28th).
5. Buy three or four pounds of fresh pork (January 6th); the spring or belly piece, or the hand, will be most suitable for the purpose. Make a brine by dissolving a pound of salt and half an ounce of salt prunella, pounded, in a gallon of water. Let this boil for one minute, and when cold put in the pork. It can be taken out and boiled in four days if liked, or if preferred it can remain in the pickle for ten days, then be hung up to dry. The brine can be used again and again if it is boiled occasionally. When a scum is seen on the top, it is getting weak, and should be boiled with a little more salt. Pork is very good boiled from the pickle. To boil it, see April 25th.
6. Preserve any fish that may be left. It can be warmed for breakfast.
7. Make custard blancmange for dinner to-morrow (August 4th).

Sunday, October 18th.

Breakfast.	Dinner.	Tea.	Supper.
Scalloped Cod.	Sole à la Horly.	Brown and White Bread and Butter.	Cold Beef.
Boiled Ham.	Tomato Sauce.	Greengage Jam.	Salad.
Vienna Bread.	Roast Fowls.	Hominy Cake.	Apple and Quince Pie.
Dry Toast.	Bacon Rolls.		
Brown and White Bread and Butter.	Brown Gravy.		
Mustard and Cress.	Bread Sauce.		
Bread and Milk.	Browned Potatoes.		
	Stewed Celery.		
	Custard Blancmange.		
	Lemon Syrup.		
	Cheese.		

BREAKFAST.—Scalloped Cod (January 7th); Ham boiled the day

before yesterday (Note 4, May 27th); Vienna Bread (August 26th); Bread and Milk (January 25th).

DINNER.—*Sole à la Horly.*—Fish, fowl, and the whiter sorts of game are excellent dressed à la Horly. When once the process is understood, it is not very difficult, and it possesses this advantage; one sole dressed thus will go as far as a pair of soles dressed in the ordinary way. Fillet the sole, and divide the fillets into fingers about an inch wide. Squeeze the juice of a large fresh lemon into a plate, and put with it a bunch of parsley and a slice of onion, both chopped small, and a little pepper and salt. Lay the pieces of fish in this, and let them lie for a couple of hours; turn them about two or three times in the marinade. Drain them, and dry them well by rolling them in a cloth. Have ready a little frying-batter (July 29th); this will be better if it is made two or three hours before it is wanted. Half fill a stewpan with clarified dripping (February 19th). Put it on the fire, and let it remain till it is so hot that it is quite still, and a blue smoke rises from it. Take the pieces of sole one at a time, dip them into the batter, take them out with a table-spoon, and turn the fish with as much batter as can be held in a spoon into the boiling fat. Let it remain for less than a minute, till it is a light golden brown colour. Have close at hand a dish covered with blotting-paper or kitchen-paper, put the fish fried in batter on this to free it from grease, take out any little pieces of batter that may remain with a skimmer, and finish all the pieces of fish in the same way. Pile on a dish, cover with a napkin, and garnish with fried parsley. Tomato Sauce (July 15th) is the proper accompaniment to this dish, but it may be well dispensed with. Roast Fowls (June 30th). *Brown Gravy made from Giblets.*—Clean the giblets thoroughly (February 1st). Peel and mince finely two small onions; fry these and the giblets in a slice of butter or dripping, and turn them about till all are brightly browned. Put them into a stewpan with a bunch of parsley, a sprig of thyme, a bay leaf, a blade of mace, two cloves, eight peppercorns, and two or three strips of bacon-rind, scalded and scraped. Pour over all rather more than a pint of hot stock or water. Cover closely, and stew gently for about an hour and a half. Thicken the gravy with a little brown thickening (January 6th); or failing this, by stirring into it a dessert-spoonful of corn flour mixed smoothly with a little cold water; add some sugar browning if necessary. Strain the gravy, free it from fat, pour a little of it round the birds, and send the rest to table in a hot tureen. *Bread Sauce.*—Prepare some bread-crumbs by rubbing stale bread through a wire sieve. Supposing there is half a pint of bread-crumbs, put them into about half a pint of milk. As much milk is required as the bread will soak up. Cover for ten minutes, then put the bread and milk into a saucepan with a whole onion skinned and six peppercorns. Stir the sauce over the fire till it boils, then add a pinch of salt and about an ounce of butter, and stir till the butter is dissolved. Take out the onion and peppercorns, add four table-spoonfuls of milk, or cream if it may be permitted, boil once more, and serve. It is a mistake to make this sauce very long before it is wanted. *Browned Potatoes.*—Wash and peel the potatoes, and partly boil them in the usual way (April 7th). When they are half cooked, take them up, drain them, and put them in the dripping-tin under the meat. Let them remain until they are cooked through, and equally browned all over. They will take about three-quarters of an hour. If it is not convenient to put them under the meat, they may be baked in a brisk oven till brown, being basted occasionally with dripping. Put them on kitchen paper to free them from fat before serving them. Stewed Celery (December 2nd); Custard Blancmange made yesterday (August 4th); Lemon Syrup (March 19th); Cheese (June 8th).

TEA.—Hominy Cake (October 16th).

SUPPER.—Beef prepared yesterday; Salad (March 13th); Apple and Quince Pie made the day before yesterday.

Things that must not be Forgotten.

1. Turn and rub the mutton in the pickle.
2. If the legs of the fowls have been left, prepare them for devilling at breakfast (January 14th).
3. Be sure to preserve the bones and trimmings of the fowls; they will be a valuable addition to the stock-pot.

October 19th.

Breakfast.	Luncheon.	Dinner.
Devilled Drumsticks.	Pressed Beef.	Croûte au Pot.
Boiled Ham.	Lettuce Salad, with Tomatoes.	Stewed Steak.
Vienna Bread.		Mashed Potatoes.
Dry Toast.	Stewed Cheese.	Vegetable Marrow.
Brown and White Bread and Butter.		Apple Pie.
Marmalade.		Cheese.
Milk Porridge.		

Marketing.

For the Day.—A fine Lettuce; Onions; a Small Salad; three ripe Tomatoes; Potatoes; Vegetable Marrow; three pounds of tender Steak (Marketing, January 1st), to be cut evenly and about an inch and a half thick.

For To-morrow.—Order a Neck of Mutton, not too fat; Muffins (January 29th); Sea Biscuits, if not in the house.

BREAKFAST.—Devilled Drumsticks (January 14th); Ham, served yesterday; Vienna Bread (August 26th); Milk Porridge (June 13th).

LUNCHEON.—Pressed Beef, served yesterday; Lettuce Salad with Tomatoes (March 13th): two or three tomatoes are a most excellent addition to a salad; Stewed Cheese (May 5th).

DINNER.—Croûte au Pot (May 25th); Stewed Steak (January 31st); Mashed Potatoes (May 12th); Vegetable Marrow (September 3rd); Apple Pie (August 7th); Cheese (June 8th).

Things that must not be Forgotten.

1. Turn and rub the mutton in the pickle.
2. Preserve any steak that may be left; rissoles or croquettes can be made of it for luncheon to-morrow.
3. Make a ground rice mould for to-morrow (August 7th).
4. Cut off all the meat from the ham bone and pot it for breakfast (April 15th).

October 20th.

Breakfast.	Luncheon.	Dinner.
Boiled Eggs.	Rissoles.	Milk Soup.
Potted Ham.	Ground Rice Mould.	Baked Rabbit, with Bacon.
Muffins.		Potatoes.
Dry Toast.		Boiled Onions.
Brown and White Bread and Butter.		Cottage Plum Pudding.
Honey.		Cheese.
Biscuits and Milk.		

Marketing.

For the Day.—One or, if required, two fresh young Rabbits; half a pound of Bacon in rashers; Potatoes; Onions; six ounces of firm Beef Suet.

For To-morrow.—Rolls (September 3rd); a dozen fresh Herrings with soft roes (August 25th); a bottle of Red Currants for the hydropathic pudding; Watercress; order a fine Ox-tail.

BREAKFAST.—Boiled Eggs (January 5th); Potted Ham (April 15th); Muffins (January 30th); Biscuits and Milk (June 14th).

LUNCHEON.—Rissoles made of the remains of the stewed steak (January 6th); Ground Rice Mould (August 7th).

DINNER.—Milk Soup (January 3rd); Baked Rabbit, with Bacon (July 8th); Potato Snow (April 7th); Boiled Onions (October 28th); Cottage Plum Pudding (June 6th); Cheese (June 8th).

Things that must not be Forgotten.

1. Turn and rub the mutton in the pickle.
2. Make a hydropathic pudding with the bottled red currants for dinner to-morrow (June 16th).
3. Partially prepare the rice and barley porridge for breakfast to-morrow (Note 6, June 15th).
4. Pickle the herrings bought this morning (August 20th).
5. Put a cupful of green lentils to soak all night in cold water.

October 21st.

Breakfast.	Luncheon.	Dinner.
Pickled Herrings Potted Ham. Hot Rolls. Dry Toast. Brown and White Bread and Butter. Watercress. Rice and Barley Porridge.	Stewed Ox-tail. Jam and Bread Pudding (Economical).	Sole au Gratin. Sour Mutton. Lentils. Mashed Potatoes. Hydropathic Pudding. Cheese.

Marketing.

For the Day.—A fine Ox-tail ordered yesterday; a pair of thick Soles (January 3rd); Potatoes.

For To-morrow.—Mustard and Cress for breakfast.

BREAKFAST.—Pickled Herrings (August 20th), prepared yesterday; Potted Ham (April 15th); Hot Rolls (September 4th); Rice and Barley Porridge (June 15th).

LUNCHEON.—Stewed Ox-tail (May 8th); Jam and Bread Pudding (Economical) (February 23rd).

DINNER.—Sole au Gratin (May 3rd); Sour Mutton (March 29th); Mashed Potatoes (May 12th); Lentils (March 2nd); Hydropathic Pudding (June 16th) made yesterday; Cheese (June 8th).

Things that must not be Forgotten.

1. Turn the herrings in the vinegar.
2. Boil the pork that has been in pickle (April 25th).
3. Preserve the brine in which the pork was pickled.

October 22nd.

Breakfast.	Luncheon.	Dinner.
Herrings. Pickled Pork. Hot Buttered Toast. Dry Toast. Brown and White Bread and Butter. Mustard and Cress. Milk Toast.	Scotch Collops. Macaroni à la Milanaise.	Oyster Soup. Cold Mutton. Salad. Potato Snow. Apple Fritters. Custard. Cheese.

Marketing.

For the Day.—A pound and a half of Buttock Steak (January 1st); half a pound of Macaroni; a tin of preserved Oysters, or a dozen fresh Oysters; two pounds of the Shin of Beef to make stock for clear soup; ingredients for Salad; Potatoes; Apples; two or three ripe Tomatoes; a fresh Ox-Tongue.

For To-morrow.—A jar of Anchovy Paste. Pheasants are now in season. Like partridges and grouse they are very uncertain in price, but may sometimes be obtained on reasonable terms. Especially is this the case when they are quite ready for the spit. They should never be cooked when fresh, although the length of time that they should be kept must depend upon individual taste. In French kitchens the rule is that the bird is not ready for the spit until, having been hung up by the tail, it drops down. In this condition it would most likely be considered too far gone for the taste of ordinary people. The degree of highness which the bird has obtained may be discovered by examining the vent. If the bird when sent in is sufficiently high it can be cooked to-morrow. If it wants hanging longer it must be kept for a few days.

BREAKFAST.—Herrings (August 20th); Pickled Pork, boiled yesterday; Milk Toast (June 17th).

LUNCHEON.—Scotch Collops (January 9th). *Macaroni à la Milanaise* (July 22nd).

DINNER.—Oyster Soup (October 1st); Cold Mutton, left yesterday; Salad (March 13th); Potato Snow (April 7th). *Apple Fritters.*—Cut the apples into rounds as thin as possible, stamp out the cores, pare away the skin, put them in a dish, pour over them a wineglass of brandy, and sprinkle sugar and grated lemon-rind over them. Let them lie in this for an hour. Half fill a good-sized saucepan with clarified dripping. Make it quite hot, and when it is still and a blue smoke rises from it, dip each slice separately into the batter, take it out in a table-spoon, and dip it with the batter that is in the spoon with it into the boiling fat. Turn it over lightly with a fork, and when the fritter is crisp and lightly browned it is done enough. Put it on kitchen paper to free it from grease, and fry all the slices in the same way. Sift white sugar on, and serve. Peaches, oranges, and pine-apples are frequently prepared in the same way, and are excellent. Peaches are cut into quarters, oranges into halves, and pine-apples into slices, the skins being removed in every instance before the fruit is put into the brandy or liquor. To make *Frying Batter* for fruit fritters, see July 29th; Custard (August 10th); Cheese (June 8th). *Lamb's Sweetbreads.*—Wash and trim the sweetbreads overnight, and boil them gently till firm in stock. To improve their taste, boil with them four young onions and half a blade of mace. They will take about half-an-hour, or perhaps a little less. Drain them well. Thus far they may be prepared overnight. In the morning flour them, brush them with egg, and roll them in breadcrumbs seasoned with pepper and salt. Fry three or four rashers of bacon very slowly (January 2nd). When done, put them on a hot dish, put a piece of butter in the pan with the fat, and fry the sweetbreads until browned. Lamb's sweetbreads form a superior breakfast dish.

Things that must not be Forgotten.

1. Partially prepare the rice milk for breakfast to-morrow (Note 3, June 17th).
2. Free the ox-tongue from slime (July 13th).
3. Make stock from the fresh meat bought this morning (July 30th).

October 23rd.

Breakfast.
Anchovy Paste.
Pickled Pork.
Hot Buttered Toast.
Dry Toast.
Brown and White Bread and Butter.
Marmalade.
Rice Milk.

Luncheon.
Tripe à la Coutance.
Rice Pudding.

Dinner.
Clear Soup, with Savoury Custard.
Roast Pheasant.
Brown Gravy.
Bread Sauce.
Potato Mould.
Red Cabbage.
General Favourite Pudding.
Cheese.

Marketing.

For the Day.—One pound and a half of the thin part of Tripe. Thick tripe is generally preferred, but it would not answer for the mode of cooking intended. Half a pound of lean Bacon; half a pound of lean Beef to clarify the soup; a fine Red Cabbage; Potatoes; four-pennyworth of Sponge Biscuits; four Mushrooms; German Yeast.

For To-morrow.—Watercress.

BREAKFAST.—Anchovy Paste, bought yesterday; Pickled Pork, served yesterday; Rice Milk (June 18th).

LUNCHEON.—*Tripe à la Coutance.*—The French artisans' way of dressing tripe. Wash the tripe in cold water, put it into a saucepan with cold water to cover it, bring it to the boil, then take it out and dry it well in a soft cloth. Cut it into pieces two inches wide and four inches long, and cut the bacon into thin slices the same size as the tripe. Mince finely a shalot, a small onion, and two or three sprigs of parsley. Take the tripe and sprinkle pepper and salt, and a little of the mince over each slice; lay a slice of bacon on the top, roll the two together, and be careful that the ends are straight and even, so that the little rolls can stand on end. Fasten the rolls either with twine or with a needle and thread. Put a pint of stock or water in a stewpan, wash and scrape a carrot, and cut it into pieces with a small onion, and four mushrooms. Stand the tripe round the inside of the stewpan, put the vegetables in the middle with two or three peppercorns. Bring the liquor to a boil, draw the pan back, and let its contents simmer gently for two hours. Take up the tripe and strain the gravy. Rub the carrot through a wire-sieve and keep the pulp hot, but do not shake it up, as it will look like red rice when it has just fallen. Melt an ounce of butter in a small stewpan, mix an ounce of flour smoothly with it, and stir it over the fire till it is brown. Add the strained stock and stir the sauce till it boils, then flavour with a spoonful of ketchup, and a few drops of lemon-juice. Place the pieces of tripe round a dish, and pour the sauce round the edge. The appearance of this dish is much improved if cooked vegetables are placed in the centre of the tripe. It must be remembered that the twine must not be removed from the rolls as soon as they are taken from the stock, or they will fall. When tripe is not so nice as usual, it should be rubbed with salt before being boiled in cold water. Plain Rice Pudding (February 24th).

DINNER.—Clear Soup, with Savoury Custard (July 30th). *Roast Pheasant.*—Pheasants may be trussed, roasted, and served in the same way as partridges (October 6th). A pheasant would need to roast from three-quarters to one hour. Gravy (October 6th), Bread Sauce (October 18th). *Potato Mould.*—Mash potatoes in the usual way (May 12th), then press them lightly into a handsome mould that has been well buttered inside in every part. Turn the mould out, and brown it equally all over either in the oven or before the fire. If liked, the mould can have brown bread raspings sprinkled over the inside of the mould before the potatoes are put in it. Mashed potatoes may also be pressed with a small mould, then browned before being served. *Red Cabbage, Stewed.*—Excellent served with game of all kinds or with fried pork chops. Cut up a firm moderate-sized red cabbage as for pickling. Wash and drain it, and put it in a stewpan with a little pepper and salt and two ounces of butter. Cover the stewpan closely, and stew the cabbage for two hours General Favourite Pudding (May 17th); Cheese (June 8th).

Things that must not be Forgotten.

1. Wash the tongue quickly in cold water, and put it into the brine in which the beef was pickled.

2. If it can be done, leave the legs of the pheasant untouched and prepare them to be devilled for breakfast to-morrow. Pheasant's legs are excellent devilled (January 14th).

3. Pastry is to be made to-day (April 17th): Apple and quince pies (August 7th), lemon cheesecakes (August 18th); also soda cake (August 14th), and Sally Lunns (August 26th).

4. Put a cupful of white haricot beans to soak all night in cold water.

October 24th.

Breakfast.	Luncheon.	Dinner.
Devilled Drumsticks.	Salmi of Pheasant.	Baked Hake.
Savoury Eggs.	Custard Sippets.	Brown Butter Sauce.
Sally Lunns.		Ribs of Beef, Boned and Rolled.
Dry Toast.		Haricot Beans.
Brown and White Bread and Butter.		Mashed Potatoes.
Watercress.		Wyvern Puddings.
Porridge.		Cheese.

Marketing.

For the Day.—Three or four slices of Hake: the slices to be cut about half an inch thick; two ribs of Beef, boned and rolled (September 8th); Celery; Potatoes; Apples.

For To-morrow.—Four Bloaters; a tin of Collared Tongue (January 2nd); a pair of thick Soles; Potatoes; Celery; a pound of Rump Steak to serve with the hare; materials for a Salad; a quarter of a pound of Beef Suet and two ounces of raw lean Ham for forcemeat; Sardines for Monday.

BREAKFAST.—Devilled Drumsticks (January 14th); Savoury Eggs (January 1st); Sally Lunns (June 4th); Porridge (January 25th).

LUNCHEON.—*Salmi of Pheasant.*—Cut the remains of the game into very neat pieces, and lay these, free from every particle of skin and fat, between two dishes till wanted. Collect all the bones and trimmings of the game, and put them, with a bay-leaf and one or two strips of bacon-rind, to stew in any gravy that may have been left. If there is no gravy, put the bones into ordinary stock, and add some strips of bacon-rind, an onion stuck with two cloves, a piece of carrot, a smaller piece of turnip, two or three sticks of celery, a bunch of parsley, and three peppercorns. Stew till the gravy is strong and pleasantly flavoured. Strain it and, if necessary, boil it again with a small piece of brown thickening (January 6th), or, wanting this, with a tea-spoonful of corn-flour mixed smoothly with cold water and a few drops of browning (January 2nd). Make the gravy hot, season it with salt and pepper if required, put in the pieces of game, let them heat gently by the side of the fire, and on no account allow them to reach the boiling point. Ten minutes before they are to be served put a wine-glassful of good brown sherry or Madeira with them. Arrange the birds neatly in the centre of the dish, let the sauce boil up, and pour it on them, and garnish with crumbs of bread fried in hot fat and drained. Custard Sippets (June 10th).

DINNER.—Baked Hake (September 1st); Brown Butter Sauce (February 12th). *Ribs of Beef, Boned and Rolled.*—Roast the beef, and serve it with gravy in the usual way (March 4th); Haricot Beans (June 20th); Mashed Potatoes (May 12th); Wyvern Puddings (May 9th); Cheese (June 8th).

Things that must not be Forgotten.

1. Make the apple mould for dinner to-morrow (September 15th).
2. Keep the bloaters apart from all other food.
3. For convenience the hare may be skinned and emptied to-day.
4. If any haricot beans are left, they may with advantage be reserved for the salad to-morrow evening.
5. Be sure that the ingredients for hare forcemeat are in the house (*see* recipe, October 25th).

Sunday, October 25th.

Breakfast.	Dinner.	Tea.	Supper.
Bloaters on Toast. Collared Tongue. Sally Lunns. Dry Toast. Brown and White Bread and Butter. Honey. Corn-Flour Milk.	Soles — Filleted, Rolled, and Baked. Maître d'Hôtel Sauce. Jugged Hare. Red Currant Jelly. Potao Mould. Stewed Celery. Apple Mould. Custard. Cheese.	Brown and White Bread and Butter. Soda Cake. Lemon Cheesecakes.	Cold Beef, Roasted Yesterday. Salad. Apple and Quince Pie. Cheese.

BREAKFAST.—Bloaters on Toast (March 24th); Collared Tongue, bought yesterday (January 2nd); Sally Lunns (June 4th); Corn-flour Milk (June 19th).

DINNER.—Soles—Filleted, Rolled, and Baked (March 1st); Maître d'Hôtel Sauce (May 6th). *Jugged Hare.*—This is really the best way of cooking a hare. Make the hare forcemeat (*see* recipe given below). Skin and empty the hare, and wipe it inside and out with a damp cloth. Cut it into neat pieces about the size of a small egg, and turn these about in a frying-pan over the fire with a little dripping till they are equally browned all over. Drain them from the fat, and put them into a wide-mouthed earthen jar; pour a glass of port upon them, cover the jar closely, and let the hare soak in the wine for twenty minutes. Cut the steak, bought yesterday, into very thin slices two inches long and an inch and a half wide. Spread a little forcemeat upon each slice, roll it neatly, and fasten with a small skewer. Fry the rolls in the fat till they also are brown, then put them with the hare. Have ready some good bone stock, strongly flavoured with onions. Pour a little of this into the pan in which the hare and the pieces of meat were fried, scrape the bottom to obtain all the flavour and gravy, pour the stock over the hare, adding more stock to cover it entirely. Throw in six cloves, two bay-leaves, an inch of stick cinnamon, the juice of half a lemon, and a little pepper and salt. Sprinkle a table-spoonful of forcemeat over all. Put the lid again on the jar, place it up to its neck in a stewpan of boiling water, and keep the water boiling round it for an hour and a half. Make all that remains of the forcemeat into balls the size of marbles. Fry them in hot fat, and put them into the jar a few minutes before the hare is served. Thicken the gravy with a little arrowroot. Put the pieces on a hot dish, place the forcemeat balls round, pour a little gravy over the meat, and send the rest to table in a tureen. Send red currant jelly as an accompaniment. If more convenient, the jar containing the hare can be placed in the oven in a dripping-tin filled with boiling water, care being taken to keep up the supply of water round the jar. When this plan is adopted the hare will need to be cooked two hours and a half instead of one hour and a

Y

half. The jar chosen for this purpose must be of a good size, as it is important that the pieces of hare should not be closely packed, but that there should be plenty of room for the gravy to run between the pieces of meat. It should have a tightly-fitting cover belonging to it, and if this is not at hand, two or three folds of brown paper must be tied over it. Where the family is small the beef in this recipe may be omitted. It will, however, make the hare go much further, and excellent soup can be made of the remains. To make *Hare Forcemeat*, mince finely a quarter of a pound of beef suet and two ounces of raw lean ham. Mix, and add a tea-spoonful of chopped parsley and a tea-spoonful of mixed savoury herbs. If dried herbs are used, such as are sold in bottles at the grocer's, two tea-spoonfuls will be required. Add about two inches of thin lemon-rind, chopped very small, five ounces of fine bread-crumbs, and a little pepper and salt. Bind the mixture together with the yolks of two eggs. Potato Mould (October 23rd); Stewed Celery (December 2nd); Apple Mould (September 15th), made yesterday; Custard (August 10th); Cheese (June 8th).

TEA.—Soda Cake (August (14th); Lemon Cheesecakes (August 18th).

SUPPER.—Beef, served October 24th; Salad (March 13th); Apple and Quince Pie (August 7th).

Things that must not be Forgotten.

1. Carefully preserve every bit of the hare that is left; the remnants can be turned to good purpose to-morrow.

2. When putting the collared tongue in the larder, lay the slice first cut off on the top. This will keep the meat from getting dry.

October 26th.

Breakfast.	Luncheon.	Dinner.
Sardines.	Rissoles.	Hare Soup.
Collared Tongue.	Hasty Pudding.	Fricassee of Chicken.
Sally Lunns.		Potato Snow.
Dry Toast.		Salsify.
Brown and White Bread and Butter.		Brown Bread Pudding
Marmalade.		Cheese.
Bread and Milk.		

Marketing.

For the Day.—One or, if required, two plump Fowls; half a pint of Mushrooms, or, failing these, a small tin of Champignons; Potatoes; Salsify. This vegetable is something like horseradish in appearance, but white. It is sold in bundles, and comes into the market in October and remains till May. It is not very well known, although much liked by those who do know it.

For To-morrow.—A four-pound tin of Australian Meat.

BREAKFAST.—Sardines (January 12th) ; Collared Tongue (January 2nd) ; Sally Lunns (June 4th) ; Bread and Milk (January 25th).

LUNCHEON.—Rissoles (January 6th) : made from the remains of the cold beef. Hasty Pudding (March 30th).

DINNER.—Hare Soup (January 19th) ; Fricassee of Chicken (July 28th) ; Potato Snow (April 7th). *Boiled Salsify.*—Wash the roots and brush them gently, and scrape away the outside skin. Cut them into three-inch lengths. Lay them in cold water if they are not to be cooked immediately. Put them into plenty of boiling water which has salt and a little lemon-juice in it, and boil them till tender. They will need to boil half an hour if small and young, and an hour if thick. When a fork will pierce them easily they are done. Drain them, put them into a tureen, and serve them with good melted butter (July 17th), or better still with *Sauce Blanche* (April 25th). Cold boiled salsify is very good served as a salad, or the boiled roots may be dipped in frying Batter (October 22nd), and fried like apple fritters. When prepared in this way they are a very good garnish for boiled fish. Brown Bread Pudding (July 20th) ; Cheese (June 8th).

Things that must not be Forgotten.

1. Pot all that remains of the collared tongue for breakfast to-morrow (Note 5, September 26th).
2. Make a rice mould for dinner to-morrow (October 7th).
3. Put a cupful of hominy to soak all night in cold water.

October 27th.

Breakfast.	Luncheon.	Dinner.
Potted Tongue.	Savoury Stew of Australian Meat.	Herrings au Gratin
Eggs on the Dish.		Civet of Rabbit.
Hot Buttered Toast.	Baked Apples.	Potatoes.
Dry Toast.		Spinach.
Brown and White Bread and Butter.		Rice Mould with Jam.
		Custard.
Boiled Hominy.		Cheese.

Marketing.

For the Day.—Fresh Herrings (January 3rd). One may be allowed for each person, and one over (August 25th). A plump young Rabbit, or two, if required (January 24th) ; Potatoes ; Apples ; Spinach.

For To-morrow.—Half a pound of Bacon ; a well-hung Shoulder of Mutton, not too fat ; Muffins (January 29th).

BREAKFAST.—Potted Tongue (September 26th); Eggs on the Dish (December 7th) ; Boiled Hominy (February 11th).

LUNCHEON.—Savoury Hash of Australian Meat (February 5th).

Use half of the meat in the tin for this dish. Baked Apples (February 9th).

DINNER.—*Fresh Herrings au Gratin.*—Follow the recipe for Mackerel au Gratin (May 2nd), substituting fresh herrings for mackerel. Civet of Rabbit (December 8th); Potatoes (May 12th); Spinach (May 10th); Rice Mould (October 7th), made yesterday; Custard (August 10th); Cheese (June 8th).

Things that must not be Forgotten.

1. Make mock calf's-head mould for breakfast with the remains of the Australian mutton (April 20th).
2. Preserve all that remains of the boiled hominy.

October 28th.

Breakfast.	Luncheon.	Dinner.
Mock Calf's-Head Mould.	Rabbit made hot.	Croûte au Pot.
Toasted Bacon.	Cake Pudding.	Shoulder of Mutton.
Muffins.		Browned Potatoes.
Dry Toast.		Boiled Onions.
Brown and White Bread and Butter.		Baked Batter Pudding with Jam.
Honey.		Cheese.
Fried Hominy.		

Marketing.

For the Day.—Shoulder of Mutton, ordered yesterday: Potatoes; Onions; Parsley.
For To-morrow.—Dried Haddock; Rolls (September 3rd); Watercress.

BREAKFAST.—Mock Calf's-Head Mould (April 20th); Toasted Bacon (January 19th); Muffin's (January 30th); Fried Hominy (February 12th).

LUNCHEON.—Rabbit made hot (November 13th); Cake Pudding (February 4th).

DINNER.—Croûte au Pot (May 25th); Roast Shoulder of Mutton (December 16th); Browned Potatoes (October 18th). *Boiled Onions*, Onion Sauce (October 14th) is a very usual accompaniment to roast shoulder of mutton. Sometimes for a change onions boiled whole are served instead. Skin the onions, and put them into a saucepan with boiling water to cover them. Put the lid on the pan, and let them stew gently till they are tender but not broken. When a skewer will pierce them through easily they are done. Lift them out, one by one carefully, drain them in a colander, put them on a hot dish, sprinkle pepper and salt upon them, and put a small piece of butter upon each just before serving. Baked Batter Pudding with Jam (February 5th); Cheese (June 8th).

Things that must not be Forgotten.

1. Put half a pound of Normandy pippins to soak all night in cold water.
2. Remember that the rabbit bones will be a valuable addition to the stock-pot.
3. If any cold potatoes are left they may be preserved for the salad to-morrow.
4. Make a semolina mould for dinner to-morrow (July 23rd).

October 29th.

Breakfast.	Luncheon.	Dinner.
Dried Haddock.	Cold Mutton.	Boiled Hake.
Calf's-Head Mould.	Potato Salad.	Shrimp Sauce.
Hot Rolls.	Normandy Pippins.	Broiled Steak.
Dry Toast.		Oyster Sauce.
Brown and White Bread and Butter.		Potatoes.
Watercress.		Semolina Mould.
Milk Porridge.		Cheese.

Marketing.

For the Day.—Three or four pounds of Hake (August 7th); a pint of Shrimps, or a quarter of a pint of Picked Shrimps; a slice of tender Rump Steak, not less than an inch thick (Marketing January 22nd); a dozen large Oysters, or a tin of Oysters; Potatoes; Apples; Parsley.

For To-morrow.—Three plump fresh Sheep's Kidneys; Mustard and Cress; Sea Biscuits, if not in the house.

BREAKFAST.—Dried Haddock (January 27th); Calf's-Head Mould (April 20th); Hot Rolls (September 4th); Milk Porridge (June 13th).

LUNCHEON.—Cold Mutton, roasted yesterday; Potato Salad (April 12th); Stewed Normandy Pippins (August 16th).

DINNER.—*Boiled Hake.*—Boil the hake according to the directions given for cod's head and shoulders (December 6th). It will need to boil about eight minutes to the pound. Shrimp Sauce (January 30th); Broiled Steak (January 22nd); Oyster Sauce (October 16th); Potatoes (May 12th); Semolina Mould (July 23rd); Cheese (June 8th).

Things that must not be Forgotten.

1. Turn and rub the tongue in the pickle.
2. Preserve any hake that may be left.
3. Wash a cupful of prunes, and put them to soak in cold water all night.
4. If any little pieces of broiled steak are left pot them for breakfast to-morrow (Potted Beef, January 23rd).

October 30th.

Breakfast.	Luncheon.	Dinner.
Broiled Sheep's Kidneys (à la Maître d'Hôtel). Potted Beef. Hot Buttered Toast. Dry Toast. Mustard and Cress. Biscuits and Milk.	Fish Pie. Stewed Prunes.	Fried Plaice. Dutch Sauce. Oyster Patties. Curried Fowl. Boiled Rice. Apple Gâteau. Cheese.

Marketing.

For the Day.—A Thick Plaice (April 21st); a plump Fowl, or two Fowls if required; one dozen large fresh Oysters, for Oyster Patties; Apples; Potatoes; a Bath Chap; German Yeast. Fowls and Ducks are cheap now.

For To-morrow.—Order a well-hung Leg of Mutton (January 8th), and a fine Ox-Tail to be sent first thing in the morning.

BREAKFAST.—Broiled Sheep's Kidneys (January 29th); Maître d'Hôtel Butter (April 15th); Potted Beef (January 23rd); Biscuits and Milk (June 14th).

LUNCHEON.—Fish Pie, made of the cold Hake; *see* Cod Pie (January 2nd); Stewed Prunes (February 27th).

DINNER.—Fried Plaice (April 21st); Dutch Sauce (May 14th). *Curried Fowl.*—Follow the recipe for Curried Rabbit (July 16th), substituting a fowl for the rabbit; Boiled Rice (July 21st); Apple Gâteau (September 24th); Cheese (June 8th).

Things that must not be Forgotten.

1. Soak and boil the bath chap (Note 1, August 25th).
2. Partially prepare the rice and barley porridge (Note 6, June 15th).
3. Put a cupful of green lentils to soak all night in cold water.
4. Pastry is to be made to day. Baked Custard Tart (January 19th); Apple and Quince Pies (August 7th and October 13th). *Oyster Patties.*—Make a little good Puff Paste (April 24th). If it is not convenient to make the paste, a dozen small vol au vent cases may be bought of the confectioner. These will need to be made hot in the oven a few minutes before they are to be served, then filled with the prepared oysters, which should also be hot. If puff paste is made at home, roll it out till it is the third of an inch thick. Take two round cutters, one two inches and a half across, the other an inch and a half across. Dip them into flour; stamp six rounds of the larger size, and press the smaller cutter into the centre of each one of these to the depth of the sixth of an inch. Roll out the trimmings of pastry, and stamp six of the smaller rounds; bake them separately. When the cases are baked, scoop out the centre piece from the large rounds. Fill the vacant place with

the prepared oysters, place the smaller rounds on the top to make a sort of lid, and serve on a dish covered with a hot napkin. *To Prepare the Oysters.*—Open the shells carefully, and preserve all the liquor. Cut off the beards, and put them and the liquor into a stewpan with a quarter of a blade of mace, an inch of thin lemon-rind, a grain of white pepper, and a morsel of cayenne. Boil for three or four minutes, or till the gravy tastes pleasantly, then strain it, and put with it a few drops of lemon-juice. Thicken the liquor with a little corn-flour ; cut the bearded oysters into small pieces. Put these into the boiling sauce, let them boil for half a minute, let the sauce cool a minute, add a table-spoonful of very thick cream, and it is ready for use. Teacakes (August 26th) ; and Light Tea-buns (August 14th), can also be made.

October 31st.

Breakfast.	Luncheon.	Dinner.
Ox Eyes.	Stewed-Ox Tails.	Giblet Soup.
Bath Chap.	Jam and Bread Pudding,	Roast Leg of Mutton.
Teacakes.	Economical.	Yorkshire Pudding.
Dry Toast.		Lentils.
Brown and White Bread and Butter.		Mashed Potatoes. Apple Fritters.
Marmalade.		Cheese.
Rice and Barley Porridge.		

Marketing.

For the Day.—One, or if necessary, two fine Ox Tails, ordered yesterday ; Leg of Mutton, ordered yesterday ; Potatoes ; Apples ; Parsley.

For To-morrow.—Buy one or two sets of Giblets in addition to the Goose Giblets sent with the Goose for to-morrow ; a plump young Goose (September 28th) ; a pair of thick Soles (January 3rd) ; Apples ; Potatoes ; Onions ; Bottled Red Currants for Pudding ; four pennyworth of Cream ; Sage and Onion for Stuffing ; materials for a Salad for to-morrow evening ; Sardines for Monday.

BREAKFAST.—Ox-Eyes (June 5th) ; Bath Chap (Note 1, August 25th) ; Teacakes (February 14th) ; Rice and Barley Porridge (June 15th).

LUNCHEON.—Stewed Ox-Tail (May 8th) ; Jam and Bread Pudding, Economical (February 23rd).

DINNER.—Giblet Soup (February 1st) ; Roast Leg of Mutton (March 4th) ; Lentils (March 2nd) ; Yorkshire Pudding (November 26th) ; Mashed Potatoes (May 12th) ; Apple Fritters (October 22nd) ; Cheese (June 8th).

Things that must not be Forgotten.

1. Make the hydropathic pudding for dinner to-morrow (June 16th).

2. Pluck the goose ready for to-morrow, and dry the feathers. (Note, February 28th).

3. Partially prepare the rice milk for breakfast to-morrow. (Note 3, June 17th).

FRUITS SUITABLE FOR DESSERT IN OCTOBER.

Apples: Ribstons, King Pippins, Blenheim Oranges, Orange Pippins, &c.; Grapes, Melons, Medlars, Blackberries, October Peaches, Pomegranates, Pomeloes, Plums, Pears, Shaddocks, Cobs, Filberts, Walnuts, Hazel Nuts, Crystallised Fruits.

OCTOBER.

Tomato Store Sauce.—This sauce should be made in October. Be sure that the tomatoes are ripe and red, and that they have been gathered on a dry day. Put as many as are to be used into an earthern jar, and bake them in a gentle oven till they are soft, then rub them through a fine sieve. With every pound of pulp put a quart of vinegar, an ounce of salt, and the same of white pepper, half an ounce of cayenne, and half an ounce of finely-minced shalot. Mix thoroughly, boil gently till the sauce is as thick as cream, and stir frequently to prevent burning, then put it into wide-mouthed and perfectly dry bottles, cork it closely, and keep it in a cool airy place. Where tomatoes are liked and used to any extent it is best to make sauce for home consumption.

Hams, to Cure.—Hams, especially Canadian hams, may now be bought at a very cheap rate. These hams are excellent for ordinary purposes, and it is a good plan to keep one always in the house, "in cut," as it is called. Sugar-cured hams cannot, however, compare in flavour with home-cured hams, which are a real delicacy, and would prove a welcome addition to any table. The recipe given below has been proved again and again year after year with most satisfactory results.

Procure three or four legs of fresh pork, or one leg of pork if liked. Take away the bone which lies on that part of the leg which has been cut from the loin. This can be very easily removed, and should certainly be cut away, as the ham will keep better without it. Weigh the hams, and for each fourteen pounds of meat allow half a pound of salt, a quarter of a pound of sugar, a quarter of a pound of treacle, one ounce of ground pepper, half an ounce of ground allspice, and half an ounce of salt prunella. First rub the salt into the meat, and be particularly careful to cover the shank bone. Do this for two days. The third and fourth days pour off the brine and carefully preserve it. The fifth day rub in the remainder of the dry ingredients. Measure the brine which was preserved, and boil it with three times the quantity of water and the proportion of treacle. Put the hams rind side downwards into a deep earthern pan, and turn and rub them in the pickle every day for five or six weeks, according to their size, but always leave them in the pan the rind side downwards. Boil the brine three or four times during this period. At the end of the time wash the hams lightly to free them from the pickle, which has a dark and rather unpleasant look, and hang them in a cool airy place to dry. They will be ready in about a month. If it is preferred that they should be smoked, there is almost sure to be a confectioner or provision dealer in the neighbourhood who would let them hang with his own hams for "a consideration"—fourpence or sixpence each ham. In many parts they are, however, preferred unsmoked. When done wrap each ham in a cotton bag, and hang it in a cool airy situation till wanted. The same pickle may be used for tongues after the hams are finished.

Hams are best to be cured before the weather is frosty; and anyhow the business should not be undertaken later than February. Two or three hams can very well be cured in the same pan if every day the position is changed, the top one being put to the bottom. For a small family it would be found that hams weighing from ten to twelve pounds would prove most profitable. To boil hams, *see* Note 4, May 27th.

Sunday, November 1st.

Breakfast.	Dinner.	Tea.	Supper.
Devilled Eggs.	Filleted Soles Sautés.	Brown and White Bread and Butter.	Cold Mutton.
Bath Chap.	Brown Butter Sauce.	Damson Jam.	Salad.
Teacakes.	Roast Goose with Sage and Onion Stuffing.	Light Tea-buns.	Baked Custard Tart.
Dry Toast.			
Brown and White Bread and Butter.	Brown Gravy.		
Rice Milk.	Apple Sauce.		
	Potato Mould.		
	Brussels Sprouts.		
	Apple and Quince Pie.		
	Cheese.		

BREAKFAST.—Devilled Eggs (February 27th); Bath Chap (August 25th); Teacakes (February 14th); Rice Milk (June 18th).

DINNER.—Filleted Soles Sautés (January 4th); Brown Butter Sauce (February 12th); Roast Goose (September 29th); Gravy (September 29th); Apple Sauce (September 29th); Potato Mould (October 23rd); Brussels Sprouts (*see* Cabbage, June 4th); Apple and Quince Pie (August 7th); Cheese (June 8th).

TEA.—Light Tea-buns (August 14th).

SUPPER.—Cold Mutton roasted yesterday ; Salad (March 13th); Baked Custard Tart (January 19th).

Things that must not be Forgotten.

1. Before putting the goose away, put together and preserve all the gravy, stuffing, &c., that is in the dish with it.
2. Put a cupful of white haricot beans to soak all night in cold water.

November 2nd.

Breakfast.	Luncheon.	Dinner.
Sardines.	Goose Hash.	Palestine Soup.
Mutton Collops.	Baked Batter Pudding.	Baked Rabbit with Bacon.
Teacakes.		Haricot Beans.
Dry Toast.		Potato Snow.
Brown and White Bread and Butter.		Lemon Pudding.
Honey.		Cheese.
Milk Toast.		

Marketing.

For the Day.—Three pounds of Jerusalem Artichokes ; a fine Rabbit, or two if required; a pound of Bacon in rashers, half for to-day, and half for to-morrow; six ounces of Suet ; Potatoes ; a Hand of fresh Pork (January 6th).

For To-morrow.—Watercress.

BREAKFAST.—Sardines (January 12th); Mutton Collops. If any meat still remains on the cold leg of mutton, cut it into neat slices, and proceed as directed (October 1st): the tomatoes may be omitted ; Teacakes (February 14th) ; Milk Toast (June 17th).

LUNCHEON.—Goose Hash (September 30th); Baked Batter Pudding (February 5th).

DINNER.—Palestine Soup (December 8th); Baked Rabbit with Bacon (July 8th); Potato Snow (April 7th); Haricot Beans (June 20th); Lemon Pudding (August 12th); Cheese (June 8th).

Things that must not be Forgotten.

1. Preserve all that remains of the baked rabbit.
2. Turn and rub the tongue in the brine.
3. If any haricot beans are left, they may be served with the rabbit gâteau to-morrow.
4. Boil the pork brine, and put the hand of pork into it.

November 3rd.

Breakfast.	Luncheon.	Dinner.
Poached Eggs. Bacon. Hot Buttered Toast. Dry Toast. Brown and White Bread and Butter. Watercress. Oatmeal Porridge.	Rabbit Gâteau. Haricot Beans. Rice and Cheese.	Sole au Gratin. Beef Stewed with Onions. Baked Potatoes. Nottingham Pudding. Cheese.

Marketing.

For the Day.—A pair of thick Soles (January 3rd); two pounds of tender lean Steak (January 1st); Apples; Potatoes; Onions; a dozen fresh Herrings.

For To-morrow.—Order half a fresh Ox-Kidney to be sent in good time in the morning; Mustard and Cress; Muffins (January 29th).

BREAKFAST.—Poached Eggs (February 6th); Bacon (January 19th); Porridge (January 25th).

LUNCHEON.—Rabbit Gâteau (July 9th), made of the cold rabbit; Haricot Beans (Note 3, November 2nd); Rice and Cheese (February 18th).

DINNER.—Sole au Gratin (May 3rd). *Beef Stewed with Onions.*—Rub the inside of a stewpan with good dripping. Pepper the steak, and salt it lightly. Lay it in the pan, and with it four large Spanish onions cut into thin slices. Cover the saucepan closely, place it at the side of the fire, and let it simmer *gently* for two hours. Put the steak on a dish, place the onions upon it, and pour the gravy over all. It will be found that the onions will yield sufficient gravy, so that there will be no occasion to put any sauce in the pan. Those who are very partial to the flavour of onions will like this dish; others had better avoid it. Baked Potatoes (May 4th). *Nottingham Pudding.*—Make a little good batter (*see* Toad in the Hole, January 15th). Peel and core half a dozen good baking apples. Fill the hollow in the middle with sugar, and sprinkle powdered cinnamon or nutmeg on the top. Place the apples in a buttered dish, pour the batter round them, and bake in a good oven. Cheese (June 8th).

Things that must not be Forgotten.

1. The batter will be better if made some hours before it is wanted.
2. Pickle the fresh herrings bought this morning (August 20th).
3. Preserve any beef that may be left.
4. Turn and rub the ox-tongue in the brine.

November 4th.

Breakfast.	Luncheon.	Dinner.
Pickled Herrings.	Shepherd's Pie.	Kidney Soup.
Buttered Eggs.	Baked Omelet.	Loin of Mutton, Stuffed and Rolled.
Muffins.		Boiled Parsnips.
Dry Toast.		Potatoes.
Brown and White Bread and Butter.		Rice Gâteau.
Mustard and Cress.		Cheese.
Bread and Milk.		

Marketing.

For the Day.—Half an Ox-Kidney, ordered yesterday; about four pounds of the best end of a Loin of Mutton. The butcher should be asked to bone the joint. Parsnips; Potatoes; Parsley.

For To-morrow.—A tin of Potted Grouse (January 7th).

BREAKFAST.—Pickled Herrings (August 20th); Buttered Eggs (January 16th); Muffins (January 30th); Bread and Milk (January 25th).

LUNCHEON. — Shepherd's Pie (January 12th); Baked Omelet (August 6th).

DINNER.—Kidney Soup (February 27th); Loin of Mutton, Stuffed and Rolled (April 22nd); Boiled Parsnips (September 30th). *Potato Croquettes.*—This is an excellent and tasteful way of serving potatoes. Take as many potatoes as are likely to be required, wash, scrub, and peel them. Supposing there is one pound of potatoes, boil them in the usual way (April 7th), and rub them whilst hot through a wire sieve. Melt half an ounce of butter in a stewpan, put in a dessert-spoonful of milk, and add the sifted potato. Mix smoothly over the fire, then put the stewpan on one side, and add the yolk of a fresh egg lightly beaten, a table-spoonful of chopped parsley, and a little pepper and salt. Spread the mixture on a plate, and let it stand till cold. Half fill a deep stewpan with clarified dripping, and put it on the fire to boil; it is boiling when it has ceased bubbling, is quite still, and a blue smoke rises from it. Form the potato mixture into balls, brush them over with the white of the egg which has been beaten on a plate, and roll them in finely-sifted bread-crumbs. Put them in a frying-basket, plunge them into the hot fat, and let them remain till they are brightly browned. They will be done in about two minutes. Arrange them on a dish, cover with a hot napkin, and garnish with fried parsley (January 13th). Sometimes a little flour is taken in the hands to help to form the croquettes. This should be done very sparingly, or the croquettes will burst in frying. Rice Gâteau (October 3rd); Cheese (June 8th).

Things that must not be Forgotten.

1. Turn the herrings over in the vinegar.
2. Turn and rub the ox-tongue.

November 5th.

Breakfast.	Luncheon.	Dinner.
Potted Grouse.	Minced Mutton with Poached Eggs.	Baked Hake.
Pickled Herrings.	Cauliflower au Gratin.	Anchovy Sauce.
Hot Buttered Toast.		Rump Steak and Oyster Pie.
Dry Toast.		Mashed Potatoes.
Brown and White Bread and Butter.		Macaroni Pudding.
Marmalade.		Cheese.
Corn-Flour Milk.		

Marketing.

For the Day.—Two pounds of Rump or Buttock Steak (January 1st); half an Ox-Kidney; a tin of preserved Oysters; six ounces of Macaroni; Potatoes; Cauliflowers. Late Autumn Cauliflowers last till they are cut off by frost, then their place is taken by White Broccoli.

For To-morrow.—A well-hung Neck of Mutton, not too fat; Rolls (September 3rd). Order a Fore-loin of small freshly-killed Pork.

BREAKFAST.—Potted Grouse (January 7th); Pickled Herrings (August 20th); Corn-Flour Milk (June 19th).

LUNCHEON.—Minced Mutton (January 20th); Cauliflower au Gratin (April 25th).

DINNER.—Baked Hake (September 1st); Anchovy Sauce (July 17th); Beef Steak and Oyster Pie (March 26th). A little rough Puff Pastry (May 29th) may be made specially for this pie; half the tin of oysters will probably be sufficient for the pie. Mashed Potatoes (May 12th); Macaroni Pudding (March 27th); Cheese (June 8th).

Things that must not be Forgotten.

1. Soak a large cupful of hominy in cold water.
2. If any herrings are still left turn them over in the vinegar.
3. In the north of England, Parkin is made for the Fifth of November, "Bon-fire Night." Very good Parkin may be made as follows:—Mix half an ounce of ginger and half a pound of sugar with four pounds of fine oatmeal; rub a pound of butter into this and add about two ounces of candied lemon finely chopped. Warm some treacle in a jar and stir this into the oatmeal to make a *stiff* paste. Put the preparation into greased patty pans and bake in a very slow oven. If liked, a little milk can be mixed with the warmed treacle. Keep the cakes in a tin box excluded from the air. Superior Parkin, called *Oldham Parkin*, is made as follows:—Mix together in a bowl three and a half pounds of flour and two pounds of oatmeal. Rub into this two pounds of butter, and add two pounds of sugar, two ounces of ginger, an ounce of ground mace, six ounces of candied lemon finely chopped, a small nutmeg grated, and a table-spoonful of carbonate of soda. Mix thoroughly. Warm three pounds and a half

of treacle slightly; stir a gill of cream into it, and add the dry ingredients. Leave the mixture to stand all night. Put it into a well-buttered dripping-tin, let it rise before the fire for awhile, then bake in a moderate oven. This Parkin will improve with keeping for three or four weeks.

November 6th.

Breakfast.	Luncheon.	Dinner.
Potted Grouse. Scalloped Oysters. Hot Rolls. Dry Toast. Brown and White Bread and Butter. Honey. Boiled Hominy.	The Scrag of the Neck of Mutton stewed with Vegetables. Sweet Macaroni.	Crécy Soup. Mutton Chops with Sauce Piquante. Carrots and Turnips. Mashed Potatoes. Stone Cream. Cheese.

Marketing.

For the Day.—The Neck of Mutton ordered yesterday; the Fore-loin of Pork ordered yesterday—half of this is for Sausages to make Sausage Rolls.
For To-morrow.—A pint of Shrimps to be potted for breakfast; Watercress.

BREAKFAST.—Potted Grouse (January 7th); Scalloped Oysters, made of the oysters left in the tin after making the Beef Steak Pie (April 27th); Hot Rolls (September 4th); Boiled Hominy (February 11th).

LUNCHEON.—Scrag of Mutton stewed with vegetables (January 14th); Sweet Macaroni (August 13th).

DINNER.—Crécy Soup (January 5th); Mutton Chops with Sauce Piquante (April 30th); Carrots (July 6th); Mashed Turnips (September 30th); Stone Cream (July 1st); Cheese (June 8th).

Things that must not be Forgotten.

1. Preserve any hominy that may be left. It can be fried for breakfast to-morrow.

2. *Marinade for Pork.*—Cut about four pounds from the best end of the loin of pork. Rub an earthen pan twice across with garlic. Put into it a shalot finely minced, a table-spoonful of chopped parsley, six peppercorns, a dessert-spoonful of salt, and a quarter of a pint of salad oil. Rub the mixture well into every part of the pork, lay the meat in the pickle, cover the pan, and leave it for two days.

3. Make sausages of the remainder of the loin of pork (March 18th). If the sausages which are wanted for sausage rolls can be procured of a respectable dealer, this business can be omitted.

4. Pastry is to be made to-day (April 17th). Jam Tarts (August 7th); Lemon Cheese-cakes (August 18th). *Sausage Rolls.*—Roll the pastry to the thickness of one-eighth of an inch, and cut it into pieces

six inches square. Plunge the fresh sausages into fast-boiling water, let them boil a few minutes, then remove the skins, slit them in halves lengthwise, and lay a half in the centre of each square. Fold the paste over the roll, join it neatly in the centre, and press the ends of the paste together. Place the rolls on a greased baking-tin, brush them over with egg, and bake them in a well-heated oven. Bake for about a quarter of an hour. Sausage rolls can be made of cooked or uncooked meat, or tinned meat finely minced, nicely seasoned with pepper and salt, and flavoured with a small onion and a pinch of chopped sage-leaves to half a pound of meat. When they are made of uncooked meat the rolls will need to be baked longer than when cooked meat is used. Teacakes (August 26th) and light tea-buns (August 14th) may also be made.

November 7th.

Breakfast.	Luncheon.	Dinner.
Eggs in Brown Butter. Sausage Rolls. Teacakes. Dry Toast. Brown and White Bread and Butter. Marmalade. Fried Hominy.	Toad in the Hole. Rice with Apples and Beetroot.	Croûte au Pot. Curried Rabbit. Rice. Scorzonera. Pancakes. Cheese.

Marketing.

For the Day.—A pound and a half of Steak, or the short bone of Mutton. (If any meat were left yesterday it can be used, and this need not be bought.) A fine young Rabbit, or two if required (January 24th); Apples; Potatoes; Beetroot; Scorzonera. These roots are in season at the same time that Salsify is—that is, from October to May. They are for all practical purposes the same thing, and have the same taste, but Scorzonera is black and Salsify is white. Neither of the two is to be had at all times; but when they are, they will be found excellent and delicate in flavour.

For To-morrow.—Three or four Bloaters (January 2nd); a large thick Sole, filleted (January 3rd); a pint of Chestnuts; three pounds of Brussels Sprouts; Potatoes; a quarter of a pound of French Chocolate; a tin of Prawns for Monday.

BREAKFAST.—Eggs in Brown Butter (January 6th); Sausage Rolls (November 6th); Teacakes (February 14th); Fried Hominy (February 12th).

LUNCHEON.—Toad in the Hole (January 15th); Rice with Apples and Beetroot (January 28th).

DINNER.—Croûte au Pot (May 25th); Curried Rabbit (July 16th); Boiled Rice (July 21st); Scorzonera—follow the recipe given for Salsify (October 26th); Pancakes (February 24th); Cheese (June 8th).

Things that must not be Forgotten.

1. Turn and rub the loin of pork.
2. Make a ground rice mould (August 7th) for supper to-morrow night.
3. Keep the bloaters apart from all other food.
4. Turn the ox-tongue in the pickle.

Sunday, November 8th.

Breakfast.	Dinner.	Tea.	Supper.
Bloaters on Toast. Sausage Rolls. Teacakes. Brown and White Bread and Butter. Milk Porridge.	Sole à la Horly. Pork, cooked in the French way. Potato Mould. Chestnuts and Brussels Sprouts. Chocolate Pudding. Custard. Cheese.	Brown and White Bread and Butter. Teacakes. Strawberry Jam. Light Buns.	Cold Pork. Lemon Cheesecakes. Jam Tarts. Ground Rice Mould.

BREAKFAST.—Bloaters on Toast (March 24th); Sausage Rolls (November 6th); Teacakes (February 14th); Milk Porridge (June 13th).

DINNER.—Sole à la Horly (October 18th). *Pork, cooked in the French way.*—Take the loin of pork out of the marinade in which it has been lying since November 6th. Put it to the fire and roast it well, basting it frequently, and during the last half-hour with the oil in which it was marinaded. Serve it on a hot dish with brown gravy round it, and with a sauce made as follows in a tureen :—Chop small an apple and a moderate-sized onion ; fry them in butter till they are tender, then crush them to pulp, mix a tea-cupful of stock with them, and add a little salt and cayenne, a spoonful of mustard, a spoonful of sugar, and the juice of a lemon. Stir the sauce over the fire till it boils, add a spoonful of cognac if liked, and serve. Potato Mould (October 23rd). *Chestnuts and Brussels Sprouts.*—Peel the outer skin from the chestnuts, put them into boiling water for a few minutes, throw them into cold water, and remove the second skin. Wipe them dry, put them into a saucepan, pour over them good stock to cover them, and stew them gently till they are tender without being at all broken. The time they will take will vary from twenty minutes to three-quarters of an hour, according to their quality. A bay-leaf, two or three strips of bacon-rind, and an inch of lemon-rind, with pepper and salt, should be added to the gravy in which they are stewed. Take out the chestnuts, strain the gravy, and thicken it with brown thickening or corn-flour (January 6th). It ought to be like very thick cream. Free it from fat, and add a few drops of browning (January 2nd) if necessary. Have some Brussels Sprouts boiled separately in the usual way (June 4th); drain them well, put them and the boiled chestnuts into the sauce, heat gently, and serve together in a hot vegetable tureen. This dish is seldom seen, though it is exceedingly popular with all who have tried it. Chocolate Pudding (July 24th); Custard (August 10th); Cheese (June 8th).

TEA.—Teacakes (February 14th); Light Buns (August 14th).

SUPPER.—Lemon Cheesecakes (August 18th); Jam Tarts (August 7th); Ground Rice Mould (August 7th).

Things that must not be Forgotten.

1. The fat in which the sole is fried must be so hot that it is *still* when the fish is put into it.
2. Put the pork on a clean dish as soon as it leaves the table.
3. Turn the ox-tongue in the pickle.

November 9th.

Breakfast.	Luncheon.	Dinner.
Prawns.	Minced Pork.	Mullagatawny Soup.
Boiled Eggs.	Savoury Rice.	Boiled Neck of Mutton.
Teacakes.		Maître d'Hôtel Sauce.
Dry Toast.		Mashed Potatoes.
Brown and White Bread and Butter.		Carrots.
Marmalade.		Turnips.
Biscuits and Milk.		Boiled Batter Pudding.
		Cheese.

Marketing.

For the Day.—A well-hung good-sized Neck of Mutton, not too fat (February 5th); Potatoes; Carrots; Turnips; Parsley.

For To-morrow.—Bloaters. Allow one for each person.

BREAKFAST.—Prawns (February 7th); Boiled Eggs (January 5th); Teacakes (February 14th); Biscuits and Milk (June 14th).

LUNCHEON.—Minced Pork (April 20th); Savoury Rice (June 17th).

DINNER.—Mullagatawny Soup (January 16th); Boiled Neck of Mutton (February 23rd)—the best end only to be used; Maître d'Hôtel Sauce (May 6th); Mashed Potatoes (May 12th); Carrots (July 6th); Turnips (September 30th); Boiled Batter Pudding (May 18th); Cheese (June 8th).

Things that must not be Forgotten.

1. Partially prepare the rice and barley porridge for breakfast to-morrow (Note 6, June 15th).
2. Keep the bloaters apart from all other food.
3. Put a cupful of green lentils to soak all night in cold water.
4. Turn the ox-tongue in the pickle.

November 10th.

Breakfast.	Luncheon.	Dinner.
Bloaters.	Scrag-end of Mutton boiled with Rice.	Fried Sprats.
Devilled Eggs.	Custard Sippets.	Roast Sirloin of Beef.
Teacakes.		Lentils.
Dry Toast.		Potato Mould.
Brown and White Bread and Butter.		Salsify.
Honey.		Apple Custard.
Rice and Barley Porridge.		Cheese.

Marketing.

For the Day.—Fresh Sprats. The brighter and more silvery-looking they are, the fresher they will be. Sprats are supposed to come in on Lord Mayor's Day. They are at their best in November and December. A Sirloin of Beef (March 7th); Potatoes; Apples; Onions; Salsify. Buy a little more than is likely to be wanted for to-day's dinner.

For To-morrow.—A Cow-Heel from the tripe-shop.

BREAKFAST.—Bloaters (January 3rd); Devilled Eggs (February 27th); Teacakes (February 14th); Rice and Barley Porridge (June 15th).

LUNCHEON.—Boil with rice the scrag-end of the Mutton cooked yesterday (February 21st); Custard Sippets (June 10th).

DINNER.—*Fried Sprats.*—Half fill a saucepan with frying-fat (February 19th). Put it on the fire to boil. Meantime wash the sprats quickly, lift them out of the water with the fingers and lay them on a sieve to drain. Put a cupful of flour into a cloth, throw the sprats into it, a few at a time, and shake the corners of the cloth so as to toss the sprats in the flour without handling them. Put a few at a time into a frying basket, and when the fat is so hot that it is *still*, fry as directed (January 17th). In less than two minutes, when they are lightly browned, they will done enough. Dry on paper and serve very hot. This is the best way of cooking sprats. They may also be broiled or *pickled* like herrings (August 20th). To *Broil Sprats*, run a long wire through the heads, dredge the fish with flour, put them on a gridiron that has been rubbed with mutton-fat, and broil them over a clear fire. Roast Sirloin of Beef (March 4th or March 8th); Lentils (March 2nd); Potato Mould (October 23rd); Salsify (October 26th). *Apple Custard.*—Pare, core, and cut in slices six or eight large apples. Put them into a stew-pan with a very little cold water, cover them, and stew them to pulp. Put with them a table-spoonful of preserved quince (*see* Note 4, October 13th), or, wanting this, a tea-spoonful of grated lemon-rind, and add sugar to taste. Let the mixture get cold; pour over it a pint of custard (August 10th), grate nutmeg on the top, and bake in a gentle oven. When the custard is set the pudding is done enough.. It will be better cold than hot. Cheese (June 8th).

Things that must not be Forgotten.

1. Boil the shoulder of pork that has been in pickle (Note 2, April 25th).
2. Put the beef on a clean dish as soon as it leaves the table, and preserve any red gravy that may be in the dish.
3. Preserve any salsify that may be left. It can be fried in batter (July 29th) and used to garnish the boiled cod to-morrow. It will be a great improvement.
4. Put a cupful of white haricot beans to soak all night in cold water.
5. Turn the ox-tongue in the pickle.

November 11th.

Breakfast.	Luncheon.	Dinner.
Prawns.	Cow-Heel with Parsley Sauce.	Boiled Cod.
Pickled Pork.		Salsify.
Hot Buttered Toast.	Currant Dumplings.	Oyster Sauce.
Dry Toast.		Beef Hash.
Brown and White Bread and Butter.		Mashed Potatoes.
		Haricot Beans.
Marmalade.		Town Pudding.
Milk Toast.		Cheese.

Marketing.

For the Day.—Half a pound of good Beef Suet; three or four pounds from the middle of a Cod, or from six to eight pounds of the head and shoulders; a dozen large Oysters, or a tin of Preserved Oysters; Potatoes; Apples; Parsley.

For To-morrow.—Mustard and Cress for Breakfast.

BREAKFAST.—Prawns (served November 9th); Pickled Pork (April 25th), boiled yesterday. Milk Toast (June 17th).

LUNCHEON.—Cow Heel with Parsley (February 20th). *Currant Dumplings.*—Make the mixture as for baked plum pudding (February 25th). Divide it into pieces the size of an egg, and without laying them in a cloth drop them into fast-boiling water. Boil quickly for about half an hour, and move them about at first to keep them from sticking to the bottom. Sift sugar over and serve with lemon-juice. Of course, if preferred, the mixture can be boiled all together in a cloth, but in that case it will need to boil much longer.

DINNER.—Boiled Cod (December 6th); Fried Salsify (October 26th); Frying Batter (July 29th); Oyster Sauce (October 16th). *Beef Hash, Economical.*—Cut the beef into rather thin slices; lay these in a saucepan and pour the meat gravy, or, wanting this, a little nicely-flavoured stock, upon them; there should not be enough gravy to cover the meat. Add a small piece of butter rolled in flour, and simmer very gently for about half an hour, or until the meat is hot through. It must on no account boil. Serve on a hot dish with the gravy poured over. The flavour of the dish may be varied by sprinkling a little minced pickle over the meat in the saucepan. The majority of people would perhaps prefer to have beef, especially when it has been properly carved, served cold with pickles and salad, rather than to have it warmed in this or any other way. There are others, and especially children, who have a very decided objection to cold meat, and this is a convenient and excellent though homely way of warming it up. Mashed Potatoes (May 12th); Haricot Beans (June 20th); Town Pudding (December 3rd); Cheese (June 8th).

Things that must not be Forgotten.

1. Preserve the liquor in which the cod was boiled.
2. If any fish is left, pick the flesh from the bones and make fish-cakes for breakfast (January 13th).
3. Partially prepare the rice-milk for breakfast (Note 3, June 17th).
4. Turn the ox-tongue in the pickle.

November 12th.

Breakfast.	Luncheon.	Dinner.
Fish Cakes.	Rissoles.	Lobster Soup.
Pickled Pork.	Baked Omelet.	Boiled Rabbit.
Hot Buttered Toast.		Onion Sauce.
Dry Toast.		Bacon Rolls.
Brown and White Bread and Butter.		Mashed Potatoes.
Mustard and Cress.		Stewed Celery.
Rice Milk.		Hayrick Puddings.
		Cheese.

Marketing.

For the Day.—A small fresh Lobster or a tin of Preserved Lobster; a pair of plump, fresh, young Rabbits, trussed for boiling (January 24th); a pound of streaky Bacon in rashers, half for to-day and half for to-morrow; Potatoes; Onions; Celery. Jelly is to be made for supper on Sunday night. If it is to be made of calf's-feet stock, the feet must be bought and stewed *to-day*. If gelatine is to be used, Saturday will be early enough to think about it. Excepting for the use of invalids, jelly is not often made of stock. The recipe for making calf's-feet stock is given under Jelly (November 14th).

For To-morrow.—A quart of fresh Shrimps, to be potted for breakfast; a fine plump Capon; Watercress. Buy a freshly-killed Hare and hang it (January 8th). It is intended for dinner on Sunday week.

BREAKFAST.—Fish Cakes (January 13th); Pickled Pork (April 25th) served yesterday; Rice Milk (June 18th).

LUNCHEON.—*Rissoles.* After slices have been cut from the beef for the hash, it will be found that a quantity of broken meat can still be cut from the bones, and this can be made into croquettes or rissoles (January 6th). Baked Omelet (August 6th).

DINNER.—Lobster Soup (May 20th); Boiled Rabbits (March 6th); Onion Sauce (October 14th); Bacon Rolls (July 19th); Mashed Potatoes (May 12th); Stewed Celery (December 2nd); Hayrick Puddings (March 19th); Cheese (June 8th).

Things that must not be Forgotten.

1. Carefully preserve the liquor in which the rabbits were boiled.
2. Break up the beef bone and stew it for stock (February 13th). Remember also to render down any fat that may be left.
3. As soon as the rabbit leaves the table, divide it into joints, put these into an earthen jar, cover them with the sauce, and set the jar in a cool place.
4. *Potted Shrimps.*—Shell the shrimps, put them in a dish, sprinkle a tea-spoonful of white pepper and a pinch of salt over them, and place little pieces of butter here and there on them. Put them in the oven till they are hot, but not dry. Press them into jars, and when cold cover them with clarified butter. If preferred, they can be pounded in a mortar, but they are very good done in this way.
5. Turn the ox-tongue in the pickle.

November 13th.

Breakfast.	Luncheon.	Dinner.
Potted Shrimps.	Rabbit made hot.	Palestine Soup.
Pickled Pork.	Apple Balls.	Capon, Stuffed and Roasted.
Hot Buttered Toast.		Brown Gravy.
Dry Toast.		Bread Sauce.
Brown and White Bread and Butter.		Potato Snow.
Watercress.		Brussels Sprouts.
Porridge.		Guest's Pudding.
		Cheese.

Marketing.

For the Day.—Half a pound of chopped Suet; three pounds of Jerusalem Artichokes; Potatoes; Brussels Sprouts; Apples; half a Pig's Head, and two Pig's Feet for brawn. If liked, the check can be cut away and pickled separately (Marketing, January 7th), or it may be put with the brawn, to which it will be a valuable addition. Four plump young Pigeons; and a pound and a half of tender Steak for the pigeon pie (May 15th).

For To-morrow.—Watercress.

BREAKFAST.—Potted Shrimps, prepared yesterday (Note 4, November 12th); Pickled Pork (April 25th), boiled November 10th; Porridge (January 25th).

LUNCHEON.—*Rabbit made Hot in the Sauce.*—Cut the rabbit into neat pieces, put them into an earthen jar, and pour over them sauce or gravy that is left, to moisten them. Cover the jar closely, and put it into a large saucepan of boiling water. Keep the water boiling round it till the meat and sauce are quite hot, then put it on a dish, pour the sauce over, and serve. Poultry, game, or meat warmed in this way is almost as good as when freshly cooked. It is best for the rabbit or bird to be cut into joints and placed in the jar with the sauce whilst still warm, but it may also be done when it is cold. Apple Balls (March 7th).

DINNER.—Palestine Soup (December 8th); *Capon, Stuffed and Roasted.*—Proceed in all respects as for a fowl stuffed and roasted, but allow a longer time for roasting (June 30th). Brown Gravy (October 18th); Bread Sauce (October 18th); Potato Snow (April 7th); Brussels Sprouts (*see* Cabbage, June 4th); Guest's Pudding (April 14th); Cheese (June 8th).

Things that must not be Forgotten.

1. Boil and roll the ox-tongue (July 27th).
2. Boil the brine in which the tongue was pickled, and leave it to get cold.
3. Follow the directions given in Notes 1 and 2, January 7th.
4. Pastry (April 17th) is to be made to-day; Pigeon Pie (May 15th) for breakfast to-morrow; Apple Balls (March 7th) may be made with the trimmings of the pastry; also make Scones (August 26th) and Soda Cake (August 14th).
5. If the legs of the capon were left untouched, prepare them for devilling for breakfast to-morrow (January 14th). If they are not available, the rolled tongue can be used instead.
6. Put a cupful of green lentils to soak all night in cold water.

November 14th.

Breakfast.	Luncheon.	Dinner.
Pigeon Pie.	Scotch Collops.	Croûte au Pot.
Devilled Drumsticks.	Norfolk Dumplings.	Sausages and Lentils.
Scones.		Baked Potatoes.
Dry Toast.		Wyvern Puddings.
Brown and White Bread and Butter.		Cheese.
Watercress.		
Corn-flour Milk.		

Marketing.

For the Day.—A pound and a half of buttock Steak; three pounds of best Pork Sausages, or fresh Pork to make the same (March 13th)); Potatoes; a small plump Leg of Mutton to put in pickle; Macaroni.

For To-morrow.—A good-sized Brill (January 3rd and 9th); a well-hung Leg of Mutton; half a pound of Ratafias; Potatoes; Brussels Sprouts; three heads of Celery.

BREAKFAST.—Pigeon Pie (May 15th), made yesterday; Devilled Drumsticks (January 14th); Scones (August 26th); Corn-flour Milk (June 19th).

LUNCHEON.—Scotch Collops (January 9th). *Norfolk Dumplings* (made without yeast).—Real Norfolk Dumplings are of dough made with yeast. Fresh yeast is not, however, always to be procured in towns, and very good dough may be quickly and easily made with baking powder. The dough should not be mixed until the last thing before it is to be boiled. Put a pound of flour into a bowl, and mix with it a pinch of salt, and a tea-spoonful of baking-powder (August 2nd). Mix water with it to make it into a light firm dough. Knead it quickly, and not too much, with floured hands, make it into balls about the size of a small egg, plunge these into boiling water, and boil quickly until done; they will take about twenty minutes. If preferred they can be placed in a single layer on a steamer above boiling water, and steamed instead of being boiled. Serve with the meat and gravy, or with treacle or sugar. To make *Bread without Yeast.*—Mix the dough as already described, make it up quickly in small loaves or twists; lay these on a floured baking-tin, and bake in a well-heated oven till a knife pushed into the centre of the loaf comes out bright and clean. This bread, which is very easily made, is excellent, but it soon gets dry.

DINNER.—Croûte au Pot (May 25th); Sausages and Lentils (April 4th); Baked Potatoes (May 4th); Wyvern Puddings (May 9th); Cheese (June 8th).

Things that must not be Forgotten.

1. Cleanse the pig's head and the feet (Note 2, January 8th). Lay them in the brine which was previously used for the ox-tongue, and turn and rub them every day for eight or nine days. When the brine has been used for this purpose it must be thrown away, as nothing else must be put in it after it has been used for a pig's head.

2. Make the pickle for the mutton (Note 3, March 19th), and put the mutton into it.

3. Make a mould of *Wine Jelly* for supper to-morrow night. In making *Jelly from Gelatine* it should be remembered that the only safe rule for all times and seasons is an ounce of gelatine to a pint of liquid. At the same time, when the weather is cold, the moulds are moderate in size, and the gelatine is good, nearly double the quantity may be used. Soak the gelatine in a basin with half a pint of water for an hour. Mix half a pint of boiling water with it, and stir it until dissolved. If necessary stir it over the fire for a minute or two. Let it get quite cool, then put it in a rather small stewpan with the very thin rind of one fresh lemon that has been wiped with a soft cloth, the strained juice of the lemon, an ounce of loaf sugar, two cloves, and half an inch of stick cinnamon. When lemons are dear, a little citric acid the size of half a nutmeg may be used to flavour. Break an egg, and put the yolk aside. It can be used for the Dutch sauce to-morrow, or if a dark jelly is wanted it can be put with the rest. Beat the white lightly, wipe clean and crush the egg-shell. Stir both the white and the crushed shell into the jelly, put the saucepan on the fire, and whisk the jelly till it rises in the pan. As soon as this point is reached stop stirring at once, put the lid on the pan, draw it to the side of the fire, and let it stand for twenty minutes. Make the jelly-bag hot by wringing it out of clean boiling water, put a pan or basin under it,

and pass the jelly carefully through it three or four times. The crust that will have formed at the top must on no account be disturbed, and the jelly must be poured gently upon it, a little at a time. It will act as a sort of filter, and help to make the jelly clear. When there is not a jelly-bag and stand at hand, a very effectual though simple substitute may be made out of a kitchen stool and a clean napkin (*see* April 9th). When the liquid is bright and clear add a wine-glassful of sherry and a table-spoonful of brandy, pour it into a damp mould, and put it in a cool place. A jelly made with these proportions can be varied in all sorts of ways. Various liqueurs can be used for flavouring instead of sherry or brandy, fruit juices can be added instead of water, and the jelly of course is named after the special flavourer. Thus, jelly flavoured with orange-rind and juice is orange jelly, and with maraschino is maraschino jelly.

Fruit and other additions are very often put into clear jelly, and they improve the appearance as well as the taste of the preparation. The fruits most suitable for the purpose are purple and white grapes, strawberries, cherries, raspberries, red and white currants, peaches, and apricots for summer-time; apples, pears, oranges, and preserved fruits, such as pine-apples, apricots, greengages, &c., for winter. Soft fruits, such as grapes, red currants, strawberries, and raspberries, may be put into the jelly as they are. Hard fruits should be cooked gently in syrup before being laid in the jelly, and large fruits should be cut into even-sized pieces. In preparing dishes of this kind a little jelly should be first poured into the mould to the depth of a quarter of an inch. When this is set, a layer of fruit may be arranged upon it, and *a spoonful or two of jelly should be poured in to keep the fruit in its place.* When this also is set, jelly should be poured in again to cover the fruit to the thickness of a quarter of an inch; this too being allowed to set before a further addition is made. After this the mould can be filled up to within three-quarters of an inch of the top, with alternate layers of fruit, with jelly enough to keep it in its place, and jelly to cover it to the depth of a quarter of an inch, each layer being allowed to set firmly before another one is put in. When putting in the fruit, care should be taken to contrast the colours prettily. It is astonishing what effective and delicious jellies can be made in this way for a very trifling cost.

When *Savoury* or *Aspic Jelly* is to be made, such as is used to garnish salad or to make calf's-head mould or similar dishes, the gelatine is soaked, dissolved, and clarified as before, but savoury instead of sweet flavours are boiled with the liquid. If a pint of jelly is required, the pan may be rubbed across twice with a clove of garlic, and then the liquid may be poured in, and with it a small piece of clean leek, a piece of turnip, a piece of carrot, an inch or two of celery, a shalot, half a blade of mace, a very small sprig of tarragon and chervil, two cloves, twelve peppercorns, and a little salt. The juice of a lemon, or a table-spoonful of vinegar, should also be added; the first is to be preferred. Jelly of this kind may be put into a round mould, and a gallipot may be placed in the centre to keep it hollow. Then when the jelly is turned out various savoury preparations may be put in the middle, and very pretty dishes will be produced.

If the jelly is to be made of *Calf's Foot Stock*, proceed as follows: —Make the stock the day before the jelly is to be made. Wash two calf's feet and cut each into four pieces. Put these in a stewpan with cold water to cover them, and let them boil (this is to blanch them). Take out the feet and wash them again in cold water. Pour away the water they were boiled in before, rinse out the pan, and put the pieces into it again with five pints of fresh cold water. Let this boil, skim it occasionally (if it is not well skimmed the jelly will not be clear), draw the pan back, and simmer the liquid gently for five hours. When it is reduced to one quart put a hair sieve over a basin and strain the stock. Put it aside and let it get quite cold. Next day skim the fat off the top with an iron spoon that has been dipped in hot water, and dab the stock with a cloth that has been dipped in hot water. Put it into the pan free from sediment, and clarify it according to the method adopted for gelatine jelly, remembering that the ingredients mentioned there are intended for a *pint* of liquid, and here is a *quart* of stock. Calf's-foot jelly is of course very much more nourishing than jelly made of gelatine. The moulds for jelly should be rinsed first in hot and afterwards in cold water.

4. Make a little mayonnaise (August 30th) for the celery salad to-morrow evening.

Sunday, November 15th.

Breakfast.	Dinner.	Tea.	Supper.
Savoury Eggs.	Boiled Brill.	Brown and White Bread and Butter.	Cold Mutton.
Rolled Tongue.	Dutch Sauce.	Scones.	Celery Salad.
Scones.	Roast Leg of Mutton.	Damson Jam.	Wine Jelly.
Dry Toast.	Potato Snow.	Soda Cake.	Cheese.
Brown and White Bread and Butter.	Brussels Sprouts		
Bread and Milk.	Lèche Crème Cheese.		

BREAKFAST.—Savoury Eggs (January 1st); Rolled Tongue (July 27th); Scones (August 26th); Bread and Milk (January 25th).

DINNER.—Boiled Brill (January 9th); Dutch Sauce (May 14th); Roast Leg of Mutton (March 4th); Potato Snow (April 7th); Brussels Sprouts (June 4th); Lèche Crème (May 7th); Cheese (June 8th).

TEA.—Scones (May 23rd), Soda Cake (August 14th), made on Friday.

SUPPER.—*Celery Salad.*—Be sure that the celery is perfectly *dry* (*see* Salad, March 13th). Cut the white stalks into one-inch lengths, toss them lightly in a little mayonnaise sauce (August 30th), and pour mayonnaise on the surface. Garnish with boiled beet-root, and the white of three hard-boiled eggs cut into rings; rub the yolks of the eggs through a wire sieve upon the surface of the salad, and sprinkle a little chopped parsley on the top. Celery salad is very good with thin slices of German sausage or pink ham put round it. Jelly made yesterday.

Things that must not be Forgotten.

1. Turn and rub the mutton in the pickle.
2. Rub the pig's cheek and the feet, and turn them over in the brine.
3. If any cold fish is left, preserve it. It can be scalloped for breakfast to-morrow.
4. Put a cupful of hominy to soak all night in cold water.
5. The outer sticks of celery left from the salad can be left for celery soup on Tuesday.

November 16th.

Breakfast.	Luncheon.	Dinner.
Scalloped Fish.	Toad in the Hole.	Milk Soup.
Rolled Tongue.	Sweet Macaroni.	Italian Ribs of Beef.
Scones.		Mashed Potatoes.
Dry Toast.		Stewed Endive.
Brown and White Bread and Butter.		Apple Dumpling.
Marmalade.		Cheese.
Boiled Hominy.		

Marketing.

For the Day.—Half a pound of Macaroni; one Rib of Beef, weighing about four pounds, taken from the middle ribs, to be boned and rolled; six, or if preferred, eight ounces of firm Kidney Suet (*see* Suet Crust, June 25th); Potatoes, Endive, Apples; a piece of the silverside of the Rump of Beef, weighing about eight pounds.

For To-morrow.—A tin of Oysters; Watercress; half a pound of Bacon in rashers (January 3rd); Rolls (September 4th).

BREAKFAST.—Scalloped Fish : made of the remains of the Brill (January 7th); Rolled Tongue (July 27th), boiled last Friday; Scones (August 26th); Boiled Hominy (February 11th).

LUNCHEON.—Toad in the Hole (January 15th). This can be made of the meat left on the leg of mutton, and if any sausages were left on Saturday, they can be put in also. Sweet Macaroni (August 13th).

DINNER.—Milk Soup (January 3rd); Italian Ribs of Beef (February 2nd); Mashed Potatoes (May 12th); Stewed Endive (December 5th); Apple Dumplings (July 19th); Cheese (June 8th).

Things that must not be Forgotten.

1. Turn and rub the mutton in the pickle.
2. Rub the pig's feet and the pig's head, and turn them over in the brine.

3. If any little pieces of steak are left, pot them for breakfast to-morrow (January 23rd).

4. Preserve any hominy that may be left; it can be fried for breakfast to-morrow.

5. Make fresh brine (January 13th) if necessary, and put the silverside of beef in it.

November 17th.

Breakfast.	Luncheon.	Dinner.
Potted Beef. Toasted Bacon. Hot Rolls. Dry Toast. Brown and White Bread and Butter. Watercress. Fried Hominy.	Scalloped Oysters. Macaroni and Tongue.	Celery Soup. Pork Chops with Tomato Sauce. Browned Potatoes. Stewed Red Cabbage. Rothe Grütze or Red Rice. Cheese.

Marketing.

For the Day.—Half a pound of Macaroni (January 1st); about four pounds of Pork Chops, from the Loin or Neck (January 6th); the best Chops are from the Kidney end of the Loin; the Chops should be about half an inch thick; three or four pounds of Fresh Pork to put in pickle.

For To-morrow.—A sugar-cured Ham, if Ham is not already in the house (September 17th), for to-morrow; a couple of plump young Fowls (June 29th, or August 6th).

BREAKFAST.—Potted Beef (January 23rd); Toasted Bacon (January 19th); Hot Rolls (September 4th); Fried Hominy (February 12th).

LUNCHEON.—Scalloped Oysters (April 27th). *Macaroni and Tongue.*—Follow the recipe given for macaroni and ham (April 3rd), but substitute the tongue that is still left for ham.

DINNER.—Celery Soup (December 3rd). *Pork Chops, Broiled or Fried.*—Trim the chops neatly, and cut away part of the fat. Grease the gridiron, and make it hot; lay the chops on it, at a good height over a clear fire, and turn them every two minutes till they are done. They will take about twenty-five minutes, as they must be done through. Season them with pepper and salt, and if liked, add a little powdered sage or tarragon. If liked, the chops can be fried instead of being broiled; they should then be put into a frying-pan with some good dripping made hot, fried gently, and turned occasionally, until done enough; they would be ready in about half an hour. Tomato Sauce (July 15th); Apple Sauce (September 29th); Brown Gravy (September 29th); and Piquante Sauce (May 5th), are all suitable accompaniments to broiled pork chops. Potatoes, Browned (October 18th); Stewed Red Cabbage (October 23rd); Rothe Grütze or Red Rice (December 8th); Cheese (June 8th).

Things that must not be Forgotten.
1. Turn and rub the mutton in the pickle.
2. Turn the pig's feet and head in the brine.
3. Put the fresh pork into the brine from which the hand of pork was taken last Tuesday.
4. Pluck the fowls and hang them in a cool larder; dry the feathers (Note, February 28th).
5. Turn and rub the beef in the brine.

November 18th.

Breakfast.	Luncheon.	Dinner.
Fried Ham.	Australian Meat, Cold.	Fried Whiting.
Fried Eggs.	Pickles.	Boiled Fowl with Maître d'Hôtel Sauce.
Hot Buttered Toast.	Baked Potatoes.	Bacon Rolls.
Dry Toast.	Stewed Cheese.	Potato Snow.
Brown and White Bread and Butter.		Broccoli.
Honey.		Treacle Pudding.
Milk Porridge.		Cheese.

Marketing.

For the Day.—A four-pound tin of Australian Meat; Fresh Whiting (January 17th) to be sent home ready for frying; a quarter of a pound of Bacon in rashers; a quarter of a pound of Suet; Potatoes; Broccoli; Parsley.

For To-morrow.—A Dried Haddock; three pounds of Jerusalem Artichokes for Soup; Watercress.

BREAKFAST.—Fried Ham (March 5th): for this a slice is to be taken from the middle of the sugar-cured ham; Fried Eggs (March 5th); Milk Porridge (June 13th).

LUNCHEON.—Australian Meat (February 4th); Baked Potatoes (May 4th); Stewed Cheese (May 5th).

DINNER.—Fried Whiting (January 17th); *Boiled Fowls with Maître d'Hôtel Sauce.*—Boil the fowls according to the method recommended (September 6th). Make some Maître d'Hôtel Sauce (May 6th), pour half of it over the breast of the bird, and send the remainder to table in a tureen. Garnish the dish with bacon rolls (July 19th) and branches of boiled broccoli (April 25th). Celery Sauce (December 12th); Oyster Sauce (October 16th) or Egg Sauce (April 10th), may, if preferred, be substituted for the Maître d'Hôtel Sauce in this recipe. Potato Snow (April 7th); Treacle Pudding (March 28th); Cheese (June 8th).

Things that must not be Forgotten.
1. Turn and rub the mutton in the pickle.
2. Turn the feet and the head in the brine.
3. It is not likely that the Australian meat will be finished at

luncheon to-day. Put all that remains on a clean dish in a cool larder.
4. Turn and rub the beef in the brine.
5. Partially prepare the rice-milk (Note 3, June 17th).
6. Preserve the liquor in which the fowls were boiled.

November 19th.

Breakfast.	Luncheon.	Dinner.
Dried Haddock. Devilled Eggs. Hot Buttered Toast, Dry Toast. Watercress. Brown and White Bread and Butter. Rice Milk.	Chicken Sauté aux Champignons. Plain Rice Pudding.	Palestine Soup. Roast Shoulder of Mutton. Browned Potatoes. Cabbages. Newcastle Pudding. Cheese.

Marketing.

For the Day.—A well-hung Shoulder of Mutton, not too fat; Potatoes; Cabbages; a small tin of Champignons.
For To-morrow.—A tin of Sardines (January 12th); Small Salad.

BREAKFAST.—Dried Haddock (January 27th); Devilled Eggs (February 27th); Rice Milk (June 18th).
LUNCHEON.—Chicken Sauté aux Champignons (April 2nd); Plain Rice Pudding (February 24th).
DINNER.—Palestine Soup (December 8th); Roast Shoulder of Mutton (March 4th); Browned Potatoes (October 18th); Cabbages (June 4th); Newcastle Pudding (June 12th); Cheese (June 8th).

Things that must not be Forgotten.
1. Turn and rub the mutton in the pickle.
2. Turn the pig's head and the feet in the brine.
3. Boil half of the sugar-cured ham (Note 4, May 27th).
4. Turn and rub the beef in the brine.

November 20th.

Breakfast.	Luncheon.	Dinner.
Sardines. Boiled Ham. Hot Buttered Toast. Dry Toast. Brown and White Bread and Butter. Small Salad. Porridge.	Boiled Tripe. Onion Sauce. Treacle Tart.	Half a dozen Oysters for each Person. Lemon Juice and Brown Bread and Butter. Civet of Rabbit. Mashed Potatoes. Stewed Celery. Town Pudding. Cheese.

Marketing.

For the Day.—A pound and a half of Dressed Tripe (Marketing, January 23rd); Fresh Oysters (Marketing, February 14th); a plump young Rabbit (January

24th), or two Rabbits if required; half a pound of Bacon in Rashers; Potatoes; Celery; Apples; Onions; six ounces of Suet.

For To-morrow.—Order to be sent in the morning a square piece of the thin flank of Beef, weighing about eight pounds.

BREAKFAST.—Sardines (January 12th); Boiled Ham (May 27th); Porridge (January 25th).

LUNCHEON.—Boiled Tripe (December 4th) with Onion Sauce; Treacle Tart (August 7th), to be made with the pastry to-day.

DINNERS.—Half a dozen Oysters (February 14th); Civet of Rabbit (December 8th); Mashed Potatoes (May 12th); Stewed Celery (December 2nd); Town Pudding (December 3rd); Cheese (June 8th).

Things that must not be Forgotten.

1. Turn and rub the silverside of beef in the brine, the mutton in the pickle, and also the pig's head and feet.

2. Pastry is to be made to-day (April 17th); Apple Pies (August 7th; Treacle Tart (August 7th); Baked Custard Tart (January 19th); also Sally Lunns (August 26th), and Cake. Hitherto the recipes given have been for very plain, wholesome cakes. When superior cakes are wanted the following recipe will be found excellent and not expensive:—*Gâteau Turc with Coffee Icing.*—Break four eggs into a basin, and put with them two ounces of white sugar. Have on the fire plenty of boiling water in a pan of such a size that the basin can rest on the top of it. Put the basin over the water, draw the pan back a little way, and whisk the eggs and the sugar till the mixture froths, which it will do in about twenty minutes. Take the basin off the fire and stir in lightly four ounces of Vienna flour. Pour the batter into a cake tin lined with paper, and bake in a good oven. *Coffee Icing for this Cake.*—Beat two ounces of butter to cream and work in four ounces of white sugar. Add clear, strong coffee (January 11th), to make a stiff paste. Put this on the cake with an icing tube and dry in a cool oven.

November 21st.

Breakfast.	Luncheon.	Dinner.
Boiled Ham.	Rabbit made Hot.	Victoria Soup.
Buttered Eggs.	Slices of Cold Pudding Toasted.	Boiled Silverside of Beef.
Sally Lunns.		Mashed Parsnips.
Dry Toast.		Carrots.
Brown and White Bread and Butter.		Potatoes.
Marmalade.		Apple Pie.
Bread and Milk.		Cheese.

Marketing.

For the Day.—Parsnips; Carrots; Potatoes; Parsley.

For To-morrow.—Bloaters, one for each person, and one over; three pounds of

Jerusalem Artichokes. The hare which was bought on the 12th of November will probably be sufficiently high, and may be cooked to-morrow. Ingredients for forcemeat (*see* Forcemeat for Hare, October 25th); a quarter of a pound of fat Bacon: Potatoes: Brussels Sprouts.

BREAKFAST.—Ham, boiled November 19th; Buttered Eggs (January 16th); Sally Lunns (June 4th); Bread and Milk (January 25th).

LUNCHEON.—Rabbit made Hot (November 13th); Cold Pudding Toasted (March 6th).

DINNER.—Victoria Soup (February 9th); Boiled Silverside of Beef (February 23rd); Mashed Parsnips (September 30th); Carrots (July 6th); Potatoes (April 7th); Apple Pie (August 7th); Cheese (June 8th).

Things that must not be Forgotten.

1. Turn and rub the mutton in the pickle, and the pig's head and feet in the brine.
2. Keep the bloaters apart from everything else in the larder.
3. Prepare the red rice for dinner to-morrow (December 10th).
4. As soon as the boiled beef leaves the table take the marrow from the bone in as large pieces as possible; it can be made into marrow toast for breakfast.
5. Skin the hare ready for to-morrow. To do this, cut a slit under the body, and take out the inside, break the legs at the first joint, cut the skin round the legs, and beginning at the hinder legs draw the skin off over the body, the fore-legs, and head. In doing this use a knife when necessary. Cut off the feet, skin the ears, preserving them and the tail, and take out the eyes. Wipe the hare inside and out, and if any parts look bloody, pierce them with a skewer, and wash them with tepid water.

Sunday, November 22nd.

Breakfast.	Dinner.	Tea.	Supper.
Bloaters.	Palestine Soup.	Brown and White Bread and Butter.	Cold Beef.
Marrow Toast.	Roast Hare.		Potato Salad.
Sally Lunns.	Red Currant Jelly.	Gâteau Turc.	Baked Custard Tart.
Dry Toast.	Potato Snow.	Strawberry Jam.	Cheese.
Brown and White Bread and Butter.	Brussels Sprouts.		
Corn-flour Milk.	Red Rice.		
	Cheese.		

BREAKFAST.—Bloaters (January 3rd); Marrow Toast (January 21st); Sally Lunns (June 4th); Corn-flour Milk (June 19th).

DINNER.—Palestine Soup (December 8th). *Roast Hare.*—Hare is naturally such dry meat that it is much better jugged (October 25th) than roasted. When, however, the latter method of cooking it is preferred proceed as follows :—Make some forcemeat (October 25th), fill the body with this, and sew it securely with soft cotton. Truss it with the hind legs forward and the fore legs back, and put a skewer down the mouth, and one in each ear to keep the head firmly in its right position. Put slices of fat bacon over the back to keep it moist, and put the hare in a dripping tin, put dripping on it, and place it in a *moderately* heated, not a *slow*, oven. (Roast hare is generally baked hare. It is so difficult to roast a hare equally in every part when it is hung before the fire, that cooks usually prefer to avoid the difficulty by putting it in the oven.) Baste it frequently to keep the skin moist. The time it will take to bake depends upon its size. A small hare would be done enough in an hour and a quarter, a large one would require two hours. Towards the last baste the hare with a little butter instead of dripping. Take it up, remove the skewers, and put it on a hot dish. Pour the fat from the tin, have ready some good gravy, made as directed at the end of this recipe, pour it into the tin, stir it well in the pan, pour it into a saucepan, boil it, strain a small quantity over the hare, and send the rest to table in a tureen. Red currant jelly should be served as an accompaniment. *Gravy for Roast Hare.*—Mince finely two moderate-sized onions, and fry them in a little dripping. Pour a pint and a half of stock upon them, and add the liver and heart of the hare, *if these are perfectly sweet*, a bunch of parsley, a sprig of thyme, a bay-leaf, half an inch of cinnamon, and two cloves, half a blade of mace, and an inch of thin lemon-rind. Cover closely, and stew gently for an hour and a half. Strain the gravy, free it from fat, thicken it with a dessert-spoonful of corn-flour mixed to a smooth paste with cold water, and add a little browning, a glass of port, and pepper and salt to taste. Boil up once more, and serve. Potato Snow (April 7th); Brussels Sprouts (June 4th); Red Rice (December 10th); Cheese (June 8th).

TEA.—Gâteau Turc (November 20th), made on Friday.

SUPPER.—Beef boiled (November 21st); Potato Salad (April 12th); Baked Custard Tart (January 19th).

Things that must not be Forgotten.

1. Turn and rub the mutton in the pickle, and the pig's head and feet in the brine.
2. Put a cupful of hominy to soak all night in cold water.
3. Soak a cupful of green lentils in cold water all night.

November 23rd.

Breakfast.	Luncheon.	Dinner.
Ham Toast.	Australian Meat, Cold.	Hare Soup.
Boiled Eggs.	Baked Potatoes.	Sour Mutton.
Sally Lunns.	Compôte of Apples.	Lentils.
Dry Toast.		Potatoes.
Brown and White Bread and Butter.		Cottage Plum Pudding.
Marmalade.		Cheese.
Boiled Hominy.		

Marketing.

For the Day.—A four pound tin of Australian Meat; six ounces of Beef Suet; Potatoes; Apples.
For To-morrow.—A tin of Sardines (January 12th); half a pound of prunes; about eight pounds of the thin end of the flank of Beef; Muffins (January 29th).

BREAKFAST.—Ham Toast made of the boiled ham cut from the bone (March 28th); Boiled Eggs (January 5th); Sally Lunns (June 4th); Boiled Hominy (February 11th).

LUNCHEON.—Australian Meat Cold (February 4th); Baked Potatoes (May 4th); Compôte of Apples (Note 3, September 12th).

DINNER.—Hare Soup (January 19th); Sour Mutton (March 29th); Lentils (March 2nd); Potatoes (May 12th); Cottage Plum Pudding (June 6th); Cheese (June 8th).

Things that must not be Forgotten.

1. Wash the prunes and put them to soak all night in cold water.
2. Preserve any cold hominy that may be left; it can be fried for breakfast to-morrow.
3. Boil the brine from which the silverside of beef was taken, and put the thin flank of beef into it.
4. Make brawn of the pig's head and the pig's feet (March 2nd).

November 24th.

Breakfast.	Luncheon.	Dinner.
Sardines.	Savoury Hash of Australian Meat.	Fried Cod.
Brawn.		Oyster Sauce.
Brawn Sauce.	Stewed Prunes.	Cold Mutton.
Muffins.		Celery Salad.
Dry Toast.		Baked Potatoes.
Brown and White Bread and Butter.		Pickles.
		Rice Gâteau.
Fried Hominy.		Cheese.

Marketing.

For the Day.—Four or five slices, half an inch thick, from the middle of a large Cod; a dozen Oysters, or a tin of preserved Oysters; Celery; Potatoes.

A A

For To-morrow.—A tin of Prawns (February 6th); Hot Rolls (September 3rd); Watercress

BREAKFAST.—Sardines (January 12th); Brawn (March 2nd), made yesterday; Brawn Sauce (January 15th); Muffins (January 30th); Fried Hominy (February 12th).

LUNCHEON.—Savoury Hash of Australian Meat (February 5th); Stewed Prunes (February 27th).

DINNER.—Slices of Cod Fried (January 1st); Oyster Sauce (October 16th); Mutton, roasted yesterday; Celery Salad (November 15th); Baked Potatoes (May 4th); Rice Gâteau (October 3rd); Cheese (June 8th).

Things that must not be Forgotten.

1. Preserve any fish and fish sauce that may be left, cod pie or fish cakes can be made of it for luncheon to-morrow.
2. Turn and rub the flank of beef in the brine.

November 25th.

Breakfast.	Luncheon.	Dinner.
Prawns.	Fish Cakes.	Skate with Brown Butter Sauce.
Brawn.	Stewed Ox Kidney.	
Brawn Sauce.	Suet Dumplings.	Broiled Steak à la Béarnaise.
Hot Rolls.		Fried Potatoes.
Dry Toast.		Broccoli.
Brown and White Bread and Butter.		Newcastle Pudding.
Watercress.		Cheese.
Milk Porridge.		

Marketing.

For the Day.—A fresh Ox Kidney; a quarter of a pound of Suet; about two pounds of Crimped Skate (January 10th and 3rd); a slice of Rump Steak an inch thick (January 22nd); Potatoes; Broccoli; Parsley.

For To-morrow.—Order to be sent in the morning the top side of the Round of Beef (February 3rd); Mustard and Cress; three-pennyworth of Cream for the Potato Purée, if permitted; Sea Biscuits.

BREAKFAST.—Prawns (February 7th); Brawn (March 2nd); Brawn Sauce (January 15th); Hot Rolls (September 4th); Milk Porridge (June 13th).

LUNCHEON.—Fish Cakes (January 13th); Stewed Ox Kidney (April 2nd); Suet Dumplings (October 17th).

DINNER.—Skate with Brown Butter Sauce (February 12th); Broiled Steak (January 22nd); Béarnaise Sauce (March 23rd); Fried Potatoes (February 2nd); Broccoli (April 25th); Newcastle Pudding (June 12th); Cheese (June 8th).

Things that must not be Forgotten.

1. Turn and rub the flank of beef in the brine
2. Preserve any little pieces of steak that may be left.
3. Put a cupful of white haricot beans to soak all night in cold water.

November 26th.

Breakfast.	Luncheon.	Dinner.
Prawns.	Shepherd's Pie.	Potato Purée.
Eggs on the Dish.	Custard Sippets.	Top side of the Round of Beef.
Hot Buttered Toast.		Yorkshire Pudding.
Dry Toast.		Haricot Beans.
Brown and White Bread and Butter.		Potato Mould.
Marmalade.		Brown Betty.
Biscuits and Milk.		Cheese.

Marketing.

For the Day.—Top side of the Round ordered yesterday; Potatoes; Apples.
For To-morrow.—A dried Haddock; a tin of potted Grouse; a fine Ox Tail; Watercress.

BREAKFAST.—Prawns (February 7th); Eggs on the Dish (December 7th); Biscuits and Milk (June 14th).

LUNCHEON.—Shepherd's Pie, made of the remnants of Steak (January 12th); Custard Sippets (June 10th).

DINNER.—Potato Purée (January 26th); Top side of the Round of Beef (February 3rd, and March 4th). *Yorkshire Pudding.*—Make some batter according to the recipe given with Toad in the Hole (January 15th), or if a richer batter is required, allow two eggs to three table-spoonfuls of flour, instead of one egg to two table-spoonfuls of flour. Remember always that the batter will be much lighter if it is made some hours before it is wanted. Let the tin in which the pudding is to be baked get hot through, and be well greased by being placed under the roasting joint. Pour the batter into it to the thickness of a quarter of an inch, and cook it under the joint before the fire, turning it about that it may be equally browned on all sides. When it is done enough, cut it into three inch squares, and serve these on a separate dish at the same time as the pudding. Yorkshire pudding as made in Yorkshire is thin, and browned on one side only, according to the method described here. Yorkshire pudding served in other parts of the country is half an inch thick, and is sometimes browned on both sides, being occasionally turned over when it is browned on the uppermost surface. Sometimes it is baked in the oven under a baking joint instead of before the fire under a roasting one. When this plan is adopted, it is an improvement to bake the batter in small tins, after the fashion of Wyvern Puddings (May 9th), instead of putting it in one large tin. The small puddings thus made may, if liked, be placed on the dish round the joint. Haricot Beans (June 20th); Potato Mould (October 23rd).

Brown Betty.—Pare, core, and slice six or eight large baking-apples, and prepare a large cupful of fine bread-crumbs. Butter a pie-dish, place a thin layer of bread-crumbs to cover the bottom of the dish, and put a layer of apples on this. Grate a little lemon-rind, or if preferred put a clove with the fruit, sprinkle sugar upon it, and lay two or three knobs of butter on the top. Fill the dish with these alternate layers of crumbs, apples, sugar, and butter, remembering that crumbs should form the uppermost layer. Pour a cupful of water on the top, and bake the pudding slowly for an hour and a half or more, according to the quality of the apples. The pudding is done enough when the apples have fallen, and the crumbs on the surface are brown. Of course a spoonful or two of prepared quince would greatly improve this pudding. Cheese (June 8th).

Things that must not be Forgotten.

1. Turn and rub the flank of beef in the brine.
2. As soon as the beef leaves the table put it on a clean dish, and place it in the larder.
3. If any haricot beans are left, preserve them. They will make a very good salad for dinner to-morrow.

November 27th.

Breakfast.	Luncheon.	Dinner.
Dried Haddock. Potted Grouse. Hot Buttered Toast. Dry Toast. Brown and White Bread and Butter. Porridge.	Toad in the Hole. Jam Turnovers.	Ox Tail Soup. Beef with **Sharp Sauce**. Potatoes. Broccoli. Apple Pie. Cheese.

Marketing.

For the Day.—A pound and a half of tender steak for Toad in the Hole; Apples; Potatoes; Broccoli; German Yeast; a pound and a half of Sausages, or fresh Pork to make the same (March 18th), for Sausage Rolls.

For To-morrow.—Half a pound of Macaroni.

BREAKFAST.—Dried Haddock (January 27th); Potted Grouse (January 7th); Porridge (January 25th).

LUNCHEON.—Toad in the Hole (January 15th); Jam Turnovers made to-day.

DINNER.—Ox Tail Soup (February 22nd); Beef with Sharp Sauce made of cold roast beef (December 4th); Potatoes (May 12th); Broccoli (April 25th); Apple Pie made to-day. Cheese (June 8th).

Things that must not be Forgotten.

1. Turn and rub the beef in the brine.
2. Pastry is to be made to-day (April 17th); Apple Pies (August 7th); Jam Turnovers (September 25th); and Sausage Rolls (November 6th). Also Teacakes (August 26th) may be made; Seed Cake (August 14th).

November 28th.

Breakfast.	Luncheon.	Dinner.
Potted Grouse.	Rissoles.	Croûte au Pot.
Sausage Rolls.	Italian Macaroni.	Spanish Stew.
Teacakes.		Potatoes.
Dry Toast.		Savoy.
Brown and White Bread and Butter.		Hayrick Pudding.
Milk Toast.		Cheese.

Marketing.

For the Day.—One, or if necessary two, Ostend Rabbits (January 24th); Onions; Potatoes; Savoy.

For To-morrow.—A moderate-sized Turbot (June 6th). Turbot is best and cheapest in the summer months. Nevertheless, if desired, it can usually be obtained all the year round. A shoulder of Mutton, not too fat; Potatoes; Brussels Sprouts; materials for a Salad; half a pound of Raspberry Sandwich, or Swiss Roll; and six ounces of good Suet; Sea Biscuits; a small compact leg of Pork to be pickled.

BREAKFAST.—Potted Grouse (January 7th); Sausage Rolls made yesterday. Teacakes (February 14th); Milk Toast (June 17th).

LUNCHEON.—Rissoles made of the broken remnants of the top side of the Round of Beef (January 6th); Italian Macaroni (July 7th).

DINNER.—Croûte au Pot (May 25th); Spanish Stew (April 8th); Potatoes (April 7th); Savoy (June 4th); Hayrick Puddings (March 19th); Cheese (June 8th).

Things that must not be Forgotten.

1. Turn and rub the beef in the brine.
2. The pudding for to-morrow can very well be made to-day, to save trouble on Sunday.
3. Very good stock can be made by stewing the bones and trimmings of the rabbit.
4. Rub the leg of pork all over, and very thoroughly, with salt.

Sunday, November 29th.

Breakfast.	Dinner.	Tea.	Supper.
Eggs in Brown Butter.	Boiled Turbot.	Brown and White Bread and Butter.	Cold Mutton.
Sausage Rolls.	Béarnaise Sauce.	Plum Jam.	Salad.
Teacakes.	Roast Shoulder of Mutton.	Seed Cake.	Pickles.
Dry Toast.	Potatoes.		Apple Pie.
Brown and White Bread and Butter.	Brussels Sprouts.		Cheese.
Biscuits and Milk.	Raspberry Sandwich Pudding.		
	Cheese.		

BREAKFAST.—Eggs in Brown Butter (January 6th); Sausage Rolls made on Friday; Teacakes (February 14th); Biscuits and Milk (June 14th).

DINNER.—Boiled Turbot (June 7th); Béarnaise Sauce (March 23rd); Roast Shoulder of Mutton (March 4th); Potatoes (May 12th); Brussels Sprouts (June 4th). *Raspberry Sandwich Pudding.*—Follow the recipe given for Lèche Crème (May 7th); but substitute Swiss Roll cut into slices for the ratafias. Cheese (June 8th).

TEA.—Seed Cake (August 14th).

SUPPER.—Salad (March 13th); Apple Pie (August 7th).

Things that must not be Forgotten.

1. Turn and rub the beef in the brine.
2. Put a large cupful of hominy to soak in cold water.
3. Preserve the liquor in which the turbot was boiled.
4. Turn and rub the leg of pork.

November 30th.

Breakfast.	Luncheon.	Dinner.
Fried Ham.	Minced Mutton.	Fish Soup.
Fried Eggs.	Baked Batter Pudding.	Stewed Steak.
Teacakes.		Potato Snow.
Brown and White Bread and Butter.		Jerusalem Artichokes.
Boiled Hominy.		Apple Custard.
		Cheese.

Marketing.

For the Day.—Three pounds of tender steak, cut about an inch and a half thick. Potatoes, Apples, Jerusalem Artichokes.

For To-morrow.—Bloaters. One for every two persons will probably be sufficient. Watercress.

BREAKFAST.—Fried Ham (March 5th); Fried Eggs (March 5th); Teacakes (February 14th); Boiled Hominy (February 11th).

LUNCHEON.—Minced Mutton (January 20th); Baked Batter Pudding (February 5th).

DINNER.—Fish Soup (July 13th); Stewed Steak (January 31st); Potato Snow (April 7th). *Jerusalem Artichokes.*—Wash, brush, and pare the artichokes. Put them into a saucepan with sufficient *cold* water, slightly salted, to cover them. Let the water boil, skim it well, and boil the artichokes gently till they are tender. The lid should be kept on the pan. Drain the artichokes, and serve them with melted butter poured over them. If the artichokes are left in the pan after they are done enough they will turn black. Apple Custard (November 10th); Cheese (June 8th).

Things that must not be Forgotten.

1. Turn and rub the beef in the brine.
2. Turn and rub the pork in the liquor that has run from it.
3. Preserve any boiled hominy that may be left. It can be fried for breakfast to-morrow.
4. Put a cupful of green lentils to soak all night in cold water.
5. Preserve the remains of stewed steak and pot the meat for breakfast to-morrow (January 23rd).

FRUITS IN SEASON SUITABLE FOR DESSERT IN NOVEMBER.

Apples, Pears, Shaddocks, Pomeloes, Pomegranates, Grapes, Melons, Cobs, Filberts, Walnuts, Chestnuts, Brazils, Barcelonas, Medlars, Dried and Crystallised Fruits.

NOVEMBER.

Apple Jam and Apple Jelly.—The best time for making apple jelly is about the middle of November. Almost all kinds of apples can be used for the purpose, though if a clear white jelly is wanted Colvilles, or orange pippins should be chosen; if red jelly is preferred very rosy-cheeked apples should be taken, and the skins should be boiled with the fruit. Apple jam is made of the fruit after the juice has been drawn off for jelly. Economical housekeepers will find that very excellent apple jelly can be made of apple parings, so that when apples in any quantity have been used for pies and tarts, the skins can be stewed in sufficient water to cover them, and when the liquid is strongly flavoured it can be strained and boiled with sugar to a jelly. To make apple jelly pare, core, and slice the apples and put them into a preserving pan with enough water to cover them. Stir them occasionally and stew gently till the apples have fallen, then turn all into a jelly-bag and strain away the juice, but do not squeeze or press the pulp. Measure the liquid and allow a pound of sugar to a pint of juice. Put both juice and sugar back into the preserving pan, and if liked, add one or two cloves tied in muslin, or two or three inches of lemon-rind. Boil gently and skim carefully for about half an hour, or till a little of the jelly put upon a plate will set. Pour it while hot into jars, and when cold and stiff cover down in the usual way. If yellow jelly is wanted a pinch of saffron tied in muslin should be boiled with the juice. To make *apple jam*, weigh the apple pulp after the juice has been drawn from it. Rub it through a hair-sieve, and allow one pound of sugar to one pint of pulp, and the grated rind of a lemon to three pints of pulp. Boil all gently together till the jam will set when a little is put on a plate. Apple jam is sometimes flavoured with vanilla instead of lemon.

DISHES FOR INVALIDS.

MEATS.

Mutton Chop or Rump Steak Stewed.—Trim away nearly all the fat, and put the chop in a jar that has a closely-fitting cover. Place this in a saucepan of water and keep the water simmering round it till the meat is tender. It will take about an hour and a half. For another method *see* May 29th.

Minced Meat.—Raw mutton, beef, poultry, and game can all be minced. Cut away all the fat, and skin, and sinew, and mince the flesh finely. Sprinkle a little salt upon it, put it into a delicately clean saucepan, and heat it very slowly by the side of the fire. When hot through it is done enough. It must on no account boil or it will be hard. Cooked meat should never be warmed up for invalids. Raw rump steak scraped to pulp is often ordered for weakness.

Poultry and Game of all kinds, when ordered for invalids, should be cooked and served in the usual way.

Fish should, as a rule, be plainly boiled and served with plain melted butter.

December 1st.

Breakfast.	Luncheon.	Dinner.
Bloaters.	Scotch Collops.	Fried Whiting.
Potted Beef.	Rice with Apples and Beetroot.	Lentils and Sausages.
Hot Buttered Toast.		Potatoes.
Dry Toast.		Golden Pudding.
Brown and White Bread and Butter.		Cheese.
Water Cress.		
Fried Hominy.		

Marketing.

For the Day.—A pound and a half of Buttock Steak (January 1st); Fresh Whiting (January 17th); three pounds of best Pork Sausages, or fresh Pork to make the same (March 18th); six ounces of Suet; Apples; Beetroot; Potatoes.

For To-morrow.—A pint of freshly-boiled shrimps.

BREAKFAST.—Bloaters on Toast (March 24th); Potted Beef (January 23rd); Fried Hominy (February 12th).
LUNCHEON.—Scotch Collops (January 9th); Rice with Apples and Beetroot (January 28th).
DINNER.—Fried Whiting (January 17th); Lentils and Sausages (April 4th); Potatoes (May 12th); Golden Pudding (May 4th); Cheese (June 8th).

Things that must not be Forgotten.
1. Turn and rub the beef in the brine.
2. Turn the pork over and rub it in the liquor that is around it.
3. Pot the shrimps for breakfast to-morrow (November 12th).
4. Partially prepare the rice milk (Note 3, June 17th).

December 2nd.

Breakfast.	Luncheon.	Dinner.
Potted Shrimps.	Stewed Giblets.	Crécy Soup.
Eggs on the Dish.	Cake Pudding.	Roast Capon.
Hot Buttered Toast.		Brown Gravy.
Dry Toast.		Bread Sauce.
Brown and White Bread and Butter.		Mashed Potatoes.
		Stewed Celery.
Rice Milk.		Rice Gâteau.
		Cheese.

Marketing.
For the Day.—Two sets of Giblets in addition to those of the Capon; a plump Capon (June 29th); Potatoes; Carrots; Celery.
For To-morrow.—A sugar-cured Ham if this is not in the house; half a pound of Macaroni; Fillet of Beef (January 2nd).

BREAKFAST.—Potted Shrimps (November 12th); Eggs on the Dish (December 7th); Rice Milk (June 18th).
LUNCHEON.—Stewed Giblets (February 6th); Cake Pudding (February 4th).
DINNER.—Crécy Soup (January 5th); Roast Capon (June 30th); Brown Gravy (October 18th); Bread Sauce (October 18th); Mashed Potatoes (May 12th). *Stewed Celery.*—Cooked Celery has within the last year or two risen very much in popular estimation for its purifying and nourishing qualities. Indeed, it has been declared by a well-known member of the medical profession, that the regular use of celery not only purifies the blood but makes rheumatism impossible. Celery is an exceedingly palatable dish and economical also. The strict economist, when preparing it, may cut away the outermost stalks and the leaves to be used for flavouring purposes, or for making soup; stew the coarser stalks that remain, to be served as a vegetable; and send the roots and the more delicate stalks to table

to be eaten raw with cheese or to be made into a salad. To *Stew Celery:* First, wash it well and trim it. Put it into a saucepan with boiling water, and let it boil for five minutes; drain it and put it into a stewpan with stock to cover it, and stew it gently for about half an hour, or till it is tender. Thicken the gravy with flour and butter, and add pepper and salt and a few drops of browning to make it a good colour. Boil a quarter of an hour longer and serve the celery with the sauce poured over it. If liked white stock may be used instead of flavoured brown stock, and a cupful of milk may be added when the sauce is thickened. Rice Gâteau (October 3rd); Cheese (June 8th).

Things that must not be Forgotten.

1. Turn and rub the beef in the brine.
2. Turn and rub the leg of pork in the liquor.
3. Cut the sugar-cured ham in half; soak, then boil a portion (Note 4, May 27th).
4. Stew the bones and trimmings of the capon. They will make valuable stock for the celery soup to-morrow.
5. Brush the beef over with a table-spoonful of vinegar, pepper it lightly, and hang it in a cool airy place.

December 3rd.

Breakfast.	Luncheon.	Dinner.
Savoury Eggs. Boiled Ham. Hot Buttered Toast. Dry Toast. Brown and White Bread and Butter. Porridge.	Ham and Macaroni. Custard Sippets.	Celery Soup. Fillet of Beef Roasted. Horseradish Sauce. Yorkshire Pudding. Potatoes. Broccoli. Town Pudding. Cheese.

Marketing.

For the Day.—Horseradish; Potatoes; Apples; Celery if required; six ounces of good Suet.
For To-morrow.—Normandy Pippins; Split Peas.

BREAKFAST.—Savoury Eggs (January 1st); Ham boiled yesterday; Porridge (January 25th).

LUNCHEON.—Ham and Macaroni (April 3rd); Custard Sippets (June 10th).

DINNER.—*Celery Soup.*—Wash a dozen or more outer sticks of celery and boil them till quite tender in as much of the stock made from the capon bones as will cover them. Stew with them two good-sized onions and some strips of bacon rind scalded and scraped.

Drain the celery and preserve the liquor. Take out the onions and the bacon rind, and rub the celery through a sieve. Melt two ounces of butter in a stewpan, mix a dessert-spoonful of corn-flour and a dessert-spoonful of flour smoothly with it, add a little of the liquor and the celery pulp. Boil a few minutes, and stir the soup to keep it from getting into lumps, add more liquor to make it as thick as cream, and season with pepper, salt, and a spoonful of white sugar. Pour a pint of boiling milk into the tureen, mix in the soup, and serve very hot with crusts of bread cut into dice and fried in a separate dish. If there is no white stock in the house water should be used instead, for stock is not really needed, and brown stock would spoil the colour of the soup. If a little cream were allowed the soup would, of course, be much improved; or as a substitute for cream the yolk of an egg mixed with a little milk might be put into the tureen and the soup added gradually afterwards. *Parsnip Soup*, also very good, may be made in the same way, or, if preferred, like Crécy Soup (January 5th); Fillet of Beef Roasted (February 11th). *Horseradish Sauce.*—Grate a young root of horseradish very finely; put with it a pinch of salt and a little more than a table-spoonful of vinegar, or as much as will moisten the whole. Add two table-spoonfuls of milk or cream, mix well and serve. Some people would consider it an improvement if a large table-spoonful of mixed mustard were added. This sauce should be served cold. Yorkshire Pudding (November 26th); Potatoes (April 7th); Broccoli (April 25th). *Town Pudding.*—Chop six ounces of suet finely. Mix with it half a pound of fine bread crumbs, half a pound chopped apples, weighed after being pared and cored, six ounces of moist sugar, and a little grated lemon rind. Press the mixture lightly into a buttered mould, tie a floured cloth over the top and boil the pudding for four hours. It will not need any moisture. Let it stand a minute or two, turn it out carefully, and send wine sauce (July 19th) to table with it. Cheese (June 8th).

Things that must not be Forgotten.

1. Turn and rub the beef in the brine.
2. Turn and rub the pork in the liquor that surrounds it.
3. Put six or eight Normandy pippins to soak all night in cold water.
4. Wash a pint of split peas and put them to soak all night in cold water, and take away any that float or are discoloured.

December 4th.

Breakfast.
Boiled Ham.
Eggs in Brown Butter.
Hot Buttered Toast.
Dry Toast.
Brown and White Bread and Butter.
Bread and Milk.

Luncheon.
Boiled Tripe and Onions.
Normandy Pippins.

Dinner.
Brown Soup.
Boiled Leg of Pork.
Pease Pudding.
Potatoes.
Cabbage.
Newmarket Pudding.
Cheese.

Marketing.

For the Day.—A pound and a half of dressed Tripe (see Marketing, January 23rd). If sufficient beef remains this can be dispensed with. Potatoes; Cabbage; Onions; German Yeast.

For To-morrow.—Whiting for Breakfast. The fish must be perfectly fresh, and must be put into a cool larder till wanted. Order four or five pounds of the Loin of Mutton. The butcher should be asked to bone the joint.

BREAKFAST.—Ham boiled December 2nd; Eggs in Brown Butter (January 6th); Bread and Milk (January 25th).

LUNCHEON.—*Boiled Tripe.*—Put the dressed tripe into a stewpan with boiled water to cover it, and bring the water to a boil; this is done to blanch it. Take it up, scrape it well to cleanse it, and cut it into neat pieces. Put it back into the saucepan with a pint and a half of milk, and six good-sized onions cut into quarters. Let the milk boil, then draw the saucepan back, and let its contents simmer for fully two hours, or till the tripe is quite tender when probed with a fork. Take up the tripe and the onions. Mix a table-spoonful of flour to a smooth paste with cold water. Stir this into the milk till it thickens. Chop the onions, mix them with the sauce, and return the tripe to it also for a minute to get hot. Put the tripe on a hot dish, pour the sauce over, and serve. If sufficient cold meat were left from yesterday *Beef with Acid Sauce* might be served instead of the tripe. For this, cut the cold beef into neat slices, and put them between two dishes till wanted. Supposing there is a pound of meat, peel and chop small two good-sized onions; fry them in a little dripping, dredge a table-spoonful of flour upon them, and pour on half a pint of stock, and a table-spoonful of vinegar. Add salt and pepper, a lump of sugar, and a spoonful of mixed mustard. Simmer the sauce till it is smooth and thick. Twenty minutes before the dish is to be served put in the pieces of beef, and let them get hot through, but the sauce must on no account boil after they are put in. If one or two champignons can be stewed with the sauce, so much the better. Normandy Pippins (August 16th).

DINNER.—Brown Soup (see Croûte au Pot, May 25th). *Boiled Leg of Pork.*—Put the pork on the fire in lukewarm water, bring it to the boil, let it boil for five minutes, then draw it back and simmer very gently for twenty minutes per lb. and twenty minutes over. If liked, instead of cabbage, carrots, turnips, or parsnips may be served with the pork. Some people like to have the vegetables boiled in the liquor with the pork. If not too salt the liquor can be used for making pea soup, or lentil soup; but it is scarcely suitable for any other kind of soup. *Pease Pudding* is an acceptable accompaniment to this dish. For this drain the peas that were soaked overnight, tie them loosely in a cloth, put them in cold water over the fire, and boil them for fully two hours, or till tender. Rub them through a sieve, mix with them a knob of butter or dripping, a teaspoonful of sugar, pepper and salt, and a well-beaten egg. Tie the pudding tightly in a floured cloth, plunge it into boiling water, and boil quickly for an hour. Pease Pudding is very good with boiled beef. Potatoes (April 7th); Cabbage (June 4th); Newmarket Pudding (June 2nd); Cheese (June 8th).

Things that must not be Forgotten.

1. Boil the beef that has been in pickle, and press it between two dishes (February 23rd).

2. If any pease pudding were left, it can be used for making pea soup to-morrow instead of boiling fresh peas. If there is no peas pudding, potato purée (January 26th) can be made instead.

3. Pastry is to be made to-day. Apple and Quince pies (August 7th); Jam Turnovers (September 25th); also Sally Lunns (June 4th); and Seed Cake (August 14th).

4. If the boiled ham is nearly finished, cut all the meat from the bone, mince it finely, and put it between two dishes in a cool place.

December 5th.

Breakfast.	Luncheon.	Dinner.
Fried Whiting.	Cold Pork.	Pea Soup.
Ham Toast.	Brawn Sauce.	Loin of Mutton Boned and Rolled.
Sally Lunns.	Baked Potatoes.	Potatoes.
Dry Toast.	Savoury Rice.	Stewed Endive.
Brown and White Bread and Butter.		Wyvern Pudding.
Marmalade.		Cheese.
Corn-flour Milk.		

Marketing.

For the Day.—Loin of Mutton ordered yesterday; Potatoes; two heads of Endive.

For To-morrow.—A couple of fine Ducks (July 4th); Cod's Head and Shoulders weighing about six pounds (January 1st and 6th; see also Note 4, October 16th); a dozen fresh Oysters, or a tin of preserved Oysters; eight Oranges; Onions; Sage-leaves; Apples; Potatoes; Brussels Sprouts; Chestnuts; Celery; a tin of Potted Pheasant; a quarter of a pound of Bacon in rashers; a neck of Mutton; two pounds of firm Kidney Suet for the Plum Pudding and Mincemeat to be made on Wednesday.

BREAKFAST.—Fried Whiting (January 17th); Ham Toast, made of the remnants of dressed ham (March 28th); Sally Lunns (June 4th); Corn-flour Milk (June 19th).

LUNCHEON.—Pork served (December 4th); Brawn Sauce (January 15th); Baked Potatoes (May 4th); Savoury Rice (June 17th).

DINNER.—Pea Soup (*see* Lentil Soup, April 1st); Loin of Mutton boned and rolled (April 22nd); Potatoes (May 6th). *Stewed Endive.* —Pick away the outer leaves, and wash the endive well. Put it into boiling water, and boil it like cabbage (June 4th) for a quarter of an hour, or till it is tender. Press the water from it, chop it finely, and salt it. Melt an ounce of butter in a stewpan, mix an ounce of flour smoothly with it, and add the chopped endive. Stir and toss it well over the fire, and add gradually a gill of cream, or broth if liked, and keep stirring it till the sauce is incorporated with the endive. Sprinkle a little white sugar on it, add a little butter at the last moment, and serve. Endive has a peculiar taste which is not liked by every one. Wyvern Puddings (May 9th); Cheese (June 8th).

Things that must not be Forgotten.

1. Glaze the beef boiled yesterday (March 21st).
2. Pluck the ducks to be ready for cooking to-morrow.
3. Put a large cupful of hominy to soak all night in cold water.
4. Hang the neck of mutton in a cool larder till Monday.
5. Make a little custard for supper to-morrow (August 10th).
6. Cleanse and scald the ducks' giblets. Gravy can be made of them to-morrow.
7. Make orange cream with orange garnish for supper to-morrow evening (December 6th).
8. Clear the suet from skin and fibre and chop it till it looks like fine oatmeal. Put it into a jar, cover with flour and leave it in a cool larder. To chop suet, *see* Sea Pie (March 14th).

Sunday, December 6th.

Breakfast.	Dinner.	Tea.	Supper.
Toasted Bacon.	Cod's Head and Shoulders.	Brown and White Bread and Butter.	Pressed Beef.
Potted Pheasant.	Oyster Sauce.	Apple Jelly.	Celery Salad.
Sally Lunns.	Roast Ducks.	Seed Cake.	Apple Pie.
Dry Toast.	Potato Snow.		Custard.
Brown and White Bread and Butter.	Chestnuts and Brussels Sprouts.		Cheese.
Boiled Hominy.	Orange Cream with Garnish.		
	Cheese.		

BREAKFAST.—Toasted Bacon (January 19th); Potted Pheasant (*see* Potted Grouse, January 7th); Sally Lunns (June 4th); Boiled Hominy (February 11th).

DINNER.—*Cod's Head and Shoulders.*—When the fish is sent in rub a little salt over the inside and the thick part. Next day, just before it is to be dressed, wash it quickly, cut off the gills and the ends of the fins, scrape off the scales without injuring the skin, and wipe the inside with a cloth dipped in vinegar. Dry the fish, put it on the drainer, and plunge it into plenty of well-salted boiling water, that has had half a gill of vinegar thrown into it. Boil the fish *gently* (skimming the liquor now and then) till it is done enough, which it will be when the eyes start and the flesh will leave the bone; it will take about half an hour. It can be kept hot on the drainer, if it is not to be served at once, but it will spoil if left in the water. Boil the liver and the roe in a separate saucepan, they will be wanted to garnish the fish; or if preferred, cut lemon and horseradish or parsley may be used instead; the liver must not be boiled with the fish. Send Oyster Sauce (October 16th) to table as an accompaniment. Roast Ducks (July 26th); Potato Snow (April 7th); Chestnuts and Brussels Sprouts (November 8th). *Orange Cream and Garnish* (prepared yesterday).—Peel four oranges, and put the rind in a pint of milk for an hour. Meantime soak three-quarters of an ounce of gelatine in two table-spoonfuls of milk. Boil the flavoured milk with four table-spoonfuls of sugar, stir in the gelatine, strain the cream, and let it go cold. As soon as the cream begins to set, add the strained juice of the oranges; this must not be put in before the cream is quite cold. Whisk the cream till it is in bubbles, pour it into a damp mould, and put it into a cool place till wanted. *Orange Garnish.*—Rinse the orange rind already used, it will still have flavour. When clear, throw it into half a pint of water, and simmer it till the liquor tastes pleasantly. Strain it, and boil it with loaf sugar to a clear syrup. Cut two or three of the strips of orange rind into shreds and throw them into the syrup. When the cream is turned upon a dish, garnish it with the shredded rind, and pour the orange syrup over it. If liked, the cream can be poured into a mould with a gallipot placed in the middle; a weight could be put on this to keep it down. Of course, when turned out, the cream would be hollow in the centre, and this vacancy might be filled with a *Compôte of Oranges*, prepared as follows :—Peel four oranges, and divide each orange into ten pieces. Pour over the fruit a little thick syrup made as directed for Orange Garnish. Let it soak for four hours, and it is ready for use. Or, instead of pouring syrup over the fruit, sprinkle powdered white sugar over the oranges, let them remain for three hours, then pour in three table-spoonfuls of brandy, or if preferred, port wine, and the compôte is ready. Cheese (June 8th).

TEA.—Seed Cake (August 14th).

SUPPER.—Beef boiled December 4th; Celery Salad (November 15th); Apple Pie (August 7th); Custard (August 10th).

Things that must not be Forgotten.

1. If any fish or oyster sauce is left, preserve it. It can be made into cod pie for luncheon to-morrow.

2. Preserve also the remains of boiled hominy.

December 7th.

Breakfast.	Luncheon.	Dinner.
Eggs on the Dish.	Cod Pie.	Croûte au Pot.
Potted Pheasant.	Minced Mutton.	Irish Stew.
Sally Lunns.		Potatoes.
Dry Toast.		Macaroni Pudding.
Brown and White Bread and Butter.		Cheese.
Marmalade.		
Fried Hominy.		

Marketing.

For the Day.—Potatoes; a quarter of a pound of Macaroni.
For To-morrow.—Three pounds of Jerusalem Artichokes; order four pennyworth of Cream for to-morrow.

BREAKFAST.—*Eggs on the Dish.*—When there is a close stove in use, these can be easily prepared. With an open range, the oven would need to be used for it. Butter a tin or earthenware dish that will stand the fire, that can be sent to table, and that has upright sides to keep the eggs from spreading. Butter the inside, and break the eggs in carefully to preserve them unbroken. Put the dish on the top of the stove for a couple of minutes till the whites are set; sprinkle pepper and salt over, and serve. Potted Pheasant (*see* Potted Grouse, January 7th); Sally Lunns (June 4th); Fried Hominy (February 12th).

LUNCHEON.—Cod Pie (January 2nd); Minced Mutton, made of the cold mutton left on Saturday if there were any (January 20th).

DINNER.—Croûte au Pot (May 25th); Irish Stew, made of the best end of the neck of mutton bought on Saturday (March 10th); the scrag end is to be served at luncheon to-morrow. Potatoes (May 12th); Macaroni Pudding (March 27th); Cheese (June 8th).

Things that must not be Forgotten.

1. Take one or, if necessary, two slices, the third of an inch thick, from the ham already in cut.
2. Hang the scrag end of mutton in a cool larder.
3. Make a corn-flour blancmange for dinner to-morrow (June 15th).
4. If the plum pudding and the mincemeat are to be made on Wednesday, prepare a pound and a half of currants, if there are none in the house cleaned and dried. It is a convenient plan to wash currants always as soon as they come in from the grocer. If they are washed in small quantities when wanted, they are frequently either left moist, thus making the pudding or cake heavy, or they are dried quickly before the fire, thus destroying their flavour. Wash the currants in cold water, drain them, sprinkle a little flour upon them, rub them, a few at a time, dry in a cloth, then put a small

quantity at once at the mouth of a cool oven. When quite dry, turn them over, pick out any stones there may be, and put them into a jar till wanted.

December 8th.

Breakfast.	Luncheon.	Dinner.
Fried Ham.	Scrag end of Mutton Stewed with Vegetables.	Palestine Soup.
Fried Eggs.	Baked Omelet.	Civet of Rabbit.
Sally Lunns.		Mashed Potatoes.
Dry Toast.		Stewed Celery.
Brown and White Bread and Butter.		Corn-flour Blancmange.
Milk Porridge.		Lemon Syrup.
		Cheese.

Marketing.

For the Day.—One fine Ostend Rabbit, or two Rabbits, if necessary; Potatoes; Celery; a small tin of Champignons; half a pound of Bacon. If one Rabbit only is required, part of the Bacon is for breakfast to-morrow.

For To-morrow.—Fresh Sheep's Kidneys, one for each person; Sea Biscuits; a loin of Pork to be pickled for December 11th.

BREAKFAST.—Fried Ham (March 5th); Fried Eggs (March 5th); Sally Lunns (June 4th); Milk Porridge (June 13th).

LUNCHEON.—Scrag end of Mutton (January 14th); Baked Omelet (August 6th).

DINNER.—*Palestine Soup.*—Wash and pare the artichokes and put them into a stewpan with a slice of butter, two or three strips of bacon rind, and two bay leaves. Cover the pan closely and let the artichokes sweat for ten minutes or less. Shake the pan once or twice to keep them from sticking. Pour on cold water to cover the artichokes, and boil them gently till soft. Rub them through a sieve, mix the liquor in which they were boiled with them, and add boiling milk to make the purée like gruel. Season with pepper and salt. Make the soup hot. Heat the cream separately, and mix the two at the moment of serving. If there is any stock made from rabbit bones or chicken bones it can be used instead of water. Really, however, stock is not needed, and the soup is whiter when it is not used. If the artichokes are old a little sugar should be put with them. *Civet of Rabbit.*—Wash, dry, and cut up one moderate-sized rabbit into neat pieces. Cut up a quarter of a pound of bacon also into neat rashers. Fry the bacon gently, take it up, and fry the rabbit in the same fat. Take up the rabbit, put back the bacon, and add an onion, a shallot, a small carrot, a small turnip, a bunch of parsley, a sprig of thyme, and a bay leaf. Turn all over in the fat for two or three minutes, put back the pieces of rabbit, and add a dozen champignons and a pint of stock; some of that left from the scrag of mutton will answer excellently. Season the civet with pepper and salt, and put with it a table-spoonful of flour mixed smoothly with water. Stir it till it boils and simmer for half an hour, or till the rabbit is tender. Add a glass of claret and a lump of sugar. Put the pieces of rabbit on a dish, pour the sauce over, and serve. Mashed Potatoes (May 12th); Stewed Celery (December 2nd); Corn-flour Blancmange made yesterday; Lemon Syrup (March 19th); Cheese (June 8th).

Things that must not be Forgotten.

1. Be sure to stew the rabbit bones and trimmings. They will make deliciously flavoured stock.

2. If preferred, milk can be used instead of cream in making the Palestine soup. Cream, however, is a very great improvement.

3. Make a pickle (April 15th), and put the pork into it.

December 9th.

Breakfast.	Luncheon.	Dinner.
Broiled Kidneys.	Stewed Giblets.	Skate with Brown Butter Sauce.
Toasted Bacon.	Lemon Dumplings.	Boiled Aitchbone of Beef.
Hot Buttered Toast.		Mashed Turnips.
Dry Toast.		Carrots.
Brown and White Bread and Butter.		Potatoes.
Biscuits and Milk.		Apple Gâteau.
		Cheese.

Marketing.

For the Day.—Two sets of fresh Giblets; half a pound of Suet; two pounds of crimped Skate (January 10th); Aitchbone of Beef (May 18th); Turnips, Carrots, Potatoes; materials for Plum Puddings and Mince Pies (*see* Recipes).

For To-morrow.—Speak for a Cow Heel; Rolls for breakfast (September 3rd).

BREAKFAST.—Broiled Kidneys (January 29th); Toasted Bacon (January 19th); Biscuits and Milk (June 14th).

LUNCHEON.—Stewed Giblets (February 6th); Lemon Dumplings (October 7th).

DINNER.—Skate with Brown Butter Sauce (February 12th); Boiled Aitchbone of Beef (February 23rd); Mashed Turnips (September 30th); Carrots (July 6th); Potatoes (April 7th); Apple Gâteau (September 24th); Cheese (June 8th).

Things that must not be Forgotten.

1. Partially prepare the rice and barley porridge for breakfast (Note 6, June 15th).

2. Turn and rub the pork in the pickle.

3. Boil the piece of ham that remains (Note 4, May 27th).

4. See Note 1, February 17th.

5. It is wise to make the plum puddings and mince-meat early in December, as suet is very dear at Christmas time. Good plum

puddings will keep for twelve months. Many housekeepers make half a dozen puddings, boil these, and hang them up till wanted. The quantities here given will make a good pudding for about a dozen persons. If five or six puddings are to be made the quantities will of course need to be proportionately increased.

Christmas Plum Pudding.—Take some stale crumb of bread, and rub it through a wire sieve until there are three-quarters of a pound of bread crumbs; put these into a bowl, with a quarter of a pound of flour and a tea-spoonful of salt, add three-quarters of a pound of the chopped suet, and also a pound and a half of muscatel raisins, half a pound of currants (Note 4, December 7th), picked and dried, six ounces of candied peel (orange, citron, and lemon mixed), six or eight bitter almonds blanched and pounded, and a table-spoonful of moist sugar. Prepare the raisins by cutting each one in halves and removing the pips, and the candied peel by slicing it very thinly. Mix these dry ingredients thoroughly. Whisk eight good eggs well, stir them into the pudding, and add a wine-glassful of brandy. A little milk may be put in also if required, but the pudding should be barely moistened, or it will be heavy. Take a new stout pudding cloth that has been boiled in water; wring it dry, flour it, and tie the pudding securely in it, leaving room for it to swell. Plunge the pudding into boiling water, and keep plenty of water boiling round it for eight hours. When it is necessary to add water, take care that it is boiling. After taking up the pudding hang it in the cloth in which it was boiled. If placed on a dish it will probably be heavy. To make the pudding ready for use boil it for a couple of hours till hot through. It should stand five minutes after being taken out of the water before it is turned out. For a cheaper, but very good plum pudding, *see* Cottage Plum Pudding (June 6th). The plainer pudding will be best made when it is wanted. To make mince-meat for pies, *see* December 23rd.

6. Put a cupful of haricot beans to soak all night in cold water.

December 10th.

Breakfast.	Luncheon.	Dinner.
Devilled Eggs.	Cow Heel with Parsley Sauce.	Crécy Soup.
Boiled Ham.	Apples and Tapioca.	Cold Beef.
Rolls.		Potato Salad.
Dry Toast.		Mutton Chops Stewed.
Brown and White Bread and Butter.		Haricot Beans.
Marmalade.		Cheese.
Rice and Barley Porridge.		

Marketing.

For the Day.—Cow Heel ordered yesterday; two or three pounds of Mutton Chops from the best end of the loin; Potatoes; Apples.

For To-morrow.—A dried Haddock; Watercress.

BREAKFAST.—Devilled Eggs (February 27th); Ham boiled yesterday; Rolls (September 4th); Rice and Barley Porridge (June 15th).

LUNCHEON.—Cow Heel with Parsley Sauce (February 20th); Apples and Tapioca (February 18th).

DINNER.—Crécy Soup (January 5th); Beef served December 9th; Potato Salad (April 12th); Mutton Chops, stewed in their own gravy (May 29th); Haricot Beans (June 20th). *Red Rice (Rothe Grütze.*—A Danish dish. This may be made either with the juice of fresh fruit or with dissolved red currant jelly, or raspberry jam. It is best when fresh raspberries are used for it. Take a pint and a half of red currants and half a pound of raspberries with a quart of water. Stew the currants gently till the juice flows freely, add the raspberries just before the currants are ready. Strain the juice measured, sweeten it to taste, and add corn-flour or ground rice in the same quantity as for a Blancmange (June 15th), or a Mould (August 7th). Pour the preparation into a damp mould. When cold, turn it upon a glass dish and serve cream with it, if permitted. To make red rice with jam, stew the contents of a pound jar of raspberry jam with enough water to fill a quart mould. Strain the juice, sweeten it, put a few drops of lemon juice with it, add cochineal to colour it, and proceed as before. Cheese (June 8th).

Things that must not be Forgotten.

1. Turn and rub the pork in the pickle.
2. Make a blancmange for dinner to-morrow. (*See* the recipe December 11th.)
3. Soak a cupful of lentils all night in cold water.

December 11th.

Breakfast.	Luncheon.	Dinner.
Dried Haddock.	Sheep's Head.	Fillets of Sole Sautés.
Boiled Ham.	Baked Batter Pudding.	German Pork.
Hot Buttered Toast.		Baked Potatoes.
Dry Toast.		Lentils.
Brown and White Bread and Butter.		Blancmange.
Watercress.		Cheese.
Milk Toast.		

Marketing.

For the Day.—A Sheep's Head; a pair of thick Soles (January 3rd); Potatoes; Red Cabbage; German Yeast; Bottled Cherries. Order Cream if allowed (*see* December 12th).

For To-morrow.—Sardines (January 12th); half a pound of Macaroni.

BREAKFAST.—Dried Haddock (January 27th); Ham boiled (December 9th); Milk Toast (June 17th).

LUNCHEON.—Sheep's Head (January 31st); Baked Batter Pudding (February 5th).

DINNER.—Sole, Fillets of, Sautés (January 4th); Pork, German way of cooking (April 18th); Baked Potatoes (May 4th); Lentils (March 2nd). *Blancmange.*—Soak an ounce of gelatine for an hour in a quarter of a pint of milk. Blanch ten bitter almonds and six sweet ones. Put these, with three inches of lemon rind, into a pint and a quarter of milk for a couple of hours, then pour the milk into a stewpan and add a little loaf sugar. Boil the milk, pour it upon the soaked gelatine, and strain the mixture into a jug. Let it stand, stirring it occasionally till cold. Pour the blancmange into a damp mould carefully, so as to keep back any sediment there may be, and let it stand till set. If cream, or half cream and half milk, be permitted, the blancmange will be much improved; Cheese (June 8th).

Things that must not be Forgotten.

1. Pastry is to be made to-day (April 17th); open jam tart and cherry pie made of bottled fruit (August 7th); Scones (August 26th); Gâteau Turc (November 20th).

2. Partially prepare the rice milk for breakfast (*see* Note 3, June 17th).

3. Cut all that remains from the ham bone. Ham toast, and ham and macaroni mould may be made of it to-morrow.

December 12th.

Breakfast.	Luncheon.	Dinner.
Sardines.	Ham and Macaroni.	Potato Purée.
Ham Toast.	Custard Sippets.	Pork Cutlets with Apple Sauce.
Scones.		Baked Potatoes.
Dry Toast.		Stewed Celery.
Brown and White Bread and Butter.		Brown Bread Pudding.
Rice Milk.		Cheese.

Marketing.

For the Day.—Potatoes; Apples; Celery; half a pound of Macaroni.

For To-morrow.—Bloaters. A pair of thick Soles (January 3rd); a couple of Fowls (June 29th); a quarter of a pound of Bacon in rashers; Potatoes; Apples; Celery; Brussels Sprouts; two pounds of good Pork Sausages, or meat to make the same (March 18th); a four pound tin of Australian Meat, and a tin of Collared Tongue for Monday.

BREAKFAST.—Sardines (January 12th); Ham Toast (March 28th); Scones (May 23rd); Rice Milk (June 17th).

LUNCHEON.—Ham and Macaroni (April 3rd); Custard Sippets (June 10th).

DINNER.—Potato Purée (January 26th); Pork Cutlets with Apple Sauce (January 30th); Baked Potatoes (May 4th); Stewed Celery (December 2nd); Brown Bread Pudding (July 20th); Cheese (June 8th).

Things that must not be Forgotten.

1. Pluck the fowls for dinner to-morrow, and cure the feathers (February 28th).

2. Make an apple mould for dinner to-morrow (September 15th).

3. Prepare the *Whipped Cream*, if this is to be allowed. The cream will be firmer if made the day before it is wanted. Put half a pint of double cream—that is, cream that has stood twenty-four hours—into a cold basin, sweeten and flavour it, and whisk it in a cold place with an ordinary whisk till it froths on the top. Skim off this froth and lay it at once on a fine sieve, and whisk again until the cream is finished. Take away the liquid that drains from the froth and reserve it for the celery sauce. When the froth has thus stood for some hours it will be ready for piling in the centre of a dish, or for any purpose of a similar kind. If the cream becomes very thick whilst it is being whisked, put a spoonful of cold water with it. The same remedy should be adopted if the cream should "turn," or become slightly cracked: this mischance frequently occurs, especially in hot weather. The quantity of whipped cream may be increased by beating the white of an egg to froth and adding it to the cream before beginning to whisk it.

4. The *Celery Sauce* may be partly made to-day to save time to-morrow. Proceed as for celery soup (December 3rd), decreasing the proportions for the quantity required. Celery Sauce should be thicker than soup; it should be of the consistency of very thick gruel. The outer sticks of three or four heads of celery will be needed to make sauce for a pair of fowls. When it is made of the outer sticks of celery a little cream should be stirred in to enrich and whiten it. The best part of the celery will be wanted for chicken salad. This sauce is spoiled by a mixture of seasoning.

Sunday, December 13th.

Breakfast.	Dinner.	Tea.	Supper.
Bloaters.	Sole au Gratin.	Brown and White Bread and Butter.	Chicken Salad.
Poached Eggs on Toast.	Boiled Fowls.	Strawberry Jam.	Cherry Pie.
Scones.	Celery Sauce.	Gâteau Turc.	Cheese.
Dry Toast.	Baked Sausages.		
Brown and White Bread and Butter.	Potatoes.		
Corn-flour Milk.	Brussels Sprouts.		
	Apple Mould.		
	Whipped Cream.		
	Cheese.		

BREAKFAST.—Bloaters (January 3rd); Poached Eggs on Toast (February 6th); Scones (May 23rd); Corn-flour Milk (June 19th).

DINNER.—Sole au Gratin (May 3rd). *Boiled Fowls with Celery Sauce.*—Follow the recipe given (September 6th), but use celery instead of egg sauce. Pour a little of the sauce over the birds and send the rest to table in a tureen. *Baked Sausages.*—Sausages are excellent baked instead of being fried. They should be put into a greased dripping tin and cooked in a *gentle* oven for about an hour and a half, when they will be done through without being burnt. For Gravy, see Liver and Bacon, January 17th; Potatoes (May 12th); Brussels Sprouts (June 4th); Apple Mould (September 15th); Whipped Cream (December 12th); Cheese (June 8th).

TEA.—Gâteau Turc (November 20th).

SUPPER.—Chicken Salad made of the remains of boiled Fowl, and the Celery reserved from Celery Sauce (August 30th); Cherry Pie (August 7th).

Things that must not be Forgotten.

1. Preserve the liquor the fowls were boiled in, and also the bones and trimmings of the fowls.
2. Put a cupful of German lentils to soak all night in cold water.

December 14th.

Breakfast.	Luncheon.	Dinner.
Collared Tongue.	Australian Meat, Cold.	Gravy Soup.
Toasted Bacon.	Baked Potatoes.	Stewed Steak.
Scones.	Savoury Rice.	Potatoes.
Dry Toast.		Boiled Lentils.
Brown and White Bread and Butter.		Apple Dumpling.
Milk Toast.		Cheese.

Marketing.

For the Day.—Three pounds of tender Steak (January 1st), cut evenly, and about one and a half inches thick; half a pound of Suet; Potatoes; Apples.

For To-morrow.—A dried Haddock.

BREAKFAST.—Collared Tongue (Note 2, January 3rd); Toasted Bacon (January 19th); Scones (May 23rd); Milk Toast (June 17th).

LUNCHEON.—Australian Meat (February 4th); Baked Potatoes (May 4th); Savoury Rice (June 17th).

DINNER.—Gravy Soup (September 22nd); Stewed Steak (January 31st); Potatoes (April 7th); Boiled Lentils (March 2nd); Apple Dumpling (*see* Red Currant Dumpling, July 19th); Cheese (June 8th).

Things that must not be Forgotten.

1. Put half a pound of prunes to soak all night in cold water.
2. Reserve any pieces of steak, and any cold potatoes that may be left.

December 15th.

Breakfast.	Luncheon.	Dinner.
Dried Haddock.	Savoury Hash of Australian Meat.	Croûte au Pot.
Collared Tongue.	Stewed Prunes.	Civet of Rabbit.
Hot Buttered Toast.		Potatoes.
Dry Toast.		Stewed Celery.
Brown and White Bread and Butter.		Lèche Crème.
Oatmeal Porridge.		Cheese.

Marketing.

For the Day.—One fine Ostend Rabbit, or two Rabbits if required (January 24th); half a pound of Ratafias; Potatoes; Celery.

For To-morrow.—Muffins (January 29th); half a pound of Macaroni; Dried Sprats, a bundle for each person; a well-hung Shoulder of Mutton, not too fat.

BREAKFAST.—Dried Haddock (January 27th); Collared Tongue (Note 2, January 3rd); Porridge (January 25th).

LUNCHEON.—Savoury Hash made of the remains of Australian Meat (February 5th); Stewed Prunes (February 27th).

DINNER.—Croûte au Pot (May 25th); Civet of Rabbit (December 8th); Potatoes (April 7th); Stewed Celery (December 2nd); Lèche Crème (May 7th); Cheese (June 8th).

Things that must not be Forgotten.

1. Excellent stock can be made of the rabbit bones.
2. Pot all that is left of the collared tongue; it can be served at breakfast to-morrow (Note 5, September 26th).

December 16th.

Breakfast.	Luncheon.	Dinner.
Potted Tongue.	Scotch Collops.	Haddock Stuffed and Baked.
Dried Sprats.	Italian Macaroni.	Roast Shoulder of Mutton.
Muffins.		Brown Gravy.
Dry Toast.		Potatoes.
Brown and White Bread and Butter.		Savoys.
Marmalade.		Rice Gâteau.
Bread and Milk.		Cheese.

Marketing.

For the Day.—A pound and a half of Buttock Steak (January 1st); a good-sized fresh Haddock (September 4th); a quarter of a pound of Suet; Potatoes; Onions; Savoys.

For To-morrow.—Small Soles "Slips" for breakfast (January 3rd); Hominy, if not in the house (February 10th).

BREAKFAST.—Potted Tongue (September 26th); Dried Sprats (February 28th); Muffins (January 30th); Bread and Milk (January 25th).
LUNCHEON.—Scotch Collops (January 9th); Italian Macaroni (July 7th).
DINNER.—Haddock Stuffed and Baked (September 4th). *Roast Shoulder of Mutton.*—When the family is small, a shoulder of mutton may, with advantage, be served hot twice. The first day, roast, and serve it in the usual way (March 4th), and get the carver to cut the meat from the shank end, not higher than that part of the joint where the bone juts out. The next day trim away the fat on the outer edge to make the joint a neat oval shape. Remove the skin, brush the surface of the meat with beaten egg, and sprinkle nicely seasoned bread-crumbs thickly over it. Bake it in a moderately heated oven till it is hot through. It will take about an hour and a quarter. Make some good well-flavoured brown gravy of stock (October 6th); pour a little of this round the joint, and send the rest to table in a tureen. Potatoes Browned (October 18th); Savoy (June 4th); Rice Gâteau (October 3rd); Cheese (June 8th).

Things that must not be Forgotten.
1. Put a large cupful of hominy to soak all night in cold water.
2. Soak also a cupful of white haricot beans in cold water.

December 17th.

Breakfast.	Luncheon.	Dinner.
Baked Slips.	Stewed Giblets.	Haricot Purée.
Boiled Eggs.	Rice and Cheese.	Shoulder of Mutton.
Hot Buttered Toast.		Brown Gravy.
Dry Toast.		Boiled Broccoli.
Brown and White Bread and Butter.		Potato Snow.
		Apple Gâteau.
Boiled Hominy.		Cheese.

Marketing.
For the Day.—Two, or if required, three, sets of Fowls' or Ducks' Giblets: these must be quite fresh; Broccoli; Potatoes; Apples; a quarter of a pound of Suet.
For To-morrow.—A tin of Sardines (January 12th); Potted Grouse (January 7th); a two pound tin of Tomatoes; Watercress.

BREAKFAST.—Baked Slips (January 7th); Boiled Eggs (January 5th); Boiled Hominy (February 11th).
LUNCHEON.—Stewed Giblets (February 6th); Rice and Cheese (February 18th).
DINNER.—Haricot Purée (March 9th); Shoulder of Mutton (December 16th); Broccoli (April 25th); Potato Snow (April 7th); Apple Gâteau (September 24th); Cheese (June 8th).

Things that must not be Forgotten.
1. Preserve any boiled hominy that may be left.
2. Render down all that is left of mutton fat (February 19th).

December 18th.

Breakfast.	Luncheon.	Dinner.
Sardines.	Toad in the Hole.	Sliced Cod.
Potted Grouse.	Tomatoes on Toast.	Pork à l'Italienne.
Hot Buttered Toast.		Stewed Celery.
Dry Toast.		Potato Mould.
Brown and White Bread and Butter.		Apple Pie.
		Cheese.
Fried Hominy.		

Marketing.

For the Day.—One pound and a half of Buttock Steak; three or four slices of Cod (January 1st); a small Leg of fresh Pork, weighing not more than four pounds; Celery; Potatoes; Apples; a pennyworth of German Yeast.

For To-morrow.—Watercress. If a turkey is to be cooked on Christmas Day, it should, if the weather be cold, be bought at once, and allowed to hang in a cool larder; a young plump bird should be chosen. Hen birds are to be preferred for boiling, cock birds for roasting. Suet for the Forcemeat should also be bought. If a Sirloin of Beef is to be served on Christmas Day, it should be ordered of the butcher in good time. A Hare for the Sunday after Christmas Day.

BREAKFAST.—Sardines (January 12th); Potted Grouse (January 7th); Fried Hominy (February 12th).

LUNCHEON.—Toad in the Hole (January 15th); Tomatoes on Toast (March 16th); half the contents of the tin will probably be sufficient for this dish.

DINNER.—Sliced Cod (January 1st). *Pork à l'Italienne.*—Roast the pork in the usual way (March 4th), and serve it with sauce à l'Italienne prepared as follows:—Rub a small saucepan with garlic, melt an ounce of butter in it, and throw in two shallots finely minced. Shake them over the fire till soft, then dredge a dessert-spoonful of flour over them, and add a quarter of a pint of stock, a table-spoonful of vinegar, a tea-spoonful of bruised capers, half a spoonful of mixed mustard, six peppercorns, and six drops of anchovy essence. Simmer the sauce gently for a quarter of an hour, strain it, put a spoonful of sherry into it, and serve in a tureen. Stewed Celery (December 2nd); Potato Mould (October 23rd); Apple Pie, made to-day. Cheese (June 8th).

Things that must not be Forgotten.
1. Put a cupful of German lentils to soak all night in cold water.
2. Partially prepare the rice milk for breakfast to-morrow (Note 3, June 17th).
3. Pastry is to be made to day (April 17th); Apple and Quince Pies (August 7th); also Seed Cake (August 14th), Vienna Bread (August 26th).

December 19th.

Breakfast.	Luncheon.	Dinner.
Eggs in Sunshine. Potted Grouse. Vienna Bread. Dry Toast. Brown and White Bread and Butter. Watercress. Rice and Barley Porridge.	Minced Pork. Yorkshire Pudding baked in tins.	Crécy Soup. Sausages and Lentils. Potatoes. Brown Bread Pudding. Cheese.

Marketing.

For the Day.—Three pounds of the best Pork Sausages, or fresh Pork to make the same; Potatoes; Carrots.

For To-morrow.—Fresh Sheep's Kidneys; two ribs of Beef, boned and rolled (January 10th); Jerusalem Artichokes; Potatoes; Endive; materials for a salad for supper on Sunday; six ounces of firm Suet; a Melton Mowbray Pork Pie for Monday.

BREAKFAST.—Eggs in Sunshine (July 15th). This can be made of the remains of tinned tomatoes. Potted Grouse (January 7th); Vienna Bread (August 26th); Rice and Barley Porridge (June 15th).

LUNCHEON.—Minced Pork (April 20th); Yorkshire Pudding (November 26th).

DINNER.—Crécy Soup (January 5th); Sausages and Lentils (April 4th); Potatoes (October 23rd); Brown Bread Pudding (July 20th); Cheese (June 8th).

Things that must not be Forgotten.

1. To save time to-morrow, stew the artichokes to-day and rub them through a sieve.
2. For the same purpose chop the suet and prepare the breadcrumbs for the Golden Pudding.
3. The remains of cold pork or of any cold meat may be made into a mould for breakfast, following the recipe given for Calf's Head Mould (April 20th).

Sunday, December 20th.

Breakfast.	Dinner.	Tea.	Supper.
Broiled Kidneys. Savoury Eggs. Vienna Bread. Dry Toast. Brown and White Bread and Butter. Milk Porridge.	Palestine Soup. Rolled Ribs of Beef. Mashed Potatoes. Stewed Endive. Golden Pudding. Cheese.	Vienna Bread. Brown and White Bread and Butter. Plum Jam. Seed Cake.	Cold Beef. Salad. Apple Pie. Cheese.

BREAKFAST.—Broiled Kidneys (January 29th); Savoury Eggs (January 1st); Vienna Bread (August 26th); Milk Porridge (June 13th).

DINNER.—Palestine Soup (December 8th); Roast Beef (March 4th); Mashed Potatoes (May 12th); Stewed Endive (December 5th); Golden Pudding (May 4th); Cheese (June 8th).
TEA.—Vienna Bread (August 26th); Seed Cake (August 14th).
SUPPER.—Salad (March 13th); Apple Pie (August 7th).

Things that must not be Forgotten.

1. Put any Golden Pudding that may be left on a clean dish. It can be served at luncheon to-morrow.

2. If there is any mashed potato remaining it also should be preserved.

December 21st.

Breakfast.	Luncheon.	Dinner.
Melton Mowbray Pork Pie. Eggs on the Dish. Vienna Bread. Dry Toast. Brown and White Bread and Butter. Milk Toast.	Shepherd's Pie. Golden Pudding Réchauffé.	Croûte au Pot. Whole Neck of Mutton stewed with Vegetables. Potato Snow. Lemon Pudding. Cheese.

Marketing.

For the Day.—A whole Scrag of Mutton (February 9th); Turnips; Carrots; Potatoes; Onions; six ounces of Suet.
For To-morrow.—Bloaters; half a pound of German Sausage; Watercress.

BREAKFAST.—Pork Pie bought on Saturday; Eggs on the Dish (December 7th); Vienna Bread (August 26th); Milk Toast (June 17th).
LUNCHEON.—Shepherd's Pie (January 12th); Golden Pudding (March 6th).
DINNER.—Croûte au Pot (May 25th); Mutton Stewed (February 10th); Potato Snow (April 7th); Lemon Pudding (August 12th); Cheese (June 8th).

Things that must not be Forgotten.

1. If any mutton be left it can be cut from the bone, and minced for luncheon to-morrow.

2. Be sure to keep the bloaters apart from everything else in the larder.

December 22nd.

Breakfast.	Luncheon.	Dinner.
Bloaters.	Minced Mutton.	Baked Cod.
German Sausage.	Custard Sippets.	Boiled Rabbit.
Hot Buttered Toast.		Liver Sauce.
Dry Toast.		Bacon Rolls.
Brown and White Bread and Butter.		Potatoes.
Watercress.		Baked Batter Pudding with Jam.
Corn-flour Milk.		Cheese.

Marketing.

For the Day.—About three pounds of Cod from the middle of the fish; two fine Ostend Rabbits (January 24th); a pound of Bacon in rashers; Potatoes.

For To-morrow.—A Bath Chap; Anchovies, if not in the house; Muffins; a pennyworth of small Salad.

BREAKFAST.—Bloaters on Toast (March 24th); German Sausage (June 6th); Corn-flour Milk (June 19th).

LUNCHEON.—Minced Mutton (January 20th); Custard Sippets (June 10th).

DINNER.—Baked Cod (*see* Baked Hake, September 1st). Boiled Rabbits (March 6th). *Liver Sauce.*—Onion sauce (October 14th) is usually served with boiled rabbit, but when the flavour of onion is objected to liver sauce may be taken instead. Of course the livers must be perfectly sweet, but so also must be the rabbits. Wash the livers, boil them gently for half an hour, then chop them finely, or rub them through a sieve. Season the pulp with pepper and salt. Melt an ounce of butter in a small stewpan, mix half an ounce of flour smoothly with it, and add the third of a pint of milk and water. Stir the sauce till it boils, add the chopped liver, and serve. When good sauce is wanted, milk alone may be used instead of milk and water, or two or three table-spoonfuls of cream may be stirred into the sauce. Bacon Rolls (July 19th); Potatoes (May 12th); Baked Batter Pudding (February 5th); Cheese (June 8th).

Things that must not be Forgotten.

1. Preserve the liquor in which the rabbits were boiled. Excellent soup may be made from it.
2. Soak and boil the Bath chap for breakfast (Note 1, August 25th).
3. Fillet the anchovies, and pick and dry the small salad (Note 4, January 17th).
4. Take care of any cold fish that may be left.
5. Soak two table-spoonfuls of tapioca in water.

December 23rd.

Breakfast.	Luncheon.	Dinner.
Bath Chap. Anchovies and Hard-boiled Eggs. Muffins. Dry Toast. Brown and White Bread and Butter. Porridge.	Fish Cakes. Tapioca and Apples.	Celery Soup. Irish Stew. Potatoes. Newmarket Pudding. Cheese.

Marketing.

For the Day.—A Neck of Mutton, not too fat; Potatoes; Apples.
For To-morrow.—Dried Haddock.

BREAKFAST.—Bath Chap (Note 1, August 25th); Anchovies and hard-boiled Eggs (January 18th); Muffins (January 30th); Porridge (January 25th).

LUNCHEON.—Fish Cakes made of the cold baked Cod (January 13th); Tapioca and Apples (February 18th).

DINNER.—Celery Soup (December 3rd); Irish Stew (March 10th); Potatoes (April 7th); Newmarket Pudding (June 2nd); Cheese (June 8th).

Things that must not be Forgotten.

1. Put a cupful of green lentils to soak all night in cold water.
2. If the mincemeat is not already made (December 9th), make it, and mince pies to-day. To make *Mince Meat.*—Chop a pound of suet till it looks like oatmeal, put with it four ounces of lean beef that has been gently stewed till tender, then minced, a pound of muscatel raisins, stoned and chopped, three-quarters of a pound of currants, a pound of moist sugar, four ounces of mixed candied peel finely shred, a lemon freed from the white pith and chopped small, one pound of apples chopped, a tea-spoonful of mixed spice, made up of powdered cinnamon, powdered cloves, and grated nutmeg, a glass of brandy, and a glass of port; the brandy and port should be added last of all. Mince meat that is to be kept some days should be put into a stone jar, and have a brandied paper placed on the top. It should be stirred up every three days, and kept in a cool place. To make *Mince Pies.*—Make a little rough Puff Paste (May 29th), roll this out till very thin, with it line some small patty pans that have been well buttered, moisten the edges with water, place a spoonful of the mince in the middle, and cover this with pastry again. Press the edges together, ornament them by pressing the prongs of a small fork upon them, and make a slit in the middle of the patty to allow the steam to escape. Bake in a moderate oven. Before serving the mince pies, remember to make them very hot.

December 24th.

Breakfast.	Luncheon.	Dinner.
Bath Chap.	Poor Man's Goose.	Lentil Soup.
Dried Haddock.	Baked Apples.	Curried Fowl.
Hot Buttered Toast.		Boiled Rice.
Dry Toast.		Greens.
Brown and White Bread and Butter.		Marmalade Bread and Butter Pudding.
Bread and Milk.		Cheese.

Marketing.

For the Day.—A pound and a half of Pig's Fry (February 7th); a good-sized Fowl, or two Fowls, if required; Apples; Potatoes; Greens.

For To-morrow.—The Sirloin of Beef ordered some days ago; three pounds of fresh Pork Sausages; Chestnuts; Artichokes; Potatoes; Brussels Sprouts; Celery; a Pork Pie for breakfast to-morrow; the Turkey is supposed to be in the house; half a pound of Macaroni; six pennyworth of Cream for the Soup.

BREAKFAST.—Bath Chap (Note 1, August 25th); Dried Haddock (January 27th); Bread and Milk (January 25th).

LUNCHEON.—Poor Man's Goose (February 7th); Baked Apples (February 9th).

DINNER.—Lentil Soup (April 1st); Curried Fowl (*see* Curried Rabbit, July 16th); Boiled Rice (July 21st); Greens (June 4th); Marmalade Bread and Butter Pudding (June 2nd); Cheese (June 8th).

Things that must not be Forgotten.

1. Put a cupful of hominy to soak all night in cold water.
2. Pluck and truss the turkey ready for to-morrow.
3. If pastry and breakfast cakes are wanted, they should be made to-day. Fruit Pies (August 7th); Teacakes (August 26th).
4. It very often happens that plum pudding and mince pies are too rich for the digestive powers of one or two of the Christmas guests. When this is likely to be the case, a simpler dish such as Apple Mould (September 15th), may be provided, and this should be made to-day.

December 25th.
(*Christmas Day.*)

Breakfast.	Luncheon.	Dinner.
Melton Mowbray.	Macaroni and Bacon.	Palestine Soup.
Buttered Eggs.	Stewed Cheese.	Roast Turkey.
Teacakes.		Sausages.
Dry Toast.		Potatoes.
Brown and White Bread and Butter.		Brussels Sprouts and Chestnuts.
Boiled Hominy.		Plum Pudding.
		Mince Pies.
		Apple Mould.
		Cheese.

BREAKFAST.—Pork Pie bought yesterday; Buttered Eggs (January 16th); Teacakes (February 14th); Boiled Hominy (February 11th).

LUNCHEON.—Macaroni and Bacon (January 27th); Stewed Cheese (May 5th).

DINNER.—Palestine Soup (December 8th). *Roast Turkey.*—Stuff the breast of the Turkey with good veal forcemeat (June 27th). Tie a buttered paper over the breast, and hang it with the legs up before a clear fire. Baste it well (unless this is done, the flesh is apt to be dry), and roast it till the steam draws to the fire. Half an hour before it is done enough, remove the paper, and rub a little butter upon it. Send good Brown Gravy (October 18th), Bread Sauce (October 18th), and Baked Sausages (December 13th) to table. It is scarcely possible to say how long the bird would take to roast, because turkeys vary so very much in size. A small turkey would need an hour and a half, a moderate sized one, two hours and a half, a large bird would take four or five hours. If preferred, the turkey may be stuffed with Chestnut Forcemeat instead of Veal Forcemeat, and then Chestnut Sauce will be required. To make *Chestnut Forcemeat.*—Prepare about half the quantity of veal stuffing that would be otherwise needed. Take four or five dozen chestnuts, according to the size of the bird; half of these will be for forcemeat, and half for sauce. Cut the skins, and fry the nuts in a little butter until they can be easily peeled; boil them in gravy till quite tender. Mix half the quantity, whole, with the veal forcemeat, and stuff the turkey in the usual way. To make *Chestnut Sauce.*—Mix the boiled chestnuts that remain with about half a pint of good brown gravy, and rub them through a wire sieve. Make the sauce hot without letting it boil, add half a spoonful of white sugar, and a glass of sherry if permitted, and serve. Roast Turkey Glazed (March 21st), makes a very handsome dish for a supper or a cold collation. *Boiled Turkey.*—In England, turkeys are frequently boiled, instead of being roasted. The instructions given for boiling fowls may be followed (September 6th). The time required must vary with the size of the bird. In this case, Celery Sauce (December 12th), or White Sauce is served with it. To make *White Sauce.*—Melt an ounce of butter in a small saucepan, and mix three-quarters of an ounce of flour smoothly with it; add half a pint of white stock (made by stewing rabbit or chicken bones), and add a small carrot, three button mushrooms, washed, peeled, and cut into slices, and an ounce of lean ham, or two strips of bacon rind, scalded and scraped. Stir the sauce till it boils, draw it to the side of the stove, and let it simmer gently for twenty minutes. Skim the fat off as it rises; strain the sauce through a napkin, put it back into the saucepan, and let it boil again; add a quarter of a pint of cream, and the sauce is ready. These quantities will make about three-quarters of a pint of sauce. Potatoes (April 7th); Brussels Sprouts and Chestnuts (November 8th); Plum Pudding (December 9th). Let the pudding stand ten minutes after it is taken out of the water. Turn it upon a dish, cut a piece out of the top, and just before putting the dish upon the table, pour half a wine-glassful of brandy into the hole, and set this alight. The brandy should be lighted at the very last moment, not only because it quickly goes out, and also for fear of accidents. Mince Pies (December 23rd); Apple Mould (September 15th); Cheese (June 8th).

Things that must not be Forgotten.

1. Ample provision is usually made for Christmas Day. In order to prevent waste, everything that is left should, as soon as done with be put in the larder to be dealt with to-morrow.

2. If the legs of the turkey were left, prepare them for devilling (January 14th), they can be served at breakfast to-morrow.

December 26th.

Breakfast.	Luncheon.	Dinner.
Devilled Drumsticks.	Kromeskies.	Gravy Soup.
Sausages.	Jam and Bread Pudding	Turkey Sauté aux Cham-
Teacakes.	(Economical)	pignons.
Dry Toast.		Cold Potatoes Browned.
Brown and White Bread and Butter.		Elegant Economist's Pudding.
Fried Hominy.		Cheese.

Marketing.

For the Day.—A small tin of Champignons; half a pound of Bacon cut into thin rashers (January 3rd); Oranges.

For To-morrow.—Sardines; Sea Biscuits; Potatoes; Brussels Sprouts; Celery; four pennyworth of Cream; materials for Beef Steak and Oyster Pie for supper on Sunday (March 26th); Red Currant Jelly, if not at hand; the Hare is supposed to be already in the house; order for December 28th a well-hung Leg of Mutton (January 8th); a tin of Preserved Oysters; and a Collared Tongue (January 2nd); a quarter of a pound of Suet, if not in the house; Turnips; Carrots; Potatoes.

BREAKFAST.—Devilled Drumsticks (January 14th); Sausages. Put any sausages that were left yesterday on a clean dish, and garnish with parsley. If preferred, they can be made into Sausage Rolls for to-morrow (November 6th); Teacakes (February 14th); Fried Hominy (February 12th).

LUNCHEON.—*Kromeskies.*—Cut all the meat from the cold turkey. Preserve the neat slices, and put them between two dishes till it is time to prepare them for dinner. The broken remnants can be made into Kromeskies (July 29th). The bones and trimmings can be stewed for gravy soup to be served at dinner. Jam and Bread Pudding, Economical (February 23rd); to be made of pieces of bread that are left.

DINNER.—Gravy Soup (September 22nd); Turkey, Sauté aux Champignons (*see* Chicken Sauté, April 2nd). *Cold Potatoes Browned.*—Cold potatoes boiled whole may be cut into slices, laid in a tin slightly greased with dripping, and browned in a quick oven. The brisker the oven the better for this purpose. Elegant Economist's Pudding (May 12th); Cheese (June 8th).

Things that must not be Forgotten.

1. If preferred, Turkey Salad (August 30th) can be made instead of the dishes mentioned above; or the recipe given for Rabbit (November 13th) can be followed.
2. Make the Beef Steak and Oyster Pie (March 26th), and an Orange Cream (December 6th), for supper to-morrow. Scones (August 26th) and Gâteau Turc (November 20th) may also be made.

Sunday, December 27th.

Breakfast.	Dinner.	Tea.	Supper.
Savoury Eggs.	Celery Soup.	Scones.	Beef Steak and Oyster Pie.
Sardines.	Jugged Hare.	Brown and White Bread and Butter.	Potato Salad.
Scones.	Red Currant Jelly.	Damson Jam.	Orange Cream.
Dry Toast.	Potatoes.	Gâteau Turc.	Cheese.
Brown and White Bread and Butter.	Brussels Sprouts.		
Marmalade.	Viennoise Pudding.		
Milk Porridge.	Cheese.		

BREAKFAST.—Savoury Eggs (January 1st); Sardines (January 12th); Scones (May 23rd); Milk Porridge (June 13th).

DINNER.—Celery Soup (December 3rd); Jugged Hare (October 25th); Potatoes (May 12th); Brussels Sprouts (June 4th); Viennoise Pudding (July 6th); Cheese (June 8th).

TEA.—Scones (May 23rd); Gâteau Turc (November 20th).

SUPPER.—Beef Steak Pie (March 26th); Potato Salad (April 12th); Orange Cream (December 6th).

Things that must not be Forgotten.

1. Cold potatoes may be used for the potato salad.
2. Carefully preserve all the hare that is left.

December 28th.

Breakfast.	Luncheon.	Dinner.
Collared Tongue.	Scalloped Oysters.	Hare Soup.
Eggs in Brown Butter.	Cake Pudding.	Boiled Leg of Mutton
Scones.		Caper Sauce.
Dry Toast.		Potatoes.
Brown and White Bread and Butter.		Mashed Turnips.
Biscuits and Milk.		Carrots.
		Guest's Pudding.
		Cheese.

BREAKFAST.—Collared Tongue (January 2nd); Eggs in Brown Butter (January 6th); Scones (May 23rd); Biscuits and Milk (June 14th).

LUNCHEON.—Scalloped Oysters (April 27th); Cake Pudding (February 4th).

DINNER.—Hare Soup (January 19th); Boiled Leg of Mutton

(February 23rd) ; Caper Sauce (March 19th) ; Potatoes (May 12th) ; Turnips (September 30th) ; Carrots (July 6th) ; Guest's Pudding (April 14th) ; Cheese (June 8th).

Things that must not be Forgotten.
1. Be sure that the capers left in the bottle are covered with vinegar.
2. Partially prepare the rice and barley porridge for breakfast (Note 6, June 15th).

December 29th.

Breakfast.	Luncheon.	Dinner.
Collared Tongue. Poached Eggs on Toast. Scones. Dry Toast. Brown and White Bread and Butter. Rice and Barley Porridge.	Scotch Collops. Rice with Apples and Beetroot.	Baked Cod. Curried Mutton. Boiled Rice. Savoy. Queen's Pudding. Cheese.

Marketing.
For the Day.—About four pounds from the middle of a Cod ; a pound and a half of lean Beef ; Savoy ; Apples ; Beetroot.
For To-morrow.—Half a pound of Bacon in rashers (January 3rd).

BREAKFAST.—Collared Tongue (January 2nd) ; Poached Eggs on Toast (February 6th) ; Scones (May 23rd) ; Rice and Barley Porridge (June 15th).

LUNCHEON.—Scotch Collops (January 9th) ; Rice with Apples and Beetroot (January 28th).

DINNER.—Baked Cod (*see* Baked Hake, September 1st) ; Curried Mutton (May 26th) ; Boiled Rice (July 21st) ; Savoy (June 4th) ; Queen's Pudding (August 9th) ; Cheese (June 8th).

Things that must not be Forgotten.
1. If any mutton still remains after slices have been cut off for curry, let it be minced for luncheon to-morrow.
2. Partially prepare the rice milk (Note 3, June 17th).

December 30th.

Breakfast.	Luncheon.	Dinner.
Toasted Bacon. Eggs on the Dish. Hot Buttered Toast. Dry Toast. Brown and White Bread and Butter. Rice Milk.	Minced Mutton. Custard Sippets.	Croûte au Pot. Spanish Stew. Potatoes. Brussels Sprouts. Lemon Pudding. Cheese.

Marketing.
For the Day.—One fine Rabbit (January 24th), or two Rabbits, if required ; Onions ; Potatoes ; Brussels Sprouts ; six ounces of firm Suet.
For To-morrow.—Dried Sprats, one bundle for each person ; Muffins (January 29th).

BREAKFAST.—Toasted Bacon (January 19th); Eggs on the Dish (December 7th); Rice Milk (June 17th).
LUNCHEON.—Minced Mutton (January 20th); Custard Sippets (June 10th).
DINNER.—Croûte au Pot, made of the liquor the leg of mutton was boiled in (May 25th); Spanish Stew (April 8th); Potatoes (April 7th); Brussels Sprouts (June 4th); Lemon Pudding (August 12th): Cheese (June 8th).

Things that must not be Forgotten.
1. Make Custard Blancmange for dinner to-morrow (August 4th).
2. Remember that the mince must not *boil* in the gravy.

December 31st.

Breakfast.	Luncheon.	Dinner.
Dried Sprats.	Rabbit made Hot.	Milk Soup.
Ox Eyes.	Macaroni Cheese.	Broiled Steak.
Muffins.		Béarnaise Sauce.
Dry Toast.		Fried Potatoes.
Brown and White Bread and Butter.		Custard Blancmange.
Marmalade.		Lemon Syrup.
Milk Toast.		Cheese.

Marketing.
For the Day.—Half a pound of Macaroni; Rump Steak (Marketing, January 22nd); Potatoes; Brussels Sprouts.

BREAKFAST.—Dried Sprats (February 28th); Ox Eyes (June 5th); Muffins (January 30th); Milk Toast (June 17th).
LUNCHEON.—Rabbit made hot (November 13th); Macaroni Cheese (March 20th).
DINNER.—Milk Soup (January 3rd); Broiled Steak (January 22nd); Béarnaise Sauce (March 23rd); Fried Potatoes (February 2nd); Custard Blancmange (August 4th); Lemon Syrup (March 19th); Cheese (June 8th).

Things that must not be Forgotten.
1. If any little pieces of steak are left, they can either be made into Potted Beef (January 23rd), or made into a Shepherd's Pie for luncheon to-morrow (January 12th).
2. The fat in which the potatoes are fried must be boiling or the potatoes will be greasy.

FRUITS IN SEASON SUITABLE FOR DESSERT IN DECEMBER.
Oranges, Apples, Pears, Bananas, Grapes, Melons, Pomegranates, Pomeloes, Shaddocks, Cobs, Walnuts, Brazils, Almonds, Barcelonas, Dried Fruits.

APPENDIX.

FOOD FOR INVALIDS.

THERE are few homes into which sickness does not enter sooner or later, and when the misfortune occurs, a demand is made on the resources and knowledge of the housekeeper, to provide food that shall sustain and nourish the enfeebled frame of the invalid, repair the waste caused by illness, tempt the languid and capricious appetite, and be simple and easy of digestion without being insipid and unattractive. It is astonishing how difficult even clever managers sometimes find it to furnish, for any length of time, suitable food for the sick, and so often has this difficulty been experienced that it has been said that cookery for the sick is an art by itself, quite distinct from ordinary cookery. Condiments and spices are almost always forbidden in these cases; food must be simple, light, easy to digest, and very nourishing, and yet it must be varied, for a mixed diet is as necessary for an invalid as it is for the healthy. The difference between a rapid and a tardy convalescence very often depends almost entirely upon whether or not suitable food is given in sufficient quantity and properly prepared. Therefore, although a few suggestions for Invalid Diet have already been given in this volume, it has been deemed advisable to comply with a request frequently made, and in this new edition of "A Year's Cookery" to add to the number of preparations suitable for the sick and for the convalescent.

Food that is intended for an invalid should always be made to *look* inviting, so that it shall tempt the eye as well as the palate. All appointments should be daintily bright and clean; the napkin should be spotless, the silver and glass should be polished till they sparkle, and it is well worth while to bring out the best china for the invalid's tray, in order to give everything a festive look.

Whatever is intended to be served hot for an invalid should be very hot, and to prevent its going cold in its passage from the kitchen to the bed-room, the dish which contains it should be put on a hot-water dish, or over a bowl of boiling water, and covered.

Whatever is intended to be cold should be very cold, being left in the ice box or in a cool place until the moment before serving. Fresh fruits, and especially the more perishable sorts, such as strawberries and grapes, will be much more refreshing if put on a plate over a bowl filled with chopped ice.

Teachers of nursing almost always insist very strongly on the fact, that only a small quantity of food should be offered to the sick at one time, because a quantity of food is calculated to disgust the invalid. Acting on this advice it is to be feared that convalescents do not always get as *much* as they require. Excepting when the stomach is very sensitive, as after recovery from typhoid, for instance, and when there is great difficulty of digestion, it is safer to err on the side of giving too much food, than on the side of giving too little. When food can be taken in small quantities only, it ought to be taken at short intervals, and as much food as can be properly digested is generally needed. A doctor ought to be asked how much food he wishes the patient to have in twenty-four hours.

When people are very ill something warm to drink (a cup of tea or a glass of milk) should be given quite early, about five or six o'clock in the morning, then the breakfast is more likely to be enjoyed when it comes. Very few sick people can take solid food first thing. A very sick person, unless the doctor gives other orders, should be fed at least once in two hours ; a convalescent, who is not yet able to take regular meals, should have food at intervals of three hours. Beef tea, mutton broth, and similar preparations are not foods, they are stimulants, and should be regarded as extras rather than as meals. It should not be supposed that when a convalescent has had beef tea he has had a meal.

An invalid ought never to be allowed to get faint for want of food. If anything occurs to prevent the preparation of an expected meal, something else, a cup of beef tea, or a little milk, should be given to ward off faintness.

Excepting in cases of exhaustion, or when the doctor especially orders that food should be given at certain intervals, an invalid should never be wakened to be fed. Sleep is one of the best of restoratives. At the same time, during a long sleep food should always be prepared, so that it may be ready when the patient wakes.

In the day time food should never be kept in the room where the sick person lies. In the night, however, something to drink must be put where it can be taken if needed.

Water.—In almost all illnesses cold water is allowed to be given. Water that has been boiled and allowed to go cold may always be drunk with safety, but it is very flat and tasteless. The flatness will be to some extent removed if the water is passed through a filter. To keep water cold it should be put in a stone jar or jug, the vessel being wrapped in a coarse cloth kept constantly wet.

Ice is often a necessity in a sick-room. Unless, however, the nurse is quite sure that it is pure, it should not be put into the drinking water. A small quantity can be best kept by putting it wrapped in flannel into a colander or strainer, or similar dish, which will allow the water that melts to drain away, then covering it closely. Ice may be quite easily broken into chips by putting the point of a darning needle or of a strong pin near the edge of a lump, and tapping the head slightly.

Milk.—We have Miss Nightingale's authority for saying, that "milk, and the preparations of milk, are most important articles of food for the sick," and that there is nearly as much nourishment in half a pint of milk as there is in a quarter of a pound of meat. Also, there is no doubt that physicians of the present day value milk most highly, and in certain diseases they rely on it entirely. Yet there is no article of food that needs more care to keep it in good condition, for of all foods it takes up impurities most easily. Milk should not be left in the can with the cover tightly closed, but should be put into an open vessel, and disturbed as little as possible. In cases of diarrhœa it should be boiled and allowed to go cold before being drunk. Many doctors would say that *in all cases* milk should be boiled before being drunk. If the cream is to be taken off, the milk should be put in a closet opening out of a warm room in winter, and in a cool cellar in summer, because to rise well cream must either be quite warm (55° to 60°) or very cold. Milk that is to be used without the cream being taken off should be kept at 45° to 50° and stirred often.

A great many people, when ordered to take milk, object to do so, because they have found that it disagrees with them, and lies heavy on the stomach, to use a common phrase. To prevent this the milk should be largely diluted either with water or whey, or with lime water. Milk is indeed so apt to form into clots on the stomach that undiluted it is to be regarded as solid food. Mixed with lime water it is particularly valuable in cases of obstinate nausea. The proportion of lime water usually allowed is four tablespoonfuls of milk to one of lime water. The proportion of water or whey is two-thirds of the bulk of the milk. Lime water can be bought of the druggist. Soda water is sometimes substituted for lime water.

To make Whey.—Make a pint of milk lukewarm, stir into it a dessertspoonful of essence of rennet, and leave it in a warm place till the milk is firm. Boil it, when the curd will separate and can be removed, and the whey will be ready for use. Sometimes milk is rendered less objectionable to a patient by flavouring it with cinnamon, or a few drops of vanilla.

LIQUID FOODS.
BROTHS AND SOUPS.

In very serious illness, when the patient cannot or is not allowed to swallow solid foods, reliance must be placed entirely on liquid foods. For these the following suggestions are made. Recipes for Beef Tea, Veal Broth, Mutton Broth, Chicken Broth, and Barley Cream will be found on pages 95-6 of this work.

Beef Juice.—Mince finely a quarter of a pound of fresh raw lean beef. Add to it gradually a quarter of a pint of cold water, and squeeze it with the back of a silver spoon. Let it stand a few minutes, then press it through a fine wire sieve, add salt, and serve. The doctor should be asked if this proportion of water is allowable.

If undiluted beef juice is wanted, cut lean raw beef into thin strips, and squeeze in a lemon squeezer. The juice that runs from uncooked beef can, of course, be used for this purpose. As much as is wanted at one time, and no more, should be made, for beef juice will not keep.

One way of extracting beef juice is to cut the meat in squares; place these in a bottle or jar, and set in a pan of boiling water for three hours.

A little Liebig's Extract stirred into undiluted beef juice will take away the objectionable taste; a few drops of colouring will remove the objectionable colour.

Beef juice made at home is better and cheaper than any of the extracts of meat sold.

Beef Jelly.—Prepare beef tea or beef juice in the usual way, and either boil with it a pound of knuckle of veal chopped, or add a teaspoonful of soaked gelatine to each quarter of a pint of tea. The gelatine should be boiled until dissolved, and stirred into the beef tea, which may be left till firm. Beef jelly spread on toast or thin bread-and-butter is sometimes liked.

Chicken Jelly may also be made of chicken broth stiffened with gelatine.

Chicken and Rice Broth.—Stir two tablespoonfuls of cooked rice and a beaten egg into a cupful of hot chicken broth. Stir over the fire for a minute, but do not let the soup boil.

Mutton and Rice Broth.—Make mutton broth in the usual way, and allow two tablespoonfuls of boiled rice to a cupful of liquid. Stir in an egg beaten up with two table-spoonfuls of milk, and, if liked, add a little finely-chopped parsley. As there is always a little doubt whether parsley in broth will be approved, it is safest to chop the parsley and send it up separately.

Chicken Milk.—Clean a chicken carefully, and cut it into small pieces, breaking the bones thoroughly. Put it into an enamelled saucepan, with two or three peppercorns and a little salt, and the white part of a head of celery; cover it with cold water, bring it slowly to the boil, then let it simmer gently for four hours or more. Strain into a bowl and leave till cold, when the broth should form a stiff, clear jelly. Carefully remove the fat from the top by wiping this jelly with a napkin which has been dipped into hot water and squeezed dry. Take equal quantities of the jelly and milk, put into an enamelled pan, boil up three times, and strain into a cup. Serve either hot or cold, with tiny slips of dry toast.

Chicken Broth made from Giblets.—For the sake of economy chicken broth is frequently made from the giblets of the birds, that is, the feet, throat, gizzard, and liver. When this is done, the chicken itself can be used to make two separate dishes. Excellent results can in this way be obtained. Cleanse the giblets thoroughly, and be particularly careful to skin the feet, first pouring boiling water over them, and letting them lie in it for about a minute, to loosen the skin. Put the cleansed giblets into a small saucepan, with a pint of cold water, adding, if approved, a sprig of parsley, a small onion, a slice of carrot, and a little celery. Simmer very gently for two hours, then strain for use. This broth should be a jelly when cold. It may be flavoured with a tablespoonful of sherry and a squeeze of lemon-juice, or it may have a little sago, rice, or tapioca boiled in it.

Veal and Tapioca Broth.—Break into small pieces a pound of knuckle of veal and simmer in a quart of water until the liquid is reduced to one-half. Strain and skim. Turn into a clean saucepan, with two tablespoonfuls of soaked tapioca, and stew half an hour. Salt to taste. When the tapioca is clear, take off the fire, add an egg lightly beaten, and three tablespoonfuls of cream. Stir over the fire for two minutes, to set the egg, and serve. On no account must the broth boil after the egg is added.

Sometimes, when solid food is not allowed, a little soup is supporting to the invalid by way of variety. Clear soup made from meat only is generally acceptable, and it is very nourishing. Instructions for making it will be found on page 274 of this work, and it is to be remembered that the recipe may be followed, and a very small quantity of soup can be made, if water and all other ingredients are reduced in the same proportion. For the rest, almost any simple soup is available, if only it is made of good materials that are nourishing. It is not always necessary to have meat for soups. Sometimes, when the patient is tired of broths, the nourishing element may be obtained from milk or eggs. Here are suggestions:—

Celery Soup.—Wash a single head of celery; cut it up and boil it in as much salted water as will cover it. When quite tender rub it through a sieve. Mix a dessertspoonful of flour to a smooth paste with a little cold water, and pour on it three quarters of a pint of hot milk. Season with pepper and salt, add the celery-pulp, and a quarter of a pint of cream. Boil up once and serve. If liked, this soup may be flavoured with nutmeg.

Artichoke Soup may be made in the same way. Half a bay-leaf and a little lean ham, or the bone of a rasher, should be boiled with the artichokes.

Asparagus Soup.—Follow the recipe given for celery soup. Cut off and put aside the points of the asparagus, throw them into the soup, and let them boil till tender, just before serving.

Onion Soup.—Boil a large onion with two ounces of stale crumb of bread. Cook till the onion is tender. Rub the whole through a sieve, add a pint of hot milk, season with pepper and salt, and serve. Onions are to be used with caution for invalids. Sometimes they do good, sometimes they hinder digestion, but in this soup they are likely to be as little harmful as can be expected.

It is most important that soups and broths should never be sent to an invalid with globules of grease floating on the surface. Any thing of the sort would be very likely to offend a fastidious taste. It is generally quite easy to remove fat from broth by skimming. If the liquid is allowed to go cold, the fat can be skimmed off with a spoon, and, should small particles still remain, pieces of thin blotting-paper should be laid for a few seconds on the surface of the broth, and to these the grease will adhere. As the pieces of paper, one after another, become charged with grease, they should be removed until no more grease remains. When broth is hot, to plunge the vessel which contains it into cold water for a few minutes will cause the fat to rise quickly.

Broth on Toast.—Cut a slice of stale bread about half an inch thick; take off the crust and toast lightly on both sides. Lay the toast in a soup-plate, pour over a cupful of any hot soup, set in the oven for a few minutes, and serve hot.

A Poached Egg laid in half a pint of hot clear soup furnishes a very agreeable meal for an invalid.

SOLID FOODS.

FISH.

White flat fish are generally regarded as most suitable food for invalids, being less rich, and consequently more digestible than round fish, such as salmon, mackerel, and cod. As a rule, the simpler modes of cooking are to be preferred to the more elaborate ones, and rich sauces are to be avoided. Boiling, broiling, and frying are the processes most frequently approved. When fish is to be boiled, only a small quantity of water (enough to cover) should be used; much water makes the fish insipid. If the fish can be boiled in stock instead of water, so much the better; when fish is filleted, the bones may be used to make a little stock for this purpose. Well-boiled fish is almost always acceptable. Fried fish, too, is very good. It need not be in the least greasy if plenty of fat is used, if the fat is made quite hot, and if the fish be laid on *grease paper* before being served.

Oysters are frequently recommended for the use of invalids. When fine and fresh, they are best eaten raw, with pepper and lemon-juice, and a little brown bread-and-butter. Or, to make variety, they may be prepared as follows:—

Roast Oysters.—Wash the shells well, then lay them, deep shell downwards, on the bar of the stove, or on the shovel placed on the coals over a clear fire. When the shells open the oysters are done. Have ready pepper, lemon-juice, and thin brown bread-and-butter, and serve immediately in the shells. When there is an open fire in the sick-room, an invalid will sometimes quite enjoy having oysters cooked thus in his presence, and they can be served quite hot.

Stewed Oysters.—Open half a dozen oysters carefully, to save as much as possible of the oyster broth. Put with the latter enough milk to cover the oysters; then scald the oysters in the milk and broth, and remove them from the fire the moment the broth begins to boil. Strain off the oysters, and thicken the sauce with a level dessertspoonful of flour for every gill of liquor. Stir and cook well, and add a tablespoonful of cream and a little pepper. Mince the oysters, stir them into the sauce, cover closely, and cook gently by the side of the fire for three minutes, but on no account let the preparation boil. Oysters thus prepared may, if liked, be served on toast.

Scalloped Oysters.—Prepare three oysters according to the above recipe, reducing every ingredient proportionately. Take a scallop shell, butter it inside and line it with fine bread-crumbs. Put in the mixture, shake bread-crumbs over the top, and make hot in the oven. Serve in the shell.

A sole, daintily cooked, is almost invariably welcomed by a convalescent. A variety of recipes for cooking the same will be found on referring to the Index.

MEATS.

If an invalid has arrived at the stage of convalescence when solid food is allowed, the difficulty of providing variety of diet has very much diminished, yet it cannot be said that the choice of food is even yet very large. Pork and veal must, of course, be avoided; they are not easy of digestion. Beef, also, is known not to be as readily digested as is mutton; and rabbits and similar food are generally forbidden. The mode of cooking meat, too, is often a subject of doubt. Almost all authorities agree that meats which are boiled, broiled, roasted, or stewed, are more wholesome than meats which are fried. Frying is understood to be objectionable, because fat, in which the meat is cooked, produces an excess of the volatile acids, and this renders the food unsuitable for invalids. If, however, fried food is required, the portion thus cooked must on no account become greasy or burnt. It is quite easy to avoid greasiness, if a sufficient quantity of fat be employed, and if this is quite hot before the meat is put into it. When fried foods are greasy, the reason almost always is that the fat was not hot enough.

Mutton Chop.—When a small portion of animal food has to be provided, a mutton chop is always the first thing thought of, and, fortunately, it can be served in so many ways that, in itself, it furnishes abundant scope for variety. A chop taken from the middle of the loin is the best. A portion from the chump end is too large; the best end consists largely of bones and fat, and is not sufficiently meaty. Having procured the chop, be careful to trim it neatly before cooking it. It may be prepared according to one of the following recipes:—

Mutton Chop Broiled.—Have a clear, hot fire, without smoke. The best fire for broiling is made from cinders. If, about twenty minutes before the chop is to be broiled, a layer of cinders be put upon the fire, these will probably have burnt through by the time the chop is to be cooked. If a fire is not clear at the last moment, throw a little salt or sugar upon it, this will make it so. Grease the bars of the gridiron, lay the chop upon it, and set it over the fire. Let the outside brown, then turn it and brown the other sides, and turn every minute till the chop is done. On no account stick a fork into the meat, as this would let out the gravy. Have ready a very hot plate; put the chop upon it, and serve instantly. A chop from the middle of the loin, which weighs about six ounces when trimmed, will probably be done in eight minutes. When calculating the time, however, allowance will have to be made for the taste of the invalid. Some people like meat rare, some like it well done. Sauce or butter should be sent up separately; it is not wise to put any garnish upon a broiled chop. If approved, before being broiled, the chop may be dusted with pepper, but it must not be salted.

Chop Stewed.—Trim the fat entirely from a thick mutton chop, dip it in cold water, pepper it lightly, and dredge it with flour. Put it into a small earthenware jar with a closely-fitting lid, put three or four spoonfuls of water with it, cover it, and set it in a saucepan of water to stew gently for an hour and a half. Turn over when half-cooked. Carefully skim the gravy, and serve very hot. If necessary, another spoonful of gravy may be added, and for this purpose stock will be much better than water.

Chop with Oysters.—Beard half a dozen oysters, and stew the beards and trimmings in the oyster broth, to which has been added a small cupful of water, until the liquor is reduced to half. Strain and let it go cold. Trim a chop, and let it be entirely free from fat. Put it in a delicately clean saucepan; pour the oyster broth over it, and simmer very gently for ten minutes. Mix a teaspoonful of flour to a smooth paste with cold water, and add gradually a cupful of milk. Season delicately with a little salt, pepper, and a suspicion of nutmeg; put the milk with the chop, and add the bearded oysters. Let all stew together very gently two or three minutes longer, and serve.

Welsh Chop.—Put the white part of three good-sized leeks in water, and boil. Throw away the water; cover with fresh salted water, and boil till tender. The result of changing the water will be that the leeks will be rendered mellow. When thoroughly soft chop them finely or rub them through a sieve; put them into a clean stewpan, with pepper and salt, and a gill of cream, and stir the purée over the fire till thick and smooth. A little butter may be added if approved. Have ready a daintily stewed chop. Spread the prepared leeks on toast, put the chop on the top, and serve.

If liked, onion-pulp may be used instead of leek-pulp.

Pleasant accompaniments to a chop are a few green peas, a little potato mashed with cream, a few sprigs of cauliflower, or a single tomato baked. To cook the latter, cut a slice from the top and take out the pulp without breaking the skin. Mix with the pulp a few breadcrumbs, a little butter, pepper, salt, and a tiny pinch of sugar; return to the tomato case and bake. Or the tomato may be plainly baked.

Fried potatoes are, of course, most excellent accompaniments to a chop; but potatoes are not always allowed by the doctor.

Minced Mutton.—When mutton is to be minced for the use of an invalid, it is a good plan to tie three chops together, and cook the three; then use that which was in the centre, and which will be moist and full of gravy, for mincing. The two chops on the outside will be excellent also, and will be enjoyed by healthy folk; but they will not be as succulent and nourishing as the other will be.

Fillets of Beef.—When beef is preferred to mutton, the tenderest part which can be chosen is the under-cut of the rump, known as fillet steak. A slice, half an inch thick, should be neatly trimmed from skin and fat, and, if broiled or very gently stewed, will be sure to be satisfactory.

Poultry and Game are always regarded as suitable to the needs of the sick. When provided, they may be plainly cooked in the usual way. It is to be noted, however, that it is always possible to divide a bird and cook the portions differently, thus making two dishes instead of one. This plan is to be preferred to that of cooking the bird whole and serving it the second time cold or "warming it up." Cold meat, or meat made hot a second time, should never be given to invalids.

To Cook a Fowl for an Invalid.—Divide the bird into two halves by cutting it down the middle with a sharp knife. The portions may be prepared in any of the following ways:—

Broiled Chicken, if successfully managed, will be found excellent, but it requires care. Unless the bird is quite young, it should be partially cooked in the oven before being placed on the gridiron, otherwise it will be underdone in parts. Pick and singe the chicken, and divide it evenly quite through; then cleanse it thoroughly, remove the trail, cut off the head and neck, and the first joints of the feet, and if it is necessary to wash the bird, be sure to dry it perfectly afterwards with a clean napkin. This being done, put the half chicken in good position and make it as flat as possible, so that the heat of the fire may reach every part equally. Nothing looks worse than to see a broiled chicken sprawling in the dish, therefore aim at placing it neatly. A little while before it is to be cooked, oil it all over, or brush it over with warm butter, then put it on the gridiron over a clear fire, bones downwards, and keep it well basted. Turn it three or four times during the process of cooking, and begin to turn when the gravy begins to ooze out. Sprinkle with pepper and salt, and serve. It will take about twenty-five minutes. The bird will be much more easily cooked in a hanging grill placed in front of the fire than it will on a gridiron over the fire.

When chicken cannot be conveniently broiled over or before the fire, it may be baked in the oven in imitation of broiling; and there are nurses who think that a chicken thus cooked is more wholesome than chicken broiled in the ordinary way. Divide the chicken, or, if liked, simply take a wing and part of the breast from a young chicken. Should there be any doubt as to the tenderness of the bird, lay the piece on a gridiron or toaster, set over a pan of boiling water, cover it, and let it steam for half an hour before broiling. This done, lay it in a clean, warm dripping-tin, put it in a moderately hot oven, and turn it two or three times, and baste it all over by rubbing it with butter tied in muslin each time it is turned.

A piquant sauce for serving with broiled or roast chicken may be made by mixing together two teaspoonfuls of melted butter with one tablespoonful of vinegar, one saltspoonful of mustard, the same of white sugar, and a little pepper and salt. Heat to the point of boiling, pour over the chicken, and cover closely five minutes before serving.

Boiled Chicken.—Some people think that it would be impossible to boil less than a whole chicken to produce a satisfactory result. A half, or even a quarter of a fowl can, however, be prepared thus, and so both monotony and waste can be avoided. If possible, get a little second stock or veal broth to cover the chicken. If this is not at hand, an onion, a carrot, a bunch of herbs, and a few strips of bacon rind put into the water will help to give flavour. Bring the stock to the boil, put in the meat, boil for a minute, then draw the pan back and simmer gently until the chicken is tender. When it is dished, pour over it a little green parsley sauce, golden rain, or any sort of white sauce, and garnish with bacon rolls. (*See* p. 262.) If liked, the chicken can be taken up, and a sauce may be made by adding to one cupful of the stock in which it was boiled four tablespoonfuls of milk and a beaten egg. Stir the sauce over the fire for a minute or two, but do not let it boil, and serve while hot.

Fillets of Chicken.—Cut as many neat slices of meat from the breast of a fowl as it is thought that the invalid can eat. Trim them neatly and press them with the flat side of a knife that has been dipped in cool water, and put them in a shallow tin. Season them with salt and a squeeze of lemon-juice, and lay a sheet of greased kitchen paper over them. Bake in a moderate oven for a few minutes till the meat is sufficiently cooked. If the fillets are cut carefully, the fowl from which they are taken can be boiled or roasted another time.

Minced Chicken on Toast.—Stew part of a chicken till tender. Take the meat from the bones, and cut it with a sharp knife into small, neat pieces. Strain half a cupful of the stock in which the chicken was stewed, thicken it with a little flour, and add an equal measure of milk. Season pleasantly, and stir the sauce over the fire until it boils; then put in the mince, let it remain by the side of the fire till hot through, and pour over a slice of lightly buttered toast.

Stewed Chicken.—Take a half or a quarter of chicken that has been neatly trimmed. Melt a good tablespoonful of bacon fat in a stewpan which has a closely-fitting lid ; put in the portion of meat and turn it over and about till it is well browned all over. Add half a gill of good stock, cover the saucepan closely, draw it back, and cook as gently as possible for an hour. Take up the meat, clear the fat from the gravy (it will rise more readily if set in a basin of cold water), make it hot once more, and serve poured over the bird.

Stewed Pigeon with Green Peas.—A daintily cooked pigeon is a very suitable dish for an invalid. It is most important, however, that the bird should be young and freshly killed. House pigeons are generally understood to be the best, and they very quickly lose their flavour. Clean the bird carefully, and put inside it a forcemeat ball made of breadcrumbs, butter, chopped parsley, pepper and salt. Take a stewpan which has a closely-fitting lid ; melt in this a piece of butter the size of a large egg, and put in a slice of uncooked bacon cut into dice, and the bird, breast downwards, and let it roast gently, turning it from time to time. At the end of about three quarters of an hour, or when the pigeon is browned equally all over, and is almost cooked, drain away the fat ; put in its place a quarter of a pint of stock, and when this boils, put in half a pint of freshly-shelled green peas. Stew very gently until the peas are tender, and serve. If it is desired to make the pigeon more tasty, a bouquet and a few carrots turned the shape of small balls may be stewed with the bird.

If there is a fear that pigeon cooked according to the above method would be too rich for the invalid, the bird may be cut into quarters and stewed until tender in stock, without being browned in butter. The broth may then be thickened with flour, enriched by the addition of an egg and a little milk, and poured over the pigeon. Peas can be served as an accompaniment. Of course, the condition of the invalid and the orders of the doctor must always be considered when making choice of a dish.

An excellent dish for one person may also be made of the fillets of a pigeon. The fillets, it will be understood, consist of the meat from each side of the breast cut out with a sharp knife from the breastbone to the wing. A pigeon, when cooked whole, does not furnish very much meat, and this is an easy way of getting the best of what there is. After the fillets are removed, the carcase of the pigeon can be stewed for sauce. The fillets should be flattened with a cutlet bat, egged, and breaded twice, then fried in hot fat.

Broiled Pigeons make a very excellent dish. Clean a plump young pigeon and split it in two. Make the pieces flat, oil them all over, then lay on a greased gridiron over a low fire, the bones downwards. Baste well, and turn when the gravy begins to ooze out. Put each half on a slice of buttered toast.

Sweetbreads, being very delicate and easy of digestion, are generally regarded as suitable for the use of invalids. Either a lamb's sweetbread or a calf's sweetbread may be used for this purpose. However they are to be prepared, they should be used very fresh, and they should be laid for an hour in cold water as soon as they are procured. At the end of this time, put them into a saucepan, cover them with cold water ; bring this to a boil, and simmer for five minutes. Drain, put into cold water again, and, when quite cold, peel away the skin and remove the gristle.

A sweetbread of a fair size will probably be large enough for more than one dish for an invalid. The whole of it should be parboiled in the first instance. Here are two or three ways of treatment after being divided :—

The Easiest Way of Cooking a Sweetbread.—After parboiling and skinning the sweetbread, cut it into small pieces. Make some good, well-flavoured white sauce as thick as cream ; put in the sweetbread and stew gently for twenty minutes, and shake the pan occasionally. Add a little lemon-juice at the last moment, and serve on squares of toast.

Sweetbread Cutlets.—Parboil the sweetbread, lay in cold water, and peel it. Dry well, then cut into neat slices. Dust the slices with flour, brush with egg, and roll in breadcrumbs, and fry until well browned. Serve in a circle round a mound of green peas or French beans, and serve white sauce or tomato sauce as an accompaniment.

As sweetbread is rather insipid in itself, it is always advisable to try to impart flavour to it by cooking it in stock flavoured with onion, herbs, mushrooms, lemon-rind, or some other strongly-tasting ingredient. Bacon rolls are excellent served with it.

A pleasant change may be obtained by stewing sliced sweetbread in oyster broth, and adding cream and thickening thereto as for oyster sauce.

Vegetables and Fruits.

Vegetables are generally a very necessary addition to the diet of an invalid. Green peas, beans, celery, cauliflower, seakale, asparagus, onions, and spinach are all allowable when they are to be had, and tomatoes, raw or cooked, are a never-failing resource. Potatoes are not always advisable. The doctor should be consulted before they are provided. If approved, however, they are generally acceptable, especially when daintily fried. Recipes for cooking all these vegetables in various ways may be found by referring to the index.

Vegetable Purée.—When vegetables are required for health, and there is a difficulty about digesting them, they are sometimes prepared as a purée with milk, and in this form are both nourishing and easy of digestion. To make vegetable purée, boil the vegetable in the usual way, and drain it well to get the water from it. Cover it with milk, and let it simmer for a quarter of an hour, then rub as much as possible through a fine hair sieve, season with salt and pepper, and serve. Lettuces, green peas, French beans, cauliflower, cabbage, carrots, turnips, onions, and asparagus may all be prepared thus; and, if milk is not agreeable to the patient, whey or thin gruel may be substituted for it.

Fruits.—Fresh fruit, especially grapes and oranges, are often a most cooling and beneficial addition to the invalid's diet. When there is a fear that raw fruit will not agree, almost all fruits can be made into purées, following the recipe given for purée of vegetables. For the most part, however, the fruits should be boiled in water, then rubbed through a sieve, and milk should be added to make the purée thin enough for drinking. When fruit is rubbed through a very fine sieve, the skin, seeds, cores, and hard portions, which are likely to be specially difficult of digestion, are kept back. When the purée is daintily sweetened it constitutes a most acceptable and delicious food.

Eggs.

Eggs are amongst the most valuable of our resources for the use of invalids. They are most wholesome and altogether nourishing, and they can be served in all sorts of ways. Of course, it is important that they should be freshly laid.

There are one or two ways of testing the condition of eggs in this respect.

When absolutely fresh, the larger end feels warmer than the other when put to the lips.

Put the egg in the hollow of the hand, and bend the fingers round it to make a sort of frame, then hold up the hand to the light, shut one eye, and look at the sun through the egg with the other. If clear and transparent throughout it is probably good. Fresh eggs are more transparent in the centre, old eggs at the ends.

Fill a quart basin with water and dissolve therein a large tablespoonful of salt. Put in the egg. If it sinks it will probably be good; if it floats it will be bad; if it swims it will be stale.

It is generally taken for granted that an egg which is to be served to an invalid should be lightly cooked, as being more easily digested. Recipes for different modes of preparing eggs will be found by referring to the index. Soft-boiled eggs, buttered eggs, devilled eggs, eggs in brown butter, in sunshine, and on the dish, poached eggs, savoury eggs, and eggs with asparagus, and baked omelette, are all suitable for invalid use. In addition, the following recipes may be acceptable:—

Eggs and Apples.—Bake two apples, and, when soft, remove the skin and core and beat to pulp. Sweeten with sugar, and, if liked, flavour with lemon-rind or nutmeg. Add a teaspoonful of butter and a well-beaten egg. Put the preparation in a buttered cup, bake in a gentle oven till set, and serve warm.

Egg Beaten Up with Wine or Milk.—Break an egg and take out the speck. Beat the white till stiff, add the yolk, and beat again. Sweeten with a dessertspoonful of white sugar, and either a teaspoonful of brandy, a tablespoonful of sherry, or three tablespoonfuls of milk. An egg prepared thus and served with a biscuit is an excellent restorative in debility.

White of Egg and Milk.—(Of use in cases of diarrhœa, when solid food is forbidden). Beat the white of an egg and mix with it a tumblerful of milk, a teaspoonful of brandy, and half a tumblerful of soda-water. To be repeated every two hours.

Egg Lemonade.—Shake together in a bottle the white of an egg, a tumblerful of cold water, the juice of half a small lemon, and a teaspoonful of white sugar. Or,

Beat a whole egg lightly, and add a tumblerful of strong, sweet lemonade.

Egg Soup.—Beat an egg and stir it into a breakfastcupful of hot broth of any kind. Season with salt and pepper, and serve with dry toast, made without crust, and cut into fingers.

Egg Gruel.—Beat an egg, add pepper and salt, and pour on, stirring briskly the while, a teacupful of boiling water.

Egg Punch.—Beat the yolk of an egg with a teaspoonful of sugar, and add a tablespoonful of brandy. Fill the glass with half a pint of fresh milk, and, last of all, add the white of egg beaten stiff.

Egg and Coffee.—Stir the beaten yolk of an egg into a cupful of good coffee, and dilute with boiling milk. The addition of an egg makes coffee much more nourishing.

Egg Cordial.—(Very sustaining, and easily retained by a weak stomach). Take the white of an egg, beat it to a froth, and add a tablespoonful of cream and a tablespoonful of brandy. Mix thoroughly.

Egg Drink.—Mix a tablespoonful of the best arrowroot with a little cold water to a smooth paste. Add two tablespoonfuls of white sugar, the juice of a large lemon, and the whites of two eggs which have been whisked with a little water. Add boiling water to make up the quantity to three pints, boil up once quickly, and stir till boiling.

The above recipe is by Dr. Bullen, former House Physician to St. Bartholomew's Hospital. Speaking of it, Dr. Bullen says, "This drink is somewhat thick, and is often much liked by persons who complain of soreness and dryness of the throat."

PUDDINGS, CUSTARDS, JELLIES, AND CEREAL PREPARATIONS.

Spoon Pudding.—Mix a teaspoonful of flour smoothly with a little cold water; add a beaten egg, a pinch of salt, and a teacupful of milk. Stir well, turn into a teacup which has been greased well inside, lay a round of greased paper on the top, and steam gently half an hour. Turn out, and serve with a tablespoonful of sherry.

Sponge Cake Pudding.—Take a penny sponge cake, or a slice of stale sponge cake that will be equivalent thereto, and crumble over a wire sieve. Pour on a quarter of a pint of boiling milk, and beat with a fork. Sweeten, and, when cool, add a whole egg which has been whisked to a froth. Butter a cup, pour in the batter, lay a greased paper on the top, and steam till the pudding is firm in the centre. Turn out, sift white sugar over, and serve with a little wine.

Tapioca, Rice, Sago, Semolina, Ground Rice, Vermicelli, Macaroni, may all be made into excellent light puddings for the use of an invalid. Such puddings are very wholesome when eaten with fruit.

Custard Pudding.—Boil half a pint of milk with a bruised laurel leaf, and pour it, when boiling, upon a well-beaten egg. Sweeten with two good-sized lumps of sugar, pour the custard into a basin, put a round of greased paper on the top, and set in a saucepan of boiling water, to steam gently until firm in the centre. Serve with stewed fruit.

Cake Pudding.—An invalid tired of milk puddings might like cake pudding for a change. Chop a little suet till it is as fine as sand, and be most careful that no skin or fibre is left therein. Mix thoroughly three dessertspoonfuls of the suet with three of flour, three of fine breadcrumbs, three of sugar. Beat an egg, and mix it with three dessertspoonfuls of milk, and stir into the pudding. Turn into a small greased basin, put a round of paper on the top, set in a saucepan containing boiling water to come half-way up the basin, and steam for an hour.

Cake Custard.—Pour a glass of sherry over a penny sponge cake, or a slice of any light, dry cake, and let it soak, basting it occasionally until it will absorb no more. Make a custard with one egg and half a pint of milk. Sweeten and flavour, pour over the cake, and serve.

Rice Cream.—Soak half an ounce of gelatine in water. Throw an ounce of Carolina rice into boiling water and boil for five minutes. Drain, and boil in a pint of milk till tender. Rub it through a sieve, and stir the pulp thus obtained into the milk that remained in the saucepan with it. Dissolve the gelatine, mix it with the milk, and sweeten and flavour to taste. Stir the cream occasionally till cold, and, before turning it into a damp mould, put with it a quarter of a pint of cream that has been whisked till firm. Rice thus prepared, and flavoured with a laurel leaf and a tablespoonful of brandy, is excellent.

Or, soak a quarter of an ounce of gelatine. Boil half a pint of milk, pour it upon a well-beaten egg, and add sugar and flavouring. Stir into it an ounce of rice that has been boiled in milk till tender. A spoonful of cold rice pudding beaten with a spoonful of cream or milk might be used for this purpose. Dissolve the gelatine, stir it into the rice custard, being careful that the dissolved gelatine and the custard are about the same temperature, and turn into a damp mould.

Semolina Cream.—Soak an ounce of Semolina in a gill of milk, then boil it in half a pint of milk till tender. Dissolve half an ounce of gelatine, which has been soaked in water to cover it, in half a pint of milk, add sugar, flavouring, and, at the last moment, two tablespoonfuls of whipped cream. If cream is not to be had, the white of an egg whisked till firm may be substituted. When the cream is beginning to set, put it into a damp mould, and turn out for serving.

Semolina, it should be remembered, is a very valuable product, very nourishing and sustaining, and rich in flesh-forming and bone-forming material. It is, therefore, particularly excellent for sick children.

JELLIES.

Jelly.—A great many people have an idea that, although it may be allowable to make jellies and creams of prepared gelatine for household use, it is most necessary to stew down calves' feet when making jelly for an invalid. The truth is, however, that gelatine, whether it is obtained from calves' feet or from any other source, possesses very little nutritive value. It simply affords a medium for the presentation of food in an acceptable form ; and its usefulness depends upon what is put with it rather than on the nature of the stiffening material. Yet food in the form of jelly is often liked by invalids who care for nothing else. Therefore, jelly can on no account be banished from the list of foods suitable for the sick and convalescent.

Coffee Jelly.—Soak half an ounce of gelatine in half a pint of water, and, when dissolved, stir in a breakfastcup of strong, clear coffee. Sweeten to taste, and serve when firm. Jelly thus made would not be at all nourishing ; it would simply be reviving, and might serve to awaken the appetite. Yet it has sometimes proved to be very acceptable, especially when a tablespoonful of cognac is put with it. If made with milk instead of water, as it easily might be, it would be much more nourishing, and it could be still further enriched by the addition of a little cream, or whipped cream may be served with coffee jelly.

Tea Jelly is also refreshing. It is made by substituting strong tea for coffee.

Blancmange made from Cow-Heel.—Procure a dressed cow-heel from the tripe shop and cut it up into small pieces. Put it into a jar with a quart of milk, cover closely, and set it in a slow oven for three hours. Strain, sweeten, and flavour to taste, and, when cold, turn into a damp mould.

Tapioca Jelly.—Soak half a cupful of pearl tapioca in two cupfuls of water overnight. Turn into a double saucepan, or put in a jar and set in a saucepan of water, and cook gently till clear. Add sugar to taste, and a little more water if too thick, and when taken off the fire, strain into it the juice of a lemon. Serve cold, with cream or milk.

Red Tapioca.—Prepare the tapioca as in the last recipe, and, instead of lemon-juice, stir in a cupful of strawberry-juice, or red currant-juice, or raspberry and red currant-juice mixed. If liked, cooked apricots and their juice, grated pineapple and its juice, sliced bananas and orange-juice, or a few grapes can be introduced into the tapioca just before moulding. In fact, quite a series of acceptable dishes may be made from this recipe. The puddings should in every case be accompanied by cream or milk.

Tapioca Custard.—Soak half a cupful of pearl tapioca overnight in slightly salted water that will barely cover it. Next day turn into a double saucepan with two cups of milk, and cook gently, stirring frequently. When the tapioca is clear and quite tender, pour the preparation upon the yolks of two eggs, which have been beaten with two tablespoonfuls of castor sugar. Mix well, then stir over the fire for a minute or two to cook the eggs. Turn into tumblers, and serve cold.

Tapioca Cream.—Stew a brimming tablespoonful of small tapioca in half a pint of milk; sweeten and flavour with cinnamon, and set away to cool. Just before serving add a gill of cream, which has been whipped till firm, and a tablespoonful of brandy, if approved. Serve with stewed fruit.

Arrowroot Blancmange.—Blanch and bruise a quarter of an ounce of sweet almonds and five bitter ones, and boil them in half a pint of milk. Mix two heaped teaspoonfuls of Bermuda arrowroot very smoothly with a little cold milk, and strain the boiling milk over the paste, stirring to mix well. Add a teaspoonful of sugar, and return the preparation to the saucepan. Stir it over the fire for a minute or two, and serve cold. If liked, the almonds can be omitted, and when the arrowroot has cooled somewhat, a little lemon-juice can be stirred in.

Jelly of Fresh Fruit.—Draw out and sweeten agreeably the juice of any kind of fruit. Add the juice of a lemon, and half an ounce of soaked and dissolved gelatine for each pint of juice. Mould when beginning to set.

Superior Gruel.—Many invalids object very much to gruel. They acknowledge its value, but find it very distasteful. When made as follows, it is really very excellent:—Take half a teacupful of coarse Scotch oatmeal, mix it smoothly with about a pint and a half of water, pour it into a saucepan, and set it by the side of the fire to stew gently for a considerable time—two or three hours. Stir it frequently. Rub the preparation through a sieve, and keep back portions that will not go through. Boil the gruel, put with it an equal measure of boiling milk, season to taste, and serve.

For recipes for Spoon Diet, and Drinks for Invalids, refer to the index.

INDEX.

A

Acid Sauce, Beef with, 412.
Almond Syrup, 235.
Anchovies, To fillet (*see* Royal Sandwiches), 11.
Anchovies, To keep, 12.
Anchovy Butter, 17.
—— Sauce, 260.
Angelica for Garnishing, 254.
Annie's Cake, 336.
Apple Balls, 104.
—— Compote, 326
—— Custard, 386.
—— Fritters, 365.
—— Gâteau, 335.
—— Jam, 407.
—— Jelly, 407.
—— Mould, 328.
—— Sauce, 340.
Apples and Tapioca, 82.
——, Baked, 70.
——, Dried, 198.
—— Stewed with Rice and Beetroot, 50.
April, Dessert Fruits for, 170.
Aromatic Herbaceous Seasoning, 276.
Arrowroot, 206.
Artichokes, Globe, Boiled, 290.
——, Jerusalem, 407.
Asparagus, 222.
—— Served Alone, 166.
—— with Eggs, 175.
Aspic Jelly, 392.
August, Dessert Fruits for, 213.

Australian Meat, Cold, 63.
—— ——, Savoury Hash of, 64.

B

Bacon and Kidneys, Fried, 3.
—— and Liver, 31.
—— and Macaroni, 49.
—— and Tomatoes, 253.
——, To Free from Saltpetre, 188.
——, Best way of Buying, 6.
——, Boiled, 132.
——, Fat, to Use (*see* Eggs in Brown Butter), 13.
—— made Hot, 92.
—— Rind to be saved, 2.
——, Rolled, 262.
——, Toasted, 35.
——, To Choose, 6.
Bake, To, 106.
Baked Apples, 70.
—— Cod (*see* Baked Hake), 315
—— —— with Forcemeat, 61.
—— Custard Tarts, 35.
—— Gurnet, 81.
—— Hake, 315.
—— Mackerel, 151.
—— Omelette, 283.
—— Potatoes, 175.
—— Rabbit, 250.
—— Red Mullet, 302.
—— Rice and Tapioca, 98.

Baked Sausages, 422.
—— Soles ("Slips"), 15.
—— Tomatoes, 248.
—— Whiting, 298.
Barley, Cream, 96.
—— Water, 171.
—— Water, Thick, 171.
Batter, Frying, 272.
—— Pudding, Baked, 64.
—— —— Baked in Tins, 243.
—— ——, Boiled, 191.
Beans, Broad, 258.
——, French, 295.
——, Kidney, 295.
——, Haricot, 229.
——, To Sauté, 295.
Béarnaise Sauce, 124.
Beef, à la Mode, 77.
——, Fillet of the Rump of, 3.
——, Fillet of Roasted, 73.
—— Hash, Economical, 387.
——, Potted, 42.
——, Pressed (*see* Beef, To Boil), 87.
——, Olives, 319.
——, Ribs of, Boned and Rolled, 120.
——, Ribs of, Italian fashion, 60.
——, Rolled, 121.
——, Savoury Stewed, 196.
—— Stew, Economical, 122.
—— Stewed with Onions, 379.
—— Stewed with Vegetables à la Jardinière, 117.
—— Tea, 95.
—— —— quickly made, 96.
——, Thin Flank of, 38.
——, To Choose, 20.
——, Tomato, 355.
—— with Acid Sauce, 412.
Beef Steak and Mushroom or Oyster Pie, 128.
—— Pudding, 234.
—— —— Warmed, 235.
Beetroot, Remains of, To use, 103.

Beetroot with Rice and Stewed Apples, 50.
Biscuits and Milk, 222.
Bisque Soup, 329.
Black, Red, or White Currant Jelly, 241.
Blanche Sauce, 165.
Blancmange, 421.
——, Corn-flour, 223.
—— Custard, 281.
Bloaters, Broiled, 6.
—— to be kept separate, 5.
—— on Toast, 125.
Boiled Brill, 19.
—— Eggs, 10.
—— Fowls, 320.
—— Lentils, 98.
—— Meat, 87.
—— Onions, 372.
—— Ox Tongue, 270.
—— Rabbits, 103.
—— Rice, with Raisins, 61.
—— Salmon, 246.
—— Tripe, 412.
—— Turbot, 213.
—— Turkey, 432.
—— Turnips, 342.
Bone Stock, 75.
Braised Veal, 244.
Brawn, 98.
—— of Ox Cheek, 140.
—— Sauce, 29.
——, To prepare Pig's Head and Feet for, 18.
Bread Crumbs, To Store for Use, 4.
—— —— for Game, 349.
—— Raspings, 4, 58.
—— made without Yeast, 391.
——, Pulled, 307.
—— Sauce, 361.
——, Stale, can be used for :—
Apple Gâteau, 335.
Brown Bread Pudding, 263.
Cake Pudding, 63.
Croûte au Pot, 198.
Crécy Soup, 11.

Bread, Stale, can be used for (*continued*):—
  Custard Sippets, 218.
  Fig Pudding, 209.
  Guest's Pudding, 149.
  Hydropathic Pudding, 225.
  Jam and Bread Pudding, 87.
  Lentil Soup, 134.
  Macaroni Cheese, 120.
  Newcastle Pudding, 220.
  Newmarket Pudding, 208.
  Onion Soup, 39.
  Preserved Tomatoes, 116.
  Sausages on Toast, 16.
  Savoury Meat Cake, 47.
  —— Pudding, 340.
  Scalloped Cod, 47.
  Scallops, 105.
  Viennoise Pudding, 247.
Bread, Vienna, 306.
Breakfast Dishes :—
  Anchovies and Hard-boiled Eggs, 34.
  Anchovy Toast, 17.
  Asparagus with Eggs, 175.
  Baked Soles (Slips), 15.
  Biscuits and Milk, 222.
  Bloaters on Toast, 125.
  ——, Broiled, 6.
  Boiled Eggs, 10.
  Broiled Sheep's Kidneys, 51.
  Buttered Eggs, 30.
  Calf's-head Mould, 157.
  Cocoa, 33.
  Cod's Roe, 39.
  Cod, Scalloped, 16, 47.
  Collared Tongue (*see* Marketing), 3.
  Corned Beef (*see* Marketing), 83.
  Corn-flour Milk, 228.
  Cornish Pasties, 301.
  Devilled Drumsticks, 27.
  —— Eggs, 93.
  —— Salmon, 37.
  —— Lamb, 176.
  Dried Haddock, 48.

Breakfast Dishes (*continued*):—
  Dried Sprats, 94.
  Eggs in Brown Butter, 13.
  —— on the Dish, 416.
  Fried Bacon (*see* Kidneys and Bacon), 3.
  Fried Kidneys and Bacon, 3.
  —— Potatoes, 59.
  Haddock Pie, 318.
  Ham-cured Herrings, 28.
  Ham Toast, 130.
  Hot Rolls, 318.
  Kippered Salmon, 19.
  Lambs' Sweetbreads, 365.
  Marrow Toast, 38.
  Milk Porridge, 221
  —— Toast, 226.
  Mock Woodcock, 127.
  Muffins, 53.
  Mushrooms and Bacon, 322.
  Mutton Pies, 6.
  Oatmeal Porridge, 45.
  Ox-Eyes, 211.
  Pickled Herrings, 299.
  —— Mackerel, 309.
  —— Pig's Cheek, 57.
  —— —— Feet, 68.
  Pilchards, 41.
  Pork Pie, 13.
  Plum Porridge, 313.
  Potted Beef, 42.
  —— Grouse, 15.
  —— Hare, 20.
  —— Shrimps, 389.
  Rice and Barley Porridge, 224
  Rice Milk, 226, 227.
  Rissoles, 13.
  Rizzared Haddock, 323.
  Rolled Veal, 188, 189.
  Royal Sandwiches, 11.
  Sally Lunns, 210, 306.
  Sausage Rolls, 382.
  Savoury Eggs, 1.
  Omelette, 317.
  Scallops, 105.
  Scalloped Eggs, 50.
  Scones, 196.

Breakfast Dishes (*continued*) :—
  Sprats, Broiled, 386.
  ———, Fried, 386.
  Stewed Mushrooms on Toast, 120.
  Tinned Prawns, 67.
  Toasted Bacon, 35.
  Tomatoes on Toast, 116.
  Watercress and Young Radishes, 110.
Breast of Lamb Stewed with Mushrooms, 243.
Breast of Veal, Rolled, 226.
Brill, Boiled, 19.
———, To choose, 18.
Broccoli, To boil, 164.
Broiled Bloaters, 6.
—— Pork Chops, 395.
—— Sheep's Kidneys, 51.
—— Sprats, 386.
—— Steak, 40.
Broken Bread, Remarks on, 4.
Brown Betty, 404.
—— Butter, Eggs in, 13.
—— Sauce, 74.
—— Gravy for Roast Goose, 340.
—— —— from Giblets, 361.
—— Bread Pudding, 263.
—— Soup (*see* Croûte au Pot), 198.
Browned Potatoes, 362.
Browning, 5.
Brussels Sprouts, 210.
—— —— and Chestnuts, 384.
Bubble and Squeak, 40.
Buns, Hot Cross, 145.
———, Light, 294.
———, Soda, Good, 293.
Butter, Anchovy, 17.
———, Melted, 260.
———, Lobster, 214.
———, Oiled, 223.
———, To keep, in Hot Weather, 308.
Buttered Eggs, 30.
—— Shrimps, 266.

C

Cabbage, Red, Stewed, 367.
Cabbage-water, To get rid of, 211.
Cabbages, To boil, 210.
Cabinet Pudding, 254.
Cake, Annie's, 336.
———, Cheap and Good, 236.
—— Pudding, 63.
———, Savoury Meat, 47.
———, Rice, 279.
———, Sultana, 279.
———, Gâteau Turc, 398.
Cakes, Fish, 24.
———, ———, Oven for, 236.
Calf's-foot Jelly, 393.
—— Stock, 393.
Calf's-head, 155.
———, Hashed, 157.
—— Mould, 157.
Caper Sauce, 119.
Capers, To preserve, 120.
Capon, Stuffed and Roasted, 300.
Carrots, To boil, 247.
Cauliflower au Gratin, 164.
———, To boil, 164.
Celery Salad, 393.
—— Sauce, 422.
—— Soup, 410.
———, Stewed, 409.
—— Stalks to be saved, 2.
Cheap Dishes, not including Réchauffés :—
  Australian Meat, 63.
  Baked Plum Pudding, 91.
  Beef, à la Mode, 77.
  Boiled Hominy, 72.
  —— Lentils, 98.
  Bone Stock, 75.
  Brawn, 98.
  Cabbage Soup, 67.
  Cake Pudding, 63.
  ———, Cheap and Good, 236.
  Cod-fish baked with Forcemeat, 61.

INDEX.

Cheap Dishes, not including Réchauffés (*continued*):—
Cow-heel with Parsley Sauce, 84.
Dried Sprats, 94.
Eggs Stewed with Cheese, 71.
Fried Hake, 284.
——, Hominy, 74.
—— Plaice, 158.
Haricot Purée, 107.
Hasty Pudding, 132.
Jam and Bread Pudding, 87.
Lentil Soup, 134.
Liver and Bacon, 31.
Mutton, Scrag of, with Rice, 85.
—— Stewed with Vegetables, 27, 71, 149.
Norfolk Dumplings, 390.
Pease Pudding, 413.
Pig's Fry, or Poor Man's Goose, 67.
Plain Rice Pudding, 89.
—— Rolled Pudding, 116.
—— Sago Pudding, 107
Preserved Tomatoes, 116.
Rice Boiled with Raisins, 61.
—— —— with Stewed Apples and Beetroot, 50.
—— and Cheese, 82.
Savoury Hash of Australian Meat, 64.
Sheep's Head, Stewed, 54.
Stewed Beef with Vegetables, 117.
—— Giblets, 66.
—— Prunes, 93.
Stirabout Cheese, 277.
Tapioca and Rice, Baked, 98.
Tripe à la Coutance, 366.
——, Boiled, 412.
Cheese and Rice, 82.
——, Macaroni, 120.
——, Stewed, 176.
——, Stirabout, 277.
——, To serve, 216.

Cheese, Dry, To use (*see* Macaroni Cheese, 120; and Cauliflower au Gratin, 164).
Cheesecakes, Lemon, 297.
Cherry Gâteau, 253.
Chestnut Forcemeat, 432.
—— Sauce, 432.
Chestnuts and Brussels Sprouts, 384.
Chicken Boiled, 320.
—— Broth, 96.
——, Curried, 283.
——, Fricassee, 271.
—— Kromeskies, 272.
—— Pudding, 308.
——, Roasted, 239.
—— Salad, 311.
—— Sauté au Champignons, 136.
—— Stewed with Tomatoes and Mushrooms, 325.
Chicory Browning, 5.
China Chilo, 249.
Chocolate Pudding, 267.
Chops, Mutton, 189.
Christmas Plum Pudding, 419.
Civet of Leveret, 222.
—— Rabbit, 417.
Clear Soup, 143, 274.
—— —— from Fresh Meat, 274.
Cocoa, 33.
Cocoanut Pudding, 286.
Cod, Baked (*see* Baked Hake), 315.
——, ——, with Forcemeat, 61.
——, Fried, 2.
—— Pie, 4.
——, Salt, Réchauffé, 147.
——, Scalloped, 16, 47.
——, To choose, 12.
Cod's Head and Shoulders, 414.
—— Roe for Breakfast, 39.
Colcannon, 290.
Cold Cod, To use (*see* Cod Pie), 4.
—— ——, Réchauffé of (*see* Kedgeree, 21; and Scalloped Cod, 16).

Cold Meat, Réchauffés of (see Rissoles or Croquettes), 13.
Mulligatawny Soup, 39.
Mutton Pies, 6.
Rabbit Gâteau, 250.
Toad-in-the-Hole, 29.
Cold Potato (see Fish Cakes), 24.
Cod Pie, 4.
Browned Potatoes, 362.
Cold Potatoes browned, 433.
Collared Tongue, To carve, 7.
Collops, Scotch, 19.
Compote of Apples, 326.
—— of Fresh Fruit, 282.
—— of Oranges, 415.
Cook, Daily Duties of, 2.
Collops, Mutton, with Tomatoes, 343.
Corn-flour Blancmange, 223.
—— Milk, 228.
Cornish Pasties, 301.
Cottage Plum Pudding, 213.
Cow-heel with Parsley Sauce, 84.
Cream, Italian, 310.
——, Orange, 415.
——, Stone, 242.
——, Strawberry, 310.
——, Whipped, 422.
Crécy Soup, 11.
Crimped Skate, 20, 74.
Croquettes (see Rissoles), 13.
——, Potato, 380.
Croûte au Pot, 198.
Crust, Flaky, 285.
Cucumber, To serve, 192.
Curing Hams, 376.
Currant Dumplings, 387.
Curried Chicken, 383.
—— Fowl, 374.
—— Mutton, 199.
—— Rabbit, 258.
—— Veal, 264.
Curry, Rice Boiled for, 264.
Custard, 289.
——, Apple, 286.

Custard, Blancmange, 281.
——, Savoury, 275, 307.
—— Sippets, 218.
—— Tart, Baked, 35.
Cutlets, Halibut, 232.
——, Pork, with Apple Sauce, 53.
——, Salmon, 262.

D

Daily Duties of Mistress, 4.
—— —— of Cook, 2.
Dessert Fruits for January, 56.
—— —— for February, 95.
—— —— ,, March, 133.
—— —— ,, April, 170.
—— —— ,, May, 206.
—— —— ,, June, 240.
—— —— ,, July, 276.
—— —— ,, August, 313.
—— —— ,, September, 342.
—— —— ,, October, 376.
—— —— ,, November, 407.
—— —— ,, December, 436.
Devilled Drumsticks, 27.
—— Eggs, 93.
—— Lamb, 176.
—— Salmon, 37.
—— Sauce, 27.
Devonshire Junket, 330.
Dishes for Invalids :—
  Broths, 95.
  Plain Drinks, 171.
  Meats, 408.
  Spoon Meat, 206.
Dried Apples (Chips), 198.
—— Cherries for garnishing, 254.
—— Haddock, 48.
—— Sprats, 94.
Ducklings, Roasted, 269.
Dumplings, Currant, 387.
——, Fruit (see Red Currant Dumplings), 262.

Dumplings, Lemon, 350.
——, Norfolk, 390.
——, Suet (Small), 359.
Dutch Sauce, 186.

E

Eels, Stewed, 44.
Egg Sauce, 146, 320.
Eggs, Boiled, 10.
——, Buttered, 30.
——, Devilled, 93.
——, Fried, 102.
—— in Brown Butter, 13.
—— in Sunshine, 257.
—— on the Dish, 416.
——, Poached, 65.
——, Savoury, 1.
——, Scalloped, 50.
—— Stewed with Cheese, 51.
—— with Asparagus, 175.
Elegant Economist's Pudding, 184.

F

Fat for general use, 83.
—— Scraps, Use of, 2.
Feathers, To dry, 95.
February, Dessert Fruits for, 95.
Fig Pudding, 209.
Filets de Bœuf à la Béarnaise, 140.
Fillet of Beef, Roasted, 73.
—— of Veal, Baked or Roasted, 237.
—— of the Rump of Beef, 3.
Filleted Soles, à la Maître d'Hôtel, 131.
—— Sautés, 9.
—— Turbot, 230.

Fish :—
  Anchovies, 34.
  Anchovy Toast, 17.
  Bloaters, Broiled, 6.
  —— on Toast, 125.
  Brill, Boiled, 19.
  Cod-fish baked with Force-meat, 61.
  ——, Baked (*see* Baked Hake), 315.
  ——, Fried, 2.
  —— Pie, 4.
  ——, Scalloped, 16, 47.
  Cod's Head and Shoulders, 414.
  —— Roe, 39.
  Devilled Salmon, 37.
  Fish, Fried, 32.
  Flat Fish, Filleted, 9.
  Gurnet, Baked, 81.
  Haddock, Dried, 48.
  —— Pie, 318.
  ——, Rizzared, 323.
  ——, Stuffed and Baked, 318.
  Hake, Baked, 315.
  ——, Boiled, 373.
  ——, Fried, 284.
  Halibut Cutlets, 232.
  Herrings, Fresh, au Gratin, 372.
  ——, ——, Pickled, 299.
  ——, Ham-cured, 28.
  —— with Mustard Sauce, 327.
  Kedgeree, 21.
  Mackerel au Gratin, 173.
  ——, Baked, 151.
  ——, Pickled, 309.
  Oysters, Scalloped, 167.
  Pilchards, 41.
  Plaice, Fried, 158.
  Prawns, 65.
  Red Mullet, Baked, 302.
  Salmon, Boiled, 246.
  —— Cutlets, 262.
  ——, Kippered, 19.

Fish (*continued*) :—
  Salmon, Mayonnaise of, 197.
  ——, Pickled, 204.
  —— Shad, 117.
  Salt Fish, 146.
  —— Cod Réchauffé, 147.
  Scallops, 105.
  Skate with Brown Butter, 74.
  Smelts, 63.
  Soles, Baked, 15.
  ——, Filleted à la Maître d'Hôtel, 131.
  ——, Filleted, Rolled, and Baked, 97.
  ——, Filleted—Sautés, 9.
  ——, Fried, 125.
  ——, à la Horly, 361.
  —— au Gratin, 174.
  Sprats, Dried, 94.
  ——, Broiled, 386.
  ——, Fried, 386.
  Stewed Eels, 44.
  Turbot, Boiled, 213.
  ——, Filleted, 230.
  Whiting, Baked, 298.
  ——, Fried, 32.
Fish Cakes, 24.
——, Cold (*see* Réchauffés).
—— for Invalids, 408.
——, To choose, 1, 6.
——, To Egg-and-Breadcrumb, 9.
——, Salt, 146.
—— Soup, Simple, 255.
—— Stock, 53.
——, Supply of, 6.
——, To fry, 32.
——, To sauté, 9.
Flaky Crust, 285.
Flour, Vienna, 307.
Food for Invalids (*see* Appendix).
Fool, Gooseberry, 233.
——, Raspberry, 263.
Forcemeat, Chestnut, 432.
—— for Hare, 370.
—— for Veal, 237.

Forequarter of Lamb, 147.
Fowl or Chicken, Fricasseed, 271.
Fowl or Chicken, Roasted, 239.
Fowls, Boiled, 320, 396, 422.
——, Curried, 374.
Fragments of Meat Stewed for Stock, 2.
—— —— to be Saved, 2.
French Beans, 295.
—— Method of Cooking Pork, 384.
Fresh Fruit, Compote of, 282.
Fresh Herrings, 88.
—— —— au Gratin (*see* Mackerel au Gratin), 173.
Fricassee of Fowl, 271.
Fritters, Apple, 365.
Fruit Dumplings, Suet Crust for, 234.
—— Juice with Sago Mould, 351.
—— Pies, 285.
——, Preserving, 240.
Frying Batter, 272.

G

Game, Breadcrumbs for, 349.
——, Gravy for, 349.
Garlic, To store, 335.
Garnish, Orange, 415.
Gâteau, Apple, 335.
—— of Cherries, and other Fruits, 253.
—— of Rabbit, 250.
—— of Rice, 346.
—— Turc with Coffee Icing, 398.
Gelatine Jelly, 391.
General Favourite Pudding, 189.
German Pickle for Pork, 152.
German Sausage, To keep Moist, 133.

German Sausage, To serve, 212.
—— Method of Cooking Pork, 155.
Giblet Soup, 58.
Giblets, Brown Gravy made from, 361.
——, Stewed. 66.
Gingerbread Pudding, 193.
Glaze, 122.
Glazed Onions (see Beef à la Mode), 78.
Globe Artichokes, 290.
Golden Pudding, 175.
—— Rain (see Boiled Fowls), 320.
Gooseberry Fool, 233.
Gooseberry Sauce, 215.
Goose, Green, 215.
——, Hashed, 341.
——, Brown Gravy for, 340.
——, Roasted, 339.
——, Apple Sauce for, 340.
——, Brown Gravy for, 340.
——, Sage and Union Stuffing for, 340.
Gravy, 217.
——, Brown, for Roast Goose, 340.
——, Brown, from Giblets, 361.
—— for Game, 349.
—— for Roast Hare, 399.
—— for Veal, 238.
—— Soup, 313, 334.
Green Goose, 215.
—— Peas, 253.
Greens, To boil, 210.
Ground Rice Mould, 284.
—— —— Pudding, 300.
Grouse, Potted, 15.
——, Roasted, 311.
—— Salad, 311.
Gruel (two ways), 206.
Guest's Pudding, 149.
Guinea Fowl, 138.
—— —— Soup, 79.
Gurnet, Baked, 81.

H

Haddock, Dried, 48.
—— Pie, 318.
——, Stuffed and baked, 318.
——, Rizzared, 323.
Hake, Baked, 315.
——, Boiled, 373.
——, Fried, 284.
Halibut Cutlets, 232.
Ham and Macaroni, 136.
Hambro' Salad, 287.
Ham-cured Herrings, 28.
Ham, Fried, 102.
——, Minced, 207.
——, To free from Saltpetre, 188.
——, Potted, 151.
—— Toast, 130.
Hams, To cure, 376.
——, To boil, 201.
Hare Forcemeat, 370.
—— Gravy, 400.
——, Jugged, 369.
——, Roast, 399.
—— Soup, 35.
——, Suitable weather for hanging, 17.
——, To choose, 17.
——, To hang, 17.
——, To skin, 399.
Haricot Beans, 229.
—— Mutton, 148.
——, Norman, 303.
—— Purée, 107.
—— Salad, 131.
Hashed Beef (Economical), 387.
—— Calf's Head, 157.
—— Goose, 341.
—— Mutton, 190.
Hasty Pudding, 132.
Head and Shoulders of Cod, 414.
Herbs, To dry, 276.
Herbaceous Seasoning, Aromatic, 276.
Herrings, Fresh, 88.

Herrings, Fresh, au Gratin (*see* Mackerel au Gratin), 173.
——, ——, Pickled, 299.
—— with Mustard Sauce, 327.
Hominy Cake, 359.
——, To boil, 73.
——, To fry, 74.
——, To soak, 72.
Horseradish Sauce, 411.
Hotch Potch, Scotch, 251.
Hot Cross Buns, 145.
Hot Pot, Lancashire, 126.
Hot Rolls, 318.
Hot Weather, To keep Butter in, 308.
—— ——, To preserve Meat in, 270.
Hydropathic Pudding, 225.

Meats, Fish, &c. (*continued*):—
  Mutton Chops, Stewed in their own Gravy, 203.
  Rump Steak, Stewed, 408.
Spoon Meats:—
  Arrowroot, 206.
  Cocoa, 33.
  Gruel (*see* Water Gruel, two ways), 206.
  Panada, 206.
  Thick Milk, 207.
  Rice Gruel, 206.
  Sago, 206.
  Savoury Custard, 207, 275.
  Tapioca, 206.
Italian Cream, 310.

I

Icing Sugar for Puddings, 287.
Indian Pickle, 314.
Invalid's Dishes:
  Broths:—
    Barley Cream, 96.
    Beef Tea, 95.
    —— —— quickly made, 96.
    Chicken Broth, 96.
    Mutton Broth, 96.
    Veal Broth, 96.
  Drinks:—
    Barley Water, Clear, 171.
    —— ——, Thick, 171.
    Lemonade, 171.
    Linseed Tea, 171.
    Rice and Toast Water, 171.
  Food (*see* Appendix).
  Meats, Fish, &c.:—
    Fish, 408.
    Game, 408.
    Minced Meat, 408.
    Mutton Chops, Stewed, 408.

J

Jam and Bread Pudding, 87.
Jam, Apple, 407.
—— Turnovers, 336.
January, Dessert Fruits for, 56.
Jelly, Apple, 407.
——, Aspic, 392.
——, Black Currant, 241.
——, Calf's-foot, 393.
——, Fruit, 392.
——, Gelatine, 391.
——, Maraschino, 392.
——, Orange, 392.
——, Red Currant, 241.
——, Savoury, 492.
——, Wine, 391.
——, White Currant, 241.
Jerusalem Artichokes, 407.
Jugged Hare, 369.
Julienne, 143.
—— Soup quickly made, 79.
July, Dessert Fruits for, 276.
June, Dessert Fruits for, 240.
Junket, Devonshire, 330.

K

Kedgeree, 21.
Ketchup, Mushroom, 342.
——, Walnut, 276.
Kidney Beans, 295.
——, Ox, stewed, 135.
—— Soup, 93.
Kidneys and Bacon, Fried, 3.
——, Broiled, 51.
——, Sheep's, To choose, 1.
——, Stewed, 152.
——, Pork, Stewed, 152.
Kippered Salmon, Broiled, 19.
—— ——, Purchase of, 17
Kromeskies, 272.

L

Lamb, Breast of, stewed with Mushrooms, 243.
——, Devilled, 176.
——, Forequarter of, 147
——, Minced, 186.
Lamb's Fry, 188.
—— Sweetbreads, 365.
Lancashire Hot Pot, 126.
Lèche Crême, 179.
Leg of Mutton, To choose, 17.
Lemonade, 171.
Lemon Cheesecakes, 297.
—— Dumplings, 350.
—— Pudding, 291.
—— Sponge, 288.
—— Syrup, 119.
Lentils and Sausages, 138.
——, Boiled, 98.
Lentil Soup, 134.
Leveret, Civet of, 222.
——, Potted, 256.
—— Soup, 223.
Light Buns, 294.
Linseed Tea, 171.
Liver and Bacon, 31.

Liver Sauce, 429.
Lobster Butter, 214.
—— Sauce, 214.
—— Soup, 193.
Loin of Mutton, To choose, 6.
—— of Pork, 12.

M

Macaroni à la Milanaise, 265.
—— and Bacon, 49.
—— „ Ham, 136.
—— „ Mushrooms, 304.
—— „ Tongue, 223.
—— Cheese, 120.
——, Italian, 248.
—— Pudding, 129.
—— Soup, 92.
——, Sweet, 292.
——, To buy, 1.
Mackerel au Gratin, 173.
——, Baked, 151.
——, Pickled, 309.
——, Pickled, To keep good, 235.
Maître d'Hôtel Butter, 151.
—— —— Sauce, 177.
Maraschino Jelly, 392.
March, Dessert Fruits for, 133.
Marinade for Pork, 382.
Marketing :—
  Apples, Dried (chips), 198.
  Bacon, 6.
  Baker's Rolls, 317.
  Beef, 20.
  ——, Aitchbone of, 190.
  ——, Fillet of the Rump of, 3.
  ——, for Beef à la Mode, 77.
  ——, Muscle of the Leg of, 48.
  ——, Thin flank of, 37.
  ——, Top-side of the Round of, 61.
  ——, Ribs of, 20.

Marketing (*continued*) :—
  Beef, Silver-side of, 24.
  ——, Sirloin of, 104.
  Brill, 18.
  Broccoli, 164.
  Calf's Head, 154.
  Canadian Ham, 329.
  Cauliflower, 164.
  Cod, 12.
  ——, Economical way of buying, 359.
  Crabs, 297.
  Cucumber, To keep fresh, 207.
  Ducks, 245.
  Eels, 43.
  Fish, 1, 6.
  Fowls, 67.
  German Sausage, 130.
  Giblets, 65.
  Goose, 338.
  Green Geese, 212.
  Grouse, 309.
  ——, Potted, 15.
  Guinea Fowls, 77.
  Gurnets, 80.
  Haddock, 317.
  Hake, 284.
  Halibut, 219.
  —— Cutlets, 231.
  Ham (*see* Bacon), 6.
  Hare, 17.
  Herrings, Fresh, 88, 304.
  Hominy, 71.
  Indian Meal, 52.
  Italian Beef, Meat for, 59.
  Julienne, 77.
  Kippered Salmon, 17.
  Lamb, 146.
  ——, Forequarter of, 146.
  Lamb's Fry, 187.
  Leverets, 221.
  Lobster Spawn, 212.
  Lunch Tongues, Small, 62.
  Mackerel, 137.
  Meat, when tender, 1.
  Mushrooms, Forced, 119.

Marketing (*continued*) :—
  Mutton Cutlets, 169.
  ——, Neck of, 31, 61.
  ——, Leg of, 17.
  ——, Loin of, 12.
  ——, Saddle of, 19.
  ——, Scrag of, whole, 70.
  Muffins, 51.
  Ox Flare, To render, for Fat (*see* Note 5, page 83).
  —— Tails, 179.
  —— Tongue, 255.
  Oysters, 48, 77.
  Parsley, 6.
  Partridges, 347.
  Pheasants, 23, 364.
  Pigeons, 143.
  Pig's Feet for Brawn, 15.
  —— —— for Breakfast, 67.
  —— Fry, 67.
  —— Head for Brawn, 15.
  Pilchards, 41.
  Plaice, 158.
  Pork, 12.
  ——, Loin of, 12.
  ——, Leg of, 61.
  Poultry, 239.
  Prairie Birds, 94.
  Prawns, Tinned, 65.
  Ptarmigan, 85.
  Rabbits, 43.
  Red Mullet, 301.
  Rump Steak for Broiling, 39.
  —— —— for Roasting, 43.
  Salmon, 245.
  Salsify, 370.
  Sardines, 23.
  Scallops, 104.
  Shad, 116.
  Sheep's Head, 52.
  —— Kidneys, 1.
  Skate, 20.
  Smelts, 62.
  Soles, 6.
  Sprats, 386.
  Suet, 1, 71.
  Tomatoes, 248.

Marketing (*continued*) :—
  Tongues, Tinned, 3.
  Tripe, 41.
  Turbot, 212.
  Turkey, 426.
  Twist, To render, for Fat, 84.
  Veal, 90.
  ——, Fillet of, 113.
  Whiting, 31.
  Wood Pigeons, 43.
Marmalade Bread and Butter Pudding, 208.
Marrow Toast, 38.
Mashed Parsnips, 342.
—— Potatoes, 184.
—— Turnips, 342.
May, Dessert Fruits for, 206.
Mayonnaise of Salmon, 197.
—— Sauce, 312.
Meat-cake, Savoury, 47.
Meat, Cold (*see* Réchauffés).
——, Fragments of, stewed for Stock, 2.
—— in Hot Weather, 270.
—— Patties, 259.
—— Puddings, Suet Crust for, 234.
——, Tainted, 270.
—— To bake, 106.
——, To boil, 87.
——, To make tender, 1.
——, To pickle, 26.
——, To roast, 100.
——, when tender, 1.
Meats, Potted, To serve (*see* Potted Grouse), 15.
Melted Butter, 260.
Milk and Biscuits, 222.
——, Corn-flour, 228.
—— Porridge, 221.
—— Rice, 226, 227.
—— Rolls, 306.
—— Soup, 7.
——, Thick, 207.
—— Toast, 226.
Minced Ham, 207.

Minced Lamb, 186.
—— Meat, 430.
—— Meat for Invalids, 408.
—— Mutton, 37.
—— Cakes, 194.
—— Pork, 157.
—— Veal, 183.
Mince Pies, 430.
Mint Sauce, 126.
Mistress, The Daily Duties of the, 4.
Mock Turtle Soup, 114.
—— Woodcock, 127.
Monday, Marketing on, 10.
Mould, Apple, 328.
—— of Calf's Head, 157.
—— of Ground Rice, 284.
—— of Rice, 350.
—— of Sago with Fruit Juice, 351.
—— of Semolina, 266.
Moulds for Jelly, To prepare, 393.
Mountain Pudding, 332.
Muffins, 53.
Mulligatawny Soup, 30.
Muscle of Beef (*see* Stewed Beef with Vegetables), 117.
Mushroom Ketchup, 342.
Mushrooms and Bacon, 322.
—— on Toast, 120.
——, Stewed, with Breast of Lamb, 243.
—— and Macaroni, 304.
—— and Tomatoes stewed with Chicken, 325.
Mustard Sauce, 249.
Mutton à la Sauce Piquante, 132.
—— Broth, 96.
—— Cakes, Minced, 194.
—— Chops, 189.
—— —— stewed for Invalids, 408.
—— —— —— in their own gravy, 203.
——, Cold (*see* Réchauffés).

Mutton Collops with Tomatoes, 343.
——, Curried, 199.
—— Cutlets with Piquante Sauce, 170.
——, Haricot, 148.
——, Hashed, 190.
—— Kidneys, stewed, 152.
——, Leg of, To choose, 17.
——, Loin of, To choose, 6.
——, Loin of, boned and rolled, 159.
——, Minced, 37.
——, Neck of, To choose, 31.
—— Pies, 6.
——, Saddle of, To choose, 19.
——, Scrag of, stewed with Vegetables, 27, 71, 149.
——, Scrag of, with Rice, 85.
——, Shank of, To stew, 18.
——, Shoulder of, Roast, 425.
——, Sour, 131.
—— stewed with Vegetables, 27.
—— Tart, 21.
——, Top of the Loin of, stewed, 172.

N

Neapolitan Sauce, 69.
Neck of Veal rolled and roasted, 201.
Newcastle Pudding, 220.
Newmarket Pudding, 208.
New Potatoes, To boil, 147.
—— ——, To sauté, 185.
Norfolk Dumplings, 390.
Normandy Pippins, 295.
Norman Haricot, 303.
Nottingham Pudding, 379.
November, Dessert Fruits for, 407.

O

Oatmeal Porridge, 45.
October, Dessert Fruits for, 376.
Oiled Butter, 223.
Oldham Parkin, 381.
Old Potatoes, To boil, 141.
Olives, Beef, 319.
Omelette, Baked, 283.
——, Savoury, 317.
—— Tin, To clean, 28.
Onion Sauce, 356.
—— Soup, 39.
Onions, Boiled, 372.
——, Pickled, 314.
—— with Stewed Beef, 379.
Orange Cream, 415.
—— Garnish, 415.
—— Jelly, 392.
—— Marmalade, 56, 57.
Oranges, Compote of, 415.
Oven for Cakes, 236.
Ox-Cheek Brawn, 140.
—— Eyes, 211.
—— Kidney, Stewed, 135.
—— Tail Soup, 86.
—— ——, Stewed, 180.
—— Tongue, Boiled, 270.
Oyster Sauce with Fresh Oysters, 358.
—— —— with Tinned Oysters, 358.
—— Patties, 374.
—— Soup, 344.
—— Shells, Use of, 3.
Oysters, Scalloped, 157.

P

Palestine Soup, 417.
Panada, 206.
Pancakes, 89.
Parkin, 331.

INDEX

Parkin, Oldham, 381.
Parsley Sauce, 177.
——, To keep, 6.
——, To fry, 25.
——, Use of, 6.
Parsnips, Boiled, 342.
——, Mashed, 342.
—— Soup, 411.
Parson's Pudding, 280.
Partridge, Roast, 348.
Pasties, Cornish, 301.
Pastry :—
  Flaky Crust, 285.
  Kinds of, 153.
  Puff Paste, 162.
  Rough Puff Pastry, 203.
  Short Crust (two kinds), 228.
  Suet Crust, 234.
  To be made regularly, 5.
Patties of Meat, 259.
——, Oyster, 374.
Peaches, Preserved, 147.
Peas, Green, 253.
Pease Pudding, 413.
—— Soup, 157.
Pheasant, Roasted, 367.
——, Salmi of, 368.
—— Soup, 28.
Pheasant's Legs, Devilled, 27.
——, To choose, 23.
——, To hang, 23.
Pickle for Sour Mutton, 120.
—— for Fresh Pork, 360.
—— for Pig's Cheek, 18.
——, German, for Pork, 152.
——, Indian, 314.
—— or Brine for Meat, 26.
Pickled Herrings, 299.
—— Mackerel, 309.
—— ——, To keep Good, 235.
—— Onions, 314.
—— Pork, Boiled, 165.
—— Red Cabbage, 314.
—— Salmon, 204.
—— Walnuts, 276.
Pie, Beef Steak and Mushrooms or Oysters, 128.

Pie, Cod, 4.
——, Pigeon, 187.
——, Rabbit, 324.
——, Sea, 113.
——, Shepherd's, 23.
——, Spicy, 178.
——, Veal and Ham, 169.
Pies, Fruit, 285.
——, Mince, 430.
——, Mutton, 6.
Pigeons, Stewed, 281.
Pig's Brains, 16.
—— Cheek, To boil, 57.
—— Cheek, To prepare, 16.
—— Feet for Breakfast, 68.
—— Feet, To clean, 16, 18.
—— Fry, or Poor Man's Goose, 67.
—— Head, To clean, 16, 18.
—— Head and Feet, To prepare for Brawn, 18.
Pine Apple, Tinned, 142.
Pippins, Normandy, 295.
Piquante Sauce, 170, 177.
—— Stew of Veal, 345.
Pistachios for Garnishing, 254.
Plaice, Fried, 158.
Plum Porridge, 313.
—— Pudding for Christmas, 418.
—— ——, Baked, 91.
Poached Eggs, 65.
Pork à la Italienne, 426.
—— cooked French method, 384.
—— Chops, Broiled or Fried, 395.
—— Cutlets with Apple Sauce, 53.
——, Fresh, To pickle, 360.
——, German fashion, 155.
——, Kidneys, Stewed, 152.
——, Leg of, To pickle, 61.
——, To roast, 353.
——, Loin of, 12.
——, Marinade for, 382.
——, Minced, 157.

Pork, Pickled, To boil, 165.
—— Pie, To serve, 13.
——, To choose, 12.
Porridge, Milk, 221.
——, Oatmeal, 45.
——, Plum, 313.
——, Rice and Barley, 224.
Potato Chips, 160.
—— Croquettes, 380.
—— Mould, 367.
—— Salad, 148.
—— Snow, 141.
—— Soup or Purée, 47.
Potatoes à la Maître d'Hôtel, 148.
——, Baked, 175.
——, Browned, 362.
—— Cold, browned, 433.
——, Cold (see Cod Pie, 4 ; Shepherd's Pie, 23)
——, Fried, 59.
——, Mashed, 184.
——, New, To boil, 147.
——, New, To sauté, 185.
——, Old, To boil, 141.
—— Soufflées, 160.
——, Steamed, 178.
Potted Beef, 42.
—— Grouse, 15.
—— Ham, 151.
—— Leveret, 256.
—— Meats, To serve (see Potted Grouse), 15.
—— Shrimps, 389.
—— Tongue, 337.
Poultry for Invalids, 408.
Powder, Baking, 279.
Prawns, Tinned, 67.
Prairie Birds, 97.
Preserved Peaches, 147.
—— Tomatoes, 116.
Preserving Fruit, 240.
Pressed Beef (see recipe for Boiling Beef), 87.
Prunes, Stewed, 93.
Puddings :—
  Batter, Baked, 64.

Puddings (continued) :—
  Batter, Baked in tins, 243.
  —— Boiled, 191.
  Beef Steak, 234.
  Bread-and-Butter, Marmalade, 208.
  Brown Betty, 404.
  Brown Bread, 263.
  Cabinet, 254.
  Cake, 63.
  Chicken, 308.
  Chocolate, 267.
  Cocoanut, 286.
  Cottage Plum, 213.
  Elegant Economist's, 184.
  Fig, 209.
  General Favourite, 189.
  Gingerbread, 193.
  Golden, 175.
  Ground Rice, 300.
  Hasty, 132.
  Hayrick, 119.
  Hydropathic, 225.
  Jam and Bread, 87.
  Lemon, 291.
  Macaroni, 129.
  Mountain, 332.
  Newcastle, 220.
  Newmarket, 208.
  Parson's, 280.
  Pease, 413.
  Plain Rice, 89
  —— Rolled, 116.
  —— Tapioca, 217.
  Plum, Baked, 91.
  ——, for Christmas, 418.
  Queen's, 287.
  Raspberry Sandwich, 406.
  Rhubarb, Boiled, 237.
  —— Mould, 209.
  Rice and Sago, 315.
  Roly-Poly, 297.
  Sago, 107.
  Savoury, 340.
  Semolina, 110.
  Suet, 185.
  Town, 411.

Puddings (*continued*):—
 Treacle, 130.
 Vermicelli, 278.
 Viennoise, 247.
 Wyvern, 181.
 Yorkshire, 403.
Puddings, Sauces for, 262.
——, To steam, 130.
—— Pulled Bread, 307.

Q

Queen's Pudding, 287.
Quinces for Pies, 356.

R

Rabbit, Baked, 250.
——, Boiled, 103.
—— Bones, To stew, 2.
——, Civet of, 417.
——, Curried, 258.
—— Gâteau, 250.
—— made Hot in Sauce, 389.
—— Pie, 324.
——, Spanish Stew of, 142.
Radishes and Watercress, 110.
Raisins with Boiled Rice, 61.
Raspberry Fool, 263.
—— Sandwich Pudding, 406.
Réchauffés :—
 Bacon made Hot, 92.
 Beef, Hashed, Economical, 387.
 Beef Steak Pudding Warmed, 235.
 Cod Pie, 4.
 —— Scallop, 16, 47.
 ——, Salt, 147.
 Cold Meats, To re-dress, Croquettes (*see* Rissoles, 13);

Réchauffés (*continued*):—
 Kromeskies, 272; Rissoles, 13; Hash, 387; Meat Cake, as in Fish Cake, 24; Gâteau, as in Rabbit Gâteau, 250; Patties, 259; Potted Meats, 15; Meat made Hot in Sauce, 389.
 China Chilo, 249.
 Elegant Economist's Pudding, 184.
 Fish Cake, 24.
 Fowl, Fricasseed, 271.
 Kedgeree, 21.
 Kromeskies, 272.
 Lamb, Devilled, 176.
 ——, Minced, 186.
 Mutton à la Sauce Piquante, 132.
 ——, Hashed, 190.
 ——, Loin of, Stewed, 172.
 ——, Minced, 37.
 —— Pies, 6.
 —— Tart, 21.
 Rabbit Gâteau, 250.
 —— made Hot in Sauce, 389.
 Rice Mould, 167.
 Rissoles (*see* Croquettes), 13.
 Salmon, Pickled, 204.
 Savoury Meat Cake, 47.
 Suet Dumpling toasted, 103.
 Shepherd's Pie, 23.
 Spicy Pie, 178.
 Veal Cake, 202.
 ——, Minced, 183.
Red Cabbage, Pickled, 314.
—— ——, Stewed, 367.
Red Currant Dumpling, 262.
—— —— Jelly, 241.
Red Mullet, Baked, 302.
Red Rice (*see* Rothe Grütze), 420.
Rhubarb Jam, 134.
—— Mould, 209.
——, Pudding, Boiled, 237.
——, Stewed, 192.
Ribs of Beef, 20.

Ribs of Beef, Italian Fashion, 60.
Rice and Barley Porridge, 224.
—— „ Cheese, 82.
—— „ Sago Pudding, 315.
—— „ Tapioca, Baked, 98.
——, Boiled, for Curry, 264.
——, Boiled with Raisins, 61.
—— Cake, 279.
—— Gâteau, 346.
—— Gruel, 206.
—— Milk, 226, 227.
—— Mould, 350.
—— Réchauffé of, 167.
—— Pudding, Plain, 89.
——, Savoury, 226.
—— Water, 171.
—— with Stewed Apples and Beetroot, 50.
Rissoles, 13.
—— of Veal, 245.
——, to free from Grease, 14.
Rizzared Haddock, 323.
Roast Ducklings, 269.
—— Fillet of Beef, 73.
—— Fowl or Chicken, 239.
—— Goose, 339.
—— ——, Apple Sauce for, 340.
—— ——, Brown Gravy for, 340.
—— ——, Sage and Onion Stuffing for, 340.
—— ——, Savoury Pudding to serve with, 340.
—— Grouse, 311.
—— Hare, 399.
—— ——, Gravy for, 400.
—— Partridge, 348.
—— Pheasant, 367.
—— Pork, Leg of, 353.
—— Shoulder of Mutton, 425.
—— To, 100.
—— Turkey, 432.
Rolled Bacon, 262.
—— Beef, 121.
—— Breast of Veal, 226.
—— Pudding, Plain, 116.

Rolled Loin of Mutton with Forcemeat, 159.
—— Steak, 232.
—— Veal, 188.
Rolls, Hot, 318.
Rolls of Veal, 177.
Roly-Poly Pudding, 297.
—— ——, Suet Crust for, 234.
Rothe Grütze, 420.
Rough Puff Paste, 203.
Roux, 14.
—— Quickly made, 15
Royal Sandwiches, 11.
Rump Steak, Broiled, 40.
—— ——, Roasted, 46.
—— ——, Stewed for Invalids. 408.
Russian Salad, 139.

S

Saddle of Mutton, To choose, 19.
Sage and Onion Stuffing, 340.
Sago, 206.
—— and Rice Pudding, 315.
—— Mould with Fruit Juice, 351.
—— Soup, 207.
—— Pudding, 107.
Salad, 111.
——, Celery, 393.
——, Hambro', 287.
——, Haricot, 131.
——, Italian, 166.
—— of Chicken or Grouse, 311
——, Potato, 148.
——, Salmon, 120.
——, Russian, 139.
——, To serve, 210.
Sally Lunns, 306.
Salmi of Pheasant, 368.
Salmon, Boiled, 246.
—— Cutlets, 262.
——, Devilled, 37.

Salmon, Kippered, Broiled, 19.
——, Purchase of, 17.
——, Mayonnaise of, 197.
—— Salad, 120.
——, Pickled, 204.
Salsify, 371.
Salt Cod Réchauffé, 147.
Salt Fish, Boiled, 146.
Sardines, To serve, 23.
Sauce :—
  Anchovy, 260.
  Apple, 340.
  Béarnaise, 124.
  Blanche, 165.
  Brawn, 29.
  Bread, 361.
  Caper, 119.
  Celery, 422.
  Chestnut, 432.
  Dutch, 186.
  Egg, 146.
  ——, Golden Rain, 320.
  Gooseberry, 215.
  Horseradish, 411.
  Liver, 429.
  Lobster, 214.
  Maître d'Hôtel, 177.
  Mayonnaise, 312.
  Melted Butter, 260.
  Mint, 126.
  Mustard, 249.
  Neapolitan, 69.
  Onion, 356.
  Oyster, 358
  Parsley, 177.
  Piquante, 177.
  Shrimp, 53.
  Tartar, 312.
  Tomato, 257.
  —— Store, 376.
  Venison, 332.
  Whip, 263.
  White, 432.
Sauces for Turbot, 214.
——, Sweet, for Puddings, 262.
Sausage Rolls, 382.
Sausages, 118.

Sausages and Lentils, 138.
——, Baked, 422.
——, Fried, 16.
—— on Toast, 16.
Savoury Beef, Stewed, 196.
—— Custard, 207, 275.
—— Eggs, 1.
—— Hash of Australian Meat, 64.
—— Jelly, 392.
—— Omelette, 317.
—— Pudding, 340.
—— Rice, 226.
Savoys, 210.
Scallops, 105.
Scalloped Cod, 16, 47.
—— Eggs, 350.
—— Oysters, 167.
Scones, To serve, 196.
—— with Baking Powder, 305.
—— with Sour Milk, 305.
Scotch Broth, 99.
—— Collops, 19.
—— Hotch Potch, 251.
Scrag End of Mutton with Rice, 85.
Sea Kale, 223.
—— Pie, 113.
Semolina Mould, 266.
—— Pudding, 110.
September, Dessert Fruits for, 342.
Shad or Salmon Shad, 117.
Shah, Soup for the, 329.
Shallots, To store, 291.
Shank of Mutton, To stew, 18.
Sheep's Kidneys, Broiled, 51.
—— ——, To choose, 1.
—— Head, Stewed, 54.
Shepherd's Pie, 23.
Short Crust, Economical, 228.
—— ——, Superior, 228.
Shrimp Sauce, 53.
Shrimps, Buttered, 266.
——, Potted, 389.
Sippets, Custard, 218.
Skate, 20.

Skate, Crimped, 20.
—— with Brown Butter, 74.
Skin and Bones of Fish, Use of, 10.
Sliced Tomatoes, 332.
Smelts, 63.
Soda Buns, Good, 293.
—— Cake, 293.
Sole à la Horly, 361.
—— au Gratin, 174.
——, Cold (see Cod Pie, Fish Cakes, Scalloped Cod, &c.), 4.
——, Fillets of, Sauté, 9.
——, To fillet, 9.
——, Filleted à la Maître d'Hôtel, 131.
——, Filleted, Rolled, and Baked, 97.
——, To choose, 6.
——, "Slips," Baked, 15
——, Fried, 125.
Soup :—
 A la Jardinière, 144.
 Artichoke (see Palestine Soup), 147.
 Bisque, 359.
 Cabbage, 67.
 Celery, 410.
 Clear (see Soup, To Clarify), 143.
 ——, from Fresh Meat, 274.
 Colberts, 144.
 Croûte au Pot, 198.
 Crécy, 11.
 Fish, Simple, 255.
 For the Shah, 329.
 Game (see Guinea Fowl), 79.
 Giblet, 58.
 Gravy, 313, 334.
 Guinea Fowl, 79.
 Hare, 35.
 Haricot, 107.
 Julienne, 144
 ——, quickly made, 79.
 Kidney, 93.

Soup (*continued*) :—
 Lentil, 134.
 Leveret, 223.
 Lobster, 193.
 Macaroni, 92.
 Macédoine, 144.
 Milk, 7.
 Mock Turtle (Tinned), 114.
 Mulligatawny, 30.
 Onion, 39.
 Ox-tail, 86.
 Oyster, 344.
 Palestine, 417.
 Parsnip, 411.
 Pease, 157.
 Potato, 47.
 Sago, 207.
 Spring, 144.
 Tinned, 114.
 Tomato, 109.
 Vermicelli, 123.
 Victoria, 70.
Sour Mutton, 131.
—— ——, Pickle for, 120.
Spanish Stew, 142.
Spicy Pie, 178.
Spinach, 182.
Sprats, Broiled, 386.
——, Dried, 94.
——, Fried, 386.
——, Pickled (see Pickled Herrings), 299.
Steak, Broiled, 40.
——, Rolled, 232.
——, To choose, 1.
——, Stewed, 55.
Steamed Potatoes, 178.
Steam, To, a Pudding, 130.
Stew, Irish, 108.
——, Piquante of Veal, 345.
——, Spanish, 142.
——, Swiss, 212.
Stewed Apples and Rice with Beetroot, 50.
—— Beef with Onions, 59.
—— Beef with Vegetables à la Jardinière, 117.

Stewed Celery, 409.
—— Cheese, 176.
—— Chicken with Tomatoes and Mushrooms, 325.
—— Eels, 44.
—— Endive, 414.
—— Eggs with Cheese, 71.
—— Giblets, 66.
—— Mushrooms, 120.
—— Mutton with Vegetables, 71, 149, 270.
—— Ox-kidney, 135.
—— Ox-tails, 180.
—— Pigeons, 281.
—— Prunes, 93.
—— Rhubarb, 192.
—— Sheep's Head, 54.
—— Steak, 55.
—— Veal, 268.
Stirabout Cheese, 277.
Stock, Fish, 53.
——, Calf's-foot, 393.
—— from Bones, 75.
—— from fresh Meat, 274.
Stone Cream, 242.
Store Sauce, Tomato, 376.
Strawberry Cream, 310.
Stuffed Tomatoes, 266.
Stuffing for Goose, 340.
Suet Dumplings, Remains of, toasted, 103.
—— Pudding, 185.
——, To choose, 6.
——, To chop (see Sea Pie), 113.
——, To keep, 278.
Sugar Browning, 5.
—— Icing for Puddings, 287.
Sultana Cake, 279.
Sunday, Meals for, 8.
Sweetbreads, Lambs', 365.
Sweet Macaroni, 292.
—— Sauces for Puddings, 262.
Syrup, Almond, 235
——, Lemon, 119.

T

Tapioca, 206.
—— and Apples, 82.
—— and Rice baked, 98.
—— Pudding, Plain, 217.
Tarragon Vinegar, 276.
Tart, Baked Custard, 35.
——, Mutton, 21.
Tartar Sauce, 312.
Tarts, Various, 285.
Tea, 8.
Teacakes, 306.
——, To serve, 77.
Tea-cosy, 9.
Tea-pot, To keep clean, 8.
Thickening, 14.
—— quickly made, 15.
Thick Milk, 207.
Tinned Meats (see Australian Meats), 63.
—— Peaches, 147.
—— Pine Apple, 142.
—— Prawns, 67.
—— Tongues, 3.
Toad-in-the-Hole, 29.
Toast, Anchovy, 17.
——, Marrow, 38.
——, Milk, 226.
——, Sausages on, 16.
—— Water, 171.
Toasted Bacon, 35
Tomato Beef, 355.
—— Purée, 109.
—— Sauce from fresh Tomatoes, 257.
—— Sauce from preserved Tomatoes, 257.
—— Store Sauce, 376.
Tomatoes and Bacon, 253.
—— and Mushrooms stewed, Chicken with, 325.
——, Baked, excellent, 248.
—— on Toast (see Tomatoes, Preserved), 116.
——, Sliced, 332.
——, Stuffed, 266.

Tomatoes with Mutton Collops, 343.
Tongue, Collared, 3.
———, To carve, 7.
—— and Macaroni, 223.
———, Potted, 337.
———, To boil, 270.
Town Pudding, 411.
Treacle Pudding, 13.
—— Tart, 285.
Tripe, Boiled, 412.
—— à la Coutance, 366.
Turbot, Boiled, 213.
———, Filleted, 230.
———, Sauces for, 214.
Turkey, Boiled, 432.
———, Roast, 432.
Turnips, To boil, 342.
———, To mash, 342.
Turnovers, Jam, 336.

V

Veal and Ham Pie, 169.
———, Breast of, Rolled, 226.
—— Broth, 96.
—— Cake, 202.
———, Curried, 264.
———, Fillet of, Baked or Roasted, 237.
—— Forcemeat, 237.
———, Gravy for, 238.
———, Minced, 183.
———, Neck of, Rolled and Roasted, 201.
—— Rissoles, 245.
———, Rolled, 188, 189.
—— Rolls, 177.
—— Simply braised, 244.
—— Stew Piquante, 345.
———, Stewed, 268.
Vegetable Marrow, Boiled, 317.
——— ———, To store for use, 316.

Vegetables :—
Artichokes, Globe, Boiled, 290.
———, Jerusalem, 407.
Asparagus, 222.
Beans, French or Kidney, 295.
———, Broad or Windsor, 258.
———, Haricot, 229.
Beetroot, Remains of, 296.
Brussels Sprouts, To boil, 210.
Cabbage, To boil, 210.
———, Red, Stewed, 367.
Carrots, To boil, 247.
Celery, Stewed, 409.
Colcannon, 290.
Endive, Stewed, 414.
Greens, To boil, 210.
Onions, Boiled, 372.
Parsnips, Boiled, 342.
———, Mashed, 342.
Peas, Green, 253.
Potato Chips, 160.
—— Croquettes, 380.
—— Snow, 141.
Potatoes, Baked, 175.
———, Browned, 362.
———, Cold, browned, 433.
———, Fried, 59.
———, Mashed, 184, 367.
—— Soufflées, 160.
———, Steamed, 178.
Salsify, 371.
Savoys, To boil, 210.
Scorzonera, 383.
Sea Kale, 223.
Tomatoes, Baked, excellent 248.
———, Sliced, 332.
———, Stuffed, 266.
Turnips, Boiled, 342.
———, Mashed, 342.
Venison Sauce, 332.
Vermicelli for Rissoles, 14.
—— for Pudding, 278.
—— Soup, 123.
Victoria Soup, 70.
Vienna Bread, 306.
—— Flour, 307.

Viennoise Pudding, 247.
Vinegar, Tarragon, 276.

W

Walnut Ketchup, 276.
Walnuts, Pickled, 276.
Waste, To prevent, 2, 4.
Watercress and young Radishes, 110.
Whipped Cream, 422.
Whip Sauce, 263.
White Currant Jelly, 241.

White Sauce, 432.
Whiting, Baked, 298
———, Fried, 32.
———, To choose, 31.
Windsor Beans (*see* Broad Beans), 258.
Wine, Jelly, 391.
Woodcock, Mock, 127.
Wyvern Puddings, 181.

Y

Yorkshire Pudding, 403.

Selections from Cassell & Company's Publications.

Illustrated, Fine-Art, and other Volumes.

Abbeys and Churches of England and Wales, The: Descriptive, Historical, Pictorial. Series II. 21s.
A Blot of Ink. Translated from the French by Q and PAUL FRANCKE. 5s.
Adventure, The World of. Fully Illustrated. In Three Vols. 9s. each.
Africa and its Explorers, The Story of. By DR. ROBERT BROWN, F.L.S. Illustrated. Vol. I., 7s. 6d.
Agrarian Tenures. By the Rt. Hon. G. SHAW-LEFEVRE, M.P. 10s. 6d.
Anthea. By CÉCILE CASSAVETTI (a Russian). A Sensational Story, based on authentic facts of the time of the Greek War of Independence. 10s. 6d.
Arabian Nights Entertainments, Cassell's Pictorial. 10s. 6d.
Architectural Drawing. By R. PHENÉ SPIERS. Illustrated. 10s. 6d.
Art, The Magazine of. Yearly Vol. With 12 Photogravures, Etchings, &c., and about 400 Illustrations. 16s.
Artistic Anatomy. By Prof. M. DUVAL. *Cheap Edition.* 3s. 6d.
Atlas, The Universal. A New and Complete General Atlas of the World, with 117 Pages of Maps, handsomely produced in Colours, and a Complete Index to about 125,000 Names. Cloth, 30s. net; or half-morocco, 35s. net.
Bashkirtseff, Marie, The Journal of. *Cheap Edition.* 7s. 6d.
Bashkirtseff, Marie, The Letters of. 7s. 6d.
Beetles, Butterflies, Moths, and Other Insects. By A. W. KAPPEL, F.L.S., F.E.S., and W. EGMONT KIRBY. With 12 Coloured Plates. 3s. 6d.
Biographical Dictionary, Cassell's New. 7s. 6d.
Birds' Nests, Eggs, and Egg-Collecting. By R. KEARTON. Illustrated with 16 Coloured Plates. 5s.
Blue Pavilions, The. By Q, Author of "Dead Man's Rock," &c. 6s.
Bob Lovell's Career. A Story of American Railway Life. By EDWARD S. ELLIS. 5s.
Breechloader, The, and How to Use It. By W. W. GREENER. 2s.
British Ballads. With 275 Original Illustrations. In Two Vols. 15s.
British Battles on Land and Sea. By JAMES GRANT. With about 600 Illustrations. Three Vols., 4to, £1 7s.; *Library Edition*, £1 10s.
British Battles, Recent. Illustrated. 4to, 9s.; *Library Edition*, 10s.
Butterflies and Moths, European. With 61 Coloured Plates. 35s.
Canaries and Cage-Birds, The Illustrated Book of. With 56 Facsimile Coloured Plates, 35s. Half-morocco, £2 5s.
Carnation Manual, The. Edited and Issued by the National Carnation and Picotee Society (Southern Section). 3s. 6d.
Cassell's Family Magazine. Yearly Vol. Illustrated. 9s.
Cathedrals, Abbeys, and Churches of England and Wales. Descriptive, Historical, Pictorial. *Popular Edition.* Two Vols. 25s.
Celebrities of the Century. *Cheap Edition.* 10s. 6d.
Cities of the World. Four Vols. Illustrated. 7s. 6d. each
Civil Service, Guide to Employment in the. 3s. 6d.
Climate and Health Resorts. By Dr BURNEY YEO. 7s. 6d.
Clinical Manuals for Practitioners and Students of Medicine. A List of Volumes forwarded post free on application to the Publishers.
Colonist's Medical Handbook, The. By E. A. BARTON, M.R.C.S. 2s. 6d.
Colour. By Prof. A. H. CHURCH. With Coloured Plates. 3s. 6d.

5 G. 5-93

Selections from Cassell & Company's Publications.

Columbus, The Career of. By CHARLES ELTON, Q.C. 10s. 6d.
Commercial Botany of the Nineteenth Century. 3s. 6d.
Cookery, A Year's. By PHYLLIS BROWNE. 3s. 6d.
Cookery, Cassell's Shilling. 384 pages, limp cloth, 1s.
Cookery, Vegetarian. By A. G. PAYNE. 1s. 6d.
Cooking by Gas, The Art of. By MARIE J. SUGG. Illustrated. 3s. 6d.
Cottage Gardening, Poultry, Bees, Allotments, Food, House, Window and Town Gardens. Edited by W. ROBINSON, F.L.S., Author of "The English Flower Garden." Fully Illustrated. First Half-yearly Volume. Cloth, 2s. 6d.
Countries of the World, The. By ROBERT BROWN, M.A., Ph.D., &c. Complete in Six Vols., with about 750 Illustrations. 4to, 7s. 6d. each.
Cyclopædia, Cassell's Concise. Brought down to the latest date. With about 600 Illustrations. *Cheap Edition.* 7s. 6d.
Cyclopædia, Cassell's Miniature. Containing 30,000 subjects. Cloth, 2s. 6d.; half-roxburgh, 4s.
Daughter of the South, A; and Shorter Stories. By Mrs. BURTON HARRISON. 4s.
Dickens, Character Sketches from. FIRST, SECOND, and THIRD SERIES. With Six Original Drawings in each by F. BARNARD. 21s. each.
Dick Whittington, A Modern. By JAMES PAYN. In One Vol., 6s.
Dog, Illustrated Book of the. By VERO SHAW, B.A. With 28 Coloured Plates. Cloth bevelled, 35s.; half-morocco, 45s.
Domestic Dictionary, The. Illustrated. Cloth, 7s. 6d.
Doré Bible, The. With 200 Full-page Illustrations by DORÉ. 15s.
Doré Gallery, The. With 250 Illustrations by DORÉ. 4to, 42s.
Dore's Dante's Inferno. Illustrated by GUSTAVE DORÉ. With Introduction by A. J. BUTLER. Cloth gilt or buckram. 7s. 6d.
Doré's Milton's Paradise Lost. Illustrated by DORÉ. 4to, 21s.
Dr. Dumány's Wife. A Novel. By MAURUS JÓKAI. 6s.
Dulce Domum. Rhymes and Songs for Children. Edited by JOHN FARMER, Author of "Gaudeamus," &c. Old Notation and Words. 5s. N.B.—The words of the Songs in "Dulce Domum" (with the Airs both in Tonic Sol-fa and Old Notation) can be had in Two Parts, 6d. each.
Earth, Our, and its Story. By Dr. ROBERT BROWN, F.L.S. With Coloured Plates and numerous Wood Engravings. Three Vols. 9s. each.
Edinburgh, Old and New. With 600 Illustrations. Three Vols. 9s. each.
Egypt: Descriptive, Historical, and Picturesque. By Prof. G. EBERS. With 800 Original Engravings. *Popular Edition.* In Two Vols. 42s.
Electricity in the Service of Man. Illustrated. 9s.
Electricity, Practical. By Prof. W. E. AYRTON. 7s. 6d.
Encyclopædic Dictionary, The. In Fourteen Divisional Vols., 10s. 6d. each; or Seven Vols., half-morocco, 21s. each; half-russia, 25s.
England, Cassell's Illustrated History of. With 2,000 Illustrations. Ten Vols., 4to, 9s. each. *Revised Edition.* Vols. I. to VI. 9s. each.
English Dictionary, Cassell's. Giving definitions of more than 100,000 Words and Phrases. Cloth, 7s. 6d. *Cheap Edition.* 3s. 6d.
English History, The Dictionary of. *Cheap Edition.* 10s. 6d.
English Literature, Dictionary of. By W. DAVENPORT ADAMS. *Cheap Edition*, 7s. 6d.; Roxburgh, 10s. 6d.
English Literature, Library of. By Prof. HENRY MORLEY. Complete in Five Vols., 7s. 6d. each.

Selections from Cassell & Company's Publications.

English Literature, Morley's First Sketch of. *Revised Edition.* 7s. 6d.
English Literature, The Story of. By ANNA BUCKLAND. 3s. 6d.
English Writers. By Prof. HENRY MORLEY. Vols. I. to IX. 5s. each.
Æsop's Fables. Illustrated by ERNEST GRISET. Cloth, 3s. 6d.
Etiquette of Good Society. 1s.; cloth, 1s. 6d.
Europe, Cassell's Pocket Guide to. Edition for 1893. Leather, 6s.
Fairway Island. By HORACE HUTCHINSON. With 4 Full-page Plates. 5s.
Faith Doctor, The. A Novel. By Dr. EDWARD EGGLESTON. 6s.
Family Physician, The. By Eminent PHYSICIANS and SURGEONS. *New and Revised Edition.* Cloth, 21s.; Roxburgh, 25s.
Father Stafford. A Novel. By ANTHONY HOPE. 6s.
Field Naturalist's Handbook, The. By the Revs. J. G. WOOD and THEODORE WOOD. *Cheap Edition.* 2s. 6d.
Figuier's Popular Scientific Works. With Several Hundred Illustrations in each. Newly Revised and Corrected. 3s. 6d. each.
  THE HUMAN RACE. | MAMMALIA. | OCEAN WORLD.
  THE INSECT WORLD.   REPTILES AND BIRDS.
  WORLD BEFORE THE DELUGE. THE VEGETABLE WORLD.
Flora's Feast. A Masque of Flowers. Penned and Pictured by WALTER CRANE. With 40 Pages in Colours. 5s.
Football, The Rugby Union Game. Edited by REV. F. MARSHALL. Illustrated. 7s. 6d.
Fraser, John Drummond. By PHILALETHES. A Story of Jesuit Intrigue in the Church of England. 5s.
Garden Flowers, Familiar. By SHIRLEY HIBBERD. With Coloured Plates by F. E. HULME, F.L.S. Complete in Five Series. 12s. 6d. each.
Gardening, Cassell's Popular. Illustrated. Four Vols. 5s. each.
George Saxon, The Reputation of. By MORLEY ROBERTS. 5s.
Gilbert, Elizabeth, and her Work for the Blind. By FRANCES MARTIN. 2s. 6d.
Gleanings from Popular Authors. Two Vols. With Original Illustrations. 4to, 9s. each. Two Vols. in One, 15s.
Gulliver's Travels. With 88 Engravings by MORTEN. *Cheap Edition.* Cloth, 3s. 6d.; cloth gilt, 5s.
Gun and its Development, The. By W. W. GREENER. With 500 Illustrations. 10s. 6d.
Health at School. By CLEMENT DUKES, M.D., B.S. 7s. 6d.
Heavens, The Story of the. By Sir ROBERT STAWELL BALL, LL.D., F.R.S., F.R.A.S. With Coloured Plates. *Popular Edition.* 12s. 6d.
Heroes of Britain in Peace and War. With 300 Original Illustrations. *Cheap Edition.* Two Vols., 3s. 6d. each; or Two Vols. in One, cloth gilt, 7s. 6d.
Hiram Golf's Religion; or, the "Shoemaker by the Grace of God." 2s.
History, A Foot-note to. Eight Years of Trouble in Samoa. By ROBERT LOUIS STEVENSON. 6s.
Historic Houses of the United Kingdom. Profusely Illustrated. 10s. 6d.
Hors de Combat; or, Three Weeks in a Hospital. Founded on Facts. By GERTRUDE & ETHEL ARMITAGE SOUTHAM. Illustrated. 5s.
Horse, The Book of the. By SAMUEL SIDNEY. With 28 Fac-simile Coloured Plates. *Enlarged Edition.* Demy 4to, 35s.; half-morocco, 45s.
Houghton, Lord: The Life, Letters, and Friendships of Richard Monckton Milnes, First Lord Houghton. By T. WEMYSS REID. In Two Vols., with Two Portraits. 32s.
Household, Cassell's Book of the. Complete in Four Vols. 5s. each. Four Vols. in Two, half-morocco, 25s.
Hygiene and Public Health. By B. ARTHUR WHITELEGGE, M.D. 7s. 6d.

Selections from Cassell & Company's Publications.

India, Cassell's History of. By JAMES GRANT. With about 400 Illustrations. Two Vols., 9s. each. One Vol., 15s.

In-door Amusements, Card Games, and Fireside Fun, Cassell's Book of. *Cheap Edition.* 2s.

Into the Unknown: A Romance of South Africa. By LAWRENCE FLETCHER. 4s.

"I Saw Three Ships," and other Winter's Tales. By Q, Author of "Dead Man's Rock," &c. 6s.

Island Nights' Entertainments. By R. L. STEVENSON. Illustrated, 6s.

Italy from the Fall of Napoleon I. in 1815 to 1890. By J. W. PROBYN. *New and Cheaper Edition.* 3s. 6d.

Joy and Health. By MARTELLIUS. 3s. 6d. *Édition de Luxe*, 7s. 6d.

Kennel Guide, The Practical. By Dr. GORDON STABLES. 1s.

Khiva, A Ride to. By Col. FRED. BURNABY. 1s. 6d.

"La Bella," and Others. Being Certain Stories Recollected by Egerton Castle, Author of "Consequences." 6s.

Ladies' Physician, The. By a London Physician. 6s.

Lady's Dressing-room, The. Translated from the French of BARONESS STAFFE by LADY COLIN CAMPBELL. 3s. 6d.

Leona. By Mrs. MOLESWORTH. 6s.

Letts's Diaries and other Time-saving Publications published exclusively by CASSELL & COMPANY. (*A list free on application.*)

Little Minister, The. By J. M. BARRIE. One Vol. 6s.

Locomotive Engine, The Biography of a. By HENRY FRITH. 5s.

Loftus, Lord Augustus, The Diplomatic Reminiscences of, 1837-1862. With Portrait. Two Vols., 32s.

London, Greater. By EDWARD WALFORD. Two Vols. With about 400 Illustrations. 9s. each.

London, Old and New. Six Vols., each containing about 200 Illustrations and Maps. Cloth, 9s. each.

London Street Arabs. By Mrs. H. M. STANLEY. Illustrated, 5s.

Mathew, Father, His Life and Times. By F. J. MATHEW. 2s. 6d.

Medicine Lady, The. By L. T. MEADE. In One Vol., 6s.

Medicine, Manuals for Students of. (*A List forwarded post free.*)

Modern Europe, A History of. By C. A. FYFFE, M.A. Complete in Three Vols., with full-page Illustrations, 7s. 6d. each.

Mount Desolation. An Australian Romance. By W. CARLTON DAWE. 5s.

Music, Illustrated History of. By EMIL NAUMANN. Edited by the Rev. Sir F. A. GORE OUSELEY, Bart. Illustrated. Two Vols. 31s. 6d.

Musical and Dramatic Copyright, The Law of. By EDWARD CUTLER, THOMAS EUSTACE SMITH, and FREDERIC E. WEATHERLY, Barristers-at-Law. 3s. 6d.

Napier, Life and Letters of the Rt. Hon. Sir Joseph, Bart., LL.D., &c. By A. C. EWALD, F.S.A. *New and Revised Edition.* 7s. 6d.

National Library, Cassell's. In Volumes. Paper covers, 3d.; cloth, 6d. (*A Complete List of the Volumes post free on application.*)

Natural History, Cassell's Concise. By E. PERCEVAL WRIGHT, M.A., M.D., F.L.S. With several Hundred Illustrations. 7s. 6d.

Natural History, Cassell's New. Edited by Prof. P. MARTIN DUNCAN, M.B., F.R.S., F.G.S. Complete in Six Vols. With about 2,000 Illustrations. Cloth, 9s. each.

Selections from Cassell & Company's Publications.

Nature's Wonder Workers. By KATE R. LOVELL. Illustrated. 3s. 6d.
Nursing for the Home and for the Hospital, A Handbook of. By CATHERINE J. WOOD. *Cheap Edition.* 1s. 6d. ; cloth, 2s.
Nursing of Sick Children, A Handbook for the. By CATHERINE J. WOOD. 2s. 6d.
O'Driscoll's Weird, and other Stories. By A. WERNER. 5s.
Odyssey, The Modern ; or, Ulysses up to Date. Cloth gilt, 10s. 6d.
Ohio, The New. A Story of East and West. By EDWARD EVERETT HALE. 6s.
Oil Painting, A Manual of. By the Hon. JOHN COLLIER. 2s. 6d.
Orchid Hunter, Travels and Adventures of an. By ALBERT MILLICAN. Fully Illustrated. 12s. 6d.
Our Own Country. Six Vols. With 1,200 Illustrations. 7s. 6d. each.
Out of the Jaws of Death. By FRANK BARRETT. In One Vol., 6s.
Painting, The English School of. *Cheap Edition.* 3s. 6d.
Painting, Practical Guides to. With Coloured Plates :—

MARINE PAINTING. 5s.	TREE PAINTING. 5s.
ANIMAL PAINTING. 5s.	WATER-COLOUR PAINTING. 5s.
CHINA PAINTING. 5s.	NEUTRAL TINT. 5s.
FIGURE PAINTING. 7s. 6d.	SEPIA, in Two Vols., 3s. each ; or in One Vol., 5s.
ELEMENTARY FLOWER PAINTING. 3s.	FLOWERS, AND HOW TO PAINT THEM. 5s.

Peoples of the World, The. In Six Vols. By Dr. ROBERT BROWN. Illustrated. 7s. 6d. each.
Perfect Gentleman, The. By the Rev. A. SMYTHE-PALMER, D.D. 3s. 6d.
Phillips, Watts, Artist and Playwright. By Miss E. WATTS PHILLIPS. With 32 Plates. 10s. 6d.
Photography for Amateurs. By T. C. HEPWORTH. *Enlarged and Revised Edition.* Illustrated. 1s. ; or cloth, 1s. 6d.
Phrase and Fable, Dictionary of. By the Rev. Dr. BREWER. *Cheap Edition, Enlarged,* cloth, 3s. 6d. ; or with leather back, 4s. 6d.
Physiology for Students, Elementary. By A. T. SCHOFIELD, M.D., M.R.C.S., &c. Illustrated. 7s. 6d.
Picturesque America. Complete in Four Vols., with 48 Exquisite Steel Plates and about 800 Original Wood Engravings. £2 2s. each.
Picturesque Canada. With 600 Original Illustrations. Two Vols. £6 6s. the Set.
Picturesque Europe. Complete in Five Vols. Each containing 13 Exquisite Steel Plates, from Original Drawings, and nearly 200 Original Illustrations. Cloth, £21; half-morocco, £31 10s. ; morocco gilt, £52 10s. POPULAR EDITION. In Five Vols., 18s. each.
Picturesque Mediterranean, The. With Magnificent Original Illustrations by the leading Artists of the Day. Complete in Two Vols. £2 2s. each.
Pigeon Keeper, The Practical. By LEWIS WRIGHT. Illustrated. 3s. 6d.
Pigeons, The Book of. By ROBERT FULTON. Edited and Arranged by L. WRIGHT. With 50 Coloured Plates, 31s. 6d. ; half-morocco, £2 2s.
Pity and of Death, The Book of. By PIERRE LOTI. Translated by T. P. O'CONNOR, M.P.
Playthings and Parodies. Short Stories by BARRY PAIN. 5s.
Poems, Aubrey de Vere's. A Selection. Edited by J. DENNIS. 3s. 6d.
Poetry, The Nature and Elements of. By E. C. STEDMAN. 6s.
Poets, Cassell's Miniature Library of the. Price 1s. each Vol.
Portrait Gallery, The Cabinet. First, Second, and Third Series, each containing 36 Cabinet Photographs of Eminent Men and Women With Biographical Sketches. 15s. each.

Selections from Cassell & Company's Publications.

Poultry Keeper, The Practical. By L. WRIGHT. Illustrated. 3s. 6d.
Poultry, The Book of. By LEWIS WRIGHT. *Popular Edition.* 10s. 6d.
Poultry, The Illustrated Book of. By LEWIS WRIGHT. With Fifty Coloured Plates. *New and Revised Edition.* Cloth, 31s. 6d.
Queen Summer; or, The Tourney of the Lily and the Rose. With Forty Pages of Designs in Colours by WALTER CRANE. 6s.
Queen Victoria, The Life and Times of. By ROBERT WILSON. Complete in Two Vols. With numerous Illustrations. 9s. each.
Rabbit-Keeper, The Practical. By CUNICULUS. Illustrated. 3s. 6d.
Raffles Haw, The Doings of. By A. CONAN DOYLE. 5s.
Railway Guides, Official Illustrated. With Illustrations, Maps, &c. Price 1s. each; or in cloth, 2s. each.

GREAT EASTERN RAILWAY.	GREAT WESTERN RAILWAY.
GREAT NORTHERN RAILWAY.	LONDON AND SOUTH-WESTERN RAILWAY.
LONDON, BRIGHTON AND SOUTH COAST RAILWAY.	MIDLAND RAILWAY.
LONDON AND NORTH-WESTERN RAILWAY.	SOUTH-EASTERN RAILWAY.

Rovings of a Restless Boy, The. By KATHARINE B. FOOT. Illustrated. 5s.
Railway Library, Cassell's. Crown 8vo, boards, 2s. each.

METZEROTT, SHOEMAKER. By KATHARINE P. WOODS.	THE PHANTOM CITY. By W. WESTALL.
DAVID TODD. By DAVID MACLURE.	JACK GORDON, KNIGHT ERRANT, GOTHAM, 1883. By BARCLAY NORTH.
THE ASTONISHING HISTORY OF TROY TOWN. By Q.	THE DIAMOND BUTTON. By BARCLAY NORTH.
THE ADMIRABLE LADY BIDDY FANE. By FRANK BARRETT.	ANOTHER'S CRIME. By JULIAN HAWTHORNE.
COMMODORE JUNK. By G. MANVILLE FENN.	THE YOKE OF THE THORAH. By SIDNEY LUSKA.
ST. CUTHBERT'S TOWER. By FLORENCE WARDEN.	WHO IS JOHN NOMAN? By CHARLES HENRY BECKETT.
THE MAN WITH A THUMB. By BARCLAY NORTH.	THE TRAGEDY OF BRINKWATER. By MARTHA L. MOODEY.
BY RIGHT NOT LAW. By R. SHERRARD.	AN AMERICAN PENMAN. By JULIAN HAWTHORNE.
WITHIN SOUND OF THE WEIR. By THOMAS ST. E. HAKE.	SECTION 558; or, THE FATAL LETTER. By JULIAN HAWTHORNE.
UNDER A STRANGE MASK. By FRANK BARRETT.	THE BROWN STONE BOY. By W. H. BISHOP.
THE COOMBSBERROW MYSTERY. By JAMES COLWALL.	A TRAGIC MYSTERY. By JULIAN HAWTHORNE.
DEAD MAN'S ROCK. By Q.	THE GREAT BANK ROBBERY. By JULIAN HAWTHORNE.
A QUEER RACE. By W. WESTALL.	
CAPTAIN TRAFALGAR. By WESTALL and LAURIE.	

Redgrave, Richard, C.B., R.A. Memoir. Compiled from his Diary. By F. M. REDGRAVE. 10s. 6d.
Rivers of Great Britain: Descriptive, Historical, Pictorial.
 THE ROYAL RIVER: The Thames, from Source to Sea. *Popular Edition,* 16s.
 RIVERS OF THE EAST COAST. With highly finished Engravings. *Popular Edition,* 16s.
Robinson Crusoe, Cassell's New Fine-Art Edition of. With upwards of 100 Original Illustrations. 7s. 6d.
Romance, The World of. Illustrated. Cloth, 9s.
Russo-Turkish War, Cassell's History of. With about 500 Illustrations. Two Vols. 9s. each.
Salisbury Parliament, A Diary of the. By H. W. LUCY. Illustrated by HARRY FURNISS. 21s.
Saturday Journal, Cassell's. Yearly Volume, cloth, 7s. 6d.
Scarabæus. The Story of an African Beetle. By the MARQUISE CLARA LANZA and JAMES CLARENCE HARVEY. Cloth, 5s.

Selections from Cassell & Company's Publications.

Science for All. Edited by Dr. ROBERT BROWN. *Revised Edition.* Illustrated. Five Vols. 9s. each.
Science, The Year Book of. Edited by Prof. BONNEY, F.R.S. 7s. 6d.
Sculpture, A Primer of. By E. ROSCOE MULLINS. With Illustrations. 2s. 6d.
Sea, The: Its Stirring Story of Adventure, Peril, and Heroism. By F. WHYMPER. With 400 Illustrations. Four Vols. 7s. 6d. each.
Shadow of a Song, The. A Novel. By CECIL HARLEY. 5s.
Shaftesbury, The Seventh Earl of, K.G., The Life and Work of. By EDWIN HODDER. *Cheap Edition.* 3s. 6d.
Shakespeare, The Plays of. Edited by Professor HENRY MORLEY. Complete in Thirteen Vols., cloth, 21s.; half-morocco, cloth sides, 42s.
Shakespeare, Cassell's Quarto Edition. Containing about 600 Illustrations by H. C. SELOUS. Complete in Three Vols., cloth gilt, £3 3s.
Shakespeare, Miniature. Illustrated. In Twelve Vols., in box, 12s.; or in Red Paste Grain (box to match), with spring catch, 21s.
Shakspere, The International. *Edition de Luxe.*
  "KING HENRY VIII." Illustrated by SIR JAMES LINTON, P.R.I. (*Price on application.*)
  "OTHELLO." Illustrated by FRANK DICKSEE, R.A. £3 10s.
  "KING HENRY IV." Illustrated by EDUARD GRÜTZNER. £3 10s.
  "AS YOU LIKE IT." Illustrated by ÉMILE BAYARD. £3 10s.
  "ROMEO AND JULIET." Illustrated by F. DICKSEE, R.A. Is now out of print, and scarce.
Shakspere, The Leopold. With 400 Illustrations. *Cheap Edition.* 3s. 6d. Cloth gilt, gilt edges, 5s.; Roxburgh, 7s. 6d.
Shakspere, The Royal. With Steel Plates and Wood Engravings. Three Vols. 15s. each.
Sketches, The Art of Making and Using. From the French o' G. FRAIPONT. By CLARA BELL. With 50 Illustrations. 2s. 6d.
Smuggling Days and Smuggling Ways; or, The Story of a Lost Art. By Commander the Hon. HENRY N. SHORE, R.N. With numerous Plans and Drawings by the Author. 7s. 6d.
Snare of the Fowler, The. By Mrs. ALEXANDER. In One Vol., 6s.
Social Welfare, Subjects of. By Sir LYON PLAYFAIR, K.C.B. 7s. 6d.
Sports and Pastimes, Cassell's Complete Book of. *Cheap Edition.* With more than 900 Illustrations. Medium 8vo, 992 pages, cloth, 3s. 6d.
Squire, The. By Mrs. PARR. In One Vol., 6s.
Standard Library, Cassell's. Cloth, 2s. each.

Shirley.
Coningsby.
Mary Barton.
The Antiquary.
Nicholas Nickleby (Two Vols.).
Jane Eyre.
Wuthering Heights.
Dombey and Son (Two Vols.).
The Prairie.
Night and Morning.
Kenilworth.
Ingoldsby Legends.
Tower of London.
The Pioneers.
Charles O'Malley.
Barnaby Rudge.
Cakes and Ale.
The King's Own.
People I have Met.
The Pathfinder.
Evelina.
Scott's Poems.
Last of the Barons.
Adventures of Mr. Ledbury.
Ivanhoe.
Oliver Twist.
Selections from Hood's Works.
Longfellow's Prose Works.
Sense and Sensibility.
Lytton's Plays.
Tales, Poems, and Sketches. Bret Harte.
Martin Chuzzlewit (Two Vols.).
The Prince of the House of David.
Sheridan's Plays.
Uncle Tom's Cabin.
Deerslayer.
Rome and the Early Christians.
The Trials of Margaret Lyndsay.
Harry Lorrequer.
Eugene Aram.
Jack Hinton.
Poe's Works.
Old Mortality.
The Hour and the Man.
Handy Andy.
Scarlet Letter.
Pickwick (Two Vols.).
Last of the Mohicans.
Pride and Prejudice.
Yellowplush Papers.
Tales of the Borders.
Last Day of Palmyra.
Washington Irving's Sketch-Book.
The Talisman.
Rienzi.
Old Curiosity Shop.
Heart of Midlothian.
Last Days of Pompeii.
American Humour.
Sketches by Boz.
Macaulay's Lays and Essays.

Star-Land. By Sir R. S. BALL, LL.D., &c. Illustrated. 6s.
Storehouse of General Information, Cassell's. With Wood Engravings, Maps, and Coloured Plates. In Vols., 5s. each.

Selections from Cassell & Company's Publications.

Story of Francis Cludde, The. By STANLEY J. WEYMAN. 6s.
Story Poems. For Young and Old. Edited by E. DAVENPORT. 3s. 6d.
Successful Life, The. By AN ELDER BROTHER. 3s. 6d.
Sybil Knox; or, Home Again: a Story of To-day. By EDWARD E. HALE, Author of "East and West," &c. 6s.
Teaching in Three Continents. By W. C. GRASBY. 6s.
Tenting on the Plains; or, General Custer in Kansas and Texas. By ELIZABETH B. CUSTER. Illustrated. 5s.
Thackeray, Character Sketches from. Six New and Original Drawings by FREDERICK BARNARD, reproduced in Photogravure. 21s.
The "Short Story" Library.
   Noughts and Crosses. By Q. 5s. | Eleven Possible Cases. By Various Authors. 6s.
   Otto the Knight, &c. By OCTAVE THANET. 5s. | Felicia. By Miss FANNY MURFREE. 5s.
   Fourteen to One. &c. By ELIZABETH STUART PHELPS. 5s. | The Poet's Audience, and Delilah. By CLARA SAVILE CLARKE. 5s.
The "Treasure Island" Series. *Cheap Illustrated Editions.* Cloth, 3s. 6d. each.
   King Solomon's Mines. By H. RIDER HAGGARD. | The Splendid Spur. By Q.
   Kidnapped. By R. L. STEVENSON. | The Master of Ballantrae. By ROBERT LOUIS STEVENSON.
   Treasure Island. By ROBERT LOUIS STEVENSON. | The Black Arrow. By ROBERT LOUIS STEVENSON.
Tiny Luttrell. By E. W. HORNUNG, Author of "A Bride from the Bush." Crown 8vo, cloth gilt, Two Vols. 21s.
Trees, Familiar. By G. S. BOULGER, F.L.S. Two Series. With 40 full-page Coloured Plates by W. H. J. BOOT. 12s. 6d. each.
"Unicode": the Universal Telegraphic Phrase Book. *Desk or Pocket Edition.* 2s. 6d.
United States, Cassell's History of the. By the late EDMUND OLLIER. With 600 Illustrations. Three Vols. 9s. each.
Universal History, Cassell's Illustrated. Four Vols. 9s. each.
Verses Grave and Gay. By ELLEN THORNEYCROFT FOWLER. 3s. 6d.
Vision of Saints, A. By LEWIS MORRIS. *Edition de Luxe.* With 20 Full-page Illustrations. 21s.
Waterloo Letters. Edited by MAJOR-GENERAL H. T. SIBORNE, late Colonel R.E. With numerous Maps and Plans of the Battlefield. 21s.
Wild Birds, Familiar. By W. SWAYSLAND. Four Series. With 40 Coloured Plates in each. 12s. 6d. each.
Wild Flowers, Familiar. By F. E. HULME, F.L.S., F.S.A. Five Series. With 40 Coloured Plates in each. 12s. 6d. each.
Wood, Rev. J. G., Life of the. By the Rev. THEODORE WOOD. Extra crown 8vo, cloth. *Cheap Edition.* 5s.
Work. The Illustrated Journal for Mechanics. Vol. IV., for 1893, 6s. 6d.
World of Wit and Humour, The. With 400 Illustrations. 7s. 6d.
World of Wonders. Two Vols. With 400 Illustrations. 7s. 6d. each.
Wrecker, The. By ROBERT LOUIS STEVENSON and LLOYD OSBOURNE. Illustrated. 6s.
Yule Tide. Cassell's Christmas Annual. 1s.
Zero, the Slaver: A Romance of Equatorial Africa. By LAWRENCE FLETCHER. 4s.

ILLUSTRATED MAGAZINES.

The Quiver. ENLARGED SERIES. Monthly, 6d.
Cassell's Family Magazine. Monthly, 7d.
"Little Folks" Magazine. Monthly, 6d.
The Magazine of Art. Monthly, 1s.
"Chums." Illustrated Paper for Boys. Weekly, 1d.; Monthly, 6d.
Cassell's Saturday Journal. Weekly, 1d.; Monthly, 6d.
Work. Weekly, 1d.; Monthly, 6d.

CASSELL'S COMPLETE CATALOGUE, containing particulars of upwards of One Thousand Volumes, will be sent post free on application.

CASSELL & COMPANY, LIMITED, *Ludgate Hill, London.*

Selections from Cassell & Company's Publications.

Bibles and Religious Works.

Bible, Cassell's Illustrated Family. With 900 Illustrations. Leather, gilt edges, £2 10s.
Bible Educator, The. Edited by the Very Rev. Dean PLUMPTRE, D.D., With Illustrations, Maps, &c. Four Vols., cloth, 6s. each.
Bible Student in the British Museum, The. By the Rev. J. G. KITCHIN, M.A. *New and Revised Edition.* 1s. 4d.
Biblewomen and Nurses. Yearly Volume. Illustrated. 3s.
Bunyan's Pilgrim's Progress. Illustrated throughout. Cloth, 3s. 6d. ; cloth gilt, gilt edges, 5s.
Child's Bible, The. With 200 Illustrations. *150th Thousand.* 7s. 6d.
Child's Life of Christ, The. With 200 Illustrations. 7s. 6d.
"Come, ye Children." Illustrated. By Rev. BENJAMIN WAUGH. 5s.
Conquests of the Cross. With numerous Illustrations. Complete in Three Vols. 9s. each.
Doré Bible. With 238 Illustrations by GUSTAVE DORÉ. Small folio, best morocco, gilt edges, £15. *Popular Edition.* With 200 Illustrations. 15s.
Early Days of Christianity, The. By the Ven. Archdeacon FARRAR, D.D., F.R.S. LIBRARY EDITION. Two Vols., 24s. ; morocco, £2 2s. POPULAR EDITION. Complete in One Volume, cloth, 6s.; cloth, gilt edges, 7s. 6d. ; Persian morocco, 10s. 6d. ; tree-calf, 15s.
Family Prayer-Book, The. Edited by Rev. Canon GARBETT. M.A., and Rev. S. MARTIN. Extra crown 4to, cloth, 5s. ; morocco, 18s.
Gleanings after Harvest. Studies and Sketches by the Rev. JOHN R. VERNON, M.A. Illustrated. 6s.
"Graven in the Rock." By the Rev. Dr. SAMUEL KINNS, F.R.A.S., Author of "Moses and Geology." Illustrated. 12s. 6d.
"Heart Chords." A Series of Works by Eminent Divines. Bound in cloth, red edges, One Shilling each.

MY BIBLE. By the Right Rev. W. BOYD CARPENTER. Bishop of Ripon.
MY FATHER. By the Right Rev. ASHTON OXENDEN, late Bishop of Montreal.
MY WORK FOR GOD. By the Right Rev. Bishop COTTERILL.
MY OBJECT IN LIFE. By the Ven. Archdeacon FARRAR, D.D.
MY ASPIRATIONS. By the Rev. G. MATHESON, D.D.
MY EMOTIONAL LIFE. By the Rev. Preb. CHADWICK, D.D.
MY BODY. By the Rev. Prof. W. G. BLAIKIE, D.D.
MY GROWTH IN DIVINE LIFE. By the Rev. Preb. REYNOLDS, M.A.
MY SOUL. By the Rev. P. B. POWER, M.A.
MY HEREAFTER. By the Very Rev. Dean BICKERSTETH.
MY WALK WITH GOD. By the Very Rev. Dean MONTGOMERY.
MY AIDS TO THE DIVINE LIFE. By the Very Rev. Dean BOYLE.
MY SOURCES OF STRENGTH. By the Rev. E. E. JENKINS, M.A., Secretary of Wesleyan Missionary Society.

Helps to Belief. A Series of Helpful Manuals on the Religious Difficulties of the Day. Edited by the Rev. TEIGNMOUTH SHORE, M.A., Canon of Worcester. Cloth, 1s. each.

CREATION. By Dr. H. Goodwin, the late Lord Bishop of Carlisle.
THE DIVINITY OF OUR LORD. By the Lord Bishop of Derry.
THE MORALITY OF THE OLD TESTAMENT. By the Rev. Newman Smyth, D.D.
MIRACLES. By the Rev. Brownlow Maitland, M.A.
PRAYER. By the Rev. T. Teignmouth Shore, M.A.
THE ATONEMENT. By William Connor Magee, D.D., Late Archbishop of York.

Holy Land and the Bible, The. By the Rev. C. GEIKIE, D.D., LL.D. (Edin.). Two Vols., 24s. *Illustrated Edition,* One Vol., 21s.

5 B 5·93

Selections from Cassell & Company's Publications.

Lectures on Christianity and Socialism. By th Right Rev. ALFRED BARRY, D.D. Cloth, 3s. 6d.

Life of Christ, The. By the Ven. Archdeacon FARRAR, D.D., F.R.S. LIBRARY EDITION. Two Vols. Cloth, 24s.; morocco, 42s. CHEAP ILLUSTRATED EDITION. Cloth, 7s. 6d.; cloth, full gilt, gilt edges, 10s. 6d. POPULAR EDITION, in One Vol., 8vo, cloth, 6s.; cloth, gilt edges, 7s. 6d.; Persian morocco, gilt edges, 10s. 6d.; tree-calf, 15s.

Marriage Ring, The. By WILLIAM LANDELS, D.D. *New and Cheaper Edition.* 3s. 6d.

Morning and Evening Prayers for Workhouses and other Institutions. Selected by LOUISA TWINING. 2s.

Moses and Geology; or, The Harmony of the Bible with Science. By the Rev. SAMUEL KINNS, Ph.D., F.R.A.S. Illustrated. *New Edition* on Larger and Superior Paper. 8s. 6d.

My Comfort in Sorrow. By HUGH MACMILLAN, D.D. 1s.

New Light on the Bible and the Holy Land. By B. T. A. EVETTS, M.A. Illustrated. 21s.

New Testament Commentary for English Readers, The. Edited by the Rt. Rev. C. J. ELLICOTT, D.D., Lord Bishop of Gloucester and Bristol. In Three Volumes. 21s. each. Vol. I.—The Four Gospels. Vol. II.—The Acts, Romans, Corinthians, Galatians. Vol. III.—The remaining Books of the New Testament.

New Testament Commentary. Edited by Bishop ELLICOTT. Handy Volume Edition. St. Matthew, 3s. 6d. St. Mark, 3s. St. Luke, 3s. 6d. St. John, 3s. 6d. The Acts of the Apostles, 3s. 6d. Romans, 2s. 6d. Corinthians I. and II., 3s. Galatians, Ephesians, and Philippians, 3s. Colossians, Thessalonians, and Timothy, 3s. Titus, Philemon, Hebrews, and James, 3s. Peter, Jude, and John, 3s. The Revelation, 3s. An Introduction to the New Testament, 3s. 6d.

Old Testament Commentary for English Readers, The. Edited by the Right Rev. C. J. ELLICOTT, D.D., Lord Bishop of Gloucester and Bristol. Complete in Five Vols. 21s. each. Vol. I.—Genesis to Numbers. Vol. II.—Deuteronomy to Samuel II. Vol. III.—Kings I. to Esther. Vol. IV.—Job to Isaiah. Vol. V.—Jeremiah to Malachi.

Old Testament Commentary. Edited by Bishop ELLICOTT. Handy Volume Edition. Genesis, 3s. 6d. Exodus, 3s. Leviticus, 3s. Numbers, 2s. 6d. Deuteronomy, 2s. 6d.

Protestantism, The History of. By the Rev. J. A. WYLIE, LL.D. Containing upwards of 600 Original Illustrations. Three Vols. 9s. each.

Quiver Yearly Volume, The. With about 600 Original Illustrations. 7s. 6d.

Religion, The Dictionary of. By the Rev. W. BENHAM, B.D. *Cheap Edition.* 10s. 6d.

St. George for England; and other Sermons preached to Children. By the Rev. T. TEIGNMOUTH SHORE, M.A., Canon of Worcester. 5s.

St. Paul, The Life and Work of. By the Ven. Archdeacon FARRAR, D.D., F.R.S., Chaplain-in-Ordinary to the Queen. LIBRARY EDITION. Two Vols., cloth, 24s.; calf, 42s. ILLUSTRATED EDITION, complete in One Volume, with about 300 Illustrations, £1 1s.; morocco, £2 2s. POPULAR EDITION. One Volume, 8vo, cloth, 6s.; cloth, gilt edges, 7s. 6d.; Persian morocco, 10s. 6d.; tree-calf, 15s.

Shall We Know One Another in Heaven? By the Rt. Rev. J. C. RYLE, D.D., Bishop of Liverpool. *Cheap Edition.* Paper covers, 6d.

Signa Christi. By the Rev. JAMES AITCHISON. 5s.

"Sunday," Its Origin, History, and Present Obligation. By the Ven. Archdeacon HESSEY, D.C.L. *Fifth Edition.* 7s. 6d.

Twilight of Life, The. Words of Counsel and Comfort for the Aged. By the Rev. JOHN ELLERTON, M.A. 1s. 6d.

Selections from Cassell & Company's Publications.

Educational Works and Students' Manuals.

Agricultural Text-Books, Cassell's. (The "Downton" Series.) Edited by JOHN WRIGHTSON, Professor of Agriculture. Fully Illustrated, 2s. 6d. each. Farm Crops.—By Prof. WRIGHTSON. Soils and Manures.—By J. M. H. MUNRO, D.Sc. (London), F.I.C., F.C.S. Live Stock.—By Prof. WRIGHTSON.
Alphabet, Cassell's Pictorial. 3s. 6d.
Arithmetics, The Modern School. By GEORGE RICKS, B.Sc. Lond. With Test Cards. (*List on application.*)
Atlas, Cassell's Popular. Containing 24 Coloured Maps. 2s. 6d.
Book-Keeping. By THEODORE JONES. For Schools, 2s.; cloth, 3s. For the Million, 2s.; cloth, 3s. Books for Jones's System, 2s.
Chemistry, The Public School. By J. H. ANDERSON, M.A. 2s. 6d.
Classical Texts for Schools, Cassell's. (*A List post free on application.*)
Cookery for Schools. By LIZZIE HERITAGE. 6d.
Copy-Books, Cassell's Graduated. *Eighteen Books.* 2d. each.
Copy-Books, The Modern School. *Twelve Books.* 2d. each.
Drawing Copies, Cassell's Modern School Freehand. First Grade, 1s.; Second Grade, 2s.
Drawing Copies, Cassell's "New Standard." *Complete in Fourteen Books.* 2d., 3d., and 4d. each.
Energy and Motion. By WILLIAM PAICE, M.A. Illustrated. 1s. 6d.
Euclid, Cassell's. Edited by Prof. WALLACE, M.A. 1s.
Euclid, The First Four Books of. *New Edition.* In paper, 6d.; cloth, 9d.
Experimental Geometry. By PAUL BERT. Illustrated. 1s. 6d.
French, Cassell's Lessons in. *New and Revised Edition.* Parts I. and II., each 2s. 6d.; complete, 4s. 6d. Key, 1s. 6d.
French-English and English-French Dictionary. *Entirely New and Enlarged Edition.* 1,150 pages, 8vo, cloth, 3s. 6d.
French Reader, Cassell's Public School. By G. S. CONRAD. 2s. 6d.
Gaudeamus. Songs for Colleges and Schools. Edited by JOHN FARMER. 5s. Words only, paper covers, 6d.; cloth, 9d.
German Dictionary, Cassell's New (German-English, English-German). *Cheap Edition.* Cloth, 3s. 6d.
Hand-and-Eye Training. By G. RICKS, B.Sc. 2 Vols., with 16 Coloured Plates in each Vol. Cr. 4to, 6s. each. Cards for Class Use, 5 sets, 1s. each.
Historical Cartoons, Cassell's Coloured. Size 45 in. × 35 in., 2s. each. Mounted on canvas and varnished, with rollers, 5s. each.
Historical Course for Schools, Cassell's. Illustrated throughout. I.—Stories from English History, 1s. II.—The Simple Outline of English History, 1s. 3d. III.—The Class History of England, 2s. 6d.
Latin Dictionary, Cassell's New. (Latin-English and English-Latin.) Revised by J. R. V. MARCHANT, M.A., and J. F. CHARLES, B.A. Cloth, 3s. 6d.
Latin Primer, The First. By Prof. POSTGATE. 1s.
Latin Primer, The New. By Prof. J. P. POSTGATE. Crown 8vo, 2s. 6d.
Latin Prose for Lower Forms. By M. A. BAYFIELD, M.A. 2s. 6d.
Laundry Work (How to Teach It). By Mrs. E. LORD. 6d.
Laws of Every-Day Life. By H. O. ARNOLD-FORSTER, M.P. 1s. 6d. *Special Edition* on Green Paper for Persons with Weak Eyesight. 2s.
Little Folks' History of England. Illustrated. 1s. 6d.
Making of the Home, The. By Mrs. SAMUEL A. BARNETT. 1s. 6d.
Map-Building Series, Cassell's. Outline Maps prepared by H. O. ARNOLD-FORSTER, M.P. Per Set of Twelve, 1s.
Marlborough Books:—Arithmetic Examples, 3s. French Exercises, 3s. 6d. French Grammar, 2s. 6d. German do., 3s. 6d.
Mechanics and Machine Design, Numerical Examples in Practical. By R. G. BLAINE, M.E. *New and Revised Edition.* With 69 Diagrams. Cloth, 2s. 6d.

Selections from Cassell & Company's Publications.

Mechanics for Young Beginners, A First Book of. By the Rev. J. G. EASTON, M.A. 4s. 6d.
"Model Joint" Wall Sheets, for Instruction in Manual Training. By S. BARTER. Eight Sheets, 2s. 6d. each.
Natural History Coloured Wall Sheets, Cassell's New. 18 Subjects. Size 39 by 31 in. Mounted on rollers and varnished. 3s. each.
Object Lessons from Nature. By Prof. L. C. MIALL, F.L.S. Fully Illustrated. *New and Enlarged Edition.* Two Vols., 1s. 6d. each.
Perspective, The Principles of. By G. TROBRIDGE. Illustrated. Paper, 1s. 6d.; cloth, 2s. 6d.
Physiology for Schools. By A. T. SCHOFIELD, M.D., M.R.C.S., &c. Illustrated. Cloth, 1s. 9d.; Three Parts, paper covers, 5d. each; or cloth limp, 6d. each.
Poetry Readers, Cassell's New. Illustrated. 12 Books, 1d. each; or complete in one Vol., cloth, 1s. 6d.
Popular Educator, Cassell's NEW. With Revised Text, New Maps, New Coloured Plates, New Type, &c. In 8 Vols., 5s. each; or in Four Vols., half-morocco, 50s. the set.
Readers, Cassell's "Higher Class." (*List on application.*)
Readers, Cassell's Readable. Illustrated. (*List on application.*)
Readers for Infant Schools, Coloured. Three Books. 4d. each.
Reader, The Citizen. By H. O. ARNOLD-FORSTER, M.P. Illustrated. 1s. 6d. Also a *Scottish Edition*, cloth, 1s. 6d.
Reader, The Temperance. By Rev. J. DENNIS HIRD. Cr. 8vo, 1s. 6d.
Readers, The "Modern School" Geographical. (*List on application.*)
Readers, The "Modern School." Illustrated. (*List on application.*)
Reckoning, Howard's Anglo-American Art of. By C. FRUSHER HOWARD. Paper covers, 1s.; cloth, 2s. *New Edition,* 5s.
Round the Empire. By G. R. PARKIN. Fully Illustrated. 1s. 6d.
Science Applied to Work. By J. A. BOWER. 1s.
Science of Everyday Life. By J. A. BOWER. Illustrated. 1s.
Shade from Models, Common Objects, and Casts of Ornament, How to. By W. E. SPARKES. With 25 Plates by the Author. 3s.
Shakspere's Plays for School Use. 5 Books. Illustrated. 6d. each.
Spelling, A Complete Manual of. By J. D. MORELL, LL.D. 1s.
Technical Manuals, Cassell's. Illustrated throughout:—
  Handrailing and Staircasing, 3s. 6d.—Bricklayers, Drawing for, 3s.—Building Construction, 2s. — Cabinet-Makers, Drawing for, 3s. — Carpenters and Joiners, Drawing for, 3s. 6d.—Gothic Stonework, 3s.—Linear Drawing and Practical Geometry, 2s.—Linear Drawing and Projection.—The Two Vols. in One, 3s. 6d.—Machinists and Engineers, Drawing for, 4s. 6d.—Metal-Plate Workers, Drawing for, 3s.—Model Drawing, 3s.—Orthographical and Isometrical Projection, 2s.—Practical Perspective, 3s.—Stonemasons, Drawing for, 3s.—Applied Mechanics, by Sir R. S. Ball, LL.D., 2s.—Systematic Drawing and Shading, 2s.
Technical Educator, Cassell's. *Revised Edition.* Four Vols. 5s. each.
Technology, Manuals of. Edited by Prof. AYRTON, F.R.S., and RICHARD WORMELL, D.Sc., M.A. Illustrated throughout:—
  The Dyeing of Textile Fabrics, by Prof. Hummel, 5s.—Watch and Clock Making, by D. Glasgow, Vice-President of the British Horological Institute, 4s. 6d.—Steel and Iron, by Prof. W. H. Greenwood, F.C.S., M.I.C.E., &c., 5s.—Spinning Woollen and Worsted, by W. S. B. McLaren, M.P., 4s. 6d.—Design in Textile Fabrics, by T. R. Ashenhurst, 4s. 6d.—Practical Mechanics, by Prof. Perry, M.E., 3s. 6d.—Cutting Tools Worked by Hand and Machine, by Prof. Smith, 3s. 6d.
Things New and Old; or, Stories from English History. By H. O. ARNOLD-FORSTER, M.P. Fully Illustrated, and strongly bound in Cloth. Standards I. & II., 9d. each; Standard III., 1s.; Standard IV., 1s. 3d.; Standards V., VI., & VII., 1s. 6d. each.
This World of Ours. By H. O. ARNOLD-FORSTER, M.P. Illusd. 3s. 6d.

Selections from Cassell & Company's Publications.

Books for Young People.

"**Little Folks**" **Half-Yearly Volume.** Containing 432 4to pages, with about 200 Illustrations, and Pictures in Colour. Boards, 3s. 6d.; cloth, 5s.

Bo-Peep. A Book for the Little Ones. With Original Stories and Verses. Illustrated throughout. Yearly Volume. Boards, 2s. 6d.; cloth, 3s. 6d.

Bashful Fifteen. By L. T. MEADE. Illustrated. 3s. 6d.

The Peep of Day. *Cassell's Illustrated Edition.* 2s. 6d.

Maggie Steele's Diary. By E. A. DILLWYN. 2s. 6d.

A Bundle of Tales. By MAGGIE BROWNE (Author of "Wanted—a King," &c.), SAM BROWNE, and AUNT ETHEL. 3s. 6d.

Fairy Tales in other Lands. By JULIA GODDARD. Illustrated. 3s. 6d.

Pleasant Work for Busy Fingers. By MAGGIE BROWNE. Illustrated. 5s.

Born a King. By FRANCES and MARY ARNOLD-FORSTER. (The Life of Alfonso XIII., the Boy King of Spain.) Illustrated. 1s.

Cassell's Pictorial Scrap Book. In Six Sectional Vols., paper boards, 3s. 6d. each.

Schoolroom and Home Theatricals. By ARTHUR WAUGH. Illustrated. 2s. 6d.

Magic at Home. By Prof. HOFFMAN. Illustrated. Cloth gilt, 5s.

Little Mother Bunch. By Mrs. MOLESWORTH. Illustrated. Cloth, 3s. 6d.

Pictures of School Life and Boyhood. Selected from the best Authors. Edited by PERCY FITZGERALD, M.A. 2s. 6d.

Heroes of Every-day Life. By LAURA LANE. With about 20 Full-page Illustrations. Cloth. 2s. 6d.

Books for Young People. Illustrated. Cloth gilt, 5s. each.

The Champion of Odin; or, Viking Life in the Days of Old. By J. Fred. Hodgetts.	Bound by a Spell; or, The Hunted Witch of the Forest. By the Hon. Mrs. Greene.

Under Bayard's Banner. By Henry Frith.

Books for Young People. Illustrated. 3s. 6d. each.

*The White House at Inch Gow. By Mrs. Pitt.	*Polly: A New-Fashioned Girl. By L. T. Meade.
*A Sweet Girl Graduate. By L. T. Meade.	"Follow My Leader." By Talbot Baines Reed.
*The King's Command: A Story for Girls. By Maggie Symington.	*The Cost of a Mistake. By Sarah Pitt.
Lost in Samoa. A Tale of Adventure in the Navigator Islands. By Edward S. Ellis.	*A World of Girls: The Story of a School. By L. T. Meade.
Tad; or, "Getting Even" with Him. By Edward S. Ellis.	Lost among White Africans. By David Ker.
*The Palace Beautiful. By L. T. Meade.	For Fortune and Glory: A Story of the Soudan War. By Lewis Hough.

* *Also procurable in superior binding, 5s. each.*

Crown 8vo Library. *Cheap Editions.* Gilt edges, 2s. 6d. each.

Rambles Round London. By C. L. Matéaux. Illustrated.	Wild Adventures in Wild Places. By Dr. Gordon Stables, R.N. Illustrated.
Around and About Old England. By C. L. Matéaux. Illustrated.	Modern Explorers. By Thomas Frost. Illustrated. *New and Cheaper Edition.*
Paws and Claws. By one of the Authors of "Poems written for a Child." Illustrated.	Early Explorers. By Thomas Frost.
Decisive Events in History. By Thomas Archer. With Original Illustrations.	Home Chat with our Young Folks. Illustrated throughout.
The True Robinson Crusoes. Cloth gilt.	Jungle, Peak, and Plain. Illustrated throughout.
Peeps Abroad for Folks at Home. Illustrated throughout.	The England of Shakespeare. By E. Goadby. With Full-page Illustrations.

Selections from Cassell & Company's Publications.

The "Cross and Crown" Series. Illustrated. 2s. 6d. each.

- Freedom's Sword: A Story of the Days of Wallace and Bruce. By Annie S. Swan.
- Strong to Suffer: A Story of the Jews. By E. Wynne.
- Heroes of the Indian Empire; or, Stories of Valour and Victory. By Ernest Foster.
- In Letters of Flame: A Story of the Waldenses. By C. L. Matéaux.
- Through Trial to Triumph. By Madeline B. Hunt.
- By Fire and Sword: A Story of the Huguenots. By Thomas Archer.
- Adam Hepburn's Vow: A Tale of Kirk and Covenant. By Annie S. Swan.
- No. XIII.; or, The Story of the Lost Vestal. A Tale of Early Christian Days. By Emma Marshall.

"Golden Mottoes" Series, The. Each Book containing 208 pages, with Four full-page Original Illustrations. Crown 8vo, cloth gilt, 2s. each.

- "Nil Desperandum." By the Rev. F. Langbridge, M.A.
- "Bear and Forbear." By Sarah Pitt.
- "Foremost if I Can." By Helen Atteridge.
- "Honour is my Guide." By Jeanie Hering (Mrs. Adams-Acton).
- "Aim at a Sure End." By Emily Searchfield.
- "He Conquers who Endures." By the Author of "May Cunningham's Trial," &c.

Cassell's Picture Story Books. Each containing about Sixty Pages of Pictures and Stories, &c. 6d. each.

- Little Talks.
- Bright Stars.
- Nursery Toys.
- Pet's Posy.
- Tiny Tales.
- Daisy's Story Book.
- Dot's Story Book.
- A Nest of Stories.
- Good-Night Stories.
- Chats for Small Chatterers.
- Auntie's Stories.
- Birdie's Story Book.
- Little Chimes.
- A Sheaf of Tales.
- Dewdrop Stories.

Cassell's Sixpenny Story Books. All Illustrated, and containing Interesting Stories by well-known writers.

- The Smuggler's Cave.
- Little Lizzie.
- Little Bird, Life and Adventures of.
- Luke Barnicott.
- The Boat Club.
- Little Pickles.
- The Elchester College Boys.
- My First Cruise.
- The Little Peacemaker.
- The Delft Jug.

Cassell's Shilling Story Books. All Illustrated, and containing Interesting Stories.

- Bunty and the Boys.
- The Heir of Elmdale.
- The Mystery at Shoncliff School.
- Claimed at Last, and Roy's Reward.
- Thorns and Tangles.
- The Cuckoo in the Robin's Nest.
- John's Mistake.
- The History of Five Little Pitchers.
- Diamonds in the Sand.
- Surly Bob.
- The Giant's Cradle.
- Shag and Doll.
- Aunt Lucia's Locket.
- The Magic Mirror.
- The Cost of Revenge.
- Clever Frank.
- Among the Redskins.
- The Ferryman of Brill.
- Harry Maxwell.
- A Banished Monarch.
- Seventeen Cats.

Illustrated Books for the Little Ones. Containing interesting Stories. All Illustrated. 1s. each; cloth gilt, 1s. 6d.

- Firelight Stories.
- Sunlight and Shade.
- Rub-a-Dub Tales.
- Fine Feathers and Fluffy Fur.
- Scrambles and Scrapes.
- Tittle Tattle Tales.
- Up and Down the Garden.
- All Sorts of Adventures.
- Our Sunday Stories.
- Our Holiday Hours.
- Indoors and Out.
- Some Farm Friends.
- Wandering Ways.
- Dumb Friends.
- Those Golden Sands.
- Little Mothers & their Children.
- Our Pretty Pets.
- Our Schoolday Hours.
- Creatures Tame.
- Creatures Wild.

Albums for Children. 3s. 6d. each.

- The Album for Home, School, and Play. Containing Stories by Popular Authors. Illustrated.
- My Own Album of Animals. With Full-page Illustrations.
- Picture Album of All Sorts. With Full-page Illustrations.
- The Chit-Chat Album. Illustrated throughout.

Selections from Cassell & Company's Publications.

"Wanted—a King" Series. Illustrated. 3s. 6d. each.
  Great Grandmamma. By Georgina M. Synge.
  Robin's Ride. By Ellinor Davenport Adams.
  Wanted—a King; or, How Merle see the Nursery Rhymes to Rights. By Maggie Browne. With Original Designs by Harry Furniss.

The World's Workers. A Series of New and Original Volumes. With Portraits printed on a tint as Frontispiece. 1s. each.
  Charles Haddon Spurgeon. By G. Holden Pike.
  Dr. Arnold of Rugby. By Rose E. Selfe.
  The Earl of Shaftesbury. By Henry Frith.
  Sarah Robinson, Agnes Weston, and Mrs. Meredith. By E. M. Tomkinson.
  Thomas A. Edison and Samuel F. B. Morse. By Dr. Denslow and J. Marsh Parker.
  Mrs. Somerville and Mary Carpenter. By Phyllis Browne.
  General Gordon. By the Rev. S. A. Swaine.
  Charles Dickens. By his Eldest Daughter.
  Sir Titus Salt and George Moore. By J. Burnley.
  David Livingstone. By Robert Smiles.
  Florence Nightingale, Catherine Marsh, Frances Ridley Havergal, Mrs. Ranyard ("L. N. R."). By Lizzie Alldridge.
  Dr. Guthrie, Father Mathew, Elihu Burritt, George Livesey. By John W. Kirton, LL.D.
  Sir Henry Havelock and Colin Campbell Lord Clyde. By E. C. Phillips.
  Abraham Lincoln. By Ernest Foster.
  George Müller and Andrew Reed. By E. R. Pitman.
  Richard Cobden. By R. Gowing.
  Benjamin Franklin. By E. M. Tomkinson.
  Handel. By Eliza Clarke. [Swaine.
  Turner the Artist. By the Rev. S. A.
  George and Robert Stephenson. By C. L. Matéaux.

*** *The above Works (excluding* Richard Cobden *and* Charles Haddon Spurgeon*) can also be had Three in One Vol., cloth, gilt edges,* 3s.

Library of Wonders. Illustrated Gift-books for Boys. Paper, 1s.; cloth, 1s. 6d.
  Wonderful Adventures.
  Wonderful Escapes.
  Wonders of Bodily Strength and Skill.

Cassell's Eighteenpenny Story Books. Illustrated.
  Wee Willie Winkie.
  Ups and Downs of a Donkey's Life.
  Three Wee Ulster Lassies.
  Up the Ladder.
  Dick's Hero; and other Stories.
  The Chip Boy.
  Raggles, Baggles, and the Emperor.
  Roses from Thorns.
  Faith's Father.
  By Land and Sea.
  The Young Berringtons.
  Jeff and Leff.
  Tom Morris's Error.
  Worth more than Gold.
  "Through Flood—Through Fire;" and other Stories.
  The Girl with the Golden Locks.
  Stories of the Olden Time.

Gift Books for Young People. By Popular Authors. With Four Original Illustrations in each. Cloth gilt, 1s. 6d. each.
  The Boy Hunters of Kentucky. By Edward S. Ellis.
  Red Feather: a Tale of the American Frontier. By Edward S. Ellis.
  Seeking a City.
  Rhoda's Reward; or, "If Wishes were Horses."
  Jack Marston's Anchor.
  Frank's Life-Battle; or, The Three Friends.
  Fritters. By Sarah Pitt.
  The Two Hardcastles. By Madeline Bonavia Hunt.
  Major Monk's Motto. By the Rev. F. Langbridge.
  Trixy. By Maggie Symington.
  Rags and Rainbows: A Story of Thanksgiving.
  Uncle William's Charges; or, The Broken Trust.
  Pretty Pink's Purpose; or, The Little Street Merchants.
  Tim Thomson's Trial. By George Weatherly.
  Ursula's Stumbling-Block. By Julia Goddard.
  Ruth's Life-Work. By the Rev. Joseph Johnson.

Cassell's Two-Shilling Story Books. Illustrated.
  Stories of the Tower.
  Mr. Burke's Nieces.
  May Cunningham's Trial.
  The Top of the Ladder: How to Reach it.
  Little Flotsam.
  Madge and Her Friends.
  The Children of the Court.
  Maid Marjory.
  Peggy, and other Tales.
  The Four Cats of the Tippertons.
  Marion's Two Homes.
  Little Folks' Sunday Book.
  Two Fourpenny Bits.
  Poor Nelly.
  Tom Heriot.
  Through Peril to Fortune.
  Aunt Tabitha's Waifs.
  In Mischief Again.

Selections from Cassell & Company's Publications.

Cheap Editions of Popular Volumes for Young People. Bound in cloth, gilt edges, 2s. 6d. each.

In Quest of Gold; or, Under the Whanga Falls.
On Board the *Esmeralda*; or, Martin Leigh's Log.
The Romance of Invention: Vignettes from the Annals of Industry and Science.
For Queen and King.
Esther West.
Three Homes.
Working to Win.
Perils Afloat and Brigands Ashore.

The "Deerfoot" Series. By EDWARD S. ELLIS. With Four full-page Illustrations in each Book. Cloth, bevelled boards, 2s. 6d. each.

The Hunters of the Ozark. | The Camp in the Mountains.
The Last War Trail.

The "Log Cabin" Series. By EDWARD S. ELLIS. With Four Full-page Illustrations in each. Crown 8vo, cloth, 2s. 6d. each.

The Lost Trail. | Camp-Fire and Wigwam.
Footprints in the Forest.

The "Great River" Series. By EDWARD S. ELLIS. Illustrated. Crown 8vo, cloth, bevelled boards, 2s. 6d. each.

Down the Mississippi. | Lost in the Wilds.
Up the Tapajos; or, Adventures in Brazil.

The "Boy Pioneer" Series. By EDWARD S. ELLIS. With Four Full-page Illustrations in each Book. Crown 8vo, cloth, 2s. 6d. each.

Ned in the Woods. A Tale of Early Days in the West.
Ned in the Block House. A Story of Pioneer Life in Kentucky.
Ned on the River. A Tale of Indian River Warfare.

The "World in Pictures." Illustrated throughout. 2s. 6d. each.

A Ramble Round France.
All the Russias.
Chats about Germany.
The Land of the Pyramids (Egypt).
The Eastern Wonderland (Japan).
Glimpses of South America.
Round Africa.
The Land of Temples (India).
The Isles of the Pacific.
Peeps into China.

Half-Crown Story Books.

Little Hinges.
Margaret's Enemy.
Pen's Perplexities.
Notable Shipwrecks.
Golden Days.
Wonders of Common Things.
Truth will Out.
Soldier and Patriot (George Washington).
The Young Man in the Battle of Life. By the Rev. Dr. Landels.
At the South Pole.

Books for the Little Ones.

Rhymes for the Young Folk. By William Allingham. Beautifully Illustrated. 3s. 6d.

The History Scrap Book. With nearly 1,000 Engravings. Cloth, 7s. 6d.

My Diary. With 12 Coloured Plates and 366 Woodcuts. 1s.
The Sunday Scrap Book. With Several Hundred Illustrations. Paper boards, 3s. 6d.; cloth, gilt edges, 5s.
The Old Fairy Tales. With Original Illustrations. Boards, 1s.; cloth, 1s. 6d.

Cassell & Company's Complete Catalogue *will be sent post free on application to*

CASSELL & COMPANY, LIMITED, *Ludgate Hill, London.*

www.ingramcontent.com/pod-product-compliance
Lightning Source LLC
Chambersburg PA
CBHW021414300426
44114CB00010B/491